SECOND EDITION

SOCIAL INEQUALITY IN INDIA

Profiles of Caste, Class, Power and Social Mobility

Essays in Honour of
Professor Yogendra Singh

Edited by
K.L. SHARMA

RAWAT PUBLICATIONS
Jaipur • New Delhi • Bangalore • Guwahati • Kolkata

ISBN 978-81-7033-513-9 (HB)

Reprinted, 2024

Published by
Prem Rawat for **Rawat Publications**
Satyam Apts, Sector 3, Jawahar Nagar, Jaipur 302 004 (India)
Phone: 0141 265 1748 / 265 7006
E-mail: info@rawatbooks.com
Website: www.rawatbooks.com

New Delhi Office
4858/24, Ansari Road, Daryaganj, New Delhi 110 002
Phone: 011-23263290

Also at *Bangalore, Guwahati* and *Kolkata*

Printed at Nice Printing Press, New Delhi

Preface

Prof. N.K. Singhi and myself have planned five volumes on various themes such as Social Stratification, Social Change and Modernization, Village Community, Concept of Man and Theory and Method in Indian Sociology to which Prof. Yogendra Singh, our esteemed teacher, has accorded paramount importance. These volumes would be a token tribute to a teacher from whom we have learned the craft of sociological analysis and understanding. On the occasion of the XXI All India Sociological Conference, held at the Centre for the Study of Social Systems, School of Social Sciences, Jawaharlal Nehru University, New Delhi, release of the present volume of the proposed five volumes symbolizes our respect to our great teacher who is an embodiment of the highest order of human values.

Professor Singh obtained his Master's and Ph.D. degrees from Lucknow University. He had the privilege of being taught by eminent teachers like Radha Kamal Mukherjee, D.P. Mukerji, D.N. Majumdar, Baljit Singh and A.K. Saran. After teaching for a period of three years at the Institute of Social Sciences, Agra, Prof. Singh joined Rajasthan University to start a new Department of Sociology along with Prof. T.K.N. Unnithan and Prof. Indra Deva. I had the privilege of being his student at the M.A. level. In fact, I was the first student to be awarded Ph.D. degree under his supervision. After spending a decade in Rajasthan, Prof. Singh was invited to establish the Centre for the Study of Social Systems at JNU in 1971. Thirty students have so far been awarded doctorate under his guidance.

Prof. Singh has done extensive and serious work in the field of social stratification. Besides his writings on caste, class and power in the form of articles, he has authored the first and the second trend reports sponsored by the Indian Council of Social Science Research on the Sociology of Social Stratification. This volume is dedicated to Prof. Yogendra Singh with profound respects.

I am grateful to all the contributors for granting permission to include their articles in the volume and for appreciating our endeavour to bring out five volumes in honour of Prof. Singh. In particular , I am indebted to senior scholars such as Professors V.M. Dandekar, Victor S. D'Souza, Andre Beteille, A.M. Shah, Satish Saberwal, D.N. Dhanagare, K.N. Sharma and Suvira Jaiswal who made their contributions available on a short notice. My sincere thanks are due to Messrs. Rawat Publications for expeditious publication of the volume.

K.L. Sharma

Contents

Acknowledgements

We gratefully acknowledge the permission of the authors for incorporating their articles with minor editorial changes in this volume:

1. Shirirama Indradeva, 1985, *Diogenes,* 130, UNESCO, Paris, pp. 12-41.
2. Suvira Jaiswal, 1993, *The Indian Historical Review*, Volume XVI, Numbers 1&2, pp. 1-34.
3. Satish Saberwal, 1979, *Economic and Political Weekly*, Annual Number, February, pp. 243-54.
4. Andre Beteille, 1991, *Contributions to Indian Sociology*, (n.s.) Vol. 25, No. 1, pp. 3-28.
5. Sheo Kumar Lal, 1980, *Elite and Development,* by Sachchidanand and A.K. Lal (eds.), Concept Publishing House, New Delhi, pp.29- 40.
6. Dipankar Gupta, 1980, *Journal of Contemporary Asia*, 10, pp. 249-271.
7. A.M. Shah, 1988, *Division and Hierarchy*, Hindustan Publishing Corporation, Delhi, pp. 1-39.
8. Victor S. D'Souza, 1967, *Journal of Asian and African Studies*, Vol.II, Nos. 3-4, pp. 192- 211.
9. R.K. Bhadra, 1991, *Tribes, Castes and Harijans*, Ajanta Publications, Delhi, pp. 41-66.
10. Pradip Kumar Bose, 1990, *Country-Town Nexus* (ed.), K.L. Sharma and Dipankar Gupta, Rawat Publications, Jaipur, pp. 123-37.
11. V.M. Dandekar, 1978, *Arth Vijnana*, Vol. 20, No.2, pp. 102-107.
12. D.N. Dhanagare, 1987, *Economic and Political Weekly,* Vol. XXII,

Nos. 19, 20 & 21, Annual Number, pp. AN-137-AN-144.

13. Jaganath Pathy, 1975, *Economic and Political Weekly*, July 7, pp. 893-901.
14. K.L. Sharma, 1976, *Sociological Bulletin,* Vol. 25, No. 1, pp. 45-62.
15. K.N. Sharma, 1961, *Southwestern Journal of Anthropology*, Vol. 17, No. 2, pp. 146-164.
16. Pradip Kumar Bose, 1981, *Economic and Political Weekly,* February 7, pp. 191-196.
17. Vijay Kumar Vashishtha, 1992, *Proceedings* of the Indian History Congress, 52nd Session, New Delhi, pp. 717-723.
18. Nandu Ram, 1986, *Emerging Trends in Indian Sociology*, Vol. I (ed.), Ishwar Modi, Rawat Publications, Jaipur, pp. 88-107.
19. Ehsanul Haq, 1989, *International Perspectives on Education and Society*, Volume I, pp. 47-61.
20. C.Rajagopalan and Jaspal Singh, 1968, *Economic and Polticial Weekly*, Vol. III, No. 14, April 6, pp. 1-6.

Principal Works of Prof. Yogendra Singh

Articles Published in Journals

1958 'Land Reform and Social Tensions in Villages', *Journal of Social Sciences*, Vol. I, No. 2, Institute of Social Sciences, Agra University, Agra.

1959 'Group Status of Factions in Rural Community', *Journal of Social Sciences*, Vol. II, No. 1, Institute of Social Sciences, Agra University, Agra.

1959 'Institutional Factors in Land Reform Policy', paper presented at 42nd Annual Conference of Indian Economic Association and published in Conference Number of the *Journal of Indian Economic Association*.

1960 'Role of Sociology in Planning', paper presented at the Social Planning Seminar, organized by the Institute of Social Sciences, Agra University, Agra, and published in *Journal of Social Sciences Supplement*, Institute of Social Sciences, Agra University, Agra.

1960 'Social Change and Social Problems: A Study of Crime in Six Villages of UP', *Journal of Social Sciences*, Vol. II, No. 2, Institute of Social Sciences, Agra University, Agra.

1960 'Youth Problem and Welfare: A Sociological Approach', *The Economic Weekly*, Vol. XII, No. 45.

1960 'Development of Caste Consciousness in Indian Children from 4 to 10' (with S.D. Singh and K. Singh), *Journal of Research (Letters)*, Vol. VIII, Part. 1, Agra University, Agra.

1961 'Changing Caste Stratification and Problem of Integration of Indian Society', *Journal of Social Sciences*, Supplement Volume.

1964 'Cultural Integration and Changing Values', Sociological Bulletin, *Vol. XIII, No. 2, 1964.*

1965 'Processes and Problems of Social Change in India', Political Science Review, *Vol. 4, No. 1, Department of Political Science, University of Rajasthan, Jaipur.*

1965 'Disciplinary Growth of Sociology and Its Teaching in India', Sociology in India, Seminar, *109.*

1968 'Caste and Class: Some Aspects of Continuity and Change', Sociological Bulletin, *Vol. XVII, No. 2.*

1968 'Academic Colonialism: Sociological Issues', Seminar, *112.*

1970 'Indian Council of Social Science Research: Its Promise and Dilemmas', Economic and Political Weekly, *Vol. V, No. 16.*

1970 'Modernisation: Political Aspects', Seminar, *April 1970.*

1970 'For a Sociology of India', Contributions to Indian Sociology, *No. 4.*

1973 'The Role of Social Sciences in India: A Sociology of Knowledge' , Sociological Bulletin, *Vol. 22, No. 1, 1973.*

1975 'Social Contents of Scientific and Technological Revolution', Philosophy and Social Action, *Inaugural Issue, January 1973.*

1979 'Constraints, Contradictions and Interdisciplinary Orientations: The Indian Context', International Social Science Journal, Vol. XXXI, No. 1.

1984 'Relevant Sociology (I): Conceptual Issues', *Relevant Sociology*, Vol. 1, No. 1, April 1984.

1984 'Relevant Sociology (II): Conceptual Issues', *Relevant Sociology*, Vol. 1, No. 2, October 1984.

1986 'Law & Social Change in India: A Sociological Perspective', *Relevant Sociology*, Vol. III, Nos. 1-2, April-October 1986.

1988 'Quest for Relevance: Teaching & Research on Sociology', *Indian Journal of Social Sciences*, Vol. I, No. 1, January-March 1988.

— 'Literature and Social Change: A Sociological Perspective', *New Horizon*, ICCR, New Delhi.

Articles Published in Books

The Class Structure and Political Processes in Village India, M.V. Mathur and Iqbal Narain (ed.), Panchayati Raj, Planning and Democracy, New Delhi, Asian Publishing House, 1968.

Academic Role Structure & Modernisation, published in Satish Saberwal (ed.), *Beyond Village*, Indian Institute of Advanced Study, Simla, 1972.

Ideology, Theory and Method in Indian Sociology, in Stien Rokken (ed.), *Quarter of a Century of Social Sciences*, 1952-77, Concep, New Delhi, 1977.

Process of Socialisation of Education, in I.P. Desai & M.S. Gore (eds.), *Sociology of Education in India*, NCERT, New Delhi, 1967 (Reprint 1975).

The Scope and Method of Sociology in India, in T.K.N. Unnithan et al (eds.), *Sociology for India*, Prentice Hall of India, New Delhi, 1965.

Some Emerging Issues in the Indian Sociology of Social Stratification, in K.L. Sharma (ed.), *Social Stratification in India*, Manohar, Delhi, 1986.

Country-Town Nexus: Social Transformation in Contemporary Indian Society, in K.L. Sharma & Dipankar Gupta (ed.), *Country-Town Nexus*, Rawat Publications, Jaipur, 1990.

Relevance of Max Weber for the Understanding of Indian Reality, in Krishna Bhardwaj & Sudipto Kaviraj (eds.), Sage, New Delhi, 1989.

Social Process and Dimensions of Indian Nationalism (I.P. Desai Memorial Lecture), Surat, Centre for Social Studies, 1988.

Economic Development and the Changing Family System: The Indian Experience, Christian Academy of Social Sciences, Seoul, 1989-90.

Traditional Culture Pattern of India and Industrial Change, in A.B. Shah and C.R.M. Rao (eds.), *Tradition and Modernity in India,* P.C. Manaktala & Sons, Pvt. Ltd., Bombay, 1965.

Processes of Socialisation and Education, paper presented at the Seminar on Sociology of Education, organized jointly by the Tata Institute of Social Sciences, Bombay, and the Education Commission, Government of India, Winter 1965.

Modernization of Higher Education in India (review article on Higher Education in India), A.B. Shah (ed.), *Higher Education in India*, Lalvani, Bombay, 1969.

Reports

Modernisation of Syllabi in Sociology & Social Anthropology, report based on core regional workshops organized by the UGC Panel on Sociology and Social Anthropology, UGC, New Delhi, 1977.

Traditional Socio-Cultural Systems and Economic Growth in Developing Countries in Asia and the Pacific Region: the case of India, prepared for the Asian Development Bank, Manila, Philippines, 1978.

Jaipur City, A Study of Selected Sociological and Economic Aspects, Vol. I, *Ajmer City* Vol. II, and *Kota City*, Vol III, reports of a survey directed jointly with Prof. T.K.N. Unnithan for Government of Rajasthan, 1966.

Books

1. *For a Sociology of India* (ed.), with T.K.N. Unnithan et al., New Delhi: Prentice Hall of India, 1967.
2. *Towards a Sociology of Culture in India* (ed.) with T.K.N. Unnithan et al., New Delhi: Prentice Hall of India, 1965.
3. Sociology of Non-violence & Peace *(co-author) with T.K.N. Unnithan, New Delhi: Council for Social Development, 1968.*
4. Tradition of Non-Violence *(co-author) with T.K.N. Unnithan, New Delhi: Heinmann, 1972.*
5. Modernization of Indian Tradition, *New Delhi: Thompson Press, 1973.*
6. Essays on Modernization, *New Delhi: Manohar Publications, 1977.*
7. Social Stratification and Social Change in India, *New Delhi: Manohar Publications, 1978.*
8. Image of Man: Ideology & Theory in Indian Sociology, *New Delhi: Chanakya Publications, 1984.*
9. Social Aspects of Scientific & Technological Revolution *(co-author) with Ralph Dahrendorf, et al., London: Sage Publications, 1978.*
10. Indian Sociology: Social Conditioning and Emerging Concerns, *New Delhi: Vistar Publications, 1987.*
11. The Sociology of Culture *(co-author) with Boris Erasov, Moscow: Progress Publishers, 1991.*
12. *Social Change in India: Crisis and Resilience*, New Delhi: Har Anand Publications, 1993.

Introduction

K.L. Sharma

Clear and relatively stable conceptual formulations and methodological devices about somewhat dynamic formations such as caste, class and power are increasingly becoming a difficult task. Caste as a socio-religious system concerning mainly with caste endogamy and clan exogamy combining hypergamy and hierarchy has not only become visibly weak, but it has also turned into a politico-economic formation. Caste has thus acquired those dimensions that were traditionally considered outside its scope. Ritual power is being substituted by economic and political power. Conceptual schema explicating pollution-purity, organic and segmentary relations, closed and open nature of the caste system and its cultural and structural aspects not only imply one-sidedness of these devices, caste as a dynamic and resilient social formation is also undervalued. The question is not of adherence to the notions of pure and impure, hierarchy and hereditary callings, and of protecting rigid, archaic and oriental character of the caste system, but of the absorption of non-caste issues into the orbit of caste and to exploit caste for realization of political and economic goals. However, there is no one-way relationship between caste and other systems. Through caste-based mobilization access to political power is found as a common practice, and empowerment strengthens caste-based socio-cultural activities.

Adequate schema for analyzing social inequality must identify connections between its apparent and the real aspects. It may so happen that the form is not to be seen in the practice and the practice is hardly reflected in the form. The apparent distinctions may get blurred in actual life. Ritual status, pollution-purity, untouchability, hereditary callings, etc. today have not only changed considerably, they refer to contradictions, discontinuities and breakdowns in the traditional system of social stratification. A new nexus between the apparent and the real or in other words between caste, class, power and social mobility has emerged both historically and contextually. Dominant causality as well as multi-causality in ascertaining efficacy of various factors and forces over a period of time and at a given point of time should be understood. This brings in the question of 'relevance' of the categorizations, theoretic constructs, and approaches concerning the studies of social stratification and inequality. Ideological preferences, hiatus between the apparent and the hidden social reality and distortions of the real in the given frameworks and paradigms are indicative of the question of 'relevance' of the conceptual and methodological devices.

The essays included in this volume, honouring Professor Yogendra Singh who has authored the first and the second trend reports on social stratification sponsored by the Indian Council of Social Science Research, bring out the critical points relating to the structural-functional, structuralist, structural-historical and Marxist orientations and constructs in the study of social stratification. Correspondence and incongruity between caste, class and power imply a critical evaluation of the prevalent concepts, frameworks and paradigms.

The norms relating to social inequality determine the distribution of resources among individuals, families, and groups. Unequal distribution causes high and low positions and other dysfunctional consequences. Such a ubiquitous phenomenon of inequality is not uniformly intense and monocausal and monolithic. There is constant structuring and restructuring of social inequality. Inequality is a 'relational' rather an 'absolute' phenomenon. Inequality and equality may coexist in family and community. Also criteria such as income, occupation, education and competition alone cannot explain the entire gamut of social inequality. Along with 'contest', 'sponsorship' is found as a prime value in practice even in the industrially advanced societies.

Inequality in terms of a mere ideational phenomenon explains normative or valuational aspect of high and low relations, whereas inequality as a structural aspect indicates at the existential conditions and differential distribution of and access to resources. How norms relating to inequality evolve, change and influence social relations? Who play a dominating role in the production of the world of thoughts'? What are those basic aspects which are scarce and highly valued? What is the role of state in the production of 'ideas' as well as relations? Caste resilience, accretion of new dimensions, emergence of contradictions in the persisting value-frames and structures, unanticipated consequences, emergence of new middle class, embourgeosiement and proletarianization of the poor and the rich, respectively, are some of main considerations in the understanding of the structuring of social inequality as a historical process and a contextual phenomenon.

The following general patterns can be discerned from the various essays included in the volume:

(1) Continuity of tradition and emergence of modernity side by side in the realm of social inequality.
(2) Determination of social relations by the nature and direction of social change.
(3) Coexistence of the value frame, structure and process of social inequality.

A new 'rationalization' for denigrating the traditionally-oriented social relations and ideologization and 'conscientization' for a new form of society are finding their ground in India. Today, it is not the ritualistically perceived and influenced 'world of things', nor is it an 'economically conditioned' power or merely subjectivistic sensing of stratificational ramifications, but empowerment through access to positions of power, lucrative jobs, honorific statuses, a 'respectable' life-style, command on language as a social phenomenon is being perceived as the relevant instrument by the upwardly mobile sections of society. Destabilization of the entrenched through the crystallization of the emerging middle class can be gauzed in social, political and economic domains. How much a process affects caste, class, land relations, migration and mobility? Who are gainers and losers as a result of such a process of change? What is the nature of power structure in such a situation? In what way the new middle class and its empowerment are different from the pre-independence period? What is the nature of caste-class nexus, its continuity and change? Debates on the ideological and structural bases of social inequality have not only acquired new foci, alternative ideologization and paradigms are being presented. Presuppositions of the conceptual system are being reinterpreted as consciously formulated designs. New substantive concerns such as empowerment of the poor, weaker sections, women, etc. have added additional dimensions to the study of social inequality.

Let us have a look at the papers of this volume. Shrirama Indradeva analyzes that certain characteristics of the traditional pattern of social stratification in India are unique and have deep roots in peculiar ethnic constellations that existed about three thousand years ago. These features have changed from time to time over these millennia. The *varna* system, the doctrine of *karma*, the notion of Aryan supremacy, crystallization of different social orders, etc. all contributed to social stratification in the ancient India.

Observations of Indradeva are corroborated by a detailed study of the Rgvedic society by Suvira Jaiswal. She writes: "The Rgvedic society was a simple society in which the ranking of individuals depended more upon personal qualities and skills than upon inherited wealth or status by birth." The view that the Brahmana, Kshatriya and Vaishya were already 'almost a caste' or class-like categories in the Rgvedic times is found unsustainable by Jaiswal. She also differs from the view that the Rgvedic society was essentially a pastoral one. Jaiswal observes that differences between the Dasas and the Dasyus and the Rgvedic Aryans were clearly ethnic at least in the initial stages and not a matter of social hierarchy differentiating between the possessors and the non-possessors. The Arya and the Dasa were two distinct ethnic groups and not parts of one civil stratified society. "It is only towards the end of the Rgvedic period that the Dasa is completely subjugated, enslaved and assimilated and the term begins to mean a slave."

There was a lack of rigid demarcation between social echelons, it was not a purely egalitarian epoch, but it was by no means stratified. "Ranks were still largely a matter of achievement rather than inheritance." Jaiswal acknowledges that the development of a powerful priesthood and the formation of Brahmana *varna* may not be explained simply as a case of ethnic predisposition. Greater availability of surplus and enforced leisure are necessary conditions of the proliferation of rituals and the growth of a class of specialists who act as intermediaries as well between clans and ancestors and deities.

In recent times, as Satish Saberwal argues, the sociologists have become insensitive to the study of social inequalities in India. Such an insensitivity has emanated from three convergent influences. These are: (i) the prevalent public ideology drawn partly from the colonial public institutions and partly from the Indian national movement; (ii) the key premises of American cultural anthropology and the absence of countervailing insights in the other traditions; and (iii) the social backgrounds of Indian sociologists which have been limited to relatively narrow strata, and their narrow social experiences and hence their fractured personal knowledge. All these have created lean resistance to the desensitization and to the problems of poverty and social inequalities among Indian sociologists.

Papers by Andre Beteille, S.K. Lal, Dipankar Gupta, A.M. Shah and Victor S. D'Souza propose refinements relating to the approaches and paradigms for studying social inequality. Beteille observes that caste sanctions never operated in the same way at all levels of society. Today, the middle-class Indian's orientations to caste and to family are quite different. He can repudiate the demands of his caste but not his obligations to his family. Thus, caste is no longer an institution in the sense in which the family continues to be one. Caste is no longer the sole or even the main obstacle to the further advance of equality. "Caste has ceased to play an active part in the reproduction of inequality, at least at the upper levels of the social hierarchy where it is no longer an important agent of either social placement or social control." The family is indeed the main obstacle to the further advance of equality. The need is to understand the relations between family and education, family and occupation, and family and social mobility.

S.K. Lal enlists three approaches to the identification of elites: (i) positional, (ii) reputational, and (iii) issue-participation. For studying community power structure, these three approaches are found complementary to each other. Based on his study of a town in Rajasthan, Lal identifies three different types of elite commensurating with the three approaches. Different variants of reputational approach help in the identification of a variety of reputational elites. Effort is also made in the study to know respondent's awareness in identifying elites in an urban setting.

As we have seen that family and elite are found as the appropriate units for identifying social differentiation by Beteille and Lal, respectively, caste is found as a persisting social reality by Dipankar Gupta. He relates the *varna* and *jati* systems of social stratification to the Asiatic and the feudal modes of production, respectively. The fourfold division of the society into Brahmana, Kshatriya, Vaishya and Shudra is a view from the top of the hierarchy, but the view from the bottom is no more varied, and it may, in fact, appear less differentiated, because economic obligations were only directed vertically. Gupta explains painstakingly that *varna* and *jati* are reflective of specific socio-economic formations, and that the origins of the caste system should be sought in the material history of India and not in the empyrean recesses of the Hindu mind. The caste system developed in the feudal epoch and was characterized by localized exploitation, whereas the *varna* is a system in the epoch of the Asiatic mode of production.

A.M. Shah analyzes both division and hierarchy as essential aspects of the caste system. He draws upon data relating to caste in Gujarat. Orders of caste divisions are referred as hierarchical ranks. An overall view of changes in caste should include a careful study of changes in rural as well as in urban areas in relation to their past. Emphasis in Shah's paper is on the understanding of the significance of each order of division and the boundaries and mechanisms used for maintaining the same among them. What Shah suggests is that the principle of division was also an important and competing principle along with the principle of hierarchy. The holistic view of caste based mainly on the study of the village suffers from some basic limitation. In the light of the urban experience, a new view of the whole, comprising the rural and the urban and the various orders of caste divisions needs to be evolved. According to Shah, the urban situation and the complexity of horizontal units have to be the basis of the new view.

Unlike Dipankar Gupta who seeks origins of *varna* and *jati* in the material history of India, Victor S. D'Souza clearly demonstrates a dividing line between caste and class. D'Souza maintains that caste and class systems stand for different patterns of distribution of properties of individuals in hereditary groups. He writes: "These two systems can coexist in an inverse relationship and the ideal typical forms of the caste and class systems constitute the opposite poles of the caste-class continuum. This continuum refers to the rigidity-fluidity dimension of social stratification." D'Souza further observes that "the inverse relationship shows that both the systems are the extreme forms of the more inclusive system of social stratification which can be expressed as a continuum". Four indices to measure the rigidity-flexibility dimension of social stratification according to D'Souza are: (i) occupational heterogeneity, (ii) consensus about caste status, (iii) heterogeneity of individual prestige, and (iv) consensus about individual prestige.

The notions of caste and class and changes in the two when examined in the context of Assamese society provide a different view of social stratification. Coexistence of castes and tribes in Assamese society necessitates operation of two sets of norms which are apparently contradictory but in practice not so incongruent. 'Closedness' of castes and 'openness' of tribes in the same situation make the Assamese society different from the rest of India. Distinction between caste and tribe is somewhat hazy. The distinction is visible only in the case of Brahmins, Kayasthas, Kalitas, Ahoms and the Hinduized tribes. Distinctions with regard to class and power are more pronounced. A society comprising castes, tribes and Vaisnava sects, with the corresponding traditions of Hinduism, Vaisnavism and tribalism accompanied with coinciding patterns characterized by rigidity, flexibility and egalitarianism, is found as a social reality only in Assam. Such a situation calls for a paradigm different from the ones that account for caste or class or power alone.

The next four papers by Pradip Kumar Bose, V.M. Dandekar, D.N. Dhanagare and Jaganath Pathy discuss in particular the Marxian perspective of class stratification. The main point in P.K. Bose's article revolves round the transformation of class structure in contemporary India. The capital-labour relation and the conceptualization of classes are basic problems in the understanding of the transformation of class structure. Any change in class structure involves class decomposition, class transformation and class formation. Also there is a continuous dialectic between capitalism and the pre-existing social formation. Class formation, class disintegration and class conflict hence become important in the process of change in class structure. Bose identifies three approaches to the definition of agrarian classes: (i) the indigenous, (ii) the distributional, and (iii) the structural. Based on these approaches, five classes, comprising of landlord, rich peasant, middle peasant, poor peasant and agricultural labourer are proposed by Bose. A reference to relationship between the rich, middle and poor peasants is also made in terms of social status and mobility.

A critique of the orthodox Marxist theory and method is the main concern of V.M. Dandekar's paper on the nature of class conflict in the Indian society. After outlining the details of the Marxian framework, Dandekar explains that it is not able to explain many a crisis the bourgeois capitalist society has survived and it does not take into account the emergence of monopoly capitalism and the manner in which it modifies conditions of free competition. Marx thought of a perfectly competitive economy and hence failed to see that large scale industry and monopoly capitalism could develop trade unions of the proletariat in strength. Both could change the conditions of competition among the bourgeois and the proletariat. Marx did not see that with the emergence of trade unions and the collective power of the workers a perfectly competitive economy would change. Dandekar finds the modern industrial class as varied and differentiated like the pre-machine class of artisans and handicrafts-men.

Role of organizational and managerial skills of various order, hierarchy and social mobility, the new middle class comprising white-collar workers, social prestige attached to the white-collar occupations, and the life-style that goes with it, are some of the developments taking place along with capitalism. Several status groups in-between the bourgeois and the proletariat have also emerged. Three-fourth of India's population consists of people engaged in agriculture, unorganized labour and household industry, and only 9.6 per cent are blue-collar workers. Role of state as an agency working for the welfare of the proletariat is another development that has not been adequately considered in the Marxian framework. Dandekar writes: "The conditions in India are far from those postulated by Marx. Partly because the capitalist development has not gone for enough, there exists a large class, in fact as much as five-sixth of the working population, which is neither bourgeois nor proletariat and which is waiting to sink into the proletariat."

Then we have a paper by D.N. Dhanagare in which he reflects upon various studies of green revolution and social inequalities in rural India. He poses the question: "Has the green revolution succeeded in reducing socio-economic inequalities in rural India?" Dhanagare concludes that in general the findings of different studies show that the green revolution has had a contradictory impact on rural development and agricultural wages. Green revolution technology has not proved to be a measure of poverty alleviation. On the contrary, there is evidence to show that greater and greater immiseration and pauperization has surfaced with a steady growth of socio-economic inequalities in rural India due to green revolution.

Impact of capitalism in agriculture is also the main focus of Jaganath Pathy's paper—"Social Stratification in an Orissa Village". Pathy finds seven classes in the village. These are: (1) landlords, (2) rich peasants, (3) middle peasants, (4) small peasants, (5) farm workers, (6) businessmen, and (7) others. The criteria in arriving at such a classification are landownership, control over other material resources and usury. Pathy writes: "In Talapatma, we find the primordial forms of slavery and intensive sharecropping, combined with frequent fear of eviction, perpetual indebtedness of the peasantry to the landlords for consumption loans, forcible restriction of the peasantry from the capital market, predominance of exchange economy, seasonal farm labour, and poor development of commodity economy and of the productive forces. In other words, the village is a semi-feudal one."

Papers by K.L. Sharma and K.N. Sharma are again about the village community in India. K.L. Sharma discusses the nature of sources and determinants of power elite and the mobility of elites. The social background of elites and changes in the structure of elites are the focal points of study in Sharma's analysis of power elite and dominance mobility. Sharma asks: (1) How is dominance legitimized? (2) What are the basic resources which facilitate dominance of individual members in village community? (3) Are the areas of groups and individual dominance separate and distinct? (4) Is there any contradiction between individual and group dominance or are they complementary to each other? (5) Can the two types of dominance prevail simultaneously in the same setting? (6) What is the direction of dominance mobility? (7) How do different factors differently affect the nature and direction of dominance mobility? Sharma finds that group dominance has enormously eroded, and new 'dominant groups' with divergent backgrounds have emerged. The notions of 'dominance mobility' and 'downward mobility' facilitate understanding of mobility at the levels of individual and family.

The main focus in K.N. Sharma's paper is on caste and occupational mobility in a village in North India. Several questions are formulated concerning traditional occupations pursued by different castes. In general, all occupations are classified as (1) rural, (2) commercial, and (3) urban. Some occupations are 'rural-urban' as a clear demarcation seems to be difficult. Sharma concludes that a perfect correlation between castes and their traditional callings is not found. Demographic composition of different castes such as that of functionaries and patrons would considerably determine adherence to the traditional callings. Demand-supply correlation of occupations, avenues open for mobility, the pressure of population on land, availability of commercial occupations, urban contacts, etc. play an effective role in occupational mobility in relation to caste in rural India.

We have another paper by Pradip Kumar Bose—"Stratification among Tribals in Gujarat". Tribals are stratified in terms of control over resources. Bose discusses how the nature of stratification among the tribes has changed over a period of time, and the control over resources and privileges has been transferred in a few hand. Inequality and stratification are no more different among the tribals compared to the non-tribals. The tribal class structure can be seen as having rich, middle and poor peasants and agricultural labourers. Tribals are distributed among all the four classes. However, some tribes are in a better position than the others. The stratificatory process among the tribals is evident in the fields of education and political authority as well. However, for Bose, the class principle is more adequate as it provides a more meaningful and comprehensive account of structure and change in a class-divided tribal society.

Of the remaining four papers, two are concerned with the scheduled castes and the other two focus on education and social mobility. Vijay Kumar Vashishtha analyzes struggle of the Chamar peasants in a *jagir* in the princely state of Jaipur. A vivid account of social disabilities and *begar* (forced labour) imposed upon the Chamars is provided in this paper. The All India State People Bairwa Mahasabha played an effective role in ameliorating the social conditions of the Chamars of the area. Occupational and social mobility could be seen in discarding of the unclean traditional callings and adoption of agriculture and animal husbandry. Stopping of rendering *begar*, imitation of Brahminical style of life and dress pattern were some of the visible consequences of social and occupational mobility among the Chamars of a feudal state. Vashishtha reports several cases of protests against atrocities by the Chamars and its impact on the people in the region.

Based on his study of social mobility and status-identification among the scheduled castes, Nandu Ram observes the emergence of a new middle class consisting of salaried persons from among these groups. Such a middle class having the background of the scheduled castes is distinct from the old middle class or the middle class in general. The SC middle class suffers from the status-anxiety due to its nonacceptance by the non-SC middle class. Incongruity between caste rank and class position of the new middle class having lower caste background is witnessed in everyday life. Ram also suggests a framework for the measurement of social mobility and status-identification.

Ehsanul Haq observes that in Uttar Pradesh the upper castes particularly the landowning Rajputs have almost total control over the educational system. The managing committees, recruitment of teachers and administrative staff, admission of students and distribution of rewards are regulated by the Rajputs of the region. Control of educational institutions is taken as empowerment of the community. Traditional values are perpetuated by exercising such a control. Haq refers to this process as 'traditionalization of modernity'. It becomes a mutually reinforcing situation in which caste dominance facilitates control of educational institutions and the later lends strength to the perpetuation of caste-ideology and traditional practices.

Finally, C. Rajagopalan and Jaspal Singh examine the social background of the first year students of one of the five Indian Institutes of Technology (IITs) with regard to social mobility. It is observed that the awareness of the existence of technological education, appreciation of its significance, the ability to afford that education, and the quality of education previously received seem to be crucial factors. Awareness for such a higher education is found more in urban centres and that too among the upper rungs of the social hierarchy. The children of the upper strata also receive quality education.

Thus, the volume incorporates such essays that analyze historical, theoretical, structural and processual aspects of stratification and inequality in India. *Varna*, caste, class, family, and individual are discussed as units of social ranking. However, caste and class are also referred as principles of social stratification. Rural-agrarian, urban-industrial, and tribal contexts of social inequality and social mobility among the scheduled castes have been discussed in particular in this volume. Case studies analyzing social inequality in states like Gujarat, Assam, Uttar Pradesh, Rajasthan, Punjab, Orissa, etc. highlight the relevance of some of the conceptual frameworks and methodological devices relating to the study of social stratification and inequality in India.

1 Shaping of the Traditional Pattern of Stratification in India

An Analysis of Processes through the Ages

SHRIRAMA INDRADEVA

Stratification, that is, the structuring of society on the basis of differential social status of various groups, is a common feature of human societies. But the traditional pattern of social stratification in India has certain characteristics which are rather unique, and these have attracted and intrigued many scholars all over the world. The structural and cultural characteristics of the traditional pattern of stratification in India have deep roots in the past. They have stemmed from certain peculiar ethnic constellations that came into being some three thousand years ago, and they have been given many twists and turns by numerous socio-cultural currents and cross-currents through all these millennia.

The roots of the Varna system (Varna literally means colour) lie in the clash of races. Fair-complexioned Aryan hordes which started pouring into India through the north-west around 1500 B.C. vanquished and subjugated the dark-complexioned earlier settlers; and thus the foundations were laid for a class system based on birth. To begin with, the Aryans regarded the non-Aryans as non-human[1], and beyond the pale of human society. But it soon became clear to the Aryans that it was more advantageous to assign them a low position within the society and exploit them on a permanent basis. This was achieved through myths and metaphysics. The primeval myth is that of the Purusasukta[2] in which the four orders of society emerge from the four parts of *Purusa*—the original man.

But the original dispensation based solely on race could not continue for all time. The Aryans like all invading hordes were short of women, and they had to marry women of the dark-complexioned earlier settlers. Thus, their racial features were compromised. At the same time new hordes were coming from the north-west intermittently, and they had a fair skin and more pronounced Nordic features than the earlier Aryans who had already established themselves as the dominant elites. These ruling elites therefore had to play down the importance of physical features in determining social status. To take the place of racial characteristics, elaborate scruples of ritual purity were introduced. The in-coming hordes were declared to be low for being devoid of ritual, and the vast masses of pre-Aryan settlers were condemned to a low social status by being given no right to undertake rituals. This important part that ritual played in establishing and sustaining the social order perhaps explains the unique and excessive elaboration and importance of ritual in India, which has intrigued many a scholars.

The metaphysical doctrine of *karma* has provided a powerful rationalization for inequality based on birth, and made it acceptable to the wide masses. According to the *karma* doctrine, this life is just one link in the infinite chain of birth and rebirths, and each being is born in a specific position according to his own deeds in past lives. He can improve the prospects for his later births only by adhering to, and performing well, the role proper to the stratum in which he is born. Paradoxically, the doctrine of *karma*—and that of *moksa*, i.e. salvation from the cycle of births and rebirths—arose in the process of protest against Brahmanic supremacy and its extravagant ritualism.

Interesting light is thrown on the circumstances and processes which have shaped the complex features of traditional stratification of Indian society by the analysis of texts like the *Rgveda*, the *Brahmana Granthas*, *Upanisads*, Buddhist works, *Kalpasutras* and *Smrtis*. This essay is an attempt in that direction.

Rgveda: The Establishment of Aryan Supremacy

In the *Rgveda*, the world Varna clearly refers to the colour of skin and hair of the people of two different races, viz., the Aryan Varna and Krsna Varna. Nowhere in the *Rgveda* is the word Varna used for the fourfold stratification of society. Though the two classes, Brahmana and Kshatriya are mentioned often, the word Varna is not used to denote them. Even in the *Purusasukta*, where the origin of the four classes is described, the word Varna does not occur.

The Aryan hordes were quite conscious of their cultural and ethnic identity and looked down upon the dark-complexioned earlier settlers. These people are referred to in the *Rgveda* as *Dasa* and *Panis*. Both of these are described as dark-complexioned (*Krsna varna*). The word Dasa seems to be connected with the Iranian word "*Dahae*" which means "countryman".

In the beginning Aryans hunted and looted the non-Aryans. The poet Vasvamitra prays to Indra to destroy the blacks through his brilliance.[3] At one place a poet says that Indra has destroyed black armies.[4] At another place we find that Indra has killed fifty thousand blacks.[5] It appears that Dasas were a militant people. They gave a tough fight to the Aryans. A poet praises Indra for killing Dasa Sambara, a dweller of the mountains in the fortieth autumn.[6] But finally they were vanquished and were either absorbed in the lower rungs of the society or driven away from their dwellings and had to take shelter in dense forests and other inhospitable regions. A poet says: "Indra kills Dasas and increases the might of the Aryans."[7]

Some of the pre-Aryan people were city-dwellers and traders rather than warriors. The Aryans were militant and well-armed and they massacred these peace-loving people at will. The Aryan god-hero Indra is credited with demolition of ninety-nine cities of the Dasa king Sambara: "And Indra for the sake of a king Divodasa demolished Sambara's ninety-nine cities."[8]

Due to different racial features the disdain of the Aryans towards the Dasas was so great that they were called Amanusa or "non-human"[9]. And since the Dasas were considered non-human all inhuman behavior towards them was justified in the eyes of the Aryans. In a hymn of *Rgveda* we find: "You (Indra) subdued Pipru and powerful Mrgayu for Rjisvan, the son of Vidathin, you smote down fifty thousand dark ones, you shattered cities as old age shatters good looks."[10] Fire was the most effective and powerful weapon of the Aryans. They used it liberally against the Dasas.

> *"O Fire due to thy fear fled the dark races,*
> *Scattered abode, deserting their possessions,*
> *O glowing Vaisvanara, when for Puro,*
> *You burn up and rend their cities."*[11]

Thus, the Dasas had to flee, leaving behind their settlements in utter despair. Similarly at another place it is asserted that "fire drove Dasas and brought light to Aryans."[12]

The Aryans acquired the vast fertile lands of north-western India. They badly needed manpower. For them the Dasas were the most suitable source of labour. The Dasas were captured and compelled to work for them. The *Rgveda* says: "Indra binds a hundred and ten Dasas."[13] Many Dasas accepted the slavery of Aryans. In a hymn of *Rgveda* it is said: "An Aryan leads away a Dasa at will."[14] But Aryans hounded them from place to place: "The dark coloured Dasas were driven away by Indra from place to place."[15] This hymn indicates that the settlements of Dasas were demolished more than once. Ultimately, the Dasas took shelter in dark caves and dense forests: "Indra made Dasa Varna low and dweller of caves."[16] It is stated that "Dasas lived in darkness."[17] The word Dasa is used for slaves even in the *Rgveda*. In later times also Dasa has been the most common word for slave.

Panis: The Pre-Aryan City People

Other people mentioned in the *Rgveda* are the Panis. Probably, these were commercial people, and were later absorbed in the class of traders in the four-fold Varna hierarchy. The Panis are often connected with the ancient Phoenicians. Phoenicia is the ancient name of the coastal part of Syria. These Panis are portrayed as rich cattle-breeders and traders. Culturally, the Panis seem to be akin to the civilized Mediterraneans but by the time of the Aryan invasion, in terms of race, they seem to have become predominantly proto-Australoid. This is by and large true also of the people of the Indus valley civilization, who probably belonged to the category of the Panis of the *Rgveda*. The wealth of the Panis greatly lured the Aryans. The panis did not want to share their wealth with the Aryans. The tendency of the Panis to expect something in exchange for anything that they gave seemed absurd to the pastoral Aryans. Commercial values do not seem to have taken root by that time among the Aryans, and they considered this tendency reprehensible.

In the tenth *Mandal of Rgveda* we find a whole *Sukta* in which the she-dog of the hero-god Indra came to find out the hidden treasure of the Panis. In the dialogue, the Panis assert that their treasure comprising cows, horses and riches is well stored in the mountain castle, and those Panis who are excellent guards protect it well.[18] But the Aryans found the concealed treasure of the Panis and appropriated it. "Searching out everywhere, they have obtained the great treasure of the Panis hidden in the cave."[19] Fire was employed by the Aryans against the Panis also:

> "Agni, the hero, kills his enemy;
> The poet takes away the riches of Panis".[20]

The poet here refers to the eminent Aryans who composed the Vedic hymns. Fire is praised because through its help the Aryans were able to open the doors of Panis: "The fire is the wisest god who opens the doors of Panis forcefully."[21] It appears that before going on plundering expeditions the Aryans used to drink Soma. Therefore, it is quite natural for them to praise Soma too, along with Agni(fire), for the success they achieved in plundering the Panis: "O Soma and Agni, your valour is famous through which you snatched the kine and food of Panis."[22]

The Panis did not perform the Aryan sacrifices. Therefore they seemed foolish and faithless to the Aryans. The Panis spoke softly or indistinctly (in the judgement of the Aryans). They did not worship the Aryans' gods; therefore they were declared godless. The robust Aryans found no justification for allowing Panis to occupy the lands in which they were settled: "They chased the Panis to the east and turned the godless westwards."[23] Some of the Panis gave resistance to the Aryan hordes:

> *"With loud voice the people invoke thee, Indra,*
> *To aid them in the battlefield.*
> *Thou with the singers, hast pierced through the Panis;*
> *The charger whom thou aidest wins the booty."*[24]

The hoarded wealth of Panis held great attraction for the Aryans: "The men together found the Panis' hoarded wealth, the cattle horse and kine."[25] Sometimes Aryans avoided direct confrontation and stole the wealth of the Panis: "O wealthy dawn; may Panis sleep without awakening. Make us wealthy, we the rich people."[26] Similarly, at another place, we find: "They go to steal the food of Panis."[27] All those Panis who did not want to part with their wealth were looked upon as enemies by the Aryans: "O king, you yoke the ruddy horse for Agastya's nephews and defeat all the Panis who do not give."[28] Soma helped in finding out the wealth of the Panis: "O Soma you found out the wealth of Panis." After consuming Soma, plundering was easier:

> "O Soma you looted the wealth consisting of cows, (make your presence felt by) making noise in the sacrifice."[30]

Similarly:

> *"O Soma our crushing stones aspire*
> *for your friendship.*
> *Destroy the greedy Pani for he is a wolf."*[31]

The avariciousness of the Panis seemed reprehensible to the Aryans. They exhort their god Indra not to acquire this vice of the Panis:

> *"O noble elderly Indra, while gathering great riches,*
> *Do not be a pani to us."*[32]

In the course of time the Aryans settled down on the land and developed cordial relations with the Panis. A poet prays to the god Pusan: "O Pusa, one who does not want to give, make him liberal and soften the heart of Pani."[33] And we find some hymns in praise of Brbu, a leader of Panis:

> *"Among Panis, Brbu is the greatest:*
> *His heart is as large as the plains of Ganga;*
> *He who is ready to give immediately;*
> *His thousand noble gifts of cows are running like wind,*
> *Therefore all our poets praise the noble prince, the giver of thousands."*[34]

In due course it seems that the Panis were absorbed among the Vis or the Aryan countrymen. The commercial terminology in Sanskrit owes a great deal to the Panis. Among such terms are *apana* or market, *panana* or to sell, *panya* or commodity, *pana or coin, and vanik* or the trader. In the word *vanik* the sound of *pa* has changed to *va*, which is not uncommon in the evolution of languages. It is common to add the letter *ka* for making diminutives in the *Avesta* as well as in the Sanskrit language. The word *vanijya* or trade is derived from the word *vanik*.

In the Indo-Aryan social structure this whole class was given the third position; lower than the priests and the warriors. In the *Purusa Sukta* this class is called *Vaisya* or "the sons of Vis," in the *Rgveda* the word Vis is used for people. In the *Zend-Avesta* the word Vis means many families or a village.

We also find Dasas named as Balabutha and Taruksa who made gifts to an Aryan poet:

> *"I received a hundred(cows) from Dasa Balabutha and Taruksa.*
> *O Vayu these are thy people,*
> *protected by Indra, protected by gods they rejoice."*

Priests, Warriors and Commoners

In the *Rgveda* we find a society in which any individual of Aryan origin had the right to choose his profession according to his ability and achievements. He could become a priest or a warrior, or an ordinary man. The word "Brahma" means hymn and also the power inherent in the hymn. Thus Brahmana is one who is the repository of hymns. Like all ancient civilizations, in the ancient Rgvedic civilization too priesthood was considered the highest profession. A priest had precedence even over the king. But becoming a successful priest was not easy. The priest was expected to compose such hymns which would lull wealthy enemies to sleep, and swollen rivers to lower their level so that armies would cross them without difficulty. But he had also to be a master strategist and an excellent warrior himself. Naturally, there was a competition among various priests for the patronage of powerful kings. King Sudasa replaced Vasistha by Visvamitra as his priest. Many of the composers of hymns seem to be priests of one king or another. Some of their sons became composers of hymns while some others found the profession of warrior more suitable. A poet vividly describes that everybody has to do some work or other to earn his livelihood:

> *"I am a poet, my father is a physician,*
> *My mother grinds corn with stone;*
> *Striving for wealth,*
> *We follow different occupations."*[36]

Since the professions of priest and warrior were considered nobler it is not surprising that many people aspired to have these. A poet prays to lord Indra:

> *"O Indra, fond of Soma, make me a guardian of people;*
> *Or either make me a king;*
> *Would you make me a Rsi drunk with Soma?*
> *Would you not impart to me wealth that lasts forever?"*[37]

It appears that only those persons among the Aryans who were able to compose hymns were called Brahmans:

> *"Brahmans, the drinkers of Soma,*
> *Making hymns set their voices at a high pitch."*[38]

Composing hymns was not an easy task. Mere knowledge of language was not considered enough to become a good poet. A poet compares speech with a fond wife who exposes her charms only to her husband:

> *"A man though knows speech, does not know her;*
> *Though he hears her yet not hears.*
> *Like a fond well-groomed wife,*
> *She exposes her beauty to her master."*[39]

Not everyone could be a composer of hymns. The difficult process of composing a hymn is well described by a poet:

> *"The heart woven with mental brilliance,*
> *When friendly Brahmans sacrifice together,*
> *Through their attainment they leave far behind,*
> *Those who count themselves as Brahmans but are preparers of libations,*
> *Using Vak in a wrongful manner they spin out bad threads in ignorance, and*
> *Have to take ploughshares and engage in (agricultural) operations."*[40]

Thus, if a person could neither compose hymns nor become a warrior the only profession left for him was that of the agriculturist.

The profession of an agriculturist is considered lower than that of priest and warrior. These norms of considering low an agriculturist, and all those who earn their living by physical labour, have been inherited by the later tradition. The whole structure of the Varna hierarchy is based on such norms.

Entry into the rank of warrior was also quite difficult. One who failed to be a good poet could hardly be a success on the battlefield:

> *"Wandering in illusion gainlessly;*
> *The speech heard by him hears neither blossom nor fruit*
> *Dull in friendship he is called a laggard;*
> *Nobody expects him to perform deeds of valour."*[41]

From this description it becomes quite clear that the heroes of war often composed the hymns themselves.

Vis was the third rank. Nowhere in the *Rgveda* do we find a hymn in which a poet aspires to be a Vis or a common man. Obviously those who could not get entry into the two higher professions remained Vis. The Vis are described as those who give taxes to the king.[42] They were cattle breeders and agriculturists. Perhaps agriculture became a common occupation later than that of tending cattle. The poet compares the earth with a cow from whom he milks a rich harvest year after year:

> *"May Indra press the furrow down,*
> *May Pusan guide its course aright,*
> *May she be rich in milk*
> *For milking year by year."*[43]

The Fourfold Hierarchy: Organismic Analogy

In the *Rgveda* we do not find the mention of the Sudra except in the *Purusasukta*, which is considered to be of a later origin. The *Purusasukta* contains a myth about the origin of the fourfold social structure. Here all the four ranks are mentioned together. In this hymn it is asserted that all the four ranks originated from the great Purusa. The occupations of the four ranks are related symbolically to the parts of the body of the Purusa. Obviously it is an organismic analogy between man and society legitimizing the varying ranks and functions of different groups. As far as *Rgveda*, the oldest scripture, is concerned, the words Rajanya, Vaisya and Sudra occur only in the *Purusasukta*:

> *"The Brahmana was his mouth,*
> *The Rajanya was made of his two arms;*
> *His thighs became the Vaisya.*
> *From his feet was produced the Sudra."*[44]

The Brahmana has been called the mouth of the Purusa and is placed highest in society. His special function pertains to speech. Being a priest, invoking gods is his privilege. The second rank, Rajanya, is born of arms of Purusa and has the privilege of wielding arms. The thighs of the Purusa became Vaisya. The occupation of Vaisya is agriculture and trade. From his feet was produced the Sudra. Just as the feet are the lowest in the body, Sudras are the lowest in society.

The *Purusasukta* appears to be the composition of an era when the Aryans had already settled down in the Indian sub-continent. The Vis or the commoners among Aryans required agricultural labour. They employed Dasas. Gradually, the Dasas were given the generic name of Sudra. Both these words are of Iranian origin. The word Dasa is the transformed version of the Iranian word *Dahae* or common man. The word Sudra seems to have some connection with the word Kurda, the name of a pre-Aryan Iranian tribe still living in Iran.

In the *Rgveda* itself we find the tendency of considering the profession of priest and warrior higher, and the profession of the agriculturist low. The people who were employed as agricultural labourers or slaves had naturally to occupy the lowest position in society.

The composition of the *Purusasukta* and its inclusion in the *Rgveda* was probably the first attempt to systematize, justify and legitimize the exploitation of the non-Aryan masses by Aryans. The easiest way was to find some supernatural basis. This tendency of imputing divine sanction is a characteristic of the period of later *Samhitas* and *Brahmanas*. We do not find this tendency in the earlier parts of the *Rgveda*. In those parts of the *Rgveda*, the non-Aryans were considered Amanusa or non-humans and not the descendants of Manu, the primogenitor. Their subjugation was considered natural. The Vis or the agriculturists employed the non-Aryan labour. In an agricultural society, labour-force is always needed. Later, through their shrewd farsightendness the Aryan elite made an institutionalized arrangement which made cheap labour available. Sudras formed the lowest class of Aryan society. The inclusion of this hymn in the *Rgveda* sanctified this arrangement as natural and God-given. The society was conceived as an organic whole and all the classes formed its parts. Afterwards, in order to preserve the privileges enjoyed by the upper classes, and to avoid further racial admixture, it was necessary to give a more clear-cut character to various classes. Considerations of birth replaced those of individual achievement. And the classes crystallized into castes.

In the *Avesta*, the land of seven rivers is mentioned as one of the settlements of Aryans. In this land the leader of Aryan migration, Yim, married a "demoness" and gave his sister, Yimuk, to a demon. The issues born of these unions have been referred to as "abnormal" in the *Avesta*, and "monkeys and bears" in the *Pahlavi* texts. These descriptions allude to the racial admixture which took place in that early era. To avoid deformity, Yim married his sister Yimuk and thus preserved racial purity. From this myth it is quite clear that during the earliest era of settlement the Aryans married indigenous women; but when the children born of such unions had dark complexions, snub noses and other non-Aryan features, such marriages were avoided. In ancient Iran where the racial features of victorious Aryans and the subjugated people were not so different, ranks did not crystallize into endogamous groups as happened in India. In Iran, the rank of priest was hereditary but not endogamous. In India, too, caste became hereditary first. Marriages in direct order were permissible. But in the course of time castes crystallized into endogamous as well as hereditary groups.

Later *Samhitas* and *Brahmanas*: Low Status of the Sudra Institutionalized

In the later *Samhitas* hypergamy is permissible. Thus, the Aryans or men of the upper Varnas could have Sudra wives. It can also be seen in the *Taittiriya Samhita* that the Aryans used to establish illicit relations with Sudra women: "If a Sudra woman has an Aryan paramour she does not expect wealth for maintenance."[45] A Sudra could never think of marrying an Aryan woman legally. The later *Samhitas* and *Brahmanas* give a number of justifications for the low status of Sudras. In the *Taittiriya Samhita* of the black *Yajurveda*, we find: "Among men, Sudra has the same position as the horse has among animals. These two, the horse and the Sudra, are conveyances of the beings (Aryans); therefore the Sudras could not participate in a sacrifice."[46]

On the basis of the *Purusasukta*, the *Tandyamaha Brahmana* propounds: "Therefore even if a Sudra has a lot of cattle, he is not entitled to perform a sacrifice, as he is without god, no god was created after him, since he was created from the feet, he should not do anything but wash the feet (of the three higher Varnas)."[47] The *Aitareya Brahmana* puts forth another mythical justification: "He created the Brahmana ordains that the Sudra is to be ordered about by the others (three Varnas), he can be made to rise at will, he can be executed at will."[51] Thus, the Sudras were given the lowest position in the society. The elite of the society maintained a strict vigil to ensure that though the Sudras had been assigned a place in society they should not be considered as belonging to the Aryans. Their inclusion in the fourfold hierarchy was meant only for the service that they performed for the higher Varnas. They could in no way be counted as among them. To serve the three higher Varnas was the sole duty of the Sudra class. This relationship is asserted again and again in all the works of the later periods also.

Change in the Role of the Priest

By the time of later *Samhitas* and *Brahmanas*, the doctrine of four Varnas was broadly accepted by all the members of the society as God-given. We can perceive the change of the ethos in this period from the period when the hymns of *Rgveda* were composed. In the later *Samhitas* the struggle with non-Aryans no more existed. The non-Aryans, now the Sudras, accepted the superiority of the Aryans and considered serving the latter as their sacred duty. Consequently, the old militant spirit of the Aryans declined. For acquiring the comforts of life, they had to fight no more. Since priesthood was the most remunerative and respected occupation, the bulk of the Aryan people became Brahmanas or priests. The simple sacrifices were made elaborate and expensive.

The priest now was neither a military strategist nor a poet: his sole job was to preserve the humans and employ them in various complicated sacrifices which were to be performed for the fulfillment of different wishes. The character of the gods, too, changed. The militant gods lost their heroic spirit and vigour. The Aryans had by now settled down in the Indo-Gangetic plains. For the settled agricultural way of life such gods were no more needed. The gods now were expected to fulfil their mundane wishes and solve their day-to-day problems. The centres of civilization shifted further east. The land of seven rivers finds mention no more. Now the land of Kure and Pancala became the seat of the Aryan culture. The river Sarasvati in the west and the river Drasadvati in the east formed its boundary. Broadly speaking, this land comprised the modern states of Haryana and Uttar Pradesh. The secure and comfortable life of the plains made the priests self-assured and complacent.

The priestly elites preserved the highest position for themselves. There are many assertions in the later *Samhitas* which are meant to establish their supreme position. It appears that the priestly elites themselves were not quite sure of their superiority. Therefore, it was necessary for them to assert it again and again. In all the texts of the later Vedic era we find glorification of priestly elites. The *Taittiriya Samhita* declares them "the gods on earth"[52].

The sacrament of initiation, Yajnopavita, played an important part in rationalizing and strengthening the system of Varna. The first three Varnas acquired a privileged position for themselves. Though studentship is mentioned in the *Rgveda*, we do not find any mention of initiation rites. In the *Atharvaveda* for the first time we get the description of initiation. The poet conceives the sun as the child who is to be initiated into studentship by his teacher. This seems to be a forced analogy and there remain a number of incongruities. In this hymn studentship is called a second birth.

Gradually, the sacrament of initiation became much more elaborate. *Taittiriya Aranyaka* prescribed that a Brahmana should wear a Yajnopavita of antelope skin or of cloth. It asserts that the sacrifice which is performed while wearing a Yajnopavita is spread out, or become successful, whereas the sacrifices of him who does not wear a Yajnopavita would not spread.[53] And in due course Yajnopavita became the most essential part of initiation. In the *Dharmasutras* we find that the sacred cord is introduced as an option. The *Apastamba Dharmasutra* prescribes that a householder should always wear an upper garment, or in its place he may wear the sacred thread.[54]

In the *Satapatha Brahmana*, the Brahmana and Ksatriya Varnas are identified with the twin gods Mitra and Varuna: "Mitra is priesthood and Varuna is nobility; and the priesthood is the conceiver, and the nobility is the doer." It is asserted that Mitra or the priest could stand without Varuna, the nobility: but not Varuna the nobility without Mitra, the priest. It is concluded, "therefore a Ksatriya who wants to do something should seek guidance from a Brahmana, for he verily succeeds only when he is guided by a Brahmana."[55]

Upanisads: Revolt against Ritualism and Brahmanic Supremacy

Gradually, the three Varnas other than the Brahmana developed a kind of apathy for the ritualistic way of life, and a new school of thought appeared in *Aranyakas* and *Upanisads*. In these texts it is asserted that expansive, cumbersome and prolonged sacrifices do not lead to real knowledge. It was a challenge against the supremacy of the Brahmanas, and signified loss of faith in the sacerdotal science inherent in it. People began to doubt the efficacy of these sacrifices. Another interesting feature of the *Upanisads* is that, contrary to the tradition, the newer thought was marked by contributions primarily from Ksatriya, lower Varnas, and women.

The Upanisadic thought is quite different in its spirit from the *Vedas*. As a matter of fact there was implicit in it a revolt against the Varna hierarchy. The teachings of the *Upanisads* are in a simple language; therefore they earned great popularity among the people. The younger generation of the priestly class took active interest in it. In this era the importance of family and Varna also diminished. *Upanisads* contain the seeds of the systems of metaphysics which evolved later on. We come across many instances where Brahmana teachers went to learn the ultimate truth from Ksatriyas. "Brahma" which means only prayer in the *Rgveda* assumed a new mystical meaning in *Upanisads*. Now this term stood from the 'Ultimate Reality'.

In the era the supremacy of the Brahmanas was challenged in various overt and covert ways. In the *Chandogya Upanisad* we find a story in which a procession of white dogs is pictured like Brahmanas. These white dogs, one after another, each holding the tail of the preceding dog in his mouth like priests when they go to sing the Vahisapavamana hymn (in the ceremony priests have to walk in a procession, each priest holding the gown of the preceding priest). When all the dogs settled down, they began to recite, "Om, let us eat: Om, let us drink; Om, may the divine Varuna, Prajapati, Savitri bring us food; Lord of food bring hither food, bring it, Om!"[56]

Many established teachers (Brahmanas) approached kings (Ksatriyas) to acquire the ultimate knowledge. Pravahana Jaivali, king of Pancala, instructed Gautama and claimed that "Brahmanas do not have this knowledge, only the Ksatriyas possess it."[57] We find glorification of Ksatriyas in the *Brahadanayaka Upanisad* also: "The Brahmana being not strong enough, the most excellent power or Ksatriyas was created. Therefore (at the Rajasuya sacrifice) the Brahmana sits down below the Ksatriya. He confers that glory on the Ksatriya alone."[58] At another place we find that "five great householders and theologians approached king Asvapati of Kekaya carrying fuel in their hands like students to get the knowledge of Self."[59]

Even the kings sometimes approached persons of lower classes to get knowledge of Self. Jansruti Pautrayana approached a cartman named Raikva for instruction.

Before the *Upanisads* were composed, a great deal of racial admixture must have taken place. In the Vedic tradition persons of dark complexion are considered as non-humans or "Amanusa". Due to the strong patriarchal values, the birth of daughter was also considered a misfortune. In the *Upanisads* we perceive a peculiar general ethos, which is totally absent in the literature composed both before and after *Upanisads*. In the Upanisadic literature dark complexion is not considered necessarily bad. The *Brhadaranayaka Upanisad* mention rituals for having a dark-complexioned son together with that for a blond son. We find a ritual even for the birth of a daughter, which is very uncommon in the Indian elite tradition.[60]

The *Upanisads* mark a new epoch in the history of Indian thought. The ideas found in the *Upanisads* are in marked contrast to the traditional way of thinking which always looks back to the golden past. The *Upanisads* are refreshingly forward-looking. Instead of expecting people to stick to the beaten path of the past, they exhort them to move on and on. They expect the new generation to be better than the older ones. In the

Brhadarvanyaka Upanisad, the father blesses his new-born son to be more ascensive than his father, than his grandfather.

In the *Upanisads*, for the first time, the concept of rebirth is introduced. As a matter of fact it is not in consonance with the Aryan tradition. In the *Rgveda*, as well as the *Avesta*, the dead go to live with their forefathers in heaven. It is possible that the concept of rebirth has an Assyrian origin, though the idea of souls taking another birth is found in a rudimentary form in Austric tribal cultures also. As recorded by Arrian, Assyrians invaded India and ruled over its north-western part. Through continuous cultural interaction many Assyrian beliefs got entry into Indian tradition. The idea of transmigration of the soul was developed in the classical Indian systems of metaphysics specially in *Samkhya*, *Yoga* and *Vedanta*. It crystallized into the theory of Karma, which rationalized and provided the rockbed to the system of Varna hierarchy for thousands of years.

The *Upanisads* marked a revolt against Brahmanic supremacy. The wave of liberalization must have led to the adoption of ideas from non-Aryan sources; and the notion of transmigration of the soul and rebirth seems to be one of these. However, it is ironic that this very idea was turned into the most effective instrument to justify inequality based on birth. The doctrine is that one is born as a Brahmana or a Sudra entirely on the basis of his own deeds in the earlier lives; in his present life he should pursue steadfastly the duties of his own Varna in order to better his prospects in subsequent lives. Not only was this doctrine propagated by the Brahmanas as self-evident truth, but it was accepted and internalized by the most underprivileged and exploited sections also. The doctrine provided a perfect justification for gross inequality based on birth.

Sutras: The Reassertion of Varna Hierarchy

During the Upanisadic era, the Varna hierarchy and the strong patriarchal order that constituted the foundation of the ancient Indian social structure were badly undermined. The *Grhya Sutra* seem to mark the systematic and concerted efforts on the part of the priestly elites to re-establish their supremacy and resuscitate the social order in which they would have an unrivalled position. The hierarchy could no more be established on the basis of race as there had already been a great deal of racial admixture. Because of this, it seems that criteria of ritual purity were introduced by the *Grhya Sutra* to take the place of racial purity.

In the *Grhya Sutra*, for the first time, a number of sanskaras or sacraments were explicitly codified. These sanskaras are to begin before the birth of a child and this process of performing sanskaras lasts for many years even after the death of an individual. It is expected that each individual offer oblations to his father, grandfather, and great-grandfather. A professional priest has to officiate at these sacraments. All the individuals of the higher Varnas who wanted to establish themselves as respectable members of the elite had to get these sacraments performed. Non-performance of these sacraments could result even in excommunication from the community.

During the era of Aryan invasion and colonization, the victorious Aryans had to marry women belonging to subjugated people. But there is no evidence that they gave their own women in marriage to the non-Aryans. Thus, a sort of hypergamy was established. However, during the Upanisadic period some kings gave their daughters in marriage to persons belonging to a lower order in gratitude for the esoteric knowledge received from them. It seems that the Brahmanical revival marked by the *Sutras* sought to revive this trend. The *Grhya Sutra* laid down that marriages should be hypergamous, that is, in the direct order of Varnas.

As far as the Varna of the progeny is concerned, there seem to be two types of traditions which are divergent. According to one, the progeny belong to the Varna of their father irrespective of the Varna of the mother. This seems to be the earlier practice when the Aryans had no option but to marry women from amongst the non-Aryan people. The other set of norms, which is already in evidence in the *Sutras*, and is vigorously asserted in the *Smrtis*, insists that both the parents should belong to the same Varna.

This is in sharp contrast to the practice of bestowing sonhood on the children acquired in various ways. The *Gautama Dharmasutra* recognizes twelve types of sons which include besides the real son even the sons who had no biological relationship with the father or the mother. Even those whose parents are unknown have been included. The sons of all these types were given the class name which would imply also their inclusion in the Varna of their social father. It would be reasonable to surmise that such a son had to be of a fair complexion.

The *Dharmasutras* introduced many new rules about not taking food from the house of persons of lower Varnas. In the early Vedic texts, we do not find such rules. The *Baudhayana Dharmasutra*, which because of its archaic language seems to be the earliest among the *Dharmasutras*, does not contain any rules about taking food in the house of lower Varnas. Gautama introduced such restrictions in a liberal way. It is interesting to note that Gautama allows a Brahmana student to take good from the house of all the three higher Varanas;[61] but after completing his studentship he should not take food from the house of Ksatriya and Vaisya Varnas. He was expected to take food only at the house of a Brahmana householder. Apastamba further propounds that even among Brahmana householders, one should eat only in the house of a true Brahmana.[62]

It appears that the society was not prepared for the imposition of such rigid norms and many among the elites took objection to this. Apastamba refers to the opinions of "some" who allow a Brahmana to take food in the houses of Ksatriya and Vaisya householders. In times of distress a Brahmana could eat the food prepared in the house of a Sudra who was under this protection for the sake of spiritual merit. Gautama says that during distress a Brahmana may take food from a Sudra.[63]

In the Upanisadic era Ksatriyas enjoyed a position at least equal if not higher to that of Brahmans. But in the *Dharmasutras*, the priestly elites made it a point to assign a lower position to Ksatriyas. It is provided that even a king should make way for a Brahmana on the road. The gap between the two higher Varnas definitely widened. A Brahmana of ten years and a Ksatriya of a hundred years stand to each other in the relation of father and son; of the two the Brahmana is the father.[64]

Sudras constituted the fourth Varna. Apastamba and Vasistha refer to the Sudras and outcasts as burial grounds.65 Apastamba, Gautama and Vasistha provide that serving the three higher Varnas is his sole occupation. The higher the Varna he serves the greater the merit he earns.66 Gautama provided that for serving the three higher Varnas he would get remnants of their food, cast-off shoes, umbrellas, garments and mats. When a Sudra servant is unable to serve his Aryan employer due to old age or illness, the Aryan employer was expected to support him. Similarly, if the employer fell into distress, the servant was expected to look after his master. It is ordained that the savings of the servant could be used by the master.

Baudhayana and Apastamba both provide that a Sudra can cook in the superintendence of the first three Varnas. The cooks should daily have their hair cut, shave their beards and cut their nails before cooking.[67]

During the Upanisadic era, Sudras, too, participated in metaphysical discussions. In the revivalist era the priestly elites scrupulously forbade even the listening to recitation of Vedas for the Sudra—if a Sudra intentionally listens to the recitation of the Vedas his ears shall be filled with molten lead or lac. If he recites Vedic texts his tongue shall be cut off; if he remembers them, his body shall be split into two.[68] Apastamba and Gautama provide that if a Sudra tries to converse with an Aryan on an equal footing, walks on the road side-by-side with him or sits on the same couch, he should be given corporal punishment. The tongue of a Sudra who speaks evil of a virtuous person belonging to one of the first three Varnas shall be cut out.[69] If a Sudra commits homicide or theft, appropriates land, or commits similar crimes, his property shall be confiscated and he himself shall suffer capital punishment.[70] It seems that the priestly elites were quite aware that the Sudras were as capable of learning and propagating knowledge as any member of the three higher Varnas. They did not want to share the privileged position which they enjoyed on the grounds of possessing sacred knowledge even with the Ksatriya and Vaisya Varnas, and not at all with the Sudras. All the members of the Brahmana Varnas were expected to maintain a close vigil over the Sudras to prevent them even from listing to a Vedic recitation. Any kind of self-assertion on the part of a Sudra amounted to a crime according to the *Dharmasutras*.

Though it is provided in the *Sutras* that a Sudra can cook the food of a Brahmana, Apastamba and Baudhayana provide that food brought by an impure Sudra must not be eaten.[71]

The value of the life of a Sudra is assessed quite low. Apastamba provides the same penance for killing a Sudra as he provides for killing a crow, chameleon, a peacock, Brahmani duck, a swan, a frog, a mongoose, a musk-rat, or a dog.[72]

Buddhism: Challenge to the Brahmanical Order

In the eastern parts of India, however, there developed a parallel non-orthodox stream of thought through the emergence of *Upanisads* and Buddhist literature. Gradually, this became a challenge to the Vedic-Brahmanical tradition in the beginning rather covertly, but later on openly.

In these movements we find a unique synthesis of different ethno-cultural streams. Because of the complex interweaving of the varied strands, it is not easy to identify and isolate the contribution made by various cultures. Among the prominent ethno-cultural strands are the Aryan, the civilized Mediterranean, the Australoid, and the Mongoloid. In the early Rgvedic times though there existed the notion of superiority based on race, the diversion of society was not as rigid and elaborate as found in the post-Rgvedic treatises. In the Buddhist literature the people described are highly commercial, liberal, affluent and happy. It appears that in the north-eastern parts of India which became the seat of *Upanisads* and Buddhism, trade and commerce flourished extensively, and liberal ideas developed among the elite of that region. Perhaps it was these ideas that found expression in the two revolts against the Brahmanical orthodoxy. A strong plea was made for equality and fraternity in that early era of civilization, both in the monarchical and republican states of that region. The predominant position of Brahmanas, on the basis of birth, was challenged. This in a way was also a challenge to Aryan supremacy.

Though the *Upanisads* picture many respectable teachers as belonging to the lower Varnas, they do not directly criticize the Varna hierarchy. On the other hand, Buddha openly declared the Varna system unreasonable and reprehensible, as all human beings belong to a common human species, whatever be the colour of their skin. He refuted the Vedic myth of the origin of the Varna hierarchy and declared it to be false.

The social structure depicted in the Buddhist texts is not very different from the structure that actually existed in recent pre-modern times. We find in the Buddhist texts proud kings and warriors, Brahmanas who were well versed in the three Vedas, Vaisyas or rich Sresthis who liberally made gifts to the new religion, and skillful craftsmen.

In the Buddhist texts the supremacy of the Brahmanas was openly challenged. The Buddha declared that one cannot be considered superior just because of birth or lineage. He declares:

> *"By mere birth no one becomes a Brahmana,*
> *By mere birth no one becomes an outcaste.*
> *By deeds one becomes a Brahmana,*
> *By deeds one becomes an outcaste."*[73]

During a discussion with a young Brahmana, Buddha systematically argued that all Varnas whether white or black belong to one human race.

In the Buddhist literature we can witness the earlier phases of industrial and commercial society in India. Various beautiful things were produced by artisans. The artisans were organized into strong guilds. There were traders who used to take long sea voyages to sell silks, muslins, brocades, drugs, ivory and ivory work, perfumes, jewellery and gold.[74] Thus came into existence a rich, liberal middle class mainly comprising artisans and Vaisyas. It is remarkable that in the Buddhist texts we find norms and values of the rising puritanical middle class. These values promoted activism and the formation of capital. The advice given to traders in the *Digha Nikaya* brings out the commercial spirit of the Buddhist era:

> *"Making money like the bee,*
> *who does not hurt the flower;*
> *Such a man makes his pile,*
> *As an ant-hill gradually;*
> *The man grown wealthy,*
> *Thus, can help his family,*
> *And firmly bind his friends to himself.*
> *He should divide his money into four parts,*
> *On one part he should live,*
> *With two expand his trade,*
> *And the fourth he should save*
> *Against a rainy day."*[75]

These values promoted accumulation of capital which was necessary for industry and commerce.

It appears that the revolt of Buddhism against the Brahmanical system of stratification which is based on birth has much to do with the rise of the commercial class in the times of the Buddha.

Smrtis and the Brahmanical Revival

Buddhism was the greatest challenge to the priestly elites, for it gained great popularity among the masses. Many kings and Sresthis found Buddhism more suitable and they contributed to its spread in India and abroad. The religion of the pre-Aryans, too, reasserted itself among the people. The priestly elites were quite conscious of all these forces. It was clear to them that the ancient Vedic religion could not be revived in its earlier form. Many old Aryan practices had therefore to be rejected, and non-Aryan customs found entry into the revived religion. For restoring the Varna hierarchy, the backbone of the traditional Indian social structure, *Smrtis* came into existence. During the first revival of the *Sutra* period, many ancient Indo-European rituals and customs were consolidated into aphorisms or *Sutras*. We do not find much about the sanskaras (Indian *rites de passage*) in the *Rgveda*. The sanskaras were introduced in an effective manner primarily by the *Sutras*. It seems that when racial purity was compromised beyond the point of retrieval, ritual purity was substituted for it. And ritual purity itself became the hallmark of higher Varna. It was all the more necessary because during the Buddhist era marriages in the lower Varnas had no more surviving taboos. In the *Jatakas* we find many such marriages.

Since the *Smrtis* belong to the revivalist era, all the authors of *Smrtis* adopted the names of Vedic seers to get authority for what they said. *Manu Smrti* is the first attempt of the priestly elites in this direction. Therefore it was perhaps natural to attribute this *Smrti* to the primogenitor, Manu. Armed with the ancient myth of creation and various sacraments, together with the doctrine of *karma*, Manu tried to revive the bygone golden age by re-establishing the ancient system of Varna hierarchy. In this process women and Sudras were the greatest losers. The social justice they had got during the Buddhist period was taken away with a vengeance. Manu tried to assign each and every ethnic group, whether Indian or foreign, a specific place in the Varna system according to his own criteria. Many generally followed the guidelines laid down by the *Dharmasutras*. Yajnavalkya, Brhaspati, Narada and Katyayana followed the institutes of Manu.

Broadly speaking, those ethnic groups and lineages which were to be given a higher place in the social hierarchy were described to be offsprings of hypergamous unions between two Varnas, and those that were to be assigned a low status were declared to be the progeny of hypogamous unions. The social entities of various kinds (tribes, craftsmen of different types and even hordes which came from outside) were assigned a high or low position in the social hierarchy in this way. Through the myths of the origin of various castes as a result of hypergamous and hypogamous unions between men and women of different Varnas, a way was found to explain the existence of a multiplicity of castes (not just four Varnas) and each was assigned a specific status in the system of stratification.

Manu Smrti reflects the strong resentment of the Brahmanical elites against the Buddhist levelling influence. It has been categorically asserted that the dominance of priestly elites and the hierarchy based on Varna must be re-established not only through religious prescriptions but by the full might of the king and the state .The use of arms to restore their supremacy is openly commended. Manu calls: "Punishment, the son of the creator." The king is enjoined to establish Varna hierarchy through the power of punishment. Other twice-born people, too, are exhorted to resort to arms if they are in any way hindered in carrying out the duties prescribed for their particular Varnas.[76] It is obvious from these ardent exhortations and ruthless prescriptions that Manu was conscious that re-establishing the supremacy of Brahmans was no easy task-its attainment required all the power at their command, physical as well as moral.

In the *Smrti* era once again the Brahmanas ensured unquestionably the supreme position for themselves. Manu declares that "the Brahmana from the very birth is an eternal incarnation of the sacred law". Manu calls the Brahmana a great god just like fire, be he ignorant or learned. Just as the fire does not get contaminated, so also a *Brahmana*, although he may follow even a low occupation, should always be honoured and should be considered a great deity.[77]

This is in marked contrast to the theory of equality proclaimed by the Buddha. Birth in a particular Varna was considered enough for securing all sorts of privileges. It appears that by the time *Manu Smrti* was composed, norms of ritual purity had substituted those of racial purity. Many declared that the Brahmana is the lord of all Varnas because of his superiority of birth and observances of rituals and sacraments.[78] He says that a non-Aryan may have Aryan appearance, therefore one must judge a person by his acts, not by his physical appearance.[79]

The Sudras are considered lowest of all Varnas because no sacrament is prescribed for them. Following Apastamba and Baudhayana, Manu too justified the low status of Sudras. The sacrament of initiation is not permissible for the Sudras. Initiation is like a second birth because through initiation the boy becomes a full member of the Aryan society. Since the Sudras are not entitled to have initiation, they have only one birth. Manu has emphasized that their sole occupation is to serve the twice-born. Brahmanas belong to the highest Varna; serving them would be most meritorious. Manu took no cognizance of the doctrine forwarded by Buddha that the people of all the Varnas belong to one human species as all of them are biologically similar. To justify the low position of the Sudras, Manu refers to the ancient divine myth of the self-existent Brahman; since the mouth is the purest part of the body, the Brahmanas are the lords of this whole creation.[80] The Sudras were produced from the feet of of the self-existent; the service of Brahmana alone is declared to be the excellent occupation for the Sudras. In return, the Sudras are entitled to receive the remnants of food, old clothes, the refuge of grain and old household furniture. Since the Sudra has only one birth (he is not a twice born) no sin would cause loss of Varna[81] to him. Brhaspati provides that if a Sudra cannot serve the twice-born he may pursue the artisans' occupations and handicrafts.[82] In any case a Sudra must not be allowed to possess wealth.

Obviously, if a Sudra became rich he would no more serve a Brahmana or any other twice-born. Manu explicitly declares that the existence of a wealthy Sudra is painful for the Brahmanas.[83] According to commentators this is so because by accumulating wealth Sudras become proud and do not want to serve. In the Buddhist era people of all the Varnas were free to follow the occupations that they liked without attracting any social disapproval.

The fact that Manu assigns a low position to the Vaisyas and Sudras does not mean that he was not aware of their functional utility. In fact he enjoins the king to ensure that the people of the Vaisya and Sudra Varnas continue to perform the work prescribed for them. Because if these castes "swerved from their duties, the world would be thrown into confusion"[84].

The Varna hierarchy influenced the legal system a great deal. Since Brahmanas are placed highest in the social structure they enjoyed the highest privileges. The life of a Brahmana is given the highest esteem while that of the Sudras the lowest. The provisions are not based on any faith in equality before law for all. The traditional Indian legal system clearly discriminates between persons belonging to different Varnas. It is particularly harsh towards the Sudras. This system of law seems to have its roots in the ancient confrontation between the fair-complexioned Aryan hordes and the dark-skinned snub-nosed earlier settlers whom they vanquished and subjugated. In the course of time the criteria of racial purity had to be substituted by those of ritual purity, but the attitude of disdain persisted. Though this traditional system of law may not be enforced by the state today, its norms even now underline the patterns of behaviour and attitudes of a large portion of the people of India. The dictums of the *Dharmasutras* and *Smrtis* still form the basis of traditional institutions and values.

Notes

Technical reasons of composition no longer permit the case of the diacritical marks required for the transliteration of Indian words. An elementary lexicon is provided below.

1. Rgveda, X. 228.

2. Rgveda, X.XC. 12.
3. Rgveda, III.XXII. 21.
4. Rgveda, II.XX. 7.
5. Ṛgveda, IV. XVI. 13.
6. Rgveda, II. XII. II.
7. Rgveda, I. CIII, 3.
8. Rgveda, II. 19.6.
9. Rgveda, X. 22.8.
10. Rgveda, IV. XVI. 13.
11. Rgveda, VII. V. 3.
12. Rgveda, VIII. V. 6.
13. Rgveda, II. XIII. 9.
14. Rgveda, V. XXXIV. 6.
15. Rgveda, IV. XLVII. 21.
16. Rgveda, II. XX. 7.
17. Rgveda, II. XX. 7.
18. Rgveda, X, 198.
19. Rgveda, II. XXIV. 6.
20. Rgveda, VI. 13.3.
21. Rgveda, VII. IX. 2.
22. Rgveda, I. XCIII. 4.
23. Rgveda, VII. VI. 3.
24. Rgveda, VI. XXXIII. 2.
25. Rgveda, I. LXXIII. 4.
26. Rgveda, I. CXXIV. 10.
27. Rgveda, V. XXIV. 7.
28. Rgveda, X. LX. 6.
29. Rgveda, IX. CXI. 2.
30. Rgveda, IX. XXII. 7.
31. Rgveda, VI. 51. 14.
32. Rgveda, XLV. 31-33.
33. Rgveda, VI. 53.3.
34. Rgveda, XLV. 31-33.
35. Rgveda, VIII. XLVI. 32.
36. Rgveda, IX. CXIII. 3.
37. Rgveda, III. XLIII. 5.
38. Rgveda, VII. CIII. 7-8.
39. Rgveda, X. LXXI. 4.
40. Rgveda, XLXXI. 8-9.

41. Rgveda, X. LXXI. 5.
42. Rgveda, X. CLXXIII. 6.
43. Rgveda, IV. LVII. 78.
44. Rgveda, X. XC. 12.
45. Taittiriya Samhita, VII. 4.19.3.
46. Taittiriya Samhita, VIII. 1.1.6.
47. Tandyamaha Brahmana, VI. 1. II.
48. Aitareya Brahmana, V. II.
49. Satapatha Brahmana, V. XIII. 6.2.10.
50. Satapatha Brahmana, V. XIV. 1.2.31.
51. Tandya Brahmana, V. 5.14.
52. Taittiriya Samhita, 1.7.3.1.
53. Taittiriya Aranyaka, II. I.
54. Apastamba Dharma Sutra, II. 2.4. 22-24.
55. Satapatha Brahmana. IV. 1.4 1-6.
56. Chandogya Upanisad, I. 12. I-5.
57. Chandogya Upanisad, V. 3.7.
58. Brhadaranyaka Upanisad, I. 4.41. II.
59. Chandogya Upanisad, V. 11.7.
60. Brhaadaranyaka Upanisad, VI. 4.14-17.
61. Gautama Dharma Sutra, XVII. I.
62. Apastamba Dharma Sutra, I. 6.18.9-10.
63. Apastamba Dharma Sutra, 1.6; Gautama Dharma Sutra, XVII. 5.
64. Apastamba Dharma Sutra, II. 5.11. 5-6; 1. 4.14.25.
65. Apastamba Dharma Sutra, 1. 3.9.9.
66. Apastamba Dharma Sutra, I.I.I. 7-8.; Gautama Dharma Sutra, X. 56; Vasistha Dharma Sutra, II. 20.
67. Apastamba Dharma Sutra, II. 10.27.15.
68. Gautama Dharma Sutra, XII. 7.
69. Apastamba Dharma Sutra, II. 10.27.14; Gautama Dharma Sutra, XII. I.
70. Apastamba Dharma Sutra, I. 5.16.22; Baudhayana Dharma Sutra, II. 2.1.
71. Apastamba Dharma Sutra, I. 5.16.22; Baudhayana Dharma Sutra, II.2.1.
72. Apastamba Dharma Sutra, 1.9.25.13.
73. Sutta Nipata, 135.
74. Jataka, I. 108.
75. Digha Nikaya, 3.180.ff.

76. Manu Smrti, VII. 14; VIII. 346.
77. Manu Smrti, I. 98.78.
78. Manu Smrti, X. 3.
79. Manu Smrti, X. 57.
80. Manu Smrti, I. 92-94.
81. Manu Smrti, X. 123-125.
82. Manu Smrti, X. 99-100; Brhaspati Smrti, Sanskara Knada I. 530.
83. Manu Smrti, X. 129.
84. Manu Smrti, VIII. 417-418.

Lexicon

Amānusa
Apaṇa
Āpastamba
Āranyaka
Aśvapati
Balubūtha
Baudhāyana
Brāhmana
Bṛbu
Bṛhadārahayka
Bṛhaspati
Chāndogya
Dāsa
Dīgha Nikāya
Divodāsa
Draṣadvatī
Gangā
Gāyatrī
Gṛhya
Jagatī
Jāgatās
Jānśrati
Jataka
Kānda
Kātyāyana
Krṣṇa
Kṣatra
Kṣatriya
Mokṣa
Magayū
Nārada
Nipāta
Paṇa
Paṇana
Pāñcāla
Paṇi
Paṇya
Pautrāyaṇa
Piprū
Prājāpati
Pravahaṇa
Purusa
Puṣā
Puṣan
Rājanya
Rājasūya
Ṛgveda
Ṛsi
Śaṃbara
Saṃhitā

Sanskāra
Sarasvatī
Śatapatha
Sāvitri
Smṛti
Śreṣṭhī
Sudāsa
Sprime \ūdra
Sūkta
Sūtra
Taittirīya
Tāndya
Tāndyamahā
Tarukṣa
Triṣṭubh
Upaniṣad
Vahiṣapavamāna
Vaiśya
Vaiśvānara
Vāk
Vāṇijya
Vaṇik
Varṇa
Varuṇa
Vasiṣṭha
Vasvāmitra
Vāyu
Viś
Viśvāmitra
Yājnavalkya
Yajnopavīta

2 Stratification in Rgvedic Society

Evidence and Paradigms

SUVIRA JAISWAL

Ever since the application of modern historical and philological methods of criticism to the study of ancient Sanskrit texts, a large number of scholarly and not-so-scholarly works have attempted the reconstruction of early Vedic society on the basis of the *Rgveda*; yet the picture of the Rgvedic society continues to be hazy and controversial. In recent years, in a short span of five years, three eminent scholars—G.S. Ghurye, R.S. Sharma and Romila Thapar—have published monographs[1] dealing with the subject and each of them has used tools provided by history and social anthropology. Nevertheless, they arrive at very different conclusions. The work of Bruce Lincoln,[2] which is published about the same time, exemplifies the continuing interest of western anthropologists in the theme. It adds a new dimension by attempting to establish the ecological context of Rgvedic religion and society through a cross-cultural method. The multiplicity of paradigms and conflicting interpretations of evidence make an assessment of the theoretical and empirical bases of these historical-anthropological constructs an essential desideratum.

I

G.S. Ghurye belongs to that rare breed of sociologists who interfuse their knowledge of ethnography with an extensive study of historical records. His *Vedic India* is a voluminous work which uses a wide range of literary, archaeological and ethnographic data to study almost every aspect of Vedic India beginning with the cultural complex of the early Indo-Europeans to the non-literate people of the areas not covered by the Vedic people and their literature. He begins with the statement[3] that the Vedic period extends from C.2500 B.C. to 600 B.C., but modifies this view later to conclude that the Rgvedic Indo-Aryans entered India around 2200 B.C.[4] According to him, the bulk of Rgvedic hymns were composed in the latter half of the fourteenth and the first half of the thirteenth centuries B.C.; some were composed around 2000 B.C. and a few late ones around 1000 B.C. He agrees with Pargiter that the compilation of the *Rgveda* took place about 980 B.C.; and on the grounds of linguistic evidence as well as of "traditional history" culled from the Vedic and epic-Puranic sources he postulates the arrival of an earlier wave of pre-Rgvedic Indo-Europeans, who migrated to the east settling in the regions of Magadha and Kosala. The brahmanical culture of post-Vedic times, in his view, was mainly the result of interaction between these two waves of Indo-Aryans. In his discussion of the archaeological sites of the Harappa culture he leaves out those located outside India, that is, Bharat, and although he regards the early Vedic phase a late contemporary of the Harappa culture, he does not think that the latter influenced the former; for in his view the cultural environment of the two was quite different from each other.[5]

It is strange that although Ghurye's comprehensive probings into the archaeological material clearly indicate that there is hardly any trace of urban settlements[6] in the areas inhabited by the Vedic tribes, he has no hesitation in asserting, solely on the basis of his interpretations of the Rgvedic hymns, that the culture of the Rgvedic society was "essentially an urban one".[7] But these are open to questions and the hymns cited in this connection may be interpreted differently, conforming to the picture derived from the archaeological sources. Some of his inferences are quite flimsy, although they are given a lot of weight in his argumentation. Thus Ghurye argues that references to two-horse and even four-horse chariots in the *Rgveda* indicate that such vehicles were fairly numerous and this presupposes the existence of "fairly wide and good roads" and "fairly large settlements".[8] However, the use of the horse-drawn chariot as a mobile fighting platform and a vehicle for the warrior nobility spread with the Indo-Europeans both to the East and to the West; and whatever be the place of their origin, there is no doubt that they were not an urban but a cattle-tending nomadic people moving with their carts and chariots in search of better pastures. Ghurye quotes[9] Macdonell and Keith, the authors of the *Vedic Index*[10], to assert that horse-racing was a favourite pastime of the Vedic Indians. But recent researches of scholars such as Kuiper,[11] Heesterman[12] and Sparreboom[13] have established that competition and rivalry formed an intrinsic part of the original *Yajna* ritual, which was closely connected with the trekking and resettling activities of the Aryan nomads. Chariot-racing was not a form of popular festivity or sport, but a serious concern. It was interwoven with the Aryan ritual of sacrifice and played a fundamental role in resolving such issues as the question of the leadership of the band, selection[14] of a suitable site for their temporary residence in the course of their wanderings, and so on. The sacred and the mundane were completely integrated and inseparable at this stage.

Ghurye is not deterred by the fact that the excavations at Hastinapura have failed to provide any evidence of urban living in the Ganga-Yamuna region in the Vedic age and the dates of painted greyware, which are linked by some archaeologists[15] with the Vedic Aryans, cannot be pushed back beyond 1100 B.C. even at a most liberal estimate. Most PGW sites have yielded dates between 800-500 B.C. and as such are rightly associated with the later Vedic peoples.[16] In any case, the PGW sites were small settlements far from the "fairly large settlements" of Ghurye's conception. As for the copperhoard cultures of UP, Ghurye disputes the notion of their user being "uncivilized" and "nomadic", but concedes that they were not urban.[17] From Ghurye's point of view excavations conducted at Noh in Bharatpur district and Ahar in Rajasthan are more important, for in his opinion Bharatpur was occupied by the Matsyas in Rgvedic times; but these, again, do not support his urban hypothesis. The Banas culture of Ahar, dated around the eighteenth century B.C. at its earliest levels, is distinctly a copper age culture with no trace of iron. Iron objects at Noh are datable to 725 B.C.[18]. But despite these archaeological lacunae Ghurye asserts that the Rgvedic Aryans were not only familiar with iron, but even possessed or at least desired to possess iron forts.[19].

References to iron in the *Rgveda* are perceived by interpreting the term *ayas* as iron. Initially, Ghurye shows some hesitation, as he translates *ayasmaya* as made of "either bronze or iron".[20] But as he goes on visualizing a highly sophisticated sedentary urban culture of the Rgvedic period having towns adorned with beautiful statues of women in the nude, he becomes more and more convinced that the *ayas* should mean iron only.[21] However, an examination of the crucial passages in the *Rgveda* leads S.A. Dange, a Sanskritist, to conclude that *ayas* in the *Rgveda* "does not seem to indicate iron... (it) clearly indicates the reddish brown metal (copper or bronze)"[22]

A major problem in the reconstruction of a picture of the Rgvedic society stems from the fact that although it is generally accepted that the period of the composition of Rgvedic hymns spans more than five hundred years extending from roughly 1500 B.C. to 1000 B.C.—Ghurye extends it to one thousand years—few attempts have been made to sift the internal evidence on social developments on the basis of the relative chronology of the hymns. To some extent this might have been due to the fact that, as Bloomfield pointed out,[23] the Rgvedic hymns are largely epigonal in character "manufactured out of fragments of a floating anonymous literature", as is indicated by the frequent occurrence of the phrase *navyam sanyase*, "renovating the old song for an ancient god". Bloomfield warns that even the family books should not be taken as chronological units, for older and newer hymns are contained in each one of them. Nevertheless, in our opinion, these words of caution do not justify the abandonment of all attempts to establish a relative chronology of the hymns and making generalizations on that basis. An exercise of this kind would necessarily be based on certain theoretical premises which, however, have to be in conformity with the available empirical evidence. For example, Bruce Lincolon[24] shows that the myth of the killing of the primordial being in the first sacrifice and the fashioning of the cosmos from his dismembered body goes back to Indo-European times and may be traced in its Norse, Roman and Indo-Aryan versions, the last mentioned being the famous *Purusasukta* hymn in the X *mandala* of the *Rgveda*. But although the myth is undoubtedly old, it does not mean that all the ideas expressed in the *Purusasukta* hymn have an Indo-European past. This is the only hymn in the whole of the *Rgveda* which speaks of the well-known fourfold *varna* division of society and mentions the terms "Rajanya" and "Sudra". Clearly the composer of this hymn remodelled an old myth to explain and provide religious sanction to a new social situation.

It is generally accepted that the X *mandala* and the first fifty hymns of the I *mandala* of the *Rgveda* are late compositions separated from the family books, that is, II-VII *mandalas*, by about five hundred years or so.[25]. The family books comprise the earliest layer. There was also an intermediate stage when the *Samhita* collection ended with the VIII *mandala* and a supplement was attached to it after a time in the form of Valakhilya hymns. Hymns 51-191 of the I *mandala* are considered to be of the same date as the VIII *mandala* and the IX *mandala*, and are presumed to be closer in date to the X *mandala*.[26] References to agricultural activities are found mostly in Books I and X and some of these reflect a pre-plough stage as these refer to the turning of the soil with a *vrka*, that is, a digging stick or hoe, but often translated mistakenly as plough.[27] A hymn of Book IV dedicated to Ksetrapati (lord of the fields), Suna-sira (personifications of "plough" and "share" according to Monier-Williams) and Sita (furrow) is regarded as a late interpolation by Hopkins.[28] At any rate, the use of non-Aryan loan word[29] in connection with plough agriculture occurring in the later sections of the *Rgveda* suggests that the Rgvedic Aryans learnt this practice from the indigenous people, though such borrowings are not sufficient to build a theory of "the convergence of the Aryan and the non-Aryan" in the *Rgveda*, as has been ably demonstrated by Madhav M. Deshpande.[30] There is evidence of some contact, conflict and confrontation with the non-Aryans, but the *Rgveda* remains pre-eminently an Aryan document. This is also confirmed by F.B.J. Kuiper,[31] who has shown that the Boar myth occurring in the VIII *mandala* is an Aryanized version of an Austro-Asiatic myth. Kuiper states that although there is some evidence of the assimilation of non-Aryans into the brahmanical circles and adaptation of some foreign myths in the later *mandalas* of the *Rgveda*, "we have no reason to believe that such *corpora aliena* had really been naturalized already in the Rgvedic period." In his view, while the names of the priestly families who are attributed the authorship of Books II-VII are Aryan, the Kanva, attributed with the authorship of VIII *mandala*, is clearly a non-Aryan name, and the Boar myth, which retains traces of proto-Munda origin, is found exclusively in the hymns of the Kanva family. It is also interesting that the mention of cooked rice-milk (*ksirapakam odanam*) occurs only twice[32] and in connection with this myth only. Non-Aryan foreign names are more numerous among the authors of the X *mandala*, as given in the Anukramani, but the "aboriginal influence on the Rgvedic mythology has hardly been very extensive".

Thus, the long span covered by the composition and compilation of the Rgvedic hymns makes it imperative that one tries to distinguish different layers of Rgvedic evidence and weigh carefully all the arguments before concluding what constitutes an Indo-European heritage and what cannot be explained in terms of the internal dynamics of the Rgvedic society, but is to be seen as a borrowing from a non-Aryan source. The problem is compounded by the fact that words change their meanings in a changed social context and acquire new nuances quite different from their original connotations,[33] but Vedic scholarship often suffers from a static viewpoint which looks upon changes in later Vedic times as matters of detail only, an "ordered development" without any fundamental difference.[34] However, as some recent studies[35] of Vedic ritual have shown, significant changes took place both in the realm of ideas and practices, and were closely connected with the material changes taking place in the life of a semi-nomadic pastoral people who were in the process of making a transition to sedentary life and agrarian economy. Practices which were intrinsic to their earlier mode of subsistence received formalization in the later Vedic ritual and their analysis provides interesting clues to their original significance. It is pointed out that towards the close of the Rgvedic period some of the hymns had become illegible even to those who had grown in the tradition.[36] If this is the situation in the field of ritual and sacred lore, it is all the more necessary to guard against the temptation of projecting later social and economic features to an earlier past. Emile Benveniste has argued[37] that the notions of 'sale' and 'purchase' emerged among the Indo-Europeans in the context of sale by auction of men who may have been prisoners of war or may have lost their liberty in gambling. Early Vedic data confirms this.[38] Terms such as *vasna* and *sulka* which denote 'price' or 'value' in the *Rgveda*[39] are used not in connection with merchandise or goods but human beings and gods who are modelled after humans. Thus at one place[40] two *Dasas*, *Varcin* and *Sambara* are described as *vasnayanta*, "demanding ransom" apparently for having taken some prisoners of war, and are killed by Indra. At another place[41] *vasna* occurs in the context of a Hymner's bid to sell and repurchase his Indra after the latter has slain the *vrtras*, that is, demons or enemies of the one who buys him. Though the significance of the hymn is obscure, the nature of transaction is clearly modelled after the sale and redemption of human beings.[42] In a hymn of the III *mandala* Soma is requested to give salutary food to the devotees and to their 'tethered animals' (*pasave*), which terms included both the biped as well as the quadruped.[43] Reference to *rna* or debt generally pertain to those contracted at dicing and the authors of the *Vedic Index* speak of it as "a normal condition of Vedic Indians".[44] It is rightly held[45] that there is no evidence of commercial activities in the *Rgveda*. There may have been simply barter of surplus goods especially to obtain precious metal or "prestige" goods, but no merchants[46] or intermediaries playing a role in the circulation and production of wealth. Sometimes the Panis, who are described in the *Rgveda* as rich, selfish, "of hostile speech" and greedy, are taken to have been "merchants par excellence", [47] who practised usury. But this view has no solid basis.[48] One is inclined to agree with Macdonell and Keith that "it is hardly necessary to do more than regard the Panis generally as non-worshippers of the gods favoured by the singers" and the term is wide enough to cover the aborigines or the hostile Aryans as well as the demons.[49]

Thus, a more searching and rational interpretation of the Rgvedic data does not support Ghurye's view of economy and society in the early Vedic times; and his assertion that the brahmana, ksatriya and vaisya were already 'almost a caste' or class-like categories in the Rgvedic times[50] cannot be sustained. The problem is viewed from a different perspective by R.S. Sharma and Romila Thapar, both of whom look upon the Rgvedic society as essentially pastoral. Nevertheless, there are important differences in their views on the extent to which social differentiation had taken place among the Rgvedic peoples; and these will have to be examined in some detail.

II

R.S. Sharma argues that although there is some evidence of the 'band' system in the *Rgveda*, a pre-tribal stage in which a group of people not necessarily related by blood come together for food-gathering, hunting or fighting, society on the whole was 'tribal, pastoral and largely egalitarian'.[51] The main source of sustenance was cattle and not agricultural products. Apart from cattle-herding, booty capture in inter-tribal wars was a major source of livelihood. He quotes the well-known remark of Marx that man-hunting was the logical extension of animal-hunting and contends that the egalitarian ethos of the Rgvedic tribes was undermined by the unequal distribution of booty by the tribal chief.[52] The *Rgveda* refers to rich people riding on chariots and possessing a large number of cattle; but society was organized neither on differences of wealth nor on the social division of labour. It was kin-based having kin-units of various shapes and sizes to meet a variety of needs[53], and had differentiation of ranks, but no class differentiation. In short, it was a pre-state polity, which was moving gradually towards greater differentiation, as is indicated by the *danastutis* belonging to the latest stratum of Rgvedic literature. These indicate that a major share of the spoils was cornered by the chiefs and the priests leading to an inequitable redistributive system; but the phenomenon of one class living off the labour of another class was yet to emerge in 'any considerable degree'.

In its broad outline Sharma's reconstruction of the Rgvedic society is quite plausible. Recently an attempt has been made to reject the economic significance of war and 'booty-production'[54], as Sharma calls it, in the Rgvedic society on the ground that war could not have been a matter of daily routine as it involved the destruction of life and property. Nevertheless, the notion has good theoretical as well as data-based support. In their discussion of Greece of the Heroic age Marx and Engels speak[55] of 'military democracy' as a stage when the old gentile system was still full of vigour, but the decay had started and internal warfare had degenerated into systematic raids "for the purpose of capturing cattle, slaves and treasure as a regular means of gaining a livelihood". Marshall D. Sahlins develops this concept further by arguing that the segmentary lineage system was an organization of predatory expansion.[56] The term 'segmentary lineage' is the modern anthropological equivalent of the 'gens' in the narratives of Marx and Engels.

The importance of cattle raids is emphasized by Romila Thapar too, and in her monograph *From Lineage to State* she makes a pioneering attempt to apply certain anthropological models and concepts to the Rgvedic society. She avoids the use of the term 'tribal', agreeing with the criticism of those anthropologists[57] who regard this concept to be of little analytical value. But the alternative concept of 'lineage society' as used in her work seems to us no less vague and a 'holdall' concept; for she stretches it to mean not only a lineal descent group precisely defined—a position she adopts at the beginning of her work—but also clan[58] and other kin-groups, 'lineage society' becoming merely a verbal substitute for 'kin-based' or 'tribal' society. In a competent review article[59] A.M. Shah has questioned the validity of the model of 'lineage society' for the Rgvedic people from a social-anthropological perspective; but he has not given much attention to the allied concept of the lineage mode of production. Shah accepts the data cited by Thapar unquestioningly, excusing himself on the ground that he is not a historian. But in our opinion the very notion of the lineage mode of production as applied by Thapar to the Rgvedic society is seriously flawed both on account of the imprecise use of the concept and the inaccuracy of data.

Thapar begins with a precise definition of lineage as given by Middleton and Tait:[60]

> Lineage is a corporate group of unilineal kin with a formalized system of authority. It has rights and duties and accepts genealogical relationships as the binding factor. It can be divided into smaller

> groups or segments. Several unilineal descent groups go to make up a clan which traces its origin to an actual or mythical ancestor. The basic unit in such a system is the extended family based on three or four generation lineage controlled by the eldest male who represents it on both ritual and political occasions.[61]

The widest political unit in such a system is called the jural community. Thapar observes:

> The jural community takes decisions and is constituted from the dominant authentic lineage segments .... In the lineage mode of production the jural community has some control over production and its inherent exploitative tendencies differentiate it from the more egalitarian bands and ranked society. Exploitation takes the form of those in authority claiming power on the basis of kin connections and wealth and excluding those who are unrelated. This exclusion could be expressed in non-kin groups labouring for others.[62] In such a system the produce, whether acquired through labour or from raids, is divided on the basis of redistribution in which voluntary tribute and gift-giving plays a central role. Kinship relations have a genealogical base and at the same time are a unit production in accordance with lineage, segments and extended families. In a clear separation between elite groups and commoners, kinship constitutes a charter for establishing the authority of the ruling lineage through genealogical connections.[63]

Thapar acknowledges her debt to Emmanuel Terray,[64] who propounded the concept of the lineage mode of production, and the views of P.P. Rey,[65] Maurice Godelier[66] and Claude Meillassoux,[67] who commented upon it. But it is obvious that her notion of the lineage mode of production is quite different from that of the scholars cited above. For example, in Terray's model there is no room for the exploitation of "non-kin groups labouring for the others" while excluded from power and wealth. Both Terray and Meillassoux clearly state that the lineage mode of production is based on self-subsistence and short-term production techniques. Hence the units of production and consumption are homologous, constituted on the same principles through the same mechanism, and 'exploitation of labour' is conspicuously absent. Terray regards these features as "necessary condition for kinship to act as an element in the realization of the mode of production".[68] The problem of exploitation within the lineage mode of production is raised and debated in connection with the privileged position of the elders or old men vis-a-vis the junior members of their own lineage units and of men as opposed to women seen as separate classes for analytical purposes. The question of exploitation pertains more to the sphere of reproduction than to that of production and the debate centres round the role of the elders in controlling the reproduction of the social structure through their control over marriage and exchange of women. Differing positions are taken. Whereas some have tried to argue that exploitation as defined by Marx may be seen in these relationships, others have rightly asserted that groups based on the biological phenomena of age and sex can hardly be considered as classes in the same sense as the classes of the proletariat and the capitalist are in an industrialized society. But nowhere in these discussions is there any mention of the senior ruling lineages of the clan living off the tribute given by the junior lineages or 'commoners' working on clan lands and producing pastoral and agricultural items for the consumption of the former, as is the case with Thapar's paradigm. In other words, whereas the French anthropologists limit social differentiation in the lineage society to that between the elders of the lineage and the juniors, Thapar extends it to include distinctly stratified groups of the rulers and the commoners, the latter being subjected to a form of redistributive exploitation. No wonder that Thapar's narrative leads A.M. Shah to suspect that the warrior group of *rajanyas* and *vis-commoners* "were already *varna-like* strata in Rgvedic period."[69]

Thapar's concept of the lineage mode of production has more in common with the paradigm of 'chiefdom'[70] and the 'conical clan'[71] than with the lineage mode of production proposed by Terray. In a chiefdom lineages and not just a few individuals are graded in a hierarchical order, and men are 'chiefly' 'commoners' by birth regardless of their personal capabilities. Sahlins regards it as "a stage beyond primitive equalitarianism", but not yet a class society as "it is not divided into a ruling stratum in command of the strategic means of production or political coercion and a disenfranchised underclass".[72] Nevertheless, it has a structure in which rank is linked to descent—real or fictive, and access to wealth and power, claims to other's services, etc. are based on 'familial' priorities.

It has been pointed out[73] that the term *rajanya* does not occur anywhere else in the *Rgveda* with the exception of the *Purusasukta*. This is admittedly a late composition roughly of the same date as the later portions of the *Atharvaveda*, a later Vedic text. The term *rajan*, however, occurs a number of times even in the family books of the *Rgveda*, although in most cases it could simply mean the 'effulgent one', as it is applied to one or the other principal god.[74] At any rate, the occurrence of the term *rajan* in the Rgvedic hymns merely shows that the Rgvedic clans had 'big men', leaders or chiefs; it does not automatically prove that the *rajans* were representatives of the senior *rajanya* lineages. A few verses of the X *mandala* mention *rajan* in the plural. "Being foremost may we win the treasures through the chiefs (*rajabhih*) and through our band (of fighters, *vrjanena*)!"[75] Another verse speaks of the presence of the chiefs in the *samiti*, a tribal assembly.[76] But none of these references can be construed to prove the existence of senior lineage existing above the rest of the tribe.[77] The absence of the term '*rajanya*', which means kinsmen of the *rajan* and as such emphasizes the genealogical link with the chief, is crucial in this respect. Even the term *vamsa*, which is equated by Thapar to 'lineage', is conspicuous by its absence in the *Rgveda*. The term *gotra*, which signifies 'lineage' or 'clan' in later literature, is generally interpreted in the *Rgveda* in the sense of 'cowpen' rather than a patrilineal descent group. Besides, in Thapar's opinion the *gotra* system was specific to brahmanas only and the Brahmanas were an 'addenda' to the Aryan lineage society consisting of the *rajanyas* and the vis, the so-called senior and junior lineages. The institution of lineage in that case would be without any identification mark in the *Rgveda*.

It is significant that in support of her thesis Thapar is not able to produce any evidence from the *Rgveda*, but depends almost entirely on the later Vedic texts,[78] particularly the *Satapatha Brahmana*. The only Rgvedic hymn cited by her to support the view that 'those who chose the *raja* are distinct from the vis'[79]—is X.173.1. But a close examination clearly shows that no such inference can be drawn on the basis of this verse in which the priest pronounces: "I have consecrated thee (*raja*), come amongst us, be steady and unvacillating; may all these subjects desire thee (for their king) (*visastva sarva vanchantu*), may the kingdom (or ruleship? *rastram*) never fall from thee"![80]

Another argument put forward in support of the view that "the possessors of wealth were distinguished from the rest of the tribe" is based on a misunderstanding of the data produced by H.W. Bailey in his article entitled 'Iranian Arya and Daha'.[81] Thapar writes[82] that Bailey's analysis "leads him to state that *arya* (aarya) referred to the owner or possessor of wealth", but in fact Bailey attributes this meaning to the Indo-Iranian *a'rya* or *ary'a* and not to the elongated *aarya*. He states that the term *a'rya* (with a short 'a') was too narrow to denote an ethnic name, but was suitable for a rich class like vaisya in India and is explained as such in the *Nighantu* (II.6) and *Panini's-Astadhyayi* (III.I.103).[83] He further adds that *a'rya* came to have a secondary meaning of 'well-born' or 'noble' in an ethical sense. In other words, according to Bailey, *a'rya* originally denoted a nobleman who 'possessed wealth' but later came to mean one who had noble virtues. The elongated *aarya* derived by *vrddhi* from *a'rya meant* 'connected with nobles'. Bailey clearly states that as far as the term *aarya* is concerned, an early meaning 'connected with nobles' has thus derived to an ethnic name and to non-ethnic use'. Thus Bailey connects *aarya* with the secondary meaning of *a'rya* and not with its primary meaning of 'owner,possessor of wealth'. But Thapar confuses between *arya* and *aarya* and mistakenly thinks that references from the *Nighantu* and *Astadhyayi* mention *aarya*. She then proceeds to argue that since in these texts \the term '*aarya* ' (with an elongated 'a')means a possessor of wealth, or member of a nobility, this meaning is apparently a survival from the Rgvedic times and *aarya* in the *Rgveda* constituted a nobility distinct from the ordinary tribesmen-commoners. Thus she concludes that the term *Aarya* was related to "social status and wealth and not to race".

Bailey's interpretation of *a'rya* and *daha is* connected with his vision of the Aryan Great House, *a'rya* (with a short 'a') was the 'possessor', 'holder of property' contrasting neatly with the Iranian *daha* or old Indian *Dasa* meaning the 'servant' or the 'subservient one'. But the 'vision of Zoroaster', as he calls it, may not reflect the society of Rgvedic India, for the *Avesta* is far removed from the *Rgveda* in point of time. Bailey does not take into account the changes that may have taken place by the end of the early Vedic phase, and his thesis rests a good deal on the back projection of notions found in later texts.

Nevertheless, Bailey is quite convincing in tracing the *Rgvedic Dasa* and Dasyu to the Indo-Iranian base *das/daha*. In ancient Iranian *daha* means *'man', and dahyu* 'land' or 'country'. *Daha* as the ethnic name of a people is mentioned in an inscription of Xerxes, and Bailey cites several examples of words meaning 'man' or 'hero' giving rise to ethnic names. The term *dahyu*, which must have designated the habitat of the *Daha*, became "Dasyu" in the *Rgveda* and referred to the hostile Iranians who were regarded as barbarians and outsiders.[84] This suggests that the *Dasas* and *Dasyus* represented an earlier wave of the *Aryans*.[85] It is held that the term *anas*, applied to the *Dasyus* in *Rgveda* V.29.10, does not mean 'noseless' or 'flat-nosed' as interpreted by earlier scholars, but 'without a mouth', implying merely that these people spoke an alien language (not necessarily non-Aryan), and were therefore described as such contemptuously.[86] Even the epithet *mrdhravacah* applied to Dasyus[87] may not indicate their non-Aryan character, for it is applied to *Purus*,[88] too, and evidently means 'speakers of corrupt or evil tongue'. Nevertheless, the *Rgveda* speaks of the people of black skin (*tvacam krsnam*) twice[89] and at least in one of the succeeding verses it clearly shows that the Dasyus are meant as above. At another place[90], Indra, the destroyer of forts (*purandara*), is said to have scattered the black-wombed (*krsnayonih*) fortresses of the *Dasas*, and it is possible to see in it reference to the dark skin of the *Dasas*. It is suggested [91] that the *Dasas* and Dasyus were a pre-Rgvedic group of Indo-Aryan speakers and had come in contact with the people of the Harappa culture. There had been a racial and cultural fusion which explains the dark-skin colour of the *Dasas*. According to another view, at least some of the Dasyus were Austro-Asiatics.[92] A strong ethnic contrast between the Arya and the Dasa-Dasyu people is indicated by *Rgveda*, V.30.9, which informs us that 'the *Dasa* made women his weapons' (*striyo hi dasa ayudhani cakre*). Consequently, Indra remarks, "what can his feeble (*abala*) army (*senah*) do to me", and we are told that "having discovered the two female breasts of this one, (Indra) advanced to fight the Dasyu". The verse reflects the contempt of the patriarchal Aryans towards the *Dasas* and *Dasyus* whose armies contained women-warriors. This is further confirmed by another verse in which Indra asserts that without a fight he will divide the riches of his adversary, who has come with women (*stribhih*) to fight here.[93] Apparently among the *Dasas* and Dasyus women took part in warfare. They may have had certain matriarchal traits. The *Rgveda* mentions[94] only one woman warrior named Vispala who lost her leg in a "battle of thousand combats" (*sahasramilha*), elsewhere called Khela's battle.[95] The twin gods Asvins gave her a metal leg at the prayer of Agastya, enabling her to move about again. The event was important enough to be celebrated in a number of hymns.[96] Do we have here a myth of the *Dasa* origins foisted upon the Asvins? It appears significant that the myth is mentioned only in the first and the tenth *mandalas*.

However, whatever be the ethnic identity of the *Dasas* and the *Dasyus*, differences between them and the Rgvedic Aryans are clearly ethnic at least in the initial stages and not a matter of social hierarchy differentiating between the possessors and the non-possessors.[97] Prayers for the killing of the Arya as well as *Dasa* enemies and references to the fort of *Dasas*[98] indicate that the Arya and *Dasa* were two distinct ethnic groups and not parts of one civil stratified society.[99] It is only towards the end of the Rgvedic period that the *Dasa* is completely subjugated, enslaved and assimilated and the term begins to mean a slave.[100]

III

Clear evidence of a threefold social differentiation comes from Book VIII of the *Rgveda* where a prayer is offered to the Asvins to "promote (*jinvatam*) our *brahma* (prayer) and animate our thoughts, kill the demons (*raksamsi*) and drive away disease .... promote our *ksatra* (ruling power), promote our heroes (*nrrn*), kill the demons and drive away disease .... promote our milch-kine (*dhenurjinvatam*), promote our *visah*, kill the demons and drive away disease".[101] Here one can see a tripartite functional division mentioned presumably in a hierarchical order. The term *varna* is not used in this context. The *Rgveda* knows of only two *varnas*, the Arya and the *Dasa*; and Kane is right in holding that the word *varna* means 'colour' or 'light' in most passages of the *Rgveda*, and "both the Aryas and *Dasas* were designated *varnas* on account of the colour of their skins".[102] At one place[103] *Dasa* is opposed to *Varnam*, which is used to signify the Aryans apparently in allusion to their good colour or complexion.[104] However, at another place *varna* is qualified by *daasam* and Indra is praised for having placed the *Dasa Varna* in a low hiding place (*adharam guhakah*)[105]

Dumezil[106] and Benvensite[107] have argued that priests, warriors and commoners formed three distinct social groups among the Indo-Iranian and early Vedic people and the tripartite social order was a characteristic of the Indo-Europeans. However, as G.S. Kirk remarks, although the division itself is "hardly surprising", the most prominent Indo-European culture, the Greek, "is an embarrassing exception to the tripartite division of functions. The division simply does not occur at least in any form specific enough to be significant in Greek culture and mythology...".[108] On the other hand, John Brough has shown that such a threefold division may be seen in Semitic societies portrayed in Old Testament.[109] Bruce Lincoln argues[110] that the third functional category is too general to be regarded as a specialized vocation and is tantamount to "commoners"; and as far as the distinction between the priestly and warrior classes is concerned, it is found among the pastoral Nilotic tribes of East Africa too, with priests enjoying a hierarchical superiority over the warriors. He asserts that the separation of priestly and warrior groups has its roots in the ecology of the religion of cattle-keepers and goes on to build a paradigm of binary oppositions in the organization of Indo-Aryan society.[111]

However, building paradigms on inadequate and misunderstood data is a risky affair. Lincoln builds his theory on the ground that the separation of priestly and warrior groups among the ancient Indo-Iranians may be seen in its projection on the divine level in the dichotomy between what he terms as the "sovereign gods", "the *asuras*" (Skt*asura*=Av.ahura-) and "warrior-gods", the *daivas* (Skt *deva*=Av.*daeva*-Old Persian *daiva*). Among the celestial sovereigns described as *asuras* were the sky-god Dyaus, the dual deity Mitra-Varuna, the Adityas and the demiurge Tvastr. Among the warrior gods (*devas*), the most important was Indra. Others were Vayu, the personification of wind, the Maruts and the Rudras. However, recent researches[112] have convincingly shown the fallacy of building theories on the so-called dichotomy of *devas* and *asuras* in Indo-Iranian times and it is pointed out that Indra, regarded as a *deva* by Lincoln, being the warrior-god par excellence, is designated as *asura* no less than four times;[113] and at least in nine hymns of the *Rgveda* he is described as having the qualities of an *asura*[114]. This does not compare unfavourably with Varuna who is ranked as the chief 'celestial sovereign', an *asura* by Lincoln. He is called an *asura* not more than five times,[115] and the derivatives *asuryam* and *asura* are applied to him in two verses.[116] In some hymns the dual divinity Mitra-Varuna is called *asura* or attributed the quality of asuraship.[117] But so is the case with Rudra[118] and the Maruts,[119] who in the opinion of Lincoln are projections of the earthly warrior bands at the divine level.[120] Expressions such as *devanam asura*,[121] of the gods, and *mahad-devanamasuratvamekam*,[122] "great is the unique asuraship of the gods", would be difficult to explain if *devas* and *asuras* represented two mutually exclusive groups of deities belonging to different cycles of myth-making. In fact, in a Rgvedic hymn Rudra is called both *deva* and *asura* at the same time.[123] Hale is right in asserting that initially the term *asura* meant simply a 'lord',[124] human or divine, and as such was applied to the human adversaries of Indra too, such as Varcin,[125] Pipru[126] and Vrkadvara[127]. Some of these are also identified as *Dasas*.[128] But later when the historical nature of Indra's conflict with these human *asuras* was forgotten and it was attributed a mythological meaning, the term *asura* acquired a pejorative sense and began to signify a demon. Popular etymology took it to be a negative word and even invented its positive counterpart *sura*, meaning god.[129] Hale thinks that the semantic changes in the words *deva/daiva* and *asura/ahura* in India and Iran were independent of each other. The suggestion deserves further scrutiny. There appears to have been some infiltration of old Iranian ideas in later Vedic times.[130] But Hale has established quite convincingly that the *asura/deva* dichotomy cannot be traced back to Rgvedic times.

Researches of Benveniste show that although both the ancient Iranian as well as the Homeric languages draw upon Indo-European lexical roots to form words designating family, clan, tribe, etc., they are not identical and show independent development.[131] It follows that each Indo-European language group came to evolve social institutions in its own specific manner and drew upon Indo-European roots to formulate words designating them, but there could be no uniformity in this respect. The hypothesis of an Indo-European heritage would not be adequate to explain the existence or non-existence of characteristic social groupings or units of social organization. The *Rgveda* does indicate the existence of a functional grouping of priests and warriors and the evolution of an embryonic priesthood into a full-fledged specialized class of priests but, as Benveniste remarks, this grouping was not of a "political" nature or genealogically determined. Social organization proper rested on a different type of classification, that of family, clan, tribe and country in the manner of concentric circles. The problem of social stratification, on the other hand, is linked with the emergence of a specialized priestly class among the Vedic people.

There is evidence to show that although the ritual of *yajna* goes back to Indo-European times, the function of priesthood was not confined to any particular person, family or lineage. In several hymns men in general are said to be offering oblations and performing the sacrifice.[132] At one place the Five Tribes or *panca janah* are credited with bringing sacrifice to Agni.[133] It is interesting that the plural of the words 'Bharata' and 'Kuru' are given as synonyms of the term *rtvij* in the *Nighantu,*[134] and *rtvij* in Vedic Sanskrit meant "sacrificing at the proper season or regularly."[135] It seems to have been the earliest term used for a priest who officiated at a sacrifice. It has its cognate *rathwi* in the *Avesta* and may have Indo-European roots. The mention of the Bharatas and the Kurus as synonyms of *rtvij* in the traditional list of words culled from the Samhitas is rightly taken to indicate that at one time any member of these tribes could perform priestly functions.[136] Some of the Srautasutras mention a variety of the Dvadasaha sacrifice as Bharata Dvadasaha. Apparently the sacrifice was named after the Bharata *jana* or its eponymous founder. We are informed that the *Davdasaha* can be an *ahina* as well as a *sattra*, the difference between the two types of sacrifice lies in the fact that a *sattra* can be performed not only by the brahmana but any of the three upper *varnas* can perform an *ahina*.[137] However, both involve group participation. In our opinion this distinction is of later origin created with the crystallization of the *varna* system to explain away the earlier practice which may have continued among the Bharatas. In the *Mahabharata* and the Puranas, the Bharatas and the Kurus appear as ksatriya clans, but traces of the earlier custom survive in the story of Devapi and Santanu. The *Rgveda* speaks of Devapi as the *hotr*[138] of Santanu and the *purohita* (chief priest) who invoked the gods to release the rains. Yaska[139] tells us that Devapi was the elder brother of Santanu and had gone to the forest to practise austerities when his younger brother, taking advantage of his absence, usurped the throne. This transgression annoyed the gods who withheld the rains. Santanu then requested Devapi to accept the kingdom, but the latter refused and propitiated the gods on behalf of his younger brother acting as his priest. The story is repeated[140] in the *Brhaddevata*, the *Mahabharata* and several Puranas, which invent various devices to account for the unusual practice of a Kuru 'prince' acting as the priest of his brother, but the contrived efforts of the later sources to explain away Devapi's role as the priest of his brother indicates that the legend had a real basis and had to be explained away in the changed conditions when the priesthood had become the exclusive function of a hereditary class.

The case of Devapi and Santanu is not the only instance of its kind. The *Rgveda* records another case, which has somehow escaped the attention of scholars. Thus *Devasravas* and Devavata, who are regarded as composers of the twentythird hymn of the III *mandala* and are described as Bharatas, that is, belonging to the Bharata *jana* in the hymn, are said to have been brothers. As the name of Devasravas is given precedence[141] over Devavata, it may be presumed that Devasravas was the older one. The next verse urges Devasravas to praise Agni Daivavata, that is, the sacrificial fire of Devavata, which is called "the lord of the people", *jananamasad vasi*. In our opinion, the sacrificial fire of the tribe was generally identified by the name of the tribal chief and hence in this case we find that Devavata, the younger brother, was acting as the tribal chief while his elder brother officiated as his priest. *Agnim daivavatam* of the verse cited here may be compared with the expression *daivadaso agnih*,[142] fire of Divodasa, occurring elsewhere. At another place the fire of Divodasa is called *satpati*, the lord of his band.[143] It is significant that Divodasa, too, was a chief of the Bharatas. At several places Agni is called Bharata after the name of the eponymous founder chief of the Bharatas.[144] The sacrifical fire of Trasadasyu of the Puru line, too, is identified by his name as *trasadasyavam.*[145] Thus, it was customary to describe the sacrifical fire of the clan by the name of the chief and Devavata was the clan chief. This hymn speaks of him as kindling the sacrificial fire assisted by his elder brother Devasravas, who acted as his priest.

Although traditionally both Devasravas and Devavata mentioned in the hymn cited above, are regarded as brothers and composers of the hymn, only the name of Devasravas appears in the list of the Pravara *rsis* of the family of the Visvamitras given in the *Baudhayana Srautasutra.*[146] On the other hand, the *Rgveda* speaks of Srnjaya, the son of Devavata, too, as a warrior chief. He is described as kindling the fire, which in ancient times was kindled by Devavata.[147] Srnjaya, the son of Devavata, defeated the Vrcivants.[148] These references indicate that at least in some cases the succession to chiefship was hereditary. The trend crystallized by the later Vedic times and in later Vedic texts[149] the Srnjayas and the Kurus are mentioned together as Ksatriya lineages. But the earlier unity of kinship of the chief and the priest is reflected in the hymn which describes the descendants of Visvamitra, the famous priest of the Bharatas, as *bharatasya putrah*, sons of the eponymous Bharata.[150] Another Vedic seer Parucchepa, author of a number of hymns of the first *mandala*, describes himself as the clansman of Divodasa,[151] the chief of the Bharatas. Thus it seems that at least among the Bharatas the priest and the chief initially belonged to the same clan. In our opinion this lies at the root of the Puranic myth that Visvamitra was born a ksatriya prince but became a brahmana sage by practising severe austerities.

It may be argued that although at some remote period participation in the *yajna* ritual may have been an egalitarian communal activity, as is suggested by *sattra/ahina* sacrifices, the examples of Devapi-Santanu and Devasravas-Devavata suggest that the office of the priest and the chief inhered in certain privileged families,[152] which may have enjoyed higher status, as is the case with many tribal societies. Indeed the *Rgveda* applies epithet *sujata* meaning 'well-born' four times to men who are variously called *suris*,[153] *naras*[154] and *viras*[155] and are described as sitting together and tending sacrifical fire. However, in our view the term *sujata* in these passages should not be interpreted in the sense of 'high born' or 'noble lineage',[156] as is done by Griffith, but in a physical sense meaning 'well-built', 'beautiful', 'well-grown', 'tall', etc. Thus, it is said for the son of Pururavas and Urvasi that "from the waters be born a strong, young (*sujata*) hero (*naryuh*).[157] Agni is called *sujata* a number of times,[158] and at one place he is expressly described as 'well-born' (*tanva sujata*).[159] At another place the 'pure ones' (*sucayah*), apparently the Maruts, are said to have made their bodies well-developed (*tanvah sujatah*) by worshipping Agni, thus exchanging their perishable bodies for the immortal ones.[160] Apart from Agni and the Maruts, several other gods, too, such as Mitra.[161] Varuna,[162], Aryaman,[163] Bhaga[164] and Indra[165] are called *sujata* and so are the goddesses Aditi,[166] Rodasi[167] and Usa[168]. But there is no doubt that the poets had in mind the well-formed physical appearance of these deities and not their 'noble ancestry'.

Reference to *ksatra* and *ksatriya* in the *Rgvedic* hymns have often led to the conceptualization of a 'warrior aristocracy' or 'nobility' going back to proto-Indo-European times.[169] Nevertheless, it is rightly held,[170] that is, this text *ksatra* stands for 'valour' and 'ksatriya' for 'ruler' or authority, human or divine.[171] It is almost synonymous with *rajan,* but emphasizes the fighting qualities of the individual, who was no mere warrior but a person of high rank fighting along with the other members of his clan. Ordinary fighters are designated as *balam*, that is, force. There is hardly any evidence of 'ksatriya' being used to denote a compact group, class or caste in the *Rgveda*. It is significant that when the *varna/caste* structure emerges it is initially 'rajanya', which emphasizes kinship links with the *rajan* and not 'ksatriya', which is used to denote the second *varna*. Replacement of *rajanya* with 'ksatriya' in the *varna* scheme is symptomatic of a horizontal and perhaps also vertical widening of the exploitative social order both in terms of space and people and is beyond the purview of the present study.

It is held that the Rgvedic *rajan* was a tribal chief whose functions were largely confined to providing protection to his clan and its cattle and leadership in wars and cattle raids.[172] He also distributed[173] the booty or spoils of cattle raids, apparently retaining a larger share for himself. That there were persons who possessed more wealth than others is indicated by the term *maghavan. Suri* was another term of distinction and is often interpreted in the sense of 'chief' . However, Potdar points out[174] that in the prayers when long life is expected the term *suri* is used, but when food or wealth is prayed for *maghavan* is used. Both figure as the patrons of priests. In several verses the term *asura*, closely approximates to the Rgvedic *rajan*. Asuraship and *ksatra* are attained simultaneously in some cases,[175] and in one hymn the *asura* of the people is also described as the "distributor".[176] *Asura* has his own *viras (asuraya virah)*.[177] Hale's conclusions are worth noting. In his view in the earlier portions of the *Rgveda* one was an *asura* not by birth or by one's nature but one became as *asura* "by the consent and support of those who followed him". He was a chief or "lord" with some kind of military force at his command.[178]

Whereas the words *asura*, *maghavan*, *suri* and *rajan* are terms indicating high rank, warriors in general are referred to as *naras* or *viras/suviras*, which mean powerful men or heroes.[179] Apparently war was mainly the concern of young men of the patriarchal Aryan tribes. Lincoln draws[180] attention to two interesting terms signifying warrior bands, *marya* and *vrka*[181], which have their correspondence in the ancient Iranian *yasnas*. Literally, the former meant 'young men' and the latter 'wolf'. This was particularly significant in the context of the cattle-raids, since the warrior had to be a ruthless predator. The warrior band had its own characteristic emblems such as the mace (*vajra*) and the banner (*dhvaja or drapsa*).[182] Lincoln even suggests that the warrior had to go through some form of initiation. Nonetheless, he admits that it is not clear whether these bands were organized as "age-sets, secret societies, or along wholly different lines", although the fact that the Maruts are all of the same age would point to an age-set organization. The emphasis on youth would tend to make their recruitment open and not confined to certain so-called *rajanya* lineages, especially as demographically it was still a small-scale society praying for ever for the increase of its manpower.

The overall impression created by the Rgvedic data is that ranks were not closed and anyone could aspire to become a priest or a warrior chief. In an often quoted verse the poet says: "A bard am I, my dad (*tatah*) is a leech, mommy (*nana*) lays corn upon the stones. Striving for wealth, with varied plans, we follow our desires like kine".[183] In an earlier *mandala* a poet addresses Indra: "Would you make me a protector (*gopa*) of the people (*janasya*), their ruler (*rajanam*), O conquering Maghavan? Or would you make me a *rsi* having drunk the soma juice? or would you give me everlasting wealth"?[184] Such general statements may not tell us much about the organizational structure of the Rgvedic tribes, but the lack of rigid demarcation between social echelons suggests that although the social organization had progressed beyond a purely egalitarian stage, it was by no means stratified. Ranks were still largely a matter of achievement rather than inheritance.

IV

The question arises: What was the process which led to a precise defining and institutionalization of statuses, their crystallization into *varna* categories? D.D. Kosambi was of the view that the Brahmana *varna* with its gotra organization developed as "a result of interaction between the Aryan priesthood and the ritually superior priesthood of the Indus culture".[185] The survivors of the Harappa culture were absorbed at various levels in the composite Aryan society, which evolved a fourfold *varna* structure as a consequence. Most crucial was the assimilation of the Harappan priesthood. Small groups of pre-Aryan priests joined the conquering Aryan patriarchal clan-groups offering them their priestly services. This resulted in these priestly groups adopting the same clan name as that of their patrons, which in fact explains the survival of the Vedic clan names (for examples, Vikarna, Matsya, Kutsa, Vitahavya, etc.) among the Brahmanical *gotras* listed in the Srautasutras and the *Matsya Purana*. The recombined priesthood transformed the original Vedic priesthood accelerating its separation from the ksatriya elite, a structural development which was parallel to the emergence of the *Dasa/Sudra* caste and led to endogamy.[186] Individual property had not developed sufficiently among the nomadic pastoral Aryans. The subjugated Harappan agrarian population identified as *Dasas* by Kosambi, therefore, belonged to the conquering tribes as a whole while forming a separate group by themselves. This was the origin of a *Dasa/Sudra varna* and an endogamous caste system.

Kosambi's thesis is brilliant and persuasive and although some of his arguments appear far-fetched, unlike Ghurye he tries to provide a rational explanation of the origin of the Brahmanical *gotras*. Thapar acknowledges[187] her indebtedness to Kosambi in drawing up her model of a 'lineage society' in which the Brahmana and the sudra are treated as addenda; but she ignores the most important aspect of his thesis, which explains the internal stratification of the Aryan tribes as an outcome of the formation of a *Dasas/Sudras varna*, the 'surplus producing labour', and the assimilation of the Aryan and the pre-Aryan priesthood resulting in the separation of the Brahmana and the Ksatriya, a social pattern reflected in the hymns of the *Yajurveda* of the later Vedic phase and not in the *Rgveda* (with the exception of the *Purusasukta*).

One need not deny the possibility of survival of some Harappan elements and their assimilation in the expanding Aryan society, but Kosambi's assumption that the "priest class of the Aryan conquerors was largely recruited from the conquered"[188] appears to be highly exaggerated. Some of the Vedic sages such as Kavasa, Ailusa and Dirghatamas are said to have been *dasiputras*, sons of *Dasa* women, but the identification of the *Dasas* with the people of the Harappa culture remains problematic, and Kosambi's view that of the seven sages regarded as the primary founders of the brahmanical *gotra-lineage*, namely, Visvamitra, Jamadagni, Bharadvaja, Gautama, Arti, Vasistha and Kasyapa,[189] Visvamitra was "the one real indubitable Aryan", and the rest were non-Aryan—is highly speculative. One does not know why Bhrgu, the father of Jamadagni, is given a secondary position in the *gotra* lists, but so is the case with Kusika, the father of Visvamitra. However, it seems that Kosambi's only reason[190] for regarding the Bhrgu-Jamadagnis as non-Aryan is that in the battle of 'ten-kings' the Bhrgus appear as the enemies of Sudas, the leader of the Trtsus, whom Indra, "the friend of the Aryan", helps.[191] But hostility of Indra is not a sure indication of a non-Aryan identity, for at several places Indra is praised for having killed the Aryan enemies.[192] Of course, Kosambi is right in regarding the Bhrgus as 'a complete tribe' in the *Rgveda* with a full range of activities including warfare, chariot manufacture and pottery, expertise in the last-mentioned profession accounting for the word *Bhargava*, meaning a potter both in Sanskrit and Pali. It is apparent that because of this multi-dimensionality of the Bhrgus, Macdonell and Keith could not decide whether they are to be regarded as priests or warriors.[193]

Traditionally, the Angirases are closely associated with the Bhrgus. Two of the primary *gotrakaras*, Bharadvaja and Gautama, figure as Angirases in the *gotra* lists, and Vamadeva, who is attributed the authorship of the IV *mandala*, speaks of Gotama as his father. In several hymns, Angirases are described mystically as *virupas* (having various forms and sons of god (*devaputra divas putraso*).[194] But in one hymn[195] they appear as the patrons of Visvamitra and are said to have prolonged their life by giving him rich gifts at the thousand-fold *soma* pressings, that is, the horse sacrifice. The following verses[196] make it clear that it was the horse sacrifice of Sudas, the chief of the Bharatas, at which the Kusikas officiated. Visvamitra offered prayer to Indra for the protection of the Bharata *jana*. Thus, at least in this hymn the Angirases are closely allied to the Bharatas, if not identified with them, and they are mentioned as patrons bestowing riches on Visvamitra and not as officiating priests. There is hardly anything indicative of their non-Aryan origin.

Kosambi regards the myth of the miraculous birth of Vasistha mentioned[197] in the VII *mandala* as a sure sign of his adoption into an Aryan lineage and he argues that the fact that Vasistha was adopted, not in the Kusika *gotra*,"the gens of the original tribal priest Visvamitra", but into the Trtsu-Bharata tribe as the Rgvedic version shows that "Brahmanism was foreign to the original Aryan system", for Visvamitra, though a priest, was not the first brahmana. He is regarded as a ksatriya who attained Brahmanhood by practising severe austerities according to later legends, which speak of his rivalry with Vasistha. It is Vasistha who is called the first Brahmana.[198] Here Kosambi seems to imply that the very idea of a separate Brahmana *varna* was borrowed from the Harappa culture. This goes against his own view that the beginnings of the *varna/caste* organization are to be traced to changes in the relations of production and formation of a servile class of *Dasa/Sudra varna*. "Dasa" in fact became a servile category after the defeat of the *Dasas* at the hands of the Rgvedic Aryans. It was not a continuation of their pre-existing position in an earlier network of production relations. The *Rgveda* knows of several *Dasa* chiefs whose wealth was coveted by the Aryans. Besides, even if it is granted that Vasistha was a pre-Aryan priest patronized by the Bharatas, it would not explain the puzzling feature of endogamy which Kosambi tries to do with this hypothesis; for the Visvamitras and the Vasisthas, the so-called Aryan and pre-Aryan priests of Kosambi's thesis, assimilate to form one endogamous caste unit having exogamous *gotras* or clans within it. In the *gotra* system of the Brahmanas the Visvamitras occupy a considerably large space and endogamy does not mark them off from the Vasisthas; they together form one single whole constituting one *varna* separated from other occupational groups, which crystallize into distinct *varnas* and endogamous units. It is possible to argue that the description of Vasistha as the 'first Brahmana' is in the sense of his being the foremost one, or alternatively it is an allusion to his having been the first of the brahmana priest later designated as *Brahmanacchamsin* and mentioned simply as the 'brahmana' in *Rgveda* I.15.5, since he was allotted the special cup called brahmana for drinking *soma*.[199] The assimilation and accommodation of aboriginal priests within the framework of the Brahmana *varna* is a process which has taken place throughout the period of expansion of the caste system, but the emergence of endogamous subcaste within the brahmana *varna* is a post-Vedic phenomenon and presumably early medieval. Ethnic repulsion or isolation does not explain the emergence of an endogamous brahmana *varna* in the Vedic period. If there was assimilation of the Aryan and the pre-Aryan at the level of priesthood, there are stronger grounds to hold that there was assimilation at the levels of ruling lineages, the vis and the *Sudras* too; but this would not explain the origin of the *varna* system and endogamy. In our opinion endogamy should not explain the origin of the *varna* system. In our opinion endogamy should be seen as an extreme manifestation of class and gender exploitation which go together in the caste system. The system has adopted certain primitive religio-social notions of commensality and connubium to serve its own end.[200]

Identifying specific items of the socio-cultural milieu of Vedic and post-Vedic times as survivals of the Harappa culture is a hazardous exercise. It is worthwhile to keep in mind the remark of Stuart Piggott, "the observational data of prehistory seem to me in almost every way to be more ambiguous and more capable of varied interpretations than the normal run of material available to historians".[201] Theories regarding the socio-political organization of the Harappans often use the same artifacts to arrive at contradictory conclusions.[202] As for their religion, Kosambi did not have the advantage of the excavation reports of Kalibangan (Rajasthan) and Lothal (Gujarat), which have brought to light the existence of fire-altars and a fire-ritual in the Harappan cultural milieu. But it is pertinent that none of the north-western sites of the Harappa culture such as Mohenjo-daro, Harappa or Chanhu-daro provide any indication of a fire-cult. The regional divergence may be explained in terms of some intrusive Indo-Iranian or Aryan elements meeting the Harappan people, which resulted in a cultural synthesis, but it is not sufficient to warrant the supposition that the Harappan priests took charge of the Aryan fire-ritual and played a key role in the social and religious reorganization of the Rgvedic Aryans. Marshall's hypothesis[203] that the Harappans worshipped the female-principle-Sakti, in the form of a mother-goddess, as well as the male-principle, the prototype of God Siva, in both their anthropomorphic as well as aniconic forms, has been widely accepted without any critical evaluation, and elaborate theories have been built on the assumption that the Harappan religion was a direct progenitor of Hinduism. Thus Wheeler,[204] while implicitly accepting Marshall's interpretation of the data, hypothesized that the cult of the mother-goddess was observed by the lower classes and the higher classes worshipped the male-deity, the 'proto-Siva' represented on the seals. It is interesting that the case for the 'proto-Siva' identification rests mainly on the interpretation of a single seal found at Mohenjo-daro by Marshall. Two other seals discovered by Mackey[205] and regarded by him as similar to the 'proto-Siva' seal show important variations. The figure on the Mohenjo-daro seal wears a buffalo-horn headdress, numerous bracelets and, according to Marshall, it has three faces and is ithyphallic; but these features are absent on the other two seals. Referring to the views of various archaeologists and historians, Ghurye shows that there is no unanimity of opinion about the last mentioned two features even with regard to the Mohenjo-daro seal; and he concludes[206] that not only the "so-called ithyphallism of the figure is almost a fiction or an act of imagination", but the ascription of three faces to the figure, too, is quite unwarranted. He also draws attention to the fact that whereas the historic Siva is closely connected with the bull, this animal is conspicuously absent among the animals surrounding the deity on the seal. Thus Ghurye is quite justified in rejecting the thesis of the Harappan origin of the Siva-cult.

Writing more than a decade earlier, H.P. Sullivan,[207] too, has questioned Marshall's identification and assumptions regarding the religion of the Harappa people. He is quite emphatic that the figure on the Mohenjo-daro seal is neither ithyphallic nor three-headed; it is in fact a female deity, the same great Goddess of vegetation and fertility who manifested herself in the sacred tree and is shown wearing a three-pointed headdress. He points out that Marshall himself had admitted that what appeared to him to be an erect phallus could be in reality the end of the waistband. In Sullivan's view waistband and girdles are found only on the female figurines and arm bangles and necklaces adorn lavishly on the female figures in Harappan art. According to him, the coif and the pigtail worn by the two other so-called 'proto-Siva' figures resemble those worn by the female figurines and there is hardly any evidence of the worship of a male deity in the Harappa culture. The identification of the numerous conical stones found at the Indus site as phallus or *linga* is also doubtful and it has been rightly held that even if 'phallus worship' is assumed to have been a part of the Harappan religion it would not prove the prevalence of Siva-worship, for Siva's connection with the *linga* symbol is post-Vedic and perhaps later than the second century B.C.

Thus, the arguments of Sullivan and Ghurye sufficiently demonstrate the fallacy of making broad generalizations in the sphere of religious belief and practices on the basis of a few material artifacts of doubtful import. Those who trace the epic-Puranic cults of Siva and Sakti as well as the caste system to Harappa culture ignore the fact that the cults of both these deities appear to have been originally hostile to brahmanism and the *varna* system. Both Siva and the mother goddess Durga-Sakti make a late entry into the brahmanical pantheon. The story of Siva's destruction of the *yajna* sacrifice of Daksa-Prajapati and his non-inclusion among the gods who receive a share of *yajna* offering clearly establish his anti-brahmanical antecedents. Similarly the worship of the mother goddesses in Indian villages retains traces of its earlier tradition when it was free from the Brahmanical *varna* bias. Thus, it is difficult to maintain that the roots of these anti-Brahmanical cults as well as of the *varna* system go back to the Indus civilization, which was manipulated by the brahmana priests through religion and ritual. Instead of begging the questions in this manner by postulating hypothetical survivals from the Harappa culture, it would be more useful to look for explanations in the internal dynamics of the Rgvedic society.[208]

V

The development of a powerful priesthood and the formation of Brahmana *varna* cannot be explained simply as a case of ethnic predisposition; greater availability of surplus and enforced leisure are necessary conditions for the proliferation of rituals and the growth of a class of specialists who first establish their control over the great fertility rites and then assume the role of intermediaries between clans and ancestors and deities. The process may be seen in the *Rgveda*. It is generally held that the earliest terms to denote a priestly functionary are *rtvij* and *hotr*, both having their cognates in the *Avesta* as Rathwi and Zaotar. The former term is connected with seasonal sacrifices offered at regular intervals and we have already shown that initially the function of the *rtvij* was not confined to any priestly lineage. These sacrifices were performed perhaps collectively by the tribesmen in general; hence the Bharata tribe as a whole could be known as *rtvij*.[209] Later, *rtvij* became the general designation of a priest officiating at a sacrifice.[210] A similar development may be seen in the case of the *hotr*. It derives from an Indo-Eurpoean root *hu* meaning 'to pour'. Thus the original function of the *hotr* was to pour libations in the fire.[211] It also denoted one who invoked the gods by reciting the hymns and is regarded by some as the earliest priest.[212] In ancient Iran, Zaotar was the designation of a class of priests.[213] However, originally *hotr* does not seem to have belonged to a distinct priestly class but was identical with *yajamana*,[214] the sacrificer, and this position he retains in the *paka yajnas* of the *grhya* ritual. Later, with the growth of a more complicated sacrifical ritual, *hotr* becomes one of the four *rtvijs* having three priest assistants or helpers.[215] In some hymns of the *Rgveda*, the *hota* and the *yajamana* are clearly distinguished[216] and at two places he is one of the seven priests named along with *Brahman*.[217]

It is interesting that priestly specialization is related not to the monopoly of or greater expertise in worshipping certain deities or to officiating for certain specific clans or people but to certain ritual matters such as the use of specific vessels[218] for offering the *soma* drink to various divinities. This seems to suggest that elaboration of ritual, rather than assimilation of different ethnic groups, resulted in the development of a class of specialists which later crystallized as the Brahmana *varna*. The earlier terms used for the priests such as *stotr, jaritr, vipra, kavi, rsi* and *Brahman* in the masculine are connected with the function of composing or singing of the hymns or prayers. The term 'Brahmana' is of rare occurrence in the *Rgveda* and with the exception of the *Purusasukta* hymn it does not seem to have been used anywhere else to denote a member of the priestly class.[219] At least at two places it means the cup allotted to the *Brahman* priest for drinking *soma*. At several other places it is used as an adjective.[220] Similar is the case of *vipra*, a term which later came to mean exclusively a member of the Brahmana *varna* but is often used as an adjective[221] in the *Rgveda* signifying a state of exhilarated ecstasy or inspired eloquence. At one place the term seems to stand for Brhaspati[222] and at another place the *vipras* and *adhvaryus* are clearly distinguished.[223] A semantic study[224] of the four key words, *vipra, rsi, purohita* and *brahman* comes to the conclusion that a professional class of priests evolved gradually in the *Rgvedic* period "from functional notions of sacerdocy" and only towards the end of this period it became a closed order known as the brahmana *varna*.

Beginnings of this process may be seen in the hymns which clearly distinguish between the singers (*stotr*) and the bounteous patrons (*maghavans or suris*) and thank the gods for bringing food (*anadu*) to both.[225] The *vipras* create hymns[226] and are contrasted with the *naras*[227] or *viras*[228] who go to the battlefield and fight hand to hand[229] while their chief rides on a horse or, as is more likely, a chariot. So the occupational category of the composer-chanter-priest is well-marked. In a hymn of the VIII *mandala* the *vipras* claim to be 'kinless' (*abandhavah*)[230] and pray to God Indra who has 'numerous kin' (*bandhumantam*) to protect them. The statement appears significant and may show that the priestly functionaries were the first to renounce or transcend kinship ties in a society organized on kin-principle. Their activities were not confined to one clan or tribe and in a verse of the IX *mandala* the seven priests are described as "united in consanguineous brotherhood".[231] Another verse of the X *mandala* clearly distinguishes between the *vipra* and the *yajamana*.[232] Thus, in the latest stratum of the *Rgveda*, the priesthood may be said to have acquired the characteristics of a separate order claiming the highest position in society by virtue of its control over ritual. It is argued[233] that the term brahmana was preferred to other terms to indicate the generality of priesthood, for its etymon *Brahman* was more comprehensive and covered every type of priestly activity. Its use also emphasized the factor of heredity, so that whereas *Brahman* was one of the seven priests, Brahmana was an inherited status.

The transitional character of the Rgvedic society may be noticed also in the changing pattern of family system. In our opinion the Rgvedic family, as reflected in the earlier stratum of the text, was nuclear or 'elementary' consisting of not more than two generations; and it was closely embedded in a wider grouping of 'clan'. The authors of the *Vedic Index* express the view that the Rgvedic evidence does not show whether a son grows up to set up his own house or continued to stay with his father, his wife becoming a member of the father's household; perhaps the custom varied.[234] But allusions to a joint family system occur in the interpolated or latest stratum of the *Rgveda* and we are not wrong in advancing a rather uncommon view that the joint family system emerges only towards the close of the Rgvedic phase.

Although the Rgvedic society is clearly patrilineal, there is hardly any evidence of 'patriarchal' authority or control exercised by the father or the head of the family. The story of Sunahsepa is found in later Vedic texts. The *Rgveda* does not mention it and it seems to have been a later invention. The blinding of Rjrasva by his father mentioned in two hymns[235] is sometimes cited to prove a developed *patria potestas* but Macdonell and Keith are quite right in warning that "to lay stress on this semi-mythical incident would be unwise". On the other hand, they point out that there is nothing to show that a father controlled the marriage of his son or daughter. "... any excessive estimate of the father's powers over a son who was no longer minor and naturally under his control must be qualified by the fact that in his old age the sons might divide their father's property...."[236] In support they refer to a verse[237] addressed to God Agni: "Parting you, men have served you in many places as are the goods of an aged father (parted)". In our opinion, this verse alludes not merely to the division of an aged father's possessions among his sons, but also indirectly to their separate households.

References to individual couples (*mithuna dampati*) washing and pressing the *soma juice*, offering oblations together and tending the fire in their house (*dama*) are numerous in the *Rgveda*.[238] At one place Agni is called common to all, the protector of the vis and of *dampatis*.[239] Another hymn speaks of the equal age (*savayasa*) of their (*mithuna*) dwelling in the same place tending the sacrificial fire night and day.[240] Benveniste has shown[241] that the Indo-European roots *dem and * vis from which early Vedic *dampati* and *vispati* are derived were initially genealogical terms, which later assumed the meaning of physical habitat. Thus *dama* would mean family and *dampati* the master of the house qua family. In our view this was the smallest social unit, an elementary family.

Another crucial word having the sense of family or household is *grha*. In many Rgvedic passages it is clearly the material abode or place of residence.[242] The gods are described as going to the *grha* of the benefactor.[243] Elsewhere, Agni is said to be in every *dama* (house)[244]. However, at one place *grha*, too, appears to be a consanguineous unit.[245] The usage of *grhini* (housewife) and *grhastha* (householder) continues to this day in Hindi. The terms *grhapati* and *grhapatni* have been translated as the head and the mistress of the household. R.S. Sharma is of the view that *grha* in the *Rgveda* was the lowest social unit but it was a "large family containing members of four generations."[246] Thus *grhapati* would be the head of one such family, although elsewhere he suggests that the tribal chief could have been known by the title of *grhapati*.[247] Romila Thapar thinks that the *grhapatis* were of 'higher lineage' in the *Rgveda*, that is, of the *rajanya* lineage, "since the term is brought in when describing the nuptials of the daughter of Surya .... Agni is called the *grhapati* and the sacred household fire is *grhapatya*".[248] *Grhapatya* here is obviously a mistake for the *garhapatya* fire and not for *grhyagni*. The *garhapatya* fire was not a sacred 'household fire', but one of the three *srauta* or public fires, the other two being *ahavaniya* and *daksinagni*. It is always differentiated from *grhyagni*, the household fire, also called *vaivahika* or *smartagni*. The latter is meant for the purpose of daily offerings made twice, morning and evening. It is significant that the Grhyasutras speak of it as the nuptial (*vaivahika*) fire to be kindled on the day of marriage by the newly married couple, who are to keep it burning constantly. It may be allowed to go out if the wife is dead and the man wishes to remain a widower.[249] Thus the distinction between the *grhyagni* and the *garhapatyagni* lies not in the fact that one represents the 'popular' and the other 'elite' diety, but that the former is the fire of the individual household for the purpose of daily offerings, and the latter a communal fire meant for seasonal or occasional purposes. In the *yatsattras*, which were long sacrificial sessions ritualizing the eastward march of the Vedic Aryans, the *garhapatya* fire is to be built on the place where the yoke-pin of the chariot (*samya*) comes down.[250] It is contended[251] that the *grhya* ritual built around the domestic fire seems to be a 'substitute' or 'replacement' of the cumbersome and elaborate *srauta* ritual, as there is a basic similarity of structure and procedural framework. Nevertheless, the practice of making daily offerings into the domestic fire may go back to Rgvedic times. It was, however, quite distinct from the fire of the *grhapati* or *garhapatyagni*, which is mentioned in connection with the seasonal *soma* sacrifice in a Rgvedic hymn addressed to the personified season (*Rtu.*).[252]

The clue to the original significance of *grhapati* may be found in the *sattra* sacrifices. These are collective sacrifices to be performed by a band of sacrificers between the age of seventeen and twenty-four in company with their wives, who are given *diksa* along with their husbands. In a *sattra* sacrifice there are no priests, the *yajamanas* or the sacrificers themselves act as priests and they choose one among them as their *grhapati* to perform all the necessary sacred acts in the course of the sacrifice, others merely touching him. Nevertheless, the merit accruing out of the sacrifice is supposed to go to all of them equally.[253] A passage of the *Atharvaveda*[254] says that the *sattras* had become *utsanna*, that is, were no longer in vogue. This confirms their anarchic character. The rule that a *sattra* is to be performed by the brahmanas only was apparently formulated when the priestly function was confined to the brahmana *varna*. But the fact that the sacrificial utensils prepared for use in the course of the sacrifice were common to all sacrificers and also the stipulation of some sutras that all the participants of a *sattra* should belong to the same *gotra* indicates that originally the *sattras* must have been performed by bands of young men having common bonds of kinship. The *grhapati* was the leader or chief of one such band. The inference tallies with the description of *Agni-grhapati* found in the first hymn of the VII *mandala* in which well-formed men (*narah sujatah*) and brave heroes (*suvirah*) are described as sitting together around the fire in the dwelling place. Perhaps, the offering of the *grhamedha*[255] sacrifice to the Maruts, who are described as *grhamedhasa*,[256] the sharers of *grhamedha* in the *Rgveda* is a reference to a *sattra*. The connection of the Maruts with *grhamedha*, is significant, as they are all young and form one collectivity (*gana*) and as such are especially connected with *grha*.

The Rgvedic vocabulary is quite poor in kinship terms denoting an extended or joint family system. The wedding hymn found in the X *mandala*, in which it is wished that the bride may preside over a large joint family consisting of father-in-law, mother-in-law, sister-in-law and other kinsmen, appears to have been recast more than once by priestly hands and it has been pointed out[257] that the language of the latter part of the hymn, which contains allusions to the joint family structure, is more akin to modern Sanskrit than to the Vedic. The solitary description of a large household with father, mother, kinsmen (*jnatayah*) and a number of women sleeping in the courtyard is found in a hymn of the VII *mandala*, but Ghate quotes it as an example of later interpolation.[258] It is also found in the *Atharvaveda*. It is held[259] that the kin-based collectives are very prominent in the *Rgveda* although their precise nature is difficult to define. But unlike the *Atharvaveda*, the Rgvedic vocabulary is quite poor in kinship terms expressive of an extended family system. We may suggest that owing to the solidarity of clan as a social and functional unit it may not have been very necessary to have specific terms distinguishing the elders and the juniors of different generations and lineages. Hence, Rgvedic kinship terminology is classificatory. The term *pitr* stands for the father or ancestors as a whole and *janitr* is added to distinguish one's own father.[260] Similarly, while the terms *sunu, tanaya* and *putra* are used in the *Rgveda* to denote all descendants, the *Atharavaveda* uses them in a more restricted sense. The latter text has specific terms for grandfather (*pitamaha*), grandmother (*matamaha*), great grandfather (*prapitamaha*) and grandchild (*naptr*) which are absent in the *Rgveda*.[261] Kapadia has shown[262] that whereas in the *Rgveda* offerings are made to the collectivity of ancestors known as *pitrs*, the *Atharvaveda* lays down in a more specific manner that three ascendant ancestors of the ego constitute his *pitrs* and they are to receive offerings for the manas. A kinship terminology is a means of ordering relationships for social purposes. The Rgvedic social structure seems to have been what the sociologists call the Omaha type in which ancestral lineages of several generations constituted one single united group, the principle of the unity of lineage-generations being "a method of expressing and emphasizing the unity and the solidarity of the patrilineal lineage group".[263] In any case, there is nothing to warrant the assertion[264] that sons were treated as items of property for the labour power they provided for the family, for it is not shown that the family was the basic unit of production and the head of the family had patriarchal authority. References to *pitrvitta*[265] or 'patrimonial wealth' should not be interpreted in the sense of individual inheritance but related to the conception of *pitr* in the *Rgveda* and hence would mean the "wealth bequeathed by the ancestors".

The clan, also called 'sib' or 'gens', is the basic social unit among the people who are relatively settled but have not yet developed sufficient agriculture to support full political organization.[266] The use of the term 'clan' with reference to the Rgvedic people has been questioned recently on the ground that the case of exogamy is not proved. The objection is not very serious. In anthropological usage this term has been applied to societies which have gone beyond the "band"stage but have not developed a unilineal lineage structure.[267] In his definition of 'clan' Radcliffe-Brown remarks that the term clan "should be used only for a group having unilineal descent in which all the members regard one another in some specific sense kinsfolk. Frequently, *but-not-universally,* the recognition of the kinship bond uniting the members of the clan takes the form of a rule of exogamy which forbids marriage between the members of the same clan."[268] We have avoided the use of the term 'lineage' in the Rgvedic context as there is greater stress on genealogy and unilineal descent in lineage than in 'clan', though both models trace the descent from a real or mythical ancestor. In the Rgvedic vocabulary it is the term *vis* which seems to approximate to 'clan' and is generally interpreted as such by the Vedic scholars although some would prefer to interpret it simply as 'people' or 'settlement'. But the general trend of evolution being from a social entity to a physical, territorial entity, as is demonstrated in the case of *dama*, vis seems to have been a kin unit. In the ancient Iranian its cognate vis denotes 'clan' or a group of several families,[269] and it is quite likely that this was the case with early Vedic too. On the other hand, the term *jana* which could mean[270] both 'a person' as well as 'community', is also sometimes used in the sense of an exogamous social unit at least in the later Vedic sources. The *Latyayana Srautasutra* equates *sagotra* with *samanajana*[271] and the *janya* or *janyamitra* mentioned in connection with the consecration ceremony is taken to stand for a person allied by marriage.[272] The wife is called *jani* in the *Rgveda*.[273]

The case for exogamy among the Indo-Aryans has been argued by a number of scholars[274] including Benveniste,[275] who remarks that the term *ari* has a rather ambivalent meaning in the *Rgveda*; it is used in the sense of a 'friend' or 'ally' in one context and 'enemy' or 'stranger' in another. This suggests that *ari* formed a moiety in an exogamous society and hence its relationship was sometimes one of friendship and sometimes that of rivalry. 'Arya' was the common reciprocal term used by the members of moieties constituting one community to designate each other and "*Aarya*", which meant the descendant of '*ari*' or '*arya*' came to signify all those tribes which belonged to the same cultural complex, recognized the same ancestors and worshipped the same gods. Benveniste holds that the God Aryaman is the God of marriage and hospitality in the *Rgveda* and his function is to admit individuals into an exogamous community through marriage. "Aryaman intervenes when a woman taken from outside the clan is introduced for the first time as a wife into her new family." In support of his thesis, Benvensite cites a verse[276] of the *Rgveda* in which Indra's daughter-in-law states that all the *aris* have arrived but her father-in-law, Indra, is yet to come, meaning thereby that Indra was to her an *ari*, member of an exogamous clan. The meaning of the term *arillarya* continues to rouse controversy, and although some attribute to it the meaning of 'owner or possessor of wealth'. Paul Thieme's interpretation of the term as 'foreigner' or 'stranger' has given rise to a suggestion[277] that the *Arya/Dasa* dichotomy should be seen as that between the 'invader' and the 'dweller' or 'native'. Whatever the case may be, we have already shown that the contrast between Arya and *Dasa* at least in the initial stages is of an ethnic nature, the latter term acquiring a pejorative connotation due to this conflict. It could have been only with the complete subjugation of the *Dasas* that the term acquired the generic significance of 'slave' or servant and may have included such aborigines as Ibhyas, who are said to receive the reward of their labour once the charioteer is back and settled at home presumably after a hunting expedition.[278]

To conclude, the Rgvedic society was a simple society in which the ranking of individuals depended more upon personal qualities and skills than upon inherited wealth or status by birth.

Notes

1. G.S. Ghurye, *Vedic India* (Bombay, 1979); R.S. Sharma, *Material Culture and Social Formations in Ancient India* (henceforth MCSF) (Delhi, 1983); Romila Thapar, *From Lineage to State* (henceforth FLS) (Bombay,1984). Copious literature exists on the Vedas. For bibliographies, see Louis Renou, Bibliographie Vedique (Paris, 1931) and R.N. Dandekar, Vedic Bibliography, 4 vols (Poona, 1946, 1961, 1973, 1985).
2. *Priests, Warriors and Cattle: A Study in the Ecology of Religions,*

(Berkeley, 1981).
3. Ghurye, op.cit,p.1.
4. Ibid., pp.368-69.
5. Ibid., pp.173,323,324,passim.
6. The only exception is that of Kalibangan (KLB-I), which shows, according to Ghurye, "low scale of urbanization in what was or what was very shortly to be Rgvedic Aryandom" (Ibid.,p.379). He thinks that KLB-I represents a culture different from KLB-II, which was an extension of the Harappa Culture.
7. Ibid., p.318,Also see p. 284, passim.
8. Ibid., p.311.
9. Ibid., p.260.
10. A.A. Macdonell and A.B. Keith, *Vedic Index of Names of Subjects* (hereafter Vedic Index), 2. vols (London, 19:2; reprint, Delhi, 1982).
11. J.C. Heesterman, *The Ancient Indian Royal Consecration* (The Hauge, 1957); "Other Folk's Fire", in F. Staal, ed., *Agni: The Ritual of Fire Altar*, Vol.II (Berkeley, 1983), pp. 76-94; "Householder and Wanderer", *Contributions to Indian Sociology*, Vol XV (1981), pp.250-71.
13. M. Sparreboom., Chariot in the Veda *(Leiden, 1985).*
14. Ibid., pp.76,119-20. Sparreboom draws attention to the frequent equation of *yajna* with *ratha* in the Vedic and, more particularly, Rgvedic literature and thinks that the imagery had a historical connection, "...for ultimately the chariot and the sacrifice were inseparable, being the instrument for the winning of booty and the conquering of new land", Ibid., p.82.
15. B.B. Lal, "Excavation at Hastinapur and Other Explorations in the Upper Ganga and Sutlej Basins 1950-52", *Ancient India*, Nos. 10 and 11 (1954-55), pp.50-51.
16. R.S. Sharma, "The Later Vedic Phase and the Painted Grey Ware Culture", *Puratattva*, No. 8 (1975), pp.63-67.
17. Ghurye, op. cit., p. 389.
18. *Indian Archaeology: A Review*, 1971-72, p.86.
19. Ghurye, op. cit., pp. 310, 311. Also see p. 307 where Ghurye quotes the hymns referring to the loss of Vispala's leg in a battle and its restoration by an "iron leg" by the Asvins enabling her to walk again. Ghurye does not consider the possibility of this story being a mythical invention glorifying the gods' healing powers, but takes it quite literally. For him the story shows "the high state of perfection"

achieved by the science of surgery in Rgvedic times, see infra.

20. Ibid., p. 220; Rgveda, V. 30.15.
21. Ghurye, op. cit., pp. 312-13.
22. S.A. Dange, *Cultural Sources from the Veda* (Bombay, 1977), p. 42. Sometimes it is argued that the German word "eisen", which is phonetically similar to *ayas*, means iron or any instrument made of iron (ibid., p. 41). But as A.L. Basham rightly points out, Vedic *ayas* is also akin to Latin *aes*, meaning bronze and in the *Rgveda* it certainly denotes either copper or bronze, *The Wonder That Was India* (Fontana, 1971), p. 38.
The terms *krsnayasa* or *Karsnayasa*, which are used in later Vedic literature to indicate iron, do not occur in the *Rgveda*, as is assumed mistakenly by Romila Thapar, FLS, p.94.
23. Maurice Bloomfield, *Rgveda Repetitions, Harvard Oriental Series*, Vol. 20 (1916), pp.20-21; also see B.K. Ghosh, chapter XII, "Vedic Literature—General View", in *The Vedic Age*, ed, R.C. Majumdar and A.D. Pusalker (London, 1951), p. 227.
24. Op. cit., p.69f.
25. Sukumari Bhattacharji, however, envisages a minimum gap of two hundred years, Literature in the Vedic Age, Vol. I (Calcutta, 1984), p.6.
26. B.K. Ghosh, op. cit., p.228.
27. For example, *yavam vrkenasvina vapante, Rgveda*, I.117-21, is cited by Romila Thapar as an example of plough agriculture (FLS, p. 26, fn 28). But for the correct interpretation of the term *vrka*, see S.A. Dange, op. cit., pp.7-9, and M.K. Dhavalikar's review of S.A. Dange's *Cultural Sources from the Veda, The Indian Historical Review* (hereafter IHR), Vol. IV, No.I (1977), p. 115 *Vrka* also means wolf and is used in this sense at many places.
28. *Rgveda*, IV, 57. E.W. Hopkins, "Pragathikani", *Journal of American Oriental Society*, Vol. XVII (1896), p. 85. Hopkins is of the view that Book IV of the *Rgveda* is much later than the other family books and is of the same date as Book VIII, "Numerical Formulae in the Veda and Their Bearing on Vedic Criticism", *JAOS*, Vol. XVI (1896), pp. 275-81.
29. For example, *langala* (plough), a proto-Munda loan word in *Rgveda*, IV.57.4, and *ulukhala* (mortar), the Dravidian loan word in *Rgveda*, I. 28.6.

30. "Genesis of Rgvedic Retroflexion: A Historical and Socio-linguistic Investigation", in Madhav M. Despande and Peter Edwin Hook (ed.), *Aryan and Non-Aryan in India*, Michigan papers on South and Southeast Asia, No. 14 (The University of Michigan, Ann Arbor, 1979), pp. 235-315. Deshpande points out that references to the killing of the Dasyus are found mostly in Books I and X of the *Rgveda*. The influence of non-Aryan elements increase in the post-Rgvedic period.
31. F.B.J. Kuiper, "An Austro-Asiatic Myth in the Rgveda" in Mededelingan der Koninklijke Nederlandse Akademie van Wetenschappen (Afd. Letterkunde N.R. deed 13, no. 7) (Amsterdam, 1950).
32. *Rgveda*, VIII.77.10; *indro.....bhinat kanina odanam pacyamanam paro gira*, VIII. 69.14.
33. See the author's discussion on changes in the meaning of *bhagavat, bhakti* and *bhakta* from the early Vedic to post-Vedic times in Suvira Jaiswal, *Origin and Development of Vaisnavism* (Delhi, 1981), pp. 37-39, 116-18.
34. A.B. Keith, *The Religion and Philosophy of the Veda nd Upanishads*, Vol. I, Harvard Oriental Series, Vol. 31, (OUP, 1975), p. 252.
35. J.C. Heesterman, op. cit., J. Gonda, "Adhvan and Adhvaryu", *Vishveshvaranand Indological Journal* (hereafter VIJ) vol. 3 (1965), pp.163-77; also see Ganesh Thite, "Contribution of Western Scholars to the study of Vedic Tirual", VIJ, Vol. 18, pp. 43-57.
36. K.R. Potdar, *Sacrifice in the Rgveda* (Bombay, 1953), p.3.
37. Emile Benvensite, *Indo-European Language and Society* (London, 1973), pp. 105-12.
38. *Rgveda*, X. 34.4., refers to the binding and taking away of a gambler as a slave.
39. *Vedic Index*, Vol. II, pp. 278, 387.
40. *Rgveda*, VI, 47.21.
41. *Rgveda*, IV. 24-9-10. For the use of *sulka* in a similar context, see *Rgveda*, VIII.1.5, The high *sulka* of Varuna is mentioned in Rgveda, *VII. 82.6.*
42. In *Rgveda*. X. 34.3; *vasnya* qualifies a horse. The gambler laments "Like a *vasnya* (worthy) horse grown old, I find no use of the gamester".
43. Rgveda, *III. 62.14.*
44. Vedic Index, *Vol. I. p. 109.*

45. R.S. Sharma, MCSF, *p. 31.*
46. The term *vanij* occurs twice in the *Rgveda,* IN I. 112 . 11. The Asvins are requested to give sweet rain for vanij Dirghasravas, the son of *Usij,* as they had helped Kaksivan (another son of Usij and composer of several hymns) in the past. IN V. 45.6, again, there is a reference to the *vanij* who gained obstructed waters of the heavens. This, according to Sayana, is a reference to Kaksivan for whom the Asvins had sent the rains. Thus in both the passage the term *vanij* is applied to the sons of Usij. Potdar (op. cit., p 146) takes "Usij" to be proper name, but T. Burrow and H.W. Bailey are of the view that the term meant "Incantator" and "Usij" was a type of priest (quoted by Bruce Lincoln, op. cit., p. 61, fn.70). Lincoln thinks that the chief functions of the Usij priest was to assist warriors in cattle-raiding. He notes that the term appears thirty times in the *Rgveda* and in one-third of these references he is seen helping in the cattle-raiding activity. Kaksivan Ausija was a famous seer and a descendant of Pajra (*Rgveda* I. 16. 1; I.116. 7 and elsewhere). There is nothing to show that he was a merchant or trader and term *vanij* may have meant simply "wanderer".

    Madhav M. Deshpande thinks that the Skt *vanij* is related to Vedic "Pani", which in his view was the name of a non-Aryan trading tribe (op. cit., p 306, note 83). But the *Rgveda* has both *vanij* and Pani without linking the two in any way or showing their connection with trade, see footnote 48.
47. A.D. Pusalker, chapter XIII, "Aryan Settlements in India", in The Vedic Age, *p. 249.*
48. Pani is a derivative of the root *pan* which means to bet, to lay a wager, and *pana* means gaming, playing for a stake (Monier-Williams, *Sanskrit-English Dictionary,* s.v. *pan* nad *pana*). Hence it is possible that the term initially meant a person who won his riches at stakes and not through trade. Pani appears as an adjective of Dasyu in *Rgveda,* VII. 6.3. Divodasa, the son of Vadhryasva, who is described as *rnacyuta,* the cancellor of all debts, is also called the opponent of the Panis. (*Rgveda,* VI.61.1.). Debt in the *Rgveda* refers mainly to gambling debt and not to any trading practice. P.V.Kane (*History of Dharmasastra,* Vol. III, Poona, 1946, pp. 414-15) and Ghurye (op. cit. p. 246) quote two Rgvedic verses which in their view indicate the practice of usury in Rgvedic times. *Rgveda,* VIII. 66.10, says: "Indra overcomes with his power all the living *bekanatas* and Panis

(*indro visvan bekanatan ahardrsa uta kratva panirabhi*). Yaska explains that bekanata means a usurious person identical with the Panis (quoted in *Vedic Index*, s.v. *bekanata*). But it is a non-Sanskrit word of uncertain origin and meaning and it occurs only once in the *Rgveda*. The other verse, *Rgveda*, VII. 47,17, speaks of the paying of the one-eighth or one-sixteenth part of the debt. This refers to the obligation to pay back one's debt or at least a fraction in terms of the tribal norms of reciprocity which is not always one for one exchange. Ghurye and Kane see here an allusion to the rate of interest, (see Macdonell and Keith, *Vedic Index*, s.v. *rna*). Similarly, "Pramaganda" occurring in *Rgveda III*. 53. 14, means, according to Kabem, "born of a family that is extremely usurious." But as Macdonell and Keith point out, it is a proper name of the leader of the Kikatas and had nothing to do with usury (*Vedic Index* Vo. II, s.v. Parmaganda).

49. *Vedic Index* s.v. Pani; Doris Srinivasan regards the myth of Sarama and the Panis narrated in *Rgveda*, X. 108, and hints at a few other places as a "mythic intensification of an actual Pani", "Myth of the Panis in the *Rgveda*", *JAOS*, Vol. 93 (1973), PP.44-57).
50. Ghurye, op. cit., pp. 298-301. On the basis of *Rgveda*, VII. 104.13 and X. 71.81. Ghurye argues that the *Rgveda* knows even persons who made false claims to being brahmanas or ksatriyas, which shows that these were well-established categories. However, the correct interpretation of these verses is given by P.V. Kane (op. cit., Vol. II, Pt. I, Poona, 1941, pp. 31-32), who ably refutes Ghurye's contention.
51. R.S. Sharma, MCSF, p. 159.
52. Ibid., pp. 28f. Also see R.S. Sharma, "From Gopati to Bhupati", *Studies in History*, Vol. II, No. 2 (July-December 1980), pp. i-11; R. Thapar, FLS,pp.24-25.
53. Anthropologists beginning with Henri Morgan to Marshall D. Sahlins and Maurice Godelier have emphasized the dominant and multi-functional role of kinship relations in tribal societies. For an interesting discussion, see Marshall D. Sahlins, *Tribesmen* (Foundation of Modern Anthropology Series, Prentice-Hall Inc., 1968); Maurice Godelier, Perspectives in Marxist Anthropology (Cambridge, 1977), P. 70f.
54. R.N. Nandi, "Anthropology and the Study of the *Rgveda*", IHR, Vol XIII, Nos. 1-2 (July 1986 and January 1987), p. 164.
55. F. Engles, *Origin of the Family, Private Property and State* in K. Marx

and F. Engles, *Selected works*, Vol. III (Moscow, 1970), pp. 273-75.

56. Marshall D. Sahlins, "The Segmentary Lineage: An Organization of Predatory Expansion", *American Anthropologist*, Vol. 63 (1961), pp. 322-45.
57. A. Beteille, "On the Concept of Tribe", *International Social Science Journal*, Vol. 32, No. 4 (1980), pp. 825-28; M. Friend, The *Evolution of Political Society*, quoted in R. Thapar, FLS, p. 18, fn 42. Also see Maurice Godelier, "The Concept of the Tribe: A Crisis involving merely A Concept or the Empirical Foundations of Anthropology Itself", *Perspectives in Marxist Anthropology, Pt. I, Chapter 3.*
58. In another publication, Thapar clearly writes: "Vedic society of the earlier half of the first millennium B.C. can be characterized as a lineage-based society. The unit was the clan, and this formed the essential structure at many levels", "State Formation in Early India", *International Social Science Journal*, Vol. 32, No. 4 (1980), p. 656. In FLS, the gana-samghas of the sixth century B.C. and later are said to have been characterized by the "lineage system" (p. 78). Such ambiguous use of the term "lineage" brings under one heading systems whose character and functions differ widely.
59. A.M. Shah, "Towards A sociological Understanding of Ancient India", Review article on R. Thapar's FLS in *Contributions to Indian Sociology*, New Series, Vo. 22 (1986), pp. 117-33.
60. R. Thapar, FLS, p. 10; J. Middleton and D. Tait, *Tribes Without Rulers* (London, 1858; reprint, 1970), pp. 3-4.
61. FLS, p. 10.
62. Italics added.
63. Ibid, pp. 10-11.
64. Emanuel Terray, Marxism and Primitive Societies, (London, 1972).
65. P.P. Rey, "Class Contradiction in Lineage Societies", *Critique of Anthropology*, Vol. 4, Nos. 13 and 14 (1979), pp. 41-60; "The Lineage Mode of Production", *Critique of Anthropology*, No.3 (Spring 1975), pp. 27-79.
66. Op. cit.
67. "From Reproduction to Production", Economy and Society, Vol. I, No. 1 (1972), pp. 93-105.
68. Op. cit., p. 156.
69. Op. cit., p. 120.
70. Kent V. Flannery, "The Cultural Evolution of Civilizations", *Annual Review of Ecology and Systematics*, Vol. 3, (1972), pp. 399-426,

reprinted in *Ancient Cities of the Indus*, (ed.), Gregory L. Possehl (New Delhi, 1979), pp. 27-43.

71. Conical clans are "kinship units which bind their members with common familial ties but which distribute wealth, social standing and power most unequally among the members of the pseudo-family. Such kin units trace their descent back to an original ancestor, real or fictitious, but at the same time they regularly favour his lineal descendants over the junior or "cadet" lines in regulating access to social, economic or political prerogatives", Eric Wolfe, *Sons of the Shaking Earth*, (Chicago, 1959), p. 136.
72. Marshall D. Sahlins, *Tribesmen*, p. 24.
73. R.S. Sharma, "From Kin to Class", review of R. Thapar's FLS in *Economic and Political Weekly*, Vol. 20, No. 22 (June 1985), p. 961
74. R.N. Nandi, op. cit, p. 159. However, Nandi's assertion that the term *rajan* is "invariably" applied to gods only in the family books is not correct. A verse of the IV *mandala* (50.8) speaks of the people (*visah*) as paying homage of their own free will (*svayameva namante*) to the *rajan* "with whom the Brahman hath precedence" (*brahma rajani purva eti*) The following verse as translated by R.T.H. Griffith reads : "The Gods uphold that King (raja) with their protection who helps the Brahman when he seeks his favour" (the Hymns of the *Rgveda*, reprint, Delhi, 1986, p. 232). It may be argued that since the hymn is addressed to Brhaspati, it is of a later date. But Nandi's contention that the earlier family books "represent egalitarian folkdoms without a chief or king" (P.155) is confusing. Both R.S. Sharma and Romila Thapar in their works under discussion convincingly establish that the Rgvedic tribes were stateless. The tribal chief may not have been anything more than the war-leader providing protection to his tribesmen and their cattle and leading cattle raids. The term *satpati* occurring in V.27.1 would confirm this, if I. Kuhn's interpretation of this term as "the leader of the raid" is accepted (quoted by Wash Edward Hale, *Asura in Early Vedic Religion*, Delhi, 1986, p.48) No doubt there is a general absence of a centralized political organization in the *Rgveda*. For *gopa* and *gopati* as the leader of the tribe, see R.S. Sharma, *Studies in History*, Vol.II,No.2 (1980),pp.1-10.
75. In *Rgveda*, X.42.10. the verse is repeated in the following two hymns. For the various meanings of the term *vrjana*, see s.v.*vrjana*., Monier-Williams, *Sanskrit-English Dictionary*, and MacDonell and Keith, *Vedic Index*, Vol. II. Also see R.S. Sharma, MCSF, p.27.

76. *Rgveda*, X.97.6,for *samiti*, see R.S. Sharma, *Aspects of Political Ideas and Institutions in Ancient India* (3rd edn, Delhi, 1991), p.105f.
77. *Rgveda*, X.78, I, speaks of the good looks of the chief (*rajano na citrah susamdrash*).
78. See, for example, *FLS*, footnotes on pages 30 and 31.
79. Ibid., p. 35, fn. 69.
80. The English rendering is from H.H. Wilson's translation for the *Rgveda* (Delhi, 1997), p. 401. That the *vis* or the clans choose the *rajan* is mentioned in R*gveda*, X.124.8. But it is regarded as a later addition. For discussion, refer to Hale, op. cit., p.88f.
81. *Transactions of the Philological Society* (1950), pp 71-115.
82. *FLS*, p.43, Also see R. Thapar, *Ancient Indian Social History* (Delhi, 1978), p.111.
83. Bailey, op. cit., pp. 84,94.
84. E. Benveniste, op. cit., pp. 260-61.
85. M.B. Emaneau has shown that several old Indo-Aryan dialects existed in India even in the Rgvedic times; and classical Sanskrit has descended from a dialect which in some respects was even more archaic than the Rgvedic dialect. Refer to "The Dialects of the Old Indo-Aryn" in H. Birnbaum and J. Puhvel, (ed.), *Ancient Indo-European Dialects* (Berkeley, 1966), pp.123-38, quoted by Asko Parpola, in "The Pre-Vedic Background of the Srauta Ritual" in Fritz Staal, (ed.), *Agni: The Vedic Ritual of Fire Altar*, Vol II, p.43.
86. W.E. Hale, op cit., pp. 146,151. Also see S.A. Sange, op. cit., p. 37. Dange asserts that Yadu and Turvasa are clearly called *Dasas* in *Rgveda*, X. 62.10, but the verse is interpreted generally to mean that Yadu and Turvasa gave away two *Dasas* along with cattle.
87. *Rgveda*, VII.6.3.
88. *Rgveda*, VII, 18.13.
89. *Rgveda*, I. 130.8; XI.41.1 In the latter verse Soma Pavamana is said to drive the "black skin" away and the very next verse speaks of the quelling of the vowless (*avrata*) Dasyus.
90. *Rgveda*, II. 20.7.
91. Asko Parpola in the article cited in footnote 85 above. However, his main thesis identifying the Harappans as Dravidians and the *Dasas* as *Asura-worshippers* rests on weak grounds, see infra.
92. Kuiper thinks that Sambara is a proto-Munda name (op. cit., p. 177). He is called a Dasyu in *Rgveda*, IV. 31.4, and a *Dasa* in IV.30. 14 and VI. 47.21. Incidentally this shows the virtual identity of the *Dasas*

and Dasyus. Also see footnote 97 below.

93. *Rgveda*, X.27.10 Indra's claim to have taken away the manliness (*nrmnam*) from the *Dasyus* (X.48.2) may not be merely a boast, but an oblique reference to this feature of the Dasa-Dasyus.
94. I.112.10.
95. I.116.15.
96. See also. I. 117.11; I.118.8; X.39.8.
97. *Rgveda*, X.22.8, identifies the Dasyu with *Dasa* and calls him *akarman* (without rituals), unthinking (*amantu*), having other vows (*anyavrata*) and inhuman (*amanusah*). The *Dasas* had their own fortresses, which were broken down by Indra (*Rgveda*, I.103.3; II.10.7), and their own *vis* (II.11.4; IV.28.4; VI.25.2; and X. 148.2). Some *Dasas* were very rich and extolled highly by the poets. *Dasa* Balbutha Taruksa made a gift of one hundred (cows ?) to the poet of VIII. 46.32.
98. *Rgveda*, III.12.6; VI.60.6.
99. In *Sudras in Ancient India*, 2nd revised edition (Delhi, 1980, p.74f), R.S. Sharma express the view that originally Arya and *Dasa* were two separate tribal groups distinguished from each other on the basis of colour, language and religion, but later they merged to form one composite whole and some *Dasas* even obtained a high status. It is quite plausible, but *Rgveda*, VI.22.10, can hardly be regarded as indicative of this process. Sharma quotes "Sayana's interpretation to hold that the verse in question speaks of Indra convesting *Dasas* into Aryas (ibid.) p.21), but in our opinion the verse simply prays to Indra to grant vast unexhausting luck to make the Dasic, Aryan and Nahusic enemies flee" *(yaya dasanyaryani vrta karo vajrint sutuka nahusani)*, see Hale, op. cit. p. 166.
100. *Rgveda*, VII. 86.7; VIII.56.3.
101. VIII. 35.16-18.
102. P.V. Kane, op. cit., Vo. II, Pt I, p. 25.
103. *Rgveda*, I. 104.2.
104. According to Monier-Williams, *varna* means colour, especially good colour or complexion, lustre, beauty, *Sanskrit-English Dictionary*, s.v.*varna.*
105. *Rgveda*, II. 12.4. R.N. Nandi's assertion on the basis of this verse that "Already in the second book Indra is credited with the confining of the subjugated *dasa* people to a lowly place within the (*aarya*) varna" (op. cit., p. 162) is hardly acceptable as the term *varna* here

does not stand for Aryan. It is qualified by *daasam* and hence refer to the *Dasa* people. The assumption that *varna* already denoted a system of stratification with the *Dasa* occupying a lowly place is not warranted. The phrase *adharam guhakah* does not mean "a lowly place in the *varna* system of stratification", but speaks of "lowly hiding place" in a physical sense. This act of Indra may be compared with his feat of throwing down the *Dasa*-Dasyu Sambara from a lofty mountain (*Rgveda*, IV.30.14) Again, Nandi's interpretation of *janmana* and *praja* as "servants" and "*slaves*" is questionable. The Vedicists generally translate these words in the sense of "offspring", "progeny" or "descendants". One cannot simply assume that the presence of Dasyu girls must lead to the "multiplication of non-kin labour", unless it is shown too that the children of the Aryan males from the *Dasa*-Dasyu females could not be absorbed into the Aryan lineage system. But the stories of Kavasa Ailusa, Dirghatamas and Mahidasa, son of Itara, suggest that although some stigma may have been attached to such alliances, mixed parentage did not necessarily give rise to "non-kin" labour exploited by the Aryan kin-groups, at least in the Rgvedic times. On the other hand, Divodasa, the famours king of the Bharatas, may have been an adopted *Dasa* (D.D. Kosambi, *An Introduction to the Study of Indian History* (Bombay, 1956), p.89.

106. See C. Scott. Littleton, *The New Comparative Mythology; An Anthropological Assessment of the Theories of George Dumezil*, (Berkeley, 1973).
107. E. Benveniste, op. cit. p. 127.
108. G.S. Kirk, *Myth: Its Meaning and Functions in Ancient and Other Cultures* (Cambridge, 1970), p. 210.
109. John Brough, "The Tripartite Ideology of the Indo-Eurpoeans: An Experiment in Method", *Bulletin of the School of Oriental and African Studies*, Vol. 22 (1959), pp. 69-85.
110. Bruce Lincoln, op. cit. p. 51 fn. 6.
111. Ibid., p. 135f.
112. E.W. Hale, op. cit.; P.L. Bhargava, "The Word *asura* in *Rgveda*", *Annals of the Bhandarkar Oriental Research Institute*, Vol. 64 (1983), pp. 119-23. According to Bhargava, Indra is called an *asura* or is said to possess "asuraship" in sixteen hymns of the *Rgveda* (p. 120). Also see Hukum Chand Patyal, "etymology and Sanskrit Dictionary on Historical Principles", *Indian Linguistics*, Vol. 40 (1979), p. 120.

113. *Rgveda*, I. I.174.1; VIII.90.6; X.96.11; X. 29.11; In *Rgveda*, III.38.4. It is not clear whether asura is used for Indra or Tvastr.
114. *Rgveda*, IV. 16.2; IV. 20.2; VI. 30.2; VI 36.1; VII.22.5; X. 50.3; X. 54.5; X. 105; X. 105.11.
115. I. 24.14; II. 27.10; II. 28.7; VIII. 42.1; X. 132.4.
116. IV. 42.2; V. 85.5.
117. V. 66.2; VII. 36.2; VII. 65.1.,2; VII.66.2.
118. II.I.6.2; II. 33.9; V.42.11; VIII.20.17.
119. I. 64.2 In VIII. 27.20. Visvedevas are called asuras, providing protection to the pious one going to *rta* or sacrifice.
120. Lincoln, op. cit. p. 129.
121. *Rgveda*, VII. 65.2.
122. III. 55.1.
123. V. 42.11.
124. Hale, op. cit., p. 180. P.L. Bhargava thinks that the original meaning was "spirited" or "courageous", op. cit., pp. 119-20.
125. *Rgveda*, VII. 99.5.
126. X. 138.3. He is called a *Dasa* in this verse.
127. II. 30.4.
128. Varcin is called *Dasa, Rgveda*, VI. 47.21, and Pipru, along with *Dasa*-Ahisuva, figures among those who were killed by Indra in *Rgveda*, VIII. 32.2.
129. A.A. Macdonell, *Vedic Mythology*, pp. 156-57, quoted in P.L. Bhargava, op. cit., p. 123.
130. For example, the *atharvan* priest corresponds to Avestan *athravan* and makes a late appearance in the *Rgveda*. He is mentioned in three hymns, two from the IX and X *mandalas* (IIX.II.2; X.14.6) and one danastuti inserted in a hymn of the VI *mandala* (VI.47.24), see Sukumari Bhattacharjee, *Literature in the Vedic Age*, Vol. I, pp. 121-22. Unlike his Avestan counterpart, the Vedic *atharvan* is not connected with fire. Benveniste is of the view that the Vedic *atharvan* is a late borrowing from Iran, op. cit., p. 228. Similarly the three orders of old Iranian society were known as *pistra* meaning "craft", and etymologically the word meant "colour". In Iran the three classes were distinguished by the colour of their clothes-white for priests, red for warriors and blue for farmers/cattle herders. According to Benveniste, the colour classification had a profound symbolism and was related to certain cosmological concepts which associated the exercise of a fundamental activity with a certain colour (op. cit. p.227).

However, the Indian term *varna* has no philological correspondence with the Iranian pistra and although it has the primary meaning of colour it was used initially in a physical sense distinguishing two groups of people on the basis of the colour of their skin. Its use to demarcate hierarchical social categories is a later development and is found in the later Vedic texts. The Mahabharata (Critical Edn, XII. 181, 10-13) ascribes different colours to different *varnas*—red to ksatriya, yellow to vaisya and black to sudra. This is perhaps yet another evidence of the late infiltration of Iranian ideas.

131. Op. cit., p. 239f.
132. *yajnam ca manusanam,Rgveda*, I.84.2, also see VI. 2.2-5; X.150.2.
133. X.45.6. Soma pressing is said to take place among the *Pancajanas* in IX. 65.23.
134. *Nighantu*, III.18.
135. V.S. Apte, Sanskrit-English Dictionary, s.v. rtvij.
136. Padma Misra, *Evolution of the Brahman Class* (*in the perspective of Vedic Period*), Banaras Hindu University Sanskrit Series, Vol.XIII (1978),p.141.
137. P.V. Kane, op. cit., Vo. II, Pt. 2, pp. 1212-13.
138. *Hotr* is one who invokes gods and offers oblations. It is derived from the root *hve*, to call, or *hu*, to pour oblations, ibid,., p. 138, fn.4.
139. *Nirukta*, II.10.
140. J.W. Spellman, "The Legend of Devapi", JRAS (London, October, 1959), pp. 95-99.
141. *Rgveda*, III. 23.2.
142. VIII. 103.2.
143. VI. 16.19. For *satpati*, see fn. 74 above.
144. *Rgveda*, II. 7.1; IV.25.4; VII.8.4.
145. VIII, 19.32.
146. *Baudhayana Srautasutra* list quoted in C.G. Kashikar, (ed.), *Srautakosa*, Vol.I, Pt.II (Poona, 1962), pp. 1007,1008.
147. *Rgveda*, IV. 15.4.
148. VI. 27.7.
149. *Vedic Index*, Vol II, s.v. Srnjaya. *The Satapatha Brahmana*, II. 4.4.5, *states that Devabhaga Srotarsa was the purohita of the Kurus and Srnjayas.*
150. *Rgveda*, III. 53.24.
151. *Rgveda*, I. 130.10.
152. The legend of Devapi and Santanu, however, does not show that the

tribal leader "combined the functions of both priest and warlord", R.S. Sharma, *Studies in History*, Vol. II, No. 2 (1980), p.2.

153. *Rgveda*, II.2.11; V.6.2.
154. VII.1.4.
155. VII.1.15.
156. It is curious that Professor Thapar does not refer to these verses and to the term *sujata* to support her thesis regarding the existence of senior and junior lineages in Rgvedic times.
157. *Rgveda*, X.95.10.
158. I.65.2; II.1.15; II.6.2; V.21.2; VII.8.5; VIII.74.7; X.5.4; X.79.7.
159. III. 15.2.
160. I. 72.2.5. For the Maruts being described as *sujata*, also see I. 88.3; V.57.5; V. 59.6; VIII. 20.8.
161. VI. 51.3.
162. Ibid.
163. Ibid., VII.64.1.
164. VI. 51.3.
165. X.99.7.
166. V.51.3.
167. V.56.9.
168. V.79.1-10; V.123.3; VII.76.6; VII.77.6. Also see X. 172.4.
169. Bruce Lincoln, op. cit., p. 134, passim; Ghurye, op. cot., p. 300. Ghurye refers to *Rgveda*, VII. 104.13, which mentions the "ksatriya who bears false" (*ksatriyam mithuya dharayantam*), and says that if there were persons falsely assuming the title of ksatriya, it must have been "almost a caste". But as Kane points out (op. cit., Vol II, Pt.I, pp. 31-32), the verse speaks of the "ksatriya who bears false words", or a ksatriya "who has no strength as a ksatriya should have". In many later Vedic texts the term "ksatriya" is synonymous with *raja* or chief. There is no implication of *varna/caste* in this Rgvedic hymn. As Kane points out, "unless we project our notions of the later state of society and the caste system when considering this verse, it is hardly possible to hold that this verse indicates that it refers to persons making a false claim to an entrance into a compact body of ksatriyas by birth" (ibid., p.32).
170. *Vedic Index*, Vol. I, s.v. ksatriya; Potdar, op. cit., p.141; Kane, op. cit., Vol. II, Pt. I, p. 30.
171. *Rgveda*,VII,64.2; VIII.25.8; X.66.8.
172. See fn. 74 above.

173. R.S. Sharma, MCSF,p.42.
174. Potdar, op. cot., p. 171.
175. Rgveda, *V.66.2, VII.21.7.*
176. *Jananam yo asuro vidharta, Rgveda*, VII.56.24, also see VI. 36. I and VII. 21.7, where the distribution of booty is connected with asuraship, Hale, op. cit., p. 60.
177. *Rgveda*, III. 53.7, III. 56.8.
178. Hale, op. cit., pp.67,193.
179. For some interesting descriptions of the *viras/naras*, see *Rgveda*, I. 73 and VI.75. At two places (X. 47.4, and X. 104.1) powerful singers are described as vipraviras.
180. Bruce Lincoln, op.cit., p. 125f.
181. *Rgveda*, V. 59.5; VIII.43.25, also see X. 78.1.
182. S.A. Dange, "Aspects of War from the *Rgveda*", *Journal of Indian History*, Vo. 44 (1966), pp.125.38.
183. *Rgveda*, IX.112.13, Griffith's translation.
184. *Rgveda*, III.43.5.
185. D.D. Kosambi, *An Introduction to the Study of Indian History*, p.96. For a detailed discussion, see idem, "On the Origin of the Brahmin Gotras", *Journal of the Bombay Branch of the Royal Asiatic Society*, Vol.26 (1950), pp.21-80.
186. According to Kosambi, "The formation of an internal, Aryan caste system, essentially the separation of the Brahmin in function and discipline from the Ksatriya and setting of both above the householder Vaisya, after the *dasas* has been conquered, must have been accelerated by the assimilation of a subjugated priesthood; for otherwise there is no reason for demarcation into endogamous castes", JBBRAS, Vol. 26 (1950), p. 50, also *An Introduction to the Study of Indian History*, pp. 94-95.
187. Romila Thapar, "A Response to Professor A.M. Shah", *Contributions to Indian Sociology*, New Series, Vol.20, No. 2 (1986), p. 292, R.S. Sharma, MCSF,pp. 73-74.
188. JBBRAS, Vol. 22 (1946), p. 35.
189. Agastya is listed as the "eighth" and was apparently a late entrant among the primary *gotrakaras*. Interestingly, he is connected with the only female warrior mentioned in the *Rgveda*, Vispala, whose leg cut off in Khela's battle, was restored at Agastya's prayer, see. fn. 19.
190. JBBRAS (1950), p. 43, 50.

191. Rgveda, *VII, 18.6-7.*
192. Indra kills Arna and Citaratha, both "Aryas", on the banks of the Sarayu, *Rgveda*, IV. 30.17, also see VI.22.10 (fn.99 above); VI. 33.3; X.102.3.
193. *Vedic Index*, s.v. Bhrgu.
194. *Rgveda*, III.53.7; X.62.4; X. 67.2.
195. III. 53.7.
196. Ibid, verses 11-12.
197. *Rgveda*, VII. 33.10-13.
198. Kosambi, JBBRAS, Vol. 26 (1950), p. 37.
199. Henk W. Bodewitx, "The Fourth Priest (The Brahman) in Vedic Ritual", in *Selected Studies on Ritual in the Indian Religions* (Essays presented to D.J. Hoens), (ed.), Ris Kloppenborg (Leiden, 1983), pp. 33-68.
200. For further elaboration of these views, see Suvira Jaiswal, "Studies in Early Indian Social History; Trends and Possibilities", The Indian Historical Review, Vol. VI, Nos. 1-2, (July 1979 and January 1980), pp. 1-63.
201. *Ancient Europe from the Beginning of Agriculture to Classical Antiquity*, (Edinburgh, 1965), pp. 4-5, cited in Brendan O'Leary, *The Asiatic Mode of Production* (Oxford, 1989), 278-79.
202. Ibid.
203. John Marshall, *Mohenjo-daro and the Indus Civilization*, Vol. I (London, 1931), p. 52f.
204. R.E.M. Wheeler, *The Indus Civilization*, 3rd edn. (Cambridge, 1968), pp. 108-10.
205. E. Mackey, *Further Excavations*, Vol. II, pp. LXXXVII, pp. 222, 235.
206. Ghurye, op. cit. p. 157.
207. Herbert P. Sullivan, "A Re-examination of the Religion of the Indus Civilization", *History of Religions*, Vol. VI (1964-65), pp. 115-25.
208. B.P. Mazumdar was of the view that the history of technology indicates a break from Harappa to historic times. He cited *Ancient India*, No. 8 (1952, pp. 51-52) to point out that faience beads made in Harappan times reappeared after a long gap around the first century A.D. at Taxila and still later at Charsadda and Ahicchara, "Continuity and Change in Ancient and Early Medieval India", (c. 2300 B.C.1200A.D), typescript. Also see Suvira Jaiswal, "Caste in the Socio-Economic Framework of Early India", Presidential Address to the Ancient India Section, published in the *Proceedings of*

the Indian History Congress (Bhubaneswar session, 1977).
209. Supra, fn. 134.
210. *rtvijajnakrducyate*, cited in V.S. Apte, Sanskrit-English Dictionary, s.v.rtvij; also see Rgveda, *I.1.1.*
211. Bruce Lincoln, op. cit., p.62.
212. Potdar, op. cit., p. 161; Keith, *Religion and Philosophy of the Veda and Upanishads*, p. 254.
213. He is now known as Zot or Zoti, the chief priest whose sacred duty is to recite the invocation from the gatha during a ritual ceremony.
214. Henk. W. Bodevitx, op. cit., p. 35.
215. Interestingly in ancient Iran Rathwi or Rathwiskere was an auxiliary priest who assisted Zoatar, the chief priest, and did the manual work at the sacrifice, Gajanana M. Patil, "Priesthood in Avesta and Rgveda", *Bulletin of the Deccan College Research Institute*, Vol. 18, Tarporewala Memorial Volume (1957), pp. 221-25.
216. For example, III. 29.8.
217. The seven are *hotr, potr, nestr, agnidh, prasastr, adhvaryu* and *brahman, Rgveda*, II. 1.2' X. 91.10.
218. Thus *hotra, potra, nestra* and *brahman* were cups allotted to priests designated, correspondingly.
219. Padma Misra, op. cit., p. 198.
220. Ibid, p. 159.
221. In *Rgveda*, VI. 45.2 and VIII. 61.9; the term *avipra* occurs in the sense of dull, uninspired.
222. X. 67.2, W.E. Hale, op. cit., p. 72.
223. *Rgveda*, III. 7.7.
224. Padma Misra, op. cit.
225. *Rgveda*, VII. 7.7. It is repeated in VIII.7.7 for *suris* and *stotrs*; see also II. 2.12.
226. VII. 22.9.
227. I. 8.6.
228. VI. 7.3.
229. I.8.2., Indra is described as assisting them from his car (*arvata*), Griffith, *The Hymns of the Rgveda*, p.5.
230. *Rgveda*, VIII. 21.4.
231. *samicinasa asate hotarah saptajamayah*, IX. 10.7.
233. Padma Misra, op. cit., p. 200.
234. *Vedic Index*, Vol.I, pp. 526-28, s.v. pitr.
235. *Rgveda*, I. 116.16; I. 117.17.

236. *Vedic Index*, op. cit.
237. *Vedic Index* gives *Rgveda*, I. 70.10. This is, however, a misprint for I. 70.5. One may find the mistake copied in a number of publications without acknowledgement to Macdonell and Keith.
238. *Rgveda*, I. 131.3; II. 39.2; VIII. 31.5-6.
239. I. 127.8.
240. I. 144.4.
241. Benveniste, op. cit., pp. 251-54.
242. *Rgveda*, I. 49.1; I. 110.2; I. 124.11; I. 135.7; III. 60.5; IV. 49.6; VII.59.10; Also see I. 28.5; VII. 89.1; X.40.3.
243. V.11.4; also see. I. 71.4; I. 124.11.
244. V.1.5; V. 6.8.
245. *ayam nabha vadati valgu vo grhe*, "he speaks here nicely in consanguinity in your house", X. 62.4.
246. MSCF, p. 48.
247. Ibid., p. 51.
248. FLS, pp. 36-37. In this work references are often mixed up and incorrect. In this particular case, p.37, fn. 76, cites reference for the *grhapatya (sic)* fire as follows: *Rgveda*, I. 12.6; I. 36.5; I. 60.4; and VI. 48.8. These verses describe Agni as *grhapati*, but make no mention of the *garhapatya* fire. On the other hand, page 36 has fn. 75 quoting *Rgveda*. X. 85, for the occurrence of *garhpati*. Again, the word *garhpati* does not occur at all in this hymn. It has *grhapatni* once (verse 26) and *garhapatya* twice (verses 27 and 36). The latter term is generally interpreted here in the sense of "control over the household".
249. P.V. Kane, op. cit., Vol. II, Pt. I, pp. 678-79.
250. Sparreboom, op. cit., p. 80-81.
251. Brian K. Smith, "The Unity of Ritual: The Place of Domestic Sacrifice in Vedic Ritualism", *Indo-Iranian Journal*, Vol. 29 (1986), pp. 80-81.
252. *Rgveda*, O. 15.12.
253. P.V. Kane, op. cit., Vol.II, Pt. 2, p. 1241.
254. *Atharvaveda*, XI.7.7-8, quoted by N.N. Bhattarchayya, *Ancient Indian Ritual and Their Social Contents* (Delhi, 1975), p. 64.
255. *Rgveda*, VII. 56.14.
256. VII. 59.10.
257. Shakuntala Rao Shastri, *Women in the Vedic Age* (Bombay, 1954), pp. 13-18.
258. V.S. Ghate, op. cit., p. 69.

259. R.S. Sharma, MCSF, pp 48-49.
260. Irawati Karve "Kinship Terminology and Kinship Usages in *Rgveda* and *Atharvaveda*" *Annals of the Bhandarkar Oriental Research Institute*, Vol. XX (!938-39), p. 71f.
261. *Vedic Index*, Vol. I, p. 525. The *Rgveda* has no separate word for "uncle". *Abhratrvya* the negative form of *bhratrvya* is found in *Rgveda*, VIII.21.13, in the sense of "one having no rival" and is applied to Indra. The verse is repeated in *Atharvaveda*, XX. 114.1, and is certainly of late origin.
262. *Hindu Kinship* (Bombay, 1947), pp. 7-45, 222, 307-9; Suvira Jaiswal, IHR, Vol. VI, Nos 1-2, p. 55.
263. A.R. Radcliffe-Brown in Radcliffe-Brown and Daryll Forde, *African Systems of Kinship and Marriage* (London, 10th impression, 1970), pp. 33-35.
264. R.S. Sharma, MCSF,p.29.
265. Rgveda, *I. 73.1.9.*
266. Eleanor B. Leacock in introduction to F. Engels, *The Origin of the Family, Private Property and the State*, (London, 1972, reprint, 1977), Pt.II, p.ii. For the linkage between the joint family system and ownership or control of land, see Suvira Jaiswal, IHR, Vol.VI, Nos. 1-2, p. 60.
267. Marshall Sahlins, op. cit., p. 49. Sahlins also speaks of the "conical clan", which in his view were neither endogamous nor exogamous. For Polynesian clans without a unilineal lineage structure, see M. Godelier, op. cit., p. 89.
268. Radcliffe-Brown and D. Forde, op. cit., p. 40; italics ours.
269. Benveniste, op. cit.; p. 239f.
270. Stefan Zimmer, "On a Special Meaning of Jana in the Rgveda, Indo-Iranian Journal, *Vol. XXIX (1986), pp. 109-15.*
271. Quoted in P.V. Kane, op. cit., Vol. II, Pt I, p. 480.
272. J. Heesterman, *The Ancient Indian Royal Consecration*, (The Hague, 1957), pp. 118-19, fn. 24.
273. *Rgveda*, I. 71.1; I. 112.15; VII. 18.2; X. 10.3.
274. J. Brough, "The Early History of the Gotras", JRAS (1946), pp. 32-45; (1947), pp. 76-99; A.C. Banerjea, *Studies in the Brahmanas*, (Delhi, 1963).
275. E. Benveniste, op. cit., p. 303.
276. *Rgveda*, X. 28.1.
277. Bruce Lincoln, op. cit., p. 135, fn. 5.

278. *Rgveda*, X. 114.10. They are also mentioned in I. 65.4. The Ibhya, often translated mistakenly as a nobleman or rich person, was an aboriginal tribe with elephant totem, perhaps equivalent of Matanga, modern Mang, see D.D. Kosambi, "Combined Methods in Indology", *Indo-Iranian Journal*, Vol. VI (1963), pp. 181-84.

3 Sociologists and Inequality in India

The Historical Context

SATISH SABERWAL

> Given the omnipresent nature of contextual relations, it is obvious that all theories of relationship require a certain artificial closure.... But the closure evident in the theories I am criticizing is not such a necessary methodological closure. It is a closure stemming from cultural values, ideological values, or ignorance—and ignorance of the context happens to be one of our most highly developed cultural values.
>
> —*Anthony Wilden (1972:114)*

When in the early 1960s the Russian plant breeders were finally permitted to lay the ghost of Lysenkosim, the new political line allowed them to turn to genetics if that would serve them better, but not to rake up the history of Lysenkoism since the 1920s; to indulge in such embarrassing controversy would make for "disorganizing the cadres" (Joravsky 1970: Ch. 6). Though not bound by such a command politically, Indian sociologists appear to have resorted to comparable quietude; for although the paradigm which arose in the 1950s has long since fallen of exhaustion, we have never seriously asked how it came to acquire its once enormous influence and what aspects of the Indian social reality it did obscure. This essay seeks to open up these questions.

Put otherwise, I am interested in secular inequalities in India. Their importance in contemporary India struck me first with the appearance of

Dandekar and Rath's "Poverty in India" eight years ago (1971) in EPW. Apart from their demonstration that over 40 per cent of the population lived below the poverty line, their tables of distribution of income (e.g., Table 2.7: p.38) showed too that the office clerk's income put him somewhere around the 95th percentile mark; and from that plateau one could see those enormous peaks of affluence not too far away. What puzzled me greatly was why the sociological significance of this sort of income distribution went completely unnoticed in the then sociological literature.

The question was posed even more sharply the next year during a seminar on "A Cultural Policy for India". The tenor of the proceedings may be captured with a quote from Suresh Shukla (1975: 246) of Jamia Millia Islamia:

> All past experience shows that at the point of planning policy, the greatest stress is laid on universal mass education: education of women, of scheduled castes and tribes, and in rural areas. At the point of fixing quantitative targets, proportionate expansion of all sectors takes over. At the point of performance, the highest achievements are all in the field of urban education, in secondary education, upper caste education and so on.[1] The sectors of priority in policy, including adult literacy, are the laggards in performance: this is in line with, a consequence of, and a reinforcer of the pattern of distribution of political and economic power.

Clearly there was something in the structure of the wider Indian society which regularly pulled these "plans" out of shape. What was it? Why did it simply fail in register on the sociologists' analytic consciousness?

Explanations for so massive and so obvious an error of omission must necessarily be complex. The sociologists' lack of sensitivity—or at least their lack of intellectual response—to these magnitudes of poverty and to the pressures making for increasing inequalities in India, this essay will argue, can be attributed to three convergent, individually potent, and mutually autonomous influences:

(i) the prevalent public ideology, whose premises were drawn (a) partly from the colonial public institutions which, in turn, incorporated the premises of British social and political thought, and (b) partly from the ideology of the Indian national movements; I shall argue that both these strands served to desensitize the generation entering the academia in the 1940s and the 1950s to issues of exploitation and of conflicts of interest between different segments of society; and that this desensitization was aided by;

(ii) the theoretical, methodological, and substantive interests of American cultural anthropology—which came to overwhelm Indian sociology in the 1950s—and the absence of countervailing insights in the other intellectual traditions to which Indian sociologists took recourse; and finally,

(iii) the social backgrounds of Indian sociologists have been limited to relatively narrow strata, and their social experiences to relatively narrow grooves; and therefore their resources of personal knowledge have been much too lean to generate much resistance to the desensitization caused by the first two factors.

Public Ideology

Can one identify the key ideas shaping the contours of public opinion at the time of independence and since? Perhaps the most searching analysis comes from a political sociologist, Rajni Kothari (e.g., in 1976), looking for the structural flaws contributing to the crisis of early 1975. Interesting as far as it goes, it is not of much help in our particular concern here. We are interested in such elements in the public ideology as served to desensitize sociologists to the magnitudes of, and the trends in, secular inequalities. Some pointers to these elements should be available in the sociologists' own abundant writings; it would then be necessary to trace these pointers to their historical roots. Here as in any enquiry, all possible errors of judgement cannot be forestalled; the need is to define the problem and to get a debate going.

One set of possible influences concerns the variety of ideas which might be placed under the rubric "traditional". These would include the ideology of hierarchy, embodied in the caste system, and examined at length by Louis Dumont, as well as the Mughal style of imperial governance. I shall not consider these though it might be argued that their influence, operating through the culture of university departments and of the wider, quasi-political academic arenas, contributed to the otherwise inexplicably long innings of the paradigm of the 1950s. I shall bracket these off[2] because such mechanisms could only have served to *prolong* the sway of the paradigm espoused by the influentials of the 1950s; the real questions are about the particular content of this paradigm and the context which brought to its protagonists their influence.

Colonial Heritage

In propagating the paradigm of the 1950s M.N. Srinivas had a pivotal role; and our search for the beliefs which blocked the perception of secular inequalities can well begin with his "Social Change in Modern India" (1966), a sociological landmark at the time of its publication. It presents his most comprehensive interpretation of the wider social processes active in India. The terms "equality" and "inequality" are missing from the index though some related aspects are subsumed under the category "caste"; but the second chapter on "Westernization" shows exactly where Srinivas went off the rails:

> Implicit in westernization are certain value preferences. A most important value, which in turn subsumes several other values, is what may be broadly characterized as humanitarianism, by which is meant an active concern for the welfare of all human beings irrespective of caste, economic position, religion, age, and sex. *Equalitarianism and secularization are both included in humanitarianism*... (p. 48, emphasis added).
>
> Humanitarianism underlay many of the reforms introduced by the British in the first half of the nineteenth century. The introduction of British civil, penal, and procedural law put an end to certain inequalities that were part of Hindu and Islamic jurisprudence ... (p. 48).
>
> According to O'Malley[3], two revolutionary results of introducing the British judicial system were the establishment of the principle of equality and the creation of a consciousness of positive rights ...(p. 49)
>
> The principle of equality found expression in the abolition of slavery, in the opening of the new schools and colleges—in theory at least—to all irrespective of religion, race and caste... (p. 49).
>
> As British rule progressed, rationality and humanitarianism became broader, deeper, and more powerful, and the years since the achievement of independence have seen a remarkable increase—a genuine leap forward—in the extension of both. The attack on untouchability which independent India has launched provides a striking example of such extension... (p. 49).

Perhaps it would not be fair to judge Srinivas' understanding of colonialism in 1966 by today's standards.[4] Unmistakable, however, is the profound impression made upon him by British humanitarianism, seen to subsume equalitarianism. Our confidence that we have here an appropriate point of departure is enhanced by the assenting echoes of this interpretation for years in the work of eminent sociologists (e.g., in Yogendra Singh 1973).

We must recognize immediately that the belief that British rule had a strongly equalizing influence upon the highly stratified Indian society has been potent and widespread, defying the fact that the colonial order was built around the central principles of institutionalized racial inequality and of strong support for indigenous structures of power and authority—especially after 1857 (e.g., Metcalf 1965: Ch. 3ff). This potency could not have come merely from colonial spokesmen like O' Malley. It is clear that some notion of "equality" was implicit in various colonial institutional structures—the courts, the schools, the franchise—and therefore it is necessary to look for the sense in which the British used the term.

Reflecting upon the nature of "equality" before the law, equality of vote, and so forth, it becomes clear that the reference is to a certain lack of individuous discrimination in specific situations and relationships. This limited equality is fully compatible with the enormous inequalities of wealth and status all too familiar in British society. In British social and political thought this usage goes back at least to Hobbes in mid-seventeenth century. Models of the capitalist society developed in this tradition posited that everyone is subject to the rules of the market in *equal* measure and that the law is blind to the differences of status between individuals (Macpherson 1962: 74-86;199ff). (The principles perceived by Hobbes and his successors as applying to the economic market of capitalism would ultimately be extended to the political market too in the form of one man, one vote).

This notion of equality fitted closely the interest of a rising bourgeoisie anxious to ensure that, when the public law intervened in its affairs, no special allowance would be made for the entrenched landed interests with their heritable privileges. In the course of the triumph of the bourgeoisie, this somewhat esoteric sense of "equality" was built into the British legal and political institutions; and unless we remember this admittedly nebulous sense of the term, we are likely to misunderstand the implications of these institutions for the structure of Indian society.

To restate the issue more generally, the colonial regime, westernization, etc. came to be mistakenly associated in the sociological mind with a tendency towards "equality". Employing the term unreflectively, we did not notice that the term was in fact a cover for very unequal control over property—and therefore also for the associated inequalities of status, power, and so forth. These inequalities, common to capitalist societies which have not institutionalized strong and effective redistributive mechanisms, were in colonial India further reinforced by the strategies of colonial governance (see Saberwal 1979)

National Movement

One might have thought that the national movement would have scrutinized this and other aspects of the colonial institutions closely but, surprisingly at first sight, *the key ideas underlying the Indian national movement also served to direct attention away from these secular inequalities*. This movement was large and complex and is subject to much debate among specialists. After 1885, the Indian National Congress came to dominate it. Over the six decades to independence, the Congress underwent several changes in leadership, if not as much in political ideology (Bipan Chandra 1979). By 1920, Gandhi had risen to power on the national political stage and, over long spells, his was the dominant voice in the party and the movement; we may take his ideas as shaping the public ideology of the national movement importantly.

Gandhian thought in turn is a complex field of scholarship but there appears to be general agreement that, is marshalling his forces against the colonial regime, Gandhi laid great stress on a harmonious commonalty of interests among Indians of different strata (Bhattacharyya 1969: Ch. 8; Namboodiripad 1959). It is true that Gandhi brought to the movement something of a mass dimension, drawing in sections of the working class, peasantry, women and so forth (Brown 1972; Pearson 1979); yet as a good general he was careful in almost every case to direct their energies against colonial rule, defining the interests of the different classes of Indians as mutually non-antagonistic. In a society as grossly inegalitarian as India's, however, such a definition must inevitably subserve the interests of the already dominant classes. This implication Gandhi did not confront, at least not until after independence.

The foregoing is not to deny that Gandhi often said, wrote, and did things which showed his strong, genuine, and sincere personal concern for the poor. Indeed he suggested that *satyagraha* could be applied not only against the colonialists but also against the internal vested economic and other interests (Bhattacharyya 1969: 230-31). This is perfectly true, and his image of the ideal social order was a highly egalitarian one; but the unfortunate fact remains that about property relations within India, whatever his words, his actions were entirely quietest. After a spell of early hostility (Bhattacharya 1976), the more perceptive of the Indian capitalist class recognized this, seeing in him (along with others in the Congress Right) both a worthy general in the battle against the colonial regime and their best bet for a post-colonial order that would protect their interests (Bipan Chandra 1975). Many of them gave him their unstinted support, occasionally partaking also of some of his hallo (Birla 1953).

Several influential strands of the public ideology, then, served to befog the Indian social reality at mid-century. Even though the colonial courts came to be established in India largely to clear the way for British commerce, "egalitarianism" was part of the rhetoric surrounding the colonial legal order, and the rhetoric extended to other colonial institutions too. The inequalities institutionalized in the caste system had put Indians enough on the defensive to persuade some of them that colonialism had indeed brought India a more egalitarian order. The infrastructure of administration, law, communications, education, etc., designed to integrate India more closely with the colonial economy also allowed the Indian merchant castes some room to move into industrial entrepreneurship, and their pace quickened somewhat after World War I (Bagchi 1972). Simultaneously, the course taken by the national movement was very much in line with the interests of the Indian capitalist class which, over the decades, came to acquire an enduring influence over the political process (Birla 1953, makes the connection transparent). This influence would combine with wider strategic considerations to ensure that the national movement define the interests of the various classes in terms of harmony rather than conflict. It is true that Marxists writers—R.P. Dutt (1947) and A.R. Desai (1948) among them—recognized the conflicts of interest and the direction of inequalities in Indian society in all their starkness but, as we shall see, Marxist scholarship was more or less beyond the pale at least into the 1960s; its insights were at best peripheral to the public ideology at mid-century.

Cultural Anthropology

The powerful, implicit, premises of the public ideology were entirely compatible with the key premises of American cultural anthropology; and this compatibility undoubtedly helps explain something of the speed and the extent of its influence almost immediately upon contact with Indian academia. While the fields of sociology and anthropology had both come to India at about the time of the First World War, the fields did not spread much beyond Bombay, Calcutta and Lucknow (Rao 1974: xxv*f*, xxx*f*). Resources for empirical research were scant, and relations between the impoverished university departments were sometimes sour (see Ghurye 1973: 59, 131). When early in the 1950s American anthropologists began to work in India[5], with distinctive traditions in theory, method, and substantive concerns, the impression rapidly grew that they would sweep all before them.[6]

Although many leading Indian sociologists and anthropologists of the 1950s and later did their formative work in Indian, British, and Australian universities, the overall influence from the United States was much the strongest. It was felt through the very much larger number of research workers, whose work commanded general professional respect, through the vast stream of their publications, and through the large number of Indians going to the United States as students, researchers, teachers, conferees, and so forth. The intellectual premises of the British and Australian traditions, in any case, were for our purposes virtually indistinguishable from those of American cultural anthropology, and therefore I need consider here only the latter. I realize how presumptuous it is to try to force these premises into a few brief comments, but my task is made easier by my limited interest: to see how these helped further to befog the issue of secular inequalities in Indian society.

We may begin by noting that the American tradition was oriented rather loosely and inclusively towards the study of culture in contrast to the sharper concerns of British social anthropology with the social structure and, even more strongly, of the Marxian tradition with the linkages of *economic structures* with the other social dimensions. The humanistic affiliations of the American tradition were reflected in its interest in the *diversity of cultures*—in the full range of human experience— though, for practical reasons, it concentrated on, and was successful with, some parts of this experience more than with others. A liberal, rather than an ethnocentric, outlook was expressed in the doctrine of *cultural relativism*, holding that any society and culture has to be understood in terms of its own premises rather than in terms of external values, say those of Christianity, in the manner say the missionaries might be inclined to do (e.g., Benedict 1934)

There was the assumption, too, that cultures usually are *integrated wholes*; and while conflicts are part of the human situation, cultures provide for their orderly resolution: cultures are to be understood with reference not so much to be conflicts of interest as to the procedures and the norms governing their management. The road to understanding these cultural wholes, furthermore, lies through the face-to-face community—that is a residential community . An anthropologist doing field work for a year or two in an alien land could not easily cope with a community of more than about one thousand person, and therefore for a decade or more nearly every anthropologist coming to India went to study a village community. The village was seen to provide a random sample of Indian society, much as a glass of water would provide a sample from the flow of a river.

The anthropological study of the village received reinforcement from the official Indian interest in "rural uplift". Its antecedents went several decades back (Haldipur 1974:31), and in the early 1950s it came to be institutionalized as "community development" with strong encouragement from the Ford Foundation (Taylor et al. 1965). The central thrust there too was to discourage the reorganization of property relations[7], say through land reforms beyond an attack on the larger zamindars, and to stress instead the harmonious commonalty of interests, called "felt needs"; covergent here were the key premises both of the public ideology and of cultural anthropology. For some Indian anthropologists and sociologists it provided too a welcome channel to the government and to "planning", and an opportunity to acquire a personal sense of importance.

This over-commitment to the village community, for all its fecundity in print, was from the present standpoint a methodological misfortune. In mid-twentieth century, a great deal of the village community was in fact organized into the caste system which, therefore, came to be regarded as the key institutional complex of Indian society. Several generations of European scholars had already identified the caste system as a polar type in the continuum of stratificatory systems; and now the sociological mind came to equate the caste system firmly with overall inequalities in Indian society, more on the consequences of this fixation, with the caste system later.

To be fair to this tradition of scholarship, it did not limit itself to the village community entirely. A characteristic initial distinction between orthogenetic cities (the indigenous one) and heterogenetic cities (the intrusive, colonial ones) directed attention towards the links between the village community and the sanskritic tradition, the centres of pilgrimage, and the like (Redfield and Singer 1954; Marriott 1955). Such sources as western education, factories, electoral politics, etc. were recognized as acting upon the village community: but there was no analytic framework for the larger whole wherein the interlinkages of these miscellaneous sources might be located. When the scholars in this tradition thought about phenomena in that larger world, the digits of their analysis came either from their understanding of the caste system (e.g., Srinivas 1962) or from a characteristic perspective on the process of economic development—the "entrepreneurs" its prime movers (e.g., Singer 1972). The thought that the larger structure of contemporary India might have rather different patterns of internal integration and external control, worthy of inquiry in their own right, seldom touched this corpus of scholarly writing.

Before taking leave of American cultural anthropology, I would like to comment on its attitude to history. British social anthropology, when led by Malinowski and Radcliffe-Brown, or even by Firth, Gluckman, and Leach, may fairly be called anti-historical, but this will not hold for the American tradition. Their historical interests have been strong and have constituted two major clusters. One concerned the culture history of particular peoples studied. This was in some ways forced upon them, for their natural point of departure rested with the study of American Indians who had been mauled severely during the preceding century or two. To reconstruct their aboriginal way of life, recourse was necessary both to the intervening archives and to the people's collective memory. Carried to India, this sensitivity was reflected in a concern either with local history (Marriott 1953) or with the civilization (Singer 1966) or its scared texts (Orenstein 1970).

The other cluster was concerned with general culture history, with a Toynbean sweep (e.g., Kroeber 1944; Steward 1955). Here, the focus was upon the course of whole civilizations, their cyclical changes, perhaps their growth and may be decline. Missing, by and large, was a concern with the historical experience of the middle range; the rise of capitalism, the colonial expansion and its consequences, and the meaning of industrialism—or of a lack thereof. On this count until well into the sixties, the work of Bernard Cohn (e.g. 1969) and of Clifford Geertz on Indonesia (e.g., 1965) stood out as isolated exceptions. In so far as this phase entered the anthropologists' work at all, the theme song came from Redfield (1941) who, analyzing a range of communities in Yucatan in Mexico, had encapsulated the historically created differences between the structures of pre-industrial and industrial societies into the popular, but ahistorical "folk-urban continuum". All this would not have mattered had the Indian sociologists brought to their pursuits a sharper critical awareness, for correctives of a sort were then available elsewhere. These were for long ignored; the following sections explore why.

Sociological Traditions

Granted that the traditions of social and cultural anthropology gave few clues to the wider structures of societies such as India at mid-century, Indian anthropologists have since the 1950s been moving steadily over into the category of sociologists, and one might have thought that, in this new affiliation, they would seek or devise alternative paradigms for their analytic tasks; but the search has not been productive, the devising has not been vigorous. The latter will occupy us later; the unhelpfulness of much of the sociological tradition calls for enquiry now.

Britain, it will be recalled, has been the model for much academic activity in India during and since the colonial period, and sociology—as distinct from social anthropology—did not get its colours there until well after the Second World War. It is true that G.S. Ghurye, who dominated sociology at Bombay for long decades, had a Cambridge degree, but his mentor had been the anthropologist, W.H.R. Rivers. Ghurye's predecessor at Bombay, Patrick Geddes, coming from the outer fringes of British academia, had been appointed Professor of Sociology; and therefore later appointees to the department also came to be called sociologists (see Ghurye 1973: 44f). Sociology on the continent is regarded generally as having arisen as part of the attempt to comprehend the social disruption issuing from industrialization during the nineteenth century. That the process had been disruptive for British society too cannot be denied, but it would seem that it evoked an intellectual response not in the crystallization of a discipline called sociology but, among others, in the works of Dickens, Marx and Engels.

What about Marxism? To be sure, the sensitivity of this tradition to production relations and to the historic transformation of societies made it inherently the most promising potential source for insights into the structure of Indian society, and some of this promise has been realized since the early 1970s. The early work of A.R. Desai and Ramkrishna Mukherjee had offered serious, if sometimes uneven, applications of this tradition to the Indian situation. For reasons considered throughout this essay, however, Indian academia during the 1940s and the 1950s—and especially the sociologists—had been predisposed against the Marxist tradition.

Indian Marxists, furthermore, had additional burdens to carry. The public ideology at the time identified Marxism overall with Stalinist totalitarianism, with the dogmatism of much of the literature coming from Russia, and with the support given by the Communist Party of India to the British after Hitler invaded Russia (Overstreet and Windmiller, 1959: Ch. 10, discuss the context). This initial predisposition against Marxism grew stronger during the Indian sociologists' long tutelage to American cultural anthropology. A certain defensiveness was consequently induced in many Marxist scholars. Consider the case of A.R. Desai. His major work, "Social Background of Indian Nationalism", was published first in 1948. It remains, to this day, the only work by an Indian sociologist to comprehend the key dimensions of the wider structure of Indian society. His chapters concerning village India were, however, brought into question by the flood of village studies since the 1950s. Recently, I asked him why he had not responded to this literature in his much reprinted work. A.R. Desai said that he had not wanted to be identified with the common communist practice of changing one's analyses to fit the changing political winds. Confused here was the difference between a scholar's necessary autonomy vis-a-vis centre of power and his necessary openness to fresh bases of data. One unfortunate consequence of this confusion was that the anti-Marxist sociologist could readily dismiss his overall work as being merely dogmatic Marxism.[8,9]

Many Indian academics transferred their affections after 1947, from Britain to the United States, where sociology has long been burgeoning, and one can make up considerable list of Indians trained in, or strongly influenced by, various American schools of sociology: Yogesh Atal, Alfred Barnabas, Anil Bhatt, Ratna Dutta, Pradipto Roy, Lalit Sen.....Whatever the quality of individual studies, no major advance in our understanding of Indian society is associated with any of them. One gets the impression that the technology of sociology in the United States has grown to suit certain facets of a particular sort of society: one which was built on capitalist premises from the beginning and whose members, in the course of industrialization, underwent comprehensive socialization of a sort that would fit them adequately to the capitalist industrial way of life. It may be that the very technical sophistication of this sociology, fitted ever so closely to some facets of American society, renders it unproductive in societies functioning with several orders of economic organization—and their social and political correlates.

Barrier of language have stood between sociology in India and that in Europe, and until the late 1960s, the principal European influence, felt via

English translation, was that of Max Weber. His influence is explicit in Andre Beteille's work and shows through in a diluted form in much else. It is necessary to note, however, that, for all his historical depth, Weber's dominant interest in the origins of the rationality of the western industrial sort—and in the lack of such maturation elsewhere—excluded a great many other questions from his purview. Nothing in the mass of his writings would suggest that he understood very much about the implications of colonialism for societies under its sway.[10] Furthermore, although Weber distinguished between wealth, status, and power as dimensions of stratification, he did not use these distinctions to analyze any modern society on a national scale. (On both these counts the legacy of Marx is much more fertile).

Andre Beteille almost alone among the Indian sociologists has acknowledged Weber's influence explicitly, evident in his first book (1965) as well as in the most recent one (1977). The first book, a village study, established the separation of the dimensions of wealth, status, and power in the stratification of the village, but the village had, meanwhile, been integrated much more closely into the wider regional and national social, economic, and political frameworks too; disregarding this, then, did the limiting of the analysis to the village put serious limits also on one's understanding of the social process there? While Beteille has continued to write a great deal on social inequality, he has concentrated on the structure of agrarian relations (1974) and on the universal range of expressions of inequality (1977). The wider inequalities within India do flit through Beteille's writings but are seldom held in focus for very long.

A diluted form of Weber's influence pervades much of the recent literature on stratification in India (e.g., Yogendra Singh, 1974). It will be remembered that Weber had identified commensality and connubial as the two major indicators of the relative equality of status within a social stratum.[11] His reference was to societies wherein not only did the governing strata recognize themselves to be so but, furthermore, had no occasion to apologize for, nor any need to camouflage, the fact of their being in control. They did not have any pressures to tolerate commensal and connubial relations with their social inferiors; and the middle strata would in turn often follow their example.

During the decades since Weber, however, social convulsions have visited not only Russia, China, and other socialist countries but Germany itself. Certain patterns of colonial and racial dominance have had to retreat elsewhere. The old assurance of the governing strata everywhere has been somewhat jolted. They have often had to account for, if not to apologize for, the privileges associated with their being in control. It has been necessary to camouflage the reality of privilege; the governing strata almost everywhere have found it useful to proclaim that there is little difference between them and the anonymous mass.[12] Interdining between high and low is today common almost everywhere; and intermarriage is well tolerated—even on occasion publicly celebrated to suggest, at least symbolically, the openness of the social order!

The analyst's task is made even more difficult by certain widespread policy packages: "progressive" income taxation, state subsidies for the unemployed, health services, and the like.[13] Policy packages whose form, if not their content, has been similar came into widespread use in India under Nehru and since. Alongside this came the uncritical use of concepts arising in the structures of western industrial societies. Together these generated powerful optical illusions among social scientists working on India, and it would be useful to trace this process in one case in some detail.

The first step in generating this illusion was the implicit assumption that the caste system was the traditional matrix of stratification not only in village India but also elsewhere.[14] It is true that much of precolonial urban India would have been organized residentially into caste groups or their analogous, but, the principles underlying the supra-village distribution of resources in, say, Mughal India had very little to do with the caste system (see Habib 1963). Put differently, a limited dissociation between caste and occupation in the urban milieu did not in fact represent a decisive change in Indian social structure.

Having assumed however that the link between caste and occupation had been central to the society, the second act in the rise of the illusion was the perception that this link was in fact being violated. The evidence for this violation could come from several directions. At least some aspects of the caste system had drawn fire from the national movement, and this hostility was embodied in the Constitution (piloted by an ex-untouchable) and in the subsequent legislation providing for reverse discrimination favouring the scheduled castes and the like. Through politics, educational institutions, and the job quotas, a few members of the scheduled castes moved into non-caste occupations, and this limited dissociation between caste and occupation was acting upon other castes in the urban bureaucratic and industrial sectors also. It was easy enough in this situation to document some erosion of the caste order in certain urban areas (e. g., Saberwal 1976b).

It should be remembered that pressures to accept the lower castes commensally had been active since late nineteenth century at least (e.g., Jones 1976), and here and there marriages too would cut across the caste boundaries. Over the decades, evidence came too of a variety of challenges being mounted against, and of some decline in, caste ideology in regions as far apart as Punjab, Tamil Nadu, Kerala, and Maharashtra.

Having concluded that the caste system was declining, we cast about for another label for the new order, and the illusion was complete when the label 'class' was put on the new situation (e.g. D'Souza 1967; Bhatt 1975). What the term "class" meant was drawn from its use in relation to western industrial societies with their greater mobility and, in Srinivas's term, equalitarianism; the implication that inequalities in India were declining was thus smuggled into the terminology. Questions concerning class *relations* and the associated control over resources were seldom posed. Typically, the whole argument was fastened to a community study—or to questionnaire data from a sample survey; wanting entirely were the wider perspectives both of historical development and of the contemporary social framework.

Sociologists' Interests

We move now to the third of the elements which have tended to veil secular inequalities from the sociological consciousness; it concerns us sociologists ourselves. While we have been aware of the cultural variation as between regions, our intellectual energies appear to have been more or less fully absorbed in documenting the variations in the caste system or, say, in kinship (Karve 1953). The wider structures of Indian society either did not seem to be problematical or, when attention was directed to them, as we have seen, the digits of discourse were extraneous, these did not emerge from the logic of these wider structures themselves.

One can only speculate why these wider structures did not seem to be problematical. There is some evidence that the first wave of sociologists, like the intelligentsia generally, tended to come from propertied, upper caste background; and one may surmise too that, as with this stratum generally, their socialization would *not* normally have pushed them towards exploring their social environment extensively. If this was indeed so, and given the desensitization coming from the public ideology and from American cultural anthropology, the consensual picture of Indian society emerging from the village studies would not be quickly challenged on the basis of the Indian sociologists' personal experiences elsewhere in the social space.

On the other hand, the 1940s, 1950s, and 1960s were periods of considerable opportunity for them even with the consensual picture, with all its flaws. In universities and in the research institutes the field of sociology expanded spectacularly, offering its members a comfortable living if not always affluence. Compared with pervious generations, opportunity and mobility were very much a part of these first generation sociologists' own experience, consciousness, and perception. It seemed to be appropriate for them to focus on similar situations of mobility and change elsewhere. (For a late example of this temptation, see Saberwal 1976b). It enabled one to document the decline of the caste system, something we Indians had long been defensive about; and in any case the accounts of mobility and change made for much more interesting reading than those of immobility and stagnation. In early 1976 a young Swedish anthropologist, Stefan Molund, who had been working in a stagnant, poor neighbourhood in Kanpur expressed his puzzlement to me: reading the literature, everywhere he encountered evidence of mobility, of entrepreneurial success, of caste organizations bargaining effectively with political parties, and so forth. He had not found much evidence of any of this in his area of study; this worried him: how would his thesis hold together? What he did not know was that a whole generation of Indian sociologists had unwittingly misread the course being taken by Indian society, regularly though unconsciously emphasizing achievement, mobility, mobilization, reverse discrimination, egalitarianism, and the like, and neglecting the masses of poverty and the *growing* inequalities as well as the processes which made this permanently so!

In this essay I have argued that both the public ideology in the late 1940s and American cultural anthropology combined to desensitize us to the magnitudes of inequality, and the associated magnitudes of deprivation, which strike visitors as such stark features of the Indian social landscape; and nothing in our social backgrounds or personal experiences would persuade us to challenge the emerging consensual picture. The literature was not entirely wanting in references to bonded labourers (Harper 1968) or to destitute tribal groups (Gardner 1966); but lying beyond the dominant analytic frame, these tended to be dismissed as marginal.

From the earlier sociological concern with the sacred texts, the paradigm of the 1950s did move attention to the *social context* for interpreting behaviour, but this context was largely bounded by the local community.

This has turned out to be misleading, indeed falsifying, for the local has long since been integrated into the larger mechanisms of appropriation, deprivation, and exclusion, during the colonial period and since. In the immediate future the pointers to these large mechanisms may have to be taken from historians and economists. To continue to ignore that context is epistemologically deeply flawed; and this essay has sought to demonstrate this by placing the paradigm of the 1950s itself in that socio-historical context.

Notes

1. Cited here is John A. Laska "Planning and Educational Development in India", Teachers College Press, New York, 1968.
2. For an earlier consideration of these issues see Saberwal (1976a).
3. Cited here is L.S.S. O'Malley (1941:59). While the British administrators' reports are an invaluable source of data for much of the colonial period, their views on the colonial encounter have to be handled with considerable discretion. O'Malley's own stock among modern Indian historians is quite low.
4. My forthcoming "Inequality in Colonial India" (1979) offers what I hope will be a somewhat less vulnerable interpretation.
5. See Saberwal (1970) on political context for this sharp expansion in the overseas interests of American anthropology.
6. During the 1920s and later, the vigorous organs of a native German intellectual tradition had enabled the Frankfurt School to digest the Anglo-American empiricism into its own system (see Jay 1973); but nowhere in sociology were the Indian traditions able to muster the sense of mastery and of critical awareness requisite to the task of appropriating this empiricism. We succumbed to it; we did not have and did not seek the critical apparatus needed to examine its credentials and claims autonomously.
7. Interview with Erich Jacobi, Stockholm, November 28, 1978. During the 1950s Jacobi watched the scene in India closely as a senior member of FAO.
8. Desai wrote his thesis under Ghurye. While the latter's autobiographical account (1973) is replete with details of the theses of his many minor students, the name of A.R. Desai is not so much as

mentioned!

9. The case of Ramkrishna Mukherjee is more enigmatic, but this defensiveness may in his case have led to his heavy concentration, since the 1960's, largely on methodological issues. His recent, wide-ranging, and erudite survey of the field over the past quarter of a century (1977) is silent on this change of direction in his own work.
10. This lack of interest in colonialism by itself, in the judgment of Romila Thapar (in press), led Weber to misconstrue the complex antecedents of industrial capitalism; she has argued that, without the colonial loot, fluid capital would in England have been so much scarcer that the pace and the course of industrialization would have been very different. The argument is interesting even through, I think, Romila Thapar has misread the evidence somewhat.
11. Gerth and Mills, 1946; 188, 191, 400; the indicators are applied to the caste system on pp. 405-9.
12. The issue here admittedly bristles with complexity. On one side is Ralf Dahrendorf who, for the industrial West, stresses the high rate of social mobility and the expansion of the "social rights of citizenship", so that only "the inequality of power and authority which inevitably accompanies social organization" remains—or will remain—as the "fundamental inequality of social structure" (1959:64). On the other side is Raymond Boudon (1974) who sees this much vaunted social mobility as being principally *lateral*, implying that the structure is very much less open that Dahrendorf suggests.

    These arguments are peripheral for India. Inequality here is scarcely a matter of interpreting complex statistical data. The suppression of its awareness here is much more direct; one among many examples concerns the Director of a private sector social research centre, a very highly paid, affluent man (in fact *not* a social scientist at all!) who responded to a staff member's proposal to study urban poverty with the comment, "Poverty? What poverty? I'm also poor."
13. For one attempt to de-mystify their consequences for inequalities in England, see Titmuss (1962).
14. Fuller (1977) has argued that the caste system in a tightly organized village structure was not so much the traditional— precolonial—pattern as the outcome of the economic and political processes in the colonial order. (Uif Hannerz gave me this essay.)

References

Bagchi, A.K., 1972, "Private Investment in India 1900-1939", Cambridge University Press.

Benedict, Ruth, 1934, "Patterns of Culture", Mentor (1946).

Beteille, A., 1965, "Caste, Class and Power", University of California Press.

—, 1974, "Studies in Agrarian Social Structure", Oxford University Press.

—, 1977, "Inequality among Men", Oxford University Press.

Bhatt, Anil, 1975, "Caste, Class and Politics: An Empirical Profile of Social Stratification in Modern India", Manohar, Delhi.

Bhattacharyya, Buddhadeva, 1969, "Evolution of the Political Philosophy of Gandhi", Calcutta Book House, Calcutta.

Bhattacharya, S., 1976, "Cotton Mills and Spinning Wheels: Swadeshi and the Indian Capitalist Class, 1920-22", *Economic and Political Weekly*, 11: 1828-34.

Birla, G.D.,1953, "In the Shadow of the Mahatma", Orient Longmans, Bombay.

Boudon, Raymond, 1974, "Education, Opportunity, and Social Inequality: Changing Prospects in Western Society", Wiley, New York.

Brown, Judith, 1972, "Gandhi's Rise to Power: Indian Politics 1915-22", Cambridge University Press.

Chandra, Bipan, 1975, "Jawaharlal Nehru and the Indian Capitalist Class, 1936", *Economic and Political Weekly*, 10:1307-24.

—, 1979, "Elements of Continuity and Change in Early Nationalist Activity", *Studies in History*, 1: 73-88.

Cohn, Bernard C., 1969, "Structural Changes in Indian Rural Society 1596-1885", In "Land Control and Social Structure in Indian History", R.E. Frykenberg (Ed.), University of Wisconsin Press.

Dahrendorf, Ralf, 1959, "Class and Class Conflict in Industrial Society", Routledge and Kegan Paul, London.

Dandekar, V.M., and N. Rath., 1971, "Poverty in India", *Economic and Political Weekly*, 6:25-48, 106-46.

Desai, A.R., 1948, "Social Background of Indian Nationalism", Popular Prakashan, Bombay.

D'Souza, V.S.,1967, "Caste and Class: A Reinterpretation", *Journal of Asian and African Studies*, 2:192-211.

Dutt, R.P., 1947, "India Today", Manisha, Calcutta (1970 ed).

Fuller, Chris, 1977, "British India or Traditional India? An Anthropological Problem", *Ethnos* (Stockholm), 42:95-121.

Gardner, Peter, 1966, "Symmetric Respect and Memorate Knowledge: The Structure and Ecology of Individualistic Culture", *Southwestern Journal of Anthropology*, 32: 389-415.

Geertz, Clifford, 1965, "Social History of an Indonesian Town", MIT Press.

Gerth, H.H. and C.W. Mills, 1946, (eds.) "From Max Weber: Essays in Sociology", Oxford University Press.

Ghurye, G.S., 1973, "I and Other Explorations", Popular Prakashan, Bombay.

Habib, I., 1963, "Agrarian System of Mughal India (1556-1707)", Asia, Bombay.

Haldipur, R.N., 1974, "Sociology of Community Development and Panchayati Raj (Part-I)". In "A Survey of Research in Sociology and Social Anthropology", Vol. II, Indian Council of Social Science Research (sponsor), Popular Prakashan, Bombay.

Harper, Edward, 1968, "Social Consequences of an "unsuccessful" Low Caste Movement". In "Social Mobility in the Caste System in India", James Silverberg (ed.), Mouton, The Hague.

Jay, Martin, 1973, "The Dialectical Imagination", Heinemann, London.

Jones, Kenneth, 1976, "Arya Dharm: Hindu Consciousness in 19th Century Punjab", Manohar, New Delhi.

Joravsky, David, 1970, "The Lysenko Affair", Harvard University Press.

Karve, Irawati, 1953, "Kinship Organization in India", Asia, Bombay (3rd ed., 1968).

Kothari, Rajni, 1976, "Democratic Polity and Social Change in India", Allied, Bombay.

Kroeber, A.L., 1944, "Configurations of Cultural Growth", University of California Press.

Macpherson, C.B., 1962, "Political Theory of Possessive Individualism: Hobbes to Locke", Oxford University Press.

Marriott, McKim, 1953, "Village Structure and the Punjab Government: A Restatement", *American anthropologist*, 55: 137-43.

—, 1955, "Little Communities in an Indigenous Civilization", In "Village India," M. Marriott (ed.), University of Chicago Press.

Metcalf, Thomas, 1965, "The Aftermath of Revolt: India, 1857-70", Princeton University Press.

Mukherjee, Ramkrishna, 1977, "Trends in Indian Sociology", *Current Sociology*, Vol 25, No. 3.

Namboodiripad, E.M.S., 1959, "The Mahatma and the Ism", Peoples

Publishing House, New Delhi.

O'Malley, L.S.S., 1941, "The Impact of European Civilization", in "Modern India and the West", L.S.S. O'Malley. (ed.), Oxford University Press.

Orenstein, Henry, 1970, "Logical Congruence in Hindu Sacred Law: Another Interpretation", *Contributions to Indian Sociology* (n s), 4:22-35.

Overstreet, Gene D. and Marshall Windmuller, 1959, "Communism in India", University of California Press.

Pearson, Gail O., 1979, "Women in public life in Bombay city with special reference to the Civil Disobedience Movement", Jawaharlal Nehru University, Ph D. thesis, New Delhi.

Rao, M.S.A., 1974, "Introduction" . In "A Survey of Research in Sociology and Social Anthropology", Vol. I, ICSSR (sponsor), Popular Prakashan, Bombay.

Redfield, Robert, 1941, "The Folk Culture of Yucatan", University of Chicago Press.

—, and Milton Singer, 1954, "Cultural Role of Cities", *Economic Development and Cultural Change* 3:53-73.

Saberwal, Satish, 1970, "International Social Science: Some Political Aspects", *Economic And Political Weekly*, 5:1043-51.

—, 1976a, "For Academics to Read", *Indian Book Chronicle,* 1:225-27.

—, 1976b, "Mobile Men: Limits to Social Change in Urban Punjab", Vikas, New Delhi.

—, 1979, "Inequality in Colonial India", *Contributions to Indian Sociology* (ns), 13: 241-64.

Shukla, Suresh, 1975, "Educational Elements in Cultural Policy-A Socialist perspective", In "Towards a Cultural Policy", S. Saberwal (ed.), Vikas, Delhi, pp. 230-48.

Singer, M., 1966, (ed.), "Krishna: Myths, Rites and Attitudes", East-West Centre, Honolulu.

—, 1972, "Industrial Leadership, the Hindu Ethic, and the Spirit of Socialism", In his "When a Great Tradition Modernizes", Vikas, Delhi.

Singh, Yogendra, 1973, "Modernization of Indian Tradition", Thomson, Delhi.

—, 1974, "Sociology of Social Stratification", In "A Survey of Research in Sociology and Social Anthropology", Vol. I, ICSSR (sponsor), Popular Prakashan, Bombay.

Srinivas, M.N., 1966, "Social Change in Modern India", University of California Press.

—, 1962, "Caste in Modern India", In his "Caste in Modern India and Other Essays", Asia, Bombay.

Steward, Julian, 1955, "Theory of Culture Change", University of Illinois Press.

Taylor, Carl, *et al.*, 1965, "India's Roots of Democracy", Orient Longmans, Bombay.

Thapar, Romila, 1980, "Durkheim and Weber on Theories of Society and Race Relating to Precolonial India", in *Sociological Theories: Race and Colonialism*, UNESCO, Paris, pp. 93-116.

Titmuss, Richard M., 1962, "Income Distribution and Social Change", George Allen and Unwin. London.

Wilden, Anthony, 1972, "System and Structure", Tavistock, London.

4 The Reproduction of Inequality

Occupation, Caste and Family

ANDRE BETEILLE

The Problem

"The spirit of the age is in favour of equality", Nehru (1961: 521) wrote on the eve of India's independence, "though practice denies it almost everywhere". That was characteristic of Nehru's sense of history and of his desire to keep his thoughts on India in tune with it. He was calling for a change in the existing order of things to make it more consistent with the new spirit. In India, imperialism was still a reality, and so was the hierarchy of castes and communities based on immemorial tradition; but these were beginning to appear increasingly anachronistic to many who had caught something of the new spirit of which Nehru spoke.

"Yet", continued Nehru, "the spirit of the age will triumph". He was not alone in his enthusiasm for equality, for Tagore and Gandhi, to name only two, had both expressed themselves in its favour. The members of the Constituent Assembly, representing different sections of Indian society, clearly wanted equality to be the basis of the new legal and political order in India. Finally, in the last several decades, the commitment to equality has been repeatedly expressed in public life; politicians, judges, civil servants, lawyers, religious leaders, journalists, scholars and social workers have all spoken in one voice in its favour. It may safely be said that in India today, everyone is prepared to speak publicly in support of equality, but none in support of hierarchy or inequality.

Close to half a century after Nehru wrote, the contradiction between the ideal of equality and the practice of inequality still remains deeply and firmly lodged in Indian society. Why has "the spirit of the age" failed to triumph? If indeed the commitment to equality has spread and grown stronger in these years, why has it made so little difference to social practice? Where, specifically, do the obstacles to the further advance of equality lie?

We must not minimize the change that takes place when hierarchy is replaced by equality as the social ideal of a nation. The hierarchical conception of society was not unique to the Indian past, but it was carried much further and prevailed much longer there than in the West. This is not to say that equality meant nothing at all to Indians in the past, but rather, that religion, morality, law and custom combined to severely restrict its scope in the social domain, particularly in the relations between upper and lower castes, and between men and women.

Today, Indians no longer idealize hierarchy; what they, or at least the more articulate among them, idealize is equality. It may well be that some of this is make-believe, or merely for show, or a concession to liberal opinion in the West which enjoys cultural hegemony in the contemporary world. Be that as it may, our constitution, our laws and the programmes of all our political parties stress equality clearly and persistently; and they are an ineluctable part of the social reality of contemporary India.

We know that the modern conception of equality as a social ideal first emerged and became established in western countries such as Britain, France and the United States, and then spread to other parts of the world. The laws and constitutions of the former countries acted as models for others to emulate in their movement towards equality acted as models for others to emulate in their movement towards equality. No less significant than the legal and the constitutional changes in the West are those that have taken place in the rules and conventions of everyday life; if social equality has come to signify so much in the West, it is due in no small measure to these unwritten rules and conventions.

While it is true that equality is a reasonably effective social ideal in western countries, one can find from each of them many examples of inequality in social practice in virtually every domain. Further, although particular forms or instances of inequality may be condemned by some or many, there is general recognition that inequality as such cannot be eradicated from social life, but has to be accommodated or even encouraged up to a point (Jencks 1975; Letwin 1983; Rawls 1973). It is the Indian, and not the western, intelligentsia that is likely to adopt the more intransigent public position on inequality. But how can we expect to eradicate inequality root and branch when countries that started on the road to equality long before us and have advanced much further along it are prepared to live with it in some measure?

There are, of course, those who could argue that the true exemplars of equality in the contemporary world are not countries like Britain, France and the United States which have chosen the path of capitalism with its inevitable division into classes, but the USSR and other East European countries which have advanced much further towards equality along the path of socialism. It is true that in the 20th century, it is socialism and not capitalism that has stood for equality, at least in the countries of Asia, Africa and Latin America. But it is no longer possible to view the achievements of real socialism in the same light as before. The record has to be reinterpreted, and in part rewritten. Suffice it to say that throughout Eastern Europe, including the USSR, there is today wide and open acknowledgement of the need to accommodate a measure of economic inequality if only to moderate the extremes of political inequality.

While assigning to the social ideal of equality the importance it deserves, we must recognize that it is an equivocal ideal. As one of the great sociologists of our time has reminded us: "In every century it has been defined by negating some form of inequality"(Aron 1968:3). This only means that it cannot be expected to negate every form of it. In what follows I will show that some forms of inequality are constitutive of certain arrangements in all modern societies, and that inequalities of income, esteem and authority have to find accommodation within the prevalent ideal of equality. But the matter does not end there, for we must deal not only with the prevalence of inequality but also with its social reproduction. We have to ask not only why social positions should be graded and ranked, but also how it comes about that the same sorts of persons occupy the same sorts of positions from one generation to the next. I shall concentrate on only one sector of Indian society, conceived broadly as the service class, and argue that certain fundamental changes are taking place in the social mechanism of the reproduction of inequality in which the family and not caste now plays the active part. While on the surface present inequalities appear much like past ones, the internal mechanisms of their reproduction are undergoing significant change. I try to shift attention in this paper from the macro-structure of society to its micro-processes; but those processes can be closely examined only after a general discussion of the structure of inequality.

Professions and Institutions

Modern societies are characterized by the presence of a number of professions whose members perform a variety of specialized functions. These include doctors, lawyers, accountants, engineers, scientists, journalists and a host of others. Although we can find their counterparts in earlier societies, they are far more numerous today than in any previous historical epoch. Moreover, their social importance far exceeds their numerical strength (Parsons 1968). It has been pointed out that the expansion of these professions was historically linked to the expansion of bourgeois society (Perkin 1989). But their importance today is not confined to any particular type of society; doctors, engineers, scientists and economists are as important in the Soviet Union as they are in the United States or Great Britain.

In modern India, the professions have come to acquire not only great functional importance but also high social prestige. I hardly need to point to the significant part played by members of the liberal professions in the leadership of the nationalist movement. That apart, it is difficult to visualize an India of the future without doctors, engineers, scientists, journalists, lawyers, and so on. Not only has there been an enormous expansion in these professions since independence but also a more or less continuous demand for their further expansion (Gandhi 1982; Madan 1980).

For all their great and increasing variety, modern professions have certain features in common. Entry into such a profession is typically based on formal qualifications that can in practice be secured by only some and not all members of society. A high level of education, or specialized training, or both are required, and these involve the expenditure at least of time and usually also of money. Among the various professions, some are more exclusive than others, and there are variations from one society to another in the procedures that regulate entry into them.

Doctors, engineers, academics and other professionals enjoy greater esteem than most other members of society. It is difficult to explain fully why this should be so, and, certainly, an explanation that takes only income into account will be unsatisfactory, for, one can argue as well that income differentials are the result of unequal esteem as that they are the cause of it. It is true that many professionals earn very high incomes in capitalist countries such as the United Sates, but their counterparts in the USSR enjoy the same sort of esteem, despite their much lower income.

Comparative studies have established conclusively the remarkable similarity in the esteem enjoyed by the professions in capitalist and socialist societies. And one can argue without much fear of contradiction that they enjoy very high esteem in India.

Important factors behind the esteem enjoyed by the professions in all modern societies are the high levels of education required for entry into them and their real or presumed association with specialized knowledge and technical ability. Specialized knowledge and technical ability are valued in themselves and not merely for the material returns their possession undoubtedly secures. Perhaps they are especially valued—some might say overvalued—in our society where even literacy and primary education are beyond the reach of many.

In our society, as in any other, while doctors as a whole enjoy high esteem, some among them enjoy higher esteem than others. Professional reputation and success are determined by a complex of factors, including some that are extrinsic to professional requirements. The esteem enjoyed by a doctor is determined partly by his personality, but also by such impersonal factors as qualification, skill and experience. Very broadly speaking, specialists are more highly esteemed than general practitioners, mainly because they are presumed to be more highly qualified and to possess superior skills.

One might ask whether it is possible or even desirable to have a social order in which all doctors—or all engineers, or all scientists—will be treated as equal. Apart from its effect on efficiency, such a state of affairs will bespeak complete indifference to all distinctions of knowledge, skill, experience and ability. One must doubt whether a society that is indifferent to the quality of what it professes to value can be regarded as a good society, let alone the question of its being an efficient one.

Where there are wide disparities among doctors, or among members of any other profession, it would be unreasonable to expect equality of treatment towards them. One would expect some inequality of rewards where it is recognized that such disparities exist. The very recognition of such disparities, to the extent that it is a social and not merely an individual fact, entails unequal esteem. Of course, inequality of esteem is difficult to measure, or even agree upon, in every case, so people tend to go by inequality of income which is a general, though by no means always a reliable, index of it.

We must distinguish the acceptance in principle of income differentials between members of a profession from satisfaction with the existing differentials at any given place or time. There is indeed wide public dissatisfaction over the large and sometimes extortionate fees charged by members of the medical, legal and some other professions in India. These developments are viewed with misgiving by professionals themselves as breaches of professional norms, and there are pressures for the regulation of professional incomes by the state or some other public agency. Such regulation works better in some cases than in others, and generates problems of its own. Moreover, even the strongest advocates of the regulation of professionals' incomes must stop short of recommending equal incomes for all doctors—or all engineers, or all accountants—when they reflect on the Soviet or the Polish experience.

The older professions such as law, medicine and accountancy were known as "independent professions"; lawyers, doctors, accountants and others practised independently and received fees rather than salaries. This has changed substantially throughout the world, though not to the same extent everywhere and not equally in all professions. Most professionals, and particularly those in the new ones, now work in institutions, and the terms and conditions of their work, including their emoluments, are regulated by the institutions in which they are employed. These institutions vary enormously in nature and type. Some are very large and others are small; some are privately controlled and managed, and other are of a public or semi-public nature.

The increasing bureaucratization of professional activities means that more and more professionals—doctors, accountants, engineers, and so on—have to work in and through administrative hierarchies of various kinds. One has only to glance at a list of engineers in a public works department to get an idea of their hierarchy of ranks. There is a similar hierarchy of ranks among the medical personnel in a large public hospital, and of scientists in a large scientific establishment such as the National Physical Laboratory or the National Chemical Laboratory (Visvanathan 1985).

Bureaucratization reduces the disparities of income to a large extent, as can be seen by comparing doctors in private practice with those in a public hospital. But it introduces a new kind of inequality associated with the rank and authority of office. In private practice, a meagrely-qualified GP may have a very much lower income than a highly-qualified specialist, but he is nobody's subordinate. In a public hospital there are chief and subordinate medical officers, and although this is partly a matter of age and experience, it is not entirely so. Sometimes the chain of command in a public institution can be quite long, and junior professionals in a scientific establishment typically complain of the arbitrary restrictions imposed on their work by superiors who have lost touch with their discipline.

There is probably a good deal of bureaucratic fat in many public institutions performing specialized functions, and some of this can be cut down to the advantage of both the professionals and the publics they serve. I have so far spoken only indirectly of the bureaucracy and deferred a consideration of its prototype which is the administrative bureaucracy whose *locus classicus* is the secretariat. In view of the central place of the administrative bureaucracy in modern Indian society and culture, I would like to make a few observations on its hierarchical structure.

The classic account of bureaucracy as an ideal type is to be found in the work of Max Weber who also described in detail its historical origin and gradual expansion in all modern societies (Weber 1978). We need not enter into a comprehensive discussion of bureaucracy but will only enumerate some of its principal features. These are: (i) the adherence to impersonal rules, (ii) the concept of the office as a distinct sphere of activity, (iii) the delimitation of areas of competence within the office, and (iv) an established order of superordination and subordination of official ranks.

Max Weber stressed the "rational-legal" character of bureaucracy and its functional efficiency. Later sociologists, while accepting his basic ideas, have also discussed the dysfunctions of bureaucracy, as a result of which we are now more aware of its features (Crozier 1964; Merton 1957). These negative features are very conspicuous in contemporary India, and one can certainly argue that a great deal of the hierarchy associated with the Indian bureaucracy is dysfunctional.

Although it had its counterparts in Mughal India, the framework of modern bureaucratic administration was laid by the British in this country with the Indian Civil Service (ICS) as its "steel frame". As an important part of an imperial system, the British Indian bureaucracy acquired and maintained a markedly hierarchical character; the Indian civil servants were known as "the heaven born", and were concerned as much about exercising power as about maintaining an image. The metaphor of caste was frequently used to describe the rigid and ceremonial nature of the official hierarchy in India, and in the south it became common to compare and contrast the "British bureaucracy" with the "Brahmin oligarchy".

When India became independent, there were pressures to jettison the ICS because of its association with imperial rule. Both Nehru and Patel withstood these pressures, for they felt that India needed a strong and capable administration in the interest of stability and progress. They also felt that the administration could be made more sensitive to the needs of the people by being brought into closer contact with them. The most notable change in the administration since independence has been a quantitative one; it has grown enormously in size. Some say that it is now more in tune with the needs of the people, and others that it has become more callous. It has certainly lost some of its ceremonial rigidity and is now more exposed to public criticism. It is difficult to say whether, with all these changes, administration in India has become less or more hierarchical. Clearly, there is much scope for streamlining in the interest of both equity and efficiency, but it is difficult to see how administration can work in a modern society without some superordination and subordination among officials.

If the market is the nightmare of egalitarians under capitalism, under socialism it is the bureaucracy. It should by now be abundantly clear that no modern society can succeed in eliminating either; they can be dissolved by the force of ideas only in the world of fantasy. They are realities that shape our lives as much as what has been described as "the spirit of the age". We cannot turn away from the real change of orientation in our norms and values in the direction of equality, nor can we ignore or wish out of existence the many social arrangements of which inequality is a constitutive part.

Occupational Ranking and Mobility

The inescapable reality that I have briefly described and that coexists in a kind of dialectical relationship with the spirit of equality, falls within the broad category of social stratification. This is a very broad domain, and I have dwelt mainly on inequalities attached to positions and offices open to all. They are the inequalities characteristic of the modern world, associated with modern institutions, modern professions, and the modern occupational system in general. They are very different from the inequalities of caste, attached to positions not open to all in either practice or principle.

New occupations have grown and expanded enormously in India since independence, and there are now millions of persons in every part of the country who secure their livelihood from them. It is true that many more are still engaged and will probably continue to be engaged in agriculture and other occupations in settings that may be broadly described as "traditional". The new occupations are of many different kinds; professional, administrative, managerial and other non-manual occupations; and skilled, semi-skilled and unskilled manual ones. These occupations, and particularly the former, are very important, not only because of their numbers but also because of the high value placed on them by all sections of society.

Sociologists have noted the significance of the occupational system in all modern societies (Blau and Duncan 1968; Parsons 1954; Treiman 1977). The individual's position in society—his social identity—his economic standing, his social status, his own self-esteem are all to some extent dependent on his occupation. A large part of his adult life is devoted to it, and much of his early life is a preparation for it. This is not to say that occupation alone shapes a person's social identity; race, religion and provenance are important in many societies, and gender is an important basis of identify in every society. In India, caste is a very important basis of social identity, although we can no longer assume that it is always more important than occupation in every sector of society.

I turn briefly to two related aspects of modern occupational systems: occupational ranking and occupational mobility. Studies conducted in different parts of the world show a fair measure of consistency in the ranking of occupations in every society; this does not mean that all the individual members of a society rank all occupations in identically the same way, but that there is considerable agreement about their ranks (Svalastoga 1959). Second, despite the displacement of old occupations by new ones due to rapid technological change, the prestige structure of occupations retains a fair degree of stability over time (Hodge *et al.* 1966). Finally, comparative studies tend to show that, despite historical and cultural variations, similar occupations tend to be similarly ranked across a wide range of contemporary societies in different parts of the world (Treiman 1977).

The differentiation and ranking of occupations go hand in hand with mobility between occupations, both within a lifetime and between generations. Occupational ranking and occupational mobility are two important and closely-related features of all modern societies. While there is no necessary relationship between the span of occupational ranking and the rate of occupational mobility, one can speak meaningfully about upward and downward mobility only within a generally-accepted framework of ranks. It does not appear that many persons would actually wish to see all ranks abolished; for them the requirement of "practical equality" (Tawney 1964: 106) would be reasonably satisfied if there were relatively free movements across the ranks of the occupational hierarchy.

There is a large body of literature on occupational mobility in the advanced industrial societies (Robinson 1985; Treiman and Robinson 1981), and, although we do not have many systematic studies of the subject in India, a beginning has been made (Pande 1986; Rao 1989). The facts relating to occupational mobility are extremely complex, and there are disagreements about their correct interpretation. Although sociologists have tried to measure and compare rates of mobility, it is difficult to do so in a direct and straightforward manner. One has to distinguish between intra-and inter-generational mobility; between absolute and relative mobility; and between mobility under different rates of occupational change (Goldthorpe 1987).

Despite all the difficulties of accurate measurement and reliable comparison, it is now clear that there is widespread occupational mobility, both intra-and inter-generational, in all advanced industrial societies. Further—and this is of particular importance—in countries such as Britain and the United States, the secular trend in the present century has been towards greater upward than downward mobility (Goldthorpe 1987). This paradox of a net balance of upward mobility is resolved when we take into account changes in the occupational system in these societies, leading to an aggregate displacement of occupations with lower status by those with higher prestige. In a very broad way, agricultural occupations have been displaced by non-agricultural ones, and inferior manual occupations by superior non-manual ones.

The relation between occupational mobility and the class structure is a controversial subject on which there is much disagreement (Giddens 1973). Much depends on how one defines classes, and it is possible to define them in such a way as to make changing rates of mobility irrelevant to their structure (Poulantzas 1976). The old definition of classes in terms of distinctions among the "owners merely of labour power, owners of capital, and landowners' (Marx 1959: 885) cannot take us very far without substantial modification to accommodate the differentiation of occupations. Some sociologists are inclined to the view that, particularly in the United States, the combined effect of high occupational differentiation and extensive occupational mobility has been the obliteration of classes as well marked features of the social morphology (Blau and Duncan 1968).

It would, however, be premature to maintain that classes have disappeared from advanced industrial societies. The working class still has a clear social identity, although one may wonder about the utility of the old concept of the bourgeoisie. A recent important study has described three broad classes that occupy a prominent place in British social structure, despite occupational differentiation and mobility. These are:(i) the service class, (ii) the intermediate class, and (iii) the working class (Goldthorpe 1987).

The service class, which has been studied in detail in Germany, Britain and other western countries, has its counterpart in India. Professional, administrative and managerial occupations are of crucial importance in Indian society, but their sociological study is still in its infancy. In what follows I shall make some general observations on stratification and mobility in contemporary Indian society on the basis of the little that we know about these occupations.

Reproduction of Inequality

When people in India or elsewhere say that they are opposed to inequality or to extreme forms of it, they have in mind two distinct things whose mutual relationship is not always clear to them. They might feel that the disparities between the top and the bottom in society as a whole or in its various institutions and organizations are too large; for instance, they might say that in Indian hospitals the disparities of income, authority and esteem between senior and junior medical personnel, or between them and sweepers, cleaners and attendants are much larger than in hospitals elsewhere, and that these can and should be reduced. Alternatively, they might point out that access to the medical profession is so severely restricted in India that only some sorts of persons can possibly expect to reach senior positions in a hospital, whereas most others can expect at best to become sweepers, cleaners and attendants. The first relates to the extent of disparity, and the second to the rate of mobility; it does not follow that where disparities are high, the rates of mobility must always be low.

It is frequently maintained that our public institutions are too hierarchical, that they have too many ranks in them, and that there is too much distance between the top and the bottom. Civil servants themselves often say this about the administrative bureaucracy, and then point out, not without reason, that in India most public institutions tend to model themselves on the administrative bureaucracy. It is difficult to form a clear judgement on this, because public institutions in general and administrative bureaucracies in particular are favourite targets of attack for egalitarians throughout the world. No doubt, public institutions often show larger inequalities in India than elsewhere, but they are also undergoing change. To take one example, the hierarchy of academic ranks has undergone considerable change in the last two decades, so that university departments in India are less hierarchical, at least in their internal organization, than they were in the past and than they are in some western countries (Beteille 1981, 1990a). But this does not mean that access to academic positions is in practice as open to the different sections of society as it is in those countries.

There is no society in which access to the service class is in practice equally open to persons from all sections of society; social origin and background play some part in restricting or facilitating such access in all societies. All that we can say is that it is more open in some societies than in others. It would be reasonable to maintain, even without exhaustive enquiry, that in India such access is severely restricted by social origin and background (Navlakha 1989). This is markedly at odds with the strong provisions on equality, including equality of opportunity, in the Constitution of India.

I shall take for granted the fact that positions in society carry unequal rewards in terms of income, esteem and authority, and also the continued existence of a service class whose members enjoy a high position in society. The question to which I would like to address myself here relates to the reproduction of the service class from one generation to another, and the unequal distribution of life chances among members of society in terms of their access to it. Why is access to the service class almost automatically ensured for some members of society whereas others find it very hard, if not impossible, to enter it, despite the removal of all legal barriers to entry and despite the extensive concern expressed in our society for equality of opportunity?

There are marked disparities of wealth and caste in India, and these two disparities reinforced each other in the traditional order (Beteille 1972). Disparities of wealth are related to the inequalities to which I have referred, though not as closely as one might assume; sons and daughters of landowners do not necessarily have better prospects of entering the professions or the civil service than those of school teachers or section officers. There is also a marked correlation between caste status and occupational position, but the direct influence of caste on the distribution of life chances is changing; one no longer has automatic access to particular occupation by virtue of one's caste as was largely the case in the past.

In every society some measure of continuity from one generation to the next is maintained through what is described by means of a biological metaphor as social and cultural reproduction. Indeed, what we describe as a society or a culture would be incomprehensible without some continuity and reproduction. It is my central argument that the family plays a crucial, if not decisive, role in the reproduction of social structure, including the structure of inequality. To be sure, the family as an institution is not equally effective everywhere, and it does not act in isolation from other institutions anywhere. But all things considered, it will be safe to say that the family plays a far more active role than caste in reproducing the inequalities associated with the new occupational system. The retreat of caste as an active agent for the reproduction of inequality at the upper levels, and the continuing, if not increasing , importance of the family constitute two of the most striking features of contemporary Indian society.

Since I assign such crucial significance to the active role of the family in reproducing inequalities in the new occupational system in India, I would like to make a few general observations on it. The family is the one social institution that is universally present in all human societies. Nineteenth century anthropologists commonly believed that it did not exist in the earliest stages of social evolution, and this led some to speculate that it might cease to exist in some future historical period (Engels 1948). These beliefs, at least as far as early societies are concerned, have been proved to be false. However, we must be careful not to repeat the mistake, made by many in the past, that the family has everywhere the same form as in middle-class western society. In fact, it takes a variety of different forms, although one is stuck by the regularity with which it takes the form of the nuclear family of parents and unmarried children in the service class in virtually every part of the world (Goods 1970).

Much has been written about the place of the joint or extended family in Indian society. A recent influential study of personality formation among Hindus (Kakar 1978) takes for granted the universal presence of the extended family in all strata of society. This is plainly misleading. Nuclear families outnumber extended ones in many social settings (Narain 1975). It is of course true that the same individual might live in both types of family during different phases of his life. Moreover, grandparents, uncles, aunts and cousins continue to play an important part in the individual's development, whether from within or outside the family, in all sections of Indian society. Nevertheless, we should not discount the importance of the nuclear family in the service class in large metropolitan cities. In any case, my argument about the displacement of caste by family remains substantially true whether the family is of the extended or the nuclear type.

Without denying variations in morphological form, I shall be more concerned with such questions as the strength, effectiveness and adaptability of the family in modern societies. Both popular and professional opinion is divided on these questions in the West (Berger and Berger 1983; Morgan 1975). Writing in the mid-1950s, Talcott Parsons had noted the view widely expressed in the preceding years that the family was on its way out in western society and particularly in the United States (Parsons and Bales 1956). Arguing vigorously against the view, he had maintained that a closer look at the evidence would show that the family in America was becoming stronger and not weaker. More recently, the women's movement has reopened the question of the durability of the western family. Changes in gender roles will no doubt have an impact on the family, but there is as yet little evidence to suggest that the family as such is likely to disappear or even to lose its vitality in the foreseeable future.

The family plays a crucial part in the socialization of its children, particularly in the early years (Erikson 1965; Kakar 1978). Although the learning process, broadly conceived, continues throughout life psychologists have stressed the significance for the child for the first three years of it. The family acts in conjunction with others—kin, neighbours, and so on—in the socialization of the child. The extent to which it shares the responsibility for the socialization of the child with other agencies varies from one society to another, and from one phase of the child's life to the next. It is likely that the family's role in the socialization process, particularly in the early years, has been enlarged in the modern western type of society where the nuclear unit insulates the infant from other kin and neighbours to a greater extent than in other types of society. It is also likely that this happens to some extent in all societies or all social classes where the nuclearization of the family is at work.

Indians of all social classes have a markedly conservative attitude towards both marriage and parenthood. This is in contrast to the relatively more experimental attitude towards domestic arrangements in the West and towards some other social arrangements in India. Among Indians, in the upper social strata, divorce is rare, and experimentation in the choice of partners by adhering to the practice of arranged marriages persists. Parents not only select spouses for their children, but also play a large part in guiding them towards their careers. The conservative attitude towards marriage and parenthood is able to survive the change from the extended to the nuclear type of family.

The modern Indian family among professionals, civil servants and others is not a mere replica of the traditional family of the classical texts either in its morphology or in its norms and values. It has its own norms and values. Nor are they identical with those characteristics of the nuclear family in the West. Despite nuclearization, the Indian family remains distinctive in its orientation to marriage, parenthood and siblingship, and in its involvement in wider kin ties.

In the West, the family surrenders a part of its monopoly over the child when he or she enters school. The experience of school is very important in all societies or social classes where schooling is universal and starts at an early age. The relationship between family and school is a subject in itself to which I shall advert, though only in passing, a little later; suffice it to say here that the influence of the family on the child continues through school and beyond, although here again there are bound to be variations from one society to another and from one social class to another.

Now, in all modern societies, different families are very differently endowed as to both means and motivations. The atmosphere in which a child grows up in the home of a doctor or a civil servant is very different from the atmosphere in the home of a clerk or a watchman. Children have access to very different kinds and amounts of resources in these homes. It is essential to have a broad view of these resources and not define them narrowly in terms of the economic criteria of wealth and income. In recent years the problem of the reproduction of inequality has been greatly illuminated by the extension of the concept of capital to include cultural and social capital in addition to material capital in the conventional sense (Bourdieu 1984; Bourdieu and Passeron 1977).

To be sure, the unequal distribution of private wealth in the form of land and other material assets is a major constituent of the disparities between families, but there is more to these disparities than that. Apart from its material capital, and to some extent independently of it, each family has a stock of cultural capital, comprising its command over knowledge, skills, tastes, etc., that are a part of its distinctive way of life. It has also its own social capital in the form of networks of relationships, partly acquired from the past and partly constructed through the initiative of its members.

I do not wish to enter into a discussion of the many conceptual difficulties in defining cultural and social capital, and I am concerned here mainly with their variability between families. The attraction of the concept of capital as conventionally used in economic analysis is its amenability to quantitative treatment. Although Pierre Bourdieu (1984: 114), who has played a large part in popularizing the concept, has spoken of different volumes of cultural capital, it is difficult to extract from his work any clear procedure for measuring it; and the same is true for social capital in the sense in which I use it here. Second, although we can think of procedures, at least in principle, for nationalizing, expropriating or re-distributing physical or material, or economic capital, it is difficult to see how this can be done for cultural or social capital. Only some of the recourses of the family can be seen as entitlements that are at least in principle separable from it; others are embedded in its very nature and constitution.

The family forms a very important part of the social environment of the infant, the child and the adolescent, although it would be absurd to maintain that what a person is in adult life depends entirely on his family environment or his social background. We know very well that many individuals overcome the disadvantages of family and social background; and others move downwards because of failures of one kind or another, sometimes within the family itself. The family has its own internal dynamics, and these are not dependent entirely on its capital, even in the broad sense that we have given to the term. What is remarkable, however, is the extent to which the family, particularly in the service class, does succeeded in transmitting its cultural and social capital to its younger members, despite psychological failures of many kinds.

I would like to stress that there is nothing mechanical about the transfer of cultural capital from one generation to another within the family. This transfer is guided by complex social and physiological processes whose outcome can never be guaranteed in the individual case. In families that start with substantial social and cultural advantages, there may be major psychological failures that wipe out the advantages of the first generation for the second. Conversely, children from families with slender resources may benefit more than proportionately from an emotionally supportive home environment. The modern educational and occupational systems are highly dynamic and the personality traits favoured by them are not determined in a straightforward way by social and cultural circumstances.

The family has been and continues to be one of the strongest institutions of Indian society, in all regions, among all communities and in all social classes. This is not to deny the very great range of variation in family types in India, but only to draw attention to its continued strength as an institution in and through which the individual acquires his capabilities and orientations as a member of society. In what follows, I shall be concerned with the family's role in social reproduction, mainly at the upper levels of the new occupational hierarchy.

Despite the persistence of a basically conservative attitude to marriage and parenthood, some changes are taking place in the Indian family. There is reason to believe that it is undergoing a process of nuclearization, at least in the sense that the small group of parents and unmarried children is acquiring a sharper identity within the wider kin group. Important demographic changes have begun, and are probably quite widespread in the higher occupational strata. The age at marriage is rising for both men and women, and the limitation of family size has become a common strategy. These demographic changes are probably being accompanied by more subtle changes in the relations between spouses, between parents and children, and between siblings. Despite these changes, the Indian family is at this social level much more stable than its counterpart in the West.

The upper-middle class Indian family has shown its strength by the manner in which it has adapted to and retained control over a changing social environment. A very remarkable aspect of this is the manner in which it has shifted its focus of attention away from caste and sub-caste and towards school, college and office. It would be safe to say that in metropolitan cities like Delhi, Bombay and Calcutta, doctors, engineers, professors, civil servants and others take much less account of their caste and sub-caste when planning for the future of their children than of the schools to which they might secure admission for them.

I would like to stress the active role of the family in transmitting to its younger members all the advantages it has at its command. Among doctors, engineers, accountants, civil servants, managers and others, parents do not simply wait for their children to soak up the cultural capital that is a part of the domestic environment. They take an increasingly active part in their education and training. Middle-class parents have become increasingly career conscious, and this consciousness is implanted in their children at a young age. The idea that the child will step automatically or effortlessly into his parent's occupation has ceased to be a secure basis for socialization: a different kind of preparation is now required for his success in the future. The school has emerged as a major institution for mediating the relationship between the family and the new occupational system, and it also plays a major part in the reproduction if inequality. (Coleman 1990; Jencks 1975). Schools are of many different kinds, and they are ranked. As the scholastic agent in Evelyn Waugh's novel(1937:17) points out: "We class schools, you see, into four grades: Leading School, First-rate School, Good School, and School." "Frankly", said Mr. Levy, "school is pretty bad". In India, the major distinction is between fee-paying schools that are very expensive and government schools where the charges are nominal. The best schools are not only very expensive but also very difficult to get into, and here the status and "personality" of the parent counts as much as the aptitude of the child (D'Souza 1974).

It is, of course, well known that schools differ vastly in their quality, and much public animosity is directed against the elitist character of the Indian school system. But those who are most articulate in their criticism of the system take good care to select the best schools for the education of their own children. The moral implications of this contradiction, by no means unique to Indian society, are not always clear. There is no doubt that the Indian school system leaves much to be desired, and a great deal can be done to expand the opportunities for better schooling in the interest of children who are now effectively denied such opportunity because their families are devoid of all resources.

At the same time, the elimination of all disparities between schools does not appear to be a feasible objective. The reduction of disparities will make some contribution to the equalization of life chances, but that contribution may not be as large as one might expect. At the top, the school system is highly competitive and likely to become more so. Middle-class parents have begun to feel increasingly that they cannot leave it entirely to the school to train their children for success in competitive examinations. They take an increasing part in helping their children with their lessons at home; here the cultural capital of the family is extremely important in the development of both skill and motivation. Nor do parents rely entirely on their own abilities to prepare their children for success in examinations. Where they have the means , they engage tutors or send their children to coaching classes. Networks of tutors and coaches have become familiar features of the urban social landscape in contemporary India.

The involvement of parents in the educational progress and career prospects of their children has to some extent altered the atmosphere of the family, at least among those in professional, administrative and managerial occupations. The rapid expansion of college education among women in these groups is likely to alter it further. Already, women are taking an increasingly active part in the school-work of their children; this can be seen from the number of active mothers in what are called "public schools" in India on occasions such as parent-teacher meetings, prize-giving ceremonies, sports competitions, and so on. Second, change is also coming about in attitudes towards the education of girls; certainly, they continue to be prepared for marriage, but more and more of them are being prepared simultaneously for careers.

Families have variable amounts not only of cultural but also of social capital. The social capital of the family consists of the networks of relations that may be activated for maintaining and furthering the interests of the family as a whole or of its individual members. These networks are made up of many strands. Ties of kinship and marriage are important everywhere. In addition, and particularly in the service class, other ties, developed in school or college, office or profession, and associations of diverse kinds also play an important part (Srinivas and Beteille 1964).

The nature and span of the networks available to Indians varies enormously from one level of society to another. In the traditional order, social networks operated within a more or less fixed framework of village, caste and lineage, and this still survives to a large extent in the rural areas and at the lower levels of the social hierarchy. But in the urban areas and at the levels with which I am concerned, networks are much more flexible and dynamic; old links are discarded and new ones created to meet the demands, real or perceived, of a changeable environment. This is a social world in which many people are or appear to be on the move; but not many change places or move very far relatively to others.

It is difficult to assess and compare the parts played by family contact and social influence in the successes of individuals from different backgrounds. That they operate extensively and unequally is well known. So far as it concerns the careers of their children, doctors, lawyers, professors, civil servants and managers have more extensive and more useful contacts than clerks, electricians, plumbers, road-menders and masons. In a society in which family commitments are of such strength, it would be remarkable if children did not benefit from the social contacts of their parents.

The extensive use of the social capital of a family for furthering the prospects of its individual members raise analytical and normative questions whose nature can only be indicated here. It is both extremely important and extremely difficult to keep consistently in view the distinction between the private and the public domains. It would be a mistake to declare unequivocally against the use of social contacts in every case. For instance, they are of crucial importance in securing information essential to career planning, and little can be said against that. Second, in the independent professions and in private enterprises, personal relations are considered to be an important basis of trust, and it is difficult to see how they can be excluded from professional and business activity. The case of public institutions is different, but even here some legitimate ground exists for the use of recommendations based on personal knowledge from responsible members of society. One can easily see that that ground will be repeatedly crossed in a society in which family and kin ties have compelling force and where at the same time independent or private enterprise is progressively displaced by governmental organization.

Family, Class and Caste

I have described how inequalities are maintained in societies in which careers are, or are believed to be, open to talent. In my account I have drawn attention to the crucial part played by the family in the maintenance of the system. I must emphasize that my purpose was not to explain how inequalities come into existence, but rather to show how existing inequalities are reproduced, not in exactly the same form as before but in recognizably similar forms.

In drawing attention to the crucial part played by the family, it was not my intention to suggest that other institutions, resources, ideas, beliefs and values play no part in maintaining the system of inequality. However, one must make a distinction between patterns and forms that exist as residues from the past in a more or less passive way, and institutions that play an active part in reproducing the structure of inequality. It is the active role of the family in reproducing the structure of unequal life chances, not always clearly perceived, that I have tried to emphasize, for the problem is not simply why inequalities come into being, but why, despite efforts of many kinds, they refuse to disappear.

An important tradition in social theory views the structure of inequality in terms of wealth and property. There are large disparities of wealth and property in Indian society, and these are of great importance in the agrarian system where landownership and landlessness are the two poles between which inequalities are structured (Beteille 1974). Although in the form in which it now exists is not of very great antiquity, private property in land is today an institution of great strength in rural India. Agrarian reform has altered the distribution of land to some extent, but it has not weakened the institution of property (Herring 1983; Joshi 1975). The two institutions of property and the family are today intimately linked in rural India: what link property had in the past with lineage and sub-caste it has largely lost. The meagre success of land reform has repeatedly demonstrated the exceptional strength of the landowning family.

Property and wealth also have a significant place in the system of stratification outside agriculture to which I have mainly devoted my attention. But that system as a whole cannot be understood without taking into account the growth of a new occupational structure. The inequalities in the latter, which enjoys a position of great importance in all modern societies, cannot be easily understood in terms of the traditional definition of capital, and certainly not in terms of one that sharply separates "capital" and "labour". We require a more extended concept of capital, one that incorporates both cultural and social capital in addition to capital in the old sense, but that in turn calls for a considerable change in our analytical strategy. I have in the preceding tried to explore some of the possibilities opened up by such a strategy. My objective was not to deny the great importance of private wealth in the reproduction of inequality, but to draw attention to other resources that are also important in its reproduction.

There remains the structure of caste. No enquiry into inequality can ignore caste which has been widely regarded as the fundamental institution of Hindu, and indeed, Indian society. It has stood as the watchword for the most elaborate, the most rigid and the most comprehensive system of social hierarchy. It exists as a salient feature of the social morphology in contemporary India, and, although caste is no longer enumerated in the decennial census, a multitude of social survey and case studies bear witness to its continued existence in all parts of India, not only among Hindus, but among Muslims, Christians, Sikhs and other religious denominations.

When we say that caste was the fundamental institution of Hinduism, we mean not only that it was a central part of religion, morality and law among the Hindus. It will be impossible to explain the remarkable continuity of the institution of caste, till almost our own time, solely in terms of social morphology, without taking any account of religion, morality and law. To be sure, there were many changes, and sometimes important ones, in the system till the end of last century; but through all these changes, and in the long run, both the social morphology and the legal, moral and religious foundations of caste remained recognizably the same.

Caste not only remains a salient feature of the social morphology, it is still manifestly correlated with every form of social stratification, whether based on wealth, occupation, income, education, or some other criterion. In all public institutions, those in superior positions are likely to be of higher, and those in inferior positions of lower caste. Some take this kind of manifest correlation as proof that caste is at bottom the cause of the ranks that we observe in public life. This is plainly mistaken, for, as we have seen, doctors, scientists, civil servants and others are ranked in all societies, including those that have had nothing to do with caste. While the ranking of occupations may be somewhat more elaborate and more rigid in our society than in others, the logic of ranking among doctors, scientists or civil servants is quite different from the hierarchical logic of caste.

The fact that the morphological side of caste still remains salient should not lead us to conclude that the other side of it, having to do with law, morality and religion, has also remained unchanged. Indeed, it is my argument that profound changes have taken place and are taking place in the religious, legal and moral foundations of caste, and that these are bound in the long run to alter its social morphology as well.

It cannot be too strongly emphasized that at least among Hindus, the distinctions among castes as well as their ranks were acknowledged, upheld and reinformed by both shastric and customary law for two thousand years (Sivaramayya 1984). The legal code of the Dharmashastra gave primacy to *varna* and *ashrama,* and as such, it was for the most part *varnashrama-dharma*; customary law, which departed on many points from shastric law, was at one with it in giving due recognition to the distinctions of caste. Undoubtedly, many changes took place through the centuries in both law and custom, but they were not of the same significance as those that were initiated with the Removal of Caste Disabilities Act in 1850.

The privileges and disabilities of caste were slowly but progressively whittled down between 1850 and 1950 when the constitution was adopted (Ghurye 1961). The new constitution repudiated the hierarchical structure of caste, and it is now impossible to use the law to uphold the age-old privileges and disabilities of caste. It is true that custom still takes account of caste distinctions, particularly in the rural areas, but here custom is at variance with the law, whereas in the past it was in harmony with it.

Changes have also taken place in Hindu religion that have a bearing on caste, although it is more difficult to assess the nature and significance of these changes. Scholars are generally agreed that caste was in the past an integral part of the Hindu religion. The fact that this view has been challenged by a large number of Hindu reformers in the last hundred years itself shows that a change of orientation has come about in modern Hinduism. Every important modern reformer of Hinduism, including Vivekananda and Gandhi, has attacked caste or at least the hierarchy of caste, and it will be difficult to find any today who will defend it as an institution.

It is instructive to compare and contrast the attitudes of reformers of Hinduism towards its two most fundamental institutions—caste and the family—in both of which social life was deeply tinged by religion. Now, while many have attacked caste, and come very severely, it will be difficult to find any who have attacked the family as an institution. It is the central argument here that modern Hindus, whether of a secular persuasion or not, are no longer committed to caste, as Hindus were in the past, but that they continue to be committed to the family. This is not to say that the Hindu undivided family is not changing or that it will not change further. It is obvious that many modern Hindus find it possible to visualize their society in the future without the Hindu caste system; it is difficult to say how many of them are able to visualize it without the Hindu family.

It is even in the best of circumstances difficult to demonstrate a change in the moral values of a society, and I will not attempt to do so systematically here. But what we should not forget is that the traditional order of caste had its own morality, centred on a specific sense of duty associated with one's station and stage in life. It is possible that in the rural areas a sense of duty still survives towards the occupation and way of life of one's caste among artisans and cultivators, but that sense of duty has little place in the new occasional order. Modern Indians have at best an ambivalent, if not negative, attitude towards the morality of caste, and some at least would be surprised to learn that such a thing ever did or could exist.

In the last forty years, whenever caste has come up for public discussions, it has invariably been subjected to censure. How does one account for the continued existence of a social arrangement which everyone is eager to attack and no one is prepared to defend? The recent agitations over the recommendations of the Mandal Commission have brought this out clearly. Those who opposed caste quotas argued that quotas would give a new lease of life to caste whose revival or reinforcement they condemned. But those who supported quotas were no less vocal in their condemnation of caste; they felt that certain measures were needed in the short run to secure more effectively the removal of caste in the long run. It is another matter that the unintended consequences of their actions might be, as their opponents believe they must be, to strengthen and not weaken the identities of caste.

Social institutions such as the family or the school reproduce themselves partly through the conscious actions of individuals who desire their continued existence. But besides these, there are social patterns whose reproduction is the unintended consequence of actions directed to other ends. In the traditional order, caste and sub-caste were not only active agents of social placement, they were active agents of social control as well. In the modern occupational system about which I have spoken, there is still a relationship between caste and social placement, it is a relatively passive one, and caste has ceased to be a significant agent of social control. By contrast, in the same sector, the family is not only an active agent of social control, it is also an active agent of social placement. Further, it continues to be so despite such changes as are coming about in its composition and form.

The doctor in his clinic, the lawyer in his chamber, the civil servant or even the clerk in his office is no longer bound by the moral authority of his caste or sub-caste in the way in which the Brahmin, the Rajput, the Nai or the Dhobi was in the traditional village. The emancipation of the individual from the demand of caste and sub-caste has been a complex and longdrawn process that is by no means complete as yet. It has been due partly to conscious action, both individual and collective, and partly to social and economic forces whose consequences no one fully foresaw. The emergence of a new educational and occupational system gave individuals an increasingly secure basis for freeing themselves from the demands of caste and sub-caste.

We must avoid hasty conclusions about a development that is complex, uneven and not free from contradictory tendencies. Even today, the extent to which the individual can repudiate with impunity the demands made on him by his caste or sub-caste varies from one sector to another, and from one social stratum to another. We need far more systematic information about the strength and mode of operation of caste sanctions in contemporary India than we have.

Caste sanctions never operated in the same way at all levels of society. It is well known that only some castes had active caste panchayats, whereas others did not (Rowe 1973). Such studies as we have tend to show that caste panchayats are in decline in most parts of the country and at all levels of the hierarchy (Dube 1955; 222; Hutton 1961; 99,102). However, there are also reports of panchayats becoming activated in response to particular issues thrown up usually by regional or national politics. These and, in particular, caste associations that are activised by the demands and opportunities of modern electoral politics are clearly different in their range and mode of operation from the traditional agencies through which caste and sub-caste exercised social control (Kothari 1970). It is not at all clear how far the individual members of a caste or sub-caste feel morally or even politically bound by the demand for electoral support made on them by the leaders of their caste associations, or what sanctions such leaders can enforce against those who ignore their demands.

What is clear, however, is that increasing numbers of professionals, civil servants, managers and others feel free to repudiate such moral claims as may be made on them in the name of the caste to which they happen to belong. Some individuals may feel free to use on occasions their caste connexions to further their individual or domestic interests, but this does not generally bind them morally to the demands of their caste; this has now become an instrumental, not to say an amoral, domain of action, used by many and condemned by all. It is in this sense that the middle-class Indian's orientations to caste and to family are quite different. He cannot repudiate his obligations to his family even when he finds them irksome; nothing is easier for him than to repudiate the demands of his caste if he finds them inconvenient.

It will now be clear what I mean when I say that at this level of society caste is no longer an institution in the sense in which the family continues to be one. An institution is not merely a convenient arrangement for individuals to use it from time to time in the pursuit of their interests; nor is continuity over time or mere antiquity a test of its effective strength. Above all, an institution must be able to command the loyalties of its individual members who should be prepared to sacrifice their interests, at least to some extent, to secure its well-being and continuity. The plain fact is that modern Indians are prepared to sacrifice many things to protect and promote their family in the narrow or broad sense; they are not prepared to make the same sacrifices for their caste.

I return finally to public-spirited Indians and their frustrations over the persistence of widespread inequality. As I have shown, there are two kinds of response to the latter. The first, which one many call the radical response, is directed against inequality as such, and would wish to see it reduced in every sphere, if not eliminated altogether. The second, which is a more moderate response, is troubled not so much by inequality as such as by its manifest correlation with caste which has somehow come to be viewed as its ultimate cause. It is remarkable how many well-meaning Indians have recently discovered in caste the root of every form in inequality in contemporary India.

It is understandable that those who have formed a commitment to equality should find it difficult to reconcile themselves to so much inequality in their own environment. At the same time, it will be naive to believe that all these inequalities can be removed at no social cost. Hence, it is necessary to attempt some assessment of the costs, no matter how difficult that attempt may be. The difficulty is that there are many different kinds of obstacles to the further advance of equality in the distribution of benefits and burdens, and that they operate at many different levels.

I have argued that it is a mistake to believe that the sole or even the main obstacle to the further advance of equality in social practice today is still caste, however natural that belief may appear. Caste has ceased to play an active part in the reproduction of inequality, at least at the upper levels of the social hierarchy where it is no longer an important agent of either social placement or social control.

The recent attack on caste by egalitarians of both radical and liberal persuasions is misdirected even where it appears well-meaning. Caste should be attacked for its divisive role in electoral politics rather than its active role in th reproduction of inequality which is relatively small and clearly declining. The role of caste in politics is neither small nor declining. caste is no longer an institution of any great strength among the influential urban intelligentsia; but it is still an instrument of great force in mobilizing political support in the country as a whole. If we remember Nehru's description of the spirit of the age, we will see why all parties that use caste for mobilizing political support say that they are acting in the cause of equality.

Equality, at least at the higher levels of society, can no longer be significantly advanced by attacking caste. Much of the anger that is publicly expressed against the hierarchy of caste—in the newspapers, on television, in conferences—is purposeless if not insincere. Those who are serious about carrying the advance of equality further, particularly in the domain that I have discussed must direct their attention to the institutions that are the real obstacles in the path of the advance. The two most important ones are the family and the school.

A dispassionate and critical examination of the middle-class family and its role in the reproduction of inequality may turn out to be more disturbing than one might expect. For, if the result of such an examination shows, as I believe it must, that the family is indeed the main obstacle to the further advance of equality, what conclusions for policy can we then draw? Nothing is easier than to get government and opposition together in parliament to denounce the caste system and ask for its abolition. Who will denounce the Indian family, and ask for that to be abolished? It may not be too fanciful to suggest that both radicals and liberals have found a perfect alibi in caste to draw attention away from those institutions through whose agency inequality is reproduced in the strategic domains of society.

The Indian sociologist engaged in the study of his own society lives much more closely with his family than with his caste. He not only experiences life in his own family but is also more or less actively involved in its changing fortunes; his personal involvement in his own caste is by contrast marginal or atypical. Yet, the sociological literature on caste is voluminous, while that on the family is meagre. The few standard works that we have on the subject refer either to the family as traditionally conceived (Kapadia 1958) or to the rural family (Madan 1988; Shah 1973). The emphasis in these works, with some notable exceptions, is overwhelmingly on family and kinship, family and caste, and family and religion. The point of departure is the Hindu extended family as both social fact and social ideal. Not much can be learnt from them about the interface between the family and the new institutions of society. We need to give a more central place to the family in the sociology of India, and we need to examine more extensively its distinctively contemporary features, for example, the relations between family and education, family and occupation, and family and social mobility. I have argued elsewhere (Beteille 1990b) that the sociological, as opposed to the Indologial, approach must take its orientation from the lived experiences of the present rather than the presumed ideals of the past. There is no better way of finding out what is modern and at the same time Indian in our contemporary society and culture than by examining the family in the kind of context that I have outlined above.

References

Aron, R., 1968, Progress and disillusion, London: Pall Mall Press.

Berger, B. and P.L. Berger, 1983, The war over the family, New York: Doubleday.

Beteille, A., 1972, *Inequality and social change, Delhi: Oxford University press.*

—, 1974, *Studies in agrarian social structure,* Delhi: Oxford University Press.

—, 1981, The Indian university, Minerva, 19.2: 282-310.

—, 1990a, A career in a declining profession, Minerva, 28, 1: 1-20.

—, 1990b, Race, caste and gender, Man 25: 485-504.

Blau, P.M. and O.D. Duncan, 1968, *The American Occupational system*, Glencoe: The Free press.

Bourdieu,P., 1984, *Distinction, Cambridge, Mass*: Harvard University Press.

Bourdieu, P. and J.C. Passeron, 1977, *Reproduction in education, society and culture,* Beverley Hills: Sage.

Coleman, J.S., 1990, *Equality and achievement in education*, Boulder: Westview Press.

Crozier, M., 1964, *The bureaucratic phenomenon,* Chicago: University of Chicago Press.

D' Souza, A., 1974, *Indian public schools, New Delhi: Sterling.*

Dube, S.C., 1955, *Indian village*, London: Routledge and Kegan Paul.

Engels, F., 1948, *Origin of the family, private property and the state*, Moscow: Progress Publishers.

Erikson, E., 1965, *Childhood and society*, London: Hogarth Press.

Gandhi, J.S., 1982, *Lawyers and touts*, New Delhi: Hindustan.

Ghurye, G.S., 1961, *Caste, class and occupation*, Bombay: Popular.

Giddens, A., 1973, *The class structure of advanced societies,* London: Hutchinson.

Goldthorpe, J.H., 1987, *Social mobility and class structure in modern Brit-*

ain, Oxford: Clarendon Press.
Goode, W.J., 1970, *World revolution and family patterns*, New York: The Free Press.
Herring, R.J., 1983, *Land to the tiller*, New Haven: Yale University Press.
Hodge, R.W., P.M. Siegel and P.H. Rosst, 1966, *Occupational prestige in the United States*: 1925-63, In R. Bendix and S.M. Lipset, eds. *Class, status and power*, pp. 322-34, Glencoe: The Free Press.
Hutton, J.H., 1961, *Caste in India*: London: Oxford University Press.
Jencks, C., 1975, *Inequality*, Harmondsorth: Penguin Books.
Joshi, P.C., 1975, *Land reforms in India*, Bombay: Allied Publishers.
Kakar, S., 1978, *The inner world*, Delhi: Oxford University Press.
Kapadia, K.M., 1958, *Marriage and family in India*, Bombay: Oxford University Press.
Kothari, R., (ed.), 1970, *Caste in Indian politics*, Delhi: Orient Longman.
Letwin, W., (ed.), 1983, *Against equality*, London: Macmillan
Madan, T.N., 1980, *Doctors and society*, Delhi: Vikas.
—, 1988, *Family and kinship*, Delhi: Oxford University Press.
Marx, K., 1959, Capital, vol. 3, Moscow: Progress Publishers.
Merton, R.K., 1957, Bureaucratic structure and personality, In R.K. Merton, *Social theory and social structure*, pp. 240-60, Glencoe: The Free Press.
Morgan, D.H.J., 1975, *Social theory and the family*, London: Routledge and Kegan Paul.
Narain, D., (ed.), 1975, *Explorations in the family and other essays*, Bombay: Thacker.
Navlakha, S., 1989, *Elite and social change*, New Delhi: Sage.
Nehru, J., 1961, *The discovery of India*, Bombay: Asia Publishing House.
Pande, S., 1986, *Trends of occupational mobility among migrants*, Jaipur: Rawat.
Parsons, T., 1954, *Essays in sociological theory*, Glencoe: The Free Press.
—, 1968, Professions, in D.L. Sils, (ed.), *International encyclopaedia of the social sciences*, Vol. 12, pp. 536-47, New York: Macmillan.
Parsons. T. and R.F. Bales, 1956, *Family*, London: Routledge and Kegan Paul.
Perkin, H., 1989, *The rise of professional society*, London: Routledge.
Poulantzas, N., 1976, *Les classes sociales dans le capitalisme aujourd'hui* Paris: Seuil.
Rao, A.V.P.R., 1989, *Urbanization, occupational mobility and integration*, Delhi: Deep and Deep.

Rawls, J., 1973, *A theory of justice*, London: Oxford University Press.

Robinson, R.V., (ed.), 1985, *Research in social stratification and mobility*, vol. 5, Greenwich, Conn: Jai Press.

Rowe, W.L., 1973., *Caste, kinship and association in urban India*, in A. Southlall (ed.), *Urban anthropology*, pp.211-49, New York: Oxford University Press.

Shah, A.M., 1973, *The household dimension of the family in India*, New Delhi: Orient Longman.

Sivaramayya, B., 1984, *Inequalities and the law*, Lucknow: Eastern Book Co.

Srinivas, M.N. and A. Beteille, 1964, Networks in Indian social structure, Man, 66:165-68.

Svalastoga, K., 1959, *Prestige, class and mobility*, Copenhagen: Glyndendal.

Tawney, R.H., 1964, *Equality*. London: Unwin books.

Treiman, D.J., 1977, *Occupational prestige in comparative perspective*, New York: Academic University Press.

Treiman, D.J. and R.V. Robinson (eds.), 1981, *Research in social stratification and mobility*, Vol.I, Greenwich, Conn: Jai Press.

Visvanathan, S., 1985, *Organizing for science*, Delhi: Oxford University Press.

Waugh, E., 1937, *Decline and fall*, Harmondsorth: Penguin Books.

Weber, M., 1978, *Economy and society*, vol. 2., Berkeley: University of California Press.

5 Approaches to the Identification of Elites

SHEO KUMAR LAL

The problem of identifying elites is not a new one to social scientists today. Studies in this sphere have mostly been conducted in western communities following three approaches in the main: (a) positional, (b) reputational, and (c) issue participation. In this paper, an attempt has been made to describe briefly each of these approaches.

Positional Approach

Prior to 1953, the positional approach was very popular. The basic assumption of this approach is that "those holding positions of authority actually make key decisions while those who do not occupy such positions do not make key decisions".[1] Followers of this approach adopted different criteria in selecting important positions. For instance, following Marx, both Lynds and Mills maintained that those who were at the apex of the economic concerns were better situated to decide and thus economic dominants were regarded as positional elites. Stouffer did not take top economic position into consideration; he selected top civic and political statuses instead.[2] Schulze and Blumberg chose economic dominance and such other objective criteria to determine positional elites.[3] Jennings selected government officials, civic staff personnels and economic dominants as their positional elites.[4] This approach has been criticized because of the variation in terminology characteristics of different associations in designating similar offices.[5]

Reputational Approach

In the study of social stratification, Warner, Hollingshed and several others used the reputational approach. Weber and Lasswell provided the theoretical framework for it. However, in the context of the community power structure, this approach was first used by Hunter[6] and by Angell[7]. There are several variants of this approach but irrespective of those variants, the respondents desired to name influential persons in the community who play a significant role and can get things done for the community. The basic assumption of this approach is that the respondents understand the question well and they are able to perceive the power structure accurately. The respondents may form a panel of knowledgeables or they may be selected through a "snow-ball". At times heads of organizations are asked to nominate people to these panels. They may also be randomly selected from a cross-section of the population. Nominations are secured from the respondents, and then a cut-off point is decided; and those who obtain a larger number of nominations above the cut-off point, are considered to be elites. Though this approach has been widely used, it has been criticized on various grounds. It is considered subjective and indeterminate. It is pointed out that it measures reputation for power and not the possession of actual power. It locates the existence of a monolithic power structure, the respondents are unable to perceive the power structure accurately, that there is no correspondence between the researcher and the respondent about the use of the term.[8]

Issue Participation Approach

The issue participation approach is also well known as the "event-analysis" or "decision-making" approach. This approach is based on the assumption that those who actually participate in the decision-making process are the elites because they have shown their influence in real-life situations. The first task, according to this approach, is to specify those decisions which are considered vital for the community at large. Once the decisions are specified, attempts are made to find out those who are the active participants in the decisions. The elites, according to this approach, are those who actually shape the decisions.[9]

This approach is likely to identify overt power rather than the power potential and thus it provides a more realistic viewpoint of power relations. But this too did not escape criticism and it is considered to be less expedient than the others.

The basic assumption of the various approaches and the various points of criticism have very ably been rephrased by Danzger and in his opinion the following questions are open to investigation and research:[10]

1. Does the informant's perception of power actually correspond to the power structure as measured by some objective means?
2. If the informant's perception is "incorrect" or if objective "correctness" cannot be determined, then what is the relation between the power structure as perceived through the reputational technique and as perceived through other techniques?
3. What do "informed" informants mean by the term "power"? Do they understand this term in the same sense as the researcher?
4. Do the leaders identified through the use of the reputational technique lead in "several scopes of power" or is their leadership restricted to one or few scopes?
5. Is the power structure as described through the use of the reputational technique stable over time or is it merely a description of power based on the highly variable "popularity" of certain individual at a particular moment?

A comparison of elites identified by reputation, position and issue participation approaches can answer the questions raised. If reputational elites are also identified by positional and issue participation approaches, then it can be said that: "(a) reputation for power corresponds to the realities of the power distribution, (b) that the respondents understand the term power or use it in a way similar to the usage intended by the researcher, (c) that once research techniques have located informants whose perception of the power structure is indeed accurate."

The present paper tries to answer some of the questions raised here. The objectives of the study may be spelled out in brief:

1. to identify elites through positional, reputational and issue participation approaches;
2. to examine the extent of correspondence of elites identified through different variants of reputational approach;
3. to examine whether or not randomly selected respondents from a cross-section of the population are able to identify elites of the community; and
4. To explore the relative adequacy of the three basic approaches— positional, reputational, and issue participation.

Method of Identifying Elites

Positional Approach

In our study, the determination of elites on the basis of position was done by selecting persons who were occupying the objectively defined top formal offices.[11] To check the salability and validity of these positions, a list of top positions was circulated among a panel of knowledgeables who were in substantial agreement with the list. In all, 41 persons were identified as positional elites. Persons holding these positions were supposed to wield influence.

Reputational Approach

To identify elites through the reputational approach, different variants were taken into account. Nominations were sought from three different panels of knowledgeables. One panel of knowledgeables consisted of the heads of the voluntary organizations; another was constituted through snow-ball; and the third panel was of such persons who came from different walks of life. We also selected respondents from a cross-section of the population to give nominations. In all, four variants of reputational approach were employed. Variant first identified 23 persons as elites, whereas variant second and third identified 21 and 23 persons, respectively. And lastly, in all, 21 elites were selected by a cross-section of the population.

A group of researchers maintain that randomly selected samples are not in a position to perceive the power structure accurately and instead they suggest the nomination from the panel of knowledgeables. However, this may be treated as an empirical question and it can be seen here whether the elites being perceived by the knowledgeables are the same as those perceived by randomly selected samples.

The overall selection of these variants reveals a high degree of consensus among all the four categories of respondents. Eighty per cent of the elites identified by samples were also identified by the first panel of knowledgeables. A large proportion (76%) of the elites selected by samples were also specified by the second panel of knowledgeables, and 71 per cent of them were also identified by third panel of knowledgeables. Only three of the 21 elites identified by sample failed to be included in the list selected by the knowledgeables.

Even more significant was the degree of agreement among the nominations with regard to the uppermost range of community power. Nine of the ten persons most frequently considered influential by all the four sets of the respondents were common to all. The individual first ranked of all the categories was the same.

The data show that despite different sets of nominators each set perceived substantially the same set of persons as influential in community affairs.

Still more interesting is the fact that even a cross-section of population was also able to perceive members of power structure as was done by the panels of knowledgeables invalidating the assumption that randomly selected samples are not expected to perceive power structure accurately. We found in all 34 persons, who could be considered elites in terms of the reputational approach.

Issue Participation Approach

To identify the issue participants, it is essential to identify the important community issues. Five major issues were: (1) retention of the unified seat of High Court at Jodhpur, (2) levy of octroi, (3) opening and location of Medical College, (4) urban identity, and (5) introduction of city bus service.

In all, 64 elites were identified as issue participants. When the elites were identified with the help of three approaches the names were analyzed for duplication and reduced to a total of 30 elites.

The empirical work based on the simultaneous use of all the major approaches for the identification of elites provided an opportunity for a comparative testing of these approaches themselves.

As indicated earlier, the adequacy of the positional approach has been doubted by many scholars and its basic assumption that "those who hold positions of authority are actually in a position to make important decisions and those who do not hold such positions do not do so"—has seriously been challenged. In the light of the above statement, an attempt was made to ascertain whether the assumption of this approach came true in an Indian urban community or the data supported the view of the opponents of this approach that it was not likely that position—holders would necessarily be issue participants.[12]

On the basis of this assumption, one may expect that position-holding is associated with decision-making. The data of this study with regard to the positional approach suggest that 51 per cent of the positional elites were also issue participants and they constituted only 37 per cent of all the issue participants. This suggests a reluctance in accepting the view that office-holding is necessarily related to issue participation. There is no one-to-one correlation between top positions and issue participants but we found that out of every two positional elites, one was also an issue participant. It may be taken to follow that a moderate relationship exists between position holding and issue participation, and thus one aspect of the basic assumption of the positional approach, i.e., those who hold positions are necessarily the issue participants, does not stand true in this study. As mentioned earlier, the advocates of the positional approach also hold that those who do not hold top positions are not supposed to be issue participants; but contrary to their expectation, a large section (63%) of the issue participants do not hold such positions, as might have been included in our study. Thus, it would be rather inaccurate to say that the issue participants are necessarily the positional elites. Some studies, however, have lent at least some support to the idea that there exists a relationship between position holding and decision-making[13], but some others have clearly contradicted the relationship.[14]

Having examined the assumption, we now turn to examine whether the positional elites have been perceived influentials in terms of the reputational approach. It would show as to what extent the positional elites were perceived as influentials. Our data reveal that 49 per cent of them were also perceived influentials. Thus, it may be inferred that out of every two positional elites one was also a reputational elite. Further, the data suggest that 59 per cent of the reputational elites were holding one or the other positions. This again suggests a moderate relationship between position and reputation. Some other studies that found relationship between position and reputation more particularly in small communities and accordingly hold that positional approach is a quicker and dependable approach to identify elites in small communities.[15] But contradicting the view two other studies have shown that this approach is not applicable even in small communities, and there too the relationship does not exist.[16]

Thus, the analysis leads us to conclude that office-holding is not necessarily related to issue participation and reputation. In short, the positional approach taken alone can identify only partially the members of the power structure; hence this approach by itself may not be valid.

We now turn to the reputational approach. When the list of elites identified by reputational approach was compared with that of the positional elites, it was found that 59 per cent of the reputational elites also had their place in the list of positional elites. That is to say that 59 per cent of the reputational elites were holding one or the other important offices. Similarly, the data suggest that 76.5 per cent of the reputational elites were also issue participants, which shows that a significantly large proportion of the reputational elites does not only have reputation for power, but they have expressed it in real-life situations and are more powerful participants than others. Further, they are not confined to only one issue. The two persons who had participated in all the five issues, another one who had participated in four issues, and all those persons who had participated in three issues, were reputational elites as the data suggest that on an average they had participated in more issues than others.

The overlapping of reputational elites in the list of positional elites and issue participants showed beyond doubt that the respondents were able to perceive the power structure accurately, and that there was a correspondence in the understanding of the respondents and the investigator about the meaning of the term "power". Another index was used to further establish this point. The opponents of the reputational approach criticize it on the ground that respondents, more particularly the randomly selected are not able to perceive the power structure, accurately. Surprisingly enough, this does not hold true in our study. As mentioned earlier, the randomly selected respondents had identified almost the same set of persons as panels of knowledgeables, and most of them were also identified by the other two approaches. In the face of such evidence, it is difficult to agree with the view that respondents do not understand the term 'power' and are not in a position to locate power structure accurately. No doubt this approach had left out a number of positional and issue participants, but data clearly indicate that these unidentified positional elites were not being perceived as important position holders as those who had been identified by the reputational approach also. The reputational approach identified generally persons holding elective political posts, heads of Chambers of Commerce, the Rotary Club, welfare organizations and chairmen of semi-governmental organizations. Only one of the government officials had been identified who was a highly placed judicial officer. Government officers were apparently not held in high esteem by the community leaders. Similarly, those issue participants who were not identified by the reputational approach had less participation in comparison to those who had been identified so. This shows that the upper layer of both positional and issue participants had been identified by the reputational approach.

After examining these aspects, we now turn to the scope of influence of these reputational elites. It is interesting to note that the elites identified by the reputational approach excel other elites in issue participation, organizational membership and area of influence. The data reveal that reputational elites had more organizational membership than that of others which indicates that their participation in organizations was more varied than the remaining elites. Similarly, reputational elites were active in several areas. This fact may further be corroborated by the perception of one elite about the other. A question was asked to indicate the areas of influence of these elites. For a larger section of reputed elites (22), it was reported that they were influential in two or more areas. It may be re-called here that in this study only 29 elites were perceived influential in two or more areas, and out of them 22 were reputational elites showing beyond doubt that the reputational elites were generally influential and they were not confined to a particular field. Thus, on the basis of empirical evidence it may be said that:

1. reputational elites are generally influentials;
2. respondents, even randomly selected, perceive the power structure as well as knowledgeables; and
3. reputational elites are active participants in issues and organizations.

Our data do not suggest, however, the existence of a stable group over a period of time. This can be possible only when a study of this kind is conducted again after some lapse of time.

The issue participation approach has identified 64 elites but the analysis is based on 56 elites.[17] Out of these 56 participants, 37 per cent and 46 per cent were found in positional and reputational lists, respectively, and on the whole 45 per cent of the issue participants were not identified by either of the two approaches. This clearly suggests that the issue participants are also not necessarily reputational whereas the reputational elites are generally issue participants.

Resolving Methodological Issues

The simultaneous use of the three approaches reveals that these three approaches are supplementary and complementary in identifying the community power structure. None is infallible. We thought that the issue participation approach would identify those who had real influence because of their active participation in community issues. We were surprised as to why as many as 53 per cent of them were not identified as reputational elites. This led to a further analysis of the data and a deeper understanding of the situation. We then came to know that as many as 10 of these issue participants performed only official routine duties and that their roles were not very important. Since they were the officers through whom the decisions were to be routed, they were reported to be issue participants. Similarly, there were two persons who were ranked high by the reputational approach but they had taken part only in one issue, whereas there were some who participated in two issues but were not nominated as reputational. This became somewhat perplexing. When their levels of participation were examined in terms of weighted criteria, it became clear that though they had participated in two issues, their roles were peripheral, whereas the one-issue participants who were ranked high through the reputational approach had played a very critical role in a very significant community issue. If we had depended on the issue participation approach exclusively, those who had participated in two issues but had played marginal roles would have been ranked high in power attribution. This aspect could become clear only when issue participation was examined against the result of the reputations.

Most of the remaining issue-participants were just followers of the reputational elites. Their roles were not very crucial either. What we want to suggest here is that the issue participation approach identified even those who performed just ministerial and formal roles. To illustrate, we may mention an official saying that he moved the paper for the introduction of a city bus service because his minister wanted it to be done, i.e., these officers generally legitimized the decisions merely as part of their duties.

On the other hand, we saw some shortcomings in the reputational approach as well. It did identify some persons on the basis of their position, status and sociometric relations. But the proportion of such persons is not large. It may further be noted that some of these did not participate in the issues not because they were not in a position to do so but because they thought that there were others to do it and their own social and official positions forbade them from taking an active part.

The use of the positional approach brought out the fact that it was not necessary for position holders to be issue participants and to be perceived as influential in society.

In short, the use of the three approaches has helped us in bringing out the subtleties of the power structure which could have remained concealed had we used only one of the approaches. Each one was a check against the other. It is possible to find better results if we use more than one approach.

Notes

1. C.M. Bonjean and D.M. Olson, "Community Leadership: Direction of Research", *Administrative Science Quarterly*, Vol. 9, No. 3, December, 1974, page 282.
2. S.A. Stouffer, *Communism, Conformity and Civil Liberties*, Garden City: Doubleday, 1955.
3. R.O. Schulze and L.U. Blumberg, "The Determination of Local Power Elites", *The American Journal of Sociology*, Vol. LXIII, No. 3, November, 1957, pp. 290-296.
4. M.K. Jennings, Community Influentials, *London: The Free Press of Glencoe, Collier-Macmillan Ltd., 1964.*
5. J.E. White, "Theory and Method for Research in Leadership", American Sociological Review, *Vol. 15, 1950, pp. 50-60.*
6. F. Hunter, Community Power Structure, *Chapel Hill: University of North Carolina Press, 1953.*
7. R.C. Angell, "The Moral Integration of American Cities", American Journal of Sociology, LXI, July, 1951, part 2.
8. W.V.D. Antonio and M.J. Ehrlich, *Power and Democracy in America*, North Darue: Ind., 1961, pp. 92 and 132.
   R.E. Wolfinger, "Reputation and Reality in the Study of Community Power", *American Sociological Review*, Vol. 25, 1960, pp. 636-644.
9. R.A. Dahl, *Who Governs?* New Haven: Yale University Press, 1961.
10. M.H. Danzger, "Community Power Structure: Problems and Continuity", *American Sociological Review*, Vol. 29, 1964, pp. 707-717.
11. For instance, Ministers, MPs, MLAs, Presidents of Civic Bodies, Presidents of Chamber of Commerce, Large Trade Union Organizations, Political Parties, Professional organizations, Service clubs, and other social and cultural organizations.
12. Counts was the first to draw attention to this fact. George S. Counts, *Society in Chicago*, New York: 1928.
13. J.E. White, "Theory and Method of Research in Community Leadership", *American Sociological Review*, vol. 15, 1950, pp. 50-60.
14. Hunter, op. cit., Schulze and Blumberg, op. cit., R.O. Schulze; "The Role of Economic Dominants in Community Power Structure", *American Sociological Review*, vol. 23, 1958, pp. 3-9; *Robert Presthus, Men at the Top: A Study in Community Power*, New York: 1964.
15. R. Laskin, et al., "Formal Versus Reputational Leadership", paper read at the annual meeting of the Pacific Sociological Association,

Portland, Ore., April, 1963.

16. Laskin et al., "Formal Versus Reputational Leadership" identification: A re-evaluation", paper read at the annual meeting of the Pacific Sociological Association, Portland, Ore., March 1964.
17. The remaining eight have been left out because they have either expired or left the city for long and as such they were not likely to be included in the list of present reputational and positional elites.

6 From Varna to Jati

The Indian Caste System, from the Asiatic to the Feudal Mode of Production

DIPANKAR GUPTA

Unfortunately, there has as yet been no attempt to identify the historical and material roots for the four-fold classificatory *varna* scheme, on which the present-day Indian caste system rests. This paper seeks to make a beginning in that direction by placing the problem of *varna* in the material history of period in which it was manifest, i.e. in the Vedic age, and then to trace the course of its fate through history. The objective is to explain the possible social and material factors responsible for the *varna* scheme of stratification. It is, therefore, intended to relate *varna* and *jati* to their respective epochs and to the modes of production to which these two forms of stratification correspond, namely, the Asiatic and feudal modes of production, respectively.

At the outset we should like to make it clear that, following Marx, we believe that the mode of production can be typified by its relations of production, or by the character of its exploitative structure which defines the parameter of expansion of the productive forces of the epoch. And that a particular mode of production defines the internal logic and coherence of a particular social structure, and allows for variations between societies characterized by the same mode of production. Therefore, a correct application of the Marxist conception of history, that basis determines superstructure, would demand an examination of the specific formation of a mode of production in a particular society. In other words, it is imperative to study the manner in which contingent and historical factors are conditioned by a particular structure of exploitation.

As Marx said in the *Grundrisse*: "It (a specific mode of production) is a general illumination which bathes all other colours and modifies their particularity. It is a particular ether which determines the specific gravity of every being which has materialized within it" (1973: 107). The other advantage, therefore, of relating the study of *varna* and *jati*, to the mode of production methodologically follows this other aspect. In order to account for the singular features, of *varna* and *jati*, we must be sensitized and alerted to the specificities of the social formations of the respective modes of production in which these systems of stratification were manifested.

To examine the hypothesis that the *varna* system was reflective of a material order and not merely fiction, we must consider the possibility of drastic epochal changes, so drastic that the *varnas* which corresponded to an earlier epoch were completely out of step in a later epoch, i.e., when the *jatis* were in the forefront. This would run counter to the proposition that Indian society has been stagnant and has remained unchanged from ancient to medieval times. Because the possibility of such epochal changes was not entertained in the past, the *varna* system was rendered incomprehensible and mystical.

Our primary focus then will be to relate the *varna* and *jati* systems of stratification to the Asiatic and feudal modes of production, respectively. This paper does not claim to be exhaustive, nor does it pretend to bring to light fresh material, though there is some reinterpretation of data. It merely presents a preliminary framework by systematically arranging the facts most pertinent to *varna, jati* and the socio-economic formations in which they found expression. It is hoped that this attempt will at the very least dispel myths surrounding the concept of caste.

The Asiatic Mode of Production

Apart from raising the possibility of the *varna* system as a viable historical category, we are forced concurrently to delve into another controversy—that of the Asiatic mode of production.

Marx found the concept Asiatic mode of production useful in understanding Asiatic societies, particularly India. According to Marx (1965: 69-70), the Asiatic mode of production "is quite compatible with the fact that the all-embracing *unity* which stands above all these small common bodies may appear as higher or sole *proprietor*.... It therefore follows that the surplus product (which, incidentally, is legally determined in terms of the real appropriation through labour) belongs to this highest unity... which ultimately appears as a person. This surplus labour is rendered both as tribute and as common labour for the glory of unity". As Godelier (1965a: 34-35) elaborates, "the exploitation of man by man assumes within the Asiatic mode of production, a form which Marx called 'general slavery', distinct in essence from Graeco-Latin slavery as it does not exclude the personal liberty of the individual, is not *relationship of dependence vis-a-vis one another, and is achieved by the direct exploitation of one community by another*" (see also Marx 1965:5; emphasis added). In other words, general exploitation of the people directly by the superior community or the state is the crucial feature of the Asiatic mode of production. This direct and general exploitation of one community by another in turn precludes any relationship of dependence and exchange at the lower levels.

The Asiatic mode of production is not necessarily tied to a powerful state, as Marx (1965:70) himself had shown (see also Godelier 1965:101), nor to a hydraulic society, as Habib (n.d.: 61) has demonstrated. It should be mentioned in this connection that Marx's characterization of the Asiatic mode of production does not in any way assume that the exploited community in these societies is an undifferentiated peasant mass (Hindess and Hirst 1975: 196-198). Stratification and differentiation among the exploited, as we shall see, in no way militates against the concept of the Asiatic mode of production, nor does it contradict the principles of general exploitation.

Much of the controversy about the Asiatic mode of production can be traced to Marx's writing on the subject and to the several inconsistencies in his treatment of Asiatic societies.

What is often overlooked is that Marx substantially revised his position on the Asiatic mode of production between 1853 and 1858. This has been pointed out by Hobsbawm (1965) and Mukherjee (1975), but has generally been glossed over by Marxists and other sociologists. Until 1853, Marx's writing on India, which include his despatches to the *New York Daily Tribune*, were largely derived from reports of European travellers like Bernier. This is perhaps what led Marx to exaggerate the "stagnation" and "despotism" in Oriental societies (Hobsbawm 1965: 33; Mukherjee 1975: 98-99). For instance, in the *Future Results of British Rule in India,* Marx wrote: "India has no history at all, at least no known history. What we call its history is but the history of successive intruders who founded their *empires* on the passive basis of that unresisting and unchanging society" (see Mukherjee 1975:98).

But later, around 1858, when Marx was preparing his *Critique of Po-*

litical Economy and *Capital*, he undertook a more intensive study of Indian history. This led him to reject, or at least to modify, some of his earlier position on Asiatic societies. He no longer considered despotism and stagnation to be the essential features of societies characterized by the Asiatic mode of production. We also find that Marx became more preoccupied with the Asiatic mode of production on an analytical rather than on a descriptive level. He eventually defined the Asiatic mode of production, as he had defined other modes of production, on the basis of its production relations and its character of surplus appropriation. He found that the essential feature of the Asiatic mode of production was the direct and generalized exploitation by the state (or the superior community) of the inferior community. This provided Marx with greater flexibility in his study of Asiatic societies. No longer did he pivot his examination of Oriental societies on purely epiphenomenal features like "despotism", or the large centralized water works operated by the state. By focusing on the relations of production and on generalized exploitation, Marx allowed for variations in the social formation of economies characterized by the Asiatic mode of production. He now accepted the idea of "either a more despotic or more democratic" from of authority (Marx 1965:70). He also acknowledged the possibilities of orthogenetic sources of change and dynamism in Asiatic societies, to such an extent that he discussed the possibility of development from the Asiatic mode of production to feudalism (Ibid.).

We have highlighted this change of Marx's position on Asiatic societies because all too often scholars uncritically base their study of the Asiatic mode of production on some of the descriptive superstuctural features Marx had sketched of Asiatic societies prior to 1853. This inhibited any meaningful discussion of the Asiatic mode of production, for scholarship on the subject centred around such trivia as whether the Asiatic mode of production should be defined on the basis of a despotic state, or large public water works, etc. (see, for instance, Wittfogel 1970). All this prompted Perry Anderson (1974: 424) to remark that the utilization of the concept "Asiatic mode of production" has generally resulted in "blending features found in distinct social formations into a single blurred archetype".

Recently, however, there have been several attempts by Marxist scholars like Godelier and Jean Chesneaus, among others, to apply Marxism more scientifically to the problem of the Asiatic mode of production, in terms of its central or essential features, i.e., its relations of production, and its character of exploitation. Such an approach is steadily gaining ground and this paper is largely indebted to it.

Even so, the status of the Asiatic mode of production, as a determinate historical category, is still extremely precarious. Several Indian historians have substantially revised and improved upon much of Marx's writing on Asia without arriving at a consensus on whether any epoch in Indian history can be characterized by the Asiatic mode of production. This, in turn, compounds the difficulty in accounting for the sources of contradiction and change in the Asiatic mode of production, without which it falls short of being a true and demonstrable Marxist category. Therefore, if the Asiatic mode of production is not to remain a purely mythical concept, as it has for some time now for several Marxists, any investigation involves the two-fold task of identifying the era of the Asiatic mode of production and locating its dynamic potential. We shall touch on these two areas with what little evidence we have from the Indian situation. Our treatment ought not to be regarded as definitive, but we hope to shed some light on these two very complex and urgent issues.

Varna as Colour

The first sacred book of the Aryans—the *RgVeda*—was composed around 1500-1400 B.C. in the region between Kabul and Ganges. It is from the perusal of this and three later *Vedas* that historians have been able to reconstruct the socio-economic conditions of that society until approximately 500 B.C., when the Vedic age is said to end. The *varna* system came into being only after the Aryans settled in the vast Indo-Gangetic plains. There seems to be no doubt that they were racially of a different stock from the indigenous population which they subjugated.

It is said that the Aryans entered India around 1750 B.C. and were the marauders of the Indus Valley civilization. Though there is no proven Aryan skull form, according to Kosambi (1975: 173), "certain tribes among the whole Indo-European group were conscious of being Aryans in some ethnic sense. For example, Darius I of Persia proclaimed in his grave inscription (486 B.C.) that he was "*parsu, parachaya puthra, Arya Arya cithre*", i.e., a Persian, son of a Persian, an Aryan of Aryan descent". The European origin of the Aryans is suggested by Ghosh (1951:202) on the basis of the geographical distribution of the idioms of the Indo-European speech family. He suggested that "the original home of the Aryans should be sought in Europe rather than in Asia". S.K. Chatterji (1951: 142-43), after reviewing both Hutton and Guha on the race movements in India, agrees that the Aryans were racially vastly different from the indigenous stock who were of a darker complexion and had probably in them strains of the Negrito and the Proto-Australoid (from the Mediterranean) (see also Pusalker 1951a: 195-92; Kosambi 1975-98).

This racial differentiation needs to be emphasized; historically, perhaps in no other society did two racially dissimilar communities co-exist for such extended periods. Moreover, the superiority of the conquerors did not result from superior technological or cultural achievements, but more likely from their superior martial prowess. This necessitated close interaction between the Aryans and the original inhabitants. In order to preserve and rationalize their superiority, the Aryans had to emphasize and maintain their racial distance from the indigenous community. Likewise, the *RgVeda*—the oldest Vedic text—mentions the difference between the Arya and the Dasa *varna*, and that differentiation between the conquerors and the vanquished was expressed in the idiom of colour. *Varna* literally means *colour*. This fact gives us the clue to the origin of the myth of "natural superiority" which rationalizes the *varna* scheme and contributes to the peculiarities of the caste system. Later development did not go against this rationale, and it became well-entrenched and ritualized by the end of the Vedic period.

The expansion of the Aryans in the early Vedic period did not occur by conquest alone. Some adventurous Brahmans and Kshatriyas from different Aryan kingdoms helped to clear jungles and make the land arable (Chanana 1960:24; Kosambi 1975: 123). They also set up new hermitages. The *close co-operation* between the Brahmans (priests) and the Kshatriyas (warriors) made this possible, and they consolidated their exploitative status in tandem.

> Brahman missionaries who accompanied the Kshatriya introduced the essentials of Aryan culture and tradition to the masses, converted the principal figures and paved the way for social and cultural contact by allowing high-born Aryans to marry non-Aryans (Pusalker 1951b:314).[1]

The primitive economy of the early Vedic period did not allow the Aryans to maintain a profound distance from the indigenous and subjugated communities in day-to-day activities. Even the Brahmans and Kshatriyas worked on the land and did other manual jobs essential in this phase of Aryan expansion. Therefore, for the conquering Aryans, the religious conversion of the non-Aryans into the Vedic fold was the most effective guarantee of their superiority. The ascetic Brahmanical or the priestly side of Aryan expansionism was used to full advantage in this period by the Aryans. The esoteric sacred Vedic texts and religious rites were emphasized to bring about a peaceful acquiescence of non-Aryans to Aryan supremacy. Concomitantly, the myths and rituals which sanctified the Vedic differentiation on the basis of colour found extended application with each phase of Aryan expansion and consolidation.

Varna System and Generalized Exploitation

The four strata of the *varna* scheme did not emerge full blown from the very inception of the Aryan settlement in India. It is true that in the *RgVeda* the main division is between the Arya and Dasa *varna*. But the Aryans themselves were not an undifferentiated community. They were divided into elites and commoners. The latter were called *vis* in the *RgVeda*. This category later largely constituted the Vaishya community, the third stratum of the fully developed *varna* scheme. The Vaishyas were the common peasants engaged primarily in agricultural practice. The Aryans tried to absorb the indigenous local tribes and communities and establish a workable relationship with them, but naturally from a position of strength. Some friendly tribes like the Sutas were even considered respectable (Jha 1975:15). Rituals were profitably utilized to make allies for the Vedic Aryans from among the non-Vedic people (Sharma 1975:9-11).

Members of several weak or unfriendly tribals who were unable to withstand the Aryan onslaught were enslaved by the Aryans or became a servile class in the Vedic economic structure. They were called the *dasas*. The *dasa* thus later came to mean, according to Kosambi, a helot of some sort. He had "not the right to initiation, nor to bear weapons: he had no property of the Aryan tribes as a whole, much in the same way as cattle" (Kosambi 1975:97) and like cattle[2] both the male and female *dasas* were objects of gift to the superior community (Chanana 1960:21). The *evidence* that Kosambi and other historians have cited to show the absorption of the *dasas* into the Aryan-fold leads one to believe that the Shudras (the lowest rung of the *varna* order) arose out of this servile population "augmented also by such Aryans as were subjugated and enslaved in internecine warfare" (Habib 1965:23).

A clear delineation of the four *varnas* is not evident in the *RgVeda*, but appears in the *Purusasukta* which is a later addition. Further, as Muir opines, the Brahmans, or the priestly class, did not constitute an exclusive community. In the Vedic age priestly duties were not necessarily fulfilled by men of priestly families (Apte 1951a:388). Even in the *Yajurveda*, where we find the Vedic Aryans in a settled community (i.e., in the later Vedic age), where the full elaboration of the four orders of the *varna* scheme has taken place, a conflict for supremacy exists between the Brahmans and Kshatriyas, as well as a considerable overlapping of duties. Sharma (1975:10) notes that the *Pancavimsha Brahmana* records the conflict between Sudas and his priest Vashist. Throughout the later Vedic age and up to the Upanishadic period, we find several instances of a Kshatriya's thirst for knowledge and increasing inquisitiveness to know the essence of nature and the world. Thus, through the priest-king/warrior groups combined to form a composite ruling class, the distinctions between them were nebulous.

From the ancient texts it appears that the basic unit of Aryan social life was the patriarchal family. Their chief god was Agni (fire) while their other anthropomorphic deities were male, headed by the hard-drinking Indra (Kosambi 1957:87). The Aryans were also pastoral people who had domesticated the horse and, as a result, had gained much mobility. Their indices of wealth accordingly were associated with cows, horses and other animals. The Aryans had also sought to combine pastoralism with agriculture and are said to have used the wooden plough to cultivate barley and other cereals. There were, however, no towns at this stage and the Aryans were in fact rather proud of the great destroyer Indra who had allegedly demolished the earlier pre-Aryan towns (Habib 1965:23).

The Aryans in this stage had a simple social structure. They were divided among tribes which they called *jana* and lived in villages (Ibid:30). *Bali* was the recognized form of payment to the Brahman-Kshatriya combine and was more in the nature of an offering than a tax. There does not seem to exist any overlordship of land, but cattle and horses were owned by the Brahmans and Kshatriyas.

It appears that most of the land was divided into fields cultivated by individual peasants who were regarded as *kshetrapati* or holders of the land. Lands, as Kosambi (1975:111) said, "were allotted to groups in rotation and within the group by rank....Agriculture was so crude in any case that ploughed land had to be changed every year". According to Habib (1965:24), as the Aryans lived in "semi-nomadic conditions, the conception of permanent occupation, let alone ownership of particular fields could not have possibly developed".

In contrast to the earlier nomadic RgVedic stage, the later Vedic phase, i.e., when the other three *Vedas* as well as the early *Brahmanas* were composed, denoted a phase of great Aryan expansion (Ibid.:23). According to Kosambi (1975:111), this period, beginning more specifically from the Yajurvedic stage,

> ".....seems nearer to that of Caesar's Gauls, who were Aryans too, softened from a recent martial past. They had developed settled agriculture, some trade and strong class structure within the tribe..... (The) existence of a still lower class of menials, the Sudras, made the position of the Vaishya easier. The two privileged class of druids and knights correspond exactly (sic) to Brahmans and Kshatriyas."

Also unlike the RgVedic period, the Aryans now produced wheat, several kinds of pulses, rice (Sharma 1975:1) and even sugarcane (Habib 1965:66). Society was not pastoral as in the RgVedic age and peasants now "produced surplus to maintain priests, princes and their retinues" (Sharma 1975:1), though the wooden plough was still in use.[3] The peasants, Vaishyas, became increasingly subject to the exactions and oppressions of superior class. Behind this class differentiation can be traced "the growth in the power and pretensions of the ruler or chief" (Habib 1965:27). The gain tithe of the Vaishyas served to maintain the Brahmans and Kshatriyas, while the Shudras performed essentially menial tasks and were a domestic adjunct, small in number at this stage (Sharma 1975:4).

In spite of the sharp differentiation, monarchy did not develop. Tribes took the form of oligarchies, where the undifferentiated superior community was maintained by the efforts of the Vaishya commoners and Shudra menials and helots (Habib 1965:28). The Vaishya community also served as artisans and provided the nobility with such services as carpentry, smithery, chariot-making, etc. (Apte 1951a:397). The tax collectors were generally related to the king, and force was used to collect taxes, the royal share being one-tenth or one-twelfth of the total produce (Sharma 1976:6-8). Nevertheless, the state apparatus did not crystallize until the end of the Vedic age. "The Vedic communities had neither a regular taxation system nor a standing army which was permanent, though one hears of *sena, senapati* etc." (Ibid.:12.)

Neither had the distinctions between artisans and peasants developed. They belonged to the undifferentiated Vaishya category of the *varna* scheme. This was probably due to the low level of productive forces of that period. Some iron weapons were made by smiths for the nobility, but they were few and of an inferior quality. This suggests that these artisans probably also had an additional stable means of livelihood, namely, agriculture. The utilization of wooden implements produced limited surplus, and this did not favour greater class differentiation either. However, the priest-warrior/king combine undoubtedly constituted the nobility and there was no question of their paying any taxes (Ghoshal 1972:170). The Brahmans could hold land in the form of villages and fields without invoking the authority of the tribe and the clan (Kosambi 1975:139).

The differentiation of the *varna* scheme into four broad categories was a reflection of the socio-economic formation of that period, namely, small peasant predominating villages which used pre-iron agricultural equipment and gave up the surplus to the Brahman-Kshatriya combine. The latter directly collected the surplus from the peasantry and took advantage of the artisans' rudimentary skills. Exploitation, in other words, was general. As the *Shatapatha Brahmana* states: "The state authority feeds on the people. The state is the eater and people are the food: the state is the deer and people are the barley" (see Sharma 1975:6). Likewise, the principal aim in the later Vedas is to sanction this exploitation. It is made clear that man is born with certain *rinas* (debts) and he can overcome these *rinas* by following the injuctions laid down in the Vedic scriptures, by paying homage to the gods and the Brahman *rishis*, and by swearing allegiance solely to the law-makers and the law-enforcers (Apte 1951b:445).

The entrenchment of the *varna* scheme may in no small measure be attributed to the fact that until the first half of the first millennium B.C., the settled phase of Aryan society was prolonged on account of the persistence of pre-iron agriculture. In Greece and Iran, iron-based craft and agriculture appeared approximately four centuries and two centuries, respectively, earlier than in India. "Hence on account of low agricultural productivity, ritualism and ritualist class grew far more rapidly in India" (Sharma 1975: 13), *rigidifying* the ritual bases of the *varna* classification as well. The tools and implements of the period throw light on the nature of the economic formation which, in turn, influenced the relations of production of that epoch, and profoundly affected the superstructure. As Emmanuel Terray (1972:103) states:

> "It is not articles made, but how they are made, or by what instruments, that enables us to distinguish different economic epochs. Instruments of labour not only supply a standard of the degree of development of which human labour has attained, but they are also indicators of the social conditions under which labour is carried on."

It may appear that the four-fold *varna* scheme was an outcome primarily of the low development of productive forces and the absence of extensive division of labour, and had nothing to do with *generalized exploitation*. But, as we hope to show, even in the succeeding post-Vedic Mauryan period which saw quite an extensive division of labour, the four-fold categories of the *varna* scheme still sufficed to guide social intercourse and ranking. So obviously the *varna* scheme was rooted in a deeper reality, namely, the relations of production or the character of exploitation, which as we shall see, remained largely unaltered from the later Vedic period to the Mauryan period. There is nothing inherently contradictory between the existence of extensive differentiation and division of labour and a simple four tiered stratification system such as *varna* system. The two can be reconciled, as it is here hypothesized they were in the Mauryan period, if the logic of generalized exploitation is followed through. The following section hopes to deal with this problem.

The Mauryan Empire: The Climax of Asiatic Society

The second phase of iron age which began approximately around 550 B.C. made greater surplus expropriation possible by intensifying the prevailing structure of exploitative relations. The artisans and peasants, i.e., the Vaishyas in their dual role, were still tied to the nobility, with the difference that the petty oligarchies of the Vedic Aryans had given way to powerful kingdoms beginning from the Magadha and climaxing with the Mauryan empire. The release of productive forces with the more intensive utilization of iron crystallized the formation of the state and its apparatuses such as the royal bureaucracy and a standing army.

For the appropriate utilization of this technological breakthrough, the state grouped different categories of artisans in separate guilds and directed their energies solely towards the production of superior agricultural tools and weapons. While the former augmented the agricultural surplus, the latter enhanced the instruments of coercion at the hands of the Mauryans. Several *srenis* were also composed of certain communities and tribes outside the empire who had been subjugated by the state. Through the *srenis* they rendered myriad services to the state. Book 2 of the *Arthashastra*[4] mentions *srenis of vratya* (non-Vedic) Aryans as well. These guilds, or *srenis*, functioned primarily to meet the needs of the state and the nobility for their personal consumption, warfare and trade.

> "The king as the successor to chiefs of many different tribes and as the recipient of great revenues in kind from harvested grain and from local manufacture, had to convert a substantial part of the grains into commodities to pay the army and the bureaucracy. The state was

therefore the great trader, the supreme monopolist" (Kosambi 1975:216).

Exploitation, thus, still continued to be general. The artisans in the guilds or *srenis* of the Mauryan period were probably members of the Vaishya community, who were alienated from agricultural practice as the art of smelting became widely known. But even so it included only a minority of the artisans in the Mauryan empire. Evidence suggests that certain artisans, such as smiths and carpenters, settled in villages composed of only members of their caste, and where they also had to quite naturally, cultivate land for themselves (Habib 1965:29). The artisans in the *srenis* were probably drawn from these villages. Such manufacturers' villages were a peculiarity of this period and may be explained by the fact that the artisans would not have been able to feed themselves without engaging in agriculture, indicating once again that strict occupational specialization resulting in exchange at the local level did not exist to a significant degree. Handicraft production had therefore not yet moved to the village, in the sense that artisans as a distinct occupational group had not yet emerged, nor had they been integrated into a web of exploitation and exchange at the local village level. In subsequent epochs, when this was to come about, the possibility of artisans engaging in agricultural production was not considered either by the peasantry or by the ruling classes (Chichirov 1971:31).

But where do these guilds fail in the *varna* scheme? There is a tendency among certain scholars to dismiss every other group, tribe or community, and to believe that the four categories of the *varna* scheme were the only social divisions that existed. And on the other hand, because of this differentiation, others believe that the *varna* system was not applicable at all. As we have already pointed out, there were numerous tribes, other than the Vedic, which were integrated in the Vedic Aryan society. Nevertheless, the four-fold *varna* scheme was still the dominant model of status and economic differentiation. As each community was largely self sufficient, because agriculture was still open to all communities, as exploitation was general, and as hardly any economic interaction existed among different groups and communities at the local level, further elaboration of the four-tiered *varna* scheme was unnecessary. Other groups, tribes and *srenis* found their place in one of the four categories (more often at the bottom, but sometimes in the Kshatriya category) through various occupations prevalent in the epoch and necessary for the ruling community or the state.

It is widely believed that these guides crystallized into *jatis* (Ghurye 1969:114). The beginning of occupational specialization may have originated here. But to believe that it was just a matter of time before guilds became rigid caste groups is incorrect. The complete elaboration and strict separation of the various orders denoting the rules of intercourse and exchange had to await a further development in the socio-economic structure. The ramifications of caste ranking among artisans, peasants and traders had not yet developed, nor had the notions of superiority and inferiority bordering on competition amongst the erstwhile constituents of the Vaishya and Shudra communities, as they were all exploited by the state and had few, if any rights and obligations towards each other.

From the Vedic age to the Mauryan period, we find the gradual development of a monolithic, centralized authority. Though productive forces increased in this period, with the second phase of iron, they did not bring about a qualitative change in the relations of production. Authority and ownership still lay with the state, and with the growth of powerful empires, exploitation became more general and more intensive. The Vedic rationale of superiority on an ascriptive criterion continued to serve in this period as well. It was a very vital element of the superstructure and its dominance was an outcome of the protracted stagnant economy with low rates of production in the pre-iron Vedic age. It is necessary to emphasize this aspect of the *varna* classification if one is to understand the peculiarities of the caste system as it developed over the ages.

This phase, beginning from the Yajurvedic age to the fall of the Mauryan empire, is in essence similar to Marx's Asiatic mode of production, namely, that ownership and authority over land are vested with the state, which results in the second crucial characteristic, that of the general exploitation of the peasantry and artisans by the state via the royal bureaucracy, or directly by the oligarchs of the Vedic era.

Though several Indian historians and sociologists have detailed this system of generalized exploitation, and the centralization of property rights by the state, the implications of this have not been realized in terms of their relation to the Asiatic mode of production, obfuscating, among other things, a correct understanding of the *varna* system. It was this system of generalized exploitation that brought about the *varna* order of differentiation wherein the various distinctions between the artisans and peasants had not yet developed. This was because each community was largely self-sufficient, as agriculture was open to all, and secondly, because they were all exploited by the superior community or the state. These, in turn, did not demand further elaboration of rights and duties beyond the four-fold *varna* scheme, which adequately defined the status and privileges of numerous communities and groups which were accreted over a period of time to the Vedic and Mauryan societies. This four-tiered differentiation is admittedly, a view from the top of the hierarchy, but the view from the bottom is no more varied, and may, in fact, appear less differentiated, because economic obligations were only directed vertically.

Transition to Feudalism

We shall try to highlight some of the contradictions and forces of change within the Asiatic mode of production, in the specifics of its Indian variant, which led to its gradual dissolution, albeit over centuries, resulting in far-reaching changes in the forms of stratification and property rights. What also seems analytically important in this connection is not to mistake a slow pace of change (as compared to the West) for no change at all.

The period ending approximately with the Mauryan empire was characterized by substantial trade and mercantile activity. This is evident from the large number of coins available from the period, as well as by the presence of merchants, who, though despised by the state (*Arthashastra* 4:1), were nonetheless quite powerful, and some even bore arms. Between the peasant mass and the monarchs were the *pauri janapadas* who were leaders of erstwhile tribal formations (Kosambi 1975:223). These *janapadas* were in charge of certain districts, and were also ministers of the royal courts. According to the *Arthashastra*, they were paid salaries. The *janapadas* at this stage, did not resemble feudal or private landlords. According to Kosambi, " (by) tribal custom land had been apportioned by the chief or a council of *elders whose authority had now passed to the king*" (Ibid.:222: emphasis added). Authority had not devolved to the *janapadas*, even though they converted surplus produced by men in their jurisdiction into private property. Moreover, the royal *sita* lands which were very large belonged to the king and formed the bulk of arable land which "could adequately explain the Greek report that in India all land belonged to the king" (Habib 1965:31).

Mauryan society did, however, contain within itself the makings of its own destruction which in its wake brought about a qualitative change in the production relations. The disintegrating forces of the preceding period were, firstly, the contradiction between private property and the property of the state. The seeds of landlordism were sown in the Mauryan period as the *janapadas* were able to convert surplus to private property, though during the reign of the Mauryas this contradiction was not allowed to develop (Kosambi 1975:225). Moreover, the Mauryan empire, due to its size, was susceptible to fissiparous tendencies where local officials began to assert themselves once the period of expansion and of powerful emperors was over. Secondly, "the population of craftsmen increased and certain skills like smelting became widely known under the impetus of the growth of commerce and the centralized administration of the Mauryas, and individual artisans could begin moving to villages" (Habib 1965:32). Thirdly, the forcible settlement of the Shudras as cultivators, advocated by Kautaliya, transformed a large number of Shudras from pure menials and servants of the nobility to peasants and rural labourers (Habib 1965:33; Kosambi 1975:301; Ghoshal 1972:194). This transformation also helped the subsequent growth of a village-based economy which characterized the period beginning around 200 A.D. These peasant villages were subordinated to local chiefs who had begun to assert their local authority and whose links with the emperor were tenuous and much weaker than in earlier times. This development is often characterized as *feudalism* which took on a more pronounced form during the Gupta (circa 400-500 A.D.) and Harsha (700 A.D.) empires, and continued down through the medieval age under different local economic formations.

According to R.S. Sharma (1965:1), certain political and administrative developments tended to feudalize the state apparatus after the Mauryan period. The most striking development, he believes, is the practice of land-grants made to Brahmans (Brahmadaya) which was sanctified by the injunctions in the *Dharmasastras*. The *Mahabharata* which was written just prior to the Gupta period devotes an entire section to praising such gifts of land (Ibid.:2). The practice of giving up administrative rights to the grantees was started probably during the reign of Guatamiputra, the Satavahana ruler in the second century A.D. This became more frequent by the Vakataka period around the fifth century A.D. (Ibid.:3). The Gupta period also affords instances of such transfer of powers to the grantees, especially during the reign of the Gupta period, who were, however, not always Brahmans. They were also officers of the state (Ibid.:7). Though there is no direct evidence about the conditions on which these grants were made, from extant information, it appears that the office of the *bhogikas*, or administrative officer of the Gupta period, had become hereditary in some localities. Moreover, "the village headman" (*gramadhipati ayuktaka* is represented in the *Kamasutra* (c.400-500

A.D.) as "exacting unpaid labour from peasant women and compelling them, among other things, to fill his granaries and work on his own fields. The officials thus appear as having land of their own and enjoying semi-feudal rights over the peasantry" (Habib 1965:38). According to the *Arthashastra*, the officials in the Mauryan period were paid salaries in cash, but by the time of Manu (circa 200 A.D.), they were paid in land-grants, while in Harsh's time, they were paid a percentage of revenues (Sharma 1965:11).

It is a reasonable assumption that by this time individual ownership of land was quite prevalent. The *Manusmriti* (9:44)[5] also declares: "The land belongs to him who first clears it, as the deer to him who gets in the first arrow." This is in substantial agreement, as Kosambi (1975:257) points out, with the earlier *Milindipanha* text which states: "When a man clears away the jungle and sets free (*niharti*) a piece of land... people say it is his land. It is because he has brought this land into use that he is called the owner of the land". This would certainly not have been entertained in the *Arthashastra*.

A statement such as that in *Manusmriti* might lead one to believe that as land was abundant, it could be cleared and occupied directly by individual peasants. This, however, seems unlikely for a number of reasons. Firstly, an individual peasant would be far too ill-equipped to clear the jungle without the help of the king or the superior class. According to Ghoshal (1972:170-171): "In so far as the settler of new lands are concerned, it will be seen that they are required necessary capital in the shape of provisions, implements and the like... (It) requires the king to make advances of money to the new settlers ". Secondly, as Kosambi (1975:257) argues: "The individuals who cleared a patch of land would in general be a member of some community, based upon kinship and upon a village...A solitary cultivator in completely virgin wilderness is difficult to imagine". It would appear then that the superior class cleared the forest land with the help of the general peasantry and menials, and exercised property rights over it by siphoning off the surplus produced, a portion of which was paid to the king.

The *Jati* System and Localized Exploitation

From the seventh to the twelfth century A.D., these features crystallized. Serfdom became a widespread phenomenon (Sharma 1965:57-60). The erstwhile officials of the king now began to keep the entirle revenue and for all practical purposes severed their ties with the monarch by totally usurping his administrative authority. The feudal elites such as the *samantas*, petty village chiefs and lesser landholders began to exert greater rights over lands (Yadav 1976: 45). This brought about the division of the entire territory of the kingdom, leading to several sub-divided clan monarchies of the Gujara Pratihara kind between the eighth and the tenth century A.D., and the Cahamanas from the middle of the eighth century to the early fourteenth century A.D. (Chattopadhyay 1976:64-69).

> "Here the territory was parceled out by the ruler after retaining his own share among his kinsmen and clan chiefs. Each of the latter then set about dividing his territory among his own clansmen while retaining his own share, until by this process, every village was assigned to a particular man in return for a supply of troopers when needed by the assignor....The most common titles of the potentrates (i.e., the new landed aristocracies) are *samantas, ranaka, rauta, thakkurra*...and *rajaputra*" (Habib 1965:41-42).

The distribution of land among royal kinsmen and officers was a widespread phenomenon of this period (Gopal 1963-64: 75-103). The Harsa inscriptions of 973 A.D. at Jaipur are considered to be the earliest evidence of such distribution (Chattopadhyay 1976:71).

This period is also characterized by the breakdown of large-scale commerce and trade which is evident from the paucity of coins of the era (Sharma 1965:270). The towns and large trading centres which dotted the earlier Buddhist and Mauryan empires had also disappeared. The ruralization of the ruling class was accompanied by the ruralization of the artisans and handicraft workers. Never before had the peasants and craftsmen been subject to such direct control by local chiefs, his intermediaries and clansmen. As Sharma (1965:271-272) said:

> "The main characteristics of European feudalism, the self-sufficient economy, buttressed by lack of commercial intercourse and the rise of intermediaries leading to the subservience of the peasantry prevailed in India....(and) the possessing class appropriated the surplus produce of the peasants by exercising superior rights over land and persons."

Moreover, in the feudal structure of exploitation, the subordinate communities were not generally related directly to the state, but to the various local intermediaries and to the feudal lord. The officials of the Mauryan empire were officials of the royal court, and the benefits they derived from the structure of generalized exploitation was routed via the state. In the feudal period, however, the intermediaries and clansmen of the overlord were paid not so much in cash by way of salaries—as in land grants. This led to a hierarchy of direct exploiters in feudal societies as the noblemen held differential sizes of land, depending on their rank and closeness to the overlord, and a right to differential shares of the produce of the peasants, which they extracted through extra economic coercion in their respective demesness.

In feudal societies, all the land generally did not belong to the overlord or to his intermediaries and clansmen. Some land was distributed to particular groups in return for their services during military campaigns, The rest was given over for peasant (*ryot*) cultivation. The landlord's own land was either cultivated by serfs, or by ryots, who in addition to giving up part of the surplus on their own allotments, were forced to render labour service by the lords.

This localization of exploitation had several consequences. First, as we have already mentioned, was the decline of trade. Second, the exactions by the overlords and the nobility of the serfs, peasants and artisans increased. This was possible as the former held juridical rights over their area. Third, as land became the index of wealth and power it was highly prized and cultivation emerged in this period as the only viable occupation for the people. Those peasants who had enough land to make a living out of agriculture were as a consequence held in greater esteem, than those who had to supplement agriculture by crafts and artisanry. This tied the ryot to the nobility. The nobility also took care not to dispossess or ruin the peasants uniformly, as they formed a guaranteed pool from where they could draw labour services. As Lenin (1960:194) said, large pre-capitalist landlords need peasants attached to small pieces of land as they then become dependable sources of labour. Fourth, not only did stratification increase and deepen among the ruling class, but it also in turn differentiated the subordinate community who served them. The peasants are split into grades depending on the types of allotment, differing amount of payment, whether state peasant or tied and taxed by the feudal lord (Sharma 1966:183), and also on the status of their feudal overlord (Breman 1974:19).[6]

Artisans were also ranked depending on the rank of their patrons or of their customers. An ironsmith, therefore, was lower than a goldsmith, a weaver even lower than an ironsmith, and so on. The other side of this tendency towards greater stratification in feudal societies is the greater integration and interdependence in the local village milieu between different communities. We no longer hear of villages belonging to any one artisan community. Each village now had not only its lords and nobles, its *ryots* and officials, but also its complement of goldsmith, weavers, ironsmith, potters, etc.

It was the progressive development of this economic structure of localized exploitation within the village nexus which brought about the elaboration of the *jati* or what is popularly known as the Indian caste system. The dependence of the lower exploited classes on each other and on their masters in a closed society and market necessitated a greater elaboration of the rules of exchange and intercourse. The rationale of "natural superiority" which served the *varna* scheme so well was not abandoned but on the other hand utilized fruitfully by the exploiting classes. This percolated right down the ranks, enabling the peasants and artisans to interact on the basis of the ruling class ideology. The general exploitation of the Asiatic mode of production of the previous epoch whereby the rights and duties of the artisans and peasants vis-a-vis each other had not been elaborated now gave way to more clearly specified patterns of interaction due to the exigencies of localized feudal exploitation. Also the notion of "untouchability" originates around 200 A.D., especially in association with the *chandalas*. This institution takes on an extreme from by the twelfth century A.D., as revealed in the *Parasasmriti*.

It is not merely the proliferation of numerous occupational groups that distinguishes *jati* and *varna*. As we have pointed out, the belief that the Vedic age had only four orders of the *varna* scheme is incorrect. This belief led one to question the veracity of the various occupational groups in Megasthenes *Indica* (Kosambi 1975:193). The Vedic society, however, did try to fit these diverse groups and communities into the Procrustean bed of the *varna* scheme, though not always successfully. The failure to do so did not create any problems of controlling social relations of the period because exploitation was general and the exploited classes served only the superior community with few or no rights, obligations and economic intercourse among themselves. The status of the numerous occupational groups of peasants, artisans, menials, etc., correspond generally to that of either the Vaishya or the Shudra. Further delineation of status and position among them was not necessary. The essential difference between *varna* and *jati* is precisely this aspect which was brought about by a closed village economy.

With the level of productive forces remaining stagnant, any rise in population was accommodated in the feudal structure of medieval India at the cost of greater rigidification and further stratification of the *jatis*. As the facilities to utilize land were limited, and property rights over land were monopolized by a minority, population pressure did not expand the frontiers of land utilization, but led instead to greater differentiation within the confines of the feudal economy.[7] This resulted in a plentiful supply of skilled labour which was intensively utilized for the expropriation of use values and also for commodity production (Habib 1971:41). This inhibited in turn the use of labour saving devices and the manufacture of tools with higher productivity. Habib (Ibid.:38) quite rightly says:

> "(While) it is true that extensive development in technology can only occur when metal, particularly iron, replaces other materials, this change can be delayed in a particular situation for no other reason than that a tool of lower efficiency can be used to manufacture the same commodity by employment of cheap skilled labour."

Besides the abundance of skilled labour in a labour-intensive economy, the number of *jatis* was also enhanced by the continuing absorption of tribals, whose lands were annexed by the might of the nobility into the village nexus. They were forced to render certain services to meet local needs,[8] and were likewise placed in the hierarchy, usually at the bottom. Conversely, those tribes not within this nexus, due to either their inaccessibility or their indomitability, were driven to the extremities of established society and to the brink of survival. This can be seen even today in the tribal belts of India (Breman 1974:7).

When trade resumed on a large scale in the eleventh century A.D., it did not disturb this village structure. Indeed, the needs of trade very often brought about new occupational groups, like the diamond miners of Karnataka (Habib 1971:38). Similarly, during the Muslim period, the regeneration of powerful royal bureaucracies did not dismantle this feudal set-up (Singh 1973: 200), and contrary to popular British myth, as Alavi (1975: 186) has pointed out, all land did not belong to the great Mughal emperor. These royal officials of the Muslim court were alternately paid salaries in cash, or were assigned the revenues of a particular area over which they exercised superior authority much in the manner of a feudal overlord. Such changes were rather by his successor, which usually left the existing village structure undisturbed (Siddiqui 1970:17-40; Habib 1965:54-55; Habib 1971: 14-15; Hassan 1963:118). Therefore, the apparent similarity between the royal bureaucracies of the Muslim rulers and the notion of an "oriental despot" of the Asiatic mode of production should not mislead one, as Marx himself had been at one time, to identify the Muslim period with the Asiatic mode of production. To quote Marx (1945:58): "Bernier rightly considered the basis of all phenomena in the East—he refers to Turkey, Persia and Hindostan—*to be the absence of private property* in land. This is the real key, even to the Oriental heaven." Bernier was misinformed to say the least. As we have noted earlier, the absence of private property rights in land is characteristic of the period prior to the Gupta empire, after which the accumulated contradictions of the epoch over many centuries slowly led Indian society towards feudalism. During the period in which Bernier lived and wrote of India, i.e., in the height of the Mughal period, private property rights in land were widespread.

Unfortunately, Marx had to depend on these wildly exaggerated accounts of European travellers, and if Bernier chose to misunderstand the situation, Marx cannot be held responsible. But the later-Marxists cannot claim such extenuating circumstances in their favour, since several noted Indian historians have more than adequately detailed the socio-economic conditions of India during the Muslim period. And yet we find several European Marxists like Shlomo Avineri (1969-29) still clinging to the antiquated notions of Medieval India.

Ritual Status and Political Power

Vertical mobility which took place within the *varna* and *jati* schemes did not contradict the principal rationale behind the *varna* scheme, which was based on the myth of "natural superiority". For instance, all powerful monarchs and all landowning communities were not always of Kshatriya origin. Several powerful warrior kings from Chandragupta Maurya to Shivaji as well as "those who became landholders by force or royal pleasure could hide their low origins by paying enough priestly Brahmans to support their claim" (Kosambi 1975:33).

Moreover, superior ritual status as depicted in the *varna* scheme did not always entail superior economic and political power. Only in the Vedic age can it be said that the two coincided as the warrior-priest ruling class amalgam working in close collaboration to clear virgin lands and to subjugate hostile tribes which were threat to the Vedic Aryans who were quite primitive themselves. The amalgam came apart in the years to follow. The growth of the Mauryan empire in a sense crystallized this distinction. The growth of large empires, the emergence of a developed state structure with a standing army and a large royal bureaucracy necessitated greater preoccupation with administrative and political control. The list of duties of the king as prescribed in the *Arthashastra*, along with the multifarious activities for the officials of the bureaucracy detailed therein testify to this. This explicitly compartmentalized and segregated the activities of the warrior/king from the poet/priest. Operative political and social control was exerted exclusively by the non-priestly warrior class. But the Brahmans continued to exercise their influence through clever manipulation of religion and rituals, and were also generously endowed with land, such as with the Brahmadaya lands.

During the feudal period in which to quote Sharma (1965: 272) again, "the possessing class appropriated the surplus product of the peasants by exercising superior rights over land persons", social and political power stemmed from these superior rights over land. Hence, those Brahmans who did not own land or were impoverished were not dominant in terms of the operative exercise of political power. Yadav (1976:45) draws over attention to *Kathakosa Prakarama* of Jinesvara Suri to show that landed property in this age emerged as the most "tangible basis of social and political status". We find here that "the ruling landed aristocracy composed of two strata-paramount rulers and the different grades of the feudal elite actually enjoyed the highest status in society and emerged as a chief socio-economic class"—were placed below the landed aristocracy (Ibid.).

The priests, however, were given superior ritual status, as in all other pre-capitalist societies, because they were the ideological fountainhead on which the myth of "natural superiority" legitimized feudal exploitation.[9] But this ritual superiority does not necessarily subsume actual dominance in secular affairs. For instance, the rise of the Lingayat community of Mysore to dominance was challenged by Brahmanical orthodoxy, as a result of which the Lingayats employed their own non-Brahman priests to perform identical functions (Manor 1977: 177)—a measure that the "high" caste Brahmans could do nothing to prevent.

Similarly, it should be remembered that social and political power emanated not from wealth alone but from the role of the individual and of his community in the system of production. Several merchants were wealthy even during the Mauryan times, but they were not able to elevate themselves above the nobility. As Habib (1971:33, 55-56) has shown, the merchants were closely tied to the landed nobility and their fortunes depended upon the fate of their immediate feudal patrons. It was only after the degeneration of feudalism in the middle of the nineteenth century, when first gradually and then increasingly, the feudal apparatus in India lost its stranglehold (without of course relenting completely), that the merchants-turned capitalists could become a dominant power in the state structure.

Varna and *jati*, as we have tried to show, are systems of stratification based upon exploitation under the Asiatic and feudal modes of production, respectively. The capitalist order brings about, ideally, a new order of differentiation based on the exploitation of labour by capital. But very rarely do societies exhibit a single mode of production to the total exclusion of other modes, i.e., in its "pure" form. Several modes of production can and do exist side by side in a society, as in India, "one being dominant, i.e., governing the basic relations of the society" (Meillasoux 1972: 98). Therefore, it would be too much to ask for a casteless system in modern India where the introduction of capitalism was not accompanied by an industrial revolution (either capitalist or socialist) and where, as a result, pre-capitalist remnants are still prevalent. These pre-capitalist structures are used by capitalists in underdeveloped countries for "super exploitation", as Meillassoux has admirably demonstrated, because they prefer not to assume "the functions of social security" (Ibid.:102). Hence, the traditional ties with the village, clan, caste and feudal lord were not severed but actually reinforced by the uncertainties of capitalist exploitation.

Summing up the Two Orders

We have already stressed that this paper touches on a complicated issue which requires more intensive and in-depth treatment before any definitive arguments can be made. Furthermore, as the contours of this paper have been sketched on a broad historical canvas going back to that Vedic age, we can only describe the most general trends in Indian history. We hope, however, that it will help to demonstrate that *varna* and *jati* are reflective of specific socio-economic formations, and that the origins of the caste system should be sought in the material history of India and not in the empyreal recesses of the Hindu mind.

What distinguishes *varna* and *jati* as forms of differentiation is not that the latter subsume greater internal stratification than the former, which is only stratified into four categories, as Srinivas assumes (Srinivas 1962:65), nor that the *varna* is merely the "theory" behind *jati*, which may be true but only in very general sense.[10]

The crucial distinction between *varna* and *jati* is that, whereas *varna* is a system of differentiation in the epoch of the *Asiatic mode of production*, which was characterized by *general exploitation* the *jati* system developed later in the epoch of *feudalism* and was characterized by *localized exploitation* in a closed village economy, where the ruling class lived off the land. The ownership of land under feudalism was concentrated in the hands of a minority landowning class, and the land became an index of wealth and the basis of socio-political authority. This necessitated the elaboration of rules of interaction and economic intercourse among the middle and lower orders and also bought about greater occupational specialization. On the other hand, in the epoch of the *varna* system, as exploitation was general, rights and obligations were detailed in one direction only, i.e., to the service of the superior community and the state. Hence, even though there were numerous other tribes and groups, once they were evolved in the Vedic-fold, they found their place in the prevalent four-fold *varna* hierarchy, according to their respective occupations. This did not create any imbalance or confusion in the existing social relations, as they all served the state or the superior community, and had no rights or obligations amongst themselves, unlike the later *jati* system. Moreover, as agricultural operations were open to all categories of the *varna* scheme, the lower orders were quite self-sufficient and this precluded any clear demarcation between peasants and artisans.

Finally, the rigid rules of endogamy and the rationale of "natural superiority", which govern the *jatis*, can be better understood when we examine the beginning of the *varna* system, when the conquering Aryans subjugated the local indigenous communities. There was a distinct racial difference between these two communities, which provided a ready rationale for the subjugation of the indigenous tribes, namely, in the metaphor of colour. This rationale of differentiation enjoyed centuries of uninterrupted domination because of the extended period of stagnation in the level of productive forces due to the protracted existence of pre-iron production in Vedic India. It is primarily for this reason that the myth of "natural superiority" and the rituals that sanctified this myth became deep-seated and well-entrenched in Indian society, the significance of which has often been underestimated.

A Review of Literature

We have attempted to relate *varna* and *jati* to the mode of production for the purpose of understanding the origins and peculiarities of the caste system in India, and to throw some light on the principal reasons behind its peculiarities and its persistence. Our study also demonstrates that in order to understand the *varna* system, and especially the rigidity and ritualism of the *jati*, it is necessary to relate its ideological structure to the peculiarities of the socio-economic formations of its epoch. We therefore, disagree with Srinivas' approach that the caste system can be understood by disregarding the *varna* scheme, although, "they are an integral part of the society" (Srinivas 1962:65).

This point needs some clarification. Untouchability, as Jha has shown, only emerged around the second century A.D., gaining importance after the Gupta period and firmly entrenching itself by the eleventh century A.D. (1975:15-20), i.e., in the heyday of feudalism, characterized not by the *varna* form of differentiation, but by the *jati* variant. In Vedic and Mauryan societies, on the other hand, because of the generalized form of exploitation no community could be strictly segregated nor could prohibitions on social intercourse develop. The Shudras, as we found in Kautilya's *Arthashastra*, were employed as agricultural labourers. It was only later in the feudal epoch when certain communities were restricted solely to "unclean" occupations that the notion of untouchability developed. In the Vedic period, as Jha has demonstrated, some communities were abhorred, but they were not untouchables (Ibid.:15).

This attempt to relate the peculiarities of the *varna* and *jati* to the specificities of the socio-economic formations of the modes of production provides an alternative approach to a rather popular view recently blostered, albeit in round about manner, by the structuralist school headed by Dumont (1971). The contention of this school is that the Indian mind, as revealed in the ideology of the caste system, has a peculiar propensity for thinking in hierarchical terms, and is incapable of overcoming this. We have attempted to counter this view by positing the epochal and contingent factors responsible for the rigid ideology of caste. The logical outcome of this structuralist bias is that the caste system is seen as emerging full-blown from the very inception of the Vedic society. Weber (1958: 101-129), no less, is the hallowed mentor of this view. In fact, nothing could be further from the truth.

Several authors have explored the exploitative dimensions of the caste system, and besides Kosambi whom we have cited extensively, the names of Gough (1969), Chanana (1961), Singh (1969), Breman (1974), and Mencher (1974) come readily to mind. Though the focus of their research is not identical to ours, their works have provided us with critical insights, and our indebtedness to them lies in their successful "demystification" of the concept of caste.

However, we are forced to take issue with Mencher in particular as her work has a direct bearing on the subject-matter of this paper. We have some misgivings regarding her structural view of caste. She tends to undermine the peculiarities of this phenomenon, and equates the untouchables and Harijans with the Blacks of America (Mencher 1974:478). Though it is true that there is a certain similarity in the manner in which both the Blacks and the lower castes are treated, there is a vast difference in the structural configurations which determined their debasement. One instinctivitely sympathizes with the position that Mencher takes, which in itself is a reaction to the narrow, biased, Eurocentric, anthropological investigations of caste. Yet, it should be stressed that the peculiarities of the caste system are so pronounced that they set it apart from other forms of stratification. Therefore, rather than deny the peculiarities of the caste system, the more scientific and fruitful approach would be to explode the myth that the Indians have a mystic predilection for constructing rigid hierarchical structures. To do so, it is important to relate the peculiar contingent conditions of India which, under the different economic epochs known generally as the Asiatic and feudal modes of productions, brought about specific economic formations which were the bases of *varna, jati* and the caste system as such. This approach would less prejudicially expose the Eurocentric endeavours to consign Indian society forever to the limbo of timelessness and stagnation. Finally, it is hoped that this study might provoke a re-examination of the Asiatic mode of production and its domination of the social structure at a crucial time in Indian history.

Notes

1. Such unions were generally hypergamous.
2. The word *pasu* which applies to both beast and cattle is applied in the *RgVeda* to the dasas also (Kosambi 1975:98).
3. Only in the second phase of iron in India, i.e., circa 500-200 B.C. in the Vedic age, do we encounter iron agricultural implements.
4. Kautilya, author of *Arthashastra*, was chief adviser to the great Mauryan Emperor, Chandragupta Maurya.

5. This work is said to have been composed by an official and law-giver, Manu, circa 220 A.D.
6. See also Lenin (1960:381) where he details an identical process in feudal Russia.
7. It is often mentioned, even by Marxist scholars, that there was a lot of surplus land in this period. See, for instance, Hamza Alavi (1975:85), Irfan Habib (1971:14-16), and Kosambi (1975-241). One fails to understand in what context they consider land to be surplus. Such a statement might be construed to imply that the economic base had room for greater expansion, and thus the increased population could be gainfully employed in agricultural occupations. This, in turn, would imply that any subordination by feudal lords was only through the medium of superior physical force (see Anderson 1974) and would underscore the fact that given the level of productive forces, and the relations of production, the availability of land and opportunities for employment were indeed restricted (see, for instance, Jan Breman 1971:11). As Lenin said, the availability of land for utilization depends not on the absolute quantum of land but on the productive forces of the epoch which utilize it. To quote him: "Speaking generally, it is impossible for human labour to supersede the forces of Nature.....Both in industry and in agriculture, man can utilize forces of Nature, when he has learned how they operate, and he can facilitate this utilization by means of machinery" (1976:11).
8. The Juang tribe of Orrisa, for instance, took to basket-making (Bose 1961:27).
9. The religious veil is rendered obsolete only with a through-going capitalist revolution. Marx and Engles deserve to be quoted in full in this context. In the *Communist Manifesto* they wrote: "It (the bourgeoisie) has pitilessly torn asunder the motley feudal ties that bound man to his 'natural superiors' and has left no doubt between man than naked self-interest ..... It has drowned the most heavenly ecstasies of religious fervour, of chivalrous enthusiasm, of philistine sentimentalism, in the icy water of egotistical calculation.... honoured and looked upon with reverent awe" (1950:486-487).
10. All that can be said in favour of this view is that the belief in natural superiority is common to both, but that is not the same as saying that *varna* is the theory behind *jati*, the empirical fact.

References

Alavi, Hamza, 1975, "India and the Colonial Mode of Production", in Socialist Register. *Edited by Ralph Miliband and John Saville, London: Merlin Press.*

Anderson, Perry, 1974, *Lineages of the Absolutist State*, London: New Left Books.

Apte, V.M., 1951a., "Political and Legal Institutions, (The age of Rik Samahita)", in *History and Culture of the Indian People*, Vol.I., The Vedic Age, Edited by R.C. Majumdar and A.D. Pusalker, London: George Allen and Unwin.

—, 1951b, "Religion and Philosophy in the Age of the Later Samahitas", in *History and Culture of the Indian People*, Vol.I, The Vedic Age, Edited by R.C,Majumdar and A.D. Pusalker, London: George Allen and Unwin.

Arthashastra, 1960, Edited by R.P. Kangle, Bombay: University of Bombay Publication.

Avineri, Shlomo, 1969, "Introduction", in *On Colonialism and Modernization*, by Karl Marx, New York: Anchor Books.

Bose, N.K., 1961, *Cultural Anthropology*, Bombay: Asia Publishing House.

Breman, Jan, 1974, *Patronage and Exploitation*, Berkeley: University of California Press.

Chanana, Dev Raj, 1960, *Slavery in India*, Delhi: Peoples Publishing House.

—, 1961, "Sanskritization and Westernization in India's North-West", *Economic Weekly* (Bombay), 8: pp. 409-414.

Chatterji, S.K., 1951, "Race Movements in Pre-Historic Culture", In *History and Culture of the Indian People, Vol. I., The Vedic Age*, Edited by R.C. Majumdar and A.D. Pusalker. London: George Allen and Unwin.

Chattopadhyay, B.D., 1976, "Origin of the Rajputs: The Political, Economic and Social Processes in Early Medieval Rajasthan", *Indian Historical Review* (New Delhi), 3:pp.59-82.

Chichirov, A.E., 1971, *Indian Economic Development in the 16th and 18th Centuries*, Moscow: Nauka Publishing House.

Dumont, Louis, 1971, *Homo Hierarchicus*, Delhi: Vikas Publications.

Ghosh, B.K., 1951, "The Aryan Proble", In *History and Culture of the Indian People*, Vol 1, *The Vedic Age*, Edited by R.C. Majumdar and A.D. Pusalker, London: George Allen and Unwin.

Ghoshal, U.N., 1972, *Contribution to the History of the Hindu Revenue System*, Calcutta: Saraswati Library.

Ghurye, G.S., 1969, *Caste and Race in India*, Bombay: Popular Prakashan.

Godelier, Maurice, 1965a, "The Notion of the Asiatic Mode of Production", in Marx and Engles", *Enquiry* (New Delhi, New Series), 2: pp. 28-48.

—, 1965b, "The Notion of the Asiatic Mode of Production in the Marxist Scheme of Evolution of Societies", *Enquiry* (New Delhi, New Series) 2:pp 76-102.

Gopal, K., 1963-64, Assignment to Officers and Royal Kinsmen in Early Medieval India (c. 700-1200A.D.), Allahabad: University of Allahabad Studies (Ancient India Section).

Gough, K., 1969, "The Social Structure of a Tanjore Village", *In Village India*, Edited by M.N. Srinivas, Bombay: Asia Publishing House.

Habib, Irfan, "An Examination of Wittfogel's Theory of Oriental Despotism." *Enquiry*, (New Delhi): 6: pp.54-73.

—, 1965, "Distribution of Landed Property in Pre-British India", *Enquiry*, (New Delhi, New Series), 2: pp. 21-75.

—, 1971, "Potentialities of Capitalist Development in the Economy of Mughal India", *Enquiry* (New Delhi, New Series), 3: pp. 1-56.

Hasan, S.N., 1963, "The Position of Zamindars in the Mughal Empire", Indian Economic and Social History Review (New Delhi), 1:pp. 107-119.

Hindess, Barry and Paul Q. Hirst, 1975, *Pre-Capitalist Economic Formations*, London: Routledge and Kegan Paul.

Hobsbawm, Eric, 1965, 'Introduction', in Pre-capitalist Economic Formations, by Karl Marx, New York: International Publishers.

Jha, Vivekanand, 1975, "Stages in the History of Untouchables", *Indian Historical Review* (New Delhi), 2: pp.14-31.

Kosambi, D.D., 1975, *An Introduction to the Study of Indian History*, Bombay: Popular Prakashan.

Lenin, V.I., 1960, *The Development of Capitalism in Russia. Collected Works* Vol. 3, Moscow: Foreign Language Publishing House.

—, 1976, *The Agrarian Question and the "Critics of Marx"*. Moscow: Progress Publishers.

Manor, James, 1977, "The Evolution of Political Arena and Units of Social Organization: The Lingayats and Okkaligas of Princely Mysore", in *Dimensions of Social Change in India*, edited by M.N. Srinivas, S.S Sehaiah and V.S. Parthasasrathy, Bombay: Allied Publishers.

Manusmriti, 1971, Translated by Arthur Coke Burnett, completed and edited by Edwar H. Hopkins, New Delhi: Oriental Books Reprint Centre.

Marx, Karl, and Engels, Frederick, 1950, *Selected Works*, 2 Vols., Moscow: Foreign Language Publishing House.

—, 1945, *Selected Correspondence 1846-1895*, Calcutta: National Book Agency.

Marx, Karl, 1973, *Grundrisse*, Harmondsworth: Penguin Books.

—, 1965, *Pre-Capitalist Economic Formations*, edited by E. Hobsbasm, New York: International Publishers.

Meillassoux, Claude, 1972, "From Production to Reproduction", *Economy and Society* (London), 1:pp-93-105.

Mencher, J.P., 1975, "The Caste System Upside Down or the Not so Mysterious East?", *Current Anthropology* (Chicago), 15: pp. 469-494.

Mukherjee, Ramkrishna, 1975, "History and Tradition in Indian Society: Null and Alternate Hypotheses?", *Sociological Bulletin* (Bombay), 24: pp. 95-108.

Pusalker, A.D,.1951a, "The Indus Valley Civilization", in *History and Culture of the Indian People*, Vol. 1,*The Vedic Age*, Edited by R.C. Majumdar and A.D. Pusalker, London: George Allen and Unwin.

—, 1951b, "Traditional History from the Earliest Time to the Accession of Parikshit", in *History and Cultural of the Indian People, Vol. 1, The Vedic Age*, Edited by R.C. Majumdar and A.D. Pusalker, London: George Allen and Unwin.

Sharma, R.S., 1966, *Light on Early Indian Society*, Bombay: Manaktalas.

—, 1976, "Class Formation and its Material Basis in the Upper Gangetic Basin (C. 1000-500B.C.)", *Indian Historical Review.* (New Delhi), 2: pp.1-13.

—, 1965, *Indian Feudalism C. 300-1200*, Calcutta: University of Calcutta Press.

Siddiqui, N.A., 1970, *Land Revenue and Administration Under the Mughals* (1700-1750), Bombay: Asia Publishing House.

Singh, Yogendra, 1973, *Modernization of Indian Tradition*, Jaipur: Rawat Publications.

—, 1969, "Social Structure and Village Panchayat", in *Rural Sociology*, edited by A.R. Desai, Bombay: Popular Prakashan.

Srinivas, M.N., 1962, *Caste in Modern India and other Essays, Bombay: Popular Prakashan.*

Terray, Emmanuel, 1972, *Marxism and "Primitive" Societies*, New York: Monthly Review Press.

Weber, Max, 1958, *The Religion of India*, Glencoe (Illinois): Free Press.

Wittfogel, Karl, 1970, *Oriental Despotism: A Comparative Study in Total Power*, New Haven: Yale University Press.

Yadav, B.N.S., 1976, "Problem of Interaction Between Socio-Economic Classes in Early Medieval Complex", in *Indian Historical Review* (New Delhi), 3: pp.43-58.

7 Division and Hierarchy

An Overview of Caste in Gujarat

A.M. SHAH

I

Hindu society is usually described as divided into a number of castes the boundaries of which are maintained by the rule of caste endogamy. There is enormous literature on these caste divisions from about the middle of the 19th century which includes census reports, gazetteers, castes-and-tribes volumes, ethnographic notes and monographs and scholarly treatises such as those by Baines, Blunt, Ghurye, Hocart, Hutton, lbbetson, O'Malley, Risley, Senart, and others. The census operations, in particular, spread as they were over large areas, gave a great impetus to writings on what Srinivas has called the horizontal dimension of caste (1952: 31f;1966: 9,44,92,98-100,114-17). What may be called the census approach influenced a great deal of scholarly work. Census officials-turned-scholars, from Risley to Hutton, wrote many of the earlier general works on caste.

With the exclusion of caste (except scheduled caste) from the census since 1951 (practically since 1941, because the census of that year did not result in much reporting), writings on castes as horizontal units greatly declined. On the other hand, there was an almost simultaneous spurt in village studies. Typically, a village consists of the sections of various castes, ranging form those with just one household to those with over a hundred. Village studies, as far as caste is a part of them, have been, therefore, concerned with the interrelations between sections of various castes in the local context. Srinivas has called the unity of the village manifested in these interrelations the vertical unity of the village (1952: 31f.), as contrasted with the horizontal unity of the caste. Indeed, a major achievement of Indian sociology during the last thirty years or so has been deeper understanding of caste in the village context in particular and of its hierarchical dimension in general.

No sooner had the village studies begun that their limitations and the need for studying caste in its horizontal dimension were realized. There are thus a few excellent studies of castes as horizontal units. In spite of them, however, sociologists and social anthropologists have not filled adequately the void left by the disappearance of caste from the census and the gazetteer. The advance made in recent years is limited and much more needs to be done. Data need to be collected over large areas by methods other than those used in village studies, castes need to be compared in the regional setting, and a new general approach, analytical framework, and conceptual apparatus need to be developed. The main aim of this paper[1] is to discuss, on the basis of data derived mainly from Gujarat, these and other problems connected with the horizontal dimension of caste. The purpose is not to condemn village studies, as is caste in a better perspective after deriving insights from village studies.

Division and hierarchy have always been stressed as the two basic principles of the caste system. In recent years, however, there has been a tendency to emphasize hierarchy as the primary principle encompassing the principle of division. This tendency reaches its culmination in the work of Dumont. He stresses repeatedly the primacy of the principle of hierarchy-epitomized in the title of his book, *Homo Hierarchicus.* I should hasten to add, however, that the open-minded scholar that he is, he does not rule out completely the possibility of separation existing as independent principle. He writes: “It is not claimed that separation, or even ‘repulsion’, may not be present somewhere as an independent factor” (1972: 346,n.55b).[2] He does not give importance to this possibility probably because, as he goes on to state, “what is sought here is a universal formula, a rule without exceptions” (ibid.). I hope to show in this paper how the principle of division is also a primary principle competing with the principle of hierarchy and having important implications for Indian society and culture.

That the sociological study of urban areas in India has not received as much attention as that of rural areas is well known, and the studies made so far have paid little attention to caste in urban areas. I hope to show that the integration of the study of caste in urban areas with that of rural areas is essential to a comprehensive understanding of caste and its implications for Indian society and culture. One of the reasons behind underplaying of the principle of division by Dumont as well as by others seems to be the neglect of the study of caste in urban areas (see Dumont's remarks in 1972: 150).

I do not propose to review the literature on caste here; my aim is to point out the direction towards which a few facts from Gujarat lead us. Nor do I claim to know the whole of Gujarat. I have done field work in two contiguous parts of Gujarat: central Gujarat (Kheda district and parts of Ahmedabad and Baroda districts) and eastern Gujarat (Panchmahals district). Together they provide a slice of Gujarati society from the sea-coast to the bordering highlands. Roughly, while in the plains area villages are nucleated settlements, populated by numerous castes, in the highland area villages are dispersed settlements, populated by tribes and castes of tribal origin. The urban centres in both the areas, it is hardly necessary to mention, are nucleated settlements populated by numerous caste and religious groups. The two areas merge gradually, and my field work covered most of the spectrum. As regards the rest of Gujarat, I have used various sources: my work on the caste of genealogists and mythographers and on the early 19th century village records; the available ethnographic, historical and other literature; and observations made while living in Gujarat.[3] Although my knowledge is fragmentary, I thought it was worthwhile to put together the bits and pieces for the region as a whole. For the sake of bravity and simplicity of presentation, I have not provided detailed documentation.

Ideally, castes as horizontal units should he discussed with the help of population figures. Unfortunately, such figures are not available for the last fifty years or so.[4] The census reports provide such figures until 1931, but it is well known that these pose many problems for sociological analysis, most of which arise out of the nature of castes as horizontal units. Nevertheless, a breakdown of the population of Gujarat into major religious, caste and tribal groups according to the census of 1931 is presented in the following table to give a rough idea of the size of at least some castes. As for the size of other castes, I shall make mainly relative statements.

Population of Gujarat by Religion, Caste and Tribe in 1931

Category	*Population*	*Percent*
Higher Castes		
Brahmin	289,796	4.06
Vania	208,739	2.96
Rajput	345,727	4.85
Others	80,321	1.13
Middle Castes		
Bharwad	143,477	2.01
Bhat, Barot	23,549	0.33
Bhoi	26,992	0.38
Kharva	13,792	0.19
Koli	1,729,039	24.22
Machhi	39,382	0.55
Kanbi,Patidar	868,030	12.16
Mali	8,669	0.12
Artisan Castes	437,762	6.13
Others	309,670	4.34
Lower Castes		
Depressed and untouchables	511,866	7.17
Other backward castes	161,381	2.26
Others		
Aboriginal	1,260,374	17.65
Muslim	609,304	8.53
Christian	52,940	0.74
Parsi	15,086	0.21
Others	3,283	0.05
Total	7,139,179	100.00

Reproduced from Ghanshyam Shah (1975: 9). He compiled this table taking figures from reports on the census of several politico-administrative units into which Gujarat was divided in 1931.

I shall first provide an analysis of caste in the past roughly during the middle of the 19th century, and then deal with changes in the modern times.

II

The Hindu population of Gujarat was divided first of all into what I have called "caste divisions of the first order"[5]. A few examples are: Brahman (priest), Vania (trader), Rajput (warrior and ruler), Kanbi (peasant), Koli (peasant), Kathi (peasant), Soni (goldsmith), Suthar (carpenter), Valand (barber), Chamar (leatherworker), Dhed (weaver) and Bhangi (scavenger). There were about three hundred divisions of this order in the region as a whole. Usually, these divisions were distinguished from one another by prohibition of what people called *roti vyavahar* (bread,i.e.,food transactions) as well as *beti vyavahar* (daughter, i.e., marital transactions). This account of the divisions is based on various sources, but mainly on *Bombay Gazetteer* (1901).

A first-order division could be further divided into two or more second-order divisions. Usually, the latter were distinguished from one another by prohibition. The Brahmans were divided into such divisions as Audich, Bhargav, Disawal, Khadayata, Khedawal, Mewada, Modh, Nagar, Shrigaud, Shrimali, Valam, Vayada, and Zarola. In all there were about eighty such divisions. It is noteworthy that many of their names were based on names of places (region, town, or village): for example, Shrimali and Mewada on the Shrimal and Mewar regions in Rajasthan, Modh on Modhera town in north Gujarat, and Khedawal on Kheda town in central Gujarat. Similarly, the Vanias were divided into such divisions as Disawal, Kapol, Khadayata, Lad, Modh, Nagar, Nima, Porwad, Shirmali, Vayada, and Zarola. In all there were thirty to forty such divisions. Many of these names were also based on place names. Although the name of a Brahman or Vania division might be based on a place name, the division was not territorial in nature.

Frequently, a division among Vanias corresponded to a division among Brahmans. For example, just as there were Modh Vanias, there were Modh Brahmans, and similarly Khadayata Vanias and Khadayata Brahmans, Shrimali Vanias and Shrimali Brahmans, Nagar Vanias and Nagar Brahmans, and so on. Sometimes a division corresponding to a division among Brahmans and Vanias was found in a third first-order division also. For example, just as there was a Shrimali division among Sonis (goldsmiths).[6] Traditionally, the Brahman division was supposed to provide the priests for the corresponding divisions. For example, the Khadayata Brahmans worked as priests at important rituals among Khadayata Vanias. All Brahman divisions did not, however, have a corresponding Vania division. For example, there were Khedawal Brahmans

ORDER OF CASTE DIVISIONS IN GUJARAT

About 300 divisions, a few of which are:

	RAJPUT	KOLI	ANAVIL	KANBI	BRAHMAN	VANIA
FIRST ORDER	*No subdivisions.* Hierarchy merging into Koli, Bhil, etc.		Hierarchy with weak *bandhos*			
SECOND ORDER		"Local" "Immigrant"		Leva Hierarchy with weak *gols* Kadva etc.	*About 80 divisions:* Khedawal, Hierarchy with weak *ekdas* Nagar, Modh, Shrimali, Khadayata, etc.	*About 30 divisions:* Nagar, Modh, Shrimali, Khadayata, etc.
THIRD ORDER					Almost every division further divided into *ekdas*	Almost every division further divided into *ekdas*
FOURTH ORDER					At least some *ekdas* further divided	At least some *ekdas* further divided

Edka, gol, bandho = small endogamous unit.

but not Khedawal Vanias, and Lad Vanias but no Lad Brahmans. And even when a Brahman name corresponded with a Vania name, the former did not necessarily work as priests of the latter.

The total number of second-divisions in a first-order division differed from one first-order division to another. One important first-order division, namely, Rajput, does not seem to have had any second-order division at all. The Kolis seem to have had only two divisions in every part of Gujarat: for example, Talapada (indigenous) and Pardeshi (foreign) in central Gujarat and Palia and Baria in eastern Gujarat (significantly, one considered indigenous and the other outsider). Usually, a single Koli division had different local names in different parts of Gujarat, but more about this later. The Kanbis (now called Patidars) had five divisions: Leva, Kadya, Anjana, Bhakta, and Matia. The Brahmans and Vanias seem to have had the largest number of divisions as mentioned earlier, about eighty in the former and about forty in the latter.

Many second-order divisions were further divided into two or three status categories. For example, among almost every Vania division there was a dual division into Visa and Dasa: Visa Nagar and Dasa Nagar, Visa Lad and Dasa Lad, Visa Modh and Dasa Modh, Visa Khadayata and Dasa Khadayata, and so on. These prefixes, Visa and Dasa, were generally understood to be derived from the words for the numbers 20 (vis)and 10 (das), which suggested a descending order of status, but there is no definite evidence of such hierarchy in action. No one knows when and how they came into existence and what they meant socially. There was also a third category called Pancha, derived from the word *panch* (meaning 5)and denoting extremely low Vania. Similarly, the Khedawal Brahmans were divided into Baj and Bhitra, the Nagar Brahmans into Grihastha and Bhikshuk, the Anavils into Desai and Bhathela, and the Kanbis into Kanbi and Patidar. Since these were all status categories rather than clear-cut divisions, I have not considered them as constituting third-order divisions.

Most of the second-order divisions were further divided into third-order divisions. For example, all Vania divisions were divided into a number of *ekdas* or *gols*. The Khadayatas were divided into about 30 *ekdas*. Literally, *ekda* meant 'unit', and *gol* 'circle', and both signified an endogamous unit. Each *ekda* or *gol* was composed of a definite number of families living in certain villages and/or towns.

The existence of *ekdas* or *gols*, however, does not mean that the divisiveness of caste ended there or that the *ekdas* and *gols* were always the definitive units of endogamy. Frequently,The *ekdas* or *gols* were each divided into groups called *tads* (split). The number of *tads* in an *ekda* or *gol* might be two or more, and each of them might be an endogamous units. The *tad* thus represented the fourth and and last order of caste divisions.

It has already been mentioned that every first-order division was not divided into second-order divisions, and that every second-order division was not divided into third-order divisions, and so on. Thus, at one end, there were first-order divisions, each of which was sub-divided up to the fourth-order, and at the other end there were first-order divisions which were not further divided at all. How many sub-divisions existed in the various divisions of the various orders is a matter of empirical investigation. I am dealing here only with certain typical situations.

If the *varna* divisions are taken into account, then this would add one more order to the four orders of caste divisions considered above. These divisions have, however, been kept out of the present analysis for reasons which have become well known to students of Hindu society since the 1950s. Briefly, while the *varna* model was significant in the total dynamics of the caste system to fit the numerous first-order divisions into the four-fold *varna* model in any part of India is impossible, and, therefore, to consider *varnas* as caste divisions as such is meaningless.

A recent tendency in sociological literature is to consider *jatis* as castes.[7] This does not, however, help describe caste divisions adequately. When divisions are found within a *jati*, the word sub-*jati* or sub-caste is used. This does not solve the problem if there are four orders of divisions of the kind found in Gujarat. If the first-order divisions are called *jatis* and castes, the second-order divisions would be called sub-*jatis* or sub-castes. For describing the divisions of the remaining two orders, it would be necessary to go on adding the prefix 'sub' but this would make the description extremely clumsy, if not meaningless. The same problems would arise in the reverse direction if, as many scholars have done, the term 'caste cluster', 'caste complex' or 'caste category' is used for divisions of a higher order and the term 'caste' or '*jati*'is used for divisions of a lower order.

To have a meaningful understanding of the system of caste divisions, there is no alternative but to understand the significance of each order of division and particularly the nature of their boundaries and maintenance mechanisms. The boundaries of caste division were fairly clear in the village community. Here, usually, what mattered was the first-order division, as for example, Brahman, Vania, Rajput, Kanbi, carpenter, barber, leather-worker, and so on. In the village strict prohibition of inter-division marriage as well as the rules of purity and pollution and other mechanisms, of which the students of Indian village communities are well aware since the 1950s, maintained the boundaries of these divisions.

In many villages in Gujarat, particularly in larger villages, one or two first-order divisions would be represented by more than one second-order division. For example, a good number of villages in central Gujarat used to have both Talapada and Pardeshi Kolis and Brahmans belonging to two or three of their many second-order divisions. Co-residence of people, belonging to two or more divisions of a lower order within a higher order was, however, a prominent feature of towns and cities rather than of villages. We shall return later to a consideration of this problem.

To whichever of the four orders a caste division belonged, its horizontal spread rarely, if ever, coincided with that of another. Also, the horizontal spread of a caste rarely coincided with the territorial boundaries of a political authority. This was because political authorities were hierarchized from little kingdom to empire and the boundaries of political authorities kept changing. In any case, the population of any large caste was found in many kingdoms. Moreover, the king himself belonged to some caste (not just to the Kshatriya *varna*) and frequently a number of kings belonged to the same caste (e.g.,Rajput). The members of a king's caste were thus found not only in his own kingdom but in other kingdoms as well. A great deal of discussion of the role of the king in the caste system,based mainly on Indological literature, does not take these facts into account and therefore tends to be unrealistic.

Inclusion of a lower-order division in a higher-order one and distinction between various divisions in a certain order was not as unambiguous. For example, there was considerable ambiguity about the status of Anavils. Many of them claimed that they were Brahmans but this claim was not accepted by most established Brahmans. The main reason was that Anavils did not practise priesthood as a traditional occupation, nor were they involved in traditional Sanskrit learning. They were involved in agriculture in one way or another. Their origin myth enshrined in their caste *purana* also showed them to be originally non-Brahman. Moreover, some leading Anavils did not wish to be bothered about Brahman status, saying that they were just Anavil. I have, therefore, considered them a first-order division and not a second-order one among Brahmans (for a fuller discussion of the status of Anavils, see Joshi, 1966;Van der Veen 1972; Shah, 1979). There was another kind of ambiguity about the

Brahman status of two other divisions—Kayatia and Tapodhan. Both were recognized as Brahman but as degraded ones. The Kayatias' main occupation was to perform a ritual on the eleventh day after death, during which they took away offerings made to ghosts: this was the main cause of their extremely low status among Brahmans. Tapodhans were priests in Shiva temples. They took away offerings made to Shiva, which was considered extremely degrading. Kayatias and Tapodhans were considered such low Brahmans that even some non-Brahman castes did not accept food and water from them. They were thus not of the same status as most other second-order divisions among Brahmans. There were similar problems about the status of a number of other divisions. We shall return to this issue later.

III

That Rajputs were one of the divisions, if not the only division of the first-order, not having further divisions, has already been mentioned. It was also an extreme example of a division having a highly differentiated internal hierarchy and practising hypergamy as an accepted norm. Since Rajput as a caste occurred all over northern, central and western India (literally, it means ruler's son, ruling son), the discussion of Rajputs in Gujarat will inevitably draw us into their relationship with Rajputs in other regions. I do not, however, have sufficient knowledge of the latter and shall, therefore, confine myself mainly to Rajputs in Gujarat.

According to the Rajputs I know in central Gujarat, the highest stratum among them consisted of the royal families of large and powerful kingdoms in Gujarat and neighbouring Rajasthan, such as those of Bhavnagar, Jamnagar, Kachchh, Porbandar, Bikaner, Idar, Jaipur, Jaisalmer, Jodhpur, Udaipur, and so on. Apparently this upper boundary of the division was sharp and clear, especially when we remember that many of these royal families practised polygyny and female infanticide until middle of the 19th century (see Plunkett 1973; Viswa Nath 1969, 1976). However, it is well known that there were subtle arguments regarding the status of certain royal families being Rajput. The marital alliances of the royal families forming part of the Maratha confederacy, and of the royal families of Mysore in south India and of Kashmir and Nepal in the north with the royal families of Gujarat and Rajasthan show, among other things, how there was room for flexibility and how the rule of caste endogamy could be violated in an acceptable manner at the highest level.

The Rajput hierarchy had many levels below the level of the royal families of the large and powerful kingdoms: lineages of owners of large and small "fiefs" variously called *jagir, giras, thakarat,thikana, taluka,* and *wanta*[9]; lineages of substantial landowners under various land tenures having special rights and privileges; and lineages of small landowners. In 1931, the Rajputs of all strata in Gujarat had together a population of about 35,000 forming nearly 5 per cent of the total population of Gujarat. Most of them were, true to their name, rulers at various levels of the political hierarchy from the kingly level to the level of dominant caste in many villages. But there were also others who did not wield any power. Hence as we go down the hierarchy we encounter more and more debates regarding the claims of particular lineages to being Rajput so much so that we lose sight of any boundary and the Rajput division merges imperceptibly into some other division. In most parts of Gujarat it merged into the various second-order divisions of the Koli division and possible also into the widespread tribe of Bhils.

Let me illustrate briefly. The Rajputs in Radhvanaj, the village I have studied in central Gujarat, had no great difficulty in establishing their claim to being Rajputs: they owned substantial amounts of land under a traditional Rajput tenure, dominated village politics and possessed certain other traditional Rajput symbols. They married their daughters into higher Rajput lineages in the local area who in turn married their daughters into still higher nearly royal rajput lineages in Saurashtra and Kachchh. Radhvanaj Rajputs were clearly distinguished from, and ranked much above local Kolis. But many Rajput men of Radhvanaj got wives from people in distant villages who were recognized there as Kolis—those Kolis who had more land and power than the generality of Kolis had tried to acquire some of the traditional Rajput symbols in dress manners and customs and had been claiming to be Rajputs.

We shall return to the Rajput-Koli relationship when we consider the Kolis in detail. In the meanwhile, it is important to note that there does not seem to have been any attempt to form small endogamous units (*ekdas, gols*) at any level among the Rajputs unlike attempts made as we shall see, among some other hypergamous castes in Gujarat.

IV

Kolis were the largest first-order division in Gujarat. In 1931, their total population was more than 1,700,000, nearly one-fourth of the total population of Gujarat. In some parts of Gujarat they formed 30 to 35 per cent of the population. They were found in almost every village in plains Gujarat and in many villages in Saurashtra and Kachchh. They co-existed in the highlands with tribes such as the Bhils, so much so that today frequently many high caste Gujaratis confuse them with Bhils, as did the earlier ethnographers. Unfortunately, although the Kolis are an important element in Gujarat's population, their earlier ethnography is confusing, and there is hardly any modern, systematic, anthropological, sociological or historical study, so that the confusion continues to persist.[10]

To obtain a clear understanding of the second-order divisions with the Koli division, it is necessary first of all to find a way through the maze of their divisional names. In central Gujarat, for example, one and the same division, freely arranging marriages within it, was known by several names such as Baraiya, Dharala, Khant, Kotwal, Pagi, Patelia, Talapada, Thakarada, and Thakor. The name, Talapada, meaning "indigenous", commonly used in the 19th century, is most clear, since it is clearly distinguished from the other division called Pardeshi, meaning "foreign", who during the last one or two centuries immigrated here from the area around Patan in north Gujarat and were, therefore, also called Patanwadias. Similarly, in Saurashtra, the Talapadas were distinguished from the Chumvalias, immigrants from the Chumval tract in north Gujarat. The Chumvalias and Patanwadias migrated possibly from the same tract and continued to belong to the same horizontal unit after migration. The indigenous Kolis in the highland area of Pal in eastern Gujarat were called Palia, but there was another smaller population of Kolis, who were locally called Baria but were actually Talapada immigrants from central Gujarat (see Shah, 1955).

The migration of the Kolis of north Gujarat into central Gujarat and those of the latter into eastern Gujarat was a process of slow drift from one village to another over a period of time. In other words, it did not involve a big jump from one place to another distant place. Thus, the result was the spread of the population of a caste division towards its fringes. For example, the Patanwadia population was spread continuously from the Patan area to central Gujarat, and the Talapada population from central Gujarat to Pal.

Today, there are two kinds of Koli areas. In an area of the first kind there are no immigrant Kolis from elsewhere, and therefore, there is no question of their having second-order divisions. The Kolis in such an area may not even be concerned about a second-order divisional name and may be known simply as Kolis. In the second kind of area, indigenous Kolis live side-by-side with immigrant Kolis from an adjoining area. I have not yet come across an area where Kolis from three or more different areas live together, excepting modern, large towns and cities.

From the 15th century onwards we find historical references to political activities of Koli chieftains. They are described by the ruling elite as robbers, dacoits, marauders, predators and the like. By the beginning of British rule in the early 19th century, a considerable number of these chieftains had succeeded in establishing petty chiefdoms, each composed of one, and occasionally more than one, village, in all parts of Gujarat. They adopted Rajput customs and traditions, claimed Rajput status, and gave daughters in marriage to Rajputs in the lower rungs of Rajput hierarchy. They also continued to have marital relations with their own folk. Thus, finding any boundary between Rajputs and Kolis in the horizontal context was impossible, although there were sharp boundaries between the two in the narrow local context.

The Rajputs' relationship with the Kolis penetrated every second-order division among them, i.e., Talapada, Pardeshi, Chumvalia, Palia, and so on. Thus, while each second-order Koli division maintained its boundaries vis-a-vis other such divisions, each was linked with the Rajputs. The Rajput links entailed the spread of Rajput culture in each Koli division and provided a certain cultural homogeneity to all the divisions.

The chiefly families constituted a tiny proportion of the total population of any second-order division among the Kolis. The bulk of the population was spread all over the villages as small landholders, tenants and labourers. This bulk also was characterized by hierarchy, with the relatively advanced population living in the plains at one end and the backward population living along with the tribal population in the highlands at the other end. Hypergamy tended to be associated with this hierarchy. The hierarchy, however, was very gradual and lacked sharpness. Marriages were usually confined to neighbouring villages, so that marriage links were spread in a continuous manner from one end of the region to another.[11] These marriage links do not seem to have allowed, among the Kolis, formation of well organized, small, endogamous units (*ekadas, gols*) as were found among some other castes. Usually, the affairs of the caste were discussed in large congregations of some fifty to hundred or even more villages from time to time.

Although I have not, during my limited field work, come across hypergamous marriages between Rajputs and Bhils, ethnographic reports and other literature frequently refer to such marriages (see, for example, Naik 1956: 18f; Nath 1960: 11-15, 57-75). It seems the highland Bhils (and possibly also other tribes) provided brides to lower Rajputs in Gujarat. The point is that the Rajput hierarchy, with the princely families at the top, merged at the lower level imperceptibly into the vast sea of tribal and semi-tribal people like Bhils and Kolis.[12]

The highland Bhils seem to have provided brides to lower Rajputs on the other side of the highlands also, i.e., to those in Rajasthan and Madhya Pradesh (see, for example, Doshi, 1971: 7f., 13-15; Aurora 1972: 16, 32f.). Rajput hypergamy seems to have provided an important mechanism for integration of the lower caste and tribal population into the Hindu society over the entire length and breadth of northern, western, central and even eastern India. Hypergamy was accompanied by sanskritization of at least a section of the tribal population, their claim to the Kshatriya *varna*, and their economic and political symbiosis with the caste population.[13] The two together formed a single complex of continental dimension.[14] The complex was provided a certain coherence and integrity—in the pre-industrial time of slow communication—by a number of oral and literate traditions cultivated by cultural specialists such as priests, bards, genealogists and mythographers (see in this connection Shah and Shroff 1958).

That there was room for flexibility and that the rule of caste endogamy could be violated at the highest level among the Rajputs was pointed out earlier. And how flexibility was normal at the lowest level has just been shown. The existence of flexibility at both the levels was made possible by the flexibility of the category "Rajput". The essential idea in the category was power, and anybody who wielded power—either as king or as dominant group in a rural (even tribal) area—could *claim* to be Rajput.[15] Once the claim was accepted at either level, hypergamous marriage was possible.[16]

V

The Rajputs, in association with the Kolis, were probably the only horizontal unit which had continuous internal hierarchy, i.e., hypergamy unbroken by any endogamous subdivisions, and which did not have discernible boundaries at the lowest level. In contrast, there were horizontal units, the internal hierarchy and hypergamy of which were restricted to some extent by the formation of small endogamous units and which had discernible boundaries at the lowest level. I describe here three prominent units of the latter type, namely, Anavil, Leva Kanbi, and Khedawal Brahman.[17]

Leva Kanbis, numbering 400,000 to 500,000 in 1931, were the traditional agricultural caste of central Gujarat. Almost every village in this area included at least some Leva population, and in many villages they formed a large, if not the largest, proportion of the population. The division had an elaborate internal hierarchy, with wealthy and powerful landlords and tax-farmers at the top and small landholders, tenants and labourers at the bottom. The Anavil, numbering 30,000 to 40,000 in 1931, were found mainly in south Gujarat. As mentioned earlier, although they claimed to be Brahman they were closely associated with agriculture. They had an internal hierarchy similar to that of the Leva Kanbis, with tax-farmers and big landlords at the top and small landowners at the bottom. The Khedawals, numbering 15,000 to 20,000 in 1931 were basically priests but many of them were also landowners, government officials, and traders.

In each of these three divisions the top stratum was clear. Usually it consisted of wealthy and powerful lineages, distinguishing themselves by some appellation, such as Patidar among the Leva Kanbi, Desai among the Anavil, and Baj among the Khedawal. The highest stratum among the Leva Kanbi tried to maintain its position by practising polygyny and female infanticide, among other customs and institutions, as did the highest stratum among the Rajput.

Within each of these divisions, small endogamous units (*ekdas, gols, bandhos*) were organized from time to time to get relief from the difficulties inherent in hypergamy. But the hypergamous tendency was so powerful that each such endogamous unit could not be perfectly endogamous even at the height of its integration. Each unit was ranked in relation to others, and many members of the lower units married their daughters into the higher units, so that almost every unit became loose in the course of time. There was a continuous process of formation and disintegration of such units. This was unlike the situation among the Rajputs who did not make any attempt to form small endogamous units.

The lowest stratum in all the three divisions had to face the problem of scarcity of brides. This stratum among the Kanbis coped with the problem mainly by practising remarriage of widows and divorced women. There was also a tendency among bachelors past marriageable age to establish liaisons with lower-caste women, which usually led the couple to flee and settle down in a distant village. The lowest stratum among the Khedawals tried to cope with the problem of scarcity of brides mainly by practising ignominious 'exchange marriage' and by restricting marriage of sons in a family to the younger sons, if not to only the youngest. The incidence of exchange marriages and of bachelors in the lowest stratum among the Anavils also was high.[18] The main point is that we do not completely lose sight of the lowest boundary among these three hypergamous divisions as we do among the Rajputs.

VI

We have analyzed the internal structure of two first-order divisions, Rajput and Anavil, which did not have any second-order divisions, and of several second-order divisions—Talapada and Pardeshi Koli, Khedawal Brahman, and Leva Kanbi—which did not have any third-order divisions. We will now analyze the internal structure of a few first-order divisions, each of which was split into divisions going down to the fourth order. A large proportion, if not the whole, of the population of many of such divisions lived in towns. And, as mentioned earlier, the co-residence of people belonging to two or more divisions of the lower orders within a division of a higher order has been a prominent feature of caste in towns and cities. A comment on the sociology of urban India would, therefore, be in order before we go ahead with the discussion of caste divisions.

It will readily be agreed that the sociological study of Indian towns and cities has not made as much progress as has the study of Indian villages. Until recently, sociologists and anthropologists described Indian society as though it had no urban component in the past. They wrote about the traditional Indian village, but not about the traditional Indian town. Fortunately, they have now started writing about it (see Rao 1974). But this is not enough. We need to formulate some idea of the nature of the Indian urban society and its relation with the rural society in the past, at least at the beginning of the 19th century. While almost all the social structures and institutions which existed in villages—religion, caste, family, and so on—also existed in towns, we should not assume that their character was the same. Even if we assume, for a moment, that the basic nature of a structure or institution was the same, we need to know its urban form or variant.

After the commercial revolution of the 16th and 17th centuries, Gujarat had a large number of traditing towns on its long sea-coast.[19] Broach, Cambay and Surat were the largest, but there were also a number of smaller ones. These coastal towns were involved in trade among themselves, with other towns on the rest of the Indian sea coast, and with many foreign lands. In addition, they carried on overland trade with many towns in central and north India. All this trade encouraged development of trading and commercial towns in the rest of Gujarat, even in the highland area.

Another major factor in the growth of urban centres in Gujarat was political. The Hindu and Muslim kingdoms in Gujarat during the medieval period had, of course, their capital towns, at first Patan and then Ahmedabad. The latter continued to be the provincial capital during Mughal rule. But during the 18th century, when the Mughal empire was disintegrating, a large number of small kingdoms came into existence, and each had a small capital town of its own.

Because of these two major factors, one economic and the other political, Gujarat at the beginning of the 19th century had a large urban population, distributed over a large number of small towns. More of them were located in the plains, than in the bordering highlands. In the plains, therefore, every village had one or more towns in its vicinity.

Although caste was found in both village and town, did it possess any special characteristics in the latter? Caste divisions of the first-order can be classified broadly into three categories. Firstly, there were divisions whose population was found almost entirely in towns. The three trading castes of Vania, Lohana and Bhatia were mainly urban. Although some of them set up shops in villages they rarely became full-fledged members of the village community. The Kayasthas and Brahma-Kshatriyas, the so-called 'writer' castes, employed mainly in the bureaucracy, and the Vahivancha Barots, genealogists and mythographers, were almost exclusively urban castes. Then there were a number of urban divisions of specialized artisans, craftsmen and servants, as for example, Sonis (gold and silver smiths), Kansaras (copper and bronze smiths), Salvis (silk weavers), Bhavsars (weavers, dyers and printers), Malis (florists), Kharadis (skilled carpenters and wood carvers), Kachhias (vegetable sellers), Darjis (tailors), Dabgars (makers of drums, saddles and such other goods involving leather), Ghanchis (oil pressers), Golas (grain and spice pounders and domestic servants), Dhobis (washermen), Chudgars (banglemakers), and Tambolis (sellers of area nuts, betel leaves, etc.). These and many other artisans, craftsmen and servants reflected the special life-style of the town.

While certain first-order divisions were found mainly in towns, the population of certain other first-order divisions was dispersed in villages as well as in towns, the population of the rural and the urban sections differing from one division to another. For example, in a Rajput kingdom the families of the Rajput king and his nobles resided in the capital town, while the Rajput landlords and cultivators resided in villages. In central Gujarat, at least from about the middle of the 18th century, the population of the wealthy and powerful Patidar section of the Kanbis also lived in towns—an extremely interesting development of rich villages into towns, which I will not describe here. A large number of priestly, artisan and service castes also lived in both villages and towns: Brahmans, barbers, carpenters, blacksmiths, shoemakers, leather-workers, scavengers, water-carriers, palanquin-bearers, and so on. Frequently, the urban population of such a division performed more specialized functions than did the rural one. It is important to note that the more literate and learned Brahmans lived in towns, more particularly in capital and pilgrim towns, which were, indeed, the centres of higher Hindu culture and civilization. They worked not only as high priests but also as bureaucrats.

The population of certain first-order divisions lived mainly in villages. The most important of them was the Koli division, which was, as mentioned earlier, the largest division and mainly included small landholders, tenants and labourers. Some of the other such divisions were Kathi, Dubla, Rabari, Bharwad, Mer (see Trivedi 1961), Vaghri, Machhi, Senwa, Vanzara, and Kharwa. The tribal groups in the highland area, such as the Bhils and Naikdas, also did not have any urban component.

The castes of the three categories—primarily urban, primarily rural, and rural-cum-urban—formed an intricate network spread over the rural and urban communities in the region. The primarily urban castes linked one town with another; the primarily rural linked one village with another; and the rural-cum-urban linked towns with villages in addition to linking both among themselves. These linkages played an important role in the traditional social structure as well as in the processes of change in modern India. Of particular importance seems to be the fact that a section of the urban population was more or less isolated—some may say, alienated—from the rural masses from generation to generation.[20]

VII

Let us now return to a consideration of the first-order divisions with subdivisions going down to the third or the fourth order. As stated earlier, co-residence of people belonging to two or more divisions of a lower order within a division of a higher order has been a prominent feature of caste in towns and cities. For example, among Vanias in a large town like Ahmedabad many of the thirty or forty second-order divisions (such as Khadayata, Modh, Porwad, Shrimali, and so on) were represented. Not only that, there were also third-order divisions (i.e., *ekdas*) in one or more second-order divisions, and finally one or more fourth-order divisions (i.e., *tads*) in one or more third-order divisions. In effect, the Vania population in a large town like Ahmedabad could have a considerable number of small endogamous units of the third or the fourth order, each with its entire population living and marrying within the town itself. Usually, it was a small population. I know some *ekdas*, and *tads* composed of only 150 to 200 households. As could be expected, there were marriages between fairly close kin, resulting in many overlapping relationships, in such an endogamous unit. It used to have a *panch* (council of leaders) and sometimes also a headman (*patel*). It owned corporate property, usually in the form of *vadis* (large buildings used for holding feasts and festivals, accommodating wedding guests, and holding meetings), huge utensils for cooking feasts, and money received as fees and fines. Frequently, each such unit had a patron deity, housed in a large shrine, with elaborate arrangements for its ownership. The unit might possess some other corporate characteristics also.

The small *ekda* or *tad* with its entire population residing in a single town was, of course, not a widespread phenomenon. Nor were *ekdas* and *tads* entirely an urban phenomenon. More common was an *ekda* or *tad* having its population residing either in a few neighbouring villages, or in a few neighbouring towns, or in both. In the past the dispersal over a wide area of population of an *ekda* or *tad* was uncommon; only modern communications have made residential dispersal as well as functional integration possible.

Although the *ekda* or *tad* was the most effective unit for endogamy, each unit of the higher order was also significant for endogamy. For example, among the Vanias the most general rule was that a marriage of a boy could be arranged with any girl who was *bhane khapati*, i.e., with whom he was permitted to have commensal relations (*roti vyavahar*). This meant that he could marry a girl of any subdivision within the Vania division. If this rule was violated, i.e., if he married a girl with whom the Vanias did not have commensal relations, the maximum punishment, namely, excommunication, was imposed. If the marriage took place within the Vania fold but outside the *tad* or *ekda*, as the case may be, the punishment varied according to the social distance between the *tads* or *ekdas* of the bride and the groom. For example, if they belonged to two different second-order divisions, such as Shrimali and Modh, the punishment would be greater than if they belonged to two different *ekdas* within the Shrimali or the Modh division. Frequently, marriages were arranged in contravention of a particular rule after obtaining the permission of the council of leaders and paying a penalty in advance. The point is that there was nothing like the endogamous unit but there were only several units of various orders with defined roles in endogamy.

Since the beginning of the modern 'reform' movement to encourage 'inter-caste' marriages—most of which are in fact inter-*tad* or inter-*ekda* marriages—the old process of fission into *ekdas* and *tads* has come to a halt, and it is, therefore, difficult to understand this process without making a systematic historical enquiry. However, on the basis of the meagre information I have, I am able to make a few points. First, since the *tads* were formed relatively recently, it is easier to get information about their formation than about the formation of *ekdas*. Second, there used to be intense intra-*ekda* politics, and *tads* were formed as a result of some continuing conflict among *ekda* leaders and over the trial of violation of *ekda* rules. Third, although two or more new endogamous units came into existence and marriage between them was forbidden thereafter, a number of pre-existing kinship and affinal relationships continued to be operative between them.

It is not easy to find out if the *tads* became *ekdas* in course of time and if the process of formation of *ekdas* was the same as that of the formation of *tads*. Some *ekdas* did come into existence in almost the same way as did the *tads*, that is to say, by a process of fission of one *ekda* into two or more *ekdas*. But there was also another process. For example, there were two *ekdas*, each with a large section resident in a large town and small sections resident in two or three neighbouring small towns. All the small towns sections in each of the *ekdas* resented that, while the large town section accepted brides from small towns, they did not reciprocate. The small town sections therefore separated themselves from the respective large town sections and formed a new *ekda*. The two former *ekdas* continued to exist with diminished strength.

While we can find historical information about the formation of *ekdas* and *tads* there are only myths about the formation of the numerous second-order divisions. Almost all the myths about the latter are enshrined in the *puranas* (for an analysis of a few of them, see Das 1968 and 1977). If, as mentioned earlier, there were Brahman and Vania divisions of the same name, the myths about both of them were covered by a single text. Besides the myths, the members of a second-order division, belonging to all *ekdas*, shared certain customs and institutions, including worship of a tutelary deity.

While we do get evidence of fission of caste divisions of a higher order into two or more divisions of a lower order, the mere existence of divisions of a lower order should not be taken as evidence of fission in a division of a higher order. While fission did occur, fusion could also occur. While some of the divisions of a lower order might be the result of fission, some others might be a result of fusion.

We had seen earlier that in the first-order division, such as that of the Rajputs, there were no second-order divisions, and no attempt was made to form small endogamous units: hypergamy had free play, as it were. In the second-order divisions of the Leva Kanbis, the Anavils and the Khedawals, while the hypergamous tendency was strong, attempts were continually made to form small endogamous units: although the strength of the hypergamous tendency did not allow these units to function effectively, they nevertheless checked its free play to some extent. In the second-order divisions of the Vanias the small endogamous units functioned more effectively and lasted longer: although the hypergamous tendency did exist particularly between the rural and the urban sections in a unit, it had restricted play.

The hypergamous tendency was never as sharp, pervasive and regular among the Vania divisions as among the Rajputs, Leva Kanbis, Anavils and Khedawals. Although the people of one *tad* would talk about their superiority over those of another *tad* in an *ekda*, and the people of one *ekda* over those of another in a higher-order division, particularly in large towns where two or more *tads* and *ekdas* would be found living together, there was no articulate ranking and hypergamy among them. There was not only no pyramid type of arrangement among the many *ekdas* in a second-order Vania division—the type of arrangement found in the Rajput, Leva Kanbi, Anavil and Khedawal divisions—but frequently there was no significant sign of hierarchical relation, except boastful talk, between two neighbouring *ekdas*. There was an emphasis on being different and separate rather than on being higher and lower.

While some hypergamous and hierarchical tendency, however weak, did exist between *tads* within an *ekda* and between *ekdas* within a second-order division, it was practically non-existent among the forty or so second-order divisions, such as Modh, Porwad, Shrimali, Khadayata and so on, among the Vanias. The prohibition of inter-division marriage was much more important than the rules of purity and pollution in the maintenance of boundaries between the lower-order divisions. The emphasis on being different and separate rather than on being higher and lower was even more marked in the relationship among the forty or so second-order divisions. This was dramatized in many towns at the *mahajan* (guild) feasts when all the members of the guild of traders would eat together.

We have seen how one second-order division among Brahmans, namely, Khedawal, was marked by continuous internal hierarchy and strong emphasis on hypergamy on the one hand and by absence of effective small endogamous units on the other. Most of the other eighty or so second-order divisions among Brahmans, however, seem to be subdivided the way the Vania second-order divisions were subdivided into third-order and fourth-order divisions. Whatever the internal organization of a second-order division, the relationship between most of the Brahman second-order divisions was marked by great emphasis on being different and separate than on being higher and lower. This was dramatized at huge feasts called *chorasi* (literally, eighty-four) when Brahmans belonging to all the traditional 84 second-order divisions sat together to eat food cooked at the same kitchen. There was also another kind of feast, called *bhandaro*, where Brahmans belonging to a lesser number of divisions (say, all the few in a small town) were invited. The very low Brahmans such as Kayatias and Tapodhans were invited but made to eat separately from the rest of the Brahmans.

Among the Kanbis, while there was hypergamy within the Leva division and possibly, similar hypergamy within the Kadva division,[21] there was no hierarchy or hypergamy between the two second-order divisions. The two considered themselves different and separate—of course, within the Kanbi fold—where they happened to live together in the villages in the merger zone between north and central Gujarat and in towns.

I have bits and pieces of information about relations between a considerable number of other lower-order divisions in their respective higher-order divisions. All of this information supports the point emerging from the above analysis, that frequently there was relatively little concern for ritual status between the second-order divisions within a first-order division than there was between the first-order divisions.

So far we have considered first-order divisions with large and widely spread populations. There were also a number of first-order divisions, mainly of artisans, craftsmen and specialized servants, with small populations. In the case of some of them the small population was so dispersed that a division such as that of barbers, blacksmiths, or carpenters, would be represented by only one or two households in each village and by a significant number of households in towns. In some other cases, mainly of urban artisans, craftsmen and specialized servants, such as Kansaras (copper and bronze smiths), Salvis (silk weavers), Kharadis (skilled carpenters and wood carvers), Chudgars (bangle-makers) and Vahivanchas (genealogists and mythographers), the small populations were so small and confined to so few towns that they had few subdivisions and the boundaries of their horizontal units were fairly easy to define. It is possible that there were a few divisions each confined to just one large city and, therefore, not having the horizontal dimension at all. James Campbell (1901: xii), the compiler of gazetteers for the former Bombay presidency comprising several linguistic regions, wrote about Gujarat: "In no part of India are the subdivisions so minute, one of them, the Rayakval Vanias, numbering only 47 persons in 1891. When Mr. H. Borradaile in A.D. 1827 collected information regarding the customs of Hindus, no less than 207 castes which did not intermarry, were found in the city of Surat alone".

Both Borradaile and Campbell were probably mixing up small endogamous units of various kinds. The significant point, however, is that there were small endogamous units which were not, like *ekdas* and *tads*, part of any higher-order division.

Systematic study of small caste divisions in villages as well as in towns still awaits the attention of sociologists and anthropologists.[22] Any one small caste may look insignificant in itself but all small castes put together become a large social block and a significant social phenomenon.

VIII

Our analysis of the internal organization of caste divisions has shown considerable variation in the relative role of the principles of division and hierarchy. At one end there were castes in which the principle of hierarchy had free play and the role of the principle of division was limited. The Rajputs, in association with Kolis, Bhils, and such other castes and tribes, provide an extreme example of such castes. At the other end were castes in which the principle of division had free play and the role of the principle of hierarchy was limited. The Vanias provide an example of such castes. The Levas, Anavils and Khedawals provide examples of castes whose internal organization had a strong emphasis on the principle of hierarchy and a weak emphasis on that of division. That the role of the two principles could vary at different levels within a first-order division has also been seen.

There was apparently a close relation between a caste's internal organization and the size and spatial distribution of its population. The castes pervaded by hierarchy and hypergamy had large populations spread evenly from village to village and frequently also from village to town over a large area. Castes pervaded by divisive tendencies had small populations confined to small areas separated from each other by considerable gaps.

There was also another important correlation. The institutions of both bride and bridegroom price (the latter also called dowry) were rampant in castes with continuous internal hierarchy—dowry mainly at the upper levels, bride price mainly at the lower levels, and both dowry and bride price among status-seeking middle level families. The small endogamous units, on the other hand, did not practise either. While the Rajputs, Leva Patidars, Anavils and Khedawals have been notorious for high dowries, and the Kolis have been looked down upon for their practice of bride price, the Vanias have been paying neither. The two categories of castes have been deeply conscious of these differences between them and have been talking freely about them.

Our analysis of caste in towns has shown how it differed significantly from that in villages. The village was a small community divided into a relatively small number of castes; the population of each caste was also small, sometimes only one or two households, with little possibility of existence of subdivisions; and there were intensive relationships of various kinds between the castes. In the city, on the other hand, the population was divided into a large number of castes and each of most of them had a large population, frequently subdivided up to the third or the fourth order. Sometimes a division could even be a self-contained endogamous unit. The larger castes and even larger subdivisions among them used to have their houses segregated on their own streets (called *pol, sheri, khadki, vad, khancho*). Frequently, social divisions were neatly expressed in street names. To give just one example, one large street in Baroda, of immigrant Kanbis from the Ahmedabad area, named Ahmedabadi Pol, was divided into two small parallel streets, Leva Sheri and Kadva Sheri, named after the two major second-order divisions among the Kanbis.[23]

The social relations between and within a large number of such segregated castes should be seen in the context of the overall urban environment, characterized as it was by co-existence of local Hindu castes with immigrant Hindu castes and with the non-Hindu groups such as Jains, Muslims, Parsis and Christians, a higher degree of monetization, a higher degree of contractual and market relations (conversely, a lesser degree of *jajmani*-type relations), existence of trade guilds, and so on. The urban community included a large number of caste groups as well as social groups of other kinds which tended to be like communities with a great deal of internal cohesion. There was considerable elaboration in urban areas of what Ghurye long ago called the community aspect of caste (1932: 179) and frequently, this led to juxtaposition rather than hierarchy between caste divisions of the same order.[24]

I am not suggesting that the principle of hierarchy was insignificant in the inter- or intra-caste relations in urban centres. Far from it,[25] I am only suggesting that its role had certain limitations and that the principle of division was also an important and competing principle. Secondly, it is necessary to study intensively the pattern of inter-caste relations in urban centres as something different—at least hypothetically—from the pattern in villages. Asking different questions and using different methods are necessary. Limitations of the holistic view of caste, based as it is mainly on the study of the village, should be realized in the light of urban experience. A new view of the whole, comprising the rural and the urban and the various orders of caste divisions, should be evolved. In particular, the implications of the co-existence of lower-order divisions within a higher-order division in the same town or city should be worked out.

In a paper on Caste among Gujaratis in East Africa, Pocock (1957b) raised pointedly the issue of the relative importance of the principles of division (he called it 'difference') and hierarchy. He stated: "...hereditary specialization together with hierarchical organization sinks into the background in East Africa" (293). Further, "...the castes there are unable to take cognizance of each other in terms of hierarchy or of occupation, and it is in this situation that they can be said to exist by virtue of their differences (296) ...it is the systematic recognition of difference which is most apparent. Systematic because castes exist and are like each other in being different" (298). Pocock goes on to observe that diminution of emphasis upon hierarchy and increasing emphasis upon difference are features of caste in modern, particularly urban, India: "...there is a shift from the caste system to individual castes and this reflects the change that is taking place in India today" (290).

The main thrust of Pocock's paper is that greater emphasis on difference rather than on hierarchy is a feature of caste among overseas Indians and in modern urban India. There would be a wide measure of agreement with him on both these counts. What I am trying to point out, however, is that greater emphasis on division (Pocock's 'difference', Dumont's 'separation', Bougle's 'repulsion') rather than on hierarchy was a feature of caste in certain contexts and situations in traditional India, and increasing emphasis on division in urban Indian in modern times is an accentuation of what existed in the past.

IX

I have discussed above caste divisions in Gujarat mainly in the past, roughly in the middle of the 19th century. I will not discuss the present situation in detail but indicate briefly how the above discussion could be useful for understanding a few important changes in modern times.

The primarily urban castes and the urban sections of the rural-cum-urban castes were the first to take advantage of the new opportunities that developed in industry, commerce, administration, the professions and education in urban centres. Early industrial labour was also drawn mainly from the urban artisan and servant castes. When the rural population began to be drawn towards the new opportunities, the first to take advantage of them were the rural sections of the rural-cum-urban castes. Many primarily rural castes, such as Kolis—the largest caste—have remained predominantly rural even today. Gujarati migrations to the nearby metropolis of Bombay the first new centre of administration, industry, commerce, education, and western culture, followed the same links. The migrants, many of whom came from heterogeneous urban centres of Gujarat, became part of an even more heterogeneous environment in Bombay. Many of them became the norm-setting elite for Gujaratis in the homeland.

One of the clearly visible changes in caste in Gujarat is the increasing number of inter-divisional or so-called inter-caste marriages, particularly in urban areas, in contravention of the rule of caste endogamy. The degree of contravention involved in an inter-divisional marriage, however, depends upon the order (i.e., first-order, second-order, etc.) to which the divisions of the marrying couple belong. The degree of contravention is less if the couple belong, let us say, to two different fourth-order divisions within a third-order division than if they belong to two different third-order divisions within a second-order division, and so on. The degree of contravention is highest if the couple belong to two different first-order divisions. Most inter-divisional marriages take place between boys and girls belonging to the lowest order in the structure of divisions.

To illustrate, among the Khadayata or Modh Vanias, an increasing number of marriages take place between two or more *tads* within an *ekda*. In fact, inter-*tad* marriages have increased so much that the *tads* have more or less lost their identity and such marriages are no longer considered as violating the rule of *tad* endogamy. The *ekdas* have not yet lost their identities. Although the number of inter-*ekda* marriages has been increasing, even now the majority of marriages take place within an *ekda*. Similarly, although the number of marriages between the second-order divisions in the Vania division, i.e., between Khadayata, Modh, Shrimali,

Lad, Vayada, etc., has been increasing, the majority of marriages take place within the respective second-order divisions. Finally, while an increasing number of marriages are taking place even across the boundaries of first-order divisions, as for example, between Brahmans and Vanias, and between Vanias and Patidars, such marriages even now form an extremely small proportion of the total number of marriages.

It is easy to understand that the pattern of change would be different in those first-order divisions (such as Rajput) or second-order divisions (such as Leva Kanbi) which did not have within them subdivisions of lower orders and which practised hypergamy extensively. In these divisions an increasing number of marriages are taking place against the grain of traditional hierarchy, i.e., girls of traditionally higher strata marry boys of traditionally lower strata. One may say that there are now more hypogamous marriages, although another and perhaps a more realistic way of looking at the change would be that a new hierarchy is replacing the traditional one. Dowry not only continues to be a symbol of status in the new hierarchy but is gradually replacing bride price wherever it existed, and dowry amounts are now reaching astronomical heights. As regards the specific case of the Rajput-Koli relationship, my impression is that, after the suppression of female infanticide in the first half of the 19th century, the later prohibition of polygyny, and the recent removal of princely states and feudal land tenures among the Rajputs on the one hand, and the increasing sanskritization as well as Rajputization among the Kolis on the other, marriage ties between these divisions have become more extensive than before.

The pattern of inter-divisional marriages shows how the idea of free marriage, which guides most of the "inter-caste" marriages, is restricted, modified, and graded according to the traditional structure of caste divisions. There is a patterned widening of the connubial field along an area chalked out historically. The idea of inter-caste marriage is, moreover, linked with the ideal of creating such a society involves a compromise with, if not subtle negation of, the ideal. The method is to remove first the barriers of the divisions of the lowest order and then gradually those of one higher order after another. As Ghurye pointed out long ago, slow consolidation of the smaller castes into larger ones "would lead to three or four large groups being solidly organized for pushing the interests of each even at the cost of the others. ...Further, during this lengthy process of slow amalgamation those who will marry in defiance of the barriers of sub-caste, will still be imbued with caste mentality" (1932: 184). The subtle manner in which the ideas of free marriage and casteless society are used by both the old and the young in modern India and how a number of new customs and institutions have evolved to cope with these new ideas is a fascinating subject of study.

Another clearly visible change in caste in Gujarat is the emergence of caste associations. Gujarat (along with Bombay) has perhaps the largest number of caste associations and they are also more active and wealthy compared to those in other regions. This reflects the high degree of divisiveness in castes in Gujarat.

The earliest caste associations were formed in Bombay in the middle of the 19th century among migrants belonging to the primarily urban and upper castes from Gujarat, such as Vanias, Bhatias and Lohanas (see Dobbin 1972: 74-76, 121-30, 227f, 259-61). They then spread to towns in the homeland and among all castes. The primarily rural and lower castes were the last to form associations and that too mainly after independence (1947). All associations originated in large towns, are more active in towns than in villages, and are led by prominent members in towns.

Caste associations have been formed on the lines of caste divisions. Among the first-order divisions with subdivisions going down to the fourth order, there are associations for divisions of all the orders. For example, among the Khadayata Vanias there are all-Khadayata associations as well as associations for the various *ekdas* and sometimes even for their *tads* (see Shah, Ragini 1978). Moreover, a single division belonging to any one of the orders may have more than one association, and an association may be uni-purpose or multi-purpose. Castes having continuous internal hierarchy and lacking effective small endogamous units, such as Rajputs, Leva Kanbis, Anavils and Khedawals, do not have active associations for lower-order divisions.

Till the establishment of democratic polity in 1947, hardly any caste association in Gujarat had manifest political functions. Gujarat did not have anything like the non-Brahmin movement of South India and Maharashtra before 1947. Caste associations in Gujarat were formed mainly among upper castes to provide welfare (including recreation), to promote modern education, and to bring about reforms in caste customs. The guiding ideas were *samaj sudharo* (social reform) and *samaj seva* (social service). Most associations continue to retain their non-political character.

The most important example of primarily political caste association is the Gujarat Kshatriya Sabha. It reflects, on the one hand, the political aspirations of Kolis guided by the importance of their numerical strength in electoral politics and on the other hand, the Rajputs' attempt to regain power after the loss of their princely states and estates. It is a coalescence of Kolis and Rajputs on the modern political plane based on the foundation of the traditional social and cultural symbiosis under the rubric of Kshatriya. Although it has been experiencing stresses and strains and has had ups and downs on account of the enormous diversity between the royal and the tribal ends, it has shown remarkable solidarity in recent years.[26]

An important idea behind the activities of caste associations is: service to one's caste is service to the nation. It is argued that the various welfare programmes of each caste association, such as provision of medical facilities, scholarships and jobs for caste members contribute, in however small a way, to the solution of the nation's problems. The associations' activities in the field of marriage, such as reform to customs, rituals and ceremonies, and encouragement of inter-divisional marriages, are also seen by the members as a service to the nation—as the caste's method of creating a casteless modern society.

The patterns of change in marriage and in caste associations are two of the many indications of the growing significance of the principle of division (or separation or difference) in caste in urban areas in Gujarat. Simultaneously, there is gradual decline in the strength of the principle of hierarchy, particularly of ritual hierarchy expressed in purity and pollution. To take one sensitive area of purity/pollution behaviour, the concern for observance of rules of commensality has greatly declined not only in urban but also in rural areas. Castes which did not sit together at public feasts, let alone at meals in homes, only 15 or 20 years ago, now freely sit together even at meals in homes. Nowadays, in urban areas in particular, very few people think of making separate seating arrangements for members of different castes at wedding and such other feasts. The change from emphasis on hierarchy to emphasis on division is becoming increasingly significant in view of the growth of urban population both in absolute number and in relation to the total population.

It has been pointed out earlier that an emphasis on the principle of division existed in the caste system in urban centres in traditional India. I would suggest that this feature of urban caste, along with the well known general tendency of urban culture to encourage innovation, provided the ground—however diffuse that ground might have been—for a favourable response to the anti-hierarchical ideas coming from the West. Significantly, a large number of social thinkers and workers who propagated against the hierarchical features of caste came from urban centres. The fact that Mahatma Gandhi came from a small third-order division in the Modh Vania division in a town in Saurashtra does not seem to be an accident.

The above brief analysis of change in caste in modern Gujarat has, I hope, indicated that an overall view of changes in caste in modern India should include a careful study of changes in rural as well as in urban areas in relation to their past. Far too many studies of changes in caste in modern India start with a general model of caste in traditional India which is in fact a model of caste in traditional rural India. (Frequently, such models are constructed *a priori* rather than based on historical evidence, but that is another story). The error is further compounded when—although this is less common—the partial, rural model of traditional caste is compared with the present urban situation, and conclusions are drawn about overall change. What is really required for a comprehensive understanding is a comparison of traditional with modern caste in both rural and urban areas (including, to be sure, the rural-urban linkages).

Frequently, the shift from emphasis on co-operation and hierarchy in the caste system to emphasis on division (or difference or separation) is described as shift from whole to parts, from system to elements, from structure to substance. A fundamental difficulty with these paradigms of change, as indicated by the above analysis, is that they are based on a partial conception of the systematic or structural whole in the past partially because it does not cover the urban situation and the complexity of horizontal units. As a consequence, the continuities of social institutions and the potentiality of endogenous elements for bringing about change are overlooked (for a discussion of some other difficulties with these paradigms, see Lynch 1977).

Sometimes castes are described as becoming ethnic groups in modern India, particularly in urban India. Such a description not only overlooks the diversity and complexity of caste divisions and the rural-urban linkages in them but also leads to placing them in the same category as Muslims, Christians, Parsis, Jains, Buddhists, and so on. The understanding of changes in caste is not likely to be advanced by clubbing such diverse groups together under the rubric of ethnic group. In any case, castes are not likely to cease to be castes in the consciousness of people in the foreseeable future. No analytical gains are therefore likely to occur by calling them by any other name.

Notes

1. The first draft of this paper was written during my fellowship at the Institute of Development Studies, Sussex, and discussed at seminars at the School of Oriental and African Studies, London, and at the University of Cambridge in 1976-77. I am thankful to the participants in these seminars and to B.S. Baviskar, Owen Lynch, N.R. Sheth and M.N. Srinivas for their comments on the paper.
2. "Repulsion" was the third of the three basic principles of caste enunciated by Bougle (1927).
3. Social science research on Gujarat is unevenly distributed. Very little research has been done on north Gujarat, Saurashtra and Kachchh, compared to that on central, south and eastern Gujarat.
4. Today the politician rather than the social scientist is the expert in the arithmetic of caste. Since caste has remained a powerful force, there is no sound academic reason why the social scientist should not study the demography of caste. The instrument of the national census may now be denied to him, but surely he can use others.
5. Ghurye considered "segmental division of society" as the first of the six features of caste (1932: 2) and devoted a whole chapter in his book to a description of the nature of caste divisions. Later, Dumont (1957: 1; 1972: 79, 100-3) and Beteille (1964) considered caste groups as forming a segmentary system, resembling in some ways the segmentary lineage systems in Africa. I have preferred to use the less specialized term "division".
6. Divisions of the same names were also found among the Jain Vanias, as for example, Mewada, Nima, Porwad, and Shrimali. There was also a further complexity: a Vania division could have both Hindu and Jain members, without restriction on inter-marriage between them, so that frequently husband and wife had different religious affiliations.

7 While the word *jati* (rather its variant, *jat*) occurs in Gujarati and is used in the context of caste, *jnati* (or one of its variants, *nyati, nyat, nat*) is the most commonly used word in this context. It is used for caste divisions of all the orders described above, and context decides to which order to division the speaker refers. I do not know if there is any relation between the pattern of caste divisions in Gujarat on the one hand and common use of *jnati* rather than *jati* on the other. The words are etymologically different (see Apte's and Monnier-Williams's Sanskrit-English dictionaries). In Bengal, at the

other end of the sub-continent, the word *jnati* is used in the sense of "kinsmen" (see Inden and Nicholas 1977: 8-15).

8. Plunkett (1973) mentions that more than half of the royal marriages in Rajasthan during the British period were arranged with spouses (mainly brides) outside of Rajasthan. One should examine how many of these marriages were arranged with royal families the ordinary members of whose caste in the local society did not have a clearly acknowledged Rajput status. See also No. 14 and 15 below.
9. For accounts of *taluka* and *wanta* villages, see Steed (1955) and A.M. Shah (1964 a, b).
10. Silverberg's two papers (1959, 1977) are concerned with Kolis almost entirely in the context of one village in Ahmedabad district and has little to say about the horizontal dimension of the caste. The same is the problem with Steed's paper (1955) on the same village. Portions on Kolis in Pocock's writings (1957, 1972, 1973) also do not add much to our understanding of this dimension. Koli population extends from south Gujarat far into Maharashtra, but there is no modern study of Kolis in Maharashtra also, except Ghurye's monograph on the Mahadev Kolis (1963).
11. The data on marriage networks of Kolis in three villages in central Gujarat presented recently by Clark (1979: 396-404) confirm the general points made here.
12. I had mainly the Rajput-Koli and Rajput-Bhil continuum in mind when in my review of Dumont (1957) (1966: 340) I commented that his monograph did not go far enough in emphasizing hierarchy. He agreed with my comments (see Dumont 1966: 343; and also later 1975: 144). However, I do not go as far as Dumont in holding hierarchy as *always* encompassing separation for division), as the following discussion will show.
13. The political symbiosis was enabled by the Rajput political institutions. For a brief account of them, see Shah and Shroff (1958), and A.M. Shah (1966). For similar accounts of these institutions in Uttar Pradesh and Rajasthan, see Fox (1971) and Stern (1977).
14. There is extensive evidence of this complex in ethnographic literature, though there is not much modern sociological work on it. Sinha (1962) provides a brief account of the complex among tribes in central India. Several sociologists who have worked in Bengal inform me in personal communications that the complex spreads as far as Cooch Behar in Bengal. As for Orissa, see Kulke (1976), for

Uttar Pradesh, Minturn and Hitchcock (1966: 16), and for a detailed account of the spread in Kangra in the far north, Parry (1979). A fuller understanding of the complex would require a lot of cooperative work by social scientists and historians of various kinds in various parts of India.

15. For an account of the category "Rajput" and its impact on personality formation in a Gujarat village, see Steed 1955.
16. In view of the basic nature of Rajput hypergamy delineated here, the general saying that among the Rajputs brides go from east to west should be interpreted as indicating only that all Rajputs aspired to get their daughters married into the highest royal families found in Rajasthan in particular and in western India in general. The saying does not preclude the flow of brides in other directions, as indeed it has been found to occur in parts of northern and central India (see Minturn and Hitchcock 1966: 57, Mayer 1960: 211, and Jain 1975: 261-67). Whether the brides go from east to west or in some other direction is not a significant issue. A more significant issue has been suggested by Mayer: "What happens at the boundaries of Rajput habitation? Is there any chain in Rajasthan, the furthest West of all, where there should then be a surplus of unmarried girls; and what happens in the South, where there is presumably a shortage of girls? It would be interesting to see whether the principle of a marriage chain has a force at the periphery equal to that in the centre of the area of habitation" (1960: 211, No. 1). I would modify these questions in terms of social hierarchy rather than of geography.
17. Some of the modern sociological writings on the Leva Kanbis are Pocock, 1954, 1955, 1957a, 1972 and 1973; Naik, 1957; and Viswa nath, 1973, and 1976; and on the Anavils, V.H. Joshi, 1966; and Van der Veen, 1972. There is no published sociological work on Khedawal hypergamy.
18. See V.H. Joshi 1966: 22, Van der Veen 1972; 143 and my review (1979) of Van der Veen's book.
19. There is now sizeable literature on the commercial history of Gujarat. Two important recent works are Pearson (1976) and Gopal (1975).
20. For a somewhat extended discussion of rural-urban relations in Gujarat, see my paper "Rural-Urban Networks in India" (forthcoming).
21. While Levas have received considerable scholarly attention, Kadvas,

an equally large and important peasant caste, have received no attention. This is part of the general neglect of north Gujarat by scholars.

22. A good beginning has been made in Beck (1979) on the boundaries of a subcaste of about 3,000 people living in about 105 villages in the Kongu region in Tamil Nadu. Beck found the subcaste boundaries "mappable and firmly defined", contrary to her hope, arising out of the prevailing theory, "to find an unbounded community, fading from one named group to another, and perhaps even stretching across regional boundaries in a disguised form". She concludes: some subcastes, at least, are "concrete, enumerable entities" and "empirically bounded units". She refers to another subcaste of about 600 families living in only four villages in the same region (p. 96). Montegomery (1977) reports on a census of a bounded subcaste of 4,522 persons (829 households) living in about 36 villages and 9 towns in Andhra Pradcsh.
23. For a detailed account of this feature of neighbourhoods in Gujarat in general and in Ahmedabad in particular, see H. Doshi (1974); Gillion (1968: 25, 26, 107, 108, 124, 127-28, 145, 150, 170); and Karve (1957). Karve's paper provides a few maps of urban neighbourhoods in Gujarat, including that of Ahmedabadi Pol.
24. The applicability, to the village society, of the view of caste as a system without competition among its components has been widely questioned. Its applicability to the urban society is even more questionable. for some useful suggestions on the nature of caste in urban areas, see the symposium on social mobility in the caste system edited by Silverberg (1968: *passim*, but particularly 103-7 of Marriott's contribution).
25. See No. 12 above.
26. The Gujarat Kshatriya Sabha has received considerable attention from political scientists (G. Shah, 1975; Kothari and Maru, 1965; 1970; Weiner, 1967).

References

Aurora, G.S., 1972, *Tribe-Caste-Class Encounters: Some Aspects of Folk-Urban Relations in Alirajpur Tehsil*, Hyderabad: Administrative Staff College of India.

Bombay Gazetteer, 1901, *Gazetteer of the Bombay Presidency, 4.1, Gujarat Population, Hindus,* Bombay: Cambridge University Press, 1971.

Das, Veena, 1988, "A Sociological Approach to the Caste Puranas of Gujarat: A Case Study", *Sociological Bulletin*, 17: 141-64.

—, 1977, *Structure and Cognition: Aspects of Hindu Caste and Ritual*, Delhi: Oxford University Press.

Dobbin, Christine, 1972, *Urban Leadership in Western India: Politics and Communities in Bombay City, 1840-1885*, Oxford: Oxford University Press.

Doshi, S.L., 1971, *Bhils: Between Societal Self-awareness and Cultural Synthesis*, Delhi: Sterling.

Dumont, Louis, 1972, *Homo Hierarchicus: The Caste System and its Implications*. London: Paladin.

Ghurye, G.S., 1932, *Caste and Race in India*, London: Kegan Paul, Trench, Trubner & Co.

Joshi, V.H., 1966, *Economic Development and Social Change in a South Gujarat Village*, Baroda: Maharaja Sayajirao University.

Kavi, Dalapatram Dahyabhai, 1851, *Jnati Nibandh* (*Essay on Caste*), Ahmedabad: Gujarat Vernacular Society.

Lynch, Owen, 1977, "Method and Theory in the Sociology of Louis Dumont: A Reply", In Kenneth David (ed.), *The New Wind: Changing Identities in South Asia*, The Hague: Mouton.

Naik, T.B., 1956, *The Bhils*, Delhi: Bharatiya Adimjati Sevak Sangh.

Nath, Y.V.S., 1960, *Bhils of Ratanmal*. Baroda: Maharaja Sayajirao University.

Plunkett, Frances Taft, 1973, "Royal Marriages in Rajasthan", *Contributions to Indian Sociology* (N.S.), 8:64-80.

Pocock, David F., 1957a, "Inclusion and Exclusion: A Process in the Caste System of Gujarat", *South Western Journal of Anthropology*, 13:19-31.

—, 1957b, "Difference in East Africa: A Study of Caste and Religion in Modern Indian Society", *South Western Journal of Anthropology*, 13:289-300.

Shah, A.M., 1955, "Caste, Economy and Territory in the Central Panchmahals", *Journal of the Maharaja Sayajirao University of Baroda*, 4:61-91.

—, 1979, "Review" of Van Der Veen, 1972, *Eastern Anthropologist*, 32:148-51.

Shah, A.M., and R.G. Shroff, 1958, "The Vahivancha Barots of Gujarat:

A Caste of Genealogists and Mythographers", *Journal of American Folklore*, 71:246-76. Reprinted in Milton Singer (ed.), *Traditional India: Structure and Change, Philadelphia*: American Folklore Society, 1959, 40-70.

Shah, Ghanshyam, 1975, *Caste Association and Political Process in Gujarat: A Study of Gujarat Kshatriya Sabha*, Bombay: Popular Prakashan.

Shah, Ragini, 1978, *A Study of Associations in a Caste in Gujarat*, Unpublished M. Litt. dissertation, Department of Sociology, University of Delhi.

Srinivas, M.N., 1952, *Religion and Society among the Coorgs of South India*, Oxford: Claredon Press.

—, 1966, *Social Change in Modern India*, Bombay: Allied.

Trivedi, Harshad R., 1961, *The Mers of Saurashtra*, Baroda: Maharaja Sayajirao University.

Van der Veen, Klass W., 1972, *I Give Thee my Daughter*. Assen: Gorcum.

Viswa Nath, L.S., 1969, *Female Infanticide in India during the British Period*, Unpublished M. Litt. dissertation, Department of Sociology, University of Delhi.

—, 1976, *Changes in Kinship and Society in Two Selected Areas in India: A Study Based on Female Infanticide Records during the Nineteenth Century*, Unpublished Ph.D. dissertation, Department of Sociology, University of Delhi.

8 Caste and Class

A Reinterpretation[1]

VICTOR S. D'SOUZA

It is generally accepted that caste and class are different forms of social stratification. At the same time it is found that both caste and class systems may coexist in the same society. This is particularly so in India. Therefore, the question about the relationship between caste and class becomes very important and yet this has not been satisfactorily explained. Most of the studies on social stratification resolve this issue in one of two ways: (i) by treating caste and class as qualitatively distinct forms of social stratification so that class system may operate within each caste group, but the two systems cannot cut across each other; and (ii) by regarding caste system as a limiting case of the class system so that the former differs from the latter only in degree. However, neither of these views helps clarify how caste system may transform itself into class system and vice versa.

Let us try to understand the nature of the problem by examining briefly the two different types of concepts of caste. One of the well-known Indian authorities on the subject, G.S. Ghurye, describes caste system by drawing attention to its six main features: (1) segmental division of society, (2) hierarchy of groups, (3) restrictions on feeding and social intercourse, (4) civil and religious disabilities and privileges of the different sections, (5) lack of unrestricted choice of occupation, and (6) restrictions on marriage. He treats these features or elements as constituting a system but finds it difficult to explain the behaviour of the elements within the system. For, in the Indian society which is to a large extent characterized by caste system, while most of the elements are changing even rapidly, the endogamous character of the caste groups is not manifesting any noticeable signs of change. Ghurye has tried to resolve this inconsistency by maintaining that endogamy is the essence of the caste system.[2] According to this view, the dissolution of endogamous groups is a necessary condition for the general transformation of caste system into class system. Until then, the functioning of the class system would be confined within each caste group.

The second variety of concepts of caste is exemplified by the description in MacIver and Page.[3] These authors derive the concept of caste from that of class. Defining class as "any portion of a community marked off from the rest by social status", they argue that in a society based on class system, the status of an individual is not fixed. But "when status is wholly predetermined, so that men are born to their lot in life without any hope of changing it, then class takes the extreme form of caste". According to their elaboration, the caste system has evolved from the class system; a caste group is endogamous and its endogamous character is derived from the predetermined and fixed status of the individual members. Consequently, a change in the caste system would entail a change in the endogamous character of the caste groups.

Both the above concepts do not satisfactorily explain the change in the behaviour pattern ordinarily subsumed under the phenomenon of caste system. They also do not explain the historical process of the formation of caste groups. It is not clear how the status of members in a caste group is predetermined. Above all, they fail to indicate the process of transformation of one form of stratification system into another.

It, therefore, seems to us that in order to resolve these conceptual problems it is necessary to reconsider and modify the concept of caste system. However, there are a few important and commonly held propositions about social stratification, including caste and class, with which we are in agreement. These are: (a) caste and class are different forms of social stratification, (b) social stratification is a "persistent system of ranking of social positions"[4] or it is simply "the objective result of rating"[5], and (c) whereas the units ranked in the class system are individuals, those ranked in the caste system are groups.[6] We have also no serious objection to the widespread notion that the groups referred to as the units in the caste system are the endogamous groups, although as will be shown presently this is not quite accurate.

On the other hand, we do not agree to the assumption which is equally widespread, that the endogamous character of castes is derived from the equal and fixed status of members. Nor do we subscribe to the proposition that the status of the members of an endogamous group is equal and fixed. We argue that there are a large number of factors like geographical, cultural, racial and kinship and other considerations, and that social status is only one of them, in the determination of endogamy. The mere existence of endogamous groups in a community does not constitute the caste system, for endogamy has been found to be a universal phenomenon in society. It is the ranking of these groups which is the essential mark of caste system.

We return to our reservation about the nature of the units in the caste system. Although generally the endogamous groups are regarded as the units in the caste system, sometimes, as it happens in some parts of India, even intermarrying groups according to the rules of hypergamy, are treated as castes. Therefore, it is not so much the endogamous character of groups but rather their hereditary nature that is important for the caste system. Because under the unilineal rules of kinship, even intermarrying groups can maintain their separate identity. Hence, we prefer to use the term "hereditary group" rather than "endogamous group" for the unit in the caste system.

The prestige ranking of individuals in the class system implies two important requirements: First, the presence of certain properties of individuals which is evaluated by the community, and second, the existence of interaction among members who rank one another. So also for the social grading of hereditary groups, the groups should have certain properties and further, they should be in interaction with one another. The need for interaction among hereditary groups can be easily understood. But there seems to be some confusion about the nature of the relevant properties of groups and the feasibility of ranking them.

In the case of the class system, it is recognized that the properties of the units or individuals which are evaluated are the individual's characteristics like education, occupation, wealth, style of living and so on. But, in the caste system, it is generally implied that there is some external factor which predetermines the status of groups. This kind of reasoning is exemplified by the time honoured Hindu view that the different castes are divinely ordained. While no one seriously considers this view now, the reasoning underlying it still lingers on. We, on the other hand, emphasize that the evaluation of hereditary groups in the caste system must be conceived in terms of the properties of the groups themselves.

There are, however, difficulties in ranking groups and according to some authors it is almost impossible to measure the prestige of groups objectively. For instance, Bergel has stated two major reasons for this difficulty. The first is the diversity of members within the group as regards age, sex, ability and achievement. The second is his assumption that the ranking of groups is "based on values, mostly derived from non-rational (frequently even irrational) considerations"[7]. But it seems to us that the objection against the possibility of the objective measurement of group prestige can be removed by explaining the logical basis of such a measurement. We have therefore to show how the properties of a group are derived and under what conditions do they result in the group being ranked.

The properties of a group are no doubt derived from the properties of its individual members. Therefore, ultimately the ranking of groups depends upon the evaluation of the properties of the individual members. But whether or not the groups will be ranked, apart from the individuals, would depend upon the degree to which the distribution of the properties of individuals in each of the group differs from their distribution in the whole community. If the distribution of individuals' properties in each group is the same, such that each group represents a microcosm of the larger community, there is no question of ranking the different groups, relative to one another. In such a situation we have the optimum degree of heterogeneity within each group with regard to the properties in question. When the distribution within each group tends to differ from the general distribution, the distribution within the group tends to be homogeneous. Therefore, we may hypothesize that for social grading of hereditary groups, the distribution of individuals' properties within each group should tend to be homogeneous and the several groups relative to one another should be heterogeneous.

Thus, there are three essential ideas in the concept of caste system: (1) the presence of two or more hereditary groups, (2) the interaction among these groups, and (3) the homogeneity of members within each group with regard to certain properties which are evaluated by the community and consequent heterogeneity of groups relative to one another. Bearing in mind these ideas we may broadly define caste system as the integration of interacting and heterogeneous but internally homogeneous hereditary groups, into a structure of status hierarchy.[8]

The relationship between caste and class can be better explained in terms of the process of change in the caste system. In studying change in the caste system, we have to focus our attention upon the hierarchical prestige relationship which renders the hereditary groups into caste groups, rather than upon the endogamous character of these groups. In other words, the concept of change in the caste system need not imply the destruction of the units, but rather a change in the properties of those units.

We may broadly conceive of two different types of change in the hierarchical relationships among caste groups. The first refers to a change in the relative positions of the groups in the caste hierarchy. This type of change does not impair the caste system as a form of social stratification. The second type refers to a change in the very tendency of hereditary groups to be ranked. This leads to a transformation of the caste system itself.

Both these types of change in the caste system are ultimately brought by changes in the properties of the individual members. In the first case, the properties of individuals change in such a way that the homogeneous character of any hereditary group is still maintained. In this case, the properties of almost all the members of a group will have risen or fallen from one level to another.[9] In the second case, the changes in the individuals' properties take place in such a way that the members within each group become heterogeneous and the various groups become similar in the distribution of the properties of members. Consequently, the tendency for groups to be ranked would tend to disappear. But the individuals in the community would still be ranked according to their individual properties, and persons within the same hereditary group would be found distributed in different prestige categories which may be termed social classes constituting the class system. The hereditary group may still continue to function in the class system in a limited manner.

It is not contended that the hereditary groups would inevitably survive even when their status connotation disappears. For that matter, it is not necessary to assume that the hereditary groups continue in the same form even in societies based on the caste system. It is here only intended to stress that the presence of hereditary groups is not inconsistent in a society based on class system.

The great importance given to social stratification in sociological studies stems from the fact that the persons who are classified as similar with regard to social status tend to have a large number of areas of social interaction in common. On the other hand, members in any social group have a more limited range of social interaction in common. In a community based on the caste system, the members of a hereditary group who have more or less equal status, have relatively large areas of social interaction in common. On the other hand, in a class society the hereditary groups, when present, control a more limited range of social interaction among members. Whereas both in the caste and the class societies, the similarity of social status of individuals forms the major basis for social interaction, in caste society individuals of similar status further confine their social interaction within hereditary groups. Therefore, the transformation of the caste system into class system would be characterized by a reduction in the potency of the hereditary group as the major basis of social interaction.

We have maintained that caste and class systems stand for different patterns of distribution of properties of individuals in hereditary groups. These two systems can coexist in an inverse relationship and the ideal typical forms of the caste and the class systems constitute the opposite poles of the caste-class continuum. This continuum refers to the rigidity-fluidity dimension of social stratification.

The coexistence of the two forms of social stratification is not of the type where class system can function only within each caste group separately, but rather it is of the type in which both the systems cut across each other. So also, the inverse relationship between the two does not imply that caste system is only an extreme form of class system in which social mobility is totally absent. As a matter of fact we have already indicated that social mobility, in so far as it relates to a change in the properties of individuals, is possible and does take place even in the caste system. The inverse relationship shows that both the systems are the extreme forms of the more inclusive system of social stratification which can be expressed as a continuum.

However, our explanation about the relationship between caste and class so far, leaves one important observation unclarified. This refers to the much publicized status discrepancy between the White and the Negro population in the United States. It is observed that while class stratification is found both among the Whites and the Negroes, given the same individual properties, a white person is ranked higher than a Negro. But this phenomenon is not difficult to explain within the framework of our present concept. The reason for the relatively lower status of the Negro in this case becomes obvious if we consider the fact that the social status of an individual is influenced not only by his individual properties, but also by the social status of the group to which he belongs. This may be schematically shown as under:

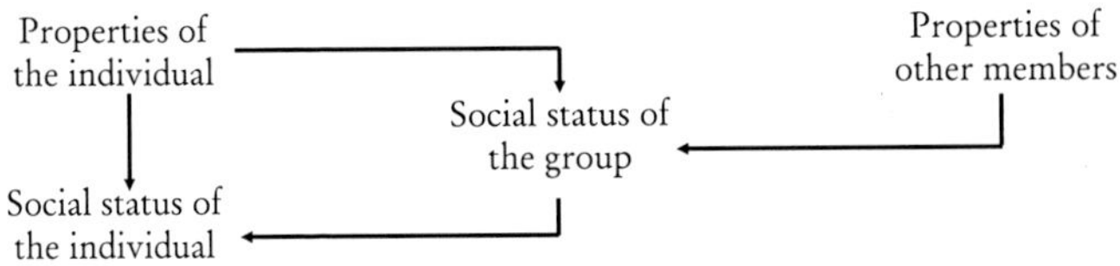

It is only when social stratification takes entirely the form of class system that the influence of the hereditary group would be neutralized and the status of an individual would be influenced solely by his own properties. Therefore, it is not necessary to assume, as is usually done, that there are parallel caste systems among the Negroes and the Whites, which operate independent of each other.

Empirical Verification

The concept of the caste system and the relationship between caste and class discussed here yield a number of hypotheses which can be empirically tested. However, to test all the important hypotheses, a wide variety of data, preferably collected under controlled conditions, are needed. But in this paper we propose to present only a limited set of data and hence the number and type of hypotheses considered here are restricted by these data.

The Hypotheses

We may now state the hypotheses by operationalizing the main variables implied in the concepts of the caste and the class systems. The data to be presented pertain to relatively small communities of two villages in India and so the operational definitions are intended to suit the study of social stratification in small communities.

To take up the concept of the caste system first, M.N. Srinivas has clarified that the Indian village is a vertical unity made up of several castes and a caste is a horizontal unity made up of members spread in several villages. The vertical unity of the village community actually represents the caste system as it operates at the local community level. However, only a segment of any caste or hereditary group is found in a given village. Therefore, the caste system in any village is the integration of the segments of several different hereditary groups into a hierarchy of social status. For the sake of convenience, we may treat the segment of the hereditary group (caste) as if it constitutes the total group.

The most important variable that we have to measure in the caste system is the social position of the hereditary group in the prestige hierarchy of groups. This variable may be termed the caste status, and it can be obtained by asking the members of the community to rank the various hereditary groups according to their social prestige. We may infer the existence of the caste system if (a) the different hereditary groups are assigned different social positions in a hierarchical order, and (b) there is a high degree of agreement on the part of the members of the community in assigning a group the particular rank.

Further, according to our concept, the caste status of different groups is based upon a differential distribution of individual properties in the different groups. The various properties which are generally evaluated in determining the prestige of an individual, such as education, occupational prestige, wealth, level of living, community participation and so on, have been found to be fairly highly intercorrelated, and the variable of occupational prestige is highly correlated with all of them. Therefore, the occupational prestige which is primarily responsible for the class status of an individual may be regarded as also responsible for the caste status of a hereditary group. If so, for the validation of our concept with regard to the prestige dimension of occupation, (c) the distribution of members in any group should differ from their distribution in the entire community, (d) the patterns of occupational prestige in the various groups should form a hierarchical order, and (e) the occupational hierarchy of groups should correspond with the hierarchy of caste status. It follows from hypotheses (c), (d) and (e) that (f) if in two communities the relative caste status of any two groups is different, their occupational status too should differ appropriately.

Our concept also implies that to form the caste system the hereditary groups should interact with one another. It therefore follows that in the absence of interaction, the members of the groups do not agree in ranking the groups in a hierarchy. Although we have other unpublished data to substantiate this hypothesis, the present data are not adequate to test it, as in each of the communities under study the hereditary groups are in interaction with one another for the most part.

The hypotheses (a) to (f) test the validity of the concept of caste system. We may now operationalize the concept of class system so as to distinguish it from caste system. Since a social class is usually regarded as a category of persons in a community having more or less equal prestige or social status, in the class system we are primarily concerned with the measurement of the prestige of individuals. This can be best done, at any rate in small communities, by asking the members themselves or a set of judges selected from the community, to rate the various individuals according to their prestige, and arrange them into convenient categories of prestige or classes.[10] The argument whether social classes are clearly distinguishable groups with identifiable boundary lines or categories with arbitrary dividing lines, need not detain us here. All the same, the operational definition of social classes in this manner does not enable us to know whether the social stratification is based either on class system or on caste system or a combination of the two. For, even in a community based on caste system, it should be possible for us to obtain measures of social prestige of individuals and to arrange the individuals into convenient classes. However, with regard to the social prestige of individuals, the distinguishing mark of the ideal typical caste system is that the members in each caste group are identical.

Thus, it is clear that it is difficult for us to have a measure of the class system independent of the measure of the caste system. We may therefore operationally define the class system as the degree to which the distribution of social prestige of members in each of the hereditary groups approximates its distribution in the entire community. Assuming that the social prestige of members is influenced mainly by their occupational prestige, we may also operationally define class system as the degree to which the distribution of the occupational prestige of members in each of the hereditary groups approximates its distribution in the entire community. We may therefore arrive at the hypothesis that (g) if the occupational prestige of members in a hereditary group varies, the social prestige of members should also vary.

Finally, we may deduce from the hypotheses (b) and (g) that (h) the greater the distribution of prestige of members in hereditary groups approximates its distribution in the entire community, the lesser is the degree of unanimity on the part of the members of the community in grading the groups according to prestige. Thus, the increasing operation of the class system would be characterized by a diminishing degree of the operation of the caste system.

Presentation of Data

We shall now test the above hypotheses with relevant data from the two Indian villages of Devigarh and Rampur. These villages are from the culturally homogeneous region of the Chandi[11] tehsil, Patiala district of Punjab. There are ten hereditary groups in each village, of which nine bear the same names in both the villages. The hereditary groups which are not repeated are Kumhar (potter) in Devigarh, and Balmiki (scheduled caste) in Rampur. Our sample consists of 88 households from Devigarh and 61 from Rampur.[12] An important limitation of the data is that except for two hereditary groups, the Jat and the Ramdasia, the number of respondents in each group is rather too small to be statistically significant. Therefore, we have not worked out any refined statistical indices for testing our hypotheses. We may, nevertheless, accept the hypotheses if the differences observed, if any, are in the direction predicted by them.

Tables 1 and 2 show the prestige ranking of the hereditary groups by the groups themselves in Devigarh and Rampur respectively. The ranking by a group is indicated by the arithmetic mean of the ranks given by all the members of the group. The ranking scores by each group are shown in columns 1 to 10. Therefore, each of the rows 1 to 10 shows the ranking scores given to a particular hereditary group by the ten groups. The arithmetic mean of these scores in a row is taken to be the general ranking score given to any hereditary group by the village as a whole. The general ranking scores are shown in the last column. The hereditary groups in each table are arranged in the ascending order of the general ranking scores which represent the descending order of the prestige.

It is evident from both the tables that the general ranking scores vary gradually, showing thereby that the groups occupy more or less distinct positions along the prestige dimension which we have designated the caste status. This evidence is in conformity with our hypothesis (a).

Hypothesis (b) may be tested with two different sets of evidence. One of these is to see if the different hereditary groups agree in giving the same relative prestige positions to one another. If we examine every column of each of these tables, we find that in three out of ten groups in Devigarh and six out of ten in Rampur, the relative order of the hereditary groups is identical with their general ranking order. In the remaining 11 columns in both the tables together, which comprise in all 110 ranking positions, there are only 16 instances in which a group has been ranked just one step higher or lower relative to the general ranking order and one instance in which a group has been ranked two steps higher. Thus, the disagreement manifested is only very slight. What is still more significant is the fact that out of 17 instances of ranking discrepancies, nine refer to the ranking of a hereditary group by itself. Since the evaluation by an individual by himself is generally termed self-esteem, we may term the

Table 1

Arithmatic means of ranking positions of caste groups by each caste in Devigarh

Name of caste ranked	*Name of caste ranking*										
	Jat	*Brahmin*	*Bania*	*Carpen-ter*	*Barber*	*Water-carrier*	*Oil-presser*	*Drum-beater*	*Potter*	*Ramdasia*	*Mean of the means*
1. Jat	1.0	2.0	1.0	1.0	1.0	1.0	1.0	1.0	1.0	1.0	1.1
2. Brahmin	2.1	1.0	3.0	2.2	2.0	2.0	3.0	2.0	2.0	2.2	2.2
3. Bania (Trader)	2.9	3.0	2.0	2.7	3.0	3.0	2.0	3.0	3.0	2.8	2.7
4. Carpenter	4.0	4.0	4.0	4.0	5.0	4.0	4.0	4.0	4.0	4.0	4.1
5. Barber	5.2	5.0	5.0	5.0	4.0	5.5	5.0	5.0	5.0	5.0	5.0
6. Water Carrier (Kahar)	5.8	6.0	6.0	5.0	6.0	5.5	7.0	6.0	6.0	6.0	5.9
7. Teli (Oil-presser)	7.0	7.0	7.0	7.0	7.0	7.0	6.0	7.0	8.0	7.2	7.0
8. Drum-Beater (Bazigar)	8.5	8.0	8.0	9.0	9.0	8.5	9.0	8.0	9.0	9.6	8.4
9. Potter	8.5	9.0	9.0	8.2	8.0	8.5	8.0	9.0	7.0	8.6	8.6
10. Ramdasia (Scheduled Caste)	9.9	10.0	10.0	9.7	10.0	10.0	10.0	10.0	10.0	8.6	9.8
No. of persons	34	1	4	5	1	3	2	3	1	34	88 (total)

Table 2

Arithmatic means of ranking positions of caste groups by each caste in Rampur

Name of caste ranked	*Name of caste ranking*										
	Jat	*Brahmin*	*Bania*	*Carpenter*	*Barber*	*Water-carrier*	*Oil-presser*	*Drum-beater*	*Potter*	*Ramdasia*	*Mean of the means*
1. Jat	1.0	1.0	1.0	1.0	1.0	1.0	1.0	1.0	1.0	1.0	1.0
2. Brahmin	2.6	3.0	2.5	3.0	3.0	2.5	3.0	3.0	2.8	2.0	2.7
3. Bania (Trader)	2.4	2.0	2.5	2.0	2.0	2.5	2.0	2.0	2.2	3.2	2.3
4. Carpenter	4.0	4.0	4.0	4.0	5.0	4.5	4.0	4.0	4.1	4.0	4.2
5. Barber	5.2	5.0	5.2	5.0	4.0	6.0	5.0	6.0	5.2	6.0	5.3
6. Water Carrier (Kahar)	5.8	6.0	5.8	6.0	6.0	4.5	6.0	5.0	5.7	5.0	5.6
7. Teli (Oil-presser)	7.4	7.0	7.0	7.0	8.0	7.0	7.0	8.0	7.8	7.0	7.3
8. Drum-Beater (Bazigar)	7.6	8.0	8.0	8.0	7.0	8.0	8.0	7.0	8.0	8.0	7.8
9. Ramdasia (Scheduled Caste)	9.0	9.0	9.0	9.0	9.0	9.0	9.0	9.0	8.2	9.0	8.9
10. Balmiki	10.0	10.0	10.0	10.0	10.0	10.0	10.0	10.0	10.0	10.0	10.0
No. of persons	16	4	3	2	1	4	2	4	23	2	61 (total)

ranking of a group by itself as in-group esteem which is shown in the diagonal cells of the tables. Invariably, the in-group esteem is either the same or higher than the general ranking and in no case is it lower. This is not surprising because even in the case of evaluation of persons, it is usually found that the self-esteem is slightly higher than the esteem of others. In the case in point, even the difference in the in-group esteem, when present, is very slight. Therefore, this part of the evidence supports our hypothesis (b).

For the other set of evidence to test hypothesis (b), we may see if members in each hereditary group agree in giving any group the particular rank. This evidence is presented in Tables 3 and 4 for the villages Devigarh and Rampur, respectively. These tables show the mean deviations of the ranking positions of groups by members in each group. Since there are ten ranking positions, if members in each group have graded any group in a perfectly random fashion, the mean deviation of the ranking score could be as high as 5. But the highest deviations we have are 0.72 and 0.69 in Devigar and Rampur, respectively, and in both cases they refer to the in-group esteem of the Ramdasia. In Rajpura, the mean deviation of the ranking score of the Oil Presser group by Ramdasia is also 0.69. In any case, the mean deviations are very small as compared to the maximum possible figure. The averages of the mean deviations in both the villages are insignificant. They range from 0 to 0.29 in Devigarh and from 0 to 0.20 in Rampur. Therefore, the hypothesis (b) is fully substantiated.

It may, however, be pointed out that although in both the villages the disagreement in ranking is very slight, it is relatively more in Devigarh than in Rampur. This is so whether we consider the agreement among groups or among individual members within groups.

From the data presented above, we can boldly conclude that social stratification in both the villages is based on caste system. We have to examine next the underlying basis for the caste system in these villages. According to our concept, the differential status of the caste groups has to be validated by a differential distribution of occupational prestige in the various groups. Before we present the relevant data in support of this idea, a brief explanation about occupational prestige under the present context may be in order.

In an earlier study of social grading of village occupations conducted in three different villages, each in a distinct linguistic region in India[13], it

Table 3

Mean deviations of ranking positions of caste groups by each caste in Devigarh

Name of caste ranked	Name of caste ranking										
	Jat	*Brahmin*	*Bania*	*Carpenter*	*Barber*	*Water -carrier*	*Oil-presser*	*Drum-beater*	*Potter*	*Ramdasia (Harijan)*	*Mean of the mean devi-ations*
1. Jat	0.00	-	0.00	0.00	-	0.00	0.00	0.00	-	0.00	0.00
2. Brahmin	2.21	-	0.00	0.35	-	0.00	0.00	0.00	-	0.31	0.12
3. Bania (Trader)	2.21	-	0.00	0.41	-	0.00	0.00	0.00	-	0.40	0.15
4. Carpenter	0.00	-	0.00	0.00	-	0.00	0.00	0.00	-	0.00	0.00
5. Barber	0.32	-	0.00	0.00	-	0.50	0.00	0.00	-	0.00	0.12
6. Water Carrier (Kahar)	0.32	-	0.00	0.00	-	0.50	0.00	0.00	-	0.00	0.12
7. Teli (Oil-Presser)	0.00	-	0.00	0.00	-	0.00	0.00	0.00	-	0.40	0.06
8. Drum-Beater (Bazigar)	0.57	-	0.00	0.50	-	0.50	0.00	0.00	-	0.42	0.28
9. Potter	0.50	-	0.00	0.35	-	0.50	0.00	0.00	-	0.66	0.29
10. Ramdasia	0.15	-	0.00	0.40	-	0.00	0.00	0.00	-	0.72	0.19
No. of persons	34	1	4	5	1	3	2	3	1	34	88 (total)

Table 4

Mean deviations of ranking positions of caste groups by each caste in Rampur

Name of caste ranked	Name of caste ranking										Mean of the mean deviations
	Jat	Bania	Brahmin	Carpenter	Barber	Water-carrier	Oil-presser	Drum-beater	Ramdasia	Balmiki	
1. Jat	0.00	0.00	0.00	0.00	-	0.00	0.00	0.00	0.00	0.00	0.00
2. Bania	0.48	0.00	0.50	0.00	-	0.50	0.00	0.00	0.33	0.00	0.00
3. Brahmin	0.48	0.00	0.50	0.00	-	0.50	0.00	0.00	0.33	0.00	0.20
4. Carpenter	0.00	0.00	0.00	0.00	-	0.50	0.00	0.00	0.19	0.00	0.08
5. Barber	0.32	0.00	0.35	0.00	-	0.00	0.00	0.00	0.49	0.00	0.13
6. Water Carrier (Kahar)	0.32	0.00	0.35	0.00	-	0.50	0.00	0.00	0.43	0.00	0.18
7. Teli (Oil-Presser)	4.48	0.00	0.00	0.00	-	0.00	0.00	0.00	0.69	0.00	0.13
8. Drum-Beater (Bazigar)	0.48	0.00	0.00	0.00	-	0.00	0.00	0.00	0.64	0.00	0.12
9. Ramdasia	0.00	0.00	0.00	0.00	-	0.00	0.00	0.00	0.69	0.00	0.08
10. Balmiki	0.00	0.00	0.00	0.00	-	0.00	0.00	0.00	0.00	0.00	0.00
No. of persons	16	4	3	2	1	4	2	4	23	2	61 (total)

has been demonstrated that villagers in India show a high degree of consensus in giving different amounts of prestige to different occupations. Persons in different villages grade similar occupations more or less in the same way. Drawing upon the experience of that study and the knowledge of persons acquainted with local conditions, the occupations in Devigarh and Rampur have been arranged in a descending order of their prestige as shown in Tables 5 and 6. Apart from the arbitrary nature of this arrangement, it is useful to bear in mind one or two other of its limitations also. While the occupation of owner-cultivator, in general may be regarded as having a higher prestige in relation to the occupations immediately following it, it is not likely that all of the four divisions of this occupation based on the size of the farm are higher in prestige than the occupations immediately following the four of them. Similarly, the occupation of shopkeeper also can be broken up into parts, depending upon the size of business and consequently the general term "shopkeeper" does not connote a single prestige position.

Since both hereditary groups and occupations in Tables 5 and 6 are arranged in a descending order of prestige, they show the relationship between caste status and occupational prestige in Devigarh and Rampur, respectively. It is abundantly clear that in both the villages the distribution of occupational prestige of members in any hereditary group differs markedly from its distribution in the village as a whole, thus supporting our hypothesis (c). Consequently, the patterns of distribution in various groups differ from one another. By and large, the occupational distribution in each group clusters around a certain point in the occupational hierarchy, showing thereby that members in any group are more or less homogeneous with regard to their occupational prestige. Therefore, it is possible to rank order the groups along the occupational prestige dimension, supporting our hypothesis (d). It is also evident from both the tables that the occupational hierarchy and caste hierarchy correspond fairly well with each other. This is in agreement with our hypothesis (e). The support for this hypothesis is even stronger if we take into account the reasons for the discrepancies which render the relationship between the variables in question less than perfect.

Where the occupational prestige position of a group is higher or lower than what is warranted by its position in the caste hierarchy, this may be due to one or more of the following reasons: There are three instances in Devigarh relating to the Brahmin, the barber and the potter

Table 5

Caste and occupational prestige in Devigarh

					Owner cultivator																							
	Quanungo	*Patwari*	*Havildar*	*Naik*	*V. Large*	*Large*	*Medium*	*Small*	*Arthia*	*Shopkeeper*	*Motor driver*	*Peon*	*Sharecropper*	*Tailor*	*Carpenter*	*Blacksmith*	*Barber*	*Midwife*	*Oil-presser, weaver, potter, water-carrier*	*Shoe-maker*	*Agricultural labourer*	*Watchman*	*Casual labourer*	*Cattle grazer*	*Scavenger*	*Unspecified*	*Total %*	*Total No.*
Jat	3	3	-	-	17	15	29	15	-	-	3	-	-	-	-	-	-	-	-	-	-	-	-	3	-	12	100	34
Brahmin	-	-	100	-	-	-	-	-	-	-	-	-	-	-	-	-	-	-	-	-	-	-	-	-	-	-	100	1
Bania	-	-	-	-	-	-	-	-	33	67	-	-	-	-	-	-	-	-	-	-	-	-	-	-	-	-	100	3
Carpenter	-	-	-	-	-	-	-	-	-	-	-	-	-	-	40	40	-	-	-	-	20	-	-	-	-	-	100	5
Barber	-	-	-	-	-	-	-	100	-	-	-	-	-	-	-	-	-	-	-	-	-	-	-	-	-	-	100	1
Kahar (watercarrier)	-	-	-	-	-	-	-	-	-	-	-	17	-	-	-	17	-	-	-	-	50	16	-	-	-	-	100	6
Teli (oil-presser)	-	-	-	-	-	-	-	-	-	-	-	-	-	-	-	-	-	-	-	-	100	-	-	-	-	-	100	2
Bazigar (drumbeater)	-	-	-	-	-	-	-	-	-	-	-	-	-	-	-	-	-	-	-	-	-	-	-	-	-	-	-	-
Potter	-	-	-	-	-	-	-	-	-	-	-	-	-	-	-	-	-	-	100	-	-	-	-	-	-	-	100	1
Ramdasia (SC)	-	-	-	3	-	-	-	-	-	-	-	3	-	6	-	-	-	-	8	3	66	-	-	3	-	8	100	35
Total %	1	1	1	1	7	6	12	7	1	2	1	2	-	2	2	4	-	-	5	1	33	1	-	2	-	8	100	-
Total No.	1	1	1	1	6	5	10	6	1	2	1	2	-	2	2	3	-	-	4	1	29	1	-	2	-	7	-	88

Table 6

Caste and occupational prestige in Rampur

Name of caste	*Occupation*																											
					Owner cultivator																							
	Quanungo	*Patwari*	*Havildar*	*Naik*	*V. Large*	*Large*	*Medium*	*Small*	*Arthia*	*Shopkeeper*	*Motor driver*	*Peon*	*Sharecropper*	*Tailor*	*Carpenter*	*Blacksmith*	*Barber*	*Midwife*	*Oil-presser, weaver, potter, water-carrier*	*Shoe-maker*	*Agricultural labourer*	*Watchman*	*Casual labourer*	*Cattle grazer*	*Scavenger*	*Unspecified*	*Total %*	*Total No.*
Jat	-	-	-	-	18	6	35	12	-	-	-	-	-	-	-	-	-	-	-	-	-	-	6	-	6	-	-	17
Bania	-	-	-	-	-	-	20	-	-	60	-	-	-	-	-	-	-	-	-	-	-	-	-	-	-	20	100	5
Brahmin	-	-	-	-	-	-	-	-	33	67	-	-	-	-	-	-	-	-	-	-	50	-	-	-	-	50	100	2
Carpenter	-	-	-	-	-	-	-	-	-	-	33	-	-	-	33	-	33	-	-	-	-	-	-	-	-	-	100	3
Barber	-	-	-	-	-	-	-	-	-	-	-	-	-	-	-	-	-	-	-	-	-	-	-	-	-	-	-	-
Kahar (water-carrier)	-	-	-	-	-	-	-	-	-	-	-	-	-	-	-	-	-	-	75	-	-	25	-	-	-	-	100	4
Teli (oil-presser)	-	-	-	-	-	-	-	-	-	-	-	-	-	-	-	-	-	-	50	-	-	50	-	-	-	-	100	2
Bazigar (drum-beater)	-	-	-	-	-	-	-	-	-	-	-	-	-	-	-	-	-	-	-	-	25	-	-	75	-	-	100	4
Ramdasia (Scheduled Caste)	-	-	-	-	-	-	-	-	-	-	-	-	10	-	-	-	-	5	-	-	38	-	42	5	-	-	100	21
Balmiki (Scheduled Caste)	-	-	-	-	-	-	-	-	-	-	-	-	-	-	-	-	-	-	-	-	-	-	-	-	100	-	-	2
Total %	-	-	-	-	5	2	11	3	-	5	2	3	-	2	-	2	2	7	-	20	2	16	7	2	8	100	-	-
Total No.	-	-	-	-	3	1	7	2	-	3	1	2	-	1	-	1	1	4	-	12	1	10	4	3	5	-	60	

groups, where the occupational positions are slightly different from their caste positions. In all the three cases, the groups are represented by just one family each. But the members of a caste group are spread in different villages and so where the number of members of any group is too small in a community, the status of that group would also be influenced by the status of the members of that group spread in the neighbouring communities. As a matter of fact, we do have information about occupations in six different villages in the same region and the combined result shows that the over all occupational prestige positions of the three groups are almost the same as their positions in the caste hierarchy. This is the extension of the principle discussed above that the prestige of an individual is influenced both by his own properties and the distribution of properties of members in his group. Accordingly, the prestige of a small group is influenced not only by the distribution of properties of its own members but also by the distribution of the properties of the members of the larger group of which it is a part.

In Rampur, the caste status of the Brahmin and the Bazigar is higher than their occupational prestige. So far as the Brahmin group is concerned, the reason described above is applicable in this case also. It may, however, be pointed out that the person who is an agricultural labourer also owns a small piece of land and the person whose occupation is unspecified owns a large farm although he does not cultivate it himself. Therefore, the occupational prestige of the Brahmin group in Rampur is higher than what is indicated in the table. Still, it would be lower than the position of the group in the caste hierarchy.

According to their occupational prestige, both in Rampur and in the neighbouring communities, the Bazigars come after the Ramdasias. But the Bazigars have been a wandering tribe and have begun to settle down only recently. They reside mostly on the outskirts of the village and the degree of their interaction with the rest of the community is relatively small. This is further indicated by the type of occupations they follow. In the six villages referred to above, both the Ramdasia and the Bazigar are engaged mainly as labourers. We have divided the category of labourers into the sub-categories of agricultural and casual labourers. The agricultural labourers are relatively more, attached to their employers. Now, of the 115 labourers among the Ramdasia, 96 are agricultural labourers and 19 casual. On the other hand, of the 61 labourers among the Bazigar, only one is an agricultural labourer and 15 are casual labourers. Thus, the interaction between the Bazigar and the rest of the community is relatively small. Therefore, the discrepancy between the caste rank and the occupational prestige in the case of Bazigar, although slight, may be attributed to a lack of adequate degree of interaction.

It may be observed further from the two tables that the relative caste positions of the hereditary groups bearing the same names are identical in both the villages except for the Brahmins. First of all, in neither case does the Brahmin group occupy the topmost position accorded to it in the traditional caste hierarchy, and this is in conformity with their occupational prestige in the region. Secondly, the Brahmin group in Devigarh is ranked second whereas in Rampur it is ranked third. Assuming that the influence of the regional Brahmin group upon the village group is constant in both the villages, the difference in their caste positions is well supported by the difference in their occupational prestige in the two villages. This is in agreement with our hypothesis (f).

The occupational prestige of Ramdasia, both in Devigarh and Rampur, is slightly higher than their caste rank. The improvement in the occupational prestige of this group has not yet made any noticeable impression on the community as a whole. But the improvement is not strikingly large. All the same, it has influenced the in-group esteem of these groups which is in greater agreement with their occupational prestige. The Ramdasias in Devigarh have on the whole a higher occupational prestige than their counterparts in Rampur. Consequently, as can be seen from Tables 1 and 2, the difference between their scores of in-group esteem and general esteem is higher in Devigarh (1.2) than in Rampur (0.7).

As an independent measure of the prestige of individuals, a selected number of heads of households in each village were asked to rank the household heads in their respective villages, into four hierarchical classes of prestige. The prestige classes were given scores 1 through 4 in the descending order of prestige. Thus, the minimum average score representing the highest prestige is 1 and the maximum score representing the lowest prestige is 4. According to their average prestige scores, the household heads have been arbitrarily divided into six prestige classes. The limits for each class are as follows: All those persons whose average score is between 1.0 and 1.50, comprise class I; between 1.51 and 2.00, Class II; between 2.01 and 2.50, Class III; between 2.51 and 3.00, Class IV; between 3.01 and 3.50, Class V; between 3.51 and 4.00, Class VI.

Table 7

Occupation and prestige class of household heads in Devigarh

Occupation	*Prestige class*							*Total*	*Total*
	I	*II*	*III*	*IV*	*V*	*VI*	*No. inf.*	*%*	*no.*
Quanungo	100.0	-	-	-	-	-	-	100	1
Patwari	100.0	-	-	-	-	-	-	100	1
Havaldar	100.0	-	-	-	-	-	-	100	1
Naik	-	-	-	100.0	-	-	-	100	1
Owner-cultivator									
1. V. large	33.3	-	16.6	33.3	-	-	16.6	100	6
2. Large	20.0	20.0	40.0	20.0	-	-	-	100	5
3. Medium	-	10.0	30.0	40.0	20.0	-	-	100	10
4. Small	-	-	33.3	33.3	33.3	-	-	100	6
Arthia	-	-	-	100.0	-	-	-	100	1
Shopkeeper	50.0	50.0	-	-	-	-	-	100	2
Motor driver	-	-	100.0	-	-	-	-	100	1
Peon	-	-	-	-	50.0	50.0	-	100	2
Sharecropper	-	-	-	-	-	-	-	-	-
Tailor	50.0	-	-	-	50.0	-	-	100	2
Carpenter	-	-	-	50.0	50.0	-	-	100	2
Blacksmith	-	-	-	100.0	-	-	-	100	3
Barber	-	-	-	-	-	-	-	-	-
Midwife	-	-	-	-	-	-	-	-	-
Oil-presser, weaver, potter, water-carrier	-	25.0	-	25.0	25.0	25.0	-	100	4
Shoe-maker	-	-	-	-	-	100.0	-	100	1
Agricultural labourer	-	-	7.0	-	20.5	72.5	-	100	29
Watchman	-	-	-	-	-	100.0	-	-	1
Casual labourer	-	-	-	-	-	-	-	-	-
Cattle grazer	-	50.0	-	50.0	-	-	-	100	2
Scavenger	-	-	-	-	-	-	-	-	-
Unspecified	14.2	-	-	28.4	-	57.5	-	100	7
Total	10.2	5.7	12.5	21.6	18.1	31.8	1.1	100	88

Table 8
Occupation and prestige class of household heads in Rampur

Occupation	Prestige class						Total %	Total no.
	I	II	III	IV	V	VI		
Quanungo	-	-	-	-	-	-	-	-
Patwari	-	-	-	-	-	-	-	-
Havaldar	-	-	-	-	-	-	-	-
Naik	-	-	-	-	-	-	-	-
Owner-cultivator								
1. V. large	100.0	-	-	-	-	-	100	3
2. Large	100.0	-	-	-	-	-	100	1
3. Medium	57.0	43.0	-	-	-	-	100	7
4. Small	-	100.0	-	-	-	-	100	2
Arthia	-	-	-	-	-	-	-	-
Shopkeeper	33.3	66.6	-	-	-	-	100	3
Motor driver	-	-	100.0	-	-	100	1	
Peon	-	-	-	-	-	-	-	-
Sharecropper	-	-	-	-	-	100.0	100	2
Tailor	-	-	-	-	-	-	-	-
Carpenter	-	-	100.0	-	-	-	100	1
Blacksmith	-	-	-	-	-	-	-	-
Barber	-	-	-	-	100	-	100	1
Midwife	-	-	-	-	-	100.0	100	1
Oil-presser, weaver, potter, water-carrier	-	-	-	-	100.0	-	100	4
Agricultural labourer	-	16.6	-	-	16.6	66.6	100	12
Watchman	-	-	-	-	100.0	-	100	1
Casual labourer	-	-	-	10.0	-	90.0	100	10
Cattle grazer	-	-	-	-	-	100.0	100	4
Scavenger	-	-	-	-	-	100.0	100	2
Unspecified	20.0	40.0	20.0	-	-	20.0	100	5
Total	16.7	18.3	3.3	3.3	13.3	45.0	100	60

The judges were able to classify all the household heads according to their prestige. As can be seen from Tables 7 and 8, the prestige of persons corresponds to a large extent with their occupational prestige. The correspondence, however, is found to a larger degree in Rampur than in Devigarh. Although occupational prestige is the major determinant of the prestige of a person, it is not the sole factor. Moreover, our occupational arrangement according to prestige is an arbitrary one. This may be borne in mind in explaining the discrepancies. For instance, the relatively low prestige of sharecroppers in Rampur may be due to the fact that their occupation has been placed by us at an unduly higher level in the occupational hierarchy. The relatively lower prestige of Naik in Devigarh may be due to the fact that he is a Ramdasia and hence his group status has depressed his individual status. On the other hand, the relatively higher status of one of the tailors in the same village, even though he is a Ramdasia, may be attributed to his leadership of his group. Such exceptions, therefore, can be satisfactorily explained.

Table 9

Caste status and prestige class in Devigarh

Name of caste	*Prestige class*							*Total %*	*Total no.*
	I	*II*	*III*	*IV*	*V*	*VI*	*No. inf.*		
Jat	17.6	5.9	26.5	35.3	8.8	2.9	2.9	100	34
Brahmin	100.0	-	-	-	-	-	-	100	1
Bania	33.3	33.3	-	33.3	-	-	-	100	3
Carpenter	-	-	-	60.0	20.0	20.0	-	100	5
Barber	-	-	-	-	100.0	-	-	100	1
Water-carrier	-	-	-	16.7	-	83.3	-	100	6
Teli (Oil-presser)	-	-	-	-	50.0	50.0	-	100	2
Drum-beater	-	-	-	-	-	-	-	-	-
Potter	-	-	-	-	-	100.0	-	100	1
Ramdasia	2.9	5.7	5.7	5.7	22.9	57.1	-	100	35
Total	10.2	5.7	12.5	21.6	15.9	33.0	1.2	100	88

Further, Tables 9 and 10 show the percentage distribution of the household heads according to hereditary group and prestige class. As indicated earlier, merely from examining the distribution of members in the various prestige classes, it is not possible to infer the degree of operation of the class system. On the whole, we find that in both the villages the distribution of the members in the prestige classes in each hereditary group is different from their distribution in the entire community. This is in conformity with our concept of caste system. But, by hypothesis, for the complete functioning of the caste system, the members in each caste must be entirely homogeneous with regard to their prestige. Since there is no complete homogeneity in both the villages, we may assume that the class system is in operation in the two villages, even though to a slight degree.

Table 10

Caste status and prestige class in Rampur

Name of caste	*Prestige class*						*Total %*	*Total no.*
	I	*II*	*III*	*IV*	*V*	*VI*		
Jat	52.9	35.3	-	-	-	11.8	100	17
Bania	20.0	60.0	20.0	-	-	-	100	5
Brahmin	-	100.0	-	-	-	-	100	2
Carpenter	-	-	33.3	33.3	33.3	-	100	3
Barber	-	-	-	-	-	-	-	-
Kahar (water-carrier)	-	-	-	100.0	-	100	4	
Teli (oil-presser)	-	-	-	-	100.0	-	100	2
Drum-beater	-	-	-	-	-	100.0	100	4
Ramdasia	-	-	-	4.5	4.5	91.0	100	21
Balmiki	-	-	-	-	-	100.0	100	2
Total	16.7	18.3	3.3	3.3	13.3	45.0	100	60

Again, a glance at the two tables would show that the homogeneity of social prestige of members in caste groups is greater in Rampur than in Devigarh. For instance, in the Jat and Ramdasia groups which are relatively the largest groups in both the villages, while the members in each group are distributed in all the prestige classes in Devigarh, they are distributed only in three classes each in Rampur. For the community as a whole the mean of the mean deviations of the distribution of prestige classes in the caste groups is 0.97 in Devigarh and 0.43 in Rampur. Consequently, we may say that the class system is functioning to a greater degree in Devigarh than in Rampur. If we refer to Tables 5 and 6, we find that the occupational distribution also is relatively more homogeneous in Rampur than in Devigarh. For instance, whereas in Devigarh the members among the Jats and the Ramdasias are distributed in eight occupations each, the members in the corresponding castes in Rampur are distributed only in six occupations each. We can obtain a crude measure of occupational heterogeneity for the community as a whole by obtaining the average number of occupational categories in which members in each caste are distributed. Castes represented by single households may be ignored. Accordingly, the average score for Devigarh is 4.2 and for Rampur 3. Therefore, the variation in the occupational prestige of members in caste groups is also associated with the variation in their individual prestige. This evidence, however, small, is in agreement with our hypothesis (g).

In the course of testing the various hypotheses, we have arrived at four different indices which measure the rigidity-fluidity dimension of social stratification. It has been shown that this dimension is ultimately dependent upon the pattern of distribution of the properties of members in hereditary groups. Insofar as occupation is an important property of the individual which is evaluated, the pattern of distribution of occupational prestige in hereditary groups may be regarded as the primary index of social stratification. This may be termed the index of *occupational heterogeneity.*

The other three indices may be regarded as indirect or secondary measures of social stratification. One of these is the degree of consensus in the grading of hereditary groups and may be termed the index of *consensus about caste status.* The second is the degree of heterogeneity of distribution of members in hereditary groups according to their individual prestige. We may name this index of *heterogeneity of individual prestige.* Finally, we have the measure represented by the degree of consensus in the grading of individuals by judges or the members themselves, which may be termed the index of *consensus about individual prestige.*

So far as the villages of Devigarh and Rampur are concerned all these four indices are consistently correlated with one another. In another paper[14], it has been shown that these indices are also intercorrelated in six different villages in India including the above two villages. Further, we have also demonstrated in that paper that the dimension of social stratification as measured by these indices is correlated with a number of other variables which are normally associated with social stratification testing thereby the validity of our concept that caste and class are the polar opposites of the rigidity-fluidity dimension of social stratification.

In conclusion, it is fairly obvious that the data presented support the conceptual interpretation of caste and class systems discussed above. However, for a conclusive evidence not only is it necessary to show that changes in the distribution of individual properties within hereditary groups bring about a change in the degree of unanimity in ranking the groups but also it is required to demonstrate that the sphere of influence of the hereditary groups in controlling social behaviour undergoes a change. The present evidence is not conclusive in this sense and more studies are needed for the purpose.

Notes

1. This is SSRC Journal Paper No. 14, I am grateful to Harold F. Kaufman and Robert C. Angell for their helpful comments, Social Science Research Center, Mississippi State University, Journal Paper No. 14. Data for this paper come from a study conducted cooperatively by the Department of Sociology, Panjab University and Social Science Research Center, Mississippi State University.
2. G.S. Ghurye, *Caste and Class in India* (Bombay: The Popular book Depot, 1950), p. 18.
3. R.M. MacIver and C.H. Page, *Society* (New York: Rinehart and Company, Inc.), pp. 348-58.
4. James M. Beshers, *Urban Social Structure* (New York: Free Press, 1962), p. 127.
5. Egon Ernest Bergel, *Social Stratification* (McGraw-Hill Book Co., Inc., 1962), p. 4.
6. Although this idea is not explicitly stated in any of the works which have come to our notice, it is implied in some of the studies on caste and class. E.G., Egon Ernest Bergel *op.cit.*, p. 4.
7. Egon Ernest Bergel, *op.cit.*, p. 8.
8. For a further explanation of these ideas, cf., Victor S. D'Souza, "Caste and Endogamy: A Reappraisal of the Concept of Caste", in the *Journal of the Anthropological Society of India* (Bombay, New Series, Vol. XI, No. 1, 1959), pp. 11-42.

9. How this may happen over a period of time has been clearly shown in F.G. Bailey, *The Caste and the Economic Frontier* (Oxford University Press, Oxford, 1958).
10. The validity of this technique has been demonstrated in the following well known studies: Harold Kaufman, *Prestige Class in a New York Rural Community* (Cornell University Agricultural Experiment Station, Memour 260, March 1944), and W. Lloyd Warner and Paul S. Lunt, *The Social Life of a Modern Community* (New Haven: Yale University Press, 1941).
11. The names of the two villages and the Tehsil are pseudonyms.
12. However, since the sample was interviewed twice, once for the social grading of hereditary groups and at another time for obtaining all the other information, the number of respondents in some tables does not exactly correspond and further in one of the investigations the members of the caste of Drum-beater in Devigarh were included in the caste of Water-carrier by oversight.
13. Victor S. D'Souza, "Social Grading of Village Occupations", in *Journal of the Gujarat Research Society* (Bombay, January/April, 1964), pp. 33-44.
14. Victor S. D'Souza, "Measurement of Rigidity-Fluidity Dimension of Social Stratification in Six Indian Villages", *Sociological Bulletin*, Vol. XVIII No. 1, March 1969.

9 Caste and Class in Assam

R.K. BHADRA

The study of caste stratification is influenced by functional theory and has generated a number of interrelated concepts. Quite often the caste system is interpreted as having "organic" relations among various castes. Such a conception has been derived from the reciprocal relationship of the *jajmani* system prevailing in the caste system. However, due to modernization of Indian society, "organic" relations have gradually been weakened in recent years. Today, although castes have become independent of each other, they have remained attached to traditional norms to a large extent. Such changes in caste stratification have been termed as "segmentation" (Bailey, 1963).

Beteille's view (1972: 15) is that the "harmonic" nature of the traditional caste society which existed in the "organic" system has been replaced by "disharmonic" relations under the emerging "segmental" system. He points out that the concept of "closed" social system is intertwined with "organic" and "harmonic" character of a traditional society. The closedness of caste stratification is also associated with the principles of "status summation" (Bailey, 1963; Beteille, 1966: 224-46). Therefore, the studies of the caste system reveal a one-sided picture of the system of stratification in India.

Substantive changes in the caste system, found in various parts of India, cannot be assumed to be changes from its "organic" character to "segmentary" character. The "organic" relations imply complete interdependence which was not always found in the traditional system.

"Segmentary" nature of relations show independence of caste groups interacting through competition. Existentially such relations cannot be found in caste society today. In reality, different castes which are hierarchically placed could not have had "harmonic" relations. Inter-caste relations, though governed by interdependence and reciprocity are largely exploitative in nature in which upper castes subordinate lower caste groups (Beidelman, 1959).

The notion of a "closed" traditional stratification system is, however, not correct. The closedness implied a static structure where summation of statuses, i.e., caste, class and power, are fixed without having mobility in any status of an individual or group. But mobility at the levels of individual and family was also found in traditional society through the acquisition of political and economic power. Numerous evidences of corporate mobility at the caste level and anti-caste movements were found in ancient and medieval India (Stein, 1968). Today, distinctions prevail at all levels: group, family and individual. Positions of a group, family and individual cannot be judged adequately by measuring status at either of these levels of mobility (Sharda, 1977). Analysis of composite status of families or units of mobility facilitates understanding of "incongruence", "segmentation" and "disharmony" as patterns of stratification. Thus, the system of stratification was both "closed" and "open" due to circumstantial and infrastructural factors. These contingent factors, however, have changed to a large extent resulting into lessening of certain inequalities. Certain new inequalities have emerged and some old inequalities have transformed into new ones. It is assumed that the stratification system did not change unilineally from "cumulative" to "dispersed" inequalities. Certain "dispersed" inequalities existed even earlier, and they might have become "cumulative" in course of time. Some of the earlier "cumulative" inequalities might have changed into new "cumulative" inequalities.

The Field of Study

In this paper, the above concepts have been examined in the context of Assamese society. The Assamese social structure consists of various castes and Hinduized tribes having two sets of norms within the same social system: norms related to caste hierarchy and norms related to tribal egalitarianism. There has been a synthesis of three religious traditions—the orthodox Hinduism (Saktaism), Vaisnava sectarianism and tribalism, these have affected differentially the stratification system of Assam. Such a situation combines "closedness" of castes and "openness" of tribes. Thus, the stratification system is different in regard to the composition of social structure and the criteria or norms of ranking of the groups and individuals compared to other regions of India. With a view to obtain a comprehensive picture of the system of stratification, three villages of upper Assam including a multi-caste village, a single-caste village and a tribal village were studied. The villages were inhabited by 333 households of both Assamese and non-Assamese people. The former comprised nine castes, a tribal group, and Muslims. The non-Assameses had seven tribal groups. The data were collected through interview, case study and observation methods. Historical records and published materials were also consulted. Heads of all the households were interviewed.

Caste, Class and Mobility in the Traditional Society

Caste system in the traditional society consisted of both castes and tribes, and social status of the latter groups was evaluated with the framework of the Hindu hierarchical system. In the hierarchical system, Brahmins enjoyed social superiority, but they were liberal in their outlook regarding occupations, social laws and commensal relations with other castes. Kshatriyas and Vaisyas were absent in Assam. Among the Sudras, the Kayasthas and the Kalitas were regarded as higher castes. Most of the Vaisnava preceptors belonged to the Kayastha caste and they were vastly learned people. They had achieved a socio-religious status equivalent to that of the Brahmins (Neog, 1958: 135). The Kalitas were agriculturists. The lower ranks among the Sudras were occupied by the Katanis, Kaibartas or Keots. The Katanis lived on spinning and agriculture while the Kaibartas were fishermen. Another caste known as Nadiyal or Dom also depended on fishing. The Haris were employed as sweepers by the Ahom kings.

In medieval Assam, a number of ruling tribes were converted into castes for higher social status in the hierarchy. The Koches were given a caste status in the sixteenth century. They subsequently absorbed many local tribes who accepted their methods of sanskritization. The Bodo-Kachari tribe was important among them. The Chutiyas, a hill tribe, was absorbed by the Ahoms. A progressive section of them came to be known as Hindu-Chutiyas by embracing Hinduism and they also enjoyed higher caste status even in the traditional society. The Ahoms—a Shan tribe, embraced Hinduism in the seventeenth century. The Kacharis were a Mongoloid tribe. The Rabhas, a Hinduized section of them, were ranked superior to the Kacharis. Miri, Mikir, and some other tribes also constituted an important section of the tribal social structure.

At the end of the fifteenth century, Sankardeva's Vaisnavite movement (1449-1569) brought considerable changes in the social structure by intensifying social mobility and changes in the caste system. Sankardeva institutionalized Vaisnavism in the form of *Satra* (temple organization) and *namghar* (temple). The spiritual bond and fellow-feelings fostered by these institutions considerably reduced caste rigidity. The Kala-Samhati, a sub-sect, preached more liberal ideology among the lower castes and tribes, and was able to place them in higher social status. Therefore, Weber's view regarding prevalence of social immobility and absolute inequality in traditional Hindu society is not correct. The caste system was already flexible and mobility was possible due to violation of norms of caste rigidity. The caste and tribes could improve their social status. A good number of instances of individual and corporate mobility are found in the traditional society. Therefore, fixidity of hereditary status was not a reality.

Sankardeva, a Sudra, was Kayastha by caste, he preached Vaisnava ideology during the first half of the sixteenth century. He became *Gosain* (religious preceptor) and succeeded in raising himself, his descendants and his Sudra followers to the status of highest spiritual and religious power equal to that of the Brahmins. Almost all the *satras* of the Kala-Samhati were headed by the Sudra *Gosains* and a good number of his Brahmin disciples became *Gosains* of the Brahma-Samhati, a sub-sect of *satras*. The Ahom rulers gave equal respect and social status to the Sakta and Vaishnava *Gosains* belonging to Brahmin and Sudra castes, whose status was further strengthened by the political relations with the kings. Such individual and family mobility was widespread in medieval Assam (Neog, 1958: 135).

Corporate mobility was also not uncommon in the traditional caste system. The Ahoms, a ruling tribe, embraced Vaisnavism and Saktaism during the seventeenth century. They rejected traditional cultural elements, prohibited food, language, Buddhist religion, etc., and assimilated themselves into Assamese society. Gradually, they were recognized as clean Hindus (Neog, 1958: 96, 206-14; Gogoi, 1971: 198-201). The Chutiyas, another ruling tribe, aspired for Hindu social status. A progressive section of them known as Hindu-Chutiyas considerably improved their social status by embracing Vaisnavism. They were regarded as a higher caste Sudra with whom Kalitas and Koches did not hesitate to interdine and intermarry (Barua, 1966: 179-83; Acharyya, 1966: 232-69; Sarma, 1966: 2). The Koches, a ruling tribe, embraced Hinduism in the sixteenth century and claimed themselves as Kshatriyas (Gait, 1967: 48-50; Barua, 1966: 191-92). Gradually, they had been accepted through inter-dining and inter-marriage by the Kalitas and were regarded as a higher caste. In the process of sanskritization they converted themselves into Vaisnavism, and adopted Assamese language, high caste customs, etc.

Medieval Assam was ruled by various tribal kings of whom the Ahoms were most powerful. During 1228 A.D. to 1833 A.D., the Ahoms extended their supremacy all over Assam and consolidated feudalism along with its class structure. In 1881, half of the indigenous population consisted of non-Hindu and Hindu tribals who still practised shifting cultivation. The tribal economy of shifting cultivation was based on egalitarian principles where inequalities did not exist. Only the Ahoms practised settled cultivation. Gradually, several tribal kingdoms were brought under the direct rule of the Ahoms where settled cultivation with its land tenure system was introduced.

Members of the royal lineage and the nobles owned large number of *khats* (estates) which were cultivated by the *Paiks* (common people belonging to lower castes and tribes) who offered services to *khats* free of wages. The nobles and high officials of the administration were mainly employed from seven Ahom clans (Barua, 1958: 52-53). Field-serfs and slaves were also commonly employed for cultivation (Acharyya, 1966: 111; Guha, 1967: 142). The Brahmin and Kayastha priests and Vaisnava *Gosains* were granted such estates by the kings. The Ahoms, Brahmins and Kayasthas constituted the upper class. The rest of the population of the country belonged to a group commonly known as *Karni-Paiks* who constituted the lower class. They were liable to render services as soldiers and labourers for the upper class and in return they used to get 2.66 acres of land free of rent. They were mainly from lower castes and tribal groups. About 30 per cent of them were attached to the nobles' estates as *Lickchous* (servants) whose status was similar to that of the slaves. The *Paiks* with specialized skill were known as *Chamua-Paiks* who offered non-manual services and were superior to the *Karni-Paiks*. The *Apaikan-Chamuas* belonged to the high castes who were entrusted with offices. Slaves were inferior to the *Karni-Paiks* and were divided into *Bandibeti* (domestic slave) and *Bahatia* (farm slave). During 1751-69, about 9 per cent of all the people were slaves and bondsmen (Guha, 1966: 232-33).

The Emerging Patterns of Caste and Class

Dynamism in caste and class relations has gained momentum during the post-independence period. Due to modernization, the traditional social structure has undergone considerable change. The feudal structure of the society has begun to decline and the caste system has been continuing in spite of some remarkable changes. The emergence of a new stratification system has been studied in three villages—a multi-caste, a single caste village, and a tribal village. The basic point in regard to the three villages is to examine how the caste and tribal groups shape social relations within their own community and with each other. The distinction between the villages on the basis of caste or tribe and economy is very thin and vague. In fact, distinction between caste and tribe itself is not very clear. Only Brahmins, Kayasthas and Kalitas can be clearly distinguished from each other and also from other groups, namely, the Ahoms and the Hinduized-tribes. In view of such a situation, our main emphasis is on a comparative analysis of the nature of social composition of the three villages. Multiplicity of groups, Hinduization of tribes, and the presence of non-Assamese people are three bases of the present study. By and large, in regard to class and power structure, similarities between tribes and castes are more than their differences. As the tribes today practise settled agriculture, they are also divided into several classes. Process of politicization also affects the tribal political institution in a similar way. In view of such a situation, emphasis is given on the nature of control and distribution of economic resources as well as distribution of power among different castes and tribes.

The Caste Structure

Caste system is characterized by its exclusiveness, inclusiveness and hierarchical relations between various groups on the one hand and the system has some other features such as endogamy, commensality, purity-pollution, hereditary specialization of occupation, cultural differences and domination of power based on hereditary principles, on the other. We have examined how and to what extent these features operate in determining relations between groups and individuals in Assamese society.

Brahmins occupy the highest position in the hierarchy and are divided into two groups—the Vaisnavities and the Saktas. The former are also sub-divided on the basis of Vaisnava sectarian affiliation. During the last few decades, they have been attracted by modern education and occupations although they mainly depend on agriculture. They practise endogamy but their socio-religious life bears some social significance which has considerably reduced social distance between them and other castes and tribes.

Kayasthas occupy a position next to Brahmins, and with the latter they constitute the upper caste group. They are *Gosains* and are religious heads of the devotees belonging to various tribes and castes including

Brahmins. Although they are Sudras, their ritual status is superior to that of Brahmins. The *Gosains* are required to take services of the Brahmin priests in marriage and death rituals while the latter are required to undergo initiation into Vaisnavism under the former.

The Kayasthas are an endogamous group, but they have hypergamous relations with the Kalitas. The practice of concubinage with women of lower castes is not uncommon among them. However, their children are not accorded the status of their father's caste.

The next position is occupied by the Kalitas. They, along with Koches, Chutiyas, Keots, Katanis and Ahoms, constitute the *intermediate caste category*. They have 'mixed' with various other castes and have lost in the process their traditional caste status. They are predominantly agriculturists, but today many of them have taken up modern occupations. The Kalitas practise endogamy, but exogamy is also not uncommon. They have marital relations with Kayasthas, Koches and Chutiyas. Marriage with Ahoms is not uncommon.

The Koches occupy a position just below the Kalitas. They were originally a tribe but have transformed themselves into a caste. They are agriculturists. Koches are basically endogamous, but today their marriages with Kayasthas, Kalitas, Keots and Chutiyas have become a common feature. Katnis and Ahoms, though not frequently, are also accepted by them for marriage.

The Chutiyas, originally a tribe, come next in the hierarchy. They generally practise endogamy, but have exogamous relations with Kalitas, Koches, Keots and Katanis. The Ahom-Chutiyas have marital alliances with the Ahoms. They cremate dead bodies, and practise widow re-marriage. They observe Vedic rites and rituals in marriage and death ceremonies in which Brahmin priest presides. Occasionally, marriages between Chutiyas and Kacharis also occur.

The Keots occupy position below the Koches. Their status is somewhat ambiguous as they feel superior to the Chutiyas. They have two sub-groups—Halowa-Keots and Jalowa-Keots. The former is agriculturist and enjoys superior position by practising exogamy with some higher castes, such as Koches. Exogamous relations with Ahoms are also socially accepted. The Jalowa-Keots have marriage alliance with Kaibartas—a fishing caste.

Next to the Keots, there are Katanis who are agriculturists. About twenty years ago, they left their traditional occupation of spinning and weaving and considerably improved their social status. Occasionally, they enter into marital relations with Chutiyas, Keots and Ahoms.

The position of the Ahoms, formerly a ruling tribe, is next to the Katanis. They think themselves superior to other castes except the Brahmins. They never practise endogamy in the true sense. During the last twenty years, they have been practising exogamy with Kalitas, Koches, Keots, Chutiyas and Katanis. Marriage with the Kacharis is also accepted. Still they have retained many of their traditional customs like the practice of widow re-marriage, levirate, burial of dead bodies, etc. Their socio-religious life represents a mixture of both tribalism and Vaisnavism. They never accept services of a Brahmin priest. These factors have, however, created an ambiguity in identifying their rank in the caste hierarchy.

The Kacharis, a scheduled tribe, are ranked next to the Ahoms, but above the Kaibartas. The Sonowal-Kacharis, a Vaisnavite section, think themselves as clean Sudras. They regard themselves as inferior to the Brahmins, Kayasthas, Kalitas and Koches, but superior to the Keots, Katanis, Ahoms and Kaibartas. Today, they have left gold-washing and have become peasants. They are an endogamous group, but exogamy is not uncommon among them. With the process of Vaisnavization they have been losing tribal characteristics. Their culture is a mixture of both Hindu and tribal cultural elements. Therefore, their status is ambiguous.

The traditional calling of the Kaibartas is fishing, but today a majority of them are agriculturists. They are an endogamous group and can accept members of any caste as affinal kin. It indicates their lowest social status. The Brahmins who serve them have lower status than their counterparts who serve the higher status groups because of the Kaibarta's lowest social status.

The non-Assamese communities consist of various tribes and a few lower castes whose forefathers migrated to Assam as tea plantation labourers from Bihar, Orissa and Madhya Pradesh during the British period. Their present generation includes agriculturists or ordinary labourers. They have lost many of their traditional customs, but have still retained their dialect and animistic religion. Culturally, they are distinct from the indigenous people and are called "collies" by the Assamese people. Though commensal and marital rules suggest prevalence of endogamy in theory but in practice dominance of inter-community marriage is found. A combination of rigidity and flexibility dimensions of societal norms can be seen through the rules of marriage. The Kayasthas have normal marriages with the Kalitas and Koches. In Dumont's (1970: 118) words, it coincides with the "optional hypergamy". But the Kalitas and Koches generally avoid marrying daughters of Kayasthas as the latter are their *Gosains*. Considerable flexibility is found in marital relations among the castes occupying middle position. The Kalitas, Koches and Chutiyas practise inter-caste marriages. The Koches, Chutiyas, Keots and Katanis also have marital relations with each other. Under such a situation how these caste groups maintain exclusiveness and separateness? This leads to the discussion on commensal behaviour. In the case of hypergamy, a woman is raised to her husband's caste-status, and she stops commensal relations with the caste of her parents. Members of her husband's caste accept food from her, and children born out of such union enjoy the status of their paternal caste.

The rules of commensality are not very important in the society. Only among the upper and lower caste groups commensal norms are observed regularly. The intermediate castes frequently violate such norms and do not strictly observe commensal restrictions. Such a wide range of commensal relations do not permit any sharp commensal hierarchy as well as hierarchy of relative exclusiveness of caste groups. This is not fully in tune with Dumont's (1970:43) view that in commensal hierarchy, exlusiveness is the organizing principle. He refers to "groups who are in the process of transition from tribe to untouchable caste". But in Assam, those tribes who have transformed themselves into castes have always enjoyed considerably superior status among the Sudras.

Some of the intermediate castes, namely, Koches, Chutiyas, Keots and Ahoms have gradually been able to change their status from tribes to castes. Today, they are regarded as clean castes. This fact contrasts with Dumont's view of inclusion of foreign groups into a territorial set of castes.

The wide range of commensal and connubial relations practised by these groups reflect the presence of egalitarian principle among tribes, and the concept of purity-pollution of the caste system has affected the tribal groups. Their affiliation to the Vaisnavite sub-sects has made them liberal as well as strict in their outlook regarding norms of caste hierarchy and inter-caste relations in a similar way. In this way, they are integrated into the caste society and maintain separateness at the same time. Therefore, exclusiveness is not the most distinctive feature of caste society as it is mentioned by Dumont. Moreover, Dumont's (1957: 7-22) thesis has always kept the Indian tribes outside the main sphere of his interest as if they are not part of the Hindu social structure. Therefore, it would be misleading if one places the tribes outside the caste system.

The Class Structure

Since we are investigating the rural class structure, our main emphasis is on the agrarian class relations. Agriculture is the primary occupation of the villagers and it is associated with service, trade and wage labour. The mode of agricultural production is not yet mechanized as simple iron-blade plough, sickle and bullock are used by the villagers. Only one big landowner has recently purchased a tractor. The villagers grow summer paddy extensively and approximately 840 kg of paddy is grown per acre. The winter paddy is cultivated by a very few peasants, although it provides better yield, i.e., approximately 1400 kg per acre. Cultivation of areca nut and betel leaf is done by every household. No other crop is cultivated.

The agrarian mode of production involves three classes of people, namely, landowner, sharecropper and agricultural labourer, and they are not exclusive ones. These classes are further divided into 14 sub-classes on the basis of economic diversification, and they bear considerable social significance. There are also five absentee landowners. Two families, one Brahmin and one Kayastha depend upon priestly occupation. They do not have any land, and are, therefore, excluded from the agrarian structure (Table 1).

Table 1
Class and landholding

Class	*No. of household*	*No. of landless households*	*Average landholding (in acres)*
Landowner	129 (38.73 %)	0	6.07
Sharecropper	70 (21.4 %)	2	1.5
Agricultural labour	132 (39.63 %)	42	7

The absentee landowners have an average of 206 acres of land. They belong to both the upper and the lower caste groups. The 129 (38.73%) resident landowners have land as their primary source of income and livelihood but some of them also have income from subsidiary sources. Service, trade, priesthood, etc. are such subsidiary occupations. The non-cultivating landowners are very few. It is mainly the supervisory landowners who have other sources of income. Their average landholding is much bigger than that of other landowners. However, families having a small amount of land also belong to this category. The average landholding of the landowners is 6.07 acres per family. The largest landholding is found among the Ahoms. They have become supervisory landowners, particularly due to their high caste position, modern education and professional status. Socially and culturally, they are diversified. This diversification explains some degree of incongruence between caste and class. Generally, they do not have interest in expanding agricultural production. The supervisory owners generally get their land cultivated by agricultural labourers. But today some of them do not hesitate to participate in agricultural operations.

The small landowners mainly depend upon family labour. Those who are well-off, employ agricultural labourers to cultivate their land. Thus, there is a tendency for labour employment. Hence, a clash of interests with the labour force remains a potent possibility. Such a situation explains differentiation within a given class because the families belonging to this class do not have equal control over land and resources. A lack of a certain degree of class homogeneity does not permit emergence of a uniform pattern of class relations and class consciousness. The condition of the marginal landowners, living on bare subsistence, is not better than that of sharecroppers and agricultural labourers. Generally, they are found to be competing with sharecroppers for getting sharecropping contract. Therefore, absence of sharp class differences as well as consequent overlapping of economic interests discourage emergence of class consciousness.

In general, the landowning class is not an exclusive one as both the upper and middle castes and tribes belonging to this class (see Table 2). Members of this class spend their surplus on personal consumption, and do not invest in productive purposes. The agricultural production is limited and localized. Very few of them are interested in profit-making investments in land, modern agricultural technology, etc. Thus, the agrarian economy in Assam largely remains 'primitive' and feudal.

As many as 21.14 per cent of the households primarily depend upon earnings from sharecropping and have 1.5 acres of land on an average (see Table 1). However, a few of them have secondary sources of income such as service and trade. These households are economically better off than others. They have a considerable amount of land and employ labourers when they do not get a contract or cannot accept a contract due to paucity of cattle or exorbitant land-rent. This situation refers to differentiation within a given class. As land becomes scarce most of the households compete with one another to get a contract which ultimately keeps them divided. They are also distributed among various intermediate castes and tribes (see Table 2). Therefore, the sharecroppers do not constitute any concrete class.

Table 2

Caste/tribe and agrarian classes

Caste/Tribe	*No. of households of (landowners)*		*No. of households (sharecropper)*		*No. of households of (agricultural labourers)*	
Brahmin	5	(83.3)	-	-	-	-
Kayastha	4	(80.3)	-	-	-	-
Kalita	11	(47.8)	6	(26.0)	6	(26.0)
Koch	6	(40.0)	4	(26.6)	5	(23.3)
Keot	1	(25.0)	3	(75.0)	-	-
Katani	4	(50.0)	1	(12.5)	3	(37.5)
Chutiya	9	(75.0)	-	-	3	(25.0)
Ahom	39	(47.6)	14	(17.07)	29	(35.4)
Kaibarta	1	(2.5)	1	(2.5)	37	(94.8)
Kachari	49	(45.4)	40	(35.4)	24	(21.3)
Non-Assamese Communities	-	-	1	(4.3)	22	(95.7)
Muslim	-	-	-	-	3	(100.0)
Total	129	(38.73)	70	(21.14)	132	(39.63)

Figures in brackets indicate percentages.

A sharecropper's status was, in earlier times, similar to that of a wage labourer. However, as a result of the Adhiar Protection and Regulation Act of 1948 and the Assam Temporary Tenancy Acts of 1935 and 1971, their interests have been safeguarded to a certain extent. Today, though the landowners continue to harass their sharecroppers, yet the latter have been able to bring about some changes in the terms and conditions of the contracts to protect their interests.

A majority of the agricultural labourers (39.63%) are from among the lower castes and non-Assamese communities; a few are also from some intermediate castes and tribes (see Tables 1 and 2). Agricultural labourers are also a heterogeneous group due to diversities in their economic interests, as some of them accept sharecropping contracts and engage in petty trade. A few of them are basically marginal cultivators. Their women also work as daily wage earners. The peasants from among this category are found competing among themselves as well as with the sharecroppers for sharecropping contracts.

The agricultural labourers remain oppressed as they depend upon the landowners for their livelihood. Almost all of them borrow paddy from the well-to-do cultivators during July to November when price of paddy becomes comparatively higher. Payment of a loan is made in paddy or in cash or by working on the lender's land. Interest is charged on such loans, although it may appear that no interest is accepted. About half of the earnings of the harvesting season is spent on clearing their previous loan. They remain bonded to the landowners as tenurial labourers since they earn less wages than the current market rates. The system of paddy-lending and paying back loans by working on the lender's land, is contrary to the capitalist relations of production. The system helps in the continuation of the unfree labour in agriculture, a yardstick of feudal relations.

The Power Structure

Since the traditional power structure has changed, a new one has emerged. Today, power does not always go with ascriptive status. It largely depends on a variety of factors, such as economic standing, numerical strength, modern education, lucrative occupation, and contact with the government functionaries and political parties.

Our study of the *gaon-panchayat* reveals the caste and class background of the leaders and the shift of power from one caste to another. The intermediate and lower caste groups have emerged stronger in the new power structure. The upper castes have considerably lost their power in the new situation. The Kayasthas, who traditionally held power and authority, are no more powerful today. About twenty years ago, Kayastha *Gosains* held offices in the *panchayat*. Today, the multi-caste village is dominated by the intermediate caste groups, namely, Kalitas, Koches, Chutiyas and Ahoms. It has been possible because they identity themselves as a single caste group by having commensal and connubial relations as a single entity. The Kayasthas, an upper caste, try to avoid participation in the *panchayat*. However, in spite of numerical dominance, the Kaibartas, a lower caste, do not exercise influence because of their down-trodden position. Due to the reservation of a seat for the scheduled castes, a nominated member is in the *panchayat*.

Most of the well-to-do cultivators have monopolized power, whereas the agricultural labourers have not been able to acquire power. However, it is observed that marginal cultivators, sharecroppers and agricultural labourers have acquired some amount of power. In this respect, power in the multi-caste village is somewhat diffused. Today, at least a few leaders are widely recognized irrespective of their caste and class background. In the single-caste village, the Ahoms, an intermediate caste, enjoy power in the *panchayat*. The Ahom landowners, sharecroppers and agricultural labourers represent themselves more or less equally in the village *panchayat*. Since this village is part of the scheduled tribe constituency, the Ahoms cannot represent themselves in the *panchayat*. The tribal village in our study is also included in this constituency and therefore the Kacharis, a tribe, enjoys the privilege of sending their representatives to the *panchayat*. Although a few Brahmins live in this village, they do not participate in the *panchayat*. However, the *panchayat* leaders of this village are mainly sharecroppers and landowners. Therefore, instead of high caste and class background, the family background, education, personal qualities, and contacts with the influential leaders have helped them in securing a position of power.

Political parties and the village leaders provide a much wider distribution of power as they cover a large number of neighbouring villages. The Ujani Assam Rajya Parishad has considerably influenced the people of the region by giving a premium to ethnic and cultural interests of the people. However, the Congress and the Communist Party of India are the most popular political parties. The Communist Party of India, in particular, is gaining popularity among the marginal cultivators and landless people. However, the village factions and cleavages can be seen as a consequence of the competition for power, although most of the villagers have vague perceptions about the party ideologies.

In the multi-caste village, although caste roots are not so strong, affiliations to political parties are more on the line of caste and community rather than ideology or interests of the parties or of the groups themselves. However, the situation has been changing rapidly. A highly dynamic distribution of political power is found in the single-caste and tribal villages as the people here are more politicized. In the single-caste and tribal villages, political power is distributed among Ahoms and Kacharis, respectively. Political power is not determined by caste or tribe and other primordial factors. It is mainly determined by a combination of factors, such as landholding, economic position, education, occupation, social work and contacts with block and district level leaders. Therefore, political power has shifted from the traditional elites to the modern ones of various castes and tribes. Political power in the three villages is controlled to a large extent by the intermediate castes and tribal groups irrespective of their class position. The upper castes generally keep themselves away from the local politics while the lower caste people are still unable to enhance their political power in the changing situation due to their very low socio-economic standing.

In the traditional village community, religious functionaries of the *mel* (caste assembly) and *namghar* (Vaisnavite temple) were important as these two institutions informally functioned as instruments of social control. They still retain their influence in certain aspects. The religious functionaries of the *namghar* hold positions of authority, legitimation of which is based on Vaisnava tradition, while the *mel* leaders do not have any authority as such. However, today their functions are curtailed to a certain extent due to the emergence of modern forces of power. The village headman (appointed by the government) and *panchayat* leaders, educated persons, government officers, and political functionaries comprise the pool of influential persons who quite often take part in the *mel*. Thus, the *mel* has lost its traditional features and has become formal to a certain extent due to the participation of village headman and *panchayat* leaders. The study of *mel* and *namghar* provides insight into the relationships between village social structure and the distribution of power.

The traditional leaders, who dominate in the three villages are mainly from the intermediate castes. The lower castes, namely, Kaibartas, in spite of their numerical preponderance, remain subordinate to other leaders, due to their low socio-economic status. Usually, the higher castes avoid participation in village affairs. The new leaders of the *mel*, who derive strength from modern education, landholding, political patronage, personal qualities, etc., are also drawn from the intermediate castes. The traditional leaders who still exert power are more or less equally represented from all the classes. The traditional and modern leaders who are functioning side by side today are not often poles apart to each other.

Discussion

Castes, tribes and Vaisnava sects together constituted the Assamese social structure. The three traditions (namely, orthodox Hinduism, Vaishnava sectarianism and tribalism) co-existed, giving the caste system a unique form where rigidity, flexibility and egalitarianism could be found side by side. In Assam, the caste system was not so elaborate and society was overwhelmingly agrarian. There was hardly any occupation which was hereditarily monopolized by any caste. Rigidity, ritualism and purity-pollution which were the main features of the caste system were reduced in significance considerably due to the equalitarian ideology of Vaisnavism. The Vaisnavite movement opened up new avenues for social status. There was individual and corporate mobility in the society. A number of tribes transformed themselves into Hindu castes.

Weber (1958) conceived Hindu society as static where absolute inequality existed. Religious ritualism was the strongest principle of social conservatism, and change in any aspect of the society was possible only by reducing this ritualism. Such a view is misleading as no such absolute inequality existed earlier as there was mobility in the caste system, and co-existence of caste and tribe always encouraged flexibility and consequent mobility in the system. In fact, absolute inequality in Hindu society was never accepted by lower castes, classes and tribal people because of inherent contradictions in the Indian society (Davis, 1951: 170-171). In the traditional Assam, contradictions were within the "base" of the society, i.e., between primitive and feudal economic values. Superstructural contradictions were found at the ideological level of orthodox Hinduism, Vaisnava sectarianism and tribalism. Due to such contradictions, avenues for social mobility were available to lower castes and tribes. The hereditary higher status of upper castes was challenged, and this made mobility possible and acceptable. The notion of "harmonic" social system is not a useful concept, and inequality was not at all considered "legitimate", Beteille (1972: 15) is thus not right in considering in equality as a legitimate. Beteille (1972:15) is thus not right in considering inequality as a legitimate aspect of society.

Though, membership in a caste was determined by birth, but endogamy was not a rigid norm for maintaining exclusiveness of the groups. Hereditary specialization of occupations on the caste line was not a conspicuous feature. The concept of purity and pollution related to various occupations as well as hierarchy was not strongly entrenched into the traditional society. The "organic" linkages and relations, involving a group of castes, did not develop in Assam. The caste system reflected a "segmental" feature rather than an "organic" one. However, all groups maintained their exclusiveness and cultural identity in spite of flexibility in the norms of purity-pollution and hereditary occupations. In the traditional Assam, the system of stratification was relatively less "closed", and it was "open" to some extent. Due to the nature of the Assamese society, social mobility at the level of individual and family occurred in economic and political spheres. "Incongruities" existed between caste, class and power. Thus, the notion of "status summation" cannot be accepted as a frame of reference for analyzing changes in the traditional stratification system.

Class formation started with the transformation of the primitive mode of production to the feudal one but the tribal society had a quasi-feudal structure. However, the slave and serfs were negligible in the society. The royal and noble families and the upper castes constituted the dominant class who owned large estates. The *Paiks* had serfs who belonged to the lower castes and tribes and cultivated their estates. Debt-slavery was not an uncommon phenomenon. Therefore, caste ranking did not represent a corresponding hierarchy of economic relations. The upper caste and class people and also tribals had exploitative relations with the lower castes and classes.

The tribal rulers and their nobles controlled the political power in the state. Some junior administrative officers were recruited from some lower castes and tribes, but the upper castes did not enjoy such political power. Therefore, caste and power did not have a direct relationship. There were predominantly single-caste and single-tribe villages. Thus, dominance of upper castes over lower castes and tribes within the village was not a feature of the rural power structure. The lower officers of the Ahom administration or the dominant individuals of any caste or tribe usually were found to wield power in the villages.

Therefore, incongruous relationships between caste, tribe and class, and between caste, tribe and power existed in the traditional society. There were no "cumulative inequalities" or "status summation" in the traditional stratification system, rather "dispersed inequalities" characterized the system. In recent years, the system of stratification has changed to a considerable extent and it seems to have emerged through a dialectical process. Today castes have become relatively less particular about their ritual status. The principle of endogamy does not appear as an important criterion in maintaining exclusiveness of caste groups except in the case of the castes who occupy the highest and the lowest ranks in the hierarchy. Prevalence of hypergamous marriages in the society shows considerable flexibility in the marital principles. Therefore, combination of rigidity and flexibility dimensions characterizes the Assamese society.

The norm of commensality pervades over the entire social life of the people. However, the principle of commensality is not found as the important basis of distinction between caste groups on which hierarchy can perpetuate. Except for the upper and the lower castes, norms of commensality are not rigidly adhered to by other caste groups. Thus, in the commensal hierarchy, exclusiveness is not the organizing principle as thought of by Dumont (1970: 43).

Most of the occupations are not followed by the people on hereditary basis. Because the purity-pollution syndrome is not always attached to occupations, castes and occupations. Priesthood is not recognized as the highest occupation in Assam. Vaisnavism does not recognize the priestly services of the Brahmin, it advocates the ideology of equalitarianism. Almost all the castes and tribes including the upper castes are engaged in agriculture. Dumont (1970: 82, 107, 153) thinks that specialization of occupations entails separation between castes, and this is oriented towards the fulfilment of the needs of the people. While explaining the *jajmani* system, he mentions that it is an overall interdependence of caste groups on the basis of the division of labour which is encompassed by religious ideology. But in Assam such an approach is not applicable because separation of the caste groups in terms of specialization of occupations as well as consequent hierarchy does not exist as almost all the castes are involved in agriculture and allied occupations which are not embodied with the concept of purity-pollution. Thus, occupational specialization of castes does not have any meaning in Assamese society. Due to the non-existence of occupational specialization, the system of reciprocity of services did not develop.

Where rules of endogamy, principle of commensality, and specialization of occupations show considerable flexibility, caste hierarchy appears to be diluted to a certain extent. However, birth remains the only criterion by which a person's caste status is identified.

Both caste and tribe are an integral part of the hierarchical structure of the society. The commensal and marital norms practised by caste and tribal groups indicate the impact of equalitarian principle cherished by Assamese tribes. The rigidity of the caste system has also been affected by Vaisnavism. Thus, the Assamese hierarchical system is characterized by "closedness" and "openness" of the caste and tribal societies, respectively. Under such a situation the intermediate caste groups have reduced their exclusiveness while others, particularly those who occupy the highest and lowest social positions, have been able to maintain their separate identities. A caste may be accepted and absorbed by another caste group. Therefore, exclusiveness is not the most distinctive feature of caste society as it is viewed by Dumont (1970: 193). The tribes who have transformed themselves into castes are regarded as clean Sudras, and not the untouchable castes. This also contradicts Dumont's (1970: 193) view. Tribes seem to be an integral part of the Hindu caste system. Otherwise transformation of tribes into castes and their inclusion into the caste system would not have been possible. All these trends indicate mobility in the caste system.

The agrarian structure in Assam comprises three classes of people: the landowner, the sharecropper and the agricultural labourer. The upper and the intermediate castes and tribes are generally landowners. The sharecroppers are from the lower intermediate castes and tribes, while the non-Assamese and lower castes are overwhelmingly agricultural labourers. These features refer to the incongruous relations between caste and class. Classes overlap with each other, and a lack of homogeneity does not permit emergence of uniform class relations and class consciousness. Class antagonism which emerges under certain conditions is effectively dissolved due to the loyalties based on kin, caste, tribe and Vaisnavism. The agrarian structure of Assam today shows many features of feudalism, and therefore, it appears that there is no fundamental change in the economy despite a breakdown of feudal system and emergence of capitalist farming.

Today, caste and class do not coincide with power to a large extent as power is far more widely distributed among various castes and tribes than what it was before. The intermediate castes who are landowners, sharecroppers and agricultural labourers wield considerable power. In the emerging situation power is also enjoyed by the scheduled castes and the scheduled tribes. However, economic resource ownership, to a certain extent, still remains an important factor facilitating acquisition of power and prestige as the landless labourers have not yet been able to acquire considerable power. Power is, therefore, independent of caste and class.

The traditional elites have been affected by the widening of the social bases of power distribution. Some traditional elites have acquired positions of power in the new structure. The new sources of power, such as modern education, occupation, and contacts with influential political leaders have become important factors for acquiring power in the village community. Achievement is more important than ascription for acquiring power. Thus, there are "dominant individuals" rather than "dominant castes". It appears that the traditional stratification did not always have "congruence" or "cummulation" of statuses. Incongruence between various aspects of stratification was an accepted norm. Therefore, inequalities were dispersed among the various groups of people. The system was not undifferentiated. The changes that are found today are not from "cumulative inequalities" to "dispersed inequalities" as perceived by Beteille (1974:

69-73). These changes are also not from "organic" to "segmentary" nature of society as observed by Bailey (1963). The "segmentary" nature indicates complete independence of various parts which is not true for Assam. Today, there is more dynamism in regard to caste and class than before. Therefore, divergence is more noticeable between hierarchy of caste and class stratification. The change in the stratification system is, therefore, from one form of "dispersed inequalities" to another form of "dispersed inequalities".

References

Acharyya, N.N., 1966, *The History of Medieval Assam* (12th of 16th Century), Gauhati: Datta Barua and Company.

Bailey, F.G., 1963, "Closed Social Stratification in India", *European Journal of Sociology*, Vol. IV, No. 1.

Barua, A.C., 1958, *Bhumi Aru Jiban (in Assamese)*, Gauhati: Ratnaprakash.

Barua, K.L., 1966, *Early History of Kamrup (from the earliest times to the end of the sixteenth century)*, Gauhati: Lawyer's Book Stall.

Beidelman, T.O., 1959, *A Comparative Analysis of the Jajmani System*, N.Y.: Locust Valley.

Beteille, A., 1966, "Closed and Open Social Stratification in India", *European Journal of Sociology*, Vol. VI, No. 2.

—, 1972, *Inequality and Social Change*, Delhi: Oxford University Press.

—, 1974, *Studies in Agrarian Social Structure*, Delhi: Oxford University Press.

Davis, K., 1951, *The Population of India and Pakistan*, Princeton: Princeton University Press.

Dumont, L., 1970, *Homo Hierarchicus*, Delhi: Vikas Publications.

—, 1957, "For A Sociology of India", *Contributions to Indian Sociology*, No. 1.

Gait, E., 1967, *A History of Assam*, Calcutta: Tacker Spink and Company. (Earlier it was published in 1933).

Gogoi, L., 1977, *Tai Sanskriti Ruparekha (in Assamese)*, Calcutta: Sribhumi Publishing Company.

Guha, A., 1966, "Land Rights and Social Classes in Medieval Assam", *Indian Economic and Social History Review*, Vol. II, No. 3.

Guha, A., 1967, "Ahom Migration: Its Impact on Rice Economy of Medieval Assam", *Artha Vijanana*, Vol. 9, No. 2.

Neog, M., 1958, *Shri Shri Sankardev (in Assamese)*, Gauhati: Lawyer's Book Stall.

Sarma, S.N., 1966, *The Neo-Vaisnavite Movement and the Satra Institution of Assam*, Gauhati University: Department of Publications.

Sharda, B.D., 1977, *Status Attainment in Rural India*, Delhi: Ajanta Publications.

Stein, B., 1968, "Social Mobility and Medieval Indian Hindu Sect", J. Silverberg (ed.), *Social Mobility in the Caste System in India*, The Hague: Mouton Publishers.

Weber, M., 1958, *The Religion of India*, H.H. Gerth and Don Martindale (trans. and eds.), The Free Press of Glencoe.

10 Transformation of Class Structure in Contemporary Rural India

PRADIP KUMAR BOSE

Problems of Transition

A correct understanding of the transformation of class structure in contemporary India is dependent on the resolution of two theoretical problems: the capital labour relation and the conceptualization of classes. For the class structure of any society, a transition from one formation to another signifies the collapse of old classes and the birth of new ones; in other words, this period simultaneously involves the process of class decomposition, class transformation and class formation. In recent years, the literature on peasants in complex societies has dealt extensively with the nature of the articulation of capitalist with non-capitalist modes of production. Most authors[1] seem to agree that capitalist expansion and its penetration in the rural areas of the third world has not been universally successful, nor even smooth and irreversible but rather a convergence of contradictory forces. Complex forms of articulation involving both persistence and destruction reflect a continuous dialectic between capitalism and the previous social formation: class formation, class disintegration and class conflict are important elements in this process. They will be shaped both by the changes brought about by capitalism and by the specific dynamics of the pre-existing social formations.

The classical conception of the agrarian class structure implies increasing polarization where the petty commodity producer will tend to disappear, a capitalist relation of production will develop involving an agrarian bourgeois and a rural proletariat. This notion posits a class of capitalist farmers who will run their big estates with machinery and capital intensive methods of production and employ landless labourers. The polarization of the rural class structure will arise via differentiation of the peasantry. This argument on the characterization of petty commodity production as a 'transitional' stage of development and petty commodity producers as a 'transitional' class followed from the analysis of the tendency towards class differentiation within this stratum. Since petty commodity production is defined in terms of the unity of labour and capital in contrast to capitalist production which is predicated on the separation of labour and capital, eventual class polarization is assumed in capitalist agriculture. However, contemporary India presents a much more complex picture and warrants a more ingenious analysis of the transformation of class structure. The view that petty commodity production was structurally unstable due to its inherent tendency towards class differentiation is shared by many, however there are others who would argue that family-labour farms have persisted in the countryside and there are limitations to the generalization of capitalist relations of production in agriculture. Without entering into this debate, we can point out that like in other Third World countries Indian evidence also suggests the partial and incomplete nature of 'agrarian transition', that is, in terms of the real subsumption of labour by capital, and the formation of a rural capitalist class and a rural proletariat of wage labourers completely separated from the means of production.

However, there are other models like the Frank-Wallerstein's[2] conceptualization of capitalism. This model rejects the 'classical model' of agrarian transition wherein the process of internal class differentiation of pre-capitalist agriculture brings into being rural wage workers and capitalist farmers. The decisive criterion in this case is the exchange relations that pertain in the world economy. Their main concern is with relations of surplus appropriation *between* economic systems. Here, wage labour, sharecropping and tenancy become alternative modes best suited for a particular type of production as capitalism is defined only on the basis of exchange relations. But the problem with this type of analysis is that it neglects the effects of the development of commodity relations at the level of production and fails to demonstrate how an insertion into the capitalist world economy transforms the societies and determines the emergence of new class structure. Others bring out the important distinction between the formal and real subsumption of labour under capital, not developed in

Frank-Wallerstein 'trade-centered' analysis of production relations, and point out that capital can exert control over the production process without fully expropriating the direct producers. Capitalist exchange relations can be mediated through non-capitalist forms of production, such as family labour or peasant agriculture. In short, various theoretical positions challenge the notion of the 'classical model' as universal and indicate that this model of capitalist differentiation, with the expropriation of direct producers and their real subsumption by capital as free wage labour, describes a particular case or variant of the process and not "its sole or necessary form of development". General or universal formulations of agrarian transition and rural class differentiation are thus open to question. For instance, Bernstein[3] reminds us that Lenin did not restrict his attention solely to the 'class model' as outlined in this paper. Lenin also considered conditions in which the movement of capital incorporates the peasantry by a process of 'vertical concentration' with forms of capital attempting to regulate production without undertaking its direct organization. This he characterized as the subsumption of simple commodity producers by capital in peripheral social formations. Here, however, the question remains: how is one to characterize small commodity producers when their real subsumption to capital is incomplete.

The recent debate on the mode of production in Indian agriculture also attempted to explore the 'point of domination' of capitalist social relations in agrarian structures where the development of commodity relations occurred under colonialism. However, this debate still remains open since "none of the authors give the criteria for deciding when commodity production has ceased to be a peripheral activity within a mode of production and becomes instead the general form of production".[4] The generalization of commodity production if taken as the necessary and sufficient condition for the development of capitalist relations will mean that labour power and the means of production be separated and circulated as commodities. But the development towards generalized commodity production can be seen as a historical process towards a continuum. This presents major difficulties in characterizing agrarian transition because the point at which conditions of capitalist production come into existence is not easy to locate. One suggested way out of this impasse is to determine the 'point of domination' by analyzing the process of social differentiation and the development of the home market.

Problems of Class Analysis

The process of differentiation has two aspects: historical and sociological.

Sociologically coherent analysis of agrarian class formation in India is still uncommon. A clear analytical distinction in the sociological sense must derive indicators of inequality from a problematic in which 'social class' is constituted in terms of differentiation which poses class in terms of the social relations of production. However, in India, the use of a variety of criteria to define agrarian classes frustrate any comparative study of regional variation and of change through time. Though it is true that every local class structure is the product of its unique history yet the questions of ownership, of control over land and its product, and the questions of domination and power over people and their labour power are answerable only with reference to culturally constituted systems of meanings and values. Difficulties, however, are exacerbated by a failure to agree on what kinds of criteria are most important in the definition of agrarian classes.

One can delineate at least three distinct approaches to the definition of agrarian classes. The first approach focuses on categories indigenous to the society being studied. While the appeal to the indigenous categories derives its strength from the assumption that they are indeed "the categories in terms of which he (the villager) thinks and acts"[5], the problem arises because of the ideological nature of the people's images of their society which often distort the underlying structure of their relations. The other two approaches can be distinguished as the *distributional* and the *structural* approaches towards the definition of classes. In the distributional approach people are assigned to different classes depending on the association between people and things and on the basis of quantitative differences in the distribution of things. Since classification remains arbitrary and *ad hoc* in this approach it does not contain within itself any explicit directives for the historical analysis of class dynamics.

Structural studies on the other hand focus on relations between different groups of people, i.e., on social relations particularly, as these relations are themselves related to differential control of the means of production. Along with landed property, labour contribution is the other basic feature that structuralists use to differentiate agrarian classes. Their theoretical orientation also assumes that major classes are opposed to one another in a relationship of conflict. In empirical terms class distinctions are made in terms of hiring-in and hiring-out labour relative to self-employment along with the criteria of possession of means of production and economic viability.[6] On the basis of such criteria generally five classes, viz., landlord, rich peasant, middle peasant, poor peasant and agricultural labourer are proposed. However, in some cases, the structural distinctions are used not to analyze relations within and between classes, but as descriptive labels for strata that are in fact separated by distributional criteria, specifically by the amount of land held[7] or by occupational classification. Some on the other hand even though use the five class scheme they define them in terms of the combination of one or more occupational statuses. This analytic tactic of substitution subordinates the theoretical holism of the structural approach to the conveniences of empirical description, and confines the analysis within an essentially stratigraphic and atomistic framework. In any case, to assess the nature of transformation at an all-India level we have to refer to all the studies which analyze the agrarian structure in terms of classes. It is obvious that no two definitions of classes are the same and this makes comparative analyses difficult but they can still signify at a crude level the broad distinctions of classes and their transformation, which can be useful, at least, as a heuristic device.

Transformation of Class Structure

While writing in the 1950s Daniel Thorner noted: "Some parts of India, as for example Andhra, Tamil Nadu and Bihar, have to this day large absentee landlords, whose holdings are let out to tenants. In Bengal there are known to be several layers of tenants and subtenants between the zamindars and the men who actually till the soil. The former princely states still contain a great variety of *jagirdars*, *inamdars*, and other holders of large estates under especially privileged tenures."[8] He described India as having a 'unique agrarian structure' which represented a blending of remnants from the pre-British economic order together with the modern western concepts of private property. He divided rural India into three main classes: the *maliks* or proprietors, the *kisans* or working peasants and the *mazdurs* or agricultural labourers. The key to this division was the amount of actual labour contributed to the production process and the share in the product. He, however, averred that the primary aim of all classes was not to increase their income by adopting more efficient methods, but to rise in social prestige by abstaining in so far as possible from physical labour. This complex of legal, economic and social relations he characterized as the 'built-in depressor' uniquely typical of Indian countryside. In the 1960s he revised his earlier characterization of the rural scene and noted "the distinct emergence of a nation-wide class of capitalist producers".[9] In between Zamindari Abolition Acts were passed in various states in the 1950s. Though these Acts did not give land to the landless or land poor, nor they were intended to, they at least deprived the big landlords to a large degree of their village power, and turned them to farming through greater use of hired labour. This laid a basis for the richer peasants to come to power in the villages and develop as capitalist farmers. Not only was a 'new' economic class created but there was also a fresh impetus for mobility among the intermediate castes as well.

The spread of co-operative credit societies, land development banks, sugar co-operatives, government's assurance of substantial price support for farm products, subsidized inputs like water, power, fertilizer, diesel, tractors, etc., and institutional credit helped the consolidation of the rich farming class. That the rich farmers were able to claim an increasing share of government resources for itself especially after 1965 is shown by a number of studies.[10] Though empirical identification of the class of rich farmers is arbitrary, estimates show that large-size farm households cultivating holdings above 4 hectares constitute about 19 per cent of agricultural population and account for 60 per cent of cultivated area and 53 per cent of crop output.[11] Since the statistics on the development of forces of production which shaped the rise of this class is well documented, we would rather concentrate on the sociological characteristics of the classes.

The class of rich farmers includes the upwardly mobile peasant farmers with a long history of direct cultivation. They are now expanding through buying and leasing-in land from absentee or small landowners. The erstwhile non-cultivating landlords have converted themselves into active farmers with the help of new technology and active government support in terms of low taxation, high support prices, liberal provision of credits and subsidized inputs. They have now found cultivation a more profitable proposition than rack renting. Byres[12] suggests it was the medium to smaller landlords who as a result of tenancy abolition were encouraged to become direct cultivators. This involved an ejection of tenants and their replacement by wage labour. He however mentions that these tendencies within the landlord class were nowhere on a scale sufficient to suggest the possibility of widespread 'capitalism from above'. The rich peasants on the other hand were stabilized as independent proprietors in the wake of land reforms and were on their way to becoming the new dominant class in the emerging agrarian structure. There was an increase in more purely commercial as opposed to 'feudal' tenancy, and in the 1960s there was a rise in the amount of land rented in by rich peasants, who as a result gained control of a larger proportion of the tenanted area.[13]

These tendencies were more marked in *ryotwari* and *mahalwari* areas. In these regions at least the rich peasants were on their way to becoming the dominant class of the countryside. And since these were the locations of the largest concentration of marketed surpluses the rich peasants had a growing influence in the polity. They showed themselves to be eminently capable of exercising political power, not only in the village, but also at the level of district, state and centre. Many of the rich peasants also branched out into trading, transport, and other businesses and services. The establishment of tiny transport companies, flour mills, oil mills, brick kilns, cold-storages were all part of this process. With the formation of sugar co-operatives they transformed some of their wealth into capital to generate one of India's biggest industries. A typical capitalist farmer today has a competent younger generation and he systematically seeks to diversify economic activities by placing some in service, some in business, leaving one or two to manage the land. Some are even employed to take care of political pressures as well. Diversification of interests represents the investments of accumulated agricultural surplus outside agriculture; it is also a protection against the risks of pure cultivation.

While agricultural profits are invested in small business, often business profits are re-invested in agriculture and land. In spite of such tendencies, the farmer-capitalists have remained confined to small business and trade and so far have not entered the ranks of industrial capitalists. A recent study of capitalist farmers of Andhra Pradesh points out certain tendencies which are to a large extent true of other parts of India. The study notes that:

> "the new technology has led to a sharp increase in the number of rural business-cum-agricultural households as well as to a diversification in the type of investments made by them. With the spread of green revolution technology, opportunities were created for rich farmers to become dealers of fertilizers, pesticides, and agricultural machinery, a type of trade that is qualitatively different from the traditional trade in agricultural produce. Some of these who were able to get distributorships and dealerships from the manufacturing companies (mostly located in towns) prospered and expanded into other types of urban business. Contracting is another activity in which a cultivator can engage part time; if he is successful he may grow into a large-scale full-time contractor based in a town. New types of agro-industry and

> other rural-based small industries, cinema halls, and speculation in urban real estate are other 'modern' avenues of investment for the rural rich. While wealthy farmers who diversify into rural-based business may continue to be primarily cultivators, there are many others who are drawn into urban enterprises and who eventually give up agriculture."[14]

The process indicates a rural-urban connection, rural-urban kin ties and the interpenetration of business and agriculture and rural-urban property interests within this class. Rural-urban migration is not only a function of economic diversification but also of the high value that is placed on education. The switch to non-agricultural occupation and urban migration by educated children is the outcome of the high premium placed on modern education.

The Andhra study also points out that practically every medium and large landowning family in these villages (and some with small holdings), have highly educated and/or urban based members. As a result, there is a complex web of ties between rural and urban society, particularly within the elite, which has produced (or reinforced) an urban-oriented culture among the rural rich. This culture in turn reproduces the pattern of out-migration because town life and urban occupations are more highly valued by the rural elite than are rural life and cultivation. Wealthy families seem to have one foot already out of the door, and they were awaiting an opportunity to make the move to town, an opportunity that will come to their sons and daughters if not to themselves.[15] In south Gujarat Breman[16] also describes the process of rural industrialization nourished by a dynamic having its origins in the recent modernization of agriculture. Kathleen Gough[17] in her study of Tanjore villages characterizes as medium bourgeois those with landed estates producing for the market, owners of smaller mills, local transport, operators, urban real estate dealers, local traders and retail merchants. Her study shows that from the 1950s and 1980s, this class became more closely tied to imperial capital through loans and subsidies or through serving as agents for foreign, or mixed Indian and foreign, corporations and profited from its links to foreign capital.

A sizeable section of the rich farmers belong to the intermediate castes who have a long history of direct cultivation. Their attempt to establish hegemony coincided with the rise of discontent among the labouring classes. On the one hand, by demanding higher crop prices, they have unleashed their offensive to bring other classes into their fold, and on the other hand various incidents of atrocities and repression against the labouring classes also point towards their offensive against the rural poor. Their attitude can be characterized as anti-labour and their mentality as social-Darwinist on account of their brutal indifference towards those classed as being socially lower.

The middle peasants are distinguished by the fact that they are relatively little involved in the production for the market. As Alavi has pointed out, both Lenin and Mao described two distinct structures of agrarian social relations both of which were characterized by a master-subordinate relationship; and a "sector of independent peasants", namely, (1) landlords-sharecroppers (poor peasants), (2) independent small holders (middle peasants), and (3) capitalist farmers-agricultural proletariat.

Alavi's argument is that "middle peasants...do not stand between the rich peasants and the poor peasants; they belong to a different sector of the rural economy".[19] If "a different sector of rural economy" means a different mode of production, the problem is that of relationship of this mode with the social formation. On the other hand, other analyses suggest that the situation of the middle peasantry is essentially precarious. So that they eventually join the ranks of 'the exploiters' or 'the exploited'. In other words, they are quite intrinsic to the dynamics of differentiation. As Harriss in his study of northern Tamil Nadu noted: "Investigation of the process of production in Random has...shown that there is a group of independent producers which is highly 'mobile' in the sense that some of its members are significant 'exploiters' who may be on their way to becoming 'rural capitalists', whilst others are rather 'exploited'. So it might appear that in Random the 'extreme groups' are on their way to being developed at the expense of 'the middle'."[20] He, however, cautions that there can be questions as to whether the mobility which is observed results in polarization, or whether there is not simply a great deal of movement around a rather stable median position.

There are some who claim that this class of independent producers is extremely small or non-existent in India.[21] However, Bardhan's estimate for West Bengal is that they make about 30 per cent of all agricultural households. On the basis of data reported by the Farm Management Survey, he concludes that this class is relatively small in South India but quite substantial in North and North-West India. According to Bardhan, in West Bengal, the region where agricultural productivity is low, the importance of this class is highest which suggests an inverse relation between agricultural progress and proportional importance of this class. He, however, gives two contrary examples which are significant in the context of rural-urban nexus. He writes: "But the cases of two other districts, Howrah and particularly 24-Parganas, point to another significant factor. These two are among the agriculturally most stagnant districts in West Bengal, and yet the proportional importance of poor peasants and landless labourers is among the highest in the state, and that of family farmers relatively low. This may have to do with the proximity of these two districts to the urban agglomeration of Calcutta, which may have accelerated commercialization of labour transactions in agriculture even without any substantial development of the productive forces on the farm."[22]

The process of rural proletarianization is more problematic. Byres after discussing a number of studies draws up the balance-sheet as follows: "I would interpret the foregoing as, indeed, signifying the operation of a process of proletarianization of the peasantry, or depeasantization: one that is complex, but as yet partial in its impact. The 'new technology' has produced conditions in which, by a variety of means, the poor peasantry has lost an increasing share of the operated area to rich peasants. Not only that, but the poor peasantry is, in different ways, being transformed more and more into a rural proletariat."[23] The incomplete proletarianization that Byres describes boils down to the fact that increasingly more small owners surrender the working of their properties to larger farmers without giving up their own rights in them. Other studies qualify the relationship by indicating that in high rainfall, areas where population density is high, the proportion of landless or near landless is large and wage labour is cheaper to hire. The extent of proletarianization is relatively high, even though these areas are not necessarily technologically progressive. Bardhan writes: "These are historically areas of relatively secure wet agriculture where the mounting population is absorbed with an astonishing elasticity (a process described by Geertz as one of 'agricultural involution') with continuous subdivision and multiplication of rights on land leading to elaborate hierarchies with the actual manual work of cultivation done only by those who are at the bottom of the heap."[24] The situation is not the same in sparsely populated regions remotely connected with centres of commercialization. Here, the extent of use of wage labour is rather low. In other words, the extent of proletarianization is dependent, among other things, upon ecological, demographic, and institutional factors. The general indications, however, point to an increase in the use of hired labour over time along with economic growth. To the extent the increase in the number of agricultural labourers is from the eviction of erstwhile tenants, it might indicate the change in the composition of rural workers rather than proletarianization. On the other hand joining the ranks of rural workers from the class of middle and poor peasants would definitely indicate the extent of proletarianization. The statistics on small farms shows that households with ownership holdings of less of than one hectare have considerably improved their number; between 1970-71 and 1976-77 the percentage of holdings below one hectare increased from 50.9 to 54.7.[25] This has led some to suggest that as the logic of household economy is determined by the needs of simple reproduction, its economic 'behaviour' is different from that of a capitalist economy which operates on the logic of accumulation regulated by the mechanism of price of production.[26] For instance, falling prices deteriorates the terms of exchange for commodities produced relative to commodities needed for reproduction which compel such households either to reduce consumption or intensify commodity production or both simultaneously. This has been termed as simple reproduction 'squeeze'. Verogopoulos has argued that "family farming is the most successful form of production for putting the maximum volume of surplus labour at the disposal of urban capitalism. It also constitutes the most efficient way of restraining the prices of agricultural products."[27] He has argued that the family labour farms persist because they do not have to finance profits and rents. Others have emphasized the efficiency of small producers, while still others have suggested explanations in terms of the divergence between labour time and the production time inherent in natural qualities of the object being produced. Excess of production time over labour time results in the inefficient use of constant capital, lower rate of profit, labour recruitment problems and complications in the smooth realization of value in the sphere of circulation.[28] That the small producers continue to reproduce themselves is without question. New technology, because of the larger demands for agricultural inputs, has increased its dependence on bureaucracy and traders.

The class of rural workers is further internally stratified, with those having land at the top and those who are totally landless at the bottom. Political factors also influence the determinants of class positions. As Bardhan points out the class position of the tenant, for instance, depends on tenurial security. Political process plays an important part in the imposition of this security. As such two regions with two different kinds of political attitudes would have two different kinds of class structure. He writes: "A landless tenant in Kerala could have belonged to the class of 'family farmers', but were he located in Bihar, would be indistinguishable from a landless wage labour."[29] Though India has a very large agricultural labour population, they operate under a large number of restrictions and to that extent are not 'free'. As Rudra[30] has shown, the 'market' for the sellers of labour is confined to their village and neighbourhood. Marx pointed out that the buyer of labour power does not get its value immediately after the conclusion of the contract, but he has to incur some cost in harnessing it in the process of production. Therefore, 'dependability' of the worker becomes an important consideration and as Rudra has shown in many instances labour from the immediate neighbourhood is preferred even when wages are somewhat lower outside. Loyalty of the worker is ensured through regular credit and sometimes with emergency help and thus the employer is able to maintain and consolidate his social control over the labour process. So far as the rural workers are in possession of their labour power they constitute the other axis of this unequal power-nexus. This also implies that the social boundaries of a village community may significantly circumscribe the process of transfer of surplus value and thus class formation gets territorially segmented.

In other parts, however, the territorial segmentation is often broken by the capitalist farmers by importing labour from more backward areas to keep wages down. It is generally argued that the determinants of migration are the factors like increased labour intensity of the new cropping pattern, absorption of the landless labour force into expanding non-agricultural employment and unsatisfactory performance of local labourers, etc. Breman, on the other hand, shows that in the developed regions of Gujarat, labour from elsewhere is rendered mobile not for these reasons but in order to create a surplus labour force.[31] The supply of migrant labourers results in cost-cutting because of its depressive effect on local wages, and thus the bargaining position of the local landless is weakened, which also weakens his relative power. The employer can also exercise far greater control over the migrants who work in a strange environment and are not familiar with local usages. By breaking territorial segmentation the capitalist farmers have achieved two things: firstly, they are able to keep wages low; and secondly, the strong opposition of interests between the two segments of workers becomes a weapon in the hands of capitalist farmers to counter the growing consciousness of the landless workers thus preventing this section from breaking out of their dependence.

Ideology and Class

The point in capitalist agriculture can be derived from three sources: (a) greater productivity of land; (b) a protected market; and (c) a depressed wage-level which can originate from surplus wage labour or from a sizeable poor peasantry. Since India can be characterized in terms of the last alternative, the development along classical lines is to that extent complicated. Further complications are introduced by the fact that the agrarian ownership structure can be controlled and manipulated politically. The possibility of reproducing these conditions for capitalist development depends, then, on the political representation of the agrarian bourgeoisie, and its alliances with other classes.[32]

When capitalism expands and penetrates into rural areas, the dominant classes will attempt to establish the political, legal, and ideological forms necessary for its functioning and stability. In this process they will encounter ideological practices which originated in social relations now subordinate to capitalism. To explain this situation some have introduced the concept of 'ideological articulation' which allows for a dynamic and historical analysis because it does not assume that the disappearance of non-capitalist ideological practices is a precondition for modernization. In India capitalism has not yet successfully incorporated nor effectively eliminated all pre-capitalist ideological practices. Furthermore, it can be argued that all these ideological practices do not necessarily have to be eliminated in order for capitalism to be successful. Ideology of caste still remains a dominant constituent in the system of meanings through which rural people interpret the world, and this seems to give coherence to the totality of relationships. In this sense, ideology cannot be excluded from the understanding of the process of class formation. The explanation of forms of symbolic domination, "how people participate in their own repression", is necessary if one is to comprehend the constitution of class formation in India. In other words both economic and ideological aspects of the articulation of the peasantry and capitalism are called for because the problems of 'tradition' and consciousness are very much linked with the problem of the analysis and transformation of class structure. As Raymond Williams once suggested: "what we have to see is not just 'a tradition' but a *selective tradition*: an intentionally selective version of a shaping past and pre-shaped present, which is then powerfully operative in the process of social and cultural definition and identification."

Notes

1. See Barbara Bradley, "The Destruction of Natural Economy", *Economy and Society*, 4 (2), 1975; Ernesto Laclau, "Feudalism and Capitalism in Latin America", *New Left Review*, 67, 1971; C. Meillassoux, 'From Reproduction to Production: A Marxist Approach to Economic Anthropology', *Economy and Society*, 1 (I), 1972; William Roseberry, "Rent, Differentiation, and the Development of Capitalism among Peasants", *American Anthropologist*, 78 (I), 1976.
2. A.G. Frank, *Capitalism and Underdevelopment in Latin America*, New York: Monthly Review Press, 1967; I. Wallerstein, *The Modern World System* New York: Academic Press, 1974.
3. H. Bernstein, "Notes on Capital and Peasantry", *Review of African Political Economy*, No. 10, 1974.
4. D. McEachem, "The Mode of Production in India", *Journal of Contemporary Asia*, Vol. 6, 1976, p.446.
5. Andre Beteille, *Studies in Agrarian Social Structure*, Delhi, Oxford University Press, 1974, p.49.
6. See Utsa Patnaik, "Class Differentiation within the Peasantry: An Approach to the Analysis of Indian Agriculture", *Economic and Political Weekly*, 11(39), 1976; P.K. Bardhan, 'Agrarian Class Formation in India', *Journal of Peasant Studies*, October 1982; P.K. Bose, *Classes in a Rural Society*, New Delhi, Ajanta, 1984; Joan Mencher, "Problems in Analyzing Rural Class Structure", *Economic and Political Weekly*, 9 (35), 1974.
7. See, for instance, Joan, Mencher, *Agriculture and Social Formation in Tamil Nadu*, New Delhi: Allied, 1978.
8. Daniel Thorner, *The Agrarian Prospect in India*, New Delhi, Allied, 1976, pp. 8-9.
9. *Ibid*, p. 2.
10. See Ashok Mody, "Resource Flows between Agriculture and Non-Agriculture in India, 1950-1970", *Economic and Political Weekly*, 16 (10-12), 1981; Ashok Mitra, *Terms of Trade and Class Relations*, Calcutta, Rupa, 1979.
11. P.K. Bardhan, *The Political Economy of Development in India*, Delhi, Oxford University Press, 1984, p. 46.
12. T.J. Byres, "The New Technology, Class Formation and Class Action in the Indian Countryside", *The Journal of Peasant Studies*, 8 (4), 1981.
13. Kalpana Bardhan, "Rural Employment, Wages and Labour Market

in India: A Survey of Research-1", *Economic and Political Weekly*, 12 (26), 1977, p. A. 83.

14. Carol Boyack Upadhyay, "The Farmer-capitalist of Coastal Andhra Pradesh", *Economic and Political Weekly*, 23 (27), 1988, p.1381.
15. *Ibid.*, p. 1381.
16. Jan Breman, *Of Peasants, Migrants and Paupers*, Delhi, Oxford University Press, 1985, pp. 42ff.
17. Kathleen Gough, "Socio-Economic Change in Southeast India, 1950s to 1980s", *Journal of Contemporary Asia*, 17 (3), 1987.
18. H. Alavi, "Peasants and Revolution", *Socialist Register*, 1965.
19. *Ibid.*, p. 244.
20. John Harriss, *Capitalism and Peasant Farming*, Bombay: Oxford University Press, 1982, p.200.
21. K. Gough, "Peasant Resistance and Revolt in South India", in A.R. Desai (ed.), *Peasant Struggles in India*, Delhi: Oxford University Press, 1979; Ashok Rudra, "Class Relations in Indian Agriculture", *Economic and Political Weekly*, 13 (22-24), 1978.
22. P.K. Bardhan, "Agrarian Class Formation....", op.cit, p. 83.
23. T.J. Byres, "The New Technology...", p. 430, op. cit.
24. P.K. Bardhan, "Agrarian Class Formation..." p. 85, op.cit.
25. *Data on Agricultural Land Holdings*: 1976-77 Bombay: CMIE, 1981.
26. H. Bernstein, op.cit.
27. K. Vergopoulos, "Capitalism and Peasant Productivity", *The Journal of Peasant Studies*, 5 (4), 1978, p. 446.
28. S. Mann and J.M. Dickinson, "Obstacles to the Development of a Capitalist Agriculture", *The Journal of Peasant Studies*, 5 (4), 1978.
29. P.K. Bardhan, "Agrarian Class Formation...", p. 79, op. cit.
30. Ashok Rudra, "The Self-contained Village Society", *Frontier*, 13 (19-21), 1981.
31. Jan Breman, *Of Peasants, Migrants and Paupers*, op.cit.
32. See Ashok Mitra, *Terms of Trade and Class Relations*, op.cit.

11 Nature of Class Conflict in the Indian Society

V.M. DANDEKAR

I have been asked to speak on a difficult subject. I accepted the invitation not because I feel equal to the task but because I believe that, for a proper appreciation of the several problems that the Indian society is presently facing, we must understand the nature of the underlying class conflict. This sounds very Marxian. I do not at all mind. Indeed, I shall feel proud if I am ever recognized as one belonging to that great school of social analysis. As I see it, it is not a single, inviolable, unchanging doctrine but a method of analyzing social change, founded on unsparing examination of social facts and merciless pursuit of logical analysis. As late Professor Kosambi said that Marxism is a method of thinking and not a substitute for thought.

Unfortunately, Marxism has been altogether too often taken as a substitute for thinking. Baran and Sweezy, the renowned American Marxists, rightly complain that "Marxists have too often been content to repeat familiar formulations, as though nothing really new had happened since the days of Marx and Engels—or of Lenin at the latest. As a result, Marxists have failed to explain important developments, or sometimes even to recognize their existence". This has led to stagnation of Marxian social science with lagging vitality and fruitfulness.

I shall approach my subject with the Marxian method because it emphasizes the importance of studying the society as a whole, how it works and where it is going. But I shall take into account new facts and developments that have occurred since Marx wrote and also the particular circumstances of the Indian society and, in the light of these, I shall be willing to modify Marx's conclusions wherever necessary.

It will be useful to begin by examining Marx's concept of social class and of class struggle. In his historical writings, Marx referred to several social classes. For instance, in his work *The Class Struggles in France*, 1848-1850, Marx distinguished six classes: financial bourgeoisie, industrial bourgeoisie, petty bourgeoisie, peasants, proletariat and Lumpen proletariat. In this, Marx was merely adopting the concept of social class which was widely used by historians and social theorists of that time.

But social classes meant much more to Marx. As Lenin said, anything which Marx wrote was in some way concerned with the question of class. Nevertheless, Marx never defined the basic concept of social class. Lenin gave the following definition: "Social classes are large groups of people differing from each other by the place they occupy in a historically determined system of social production, by their relation (in most cases fixed and formulated in law) to the means of production, by their role in the social organization of labour, and, consequently, by the dimensions of the share of social wealth of which they dispose and the mode of acquiring it." This definition is commonly accepted as an adequate and faithful summary of Marx's views in the matter. But, it must be mentioned, it is nowhere found in Marx's writings.

It was only towards the end of his prodigious scholarship that, it seems, Marx decided to put down a systematic exposition of his concept of social class and his theory of social struggle. The evidence is in the last chapter of the third volume of *Capital*. Unfortunately, it remained unfinished and incomplete. He wrote barely a page in which he set out mainly the difficulties which he saw confronting his own concept of social class.

Marx wrote: "We have seen that this continual tendency and law of development of the capitalist mode of production is more and more to divorce the means of production from labour, and more and more to concentrate the scattered means of production into large groups, thereby transforming labour into wage-labour and the means of production into capital. And to this tendency, on the other hand, corresponds the independent separation of landed property from capital and labour, or the transformation of all landed property into the form of landed property corresponding to the capitalist mode of production. The owners merely of labour-power, owners of capital, and landowners, whose respective sources of income are wages, profits, and ground-rent in other words, wage-labourers, capitalists, and landowners, constitute then three big classes of modern society based upon the capitalist mode of production."

Because of this, it is commonly supposed that, for Marx, the social classes are distinguished by the source of their income. But, this is precisely what, it seems, Marx wanted to refute. In the above, Marx continues: "The first question to be answered is this: What constitutes a class?—and the reply to this follows naturally from the reply to another question, what makes wage-labourers, capitalists and landlords constitute the three great social classes?"

"At first glance—the identity of revenues and sources of revenue. There are three great social groups whose members, the individuals forming them, live on wages, profit and ground-rent respectively, on the realization of their labour-power, their capital, and their landed property."

"However, from this standpoint, physicians and officials, for instance, would also constitute two classes, for they belong to two distinct social groups, the members of each of these groups receiving their revenue from one and the same source. The same would also be true of the infinite fragmentation of interest and rank into which the division of social labour splits labourers as well as capitalists and landlords—the latter, for instance, into owners of vineyards, farm owners, owners of forests, mine owners and owners of fisheries."

There Marx laid his pen aside for the last time and even the preliminary question he raised, "what constitutes a social class?"—remained unanswered.

We must therefore make do with what we can lay our hands on. I suggest that we should turn to the *Manifesto of the Communist Party*. It was published in 1848 and thus is one of the early writings of Marx. It is jointly authored by Marx and Engels. But, in the Preface to its English edition, Engels makes it clear that the fundamental proposition which forms its nucleus belongs to Marx. The *Manifesto* is a little booklet of less than 50 pages and offers a concise and congent statement, not so much of a theory but of Marx's vision of the development and future of the capitalist society which remained the basis for all his later theoretical work. Whatever your personal conviction or persuasion in the matter, you will not fail to be impressed by the grandeur and prophetic quality of his vision, particularly when you note that it was written in 1848 which is more than 125 years ago. To make my points, I may have to quote from it rather extensively. It will also give you a sample of the flavour, flair and power of Marx's writings.

The *Manifesto* opens with that historic statement: "The history of all hitherto existing society is the history of class struggles" and proceeds thus: "In the earlier epochs of history, we find almost everywhere a complicated arrangement of society into various orders, a manifold gradation of social rank... The modern bourgeois society that has sprouted from the ruins of feudal society, has not done away with class antagonisms. It has but established new classes, new conditions of oppression, new forms of struggle in place of the old ones... Our epoch, the epoch of the bourgeoisie, possesses, however, this distinctive feature: it has simplified the class antagonisms. Society as a whole is more and more splitting up into two great hostile camps, into two great classes directly facing each other—bourgeoisie and proletariat."

Marx did not define these two social classes. But, Engels in a footnote in the English edition, gives the following definitions: "By bourgeoisie is meant the class of modern capitalists, owners of the means of production and employers of wage-labour. By proletariat, the class of modern wage-labourers who, having no means of production of their own, are reduced to selling their labour power in order to live."

Let me first take the bourgeoisie. What distinguishes this class? Of course, the fact is that they are owners of the means of production and employers of wage-labour. How did the class emerge? Marx explains: "...the modern bourgeoisie is itself the product of a long course of development, or a series of revolutions in the modes of production and of exchange... the means of production and of exchange, on whose foundation the bourgeoisie built itself up, were generated in feudal society. At a certain stage of development of these means of production and of exchange, the conditions under which the feudal society produced and exchanged, the feudal organization of agriculture and manufacturing industry, in one word, the feudal relations of property became no longer compatible with the already developed productive forces; they became so many fetters... Into their place stepped free competition, accompanied by a social and political constitution adapted to it, and by the economical and political sway of the bourgeoisie class."

Thus, what distinguishes bourgeoisie epoch from feudal epoch is *free competition* in place of feudal relations. Again it is worth quoting Marx: "The bourgeoisie, wherever it has got the upper hand, has put an end to all feudal, patriarchal, idyllic relations. It has pitilessly torn asunder the motley feudal ties that bound man to his 'natural superiors', and has left no other nexus between man and man than naked self-interest, than callous 'cash payment'. It has drowned the most heavenly ecstasies of religious fervour, of chivalrous enthusiasm, of philistine sentimentalism, in the icy water of egotistical calculation. It has resolved personal worth into exchange value, and in place of the numberless indefeasible chartered freedoms, has set up that single, unconscionable freedom—Free Trade. In one word, for exploitation veiled by religious and political illusions, it has substituted naked, shameless, direct, brutal exploitation."

But mistake not. In two pages, Marx pays the most glowing tribute to what the bourgeoisie, by means of free competition and free trade, has achieved. I shall quote only a brief passage. Marx says: "The bourgeoisie, historically, has played a most revolutionary part... It has been the first to show what man's activity can bring about. created more massive and more colossal productive forces than have all preceding generations together. Subjection of nature's forces to man, machinery, application of chemistry to industry and agriculture, steam-navigation, railways, electric telegraphs, clearing of whole continents for cultivation, canalization of rivers, whole populations conjured out of the ground—what earlier century had even a presentiment that such productive forces slumbered in the lap of social labour?"

What was then wrong? Nothing except that Marx believed that this could not go on for long. The reasons? Marx says: "Modern bourgeois society with its relations of production, of exchange and of property, a society that has conjured up such gigantic means of production and of exchange, is like the sorcerer who is no longer able to control the powers of the nether world whom he has called up by his spells. For many a decade past, the history of industry and commerce is but the history of the revolt of modern productive forces against modern conditions of production, against the property relations that are the conditions for the existence of the bourgeois society on its trial, each time more threateningly. In these crises, a great part not only of the existing products, but also of the previously created productive forces, are periodically destroyed. ...The conditions of bourgeois society are too narrow to comprise the wealth created by them. ...The weapons with which the bourgeoisie felled feudalism to the ground are now turned against the bourgeoisie itself." *Marx meant the weapons of free competition and free trade.*

In point of fact, the bourgeois capitalist society has survived many a crises since Marx wrote. It did this by modifying conditions of free competition. The last such crisis was the Great Depression of the 1930's. It accorded well with the Marxian theory and strengthened the belief that similar catastrophic economic breakdowns were inevitable under capitalism. Yet, in the three decades since the end of the Second World War, there has not been a single severe depression. Marxian theory is not able to explain this because it does not take into account the emergence of monopoly capitalism and the manner in which it modifies conditions of free competition.

Marx certainly recognized the tendency towards concentration and centralization inherent in the competitive system. He says: "The bourgeoisie keeps more and more doing away with the scattered state of the population, of the means of production, and of property. It has agglomerated population, centralized means of production, and has concentrated property in a few hands." But he concludes: "The necessary consequence of this was political centralization." He did not at the same time investigate how the emergence of large-scale enterprise and monopoly would affect other conditions of bourgeois production, particularly the conditions of free competition. This is of course too much to expect from one who wrote more than a hundred years ago. But probably, as Baran and Sweezy suspect, "Marx anticipated the overthrow of capitalism long before the unfolding of all its potentialities, well within the system's competitive phase."

I need not dwell on this point further because that is not germane to my theme this evening. The important point to recognize, not often explicitly understood, particularly by Marxists, is that Marx's analysis of capitalism remained confined to the case of perfectly competitive economy and hence is inadequate to explain several phenomena of the present-day capitalism.

Let me now turn to the other class, namely, the proletariat. The proletariat is a product of bourgeois society. As Marx says: "The proletariat is its special and essential product." If bourgeoisie is defined as those who own the means of production and employ wage-labour, it is obvious that it must create a class which owns no means of production and hence, in order to live, must sell its labour. Thus, the bourgeoisie creates its own enemy. Marx says: "But not only has the bourgeoisie forged the weapons that bring death to itself; it has also called into existence the men who are to wield those weapons—the modern working class—the proletarians."

Let me outline, in his own words, Marx's concept of the class struggle between the bourgeoisie and the proletariat and the ultimate inevitable victory of the proletariat.

"In proportion as the bourgeoisie, i.e., capital, is developed, in the same proportion is the proletariat, the modern working class, developed—a class of labourers, who live only so long as they find work, and who find work only so long as their labour increases capital. These labourers, who must sell themselves piecemeal, are a commodity, like every other article of commerce, and are consequently exposed to all the vicissitudes of competition, to all the fluctuations of the market.

"Owing to the extensive use of machinery and to division of labour, the work of the proletarians has lost all individual character, and consequently, all charm for the workman. He becomes an appendage of the machine, and it is only the most simple, most monotonous, and most easily acquired knack, that is required of him. Hence, the cost of production of a workman is restricted, almost entirely, to the means of subsistence that he requires for his maintenance, and for the propagation of his race. But the price of a commodity, and therefore also of labour, is equal to its cost of production. In proportion, therefore, as the repulsiveness of the work increases, the wage decreases.

"But with the development of industry, the proletariat not only increases in number; it becomes concentrated in greater masses, its strength grows, and it feels that strength more. The various interests and conditions of life within the ranks of the proletariat are more and more equalized, in proportion as machinery obliterates all distinctions of labour and nearly everywhere reduces wages to the same low level. The growing competition among the bourgeois, and the resulting commercial crises, make the wages of the workers ever more fluctuating. The unceasing improvement of machinery, ever more rapidly developing, makes their livelihood more and more precarious; the collisions between individual workmen and individual bourgeois take more and more the character of collisions between two classes. Thereupon the workers begin to form combinations (trades' unions) against the bourgeois; they club together in order to keep up the rate of wages; they found permanent associations in order to make provision before-hand for these occasional revolts.

"This organization of the proletarians into a class, and consequently into a political party...compels legislative recognition of particular interests of the workers, by taking advantage of the divisions among the bourgeoisie itself.

"Finally, in times when the class struggle nears the decisive hour, a small section of the ruling class cuts itself adrift and joins the revolutionary class ...a portion of the bourgeoisie goes over to the proletariat, and in particular, a portion of the bourgeoisie ideologists, who have raised themselves to the level of comprehending theoretically the historical movement as a whole.

"Hitherto, every form of society has been based...on the antagonism of oppressing and oppressed classes. But, in order to oppress a class, certain conditions must be assured to it under which it can, at least, continue its slavish existence. The serf, in the period of serfdom, raised himself to the membership of the commune, just as the petty bourgeois, under the yoke of feudal absolutism, managed to develop into a bourgeois. The modern labourer, on the contrary, instead of rising with the progress of industry, sinks deeper and deeper below the conditions of existence of his own class. He becomes a pauper and pauperism develops more rapidly than population and wealth. And here it becomes evident, that the bourgeoisie is unfit any longer to be the ruling class in society, and to impose its conditions of existence upon society as an over-riding law. It is unfit to rule because it is incompetent to assure an existence to its slave within his slavery, because it cannot help letting him sink into such a state, that it has to feed him, instead of being fed by him. Society can no longer live under this bourgeoisie, in other words, its existence is no longer compatible with society.

"The essential condition for the existence and for the sway of the bourgeois class, is the formation and augmentation of capital, the condition for capital is wage-labour. Wage-labour rests exclusively on competition between the labourers. The advance of industry, whose involuntary promoter is the bourgeoisie, replaces the isolation of the labourers, due to competition, by their revolutionary combination, due to association. This development of the modern industry, therefore, cuts from under its feet, the very foundation on which the bourgeoisie produces and appropriates product. What the bourgeoisie therefore produces above all, are its own grave-diggers. Its fall and the victory of the proletariat are equally inevitable."

I have quoted Marx at length so that you may have fresh in your mind his conception of the course that the struggle between the bourgeoisie and the proletariat would take leading ultimately and inevitably to the fall of the bourgeoisie and the victory of the proletariat. In this, Marx quite rightly attaches great importance to the organization of the proletariat into trade unions, gaining political power, compelling legislative recognition of their rights and interests, and above all, keeping up the wages by collective bargaining. This is the exact counterpart of the development of large-scale industry and monopoly capitalism among the bourgeoisie. Indeed, it is only to the extent that large-scale industry and monopoly capitalism develop that trade unions of the proletariat can grow in strength. One modifies the conditions of free competition among the bourgeoisie; the other modifies the conditions of free competition among the proletariat. Marx failed to see the import of this because he continued to work and think within the confines of a perfectly competitive economy.

Hence, his assertion that "wage labour rests exclusively on competition between the labourers;" or that the modern working class of wage-labourers "sell themselves piecemeal and are consequently exposed to all the vicissitutes of competition, to all the fluctuations of the market" and that, like all commodities, they get their price which is equal to the "cost of production of the worker, namely, the subsistence that the worker requires for his maintenance and for the propagation of his race." He did not see that all this would change with the emergence of trade unions and the collective bargaining power of the workers, which he clearly foresaw.

Working as he was within the confines of a perfectly free competitive economy, it was necessary for Marx to postulate a perfectly homogeneous undifferentiated class of workers. Hence, he said: "Owing to the extensive use of machinery and the division of labour, (the worker) becomes an appendage of the machine, and it is only the most simple, most monotonous, and most easily acquired knack that is required of him;" or that "the various interests and conditions of life within the ranks of the proletariat are more and more equalized, in proportion as machinery obliterates all distinctions of labour and nearly everywhere reduces wages to the same low level."

In this, Marx was clearly wrong. A worker working at a machine may appear, to an onlooker, as no more than an appendage of the machine. But, for that reason, it is not true that only the most easily acquired skills are required of him. As machines become more complex and demanding of higher precision of their output, not only specialized skills acquired through years of training but also a high degree of intelligence are required of the worker. In the range of skills which he acquires and exhibits, the modern industrial working class is at least as varied as the pre-machine class of artisans and handicraftsmen.

Large-scale industrial production also requires organizational and managerial skills of various order beginning with the shop-floor. In consequence, there emerges, even within the working class, a hierarchy of supervisors and chargemen. Men at the bottom aspire to move up in this hierarchy not only because wages there are higher, but also because the higher positions carry higher authority and because at the top there usually is a white-collar or near white-collar job accessible to the worker which carries not only higher pay and authority but also prestige and social status attaching to white-collar.

The white-collar represents the new middle class comprising office workers, supervisors, technicians and innumerable others who are essentially a product of the capitalist development. Marx did not anticipate the emergence and growth of this class. He also did not anticipate the emergence of a welfare state within a capitalist society and consequent growth of an employee class providing the many welfare services such as education, public health, railways, road transport, post and telegraph and also the growth of bureaucracy overseeing them. Members of this class also do not have any means of production of their own except the skills acquired through often expensive education. They are essentially wage-workers and may be classed with the proletariat as is commonly done. Nevertheless, we should note an important attribute of this class which distinguishes it from the proletariat narrowly defined as the industrial worker. That is the distinction between the white-collar and the blue-collar. A certain social prestige attaches to the white-collar occupations which, as Max Weber suggested, has its origins in the prestige which certain social groups such as the nobility, the officials of the state and the learned professions, enjoyed in the pre-capitalist society. The continuity is evident in the distinct life-style which the new white-collar middle class exhibits.

The social prestige attaching to the white-collar occupations and the life-style that goes with it have not left the blue-collar workers completely unaffected. Marx is not entirely correct in his assessment when he says: "The proletariat is without property; his relation to his wife and children has no longer anything in common with the bourgeois family relations. Law, morality, religion, are to him so many bourgeois prejudices, behind which lurk in ambush just as many bourgeois interests." Marx was probably right when he wrote. But, in the present-day society, even if it be true that the style and facts of proletariat life are far from those of the bourgeoisie, it is clear that aspirations everywhere are all very bourgeois. It is for this reason that the blue-collar worker strives to move up in the hierarchy not simply because it gives him higher rewards but also because it brings him close to the white-collar class. Like the serf, in the period of serfdom, raised himself to the membership of the commune, so does the blue-collar worker raise himself into the white-collar society. The bourgeois capitalist society has created the aspirations and also the opportunities. Marx did not fully appreciate the vertical mobility that bourgeois society provides.

Marx also did not anticipate the emergence of the managerial class which forms so important an element in the modern capitalist development. In general, the managerial class do not own their own means of production and are essentially wage-earners though their purse is large. Marx is quite clear that the size of the purse does not distinguish a class of his concept. In that case, the managerial class must be regarded as belonging to the proletariat. But, the size of the purse is not the only distinguishing characteristic of the managerial class. It stays close to the bourgeoisie, adopts the same style of life as the bourgeoisie, identifies its interests with those of the bourgeoisie and indeed aspires to join the bourgeoisie if opportunity presents. In its daily strife, the proletariat finds itself face to face, not with the bourgeoisie, but with the managerial class.

These several developments, which Marx either did not anticipate or, when he did, did not fully appreciate their implications to his central proposition, have belied his expectation that the development of capitalism would progressively resolve the society into just two antagonistic classes: the bourgeoisie faced by a homogeneous, undifferentiated mass of proletariat. Instead, between the two classes of Marx's conception, is interposed a hierarchy of groups vested, not necessarily with property or means of production but, with social status and prestige. This is not merely a matter of detail. It affects fundamentally Marx's theory of class conflict and final class struggle. The resolution of the society into just two antagonistic classes is a logical need of Marx's theory of class struggle. With too many classes or groups in-between, the conflict would not sharpen and the final struggle and the victory of the proletariat resulting in a classless society, would not materialize. Marx saw this clearly. The relations among a hierarchy of status groups are relations of competition and emulation, not of conflict.

Quite apart from the several status groups ranging between the bourgeoisie and the proletariat and merging one into another making a hierarchy, all creation of the capitalist system, one must examine what other groups or classes of the pre-capitalist society survive into the capitalist society. According to Marx, none. He says: "The other classes decay and finally disappear in the face of modern industry; the proletariat is its special and essential product." More specifically, Marx refers to what he calls the lower strata of the middle class and expects that it will gradually sink into the proletariat. He says: "The lower strata of the middle class—the small tradespeople, shopkeepers, and retired tradesmen, generally the handicraftsmen and peasants—all these sink gradually into the proletariat, partly because their diminutive capital does not suffice for the scale on which modern industry is carried on, and is swamped in the competition with the large capitalists, partly because of their specialized skill is rendered worthless by new methods of production. Thus, the proletariat is recruited from all classes of the population."

Marx does not give a definition of the middle class and its lower or higher strata. But judging by whom he includes in the lower strata of the middle class, it is not difficult to see the implied scheme of classification. The basic division is of course between the bourgeoisie and the proletariat: those who own the means of production, do not themselves work but employ wage-labour; and those who do not own any means of production and must work as wage-labour. In between the two, lies the middle class: those who own the means of production and also work by themselves. The middle class thus defined could be divided into higher and lower strata. In the higher strata are those with substantial means of production so that, though they are owner-operators, they may also employ considerable wage-labour. In the process of capitalist development, they would accumulate more capital and move up into the bourgeoisie. The lower strata have limited means of production and they are essentially owner-operator; if they employ any wage-labour at all, that would be only marginal. The small manufacturer, the shopkeeper, the artisan and the peasant belong to this class and Marx quite rightly put them together. His prediction that all these groups gradually sink into the proletariat and the reasons he gave for this process, namely, firstly their small capital and consequent inability to stand competition from the large capitalists and secondly their specialized skills becoming outdated by new methods of production, are well borne out by the capitalist development in the industrialized countries.

Nevertheless, we should note that the middle class, including a large lower strata, is yet very much a reality. The small shopkeeper has proved to be much more hardy than Marx imagined. The same is true of a number of professionals providing medical, legal and personal services such as tailors, launderers, hair-dressers, taximen and automobile repair and service men. Besides, the development of large-scale modern industry itself has created several ancillary areas in which a new class of small manufacturer has emerged. The capitalist development has also created new classes of professionals such as chartered accountants, insurancemen, and industrial, financial and marketing consultants. These several groups constitute the middle class, a majority of them belonging to its lower strata of Marx's conception. It is not small or negligible by size and is far from disappearing. The lower strata of the middle class of the Marx's conception also includes the peasant. As such, in the present day Indian society, it constitutes the largest single group. Of course, this is partly because the capitalist development has not as yet gone far enough in this country.

Incidentally, I should mention, that having included the peasant in the lower strata and having pronounced that, along with its class, it will sink into the proletariat, Marx, in the Manifesto, does not pay any more specific attention to the fate of the peasant.

What is the role of this lower strata of the middle class, while it survives and subsists, in the class struggle between the bourgeoisie and the proletariat? Marx says the following:

"Of all the classes that stand face to face with the bourgeoisie today, the proletariat alone is a really revolutionary class. The other classes decay and finally disappear in the face of modern industry; the proletariat is its special and essential product.

"The lower middle class, the small manufacturer, the shopkeeper, the artisan, the peasant, all these fight against the bourgeoisie, to save from extinction their existence as fractions of the middle class. They are therefore not revolutionary, but conservative. Nay more, they are reactionary, for they try to roll back the wheel of history."

Thus, the lower middle class, comprising the small manufacturer, the small shopkeeper, the artisan and the peasant, has no role in the class struggle between the bourgeoisie and the proletariat. Its historical role is to decay and disappear as a class and sink into the proletariat. Bourgeoisie assists this process by pursuing relentlessly, by merciless competition, the advance of modern large-scale industry. To the extent the lower-middle class resists the bourgeoisie, it resists the historical process and tries to roll back the wheel of history. To that extent, and in this sense, the lower-middle class is a reactionary class. It follows that all policies aimed at protecting this class, the small manufacturer, the small shopkeeper, the artisan and the peasant, are reactionary policies. One must understand the sense in which Marx uses the term, 'reactionary'. I am surprised and puzzled when I find many, who call themselves Marxists, using the term 'reactionary' in quite the opposite sense and directly or indirectly supporting policies which Marx would have labelled 'reactionary'.

How important it is for Marx's theory of class struggle to have the society resolved into just two classes—the bourgeoisie and the proletariat—is evident from Marx's reference in the *Manifesto* to yet another class. Marx says: "The dangerous class, the social scum, that passively rotting mass thrown off by the lowest layers of old society, may, here and there, be swept into the movement by a proletariat revolution; its conditions of life, however, prepare it far more for the part of a bribed tool of reactionary intrigue."

Which class is this? It owns no means of production. It also does not do wage-labour in the modern capitalist industry. In the Indian context, the description fits well the landless rural poor partly moved into the urban slums but without any wage employment. Marx's vivid description of the class as "the social scum, the passively rotting mass thrown off by the lowest layers of old society" also points to the scheduled castes of the traditional Hindu society and the bonded labour yoked to the feudal landlord-moneylender. In the present-day Indian society, this class is not numerically negligible. Yet, in the two-class schemata of Marx, this class has no place except as a handy 'bribed tool of reactionary intrigue'. The meaning and implication are not clear, at any rate to me. But I should caution and emphasize once again that the term 'reactionary' has a very special connotation when Marx uses it and it is quite different from the one in which the term is often used by vulgar Marxists. Thus conceived, distribution of land to the landless or the housesites to the bonded labour might be construed as a reactionary intrigue and the landless and the bonded labour being used as a bribed tool. May be. I do not know.

Let me now turn to the present-day Indian society. I shall first describe its class composition and then put forward before you what in my opinion is the nature of the prevailing class conflict.

First, consider the class composition. I shall present some data from the 1971 census. This is now out of date by seven years. But it is unlikely that great changes in the class composition have occurred in the past seven years. The census classifies all persons into two classes: workers and non-workers. Workers are those who are gainfully occupied; they are not necessarily wage-earners. In 1971, out of the total population of 547.9 million, 180.4 million persons were classified as workers. I now propose to classify these workers in several classes according to the relations of production in which they stand in the system of social production.

In the first instance, I shall distinguish workers whose gainful activity is conducted within the framework of household; in other words, whose relations of production are pre-capitalist. They comprise mainly three groups: cultivators that is peasants, agricultural labourers mainly landless, and persons engaged in the household industry that is artisans and handicraftsmen. In 1971, their numbers were as follows: cultivators (78.2 million), agricultural labourers (47.5 million); and artisans and handicraftsmen (6.3 million). They add up to 132 million which is more than 70 per cent of the working population.

It is only the balance of 47.5 million* workers who may be said to have entered into production relations of the capitalist economy. Even these cannot all be classified into the two Marxian classes: bourgeoisie and proletariat. There is a substantial middle class. They are neither employers of wage-labour nor are they wage-labour themselves. They own small means of production and employ themselves on them. Their number is 16 million which is one-third of the workers who may be said to be working in the capitalist system. It will be useful to note some of their major categories: 5.6 million of these are production workers such as tailors, bricklayers, transport vehicle operators and sundry labourers; 2.1 million are engaged in dairy, poultry and fishing; 1.9 million are engaged in providing various services such as restaurants, laundering and hair-dressing; and finally, 4.9 million are shopkeepers and salesmen of various description. Almost all of these are pre-capitalist occupations which are drawn into the capitalist system under somewhat different relations of production. Besides, there are new occupations which are essentially a product of the capitalist system such as professional, technical, administrative and managerial services; a little under one million workers are engaged in these occupations as independent workers.

Let me repeat. Out of the 47.5 million workers who may be said to have entered into production relations of the capitalist system, 16 million, which is one-third, are independent workers; they are neither employers nor employees and hence neither the bourgeoisie nor the proletariat. It is only the remaining 31.7 million workers who are working strictly within the employer-employee relationship: 22 million of them are employers and 29.5 million are employees. I am not sure that all of the 2.2 million employers could be called the bourgeoisie; many of them are small manufacturers and shopkeepers with small capital, themselves working and employing only a few wage-labourers. It is difficult to decide, on the basis

* The discrepancy of 0.9 million is due to the fact that the total number of workers 180.4 million is given by complete tabulation of the census while the number of workers in different occupations is estimated by a one per cent tabulation of the census.

of the data from the census, how many of them could be classified as the bourgeoisie; I presume that the number would be small. In the absence of data, I shall recognize the class of 2.2 million employers as such and equate them with the bourgeoisie.

In all, 29.5 million employees are wage-earners and constitute the proletariat in this country. However, they are by no means a homogeneous, undifferentiated mass. It will be useful to note the major categories: 11.8 million of them are wage-workers in production that is in the manufacturing industry, and transport; they also include pure labourers. We might add to these 1.9 million workers in dairy, poultry, etc., and 3.6 million workers in various service industries such as hotels and restaurant workers, housekeepers, cooks, waiters, maids, building caretakers, sweepers, launderers, hair-dressers, policemen, watchmen, etc. The three groups add up to 17.3 million workers and constitute abut 60 per cent of the proletariat. We may call them the blue-collar proletariat though some of them, such as the policemen, would prefer themselves to be classified among the white-collar.

The remaining 12.2 million constitute the white-collar workers ranging from the clerical to the managerial. Among them, 5.6 million are clerks and 1.6 million are sales workers. They constitute the lower rung of the white-collar hierarchy. The balance of 4.7 million workers comprising professional, technical, administrative, executive and managerial personnel constitute the higher strata of the white-collar hierarchy some of them with their interests aligned with the interests of the bourgeoisie than those of the proletariat.

Let me then summarize the principal classes in the present-day Indian society:

	Workers (in million)	
1. Pre-capitalist class:		
Cultivators	78.2	
Agricultural labourers	47.5	
Household industry	6.3	
	132.0	73.5%
2. Independent workers in capitalist society	16.0	8.9%
3. Employers	2.2	1.2%
4. White-collar employees	12.2	6.8%
5. Blue-collar workers	17.3	9.6%

It is in the context of this class composition, that we should examine the nature of class conflict that is evident in the Indian society. The explicit evidence and the form of the conflict are to be seen in the numerous strikes which are now a common feature of the Indian polity. They cover the white-collar workers as well as the blue-collar workers. There is evident an admirable solidarity among the workers, whether white-collar or blue-collar, whether drawing less than Rs. 200 per month or more than Rs. 2,000 per month. We should therefore recognize all employees, that is all wage-earners, to constitute a class. This accords with the Marx's concept and hence we shall call them the proletariat. Their number in the country is 29.5 million which is just about one-sixth of all workers. The proletariat in this country today is thus a small minority though a sizeable one. When, in the *Manifesto*, Marx called upon the proletariat to rise, he had a different perspective. Let me quote him: "All previous historical movements were movements of minorities, or in the interest of minorities. The proletarian movement is the self-conscious, independent movement of the immense majority, in the interest of the immense majority." I submit that the proletarian movement in India today is not a movement of the immense majority; we should ask whether it is in the interests of the immense majority.

To answer that question we should ask another question: Against whom is it directed? Marx believed that the proletariat would stand face to face necessarily only with the bourgeoisie. The situation has become somewhat complicated since then partly because of Marx's own prescription. In the ten-point programme Marx outlined in the *Manifesto of the Communist Party*, the following three appear: (1) centralization of credit in the hands of the state, by means of a national bank with state capital and exclusive monopoly; (2) centralization of the means of communication and transport in the hands of the state; and (3) extension of factories and instruments of production owned by the state. Under pressure from the proletariat, many capitalist states have made considerable progress along this path. India is one of the foremost among them. Besides, there has been a very great extension of welfare activities of the state which Marx did not anticipate. In consequence, the state is now a major employer in many capitalist countries. In India, the state is the largest employer.

As I mentioned, there were 29.5 million employees, that is, wage-workers, in India, in 1971. Not all of them faced the bourgeoisie as their employer. Some faced the state as the employer. Some faced the bourgeoisie as the employer. Others faced a small manufacturer or a small shopkeeper as their employer. If we define bourgeoisie conveniently as employers of ten or more wage-workers, the *Employment Review* gives the following figures of employment as in March 1974: Public sector (12.5 million); and private sector in establishments employing ten or more workers (6.8 million). The two together add up to 19.3 million and is often referred to as the employment in the organized sector. The balance of employment is in the private unorganized sector that is in establishments employing fewer than ten employees each. The total number of employees in March 1971 was 29.5 million. In March 1974, it would be somewhat larger. But even taking the total employees in March 1974 to be the same as in March 1971, i.e., 29.5 million, it is clear that a total of 10.2 million workers were employed in the unorganized sector.

To conclude, of about 30 million employees that were there in March 1974, more than 40 per cent were employees of the state; 35 per cent were employees of the small manufacturers and small shopkeepers; and only less than 25 per cent were the employees of the bourgeoisie even if we interpret that term liberally to include all owners of establishments employing more than ten employees each. (I recognize that one and the same owner might own more than one establishment). We should therefore examine the nature of the class struggle that the three categories of the employees are waging against their respective employers.

First, consider the employees of the state, that is, workers in the public sector. Their number is 12.5 million and they constitute over 40 per cent of the proletariat in the country. Out of these, 6.2 million, or half of the total are employed in administration and welfare services such as education and public health. Another quarter of the total, that is, 3.3 million, are engaged in various public utilities such as railways, post, telegraph, banking, insurance, electricity, gas, water and sanitary services. In all these fields, the government has exclusive monopoly. The value it puts on these services is the value that it puts on the services rendered by the employees. No surplus value arises and hence no exploitation of the workers is possible in the sense of Marx. The remaining 3 million employees in the public sector are employed in the productive sectors to which the government has extended its activities; these are: manufacturing, construction, mining and quarrying and plantation and forestry. In many of these areas, again, the government has a monopoly, a virtual monopoly or an oligopolistic position. Hardly any profits are made.

What then is the justification of the public sector employees waging a struggle against the government? One can view the situation in one of the two ways. Either the government is regarded representing the whole society. In that case, the government employees can have a genuine grievance if, and only, if, their conditions of life and work are inferior to those of the large majority of the people they are called upon to serve. This is hardly the case.

The alternative is to go back to Marx and not make any distinction between the public sector and the private sector; in other words, not make any distinction between the government and the bourgeoisie. Did not Marx say? "The executive of the modern state is but a committee for managing the common affairs of the whole bourgeoisie." Leaders of the proletariat in the country apparently take this view. In that case, we should remember that Marx also said that in developing the modern industry, "what the bourgeoisie produces, above all, are its own grave-diggers". The same would apply to the modern welfare state which undertakes planned economic development, expands its welfare services and extends its activities into production. All this requires expansion of employment in the public sector. If the employees and their leaders will not distinguish the public sector from the private sector, not distinguish the welfare state from the private capitalist, in so expanding wage-employment in the public sector, the modern welfare state would be producing, above all, its own gravediggers. In recent years, labour governments in many capitalist countries have increasingly come to realize this.

Next consider the employees of the small employer. They are about 10 million in number. The small employer suffers from many disadvantages. His turnover is small; his costs are high. He can survive the price competition from the bigger capitalists only by paying somewhat lower wages and accepting lower profits which are often less than a manager's wage. As Marx said, if he is not able to withstand the price competition, he would go down and sink into the proletariat. This is happening to many a small establishment and we find it taken under the wings of a bigger capitalist. By waging a struggle against the small employers, the workers only help them sink faster. Marx calls them reactionaries because in trying to survive in their small establishments, they are trying to roll back the wheel of history. On that consideration, the proletarian movement directed against the small employers must be considered progressive. As we shall presently see, there are independent and immediate reasons why it seems the workers would prefer the small employer to go down and be taken over by the big capitalist.

Finally, we arrive at the proletarian struggle against the bigger establishments, against the bourgeoisie. This is of course the form which Marx envisaged the proletarian struggle would universally develop into. In India, presently, it is confined to less than 25 per cent of the proletariat which itself constitutes only about a sixth of the working population. Hence, their struggle is essentially a movement of a small minority and not of the immense majority as Marx thought it would be. As I shall later explain, this circumstance gives the movement a character quite different from the one Marx postulated.

Presently, I invite attention to another noteworthy feature of this struggle, namely, that it seems to succeed better in bigger establishments. In other words, the collective bargaining power of the workers seems to increase in direct proportion to the monopoly power of the bourgeoisie. Marx saw this clearly and hence said that the bourgeoisie produced its own grave-diggers. But because his thinking remained confined to the model of a perfectly competitive economy, he could not clearly see the underlying reason why the proletariat struggle succeeds better against a monopolist. The reason is that the monopolist can pass his costs more easily to the consumer. In consequence, the workers are able to secure higher wages and better conditions of service in bigger establishments than in smaller ones. For instance, in the engineering industry in Poona, while many smaller units find it difficult to pay the statutory minimum wage, the workers in larger establishments are able to secure more than double the statutory minimum. No wonder that the workers in the smaller establishments prefer their employer to go down and be taken over by the bigger capitalist; at any rate, they do not seem to care if that happens. After all, that is the course of history as Marx saw it.

But this has serious implications. It means that the proletariat, as a class, is not homogeneous, not only because there are grades and status groups within its ranks, but also because the workers in the bigger establishments have inherently superior bargaining power than the workers in the smaller establishments. I say inherently, because the superior bargaining power of the workers in the bigger establishments comes not necessarily because of better organization or greater political skill, but simply because they face an employer who is a monopolist or an oligopolist, who does not suffer price competition in his trade. he can therefore pay higher wages and pass on the higher costs more easily to the consumer. The workers do not mind. The fact of the matter is that, under the veil of class struggle, the workers in the bigger establishments join hands with the monopoly capital and share the gains of monopoly.

This strikes at the root of the Marxian dialectic of class struggle. Marx puts it as follows:

"Proletariat and wealth are opposites; as such they form a single whole. The question is what place each occupies in the antithesis.

"Private property, as private property, as wealth, is compelled to maintain itself, and thereby its opposite, the proletariat, in existence. That is the positive side of the contradiction.

"The proletariat, on the other hand, is compelled as proletariat to abolish itself and thereby its opposite, the condition for its existence, what makes it the proletariat, i.e., private property. That is the negative side of the contradiction."

With the character that the class conflict takes under conditions of monopoly capital and monopoly labour, I do not see why the proletariat, as proletariat, should feel compelled to abolish itself. Conflict is followed by combine and sharing of common gains. If this is true of the organized labour in the private sector, it is even more true of the labour in the public sector. There, the labour constitutes a monopoly and, in the form of the state, it faces an equally exclusive monopoly. Whatever the cost can be easily passed on to the people. Marx said: "The executive of the modern state is but a committee for managing the common affairs of the whole bourgeoisie." With the emergence of monopoly capital, the bourgeoisie has found it possible and prudent to co-opt a few representatives of the monopoly labour on the executive of the state. It now manages the common affairs of the monopoly capital and the monopoly labour.

In explaining why the proletariat is compelled to abolish itself, Marx says: "All the preceding classes that got the upper hand, sought to fortify their already acquired status by subjecting society at large to their conditions of appropriation. The proletarians cannot become masters of the productive forces of society, except by abolishing their own previous mode of appropriation, and thereby also every other previous mode of appropriation. They have nothing of their own to secure and fortify: their mission is to destroy all previous securities for, and insurances of, individual property."

This is plainly not true under conditions of state and private monopoly capitalism. Under these conditions, the monopoly labour has seen that it can become, if not the master, at least the co-master of the productive forces of society. For this, it does not have to abolish its own or anybody else's mode of appropriation. It can do all this within the framework of state and private monopoly capitalism. It is also not true that monopoly labour has nothing of its own to secure and to fortify; it has a secure job with an assured minimum income on the first of every month without particular responsibility for production and performance. Its mission is to improve the quantum and security of that income. Marx said: "All the preceding classes that got the upper hand, sought to fortify their already acquired status by subjecting society at large to their conditions of appropriation." Monopoly labour is no exception. Having got the upper hand, it is seeking to combine with monopoly capital and fortify its already acquired status by subjecting society at large to its conditions of appropriation. The monopoly capital is naturally willing to co-operate as it must in order to maintain itself. That indeed, as Marx says, is the positive side of the contradiction between capital and labour.

What happens to the negative side of the contradiction? It remains latent and dormant and does not surface so long as there remains a class at whose expense the monopoly capital and monopoly labour may combine and share common gains. Marx did not envisage this possibility because his thinking remained confined to the conditions of free competition and he believed that the society would soon split itself into two classes-bourgeoisie and proletariat-leaving no other class at whose expense the bourgeoisie and the proletariat may combine and share common gains. Marxian dialectic of class struggle follows therefrom.

The conditions in India are far from those postulated by Marx. Partly because the capitalist development has not gone far enough, there exists a large class, in fact as much as five-sixths of the working population, which is neither bourgeoisie nor proletariat and which is waiting to sink into the proletariat. The process is checked because of the rise of the state and private monopoly capital and monopoly of the organized labour; these monopolies restrict the admission into the organized proletariat. Hence, conditions exist, and will persist for a long time, in which the bourgeoisie and proletariat may combine and share common gains at the expense of the rest of the society.

As I have explained, it is only the monopoly capital, whether state or private, and monopoly labour, that is organized labour, which can combine and share common gains. This organized sector comprising about 20 million workers constitutes only one-ninth of the total working population. The apparent conflict between the state and private capital on the one hand and organized labour on the other, therefore leads to the exploitation of the unorganized majority constituting eight-ninths of the society. Because a small minority exploits a large majority, the process is imperceptible but it is certain and real nevertheless.

Thus, in the Indian society of today, the Marxian class conflict is subsumed within a larger conflict between the organized and unorganized sectors. The organized sector consists of the organized labour both in the public and private sector, and private monopoly capital, the state providing an executive committee to manage the common affairs of this sector. The unorganized sector consists of the cultivator, the agricultural labourer, the artisan, the handicraftsman, the new small manufacturer, the shopkeeper, several other working with small capital and finally the unorganized labour working with them.

Can we call these two sectors social classes in the Marxian sense? That takes us back to the questions which Marx asked and left unanswered: What constitutes a social class? Marx makes it clear that the existence of classes is bound up with particular historical phases in the development of production. The historical system from which Marx derived his theoretical model was the British economy of his day and he was led to believe that perfect competition and free trade were essential and permanent attributes of that system. Within that system, quite appropriately, he discovered a criterion to define two fundamental social classes and postulated that, as the system developed, the society would split more and more into these two classes: owners of private property and of means of production and those without property and without means of production.

Circumstances have changed. Capitalism is now characterized not so much by competition but by state and private monopoly capital, and monopoly of the organized labour. Ownership of the means of production no longer provides the criterion to define basic social classes under this system. A new criterion based on the distinction between the monopolist and the rest must now define and distinguish social classes. That criterion is the distinction between the price-markers and the price-takers. The monopoly capital, whether private or public, puts its own price on its product; the monopoly labour puts its own price on itself. All others take the price that the society places on their product and their labour. The society is now divided between two classes: the price-makers and the price-takers.

The Marxian dialectic of conflict between these two classes would appear as follows: Price-makers and price-takers are opposites; as such they form a single whole. The question is what place each occupies in the antithesis.

Price-makers, for their existence, need the price-takers to take the prices they make. Hence, to preserve themselves, the price-makers must also preserve the price-takers. This is the positive side of the contradiction. It explains several policies pursued by the ruling class aimed at protecting the price-takers, namely, the farmers, agricultural labourers, artisans, handicraftsmen, and small industrymen. Such, for instance, are the policies to perpetuate small-scale farming by legislating ceilings on agricultural holdings; to protect artisans by make-believe support and assistance; and to promote small industry by supply of bank credit. What the ruling class will not do is to give these producers an assured price for their product or an assured wage for their labour.

In order to escape exploitation and privation, the price-takers must abolish themselves as a class. This they do, not by abolishing the price-makers, their opposite, but by invading the camp of price-makers and merging themselves into them. This is the negative side of the contradiction.

The process is already on. Farmers, agricultural labourers, artisans, handicraftsmen, small industry and businessmen, price-takers, all are trying to leave their trades behind and seek wage-employment in the organized sector; in other words, they are trying to join the camp of price-makers. They have nothing to lose except their petty property in land and means of production. And, they have a job to win, a job with an assured income on the first of every month, whether it rains or not, whether they produce or not, whether what they produce sells or not. With progressive exploitation of the price-takers by the price-makers, the gap between the two will widen, and the migration will accelerate until the class of price-makers reaches a critical level. The inherent contradiction in everybody trying to be a price-maker will then come to surface and the whole system will fall to the ground. I should be modest and not prophecy what will take its place.

A Restatement

I am grateful for the many comments my colleagues have offered on my analysis of the class conflict in the Indian society. It is customary to acknowledge such comments by means of a rejoinder. But, if I attempt to do it point by point, it will take far too much space. Moreover, it may take the argument away from the main focus of my analysis because, though a number of points raised in the comments deserve further discussion, in my opinion, they are not germane to the central theme of my Lecture. It is possible that, in spite of the length I have taken, I have failed to make clear my central theme. I shall therefore attempt a restatement.

I am attempting an analysis of the class conflict in the present-day Indian society within the framework of Marxian analysis modified in the light of the actual path and form in which development of capital has occurred since Marx wrote. Clearly, the development of capitalism has not proceeded quite along the lines Marx had expected. I have focused attention on a few major departures which I believe affect fundamentally certain crucial Marxian conclusions. Let me recapitulate them briefly.

Firstly, the development of capitalism has not, in general, led to a division of the society into just two sharply distinguished and antagonistic classes. Certain middle classes of the pre-capitalist society; such such as the new professions, have emerged. Secondly, the development of capitalism has not reduced the proletariat to a homogeneous class of workers requiring no more than the simplest skills. On the contrary, it has created, within the ranks of the working class, a hierarchy based on skills and experience rewarded by higher wage and status. Besides, between the bourgeoisie and the proletariat, there is now interposed a class of professional managers, with its own hierarchy, the top of which merges with the bourgeoisie and its bottom with the top of the hierarchy within the working class. Thirdly, capitalist development has not proceeded uniformly in all sectors of the economy. If we take monopoly capitalism as the highmark of capitalist development, it varies greatly between one sector and another, between one industry and another. In other words, the bourgeoisie again is not a homogeneous class. Fourthly, within the capitalist system, the state has emerged as a major employer in nationalized or state-owned enterprises, public utilities, social welfare services, and general administration. This is a complicating circumstance for the working class movement. Not to see the difference between the bourgeoisie and the state as the employer is unrealistic; but to see the difference, divides the working class. Finally, the working class is differentiated not only because of the private and the public sectors co-existing side by side but also because the bourgeoisie is itself differentiated. The workers, organized in trade unions, seem to succeed better when dealing with bigger employers with greater monopoly power, whether private or public. Hence, the workers in each enterprise or establishment prefer to go it alone with only a general support from the entire working class in the name of its solidarity. Bourgeoisie has found this convenient. It has not only conceded legislative recognition to workers' rights but also accommodated the representation of their interests, in varying degree, in the government.

In consequence, rather than organizing themselves into a single political party confronting the bourgeoisie in a single political party confronting the bourgeoisie in a revolutionary struggle, as Marx had expected, the workers have preferred to enter into agreement and arrangements with capitalism. In spite of protestations to the contrary, they have on the whole profited by this strategy.

In India, in terms of the working population, only about 10 per cent of the economy has witnessed capitalist development; 40 per cent of it is publicly owned and operated while 60 per cent is privately owned and operated. This is referred to as organized sector of the economy. Along with other features of capitalist development, the sector is characterized by the Marxian class conflict modified as described above. I ask the question: How does this affect the remaining 90 per cent, unorganized, primarily pre-capitalist sector of the economy? My contention is that, whatever the intentions and the appearances, the class struggle in the organized sector results in the exploitation of the unorganized sector by the organized sector.

I should make it clear that when I say that the organized sector exploits the unorganized sector, I do not mean, even by implication, that there is no exploitation within the organized or within the unorganized sector. There can be exploitation within each sector and nevertheless one sector can exploit the other. This for instance is the case when an imperial power exploits a colony. There is exploitation within the imperial power as also within the colony. Nevertheless, the imperial power exploits the colony and, when it does, the conflicting classes within the imperial country combine in a common cause. This is the essence of the phenomenon.

One criticism is that the organized and the unorganized sectors, or what I have called the price-makers and price-takers, do not constitute social classes in the Marxian sense. I do not know. But I shall not quarrel about words if the phenomenon of the two interest groups, one exploiting the other, is recognized. The division of the society into two classes, price-makers and price-takers, was mainly to draw the parallel with the Marxian classes and emphasize the different criterion I am suggesting to define classes. I request that, in the present phase of capitalist development, not the ownership of the means of production but the ability to dictate ones own price, should be the criterion distinguishing classes. On that basis, I would recognize not just two classes but a hierarchy of classes, one more organized, that is with more highly developed capitalism, than another; with greater monopoly power than another; and hence with greater ability to dictate ones own price than another. My contention is that in a society so stratified, each class exploits another class less organized than itself and that, in this process of exploitation, capital and labour in each class combine in a common cause.

What is the evidence? In particular, what is the evidence that the working class in the more organized sector participates in the exploitation of the working class in a less organized sector? I take this opportunity to offer some illustrative evidence.

To simplify the argument, let me confine attention to the manufacturing industry. The manufacturing industry can be clearly divided into three sectors evincing different stages of capitalist development. They are: the registered factory sector; the urban unregistered sector; and the rural unregistered sector. In the following are a few relevant figures and ratios for the three sectors pertaining to 1974-75.

Manufacturing industry (1974-75)

		Unregistered	
	Registered	*Urban*	*Rural*
Employees(million)	5.6	4.7	10.8
Wage workers (million)	4.4	1.0	0.8
Fixed capital per employee (Rs.)	12,100	1,449	601
Value added per employee (Rs.)	11,389	2,579	932
Annual wage per worker (Rs.)	3,831	1,551	822

Sources: Statistics of the Unorganized Sector.
Central Statistical Organization.
Paper submitted to the Fifth Seminar on the Data Base of the Indian Economy, Madras, May 25-26, 1978.

First notice the difference in the stages of capitalist development in the three sectors on the basis of two characteristics: (a) fixed capital per employee, and (b) proportion of wage-workers among all employees. In the registered factory sector, which is capitalistically the most developed, nearly 80 per cent of all employees are wage-workers and the fixed capital per employee amounts to Rs. 12,100. In the urban unregistered sector, only a little over 20 per cent of the employees are wage-workers, and the fixed capital per employee amounts to Rs. 1,449. In the rural unregistered sector, which is almost pre-capitalist, only about 7.5 per cent of the employees are wage-workers and the fixed capital per employee amounts to a mere Rs. 601.

Now let us compare the average annual wage per worker in the three sectors. It varies from Rs. 3,831 in the registered factory sector to Rs. 1,551 in the urban unregistered sector to only Rs. 822 in the rural unregistered sector. Thus, the wage in the urban unregistered sector is almost double than that in the rural unregistered sector; and, further, the wage in the registered sector is almost two-and-half times compared to that in the urban unregistered sector. Clearly, in sectors with higher capitalist development, the wage workers get a better wage. This needs explanation.

It will be immediately pointed out that the value added per employee is also higher in the sectors with higher capitalist development. This is quite true. Indeed, if wage per wage-worker is related to the value added per employee, it is clear that the wage per wage-worker is a smaller proportion of the value added per employee in the sectors with higher capitalist development. The wage per wage-worker constitutes only 33.6 per cent of the value added per employee in the registered sector whereas it is 66.0 per cent in the urban unregistered sector and 88.2 per cent in the rural unregistered sector. The three sectors represent successively higher stages of capitalist development and, in terms of the Marxian concept of exploitation, the exploitation of the wage-worker is clearly greater in the higher stages of capitalism. Nevertheless, the fact remains that with capitalist development, the wage-worker gets a better wage and that still needs an explanation.

It might be argued that the labour productivity as indicated by the value added per employee is higher in the sectors with higher capitalist development and that it explains the higher wage in these sectors. But the argument is patently un-Marxian. In terms of the Marx's analysis, to justify a higher wage in the more highly developed capitalist sector, one must show that the 'cost of production' of labour employed in that sector is higher than that of labour employed in the less developed sectors. Marx does not accept this either. According to Marx, capitalist development reduces the worker to a mere appendage of the machine and his own cost of production is reduced to no more than his own means of subsistence. I have argued that in this Marx is wrong, that a modern industrial worker requires several specialized skills which can be acquired only through years of training, mainly on the shop floor. The employer certainly recognizes this and is willing to pay a higher wage to an experienced worker than lose him and start all over again with a new worker. But two questions arise. One is that most of this training is at public cost and should we compensate the worker on that account? Secondly, even supposing that the training is done at the private cost of the worker, is this 'investment in himself' essentially different from private property in the means of production? And if the reward to the ownership of the means of production is not justified, how does one justify the reward to education and training sunk in the worker?

This leads us to a harder question which also is the heart of the matter. As mentioned above, workers in the more highly developed sectors are better trained. Besides, they have the advantage of working with a larger quantity of fixed capital per worker. It is clear that the higher productivity of labour in these sectors, as indicated by the higher value added per employee, is largely due to the larger quantity of fixed capital, machinery and equipment, which is combined with labour in these sectors. The focal point of Marxian analysis of capitalist development is that the bourgeoisie accumulates capital, combines it with labour, thereby improves the productivity of labour, but pays the wage-worker only his subsistence and appropriates the surplus-value for further accumulation This constitutes exploitation because, while the entire value created is the product of labour, the worker is paid only his subsistence and the surplus is expropriated by the bourgeoisie.

The bourgeoisie argue that what the worker produces over and above his own subsistence is due to the fixed capital associated with him and that therefore the surplus-value legitimately belongs to the owners of the fixed capital, that is the owners of the means of production, that is the bourgeoisie. Hence, the argument goes, the appropriation of the surplus-value by the bourgeoisie implies no exploitation of the worker. Marx does not deny that more fixed capital in better means of production improves the productivity of labour. He simply questions the legitimacy of the private ownership of the accumulated means of production which in their origin are all product of labour illegitimately appropriated by the bourgeoisie. Hence, the surplus-value being currently produced, which may quite rightly be attributed to the accumulated means of production, in the ultimate analysis, also belongs to labour. It is in this sense that all value created is the product of labour.

This Marxian proposition is often mistaken to mean that all value created in an enterprise is the product of labour currently employed in that enterprise and hence legitimately belongs to it. This is a mistake because it implies that the means of production employed in an enterprise are the product and hence the property of the workers currently employed in that enterprise. This is as un-Marxian as the proposition that the means of production are the private property of the bourgeoisie. The correct Marxian proposition is that all value created over and above the subsistence of workers is due to past labour embodied in the means of production and hence belongs to labour in the aggregate. Hence, its appropriation either for capital accumulation or for consumption over and above subsistence must be a matter for social decision. It must not be left to the bargaining between the bourgeoisie and the workers in the several enterprises. If this is agreed to, it will be hard to justify the large wage-differentials obtaining in different sectors of the economy.

My contention is that the large wage-differentials presently obtaining in different sectors of the economy are the result of the fact that the appropriation of the surplus-value generated in each enterprise is left to the bargaining between the management, private or public, and the workers in each enterprise. When this is done, the workers in the capitalistically more highly developed sectors are able to secure higher wages; firstly because, in these sectors, there is employed more fixed capital per employee and consequently is created larger surplus value per employee which, though it is due to past labour embodied in the means of production, is treated as available for splitting between the bourgeoisie and the workers; secondly because the workers in these sectors are better organized, and hence possess superior bargaining power, which power improves with every increase in wages they secure; and thirdly because the bourgeoisie in the private sector, or the state in the public sector, enjoy greater monopoly power and hence are able to pass at least part of the costs to the less developed sectors of the economy. This is the central proposition of my analysis and, in my view, this constitutes exploitation of the less organized sector by the more organized sector in which process the capital and labour combine.

A point is made that, in spite of all its struggle to improve its wages and living conditions, the organized labour has been able barely to protect its real wage and that in some sectors, such as the public administration, the real wages have in fact declined. I shall not dismiss this point. But, even if it sustains, I do not see that it refutes my contention regarding exploitation of the less organized by the more organized. As I have argued, the evidence for the exploitation is the large wage differentials between different sectors; so long as they persist, the exploitation continues. If this is accepted, we can discuss independently whether the exploitation has progressively increased in the last one or two decades.

In evidence, we may enquire whether the real wages in the organized sector have increased or, more appropriately, whether the wage differentials between organized and the unorganized sectors have widened. To examine this will require a much disaggregated analysis of wages. Such an examination, I suspect, will show that, in enterprises where capitalist development has proceeded faster, along with such development, the workers have improved their real wages. In other words, in enterprises where, because of increased capital intensity and improved organization and management, the productivity of labour has increased, the workers have benefited by a share in the gains in productivity. But this is no more than a conjecture based on a general impression. It needs and deserves careful analysis.

If it shows that the wage differentials between different sectors have not widened, what are its implications? Does it mean that the gains of development are being shared by the organized and unorganized sectors equally or at least proportionately? This is hardly the case; nor is it the contention of my critics. Their contention, I presume, would be that all the gains of development are being appropriated by the bourgeoisie leaving the unorganized sector as also the wage and salary workers in the organized sector where they are. Subject to what I have said above and what I have to say in the following, I accept this contention. The bourgeoisie, supposing they do not dispute it, may say that only a small part of the surplus-value they appropriate goes into their luxury consumption but a large part goes into capital accumulation which provides the basis for expansion of wage and salary employment in the organized sector. I suppose this will be agreed to. What does it mean? It only means that the surplus-value is used, if not for widening the wage-differentials between the organized and the unorganized sectors, for expanding the organized sector in which the wage and salary workers, by drawing much higher wages compared to those in the unorganized sector, combine with the bourgeoisie and the state in the exploitation of the unorganized sector. It is thus that, even if the wage differentials between the organized and the unorganized sectors might not widen, the process of exploitation of the unorganized by the organized progressively increases.

It might be said that the industrial employment has not increased in proportion to the increase in industrial production. This is true but is besides the point. For the process I am describing above, it is enough that industrial employment, with wages much above those obtaining in unorganized sector, is expanding at all. That the employment is not expanding in proportion to the expansion of production only means that capitalist development is proceeding further and, with increased capital intensities, and improved organization and management, is strengthening the basis for continued exploitation. It does not affect my contention that the industrial workers, either by improving the real wages of their class or by numerically expanding their class, combines with the bourgeoisie or the state to keep all the direct and indirect benefits of surplus-value to that class and thus to exploit the unorganized class.

More than the expansion of industrial employment, or more generally what Marx would call productive employment, is of concern the expansion of what Marx would call the unproductive employment such as in general administration and welfare services. The modern state appropriates a substantial part of the surplus-value and uses it for the purpose of general administration and welfare services. India is no exception. Indeed, in India, the expansion of such unproductive employment has been much faster than the productive employment in the organized sector. The wages and salaries in this sector are as high as, if not higher, than those in the productive organized sector. Clearly, these workers are a party to the exploitation of the unorganized sector. Moreover, the general administration functions largely in the interest of the organized sector and the welfare services which the state provides are also used largely by this sector. Thus the general administration and welfare services of the state further strengthen the process of exploitation of the unorganized by the organized.

What does the unorganized sector do to escape this exploitation? It does not try to destroy the organized sector; being unorganized, it has no such power. Indeed, being unorganized, it does not even react as a class. Instead, its individual members try desperately to leave their class and join the other class. Their motivation, I said, is a job with an assured income on the first of every month, whether it rains or not, whether they produce or not, whether what they produce, sells or not. I should have made a distinction between a productive job and an unproductive job in the sense of Marx. Thus distinguished, the phrase, 'whether what they produce, sells or not' applies to the productive job; the phrase, 'whether they produce or not', applies to the unproductive job; 'a job with an assured income on the first every month, whether it rains or not' applies to both.

12 Green Revolution and Social Inequalities in Rural India

D.N. DHANAGARE

The green revolution has been the dominant orientation for rural development programmes in India for over two decades now. As a strategy it implied the introduction of high yielding varieties, extensive use of farm machinery, energized well-irrigation, use of high doses of fertilizers and pesticides directed at improving farm production. It was optimistically reckoned that from this would emerge lasting solutions to the perpetual problem of rural poverty and hunger. This paper examines the extensive literature which has accumulated about the green revolution with a view to determine the nature of impact of the developmental strategy on different sections of rural society. Has the green revolution succeeded in reducing socio-economic inequalities in rural India?

Since 1967 when the High Yielding Varieties (of seeds) Programme (HYVP) was consciously introduced in Indian agriculture, a lot has been written for and against the green revolution. It would, however, be erroneous to equate the green revolution with HYVP alone. The green revolution has to be understood more as a broader ideology of rural transformation whereas programmes such as HYVP, IRDP (Integrated Rural Development Programme) and the like are specific institutionalized mea-

This is a revised version of the paper presented at the Indo-German Colloquium on 'Equality-Inequality' organized by the Max Mueller Bhawan, New Delhi, August 27-29, 1986. The author is grateful to Andre Beteille, Co-ordinator and other participants of the colloquium for their comments and suggestions. However, only the author is responsible for the facts cited and views expressed in this paper.

sures for translating the green revolution ideology into practice (Parthasarthy, 1970: 1-8). Even at the risk of appearing to be stating the obvious rather simplistically, it is necessary to emphasize that the green revolution as a package (ideology and programme) is to be defined as "large scale application of modern science and technology to agriculture". The green revolution technology involved extensive use of farm machinery (as labour saving efficient devices), hybrid (high yielding) seeds, energized well irrigation (and lift irrigation), use of high fertilizer doses and pesticides, and the like. In short, "extensive and intensive use of improved production technology and high yielding varieties of seeds" has been the essence of the green revolution (CSSC, 1974: 3-9).

Though with a difference of degrees different parts of rural India have been humming with developmental activity. The initial measures for rural development in the form of community development programme, land reforms and co-operative institutions, introduced in the first two decades (1947-67) of the independence, had not been particularly effective either in increasing farm productivity substantially or in removing the spectre of rural poverty, unemployment and also of the ever-growing socio-economic inequalities (Dhanagare, 1984: 178-93). The green revolution—the US-sponsored technological package for agricultural development—was accepted in India somewhat overenthusiastically and also uncritically. It was hoped that with improved farm production, not only a lasting solution would be found for the perpetual problems of rural poverty and hunger but also it would generate a new resource base—a launching pad for rural industrialization that would create new employment opportunities and would improve the quality of life at the grassroots in an appreciable measure.

The green revolution—theory and practice—has been the dominant, and also much-talked-about, orientation for rural development programmes in India for nearly two decades now (since 1967). Meanwhile, two mid-term reviews of the net outcome and impact of the green revolution on the Indian countryside were attempted by two separate voluntary institutions in the early 1970s, i.e., within just five years of the introduction of HYVP and similar other programmes. One of these was in the form of a symposium organized by the Centre for the Study of Social Change in 1973 (CSSC, 1974). It had highlighted both the positive and negative aspects of the green revolution. On the positive side it was claimed that the impact of green revolution was visible in the food grain production which had increased in India in the post-HYVP period

(1967-73) by 19.1 per cent over the pre-HYVP period (1961-65). This increase was 87.2 per cent in Punjab, and 64.90 per cent in Haryana where the gains in production performance were impressive (Vyas, 1974: 67-70). Hence, some scholars believed then that to improve the backward regions in general, and agriculture in particular, there was no other alternative to the green revolution (CSSC, 1974: 71).

This rosy picture was, however, not endorsed even by its staunch protagonists. For example, it was asserted at the CSSC symposium that the green revolution was really not taking place, that the new agricultural technology was accessible only to the large farmers and that the prosperity unleashed by the green revolution was distributed differentially to different categories of farmers putting the small and marginal farmers at a relative disadvantage. The reasons for differential distribution were obvious. The high cost/high yield cereal technology of the green revolution called for substantial capital investments generally beyond the means of a majority of small and marginal farmers.[1]

The second review was attempted in 1973 by the London-based Halslemere Declaration Group (HDG). Its report assailed the green revolution as a propagandist and a highly misleading way of describing an annual growth rate of 5 per cent in wheat achieved in Punjab and Haryana from 1967 to 1973 with the introduction of HYVP when the annual compound growth rate of food grain in India, using locally improved varieties of seeds, was about 3 per cent. The HDG (1973: 3-9) further criticized the Indian government for making institutionalized subsidies and cheap credit as well as similar other facilities relatively more accessible to big landowners/rich farmers than to small and marginal farmers. The HDG report did admit that in Punjab and Haryana the trickle down effect of the green revolution was partially visible in the improved daily wages (for agricultural labour) which increased by 89 per cent from 1961 to 1968. However, this 'so-called' gain was totally offset by the rise in prices (by about 93% over the same period) in spite of substantial increase in agricultural production (HDG, 1973: 7).

In our view, both the reviews discussed above were somewhat premature assessments of the green revolution in India. Till 1973, the green revolution measures had been introduced only in a few selected areas whose proneness to adopt new farm technologies was an established fact. Moreover, the trial period of five years (from 1967 to 1973) was too short for any assessment to be fair. Thereafter, several studies have reported their findings revealing the complexity of the precise impact of the green revolution measures, on farm output per acre, on wages, on total household incomes of different categories of farmers, on consumption patterns and also on rural poverty alleviation in general. This research literature has grown into a massive body.

In this paper, an attempt is made to sift some of this material with a view to examining the nature of impact of the green revolution on different sections of the rural society. It is aimed at finding out whether or not this developmental strategy has succeeded in lifting a sizeable section of the rural poor above the poverty line and in reducing socio-economic inequalities in rural India. The exercise is based on the use of secondary source material. Of course different researchers have used different measures to qualify 'growth' or 'impact'. Since such quantitative measures evoke disagreements among economists more often than they evoke unanimity of opinions, same sets of data are and can be used to support and sustain different standpoints or interpretations. Furthermore, studies on impact of the green revolution have been reported from different geo-political regions of India. Not all the regions are at the same level of development.

Regional variations in agrarian social structures—land control and land use patterns, agro-climatic conditions and other socio-cultural as well as historical specificities can at least partly account for some of the inequalities in rural India discussed in this paper. It is, therefore, not suggested here that all rural inequalities across different regions of India could be attributed to the green revolution. Hence, only those which could be decisively attributed to uneven implementation of the state directed measures are discussed in this paper. It would also be difficult to defend a claim that such an exercise is, or even, can be, totally value-free. Nonetheless, we have tried this assessment of the green revolution in the hope that it would provide us with at least qualitative answers to our questions and would suggest future lines for rural developmental strategies in India.

Initially, the green revolution measures were considered to be 'scale-neutral'. It was, therefore, expected that whether it is HYV seeds, pesticides, insecticides and fertilizers, or whether it is lift irrigation, mechanization of farm operations and other farm subsidies, small landholders would benefit as much as larger landowners would, if not more. The agricultural development bureaucracy working at the grass roots, however, has had different perceptions. Their understanding rarely conformed to the notion of scale-neutrality and their actions almost always reflected a tacit pro-rich policy of rural development. Joan Mencher (1978), for example, has reported that most of the agricultural officers she had interviewed in the Chingleput district of Tamil Nadu appeared to be far from neutral. "What they thought was needed to further green revolution was to forget about small farmers (i.e., holders of less than 5 acre of irrigated land—defined as uneconomic holding), because they could not really contribute to increased production. To these officials progressive farmers are those who have viable farms and who are fairly well-off" (Mencher, 1978: 239-40). However, the reality was to the contrary. Mencher found that some of the small holders in Chingleput were as interested in trying new inputs and were as innovative as the rich landowners were. But the former often lacked facilities to try new methods, and seldom received encouragement from the development bureaucracy.

The National Seed Project, started in India with World Bank assistance in 1976 as a part of the green revolution measures, is yet another example of how rural development strategy is founded on similar (pro-rich) assumptions. Production and marketing of HYV of seeds to augment production in agriculture has been the professed aim of this project. The actual implementation of this scheme—an integral part of the green revolution—has been critically investigated by Satya Deva (1980) taking a specific case of the Haryana Seeds Development Corporation. The policy underlying this project was to support the expansion of the private sector to maintain a reasonable balance between the public and private sectors in agriculture.

The farmers in the project area (9 blocks of about 100 villages each) were to buy two shares of Rs. 100 each per acre of seed producing land; share money was paid over five crops (Deva, 1980: 263-65). Within four years of establishment of the Seeds Corporation in Haryana, there were 285 shareholder seed growers. About one-third of these were growing seeds in plots of 5 acre each; another one-third in plots of 5-10 acre; the remaining third used larger plots ranging between 10 and 100 acre (Deva, 1980: 265). Since seed was being grown generally in only parts of their larger landholdings, obviously mainly rich farmers with substantial holding were benefiting from the project. After all, the very agreement terms requiring a farmer to buy two shares (of Rs. 100 each) per acre favoured the rich farmers. And at any rate, even the smallest seed grower (with a 5 acre plot under seed cultivation) required an initial investment of Rs. 1,000 in share capital if he wanted to benefit from this scheme. As regards utilization of seeds, a survey of 60 users and 73 non-users of certified wheat seeds also brought out some interesting facts of growing disparities in green revolution areas. "It was found that users came only from among landowners and high caste farmers and not even one came from among tenants or low (scheduled) caste ones" (Deva, 1980: 268).

Unmistakably, Satya Deva's conclusion suggests that the agricultural development through the application of new scientific knowledge was just a euphemism for using the public sector to promote the private seed industry in which the benefit of the new scientific knowledge went invariably to the upper caste rural rich farmers; it seldom reached poor tenants and low caste farmers who needed it most (Deva, 1980: 269). Introduction of high yielding variety seeds as inputs in green revolution area was thus yet another measure that created new kinds of inequalities, and at times augmented the old ones.

Pro-Rich Peasant Bias

The pro-rich peasant bias of the Indian rural development planning draws its justification from a fallacy that the green revolution technology, being capital intensive, suits rich farmers much better than small and marginal farmers because the rich farmer alone has adequate resources to afford that technology of production, and that expensive inputs are within the reach of only more affluent farmer; therefore, the latter is better placed to derive its benefits. This assumption is then developed into an argument, somewhat hypothetical, that overall yield-rates as well as productivity per acre would be positively correlated to farm-size. The built-in fallacy in this assertion has been fully exploded by the findings of a pioneering survey conducted by Bhalla and Chadha (1983) recently in Punjab.

Conducted in three separate regions of Punjab this survey selected some 180 villages following the methodology of the 30th round of the National Sample Survey and collected valuable data from 1663 cultivating households (Bhalla et al., 1983: 27-31). Its methodology of classifying households into six categories, demarcated exclusively by size of the operational holdings, does suffer from certain inadequacies since it may not get us close enough to the rural social stratification. Nonetheless, the findings of this survey are quite revealing. Analysis of the material costs (i.e., expenditure on seeds, manure and fertilizers, maintenance of bullocks, diesel and electricity, repair and maintenance of implements) has shown that in all the three regions, expenditure on material inputs per acre of cropped area was inversely related to farm-size. This is likely to create an impression that green revolution measures/inputs have truly benefited the small and marginal farmers more than the rich. But this would be quite misleading, because Bhalla and Chadha (1983: 47-49) tell us that "on marginal and small farms, a lion's share of material costs is on account of expenditure on drought cattle—some 48.63 per cent of total material cost incurred by the marginal farmers for the state as a whole". When it comes to per acre expenditure on diesel and electricity; repair and maintenance of machinery then it goes on increasing with farm size.

What is interesting and important to note is that despite their greater dependence on traditional capital inputs (such as drought cattle), small farms were found to be supplementing their own stock of productive assets by hiring on machine services. Hence, per acre expenditure on machine hiring charges is much higher on marginal and small farms compared to large size farms (Bhalla et al., 1983: 49-60). This clearly shows that marginal and small farmers do not lack the drive and initiative nor do they lack inclination to invest and take risk for effecting long-term improvements and for augmenting farm productivity.

The Punjab survey makes it abundantly clear that the small and marginal farmers for whom competing with the rich farmers is an up-hill task, do not hesitate to take risk. In fact, they are enterprising enough to make every possible effort for improving their farm inputs. However, the entrepreneurial initiatives of small and marginal farmers do not seem to have helped them substantially nor have they been able to reduce the growing inequalities in rural Punjab.

The distribution of 1,663 households in the Punjab survey unfolds some of these inequalities. Bhalla and Chadha found that in their total sample there were 140 (8.4%) households having marginal farms of the average size of 1.6 acre; at the other end of the spectrum were 74 (4.4%) large farms of the average size of 32.8 acre (Bhalla et al., 1983:34). Thus, the large-sized farms were about 20 times the size of the smallest farms (on an average). Such inequalities are then perpetuated and further reinforced by developmental bureaucracy's known preference for favouring large-farm owners on the grounds of assumed high productivity of large farms. This assumption is not, however, validated by the Punjab survey data which show that the farm business (agricultural) income per acre was Rs. 754.50 in the case of the smallest farms and Rs. 740.40 for the largest ones (Table 4.1, Bhalla et al., 1983: 78).

In other words, there is enough evidence to suggest that the smallest farmers are at least as productive if not more, as the biggest farmers are. Hence, the argument of productive potentialities and efficiency of large farms is not sustained empirically; certainly it cannot offer any convincing justification for such an inegalitarian distribution of a scarce resource like agricultural land as well as of inputs through green revolution measures as one finds in India in general and Punjab in particular (Deva, 1984: 54).

In India, the farm policies pursued by the government from the 1960s onwards have also tended to increase the degree of inequality between perennially irrigated regions and those regions which have to depend mainly on rainfall for cultivation. It is a known fact that farms in the west areas are better served and reached by the state bureaucracy which implements development programmes than it does in the dry areas. This is so because the green revolution package has been devised keeping primarily the perennially irrigated farms in mind.[2] Production of high yielding varieties of grain with heavy doses of fertilizers has mainly affected irrigated areas which are already favoured (Bagchi, 1982: 156, 175). Therefore, seen in terms of average household incomes, the inequalities in rural areas are even more glaring in the relatively more irrigated and hence prosperous areas.

Several researchers have undertaken comparative studies on the relative economic life changes in wet and dry areas. For example, Athreya and his co-researchers (1983: 4-5) have studied six villages sampled from two panchayat unions in Tiruchi district in Tamil Nadu. Their inquiry was aimed at identifying class status of individual households. As a part of a wider inquiry into production relations, this study probed comparatively the mean incomes of rural proletarian households—both poor peasants and agricultural labourers—in the wet and dry areas. For poor peasants the cash income/wages from agriculture in wet areas was Rs. 1,458 in contrast to Rs. 346 in dry areas. The income disparity in the wet and dry areas here is in the ratio of 4.2: 1.0 which suggests that in the wet areas a poor peasant household's agricultural income is more than four times the average income of a corresponding household from the dry areas (Athreya et al., 1983: 27-28). However, poor peasants from the dry areas apparently make-up by supplementing their incomes substantially through non-agricultural sources.

Even more revealing are the disparities between the economic conditions (measured by mean incomes) of the poor peasants and agricultural labourers' household. The study by Athreya and others has further discovered that the cash wages from agriculture earned by a labour household in the wet area are almost twice the wages in the dry zone. If, however, total cash incomes of agricultural labour households from all sources are taken into account, then the disparity in the dry and wet areas is somewhat reduced in the ratio of 1:1.5 which means that economic condition of wage labour in wet area on the whole still remains one and a half times better than that of labourers in the dry areas (Athreya et al., 1983: 28).

The most fascinating development on the rural scenario is not just that the gap between economic conditions in the dry and wet areas is steadily widening but also that economic returns of agricultural labour households are fast outstripping the incomes of the poor peasant families. This is as much true of the wet areas as it is of dry areas. In the Tamil Nadu study, conducted by Athreya and his associates again, it was found that the total average cash income of an agricultural labour household (from all sources) was Rs. 1,686 while it was Rs. 1,333 for a poor peasant household in the wet areas. These incomes ranged between Rs. 1,217 and Rs. 1,103 for the labourer and poor peasant households respectively in the dry areas (Athreya et al., 1983: 28). Thus, the gap is more in the wet areas compared to that in the dry areas.

Despite its somewhat mixed findings, the Tamil Nadu study by Athreya and his associates highlights an unmistakable trend in the emerging class-structure and the social inequalities or disparities attendant on it. Apparently, the size of the rural proletariat in the wet and dry area villages is not very different. However, the higher polarization in the wet area is reflected in its composition. More than 60 per cent of rural proletariat in the wet areas are not cultivating any land. Here, poor peasants are a minority while the situation is the reverse in the dry areas. There only 36 per cent of the agricultural labourers do not operate any land and poor peasants constitute a majority. Qualitative differences further reinforce the disparities between the agricultural labourers in the dry and the wet areas. Rural proletariat in the wet areas is a more specialized workforce with less non-agricultural income, with higher forms of work-organization (gang-system, etc.) which are more or less absent in the dry zone villages (Athreya et al., 1983: 57).

The most striking difference is seen in the size of the middle peasantry between the dry and the wet areas covered by the Tamil Nadu study. In the wet areas, a mere 21 per cent belonged to this category in contrast to nearly half (46%) of the agrarian population which belonged to the middle peasant category in the dry region. This polarized nature of class structure in the wet areas is also reflected in the fact that an impressive 14 per cent of the rural population in the wet areas are 'surplus appropriators' (either rich peasants, capitalist farmers, cultivating landlords or pure landlords). The proportion of 'surplus appropriators' in the wet areas was nearly three to four times higher than that in the dry area (Table 11.1, Athreya et al., 1983: 56-57).

The polarization process that accentuates the rural class differences has been further intensified by the green revolution. The number of landless labourers and their proportion to the rural population have grown in most regions. Many tenants have lost their lands as landlords were able to evict them including sharecroppers (Bagchi, 1984: 176; Dhanagare, 1984).

A micro-level longitudinal study of two villages from Mandya district of Karnataka, conducted at two different points of time—1955 and 1970—has also revealed certain growing disparities. Here, Scarlett Epstein (1978: 57-58) has found that as irrigation facilities were extended to the two villages, the average of holdings owned by upper caste Lingayat and traditional peasant castes steadily increased whereas the percentage of land belonging to Adikarnataka (untouchable, scheduled caste) households actually decreased. Wet lands had also attracted outsiders (non-agriculturists from nearby towns) to invest capital in buying farms. In the two Karnataka villages, Epstein also noticed that rural co-operative societies, particularly credit societies, were serving the "wealthy farmers better than they did poorer farmers. Rich farmers controlled co-operative institutions not for symbolic gains of 'status' but to serve their vested interests. The richest could easily get loans from co-operative societies at an official rate of 6 per cent interest which was just half the rate of what private moneylenders charged. The rich peasants were also reported to be in much better position to buy large quantities of fertilizer on credit and thereby ensure good harvest than were poorer farmers" (Epstein, 1978: 108-110).

The iniquitous income distribution among rural households from Punjab studied by Bhalla and Chadha reveals a similar or even a more striking disparity. Their survey found that the total yearly farm (business) income of the smallest farmer's household (i.e., marginal farmers having less than 2.5 acre of land) was Rs. 1,231 while that of the biggest one (with operational holdings above 25 acre) was Rs. 24,283. The disparities in the two incomes was found to be in the ratio of 1:20. (Table 4.1, Bhalla et al., 1983: 78-79). In other words, the smaller farmer who is no less productive than the biggest one, and whose entire family has to work on the farm, was much poorer than the one who hardly ever performed any manual work himself (Deva, 1984: 54-55).

It is particularly noteworthy in the findings of the Punjab study that the marginal farmers were working much harder to supplement their income through non-farm sources such as dairying, poultry farming, etc. Thus, the average non-farm income of the smallest farmer (per capita) was Rs. 392.53 but that of the biggest farmer was only Rs. 352.84. As percentage of the total household income, 64.84 (about 65) per cent of the marginal farmer's household income was from non-farm activities compared with only 12.84 per cent in the case of the biggest farmer (Bhalla et al., 1983: 79). Equally interesting is the fact that although the farm business income of the smallest farmer was twenty times lower than that of the biggest one, the former's gross investment in farm assets per acre operated was about Rs. 60 as compared with Rs. 85 for the biggest farmer (Bhalla et al., 1983: 79). Thus, the most marginal farmers in Punjab invested as much as about 5 per cent of his total household income for improvement of his farm assets; in the case of the biggest farmer however it was even less than half per cent. The risk-taking propensity of the small and marginal farmer is too evident here to need any more elaborate comment. The Punjab data have thus demonstrated that marginal and small farmers are no less enterprising than rich farmers. The former are more prone to risk-taking in their farm operations than the latter when the bulk of farmer's household income is actually derived from non-farm sources and activities. This suggests, as Satya Deva has put it, "that a more equitable distribution of land would (in fact) lead to a much larger investment in the farm sector and hence would lead to a stupendous rise in productivity. The possibility of a truly revolutionary rise in (agricultural) productivity flowing from greater equality in landownership has been all but missed (in Punjab)" (Deva, 1984: 55). Obviously, this rise in productivity would be even greater than that has been achieved so far in the so-called green revolution areas where both policies and practice have favoured the rich farmer.

Rural inequalities begin to unfold their hitherto unnoticed dimensions if we look into some statistics on electricity connections on agricultural farms which clearly indicate how only the needs of the rich farmers are catered to by electricity boards on a priority basis. For example, the Punjab Electricity Board had a system of providing priority connections on payment of Rs. 10,000 which was subsequently reduced to Rs. 7,000 a few years ago (PSEB, 1984: 30). It is interesting to note that the expert committee which went into electricity tariff for agricultural consumers in Punjab was conscious of the fact that some 67 per cent of the 10.27 lakh farm operators in Punjab have land holdings below 4 hectare, with an average holding size of 1.74 hectare only. Estimates of the department of economics and sociology of the Punjab Agricultural University for the year 1981-82 showed that this holding size (1.74 hectare) was capable of generating on an average a disposable income of Rs. 7,000 per annum—an amount which is about the bare maintenance level of income for an average family of six. But this was also the amount the Electricity Board in Punjab charged for providing connection on a priority basis. At any rate the expert committee mentioned above found that by 1983-84 there was just 3.5 lakh consumers (agricultural connections) which constituted only a little over 14 per cent of the total consumers in the whole of Punjab (PSEB, 1984: Table 6, 21-22, also p. 5). It can, therefore, be summarized that only about 35 per cent of the total farm-holders had sought service connection from the Electricity Board and that these must have been mostly rich farmers who could alone afford high costs of service connections or installation. The small and marginal farmers are at a disadvantageous position because very few of them can afford to incur expenditure on electricity connection and diesel. It is pertinent to note in this context that the Punjab survey by Bhalla and Chadha found electricity expenditure to be positively correlated to farm size (Table 3.9, Bhalla et al., 1983: 54-55).

Problems of Mechanization

Mechanization of farm operations in green revolution areas has undoubtedly strengthened the economic position of the rural rich farmers in India. However, for the landless agricultural labour, some of the fall-out effects of modernization of farm technology have been far too damaging. In some instances they are simply disastrous. The degree of farm mechanization has exceeded all expectations in Punjab so much that in 12,000 villages of the state there were as many as 2 lakh farm machines of different types mainly wheat threshers and combine harvesters (PHG, 1984: 127). But the effects of mechanization are visible in the fact that there are a total of 5,000 deaths in India resulting from farm machine accidents by 1978; of these 500 alone were from Punjab (Dongare, 1985: 12). A recent report has further revealed that every year more than 300 farm workers are incapacitated during the wheat harvesting season in Punjab. A majority of these accidents occur while workers work on wheat threshers. It is further estimated that in 1985 (one year alone) nearly 1,000 farm workers in Punjab, Haryana, and western UP lost their limbs in thresher accidents.[3] Most of the victims were invariably migratory labour. It has been estimated that by end of 1985 more than 10,000 farm labourers from Bihar, UP and Orissa have been maimed while working on such machines. According to the official information given in the Punjab Assembly on September 7, 1978, 841 cases of loss of limbs or life occurred during 1975 to 1978; eight agricultural labourers were killed and 24 lost two or more limbs.[4]

The attitude of the government towards the problems of treatment and rehabilitation of victims of accidents on farm machines is, however, that of total ambivalence. In Punjab, for example, the Workmen Compensation Act of 1923 has not been implemented properly. This Act provides for the farmers to insure their workers against accidents. Insured farm labourers are supposed to get Rs. 15,000 for the loss of a limb. Instead the government provides compensation which is usually just a third of this amount. Neither the government takes effective steps to prevent farmers from using substandard threshers nor does it prevail upon them to give rightful and adequate compensation to victims or to protect potential victims from such hazards.[5] The government clearly adopts a mothering attitude towards rich farmers whom it protects (by promptly reducing costs of electricity consumer connections as discussed earlier) but does not consider it necessary to implement rigorously as well as urgently the provisions of the Compensation Act in respect of farm labourers injured or incapacitated in machine accidents.

The health hazards for the rural agricultural labour in the green revolution belts are not confined to incapacitation resulting from machine accidents. The agricultural work in these areas has been rendered even more injurious by the increasing use of poisonous chemical sprays for plant protection on a large scale. The high yielding varieties of seeds—used as an indispensable part of the green revolution strategy—are apparently highly susceptible to diseases, and in the third world countries poisonous pesticides are used both extensively and intensively for plant protection without realizing the health hazards that follow for agricultural labour. A recent report of the International Development Research Centre, Ottawa has revealed that there were 7.5 lakh cases of acute poisoning with different varieties of pesticides. Half of these were reported from the third world countries, out of which again one-third were reported from India alone (PHG, 1984: 128-29). Victims of such poisoning are invariably agricultural labourers, and only rarely rich farmers themselves. For example, a study of 70 patients of acute poisoning reported from the civil hospitals of Vadodara and Surat (in Gujarat) in three years from 1976 to 1978 were all agricultural labourers, including two women (PHG, 1984: 129). Surprisingly, no legal protection is available to the victims of poisoning accidents on agricultural farms as the Workmen Compensation Act applies only to industrial workers in this respect.

Comparing the income distribution and consumption units of both the rural rich peasants (magnates) and agricultural labour households in 1955 and in 1970, Epstein has concluded that the rich have grown more affluent and the poor have become poorer. Agricultural real wages had declined mainly because of increase in the number of labour households, and steady price rise resulting in rises in cost of living. Wages, however, have lagged behind (Epstein, 1973: 142-82). Some other scholars, who have examined the impact of the green revolution on the weaker sections, have argued somewhat optimistically, that conditions of rural poor—particularly agricultural labour—do not necessarily deteriorate. On the contrary, general prosperity ushered in by modernization of agriculture in the green revolution areas, percolates to the grass roots in the rural society. Where this percolation process is arrested by the rich through manipulations and machinations, the agricultural labourers there tend to get better organized and more militant to fight and thereby stand to benefit through higher wages and improved working conditions (Oommen, 1971: A 99-103; also 1975: 160). Group-bargaining thus strengthens the position of agricultural labour in rural power equations (Muthiah, 1975: 52-57). However, this optimism is founded on the assumptions of perfect competition and labour market. In fact, with imperfect labour market conditions, as are obtained in India, the bargaining power of the rural labour is more apparent than real.[6] There is also another assumption that the green revolution necessarily raises the rate of agricultural growth in the affected areas. But some scholars even question this assumption. At least some economists tell us that in India agricultural production grew at best at a constant rate on an average over the period from 1950-51 to 1973-74; at best the green revolution might have just managed to arrest a tendency towards decline in agricultural production/growth rate observed in the late 1950s (Reddy, 1978), In this context it is significant that owing to the growing capitalist penetration of the countryside the process of de-peasantization has been accelerated and consequently large numbers of small and marginal farmers or poor peasants have been pushed into the ranks of landless labourers (Oommen, 1975: 175). This proletarianization process is more striking in the green revolution areas. In view of this process of proletarianization, the improvement that the green revolution is expected to bring into the conditions of wage labourers appears to be a distant mirage. At least the position of the rural poor—particularly agricultural labour—as a class is not likely to be altered substantially vis-a-vis the rich farmers who virtually monopolize economic resources and control credit institutions in the countryside (Palmer, 1976; Dhanagare, 1984: 192-93; also Bagchi, 1982: 176).

In general, findings of different studies show that the green revolution has had a contradictory impact on rural employment and agricultural wages. The pessimism of the Halslemere Group or Reddy's skepticism about the potentialities of green revolution in raising agricultural growth rate could be kept aside for a while. One may generously admit that by raising the productivity of land and by making it possible for farmers to grow two or even three crops on a piece of land, the green revolution has made it possible for rural workers to obtain more employment for the year as a whole. But then Billings and Singh have discovered that in Punjab the demand for agricultural labour went up from 51 mandays to 60.1 mandays with the introduction of the persian wheel as a means of irrigation and of fertilizers and pesticides. However, when pump-sets, wheat-threshers, corn-shellers and tractors are introduced the average demand for labour drops down to 25.6 mandays (1969: A 221-24). In certain prosperous parts such as in Haryana, the green revolution has led to replacement of paternalistic relations between capitalist farmer employer and workers by formal contracts (Bhalla, 1976); but in most other parts of the country attached labourers are simply being thrown out of work or are being converted into casual day labourers (Gough, 1977). Where mechanization of farm operations appears to brighten the employment opportunities and wages in green revolution areas, migration of workers from less favoured areas— such as Bihar, east UP, Orissa or Rajasthan—have tended to depress the bargaining position as well as wages (Bagchi, 1982; 158-59).

The pattern of consumption in the green revolution areas is also very strikingly iniquitous and figures on population below the poverty line are staggeringly high. The case of Punjab—the most prosperous state in India—once again waves a red signal. The Bhalla-Chadha study has revealed that about one-third of the marginal farmers (cultivating up to 2.5 acre), one-fourth of the small farmers (between 2.5 and 5 acre) and a fifth of the medium-level farmers (cultivating holdings between 5 and 7.5 acre) from their sample were living below the poverty line, i.e., were living on starvation diets. In the total sample of 1,663, 16.48 per cent of the farming households were living below the poverty line, and their proportion was positively correlated to the farm size in all the three regions of Punjab (Bhalla et al., 1983: 153-57, particularly see Table 5.18). If we add the 16 per cent households of landless labourers, then the proportion of rural households living below the poverty line comes to over 32 per cent which is distressing considering that Punjab is the most developed state in India (Deva, 1984: 55).

This finally raises doubts about efficacy of the green revolution technology which was originally visualized as a poverty alleviating measure. Since the green revolution was projected as the new official ideology for rural reconstruction so as to effectively fight poverty, it is pertinent to examine here whether its implementation and consequences have facilitated alleviation of poverty or whether it has arrested the process of bridging the gap between the affluent and weaker sections that represent the two extreme ends of the development spectrum in India.

In fact, all available statistics indicate greater and greater immiseration and pauperization as the green revolution technology package has spread in different parts of India. Studies on poverty, measured by per capita expenditure and consumption of calories in India, further expose the hollowness of claims often made by planners and protagonists of the green revolution. "The process of rural development during the 1960-69 decade has benefited the upper middle and the richest sections more than the middle, lower middle and the poorest sections" (Dandekar and Rath, 1971: 70). Consequently, socio-economic inequalities in rural India have been steadily growing. While Dandekar and Rath found some 45 per cent of the total population to be below the poverty line at the 1960-61 prices, Bardhan came out with even a grimmer picture. He compared the proportion of rural population below the minimum level of living (defined as Rs. 15 per month at 1960-61 prices) in 1960-61 with that in 1967-68. Without exception all the Indian states had experienced a massive increase in the percentage of rural people below the poverty line. It ranged from 80 to over 84 per cent in states like Bihar, Orissa, UP and West Bengal in 1967-68. Even in the most prosperous states it had gone up from 25.01 to 63.97 per cent in Gujarat, from 40.14 to 67.61 per cent in Maharashtra and from 13.56 to 49.98 per cent in Punjab (Bardhan, 1970: 1244). So, in the throbbing heartland of green revolution (Punjab-Haryana) this percentage had nearly quadrupled between 1960-61 to 1967-68.

This trend was confirmed a decade later (after Bardhan's study) by another study conducted by the International Labour Organization in 1979. Drawing its sample from four states of Punjab, Tamil Nadu, Bihar and UP, this survey was aimed at determining trends in absolute and relative incomes of the rural poor. It revealed a steadily worsening distribution of income and the declining real income of the rural poor. In the rich farm lands of Punjab, the real income per head was reported to have risen by 26 per cent during the 1960s (which was two and half times as fast as in India as a whole). Despite this, the proportion of rural population living below the poverty line increased in Punjab from 18 per cent in 1960 to 23 per cent in 1970 (ILO, 1979: 13-15). In Tamil Nadu, the ILO study found that the percentage of population earning less than the costs required for the minimum foodline had gone up from 36.04 per cent in 1961-62 to 48.63 per cent in 1969-70. Taking the 'basic-needs line' into account these percentages had gone up from 66.49 to 73.98 for the corresponding years (see Table 3, ILO, 1979: 18).

About the social origins of the rural poor, the ILO survey has revealed that in all the states it was the agricultural labourers—the landless and near-landless families—who constituted the core of rural poverty. For example, in Tamil Nadu in 1971, 56 per cent of all cultivators, 85 per cent of 'other workers' (mainly artisans) and 87 per cent of agricultural labourers were living below the poverty line (ILO, 1979: 9).[7]

However, some economists have provided us with a more optimistic picture. Using the data from the 32nd round (1977-78 revised) and the 38th round (1983-84) of the National Sample Survey (NSS), Hanumantha Rao has pointed out that the decline in the number of persons below the poverty line for all population is estimated around 12.5 per cent in rural areas as against 7.8 per cent in urban areas. He, however, accepts that between 1977-78 and 1983-84 this decline is less notable for scheduled castes and tribes (7.6% and 7.1% respectively) compared to 15.1 per cent for the rest of the population for whom the rate of decline in poverty ratio is more than double the rate for scheduled castes and tribes (Rao, 1985: 9). Even assuming that Hanumantha Rao's inferences are close to reality, they imply an admission that poverty alleviation programmes, whether IRDP or NREP (National Rural Employment Programme), have failed to bring about a sizeable reduction in the rural poverty ratio in a highly developed state like Punjab where between 1977-78 and 1983-84 the poverty ratio declined only by 17.1 per cent. The poor performance of Punjab in poverty alleviation programmes becomes even more striking in the light of the facts that (a) the average per capita consumption expenditure was the highest (81.69 compared to the all-India average of 70.94) in Punjab; and (b) that the expenditure on the anti-poverty (poverty alleviation) programmes like IRDP, NREP, etc., for the years 1980-84 was the highest in that state—31.22 for Punjab compared to the national average of 8.33 (Rao, 1985: 10-11, particularly Tables 3 and 5).

Two points come out clearly in Hanumantha Rao's analysis: first, that although the poverty alleviation programmes have succeeded in bringing about an appreciable decline in the proportion of rural population below the poverty line, their performance is far less impressive for the scheduled castes and tribes—the traditionally weaker sections of the Indian society; and secondly, the regional variations in the decline of rural poverty ratio clearly suggest that more developed states particularly Punjab are not performing as satisfactorily as some of the less developed states like Madhya Pradesh, Orissa and West Bengal are. The implications of these points are too obvious to need any elaboration. Agricultural growth may be a necessary but not a sufficient condition for reducing social and income inequalities. A more genuine political will and commitment to the philosophy of distributive justice must match the rising level of agricultural growth—a dictum almost discounted in the Indian planning for rural development.

There are other economists who do not share Hanumantha Rao's optimism about the impact of poverty alleviation measures nor do they accept the official versions of the 'so-called' achievements of IRDP or NREP. For example, Rath (1985: 17-21) has attempted to demonstrate the multifaceted failures of IRDP/NREP and has even commented that it should not come as a surprise if another NSS survey on consumption expenditure in the mid-1980s shows no visible impact of the IRDP on the dimensions of rural poverty in India. A similar view was expressed earlier by Raj Krishna. To him the IRDP and NREP schemes have brought only small, often negligible, benefits to the rural poor; at least these are not substantial enough to ensure that the households which are often claimed by official sources to have been lifted above the poverty line would remain permanently above the poverty line. Raj Krishna's apprehension is fully justified in the light of the fact that the Draft Plan (1978-83) had estimated the size of the rural poor as 290 million in 1978 whereas a World Bank estimate had suggested that there are as many as 327 million rural poor (Mathur, 1980: 74). In fact, Raj Krishna feared that despite the official claims about the decline in rural poverty ratio, the Sixth Five Year Plan figure of the poor population (339 million below the poverty line) for 1980 might grow to 472 million by the end of the century (Krishna, 1985: 8) which would be more than India's population at the time of independence.

For nearly two decades now the green revolution measures have been experimented with by the states in different parts of India. Not only that, in the name of spreading the green revolution technology, even the transnationals have been permitted to operate in rural areas through the official cover (Bagchi, 1982: 177). However, in most parts, the green revolution has failed to raise the incomes of rural poor appreciably, and to contribute substantially to their effective purchasing power. On the contrary, in many parts, the real earnings of agricultural labourers and poor peasants have been lower at the beginning of the 1970s than in 1960-61. Several studies of Punjab, UP, Bihar and Tamil Nadu have produced convincing data on this point (see ILO, 1977).

The main thrust of the green revolution has been towards productivity and growth. The policy makers were concerned primarily with augmenting per acre yield. The assumption underlying the planners' priorities was that growth in itself would suffice since it would show percolation effects and would in turn help in resolving problems of unemployment and poverty in rural India. This perspective now stands virtually discredited. Alternatively, another perspective is being advocated which does not treat growth and poverty alleviation as two distinct goals but believes that the latter has to be built into the growth processes. This approach advocates socialization of productive assets and more egalitarian distribution of these infrastructural facilities through the promotion of cooperative activity (Parthasarathy, 1985: 2125).

The streaks of socialistic thinking are evident in the new perspectives on rural development in India. However, ideas for reorientation and reorganization of IRDP, etc., seldom go beyond suggestions for decentralization of decision-making, entrusting panchayat bodies (zilla parishad) with responsibilities for planning and overall monitoring of anti-poverty programmes, or for altering plan allocation priorities, "for shifting from individual to group approaches"[8]—whatever that may mean. Rarely do we examine the adequacy and suitability of the constitutional framework that treats institution of private property as sacrosanct, and considers property, and not work, as a fundamental right. The pertinent question is whether and to what extent the given institutional framework is conducive to systemic changes—that are often offered as palliatives in the populist discussions on rural development and poverty. The growing domination of the new class of rich farmers is a fact to reckon with and not to be wished away. It is naive even to believe that the green revolution and the IRDP measures (for poverty alleviation) constitute a point where growth and social justice dovetail and converge and that both the goals could be targeted simultaneously without any fundamental restructuring in the institution of property. Without some rethinking on development strategies for basic changes in the system, rural inequalities would not be reduced let alone removed.

Notes

1. This is summarized from the views expressed in the papers presented by K. Mukherjee, A Thaper and S.S. Johl at the CSSC Seminar. For details see CSSC, 1984: 1-9, 21-24.
2. Since over 70 per cent of India's cultivated acreage is rainfed, it lacks assured sources of irrigation, and so it was clear from the start that these areas would not benefit from the HYVP—new cereal technology of the green revolution. See for example, Ashok Thaper's contribution in CSSC, 1974: 21.
3. See *The Times of India* (Bombay), April 14, 1986, p. 8.
4. More details of such fatal accidents on farm machines and of other health hazards resulting from use of chemical fertilizers without the mandatory use of masks by agricultural labourers in the green revolution areas are available in, PHG 1984: 127.
5. This observation has been made on the basis of an editorial comment from *The Times of India* (Bombay), April 14, 1986.
6. For a fuller discussion on "imperfect labour market", see Bardhan, 1984: 38-59.
7. The tenor of the discussion on 'Development of the Rural Poor: Intentions and Implementation' at the 24th Annual Conference of

members of the IIPA, New Delhi, also confirmed this. Particularly see Kuldeep Mathur's Theme paper in IIPA, 1980: 71-78.

8. Such suggestions have been offered by G. Parthasarathy, 1985: 2127-28.

References

Athreya, V., Boklin G., Dijurfeld G. and Lindberg S., 1983, "Identification of Agrarian Class: A Methodological Essay with Empirical Material from South India", *Arbejdspapir*, (No. 21), mimeo, Sociology Institute, Copenhagen University.

Bagchi, Amiya Kumar, 1982, *The Political Economy of Underdevelopment*, (Modern Cambridge Economics Series), Cambridge University Press.

Bardhan, P., 1970, "Green Revolution and Agricultural Labourers", *Economic and Political Weekly*, Vol. V, Nos. 29-31 (Special Number), 1241-48.

—, 1984, *Land Labour and Rural Poverty: Essays in Development Economics*, Delhi: Oxford University Press.

Bhalla, G. S, 1976, "New Relations of Production in Haryana Agriculture", *Economic and Political Weekly* (Review of Agriculture), March 1976, Vol. XI, No. 13, A 23-A 30.

Bhalla, G. S. And Chadha, G. K.; 1983, *Green Revolution and the Small Peasant: A Study of Income Distribution among Punjab Cultivators*, New Delhi: Concept Publishing Co.

Billings, M.H. and Singh A., 1969, "Labour and the Green Revolution: The Experience of Punjab", *Economic and Political Weekly*, IV (52), December 27, pp. A-221-A-224.

Centre for the Study of Social Change (CSSC), 1974, *Green Revolution: The Unfinished Task*, Calcutta: Minerva Associates.

Dandekar, V.M. and Rath N., 1971, *Poverty in India*, Pune: Indian School of Political Economy.

Deva, Satya, 1980, "The National Seed Project in India", *The Journal of Administration Overseas*, Vol. XIX, No. 4, (October), pp. 262-69.

—, 1984, "Problems of Rural Development in Green Revolution Areas", *Social Scientist*, No. 130 (March), pp. 52-59.

Dhanagare, D.N., 1984, "Agrarian Reforms and Rural Development in India: Some Observations", *Research in Social Movements, Conflict and Change*, Vol. 7, pp. 177-201.

Dongare, M.G., 1985, "Khetihar Mazadoor-Samasya Tatha Nirakaran" (Agricultural Labour: Problems and Solutions, in Hindi), Kanpur.

Epstein, T. Scarlett, 1978, *South India: Yesterday, Today and Tomorrow*, (Low Priced Edition) London: Macmillan.

Gough, K., 1977, 'Agrarian Change in Thanjavur', in K.S. Krishnaswamy et.al. (eds), *Society and Change: Essays in Honour of Sachin Chaudhuri*, Bombay, Oxford University Press.

Halslemere Declaration Group (HDG), 1973, "The Death of the Green Revolution", (prepared by M.R. Bhagwan, K. Haraksingh, Richard Payne and David Smith), London: HDG.

Indian Institute of Public Administration (IIPA), 1980, "Development of the Rural Poor: Intentions and Implementation", (Proceedings of the 24th Annual Conference of Members of the IIPA, held on October 11, 1980), New Delhi: IIPA.

ILO, 1977, "Poverty and Landlessness in Rural Asia", Geneva: International Labour Organization.

—, 1979, "Profiles of Rural Poverty", Geneva: International Labour Organization.

Krishna, Raj, 1985, "Reduction in Poverty", *Indian Express*, January 9, 1984 as reproduced in the *IASSI Quarterly News Letter*, Vol. 4, Nos. 1-2, (June 1985), pp. 7-8.

Mathur, K., 1980, "Development of the Rural Poor: Intentions and Implementation", in IIPA (2980), pp. 70-78.

Mencher, Joan P., 1978, *Agricultural and Social Structure Tamil Nadu: Past Origins, Present Transformations and Future Prospects*, New Delhi: Allied Publishers.

Oommen, T.K., 1971, "Green Revolution and Agrarian Conflict", *Economic and Political Weekly*, VI (26), June 26, pp. A99-A103.

—, 1975, "Impact of Green Revolution on the Weaker Sections", in *Changing Agrarian Relations in India* (Seminar Papers), Hyderabad: National Institute of Community Development, pp. 151-167.

Palmer I., 1976, "The New Rice in Asia: Conclusion from Four Country Studies", Geneva: UN Research Institute for Social Development.

Parthasarathy, G., 1970, *Green Revolution and the Weaker Sections*, Bombay: Thacker and Co.

—, 1985, "Reorientation of Rural Development Programmes: A Note on Some Basic Issues", *Economic and Political Weekly*, Vol. XX, No. 48, November 30, 2125-28.

People's Health Group (PHG), 1984, "Hazards of Agricultural Work: A Case Study from Punjab", *Socialist Health Review*, Vol. I, No. 3 (December), pp. 126-29.

Punjab State Electricity Board (PSEB), 1984, Report of the Expert Committee on "Level and Structure of Electricity Tariff for Agricultural Consumers in Punjab", Chandigarh; Government of Punjab—PSEB.

Rao, C.H., Hanumantha, 1985, "Changes in Rural Poverty in India: Implications for Agricultural Growth", *IASI Quarterly newsletter*, Vol. 4, (December) Nos. 3-4, pp. 7-14.

Rath, Nikant, 1985, "Limitations of IRDP as a Programme for the Poor", *IASSI Quarterly Newsletter*, Vol. 4, (June) Nos. 1-2, pp. 17-21.

Reddy, V.N., 1978, "Growth Rates", *Economic and Political Weekly*, May 13.

13 Social Stratification in an Orissa Village

JAGANATH PATHY

Capitalism in Indian agriculture has been examined by a number of Marxist scholars in recent years.[1] This paper discusses the subject in the light of material from an Orissa village, collected during 1974-75 as part of a larger study of the political structure of the village.

The author begins by reviewing the main features of the different modes of production in agriculture, as formulated by various scholars. The material on the land and credit systems of the village under study is then discussed. Finally, the particular mode of production operative in the village is considered.

Ashok Rudra and his colleagues led the way in India by approaching this issue with rich quantitative material, and concluded that capitalist farming had not appeared in Indian agriculture.[2] Their findings have provoked several others. Rudra has been attacked for being ahistorical, classifying farmers as capitalist and non-capitalist, instead of locating the trends in terms of capitalistic features.[3] Nevertheless, Rudra's findings do find considerable support in the literature.[4]

The present paper seeks to consider the above controversy at both macro and micro levels. Recognizing the inadequacy of the village as a unit for analyzing agrarian relations,[5] our analysis often extends beyond the village. Further, the data tend to be qualitative, precluding rigorous statistical operations.

We begin with the main features of the various modes of production in agriculture, followed by the material on the land and credit system in the village. Finally, the particular mode of production operative in the village is discussed.

Let us begin with the concept of feudalism. Feudalism refers to a historically conditioned socio-economic formation, wherein the production relations are based on the feudal lord's ownership of the means of production, primarily land. In this system, "an obligation is laid on the producer by force and independently of his own volition to fulfil certain economic demands of an overlord, whether these demands take the form of services to be performed or of dues to be paid in money or kind."[6] And, the relation between the owners and the serfs is predominantly socio-political, and conceals the economic contradiction.[7]

With the breakdown of the self-sufficient subsistence economy and the growth of the commodity economy, feudal relations tend to change as they are replaced by the capitalist mode of production. During this transformation there may be a transitional phase[8], which may be called semi-feudal or pre-capitalist. In this phase, the working population is exploited through land and lending. This is said to be the main feature of 'semi-feudalism'. Bhaduri writes: "The semi-feudal landowner uses *two modes of exploitation* for extracting from the tenant—he exploits the tenant through his traditional property right on land as well as through usury and the *economic basis of semi-feudalism is the combined operation of these two modes of exploitations.*"[9]

Elsewhere, in studying West Bengal villages, he narrates the main features of semi-feudal agriculture as under: The existing relations of production have more in common with classical feudalism of the master serf type than with industrial capitalism. The four prominent features of this type of agriculture are: (a) sharecropping, (b) perpetual indebtedness of the small tenants, (c) concentration of two modes of exploitation, namely, usury and landownership, in the hands of same economic class, and (d) lack of accessibility for the small tenant to the market."[10]

Likewise, Bettelheim argues that, though in today's agriculture in India, the classic Marxian categories of feudalism do not apply, there is enough evidence to note the decline of feudalism, and the new situation may be called semi-feudalism: "Typical of the situation is the absence of a labour market in a large part of the rural sector; the personal subservience of the immediate producer to the landowner; the excessive importance of land-rent; the underdeveloped marketing system, resulting in little social division of labour, a low rate of accumulation, and the use of produce mainly to satisfy immediate needs."[11]

By contrast, the emergence of capitalism in agriculture is marked by a shift to wage labour and simultaneous accumulation and reinvestment of the surplus.[12] For Rudra, a capitalist farmer will tend to (a) cultivate his land himself rather than lease it out; (b) use hired labour in much greater proportion than family labour; (c) use farm machinery; (d) market an important share of produce; and (e) organize his production to yield a high rate of return on his investments.[13] Besides, there will be increasing concentration of the means of production and thereby a development of the productive forces.[14] The agricultural wage labourers, too, will be increasingly free and unattached to the means of production.[15]

Having surveyed the different modes of production in agriculture—feudal, semi-feudal, and capitalist—we move now to the information collected from the Orissa village.

Talapatna—the village studied—is a settlement under Dharakota Panchayat Samiti, in the Ganjam district of Orissa. During the Mughal period, the entire area of the panchayat samiti was in one of the 'Northern Sirkars'. Consequently, there developed a powerful *zamindari* system here, underpinned by the law of primogeniture. In 1802-03, the Permanent Land Settlement Act was introduced in the area, entrusting the collection of revenue to the powerful zamindar.[16]

Much later, in 1898, the village of Talapatna came into existence, founded by the zamindar who provided agricultural and residential land to the settlers. These tenants were obliged to pay half the produce to the zamindar besides providing various forms of unpaid labour (*bethi*), upon demand by the zamindar's family. All the inputs and the labour necessary in production were the responsibility of the tenants. A few settlers of the artisan castes were obliged to provide certain tools and products (such as home-made cloth), and to perform other services as required by the zamindar. Still others were employed by the zamindar for looking after cattle (9 households), gardening (2 households), watchman duties (3 households), and religious functions (1 household).

By the beginning of the century, there were 74 households in the village. Today, it has 320 people in 72 households. That is, the number of households has remained more or less unchanged. The population did grow, but meanwhile in the beginning of the 1950—the time of the Orissa Estate Abolition Act of 1951[17]—several artisans and upper-caste households, who were employed by the zamindar and had no land or had very meagre land, left the village. On the other hand, the strength of the lower and exterior castes has shown rather an increase over the period (Table 1).

Table 1

Distribution of castes in Talapatna (1900-1974)[18]

Local castes (equivalents)	*Number of households in 1900*	*Number of households in 1974*
Brahmana (Brahmin)	1	0
Karan (Kshatriya)	3	2
Tanti (Weaver)	9	3
Gauda (Milkman)	5	5
Gudia (Sweetmaker)	0	1
Khandayat (Odiya)	6	5
Keota (Fisherman)	0	1
Dhoba (Washerman)	0	3
Khadal	50	52
Total	74	72

Source: Relevant records from the ex-officials of the zamindar and interview with the village elders.

Initially, the land was with the zamindar. But, in course of time, whenever he was pleased with some settler, he used to give him *patta* land (the land over which record of right exists). Accordingly, a few got land, but most not. The total cultivated land in the village is 148 acre.

In 1974, the village had an average of 2 acre of cultivated land per family. But ownership is highly concentrated. Only 17 families (23.6%) have their own land, totaling 56 acre. While of the remaining 92 acre of village land, the zamindar owns 63 acre, his ex-manager (*diwan*) who lives in a village 25 miles away owns 25 acre, and a small merchant of another village owns 4 acre. The zamindar had about 735 acre of land in 18 villages; out of which, to avoid the land laws, he transferred 300 acre to a temple which be had constructed in 1966. The *diwan* has 40 acre of land, including the land in Talapatna. We notice the distribution pattern to be very unequal. Only 7.4 per cent of the village land is left for 90.6 per cent of the households. Mention may be made that, in the calculation, we are not including the land owned by the three outside landowners from other villages (Table 2).

Table 2

Pattern of landownership in Talapatna

Land category (in acre)	*Households*			*Owned acreage*		
	Number	*Percent*	*Cumulative percentage*	*Acres*	*Percent*	*Cumulative percentage*
Landless	55	73.3	73.3	—	—	—
Upto $\frac{1}{2}$	4	5.3	78.6	1.5	1.0	1.0
> $\frac{1}{2}$-1	6	8.0	86.6	4.5	3.0	4.0
> 1-2	2	2.7	89.3	2.5	1.7	5.7
> 2-3	1	1.3	90.6	2.5	1.7	7.4
> 3-5	3	4.0	94.6	11.0	7.4	14.8
>5-10	1	1.3	95.9	8.0	5.4	20.2
> 10-20	—	—	—	—	—	—
> 20-30	2	2.7	98.6	55.0	37.2	57.4
> 30	1	1.3	99.9	63.0	42.6	100.0
Total	75	99.9		148.0	100.0	

Table 3

Castewise distribution of land in Talapatna

Castes (in equivalents)	*Households*			*Owned acreage*		
	Number	*Percent*	*Cumulative percentage*	*Acres*	*Percent*	*Cumulative percentage*
Brahmin	1	1.3	1.3	25	16.9	16.9
Kshatriya	3	4.0	5.3	93	62.8	79.7
Weaver	3	4.0	9.3	—	—	—
Milkman	5	6.6	15.9	—	—	—
Goldsmith	1	1.3	17.2	4	2.7	82.4
Sweetmaker	1	1.3	18.5	—	—	—
Odiya	5	6.6.	25.1	11	7.4	89.8
Fisherman	1	1.3	26.4	1	0.7	90.5
Washerman	3	4.0	30.4	1.5	1.0	91.5
Khadal	52	69.3	99.7	12.5	8.4	99.9
Total	75	99.7		148.0	99.9	

Though the pattern of land distribution broadly coincides with the caste hierarchy, there are exceptions too. While, among the 'high castes', 12 families are landless, among the 'low castes' 13 families do have land (Table 4).

At the same time, almost half of the unsurveyed cultivable land of the village remains waste under the categories of pasture, mango groves, cremation ground, and due to fear of the spirits. Recently, two owner-tenants cultivated 3 acre from an abandoned cremation ground, but the yield was unsatisfactory, so this year the cultivation of that ground has been discontinued.

Table 4
Distribution of castes by landownership

Land (in acre)	*Names of castes*	*Number of households*	*Total*
Landless	Kshatriya	1	55
	Weaver	3	
	Milkman	5	
	Sweetmaker	1	
	Odiya	3	
	Washerman	3	
	Khadal	41	
Upto 1	Odiya	1	10
	Fisherman	1	
	Khadal	8	
> 1-3	Odiya	1	3
	Washerman	1	
	Khadal	1	
> 3-5	Goldsmith	1	3
	Khadal	2	
> 5-10	Odiya	1	1
> 20	Brahmin	1	3
	Kshatriya	2	
Total		75	75

In Talapatna, less than 10 acre, belonging to the zamindar and lying close to the river, are irrigated; cultivation elsewhere depends on the rain.

There are two types of dryland—paddy land and the other land (*padar*) used for cultivating ragi, grams, pulses, etc. Besides, the backyard land (*bari*) is used for seasonal vegetables, lettuces, etc. This type of land is attached to houses and is neither saleable separately from the house nor is rented. Hence, we exclude *bari* land from our consideration.

In the village, a little more than 90 per cent of the cultivated land is used for paddy cultivation. And in the rest, crops like horsegram, red gram, til, mustard, etc., are harvested. However, a rough estimate suggests that the yield per acre of land is small, ranging between 300 and 400 kg of paddy (after deducting the seed).

Classes in the Village

In Talapatna, 70 households (9.13% of the population)—including the zamindar, his ex-manager, and the merchant—have agriculture as the main source of living. These may be grouped conveniently as follows:[19]

Landlords

Those who possess land, but do not engage in labour; and live exclusively by exploitation of the peasants, are here called landlords.

The village has three landlord families. The zamindar popularly known as 'Raja Saheb', does not work in his field. Of his land, 63 acre are cultivated by 17 sharecroppers. The tenancy system is such that an aging tenant goes to the zamindar and asks him to give the land to his son(s) for sharecropping. If the son is too young to undertake cultivation of the land, his father's brother or father's brother's son may cultivate it till the son(s) can do the job. This might suggest that the right to lease land is hereditary; however, in practice, the tenants can be evicted any time according to the whim of the zamindar. Actually, within the past 15 years, two tenants were evicted and two others did not get the leased-in land because they had not attained maturity at the time of their father's death. The threat of eviction keeps the tenant loyal to the landowner on all issues, including electoral support. At the same time, the zamindar, because of his capacity to replace tenants, can easily ignore the legislative dicta.[20]

The tenants are responsible for irrigating and maintaining the land; but, for large-scale operations, the zamindar provides the inputs, though the total labour is entirely that of the tenants. The tenants bear the cost of threshing and hulling the paddy. They have to pay for seed and local manure, but half the cost of the chemical fertilizer is paid by the zamindar. In the case of other landlords, the cost of local manure is also divided equally between owner and tenant. It is said that the zamindar is generally not in favour of using much fertilizer (on the land) nor is he interested in new varieties of paddy or in other crops. Only last year he allowed two of his tenants to cultivate sugarcane on five acre of wet land. In this patch of land, the total working capital was provided by the zamindar and the total labour by the tenants. Here, the tenants receive approximately 30 per cent of the produce; however, last year, both the tenants' share were taken by zamindar as part payment of their earlier debt to him. Excluding this land, in all other land, the tenant's share is two units, while the zamindar's share is three units for paddy, and for greengram and blackgram 2:3. But for crops like ragi, redgram, mustard, til, gingelly, etc., the share is 1:1.

In addition to the above crop-sharing, the tenants have several unpaid labour obligations, which not only tie the tenant to a particular landlord but also reduce the productive use of labour. To note a few such obligations:

(a) During feasts at the zamindar's house, the wives of the tenants have to work there for days together; in return, they get cooked food to eat at their homes—definitely more in quantity than one adult's single meal but lacking in various special dishes served to the zamindar's guests.

(b) Every year, the tenants have to re-thatch the cattle-sheds and the kitchen of the zamindar by their combined labour and also with their straw and fiber—the zamindar provides bamboo or wood required for the purpose. Usually the work requires one whole day of combined labour. The tenants get a meal on any day convenient to the zamindar.

(c) Every tenant, irrespective of the amount of land he sharecrops, had to give the zamindar annually a cart-load of wood for use as fuel. For the past two years, however, this obligation has been reduced, so that approximately 2.5 tenants have to provide one cart-load collectively every year. This is broadly due to the reduced needs of this fuel and its need for political support at elections.

(d) The zamindar or his relatives and office bearers can call anybody at any time to send a message or goods to nearby villages.

(e) Besides the compulsory labour, there is optional unpaid labour like sweeping the front yard of the house of the zamindar, cleaning his cowshed, grazing and bathing cattle, etc.

Regardless of age, villagers call the zamindar's father (*bapa*). His paternalism finds expression in several forms. Every year, the village has a big festival for the village deity. Though it is organized by the village elders, they discuss with the zamindar about programme and expenditure. He provides over half the expenditure, and initially joins the worship; but during the entertainment he leaves the place. This shows that his absence is needed for the villagers to make merry. Similarly, the zamindar's wife, or mother, would give any villager some food or a torn piece of clothing upon request.

At times, the disputes concerning partition of land among brothers, marriage cases, and cases of elopement are referred to him, and his decision is always final. In one case, a man insisted on remarrying while his first wife was alive, in defiance of the zamindar's decision. He was removed from the sharecropping and so, he had to leave the village. Even inter-village disputes may be referred to the zamindar. But now, due to ill health, he avoids several cases.

The zamindar deals with his tenants through two subordinates. First, the *diwan*, who was employed in 1969 to look after the land of the zamindar. Not only the tenants but also the farm labourers are afraid of him—his baseless scoldings, and his frequent beatings for petty irregularities on the part of the working people. Next to him, is the chief sharecropper, a trusted person in the house of the zamindar, who has the maximum amount of leased-in land as a single tenant. Several sorts of grievances of the tenants are conveyed to the zamindar through him.

The second landlord, who lives 25 miles away, used to be the *diwan* until 1968. He leased-out his 25 acre to seven tenants. One of them has leased-in a little land from the zamindar also. In contrast to leases from the zamindar, there is no right here of 'hereditary tenancy'. Eviction is frequent. Within five years, seven tenants were evicted, and this year three are taken in. However, four tenants have been continuing for the last six years. The shares are similar to those for the zamindar, but unpaid labour is much restricted by tradition, physical distance, and frequent evictions.

The third landlord is a small entrepreneur of the goldsmith caste. He got his 4 acre by lending to small landowners. In 1974-75, 2 acre were given on fixed rent in cash (*gutta*). The amount was fixed for Rs. 175 per acre, but since the value of the harvest, per acre, was less than Rs. 230 (at prices prevailing in the harvest season), he reduced his due by Rs. 25 per acre. The other two acre are also given on fixed rent in kind (*dhulia sanja*). Here again, he gave a concession to his tenant. He has two tenants in all.

Though they are not obliged to render him personal service, sometimes they do so voluntarily.

In the above tenancy systems (*gutta and dhulia sanja*), the tenants bear all the risk; and, given the unreliability of the monsoon, the tenants often fail to meet their dues—and so have to send a member of the family to work for the landowner just for food. In nearby villages, such cases are very common. Several informants said that this system of tenancy has recently become more common.

Rich Peasants

A rich peasant is one who has independent holdings and works in fields with the help of farm workers, while sometimes leasing-out a portion of his holding.

In Talapatna, there are two rich peasant households. The richer among the two owns 30 compact acre. The head of this household was once a primary school teacher, without any land. Somehow, the present zamindar's father was pleased with him and gave him the land. His son a trained Gram Sevak, looks after the field. He is the only son, so his father did not allow him to go for higher studies or employment. He gives hospitality to any official who comes to the village. A very orthodox Hindu, he spends more than five hours a day in worship and chanting of 'mantras'.

Out of his 30 acre, he cultivates only 7 acre with the help of two farm servants (*halia*) and his tenants' unpaid labour. The remaining land is given for sharecropping to seven tenants. Besides, out of 7 self-cultivated acre, 2 acre are cultivated by his tenants' labour. In this system (*bethi uthana*), the tenants do not get anything in return for their labour other than occasional meals. But, here, the total input and a portion (usually half) of labour during transplantation and harvesting is provided by the rich peasant. This is a recent phenomenon. Almost every year, he replaces one or two of his tenants and also changes the field from one to another.

In 1972, persuaded by his son, the rich peasant purchased a water pump. But the very next year, he sold it because of its expensive repair, and considered it less useful for the maintenance of his status. He said, "See, the Raja Saheb does not have it—how is he living? Further, what is the gain from this machine? At least, in my life time, I do not want such artificial tools..." It is observed that though his economic position does not allow him to follow the life-style of the zamindar, he tries to act like one.

The rich peasant engages his domestic servants in his self-cultivated field, puts his tenants to do household chores like gardening, selling coconuts from his 25 trees in the market, cleaning cattleshed, grazing cattle, household repairs, etc. One of his domestic servants receives his daily food and his dress annually. He has to work for five years to repay his earlier debts. The other one works a few hours a day, depending on the need of the family, and is paid annually a fixed amount of crop after harvest.

This is most powerful household in the village after the zamindar's. He gets support from his tenants, several farm labourers, and others. This faction is allied with the Congress, and the other one with the Swatantra Party. This rich farmer's hold in the village is gradually increasing, because of his greater involvement in the affairs of the people and his ability to get things done for the people through the officials. His being a staunch religious man also adds to his strength.

The second rich peasant owns 8 acre of land. He cultivates 6 acre himself, with the help of two servants of his caste. These two servants are paid monthly in paddy, and farm workers are hired on daily wages. Only 2 acre are given for sharecropping to two tenants (2: 3 share). The tenants have fewer obligations to him. His other income comes from his 30 goats.

Middle Peasants

This class includes peasants who own land but neither exploit others nor sell their own labour. Their income, in a normal year, is sufficient to give them an independent living in the village.

Only one household of an exterior caste owns 4 acre of land. The family members work in the field. But, at peak season, they hire labour. He is well-known for not drinking liquor, a habit common among his castemen. He is influential in settling disputes not only of his caste but of his village, at large. He is also the ward member of the Gram Panchayat. He is politically conscious and is an active member of CPI (Marxist). In 1974, through his caste council, he united all small peasants, tenants, and agricultural labourers, to fight against selling the village produce in the outside market before meeting the needs of the villagers. From his experience, he argued that, in the initial stage, it is better to put forth such demands through caste councils than through class organizations.[21]

Another four households can be put in this class. They own more than 1.5 acre of land each. But, since that is insufficient for their living, they lease-in a little land individually from different landlords. However, their main source of income is from their own land. All of them are relatively conscious politically.

Small Peasants

The land these peasants own is too little for subsistence. Hence, they do either sharecropping or farm labour in addition to cultivation of own land.

In Talapatna, there are 10 households with small holdings. Their distribution cuts across caste identity. Eight of the small peasants are also tenants. The other two cultivate as partners (*bhaguali)* where input, labour and produce are equally shared among the partners.

Again, 22 landless households make their living from leased-in land. On the whole, 34 tenants (*bhagachashi*) cultivate 79 per cent of the total village land. Leased-in land for the middle peasant is higher than both the small peasant and the pure sharecroppers (Table 5). And, about 59 per cent of the sharecroppers cultivate land in the range of 3 to 4 acre (Table 6). Clearly, the landlords have leased-out land to a large number of tenants. This probably helps consolidate their political power, while increasing their share through the small tenants intensive labour. If the land was given to fewer tenants, the tenants' share would have been more, and they would not have depended on the landlords for consumption loans. Thus, the practice of usury would have been weak, resulting in a weak bond between landlord and tenant. And, in course of time, it might have helped investment of capital for productive purposes. I shall return to this soon.

Table 5
Distribution of leased-in land

(per class)

Class	*Households*		*Acres leased-in*		*Average leased-in per household (acre)*
	Number	*Percent*	*Acres*	*Percent*	
Middle peasant-cum-tenant	4	11.8	21.5	18.4	5.4
Small peasant-cum-tenant	8	23.5	29.0	24.8	3.6
Pure tenant	22	64.7	66.5	56.8	3.0
Total	34	100.0	117.0	100.0	

Table 6
Distribution of leased-in land

Leased-in land	*Households*	*Acres of land leased-in*
Upto 1 acre	1	0.5
> 1-2 acre	2	3.5
> 2-3 acre	7	18.0
> 3-4 acre	20	72.5
> 4-5 acre	3	14.0
> 5-8 acre	—	—
> 8-11 acre	1	8.5
Total	34	117.0

Talapatna contains 25 ploughs. The sharecroppers have 20.5 ploughs in all. Yet, 10 of them are without ploughs and seven others have only 'half a plough' each. Hence, 10 tenants depend on the landlords' cattle, while three hire the plough, and the other four manage with the help of their relatives, preferably brothers or the father-in-law. The tenants, who use the cattle of the landlord provide straw and grass for the cattle and also do some extra unpaid work. Out of the five bullockcarts in the village, three belong to owner tenants.

And, since paddy cultivation cannot be solely undertaken by family labour, traditionally the sharecroppers hire labour—at least during transplantation and harvest. Furthermore, any Khadal tenants leasing-in over 3 acre exchange their labour among themselves. This reduces the wage burden. For such exchange of labour, the worker is given only one meal.

Among sharecroppers, the status of a person depends on (1) amount of leased-in land, (2) source of the lease—a lease with the zamindar being the most prestigious, and (3) his own caste. In 1971, when the tenants of the absentee landlord-diwan asked for a larger share, he took the help of his upper-caste tenants and suppressed the move. Still other evidence shows that, in a normal situation, uniting the tenants and labourers along class lines is difficult, mainly because of their class interests being fragmented by their allegiance to the caste and its associated hierarchy and value system. But, in times of trouble, there have been at least three occasions in the village, when they got united cutting across the caste barriers.[23] It is nevertheless essential to locate the political, social, and cultural variables which inhibit the development of class consciousness.

Farm Workers

A farm worker is one whose living is derived solely from selling his labour power in agriculture and other allied activities.

Twenty-seven households, constituting 36 per cent of the semi-employed and unemployed section of the village, belong to this category. Their distribution is also found in all the castes. They fall into two major categories: (a) labourers in permanent bondage (*halia*), and (b) labourers relatively free (*mulia*).

The *halias* are confined to the exterior castes only. They are attached to the landlords and rich peasants, mainly due to indebtedness. Only three of them are employed on the basis of monthly pay in kind, the rest work for food while repaying their debt. In practice, they are no more than serfs.

The normal wage rate for a male labourer is Rs. 2.50, for roughly eight hours of work per day—this includes an increase of 50 paisa during the last year when the price of paddy doubled. For a female farm worker, the increase during the same period was from Rs. 1.50 to Rs. 1.75. But 75 per cent of the wage is given in kind. For harvesting ragi, the labourer gets approximately one-tenth of his cutting, and for grams he gets a flat rate. The wage rate shows considerable variation during the peak seasons. The zamindar pays for his domestic work less than the regular wage rate.

Although the farm labourers constitute as much as 36 per cent of the village, at the peak of the agricultural season, there remains an acute shortage of labour owing to the nature of paddy cultivation, which needs heavy labour for specific periods. Besides, several upper castemen, more particularly women—whose economic position is below that of the small peasants or tenants—do not work in the field. Further, the farm labourers do not remain in Talapatna alone, they go to other nearby villages. However, employment is constricted to a few months in the year. During the rest of the year, the labourers subsist on collecting and selling forest produce. The forest appears to be the second main source of subsistence for them. It may be worth nothing that, especially in the lean months, kinsmen or castemen are preferred as employees.

Further, given the persistent landownership structure and the methods of cultivation, production remains stagnant. Hence, the 'surplus population' in relation to the tasks at hand; hence the insecurity of tenancy on whatever land is available.[24]

Socially, since the majority of farm labourers belong to the untouchable castes, they constitute the major section of the oppressed. It is said that they drink and spend money in gambling. Their women have low standards of 'morality'. Cases of elopement and even signs of prostitution are found in this category of people alone.

Only one man in Talapatna is a mine-labourer. He gets employment for eight months in the year but lives better than the village workers do. Whenever he is in the village, he goes to work in the fields of others. Besides, there are 12 more migrant workers to the Assam Tea Gardens and the Dhenkanal Mines (Orissa). They are not the heads of their households. Relatively speaking, they are more conscious of their rights because of their trade union experience.

Business

Talapatna has three traders in all: a goldsmith, a grocer, and a hawker of stationery. Both the grocer and the hawker of stationery and their family members work as farm labourers during the peak seasons.

Others

In Talapatna, one family lives by weaving and can be characterized as a small entrepreneur. Two persons are blind and depend for their living upon gifts from relatives and others.

More than 85 per cent of the population subsist on a mere 63 kg of paddy and ragi per person, per year, while the upper 15 per cent subsist on an average 210 kg per unit. The disparity is found from a sample of 11 households, covering all the different classes. They manage with other substitutes such as horsegram, leaves, roots, tubers, and forest mango, etc. Most of them, however, occasionally spend money on drinking to relax after tiresome labour or during festivals. Most of them have one small *dhoti* or big towel or *lungi*, and several women have cotton sarees stitched up at several places.

In this situation, the agricultural labourers and the small tenants are forced to depend on loans for consumption. Talapatna has five creditors—all the landlords and all the rich peasants—and 50 debtors. The loans are usually in kind. Twenty-one households have taken paddy on loan, eleven both staple and cash, while eighteen others have borrowed only in cash.

Interestingly, 25 tenants are indebted to their own landlords—who are also called *sahukars*, meaning moneylenders. Four more tenants are indebted to merchants and other landlords. On the whole, about 85 per cent of the tenants and 65 per cent of the agricultural labourers are indebted. In all cases, either directly or indirectly, the debt is extended against some security or other. In 16 cases, it is against gold and utensils; in eight cases against land; in one case against trade, while in 25 cases—that is, half of all the cases—the debt is attached to the sharecropping arrangement.

Table 7
Class distribution in Talapatna

Class	*Households*	
	Number	*Per cent*
Landlord	3	4.0
Rich peasant	2	2.7
Middle peasant and tenants (1+4)	5	6.7
Poor peasants and tenants (2+8)	10	13.3
Sharecropper	22	29.3
Farm, forest and mine labour (12+15+1)	28	37.3
Business	2	2.7
Others	3	4.0
Total	75	100.0

Though there are variations, the rate of interest on staple is normally 60 per cent till the next harvest. By another system, the debtor may repay twice the quantity of paddy borrowed in any year. In recent years, this second system has been giving way to the first one. The interest on cash varies from 30 to 45 per cent per annum. Most such loans are used for food and for ceremonies, and only a little (15.6%) is used for productive purposes (Table 8). Sometimes the landlords extend consumption loans to their tenants at a lower rate of interest, and they would do so even when these debtors have no further assets to offer as security. The tenant, cultivating a small parcel of land with his backward instruments, has to pay the rising land rent and to remain perpetually indebted to the landlords. The insecure tenancy, the credit nexus, and the traditional feudal culture combine to yield strong 'bonds' between the landlords and their tenants.

Table 8
Purpose of loan in Talapatna

Purpose of loan	*Percentage of the total debt*	
Cultivation expenditure	7.0	15.6
Purchase of plough	4.2	
Construction of house	3.2	
Business	1.2	
Food and other personal requirements	45.4	81.1
Social and ceremonial needs	31.2	
To repay the debt	4.5	
Others	3.3	3.3
Total	100.0	100.0

Often, as a token of gratitude the indebted households, present important forest products like honey, edible roots and rubbers, fungi, berries and also fish for the grant of the loan. Sometimes, they go for casual labour or work as farm domestic servants to pay the debt. Here, they are paid less than the wage rate of the village.

The landlords are not only the rentiers and the usurers, they are also traders in crops. This trade is carried out through the debt repaid by the tenants at harvest time in staples and cash crops (oilseeds and pulses), and their own surplus is sold chiefly when the market prices increase considerably. In 1974-75, the landlords sold approximately 10 per cent of the paddy collected at harvest time, while at the same time 25 per cent of the tenants' share was sold out (from a sample of 11 tenants). Actually, after paying a portion of the debt, the remaining crop is inadequate to meet the tenants' minimum subsistence. In the lean months, he goes again to the landlord, who provides paddy at the ruling market price at the time and collects it back at the harvest-value of the crop. Obviously, a high rate of interest is thus charged, keeping the tenant in perpetual indebtedness. Further, he is not allowed to enter into the *product-market* while he is forced to enter into the *exchange-market.*

The economic surplus extracted through land, interest bearing capital, and exchange market, is used in conspicuous and wasteful consumption, such as construction of big comfortable houses and in arranging feasts. The big landlords have not yet felt the need to transform the surplus into productive capital. Furthermore, the combined profit from moneylending and renting land is judged to be greater than that likely from the development of agricultural produce.[25]

In addition to wasteful consumption, the zamindar spends money to acquire control over elective positions in the panchayat samiti and the assembly constituency. In 1959, the second brother of the family was the sarpanch of Dharakota gram panchayat, having been unanimously elected. In 1962, he was chairman of the Dharakota panchayat samiti. In the 1967 and 1971 assembly elections, he was elected with the ticket of the Swatantra Party, and was twice deputy minister incharge of gram panchayat, community development, and agriculture. In the 1974 assembly elections, he had followed the well-known strategy of mobilization through traditional obligations including the existing owner-tenant relations plus the creditor-debtor relations. He moved the constituency with his mother, Rani Saheba. Villagers were often seen offering garlands and tributes in honour of their visit. The distribution of money and drink by him was very little compared to that by the Congress candidate, a big industrialist of the state. He had profound control in the panchayat samiti. But, for the first time, he was defeated. His defeat reveals that there is not necessarily strong relation between the institution of the panchayat and the assembly voting. A note may also be made of the role of the CPI (Marxist) in the success of the Congress. In 1973, the party for the first time organized its base in this area. It could mobilize several hundred peasants. But many people thought that CPI(M)'s hold was not a possible alternative in the election; hence they voted for the Congress. Further, out of the big four political visitors during 1974 elections, the meeting of H.K. Konar and P.D. Dasgupta of CPI(M) were more attended than those of R.N. Singh (Swatantra) and Y.B. Chavan (Congress).

Anyway, this was not the first defeat of the family. In the 1957 assembly elections, the first son of the house was also defeated, when the estate was a part of Aska constituency—which has a long-standing history of peasant movements and is not influenced by the *zamindari* system. Notwithstanding the two defeats of the family, it is noticeable that to a large extent, there is personalization of economy and of political power.

In Talapatna, we find the primordial forms of slavery and intensive sharecropping, combined with frequent fear of eviction, perpetual indebtedness of the peasantry to the landlords for consumption loans, forcible restriction of the peasantry from the capital market, predominance of exchange economy, seasonal farm labour, and poor development of commodity economy, and of the productive forces. In other words, the village is a semi-feudal one.

As is known, social progress means that the relations of production and forces of production conform with each other, and that this conformity develops the productive forces, which ultimately open the door for further social progress. But, in this case, the relations of production stand as the primary obstacle to the release of productive forces which historically demands a change in the relations of production. However, whether this situation would bring about fundamental changes in agrarian relations, cannot be said simply on the basis of the available information on a single village.

Notes

1. See, for example, the debate on the Transition from feudalism to capitalism, in *Science and Society*, between Spring 1950 to Fall 1953.
2. A. Rudra, 'In Search of the Capitalist Farmer', *Economic and Political Weekly*, 1970, Volume V, Number 26, p. 85.
3. The main critiques of Rudra's method are: U. Patnaik, 'Capitalist Development in Agriculture'?, *Economic and Political Weekly*, September 25, 1971; and, 'On the Mode of Production in Indian Agriculture; A Reply', *Ibid*, September 30, 1972. See also; P. Chattopadhyay, 'On the Question of the Mode of Production in Agriculture: A Preliminary Note', *Economic and Political Weekly*, March 25, 1972.
4. Among others, see, C Bettelheim, *India Independent*, (New York: Monthly Review Press, 1968), and A Bhaduri, 'A Study in Agricultural Backwardness under Semi-Feudalism', *Economic Journal*, March 1973, see also, Pradhan H. Prasad, 'Reactionary Role of Usurer's Capital in Rural India', *Economic and Political Weekly*, Volume IX, Numbers 32, 33 and 34, August 1974, pp 1305-1308; and Nirmal K. Chandra, 'Farm Efficiency Under Semi-Feudalism: A Critique of Marginalist Theories and Some Marxist Formulations' *Ibid*, pp. 1309-1332.
5. Among others, see, A. Beteille, *Studies in Agrarian Social Structure*, (New York: Oxford University Press, 1974), where he writes that the agrarian structure of the village cannot be understood "by considering only the internal structure of the village. Those, who

represented the top of the hierarchy,... had their hands in a number of villages without necessarily residing in any", (p 7.)

6. M. Dobb, *Studies in the Development of Capitalism*, (London: Routledge and Kegan Paul, 1946), p.35.
7. I Me'sza'res, *Marx's Theory of Alienation,* (Merlin Press, 1970), pp. 100-150.
8. See the debate in *Science and Society*, op.cit.
9. A. Bhaduri, 'An Analysis of Semi-Feudalism in East Indian Agriculture', *Frontier*, Volume 6, Numbers 25-27, September 29, 1973, p. 12, emphasis his.
10. A Bhaduri, "A Study in Agricultural Backwardness Under Semi-Feudalism" *op.cit.*, pp. 120-121.
11. C. Bettelheim, *India Independent*, *op.cit.*, p. 23.
12. U. Patnaik, 'On the Mode of Production in Indian Agriculture: A Reply', *op.cit.*, pp. 147-148.
13. A. Rudra, 'In Search of the Capitalist Farmer', *op.cit.*, p. 85.
14. K. Marx emphatically pointed out that the "Proprietorship of land parcels by its very nature excludes the development of the social productive forces of labour, social forms of labour, social concentration of capital, large-scale cattle raising, and the progressive application of science", *Capital*, Volume 3, (Moscow: Progress Publishers, 1970), p. 787. See also, V.I. Lenin, *Collected Works*, Volume 21, pp. 69-70.
15. See M. Dobb, *op.cit.*, p. 36.
16. See, for instance, R.K. Mukherjee, *Land Problems in India*, (Calcutta, 1933), p. 325.
17. In Orissa, there were altogether 425, 693 estates, and to abolish those in 1951, the Orissa Estate Abolition Act was passed. And so far 420,441 estates have been 'abolished'. See, Report of the Administrative Enquiry Committee, Government of Orissa, 1971, Volume I, p. 68.
18. The hierarchy used in both Tables 1 and 3 follows the perceptions of informants of various castes in the village. The local caste terms when translated into English appear to be a mixture of occupations, varna terms, and alternate local terms. Nevertheless, we adhere to the local perceptions for the present purpose.
19. Here, broadly we follow, Mao Tsetung, "Analysis of Classes in Chinese Society", "Report on an Investigation of the Peasant Movement in Hunan", and "How to Differentiate the Classes in Rural Areas", *Selected Works of Mao Tse-Tung, Volume I*, pp. 13-21. 23-59, and

137-143, respectively. See also, K. Gough 'Peasant Resistance and Revolt in South India', *Pacific Affairs*, Winter 1968-69, pp. 527-544.

20. However, the Tenant Relief Act, 1955, Orissa, provides that no tenant in lawful cultivation of any land on the first day of July 1954, or at any time thereafter, shall be liable to be evicted from such land by the landlords. Report on Enquiry into the Working of the Orissa Tenants Protection Act, 1948, and Orissa Tenants Relief Act, 1955, in the Five Districts of Orissa, (New Delhi, 1970).
21. Irfan Habib argues that the caste system is a framework for peasant movements, and through the caste councils peasants were able to join the peasant movements. See, *The Agrarian System of Moghul India*, (London: Asia Publishing House, 1963), p. 332.
22. K.N. Raj, 'Ownership and Distribution of Land', *Indian Economic Review*, April 1970, pp. 1-42.
23. Kathleen Gough, while analyzing peasant uprisings in India, has questioned Moore's explanation of the weakness of the peasant movement in India in terms of the caste hierarchy and values. See, *'Indian Peasant Uprisings'*, *Economic and Political Weekly*, Special Number 1974, Volume 9, Numbers 32-34, p. 1391; and also B. Moore, *The Social Origins of Dictatorship and Democracy*, (Beacon Press, 1966), p. 383.
24. The insecurity of tenancy is well described in: V.M. Dandekar and Nilakantha Rath, 'Poverty in India: Dimensions and Trends', *Economic and Political Weekly*, (January 2, 1971), pp. 106-46.
25. See Pradhan H Prasad, *op.cit.*, and Nirmal K. Chandra, *op.cit.*

14 Power Elite in Rural India

Some Questions and Clarifications

K.L. SHARMA

I

The purpose of this paper is two-fold: to examine the nature of sources and determinants of power of rural elite, and the mobility of elites. The first point deals with the social background of elites, and the second refers to the changes in the structure of elites. An effort has been made to analyze power elite and dominance mobility in the light of these two points.

The discussion relating to the sources and determinants of power of rural elite could be located in three contexts: (i) caste or group dominance (Srinivas, 1959: 1-16; Kothari, 1970: 18); (ii) dominance of individuals (Dube, 1968: 58-81); and (iii) levels of dominance and dominance statuses (Gardner, 1968: 82-97). Srinivas refers to numerical strength, economic position (land ownership) and political power as the decisive factors of caste dominance. Kothari delineates caste (group) dominance in terms of an *entrenched caste* which does not enjoy dominance on the basis of its numerical strength and dominance in the form of an *ascendant caste*, the caste which was not satisfied to work in the traditional framework of interdependence complementarity in social and economic spheres. Srinivas refers to "locally and regionally dominant caste groups". Others refer to "caste lobbies" in state politics. Dube views caste dominance as an unreal proposition in terms of its group character and distribution of power and dominance. According to him it is the individuals (families) who are dominant and not the castes. Considering these two views the most pertinent questions to be asked and answered are as follows:

(i) How is dominance legitimized (acceptance of dominance of new members)?

(ii) What are the basic resources which facilitate dominance of members in village community?

(iii) Are the areas of group and individual dominance separate and distinct?

(iv) Is there any contradiction between individual and group dominance or are they complimentary to each other?

(v) Can the two types of dominance prevail simultaneously in the same social setting?

Gardner's view regarding dominance is relevant in the analysis of dominance mobility. According to Gardner, there is a tendency to achieve group (Kshatriya) dominance status by the holders of "patron status" (dominant individuals). Gardner explicitly states that the dominant individuals would tend to communalize their dispersed dominance. It would also imply that dominance mobility from group to individual is conspicuously absent. However, my study shows that group dominance has enormously eroded in the recent years (Sharma, 1973: 59-77). New "dominant groups" have emerged recently (though they come from divergent backgrounds) and are of an amorphous nature. In fact, there is no elite group having same caste membership, economic position and other uniform social and cultural attributes. Thus, the elite group is not a "group" in terms of these characteristics, it is an amorphous set of persons who enjoy dominance at different levels of village social organization. The two pertinent questions in regard to dominance mobility then, can be formulated as follows:

(i) What is the direction of dominance mobility?

(ii) How do different factors differently affect the nature and direction of dominance mobility?

II

Srinivas (1959: 1-16; 1966: 10-16) for the first time conceptualized mobility (sanskritization) and dominance (dominant caste) as group phenomena. According to Srinivas caste dominance has the elements of numerical strength, economic and political power, ritual status and western education and modern occupations. A caste enjoying all or most of these elements has a decisive dominance. Dube (1968: 58-81) has examined the elements of caste dominance in a study of four villages in Madhya Pradesh. According to him, a caste is dominant when power is diffused in the group and is expressed in the interest of the whole group or at least a sizeable part of it. Pronounced inequalities of wealth, prestige and power are found between the members of a so-called dominant caste. The dominant individuals of such a caste exploit non-dominant members of their own caste as well as members of "non-dominant caste".

Oommen (1970a: 74-76) has raised some pertinent questions about the validity of the concept of dominant caste. According to Oommen, *alternate situations of dominance* have not been visualized by Srinivas such as "a numerically weak caste owning most of the land and wealth in a village; or a numerically strong caste which is economically deprived and ritually depressed; or a ritually superior caste which is numerically weak; and so on... It seems fairly obvious that in such situations a number of castes will share the community power" (*Ibid*., 75). Oommen also refers to two other points: (i) the context of dominance; and (ii) the aspects of power, namely, the resources available to individuals and groups for the exercise of power and the act of power exercising. According to him, there is "multiple power structure" in a multi-caste village or region having different layers and levels of leadership. Oommen refers to two other useful concepts in another essay (1970b: 226-239) in regard to community power structure, namely, "power pool" and "power dispersion". Thus, we find that:

(a) There is caste (group) dominance, hence corporate mobility or sanskritization (Srinivas, 1959: 1966).
(b) There are dominant individuals and not dominant caste or castes in the village community (Dube, 1968).
(c) "Multiple power structure" exists in a multi-caste village or region and there is "power pool" and "power dispersion" in village communities (Oommen, 1970a; 1970b).

The above formulations are singularistic in their nature and hence are incomplete. There are certain areas and aspects of social life in which a group asserts its power. There are other areas in which only families and individuals matter, and in still other domains near-monopoly of power or dispersion of power is found. Both castes and individuals are found dominant, but the areas and aspects of dominance of the two differ to a large extent. The rural power elite do not comprise a homogeneous social segment because they do not have the characteristics of a group such as unity, commonalty of interests, equality of status and economic position. An "elite group" is an aggregation of differentiated dominant individuals. To understand the process through which the elite formation crystallizes it is necessary to discuss the nature of traditional elite and dominance in the village community.

III

The traditional elites in village India were different from that of today in relation to their size, composition and recruitment etc. The "twice-born" constituted three broad categories of elites. Brahmins, Kshatriyas and Vaishyas formed religious and cultural, administrative and power, and business and economic elites, respectively. But they did not have intra-group unity and homogeneity nor all the three categories of elites enjoyed equal status and significance in the eyes of the people. These "twice-born" groups belonged to a system of hierarchy, therefore, their interrelations were determined by norms of ranking which placed them in high and low positions in different sectors such as administrative, economic, and ritual. However, in spite of differentiation of functions of the groups the Brahmins enjoyed decisive superiority over Kshatriyas and the latter over the Vaishyas.

Wealth, sanskritic education and accessibility to the rulers were some of the bases of intra-elite ranking. The study of Vedas (e.g., education) determined even nomenclature such as Dwidevi, Trivedi and Chaturvedi etc. (Ingalls, 1959: 3-9). There were Brahmins who did not study Vedas and engaged themselves in cultivation and menial works. The broad distinction of Daivik and Laukik Brahmins testifies this intra-elite hierarchy. Thus, elites were never a unified group in terms of exercise and distribution of power among the members belonging to a particular category of elite. Leach's observation (1954) that "structure of ideas" is different from that of "structure of facts" rightly applies even to the traditional Indian village community, and more so it is found today due to change from cumulative to dispersed inequalities between groups and individuals. There were Brahmins who broke traditional cultural and social sanctions and involved themselves into "anti-Brahmin movements". Some of these "deviants" strived for positions of power and privilege through such "innovative activities".

"The idea of martial Rajput" (Hitchcock, 1959: 10-17) explains the nature of the traditional power elites. It is his (Rajput's) duty to maintain law and order in the society and expect in return deference and obedience from the community members (including the members of his own clan). An elaborate hierarchy prevailed among the traditional ruling and power elites. The nature and size of landownership and rank of the "estate" determined the position of the ruling elite in the hierarchy. For example, the princes of the twenty-two princely states in Rajasthan were thought of as "supermen" of their respective estates. Below in the hierarchy were Rao Rajas, Raos, Talukedars, Jagirdars and Zamindars. Within each category of this landed aristocracy heterogeneity of rank existed as all the princes were not of equal status and so also the Jagirdars and Zamindars (Tod, 1950; Sharma, 1974).

The economic elites (e.g., Vaishyas or popularly known as Banias) must have a firsthand knowledge of economic realities and complexities (Lamb, 1959: 10-17). But they too were not a unified elite. Among the economic dominants there was a hierarchy of "Seths" (moneylenders). At the top of the economic dominants was the "Jagat-Seth" (the biggest moneylender). Below this were "Nagar-Seth" (the city moneylenders) and the "Gram-Seth" (the village moneylenders) and so on. Within each category inequality of rank prevailed because of differences of wealth, generous attitudes and relations with the rulers and the masses.

The hierarchy of cultural, power and economic elites was congruent with caste stratification. This was precisely because of its ascriptive base. The size of the traditional elite was small as it was restricted by ascription of birth (Oommen, 1970b). However, the traditional elites were specialists or professionalists in their respective fields, e.g., cultural, political and economic. This was determined by the structural requirements, and professionalization became a part of the elite culture itself. It was received by the elite through the processes of specialization and informal training.

Today, there is congruence in some aspects of elite's culture, styles of living and exercise of power, whereas in some other aspects certain amount of incongruence prevails. For instance, there is a greater possibility of political elite wielding economic power and that of less possibility of economic dominants exerting political dominance. The cultural elites may have more economic privileges than having access to positions of political power. However, professional elites continue to be a dividing line between different types of elites though the nature of professionalization today is different from that of the traditional one. The elites were never a unified group, and today also they persist in the same character to a large extent. Therefore, it is futile to talk of polarity between tradition and modernity. "Modernization is a high order integrative process" (Singh, 1975: 660) and in the wake of modern forces of change tradition has been able to maintain its identity though in a varied form in Indian society.

IV

Sociological studies and analyses of elites and dominance are a few only.

Bottomore (1965: 180-188), Beteille (1967: 223-243), Desai (1965: 150-156), Morris-Jones (1964), Srinivas (1966) and Misra (1964) have made analyses of elites at the national level, whereas Lewis (1958: 113-156), Sirsikar (1970), Somjee (1971), Carras (1972), Carter (1975) and Narain (1976) have made studies of rural elites. Most studies of the national elites are impressionistic, while the analyses of rural elites are based on empirical investigations.

Beteille refers to political elites, that is, the people in concrete political structures such as cabinets, parties and legislatures. The emphasis on the system of education and recruitment to the Indian Administrative Service is found in Morris-Jones' analysis of government and politics in India. The "new middle class" according to Misra are the products of secondary and higher education in India rather than development of industry. Shils (1961) has found continuity between the traditional intellectual elite and the modern elite. Desai also like Morris-Jones, Misra and Shils finds the new elite a product of modernization, though mainly of western education and culture, who depended on their fathers and grandfathers (who were traditionally powerful) for mobilizing people in the national movement.

These observations about the national elites do not sound valid. In addition to education and western impact a number of socio-cultural and historical factors and forces have been responsible for the emergence of a new elite structure. The new political structures and political values, at least theoretically, derecognized the traditional social networks and values. The new power elite might have been at the initial stage a noncongruent type of elite, that they did not encompass power and influence in arenas other than political. But once the political elites had its roots entrenched they started spreading their net wide. They tried to accumulate wealth and get into such positions which further enhanced their economic status. They were also influenced by the economic dominants of the country to a large extent. In the process of new elite formation, slowly the discreteness of the elite diminished and a congruent type of elite emerged.

This applies to the rural elite in India as well. The congruence as a basic feature of rural elite is not so much a result of the process of elite formation. The modern rural elites are a product of post-independence developments such as adult franchise, panchayati raj, the abolition of *zamindari* and *jagirdari* systems, education, and means of transport and communication. These changes were quite sudden for the village people, and therefore, this facilitated the continuity of the traditional upper caste and class elite in formal positions of power and authority in the new political organizations and institutions. The numerical preponderance of some caste groups in some villages in spite of their depressed economic position and lower caste rank disturbed the hegemony of the upper caste and class people. However, in most cases these groups could not become politically effective as they lacked other resources such as networks and linkages with outside leaders and money to spend on social occasions. Consequently, the incongruence which characterized the resource-base of the traditional elite continues in the case of modern elites too, the change in their resources, notwithstanding.

There are two ways to get in positions of power and authority in the village community (Oommen, 1969: 515-521). One is through one's qualities and manipulative tactics and the other is through ascription (landholding, property, high caste position and lineage etc.). For example, the ex-Jagirdars and ex-Zamindars entered into panchayati raj institutions (PRIs) to extract benefits with a view to retaining their economic superiority and styles of living which they had hitherto. However, some families from among the landed aristocracy could not face the challenge of the abolition and were forced to come down in the class hierarchy (Sharma, 1973: 59-77). Such a change I have defined as "downward mobility". Downward economic mobility is an unplanned consequence of planned social and political changes. It is a structural and historical reality observable in diverse forms and in different contexts. Such a mobility should be related to structure, ideology and behaviour of the people and its consequences should also be taken into consideration. At least two consequences are obvious: (i) the group dominance and solidarity are at stake, and (ii) this follows from the first, that corporate mobility particularly in political and economic spheres as a group endeavour does not sound as a viable proposition. I will take up these two points at a later stage of discussion in this paper.

The new institutions have provided the arenas for the power elite to manipulate benefits in their own interests, of their kinsmen, relatives and friends. It is exactly because of the scope for this type of manoeuvrability and weakness of the legislation that the elite even overcome some of the legal impediments. The ex-Jagirdars formed fake agricultural co-operative societies to retain thousands of acres of land after the abolition of the *jagirdari* and *zamindari* systems, they divided legally their landholdings among their family members and kinsmen to escape land ceiling law

(Sharma, 1974). Even servants, friends, acquaintances and some hired persons were made members of either such societies or they were given landholdings. However, in actuality, the land belonged to the ex-Jagirdars and Zamindars. A section of this landed aristocracy occupied formal positions of power in PRIs such as gram panchayat, panchayat samiti and zila parishad. The incumbents in the positions of power extended loans, grants-in-aid, subsidized equipments, fertilizer and other materials to their kinsmen, relatives, friends and supporters. In a number of cases loans were given to dig wells for irrigation, and out of those who received these loans spent it on social occasions, particularly, the marriages of their daughters and sisters. These loans have not been recovered. None of these people belonged to the "needy" or depressed sections of the village community. Innumerable instances of this kind could be found in a single district or even in a development block.

Secondly, the power elites may not be found in formal positions of power, still they influence the process of decision-making. They do not exercise power themselves but they control others who exercise power. Oommen's distinction between "power reservoirs" and "power exercisers" is useful in this context (1970: 226-239). The power reservoirs are more powerful than the power exercisers in several situations. More often than not the power reservoirs control resources of community, accumulate money and wealth and by obliging their friends, relatives and kinsmen build a strong support structure in the village community. The power exercisers are generally constrained to oblige them by offering loans, benefits and resources to ensure their continuity in the offices they hold. Some of these non-formal power elites extract benefits independent of the incumbents in the formal positions of power and authority. In case the formal power elites and real power wilders have an understanding in terms of ruling the community, factional cleavages do not seem visible and overt.

The Havik Brahmins in a Mysore village (Edward and Louise Harper, 1960: 453-70) constituted both formal and informal leaders. They were an example of unified elites. Bailey (1965: 9-13) makes observations about "elite councils" and "arena councils". The former are a ruling oligarchy. Both come in conflict with the public. "Arena council" is a standing committee of the House of Commons and a committee of the heads of the departments is an "elite council" according to Bailey. "Elite council" is formed from a minority whereas the "arena council" is formed out of diversified segments of a society. The analysis of these councils and committees by Bailey ignores the role of power reservoirs in decision-making. Power is considered as an aspect of these formal committees and councils. In fact, most studies have highlighted that the village leadership is splintered and caste and faction oriented and hence the absence of village-wide leadership (Lewis, 1959). Clearly an emphasis on the distinction between group and individual levels of dominance is lacking in most studies of power structure. One finds overemphasis on the analysis of group dominance and corporate mobility and a lack of understanding of the role of individual dominants because individual or family has hardly been accepted as units of operation independent of the caste group to which they belong in the village community. Such a preconceived notion of group dominance over the individual has led away the researcher from reality that exists at the grass roots. Whenever the patriarch of a joint family became autocratic and ignored the rights of his younger brothers, sons and other members of the family, his over-individualism was curtailed by new sanctions reinforcing corporateness. The threat to the head of the family by the sons and other dependents was averted by strengthening his hands giving him certain rights regarding property, etc. Thus, corporateness was never absolute in character. It was complimentary to individualism. Some of the recent changes have resulted into the decline of power of both individual families and particular groups. It is a very complicated phenomenon. If some families have been adversely affected by recent changes, it does not mean that the power position of the group to which these families belong would also dwindle necessarily. Similarly, if there is a general decline in the power of a group, some families or individuals still would be able to retain power and continue to dominate in the community. I do not mean that decline of power of a group does not affect its constituent units and vice-versa but the fact remains that power is not something that resides absolutely in a collectivity or a group though people have often a notion that power has corporateness. It is something which can never be equally shared even by the so-called equals, the equals also have inequality. Now I would examine the patterns of dominance with reference to the recent changes particularly resulting from the abolition of the zamindari and jagirdari systems of land tenure.

V

Dominance mobility refers to changes in the dominance structure of the community over a period of time either due to organizational changes or motivational factors pertaining to certain individuals. From Miller's data (1969: 325-340) on social mobility, four patterns of mobility could be delineated: (a) high downward and high upward mobility (+ +); (b) high downward and low upward (+ -); (c) low downward and high upward mobility (- +); and (d) low downward and low upward mobility (- -). These four combinations of patterns of mobility indicate, broadly speaking, four ideal types of societies and status systems. The traditional power structure of the village community in India was a "patrimonial" revenue-cum-administrative system, and hence feudalistic in nature. Caste council and the council of the village elders strengthened the position of the feudal patriarch. In effect, Zamindars and Jagirdars functioned as governments in themselves (Sharma, 1974). However, the Jagirdars enjoyed greater autonomy than their younger brethren (Zamindars). My aim is to see as to how group dominance has eroded today, though it was never absolute in nature in the past. Spatial mobility (Panikar, 1955) was not uncommon among certain groups and communities even in medieval India. Similarly, as Burton Stein (1968: 78-84) observes mobility at the level of individual and family was possible in medieval India.

Upward mobility of the suppressed groups has been very often understood as the sole indicator of social fluidity, but downward mobility is more indicative of social dynamics, in effect. Some of the changes have blocked continuity of sons of the privileged strata in their traditional positions of dominance. But we should not ignore the fact that changes in the society's organizational principles were not meant to bring down only a few families in the status and class hierarchy. They have not so far equally affected adversely all the units of these privileged groups nor have they equally benefited them or facilitated the process of upward mobility for the downtrodden or not-so-well-off. Thus, to think of groups sliding down or climbing up in the structure of dominance is a myth and not a reality. However, the possibility of making an analysis of the units moving upward or downward in terms of their aggregate characteristics is always there. But this aggregation of units must not be confused with concrete groups as they are found in society. There could be a "generalized decline" in case all the privileges and power extended to a group or a number of families is withdrawn abruptly. Similarly, there could be "generalized climb" in case the deprived ones are granted all the privileges and powers previously enjoyed by the dominant groups and families. Such a situation of change has not been so far a characteristic feature of Indian society. Desai (1948) observes that the class of Indian princes of pre-British period also survived due to political reasons. The decorum of royalty (feudal glamour) was maintained, hence to that extent old economy and some kind of serfdom survived in the new system. But the princes did not remain "medieval", they also invested in commerce and industry. Even after the abolition of the system of *zamindari* and *jagirdari* the landed interests continue to dominate in a qualitative sense by diversifying their activities, entering into new political arenas and aligning with the dominant political groups and parties.

One has to analyze both the directions of dominance mobility, namely, people of moderate or lower standing getting into positions of power (bourgeoisification), and people of high standing not being able to meet the challenge endangering their continuity in the present positions (proletarianization) (Sharma, 1969: 217-222). My study of six villages in Rajasthan (Sharma, 1974) shows that the Jagirdars (big landlords) came down in the status scale as they adhered to the mechanisms of traditional styles of life in the new situations which derecognized their feudal patrimony. Small Zamindars and Bhomias (grantees of Jagirdars) suffered most because of their negligent and parasitic attitude which they nourished during the hay days of the Jagirdars in Rajasthan. Consequently, their good land went out of their control due to the abolition of landlordism as they never cultivated themselves, and in fact, never considered land as property. They served their masters and catered to their requirements. In some of the villages many of them had to work as manual and agricultural labourers. These families have really been pauperized as their economic condition is not better than a number of families of ex-untouchables. This is an instance of downward dominance mobility of certain privileged families in the traditional system. This differential downward dominance mobility is basically due to the hierarchy that existed before these organizational changes and also due to the attitudes some of the Zamindars developed in regard to their styles of living and behaviour with others.

Group (caste) life represents mainly religious and cultural activities, and economic, political, educational and other such activities are determined more by the interests of specific families and individuals than the group to which they belong. I do not rule out the role of groups even in structuring some of these activities, out-group (caste) unity and activities have been generally characterized by discarding "polluted" occupations, violation of rules of marriage, birth of illegitimate child, elopement etc. Today groups striving for certain political and economic ends are drawn from different caste groups. Most studies of factions and political alliances have revealed that two or more factions existed in the same caste and the leaders of these factions drew support from other castes. Thus, a dominant individual is one who enjoys decisive dominance within or without caste or both within and outside caste simultaneously due to his acquired skills and qualities. Thus, status of a dominant individual is secular, relative rather than absolute, and based on his own progress and well-being (including his family) rather than that of the group of which he is a member. But group dominance is also not a fixed reality. Several castes have not recognized superiority of some other castes, and conflicting claims have been made by different castes for some high caste ranks (Gardner, 1968: 62-97). These moves are basically socio-cultural, implying efforts to improve caste position.

Since independence a few individuals (as we have observed earlier) from among the ex-dominant groups continue to be dominant because they have had an advanced sense of awakening, alertness, quick responsiveness to change, manoeuvrability and acceptability to new situations of dominance, though some sections of these groups have been reduced to non-dominant position. Conversely, the former non-dominant groups and families have acquired dominant status in the village community (Sharma, 1973: 59-77). Some of the well-off families from among the former tenants have acquired positions of power and influence. The confirmation of *khatedari* (ownership) right on land due to the abolition of *zamindari* and *jagirdari* systems facilitated improvement in their economic position and also inspired them to mobilize their caste members (who are generally numerically preponderant in the village community) at the time of elections to cast votes in their favour. In fact, their enhanced economic position and numerical preponderance made them politically awakened and aspirants for positions of power and prestige. Bailey (1957: 197) observed in his study of Orissa village that increased wealth made people politically more effective and also enhanced their ritual standing. Some families of the ex-tenants belonging to peasant castes have become politically influential since Independence. But this does not mean that all these families have moved up in the power hierarchy. Quite a large number of families from these groups continue to remain where they were before the abolition. And those who have gone up, have not moved up equally, and therefore, do not enjoy same influence and prestige. Thus, at both ends of the hierarchy land reforms did not have universally the same equalizing effects on the people. In fact, different land tenure systems had varying consequences in terms of transfer of land rights. For example, a Jagirdar, being an exclusive, absolute owner of his large territory, was unable to retain a substantial portion of his landholding.

This had clearly different consequences on the people: (1) In the *jagirdari* areas the landholdings got dispersed on a large scale, though the Jagirdar as an individual still remained the biggest owner but only as a Khatedar. However, the Zamindars, Bhomias and other dependents upon the Jagirdar found it difficult to cope with the new situation. Not only their influence in the community affairs declined abruptly, the process of their economic ruination also started quickly and many of them were compelled to take up lower jobs as agricultural and manual labour. Such a situation did not arise in the *zamindari* villages because the Zamindars took up *khatedari* right and moved to self-cultivation as the size of their landholdings was quite small. Consequently, Zamindar's ex-tenants were not substantially benefited, their economic position did not improve and politically too they continued to be subservient to their ex-masters. (2) These processes of change did not qualitatively alter the traditional structure. This situation prevails after the abolition of landlordism in rural Rajasthan in early 1950's. The Zamindars continue today in the garb of Khatedar cultivators and the big ex-tenants of the jagirdari areas who enjoyed certain privileges even before the abolition, have acquired the status of Khatedar self-cultivators owning bigger landholdings than the ex-Zamindars of *zamindari* villages. Thus, whatever changes we notice apparently as a result of these land reforms, have been neutralized either by retaining landholding or by gaining the status of big peasants in the *jagirdari* villages.

The question is: Who are power elites today in the village community? The power elites are not necessarily the top economic dominants, nor are the representatives of the economically depressed groups. They are the people who have viable economic standing in the community and have an adequate understanding of and interest in the village polity. Such people are also not necessarily highly educated because most of the educated people might not like to stay in the villages. Generally, power elites are those people who have political resources and understanding and also contacts with the political leaders and workers, administrators and other functionaries outside the community to whom they extend cooperation and support and in return expect the same from them. The power elites might get certain economic advantages over and above the common men but they may not be the richest in the community. However, the wealthiest man may use the power elite to enhance his interests without interfering in its activities. Economic dominants may get into positions of power but they would be constrained to keep their "economic" and "political" arenas separate at least apparently. Most of the top economic dominants would like to keep away from formal positions of power. The economic dominants who would not have/develop extra-economic links within and outside the community might not survive as power elites. Thus, power elites are either of the following in a given village community:

(1) Those people who wield political power but do not necessarily enjoy corresponding economic positions. Several factors including education, prestige or reputation of the family/parents, and other qualities such as social service, character and contacts, etc., would determine their power position. These elites would have a regular source of income including the salaries of some members of the family working in cities or elsewhere or in the village itself. Such a pattern of dominance is found in a village which has gone through a certain process of differentiation and social change.

(2) The villages which have retained their archaic character would be dominated politically by top economic dominants. Though the economic dominants may keep the two spheres separate, yet most of their political activities could be inspired by their economic interests, and also their economic activities might strengthen their political base in the community. Process of differentiation, political awakening, education and contacts, etc., would weaken the pattern of such dominance.

Until the power elite does not hamper the interests of economic dominants and the latter give economic concessions to the former, smooth functioning of the system could be found. The beginning of clash of interests between the two results into (i): the political elite trying to denigrate the economic dominant by harassing, entangling them into litigations and designating them as suckers of the blood of the people; and (ii) the economic dominants withdrawing economic support extended to the power elite and trying to overcome them by spending money on their supporters who matter a lot or on the people outside the system to get their ties snapped from them. These are hypothetical statements which could be validated only by gathering data.

Conclusion

The idea of "dominant caste" or group dominance is based on certain assumptions and these are not found valid, hence group dominance tends to be a myth rather than a reality. The new power wielders are not the same as they were in the past, however, qualitative difference between the old and the new power elites has not been much. The basic difference between the two lies in the fact that "group" rank membership as a determinant of elite position has withered away. Today elites are an aggregation and not an active functioning primordial group as the members lack group homogeneity, equality of status and rank and equal distribution of power and prestige. The elites were never unified, the man of power had always asymmetrical relations. Therefore, the idea of corporate mobility does not seem quite sound as the facts contradict this proposition.

The idea of dominance mobility makes it possible to separate the power elite from other types of elite. The concept of downward mobility facilitates a better understanding of mobility of the politically dominant individuals and families. The top power elite is not necessarily the top economic dominant and vice versa. Power elite is superior to economic dominants in all respects except wealth or money power. A one-to-one congruence between power elite and economic dominants is not a common feature in the village community. However, power elites are more resourceful in terms of networks, contacts, and education than the economic dominants. This does not mean that the power elite is drawn from the commoners, in fact, they are the people who are more resourceful and generally well-connected than the majority of the people.

References

Bailey, F.G., 1957, *Caste and Economic Frontier*, Manchester: University Press.

—, 1965, "Decisions by Consensus in Councils and Committees: with special reference to Village and Local Government of India", in Michel Banton (ed.), *Political Systems and the Distribution of Power*, London: Tavistock Publications.

Beteille, Andre, 1967, "Elites, Status Groups and Caste in Modern India", in: Philip Mason (ed.), *Indian and Ceylon: Unity and Diversity*, London: Oxford University Press.

Bottomore, T.B., 1965, "Modern Elites in India", in T.K.N. Unnithan, Indra Deva and Yogendra Singh (eds.), *Towards a Sociology of Culture in India*, Delhi: Prentice Hall of India.

—, 1967, "Cohesion and Division in Indian Elites", in Philip Mason (ed.), *op.cit.*

Carras, Mary C., 1972, *The Dynamics of Indian Political Factions*, London: Cambridge University Press.

Carter, Anthony, 1975, *Elite Politics in Rural India*, New Delhi: Vikas Publishing House.

Desai, I.P., 1965, "The New Elite", in T.K.N. Unnithan, Indra Deva and Yogendra Singh (eds.), *op.cit.*

Desai A.R., 1966, *Social Background of Indian Nationalism*, Bombay: Popular Prakashan.

Dube, S.C., 1968, "Caste Dominance and Factionalism", *Contributions to Indian Sociology*, New Series, 2.

Gardner, Peter M., 1968, "Dominance in India: A Reappraisal", *Contributions to Indian Sociology*, New Series, 2.

Edward, B. and Louise G. Harper, 1960, "Political Organization and Leadership in a Karnataka Village", in Richard L. Park and Irene Tinker (eds.), *Leadership and Political Institutions in India*, Madras: Oxford University Press.

Hitchcock, John T., 1959, "The Idea of the Martial Rajput", in Milton Singer (ed.), *Traditional India: Structure and Change*, Philadelphia: American Folklore Society.

Ingalls, Daniel, 1959, "The Brahmin Tradition", in Milton Singer (ed.), *Ibid.*

Kothari, Rajni, 1970, *Caste in Indian Politics*, New Delhi: Orient Longmans.

Lamb, Helen B., 1959, "The Indian Merchant", in Milton Singer (ed.), *op.cit.*

Leach, E.R., 1954, *Political Systems of Highland Burma*, London: G. Bell and Sons.

Lewis, Oscar, 1958, *Village Life in Northern India*, Urbana: The University of Illinois.

Miller, S.M., 1969, "Comparative Social Mobility", in Celia, Heller H. (ed.), *Structured Social Inequality*, New York: The Macmillan Co.

Misra, B.B., 1964, *The Indian Middle Classes*, London: Oxford University Press.

Morris-Jones, W.H., 1964, *The Government and Politics of India*, London: Hutchinson.

Narain, Iqbal, 1976, *The Rural Elite in an Indian State: A Case Study of Rajasthan*, New Delhi: Manohar Book Service.

Oommen, T.K., 1969, "Political Leadership in Rural India: Image and Reality", *Asian Survey*, IX (7).

—, 1970a, "Rural Community Power Structure in India", *Social Forces*, 49 (2).

—, 1970b, "The Concept of Dominant Caste: Some Queries", *Contributions to Indian Sociology*, New Series, 4.

Panikar, K.M., 1965, *Hindu Society at Cross Roads*. Bombay: Asia Publishing House.

Pareto, Vilfredo, 1935, *Mind and Society,* Vol. III, Translated by Bongiornd and Livingston, A., New York: Harcourt, Brace and Co.

Sharma, K.L., 1969, "Stresses in Caste Stratification: A Study of Six Villages in Rajasthan", *Economic and Political Weekly*, 4 (3).

—, 1973, "Downward Social Mobility: Some Observations", *Sociological Bulletin*, 22 (1).

—, 1974, *The Changing Rural Stratification System*, New Delhi: Orient Longman.

Shils, Edward A., 1961, *The Intellectuals between Tradition and Modernity: The Indian Situation*, The Hague: Mouton and Co.

Singh, Yogendra, 1975, "Historicity of Modernization", in Dhirendra Narain (ed.), *Explorations in the Family and other Essays*, Bombay: Thacker and Co.

Sirsikar, V.M., 1970, *The Rural Elite in a Developing Society*, New Delhi: Orient Longman.

Somjee, A.H., 1971, *Democracy and Political Change in India*, New Delhi: Orient Longman.

Srinivas, M.N., 1959, "The Dominant Caste in Rampura", *American Anthropologist*, 61(1).

—, 1966, *Social Change in Modern India*, Bombay: Allied Publishers.

Stein, Burton, 1968, "Social Mobility and Medieval South Indian Hindu Sects", in James Silverberg (ed.), *Social Mobility in the Caste System in India*, The Hague: Mouton and Co.

Tod, James, 1950, *Annals and Antiquities of Rajasthan*, London: Routledge and Kegan Paul.

15 Occupational Mobility of Castes in a North Indian Village

K.N. SHARMA

I

The traditional occupational structure of a village in India aims at fulfilling the religious, social, political, and economic needs of the villagers.1 There is some kind of territorial segmentation[2] or localization[3] in Indian villages. Generally, the various castes serve or are served by the residents of the village. In certain cases, a village may depend on the services of people not residing in the village. Nevertheless, the territory in which a caste operates is well-defined. The kind of service, mode of payment, and the number of families which a particular family must serve are all fixed and defined under the *jajmani* system. With occupational specialization, defined territory, and the absence of sufficient facility for spatial mobility, one may envisage an ideal situation in which there is an equilibrium between the demands for and the supply of a particular kind of service and between the total population living in a territory and the total natural resources available for exploitation. Such a community is probably not to be found in India. Even if no external factor plays a disturbing role at least the natural increase in the population of a village is likely to disturb the balance. This situation requires flexibility in the system, so that some avenues of livelihood may be open to all castes.

In modern times, increasing governmental activities, commerce, and contacts with cities have created a supply of and demand for new goods and services. New occupations have emerged. This situation has disturbed the old occupational structure and also the association between occupations and castes.

I have assumed, in this paper, that every caste is associated with one or a few traditional callings. Then on the basis of my study of a North Indian village and other rural studies made in India, I have made an effort to explore the nature of occupations and their association with castes in the modern social context. The specific questions raised in this paper are:

(1) Under what conditions the traditional callings are abandoned?
(2) Are the traditional callings of the various castes exclusive?
(3) Were and are the members of the various castes permitted to follow any occupation other than the traditionally prescribed ones?
(4) Are there certain prohibited or disapproved callings for the various castes?
(5) What are the various directions of occupational mobility for each caste?
(6) What are the limits of occupational mobility for each caste?

Answers to these questions can be provided from my own research in the village of Gamras.[4] In none of the other studies to be referred to, except Mathur's[5], were the data collected from this angle. Moreover, the number of Indian village studies is so small in comparison to the vast number of Indian villages and the significant differences among them are so numerous that safe generalization cannot be offered. It is at best an exploratory paper.

II

The village of Gamras is situated at a distance of about 10 miles from Kanpur city which is the most important industrial and commercial centre in the state of Uttar Pradesh. The total population of this village is 697 (in the year 1954), divided into 16 castes of Hindus and six castes of Muslims (see Table 1).

In this Table, I have classified the various castes found in the village of Gamras into seven categories on the basis of the nature of their traditional callings. In the first category, I have put Brahman, Mali, and Faqir (Muslim) castes, because all of them are mainly engaged in ritualistic services of one kind or another.

In the socio-religious life of clean castes in general and the *dwijas* (twice-born castes) in particular, the services of Brahmans are indispensable, yet there is no denying the fact their services are required only occasionally. In Gamras, there are 26 families of Brahmans. In 21 of these nobody within memory has followed the traditional calling. Of the rest of the families, one followed the traditional calling in the last generation but has not continued to do so in this generation. The present head of this family was employed in Kanpur and was therefore unable to perform priestly functions in the village. Now, he is retired and settled in the village, but he does not care to take up the priesthood again.

Table 1

Population and traditional callings of castes in Gamras (1954)

Categories of castes based on	*Names of castes*	*Traditional callings*	*Total no. of families*	*Total no. of persons*
A. Performance of ritualistic services	Kanyakubja Brahmans	Priesthood, teaching	26	104
	Mali	Gardening-agriculture Priestly functions	1	3
	Faqir*	Begging	1	3
B. Landownership and cultivation	Thakur	Ruling, fighting, landowning	9	36
	Lodh	Cultivation	14	50
C. Dependence on land for grazing	Ahir	Grazing of cattle	15	69
D. Dependence on business or government service	Kayastha	Secretarial service	4	28
	Pathan*	Money lending	1	2
	Kunjara*	Vegetable and fruit selling	1	4
E. Performance of regular personal services	Nai	Haircutting, Priestly functions	7	54
	Kahar	Carrying of water and palanquin	1	9
	Dhobi	Washing of clothes	7	42
F. Manufacturing of goods	Sunar	Goldsmithy	2	4
	Lohar	Blacksmithy	8	33
	Teli	Oil-pressing	19	89
	Bhurji	Grain-parching	1	1
	Julaha*	Weaving	2	7
	Bena*	Fan-making	1	3
	Kasai*	butchery	1	3
G. Unclean occupations	Chamar	Skinning, tanning	22	78
	Pasi	Pig-rearing	13	69
	Dhanuk	Scavenging, mid-wifery, pig-rearing	1	6
Total 7	22		157	697

* Muslim castes.

Table 2
Following of the traditional callings by the various castes of Gamras

Categories	Name of castes	*Following traditional callings* Exclusively	Primarily	Sub-sidiarily	Not following	Percentage of col. 6
A.	Kanyakubja Brahman	x	3	1	22	84.6
	Mali	1	x	x	x	x
	Faqir	x	x	x	x	100.0
B.	Thakur	7	2	x	x	x
	Lodh	x	6	x	8	57.1
C.	Ahir	x	x	x	15	100.0
D.	Kayastha	x	2	2	x	x
	Pathan	x	x	x	1	100.0
	Kunjara	x	x	x	1	100.0
E.	Nai	x	6	x	1	16.7
	Kahar	x	x	1	x	x
	Dhobi	5	2	x	x	x
F.	Sunar	2	x	x	x	x
	Lohar	1	4	x	3	3.75
	Teli	x	2	x	17	89.5
	Bhurji	1	x	x	x	x
	Julaha	x	x	x	2	100.0
	Bena	1	x	x	x	x
	Kasai	1	x	x	x	x
G.	Chamar	1	1	x	20	90.9
	Pasi	x	x	x	13	100.0
	Dhanuk	x	1	x	x	x
	Total	20	29	4	103	66.2

In the village of Karimpur reported by Wiser[6], out of 41 families of Brahmans only three practise their traditional callings and only one family does so exclusively. In Madhopur, of the total population of 1852, only two poor Brahman families follow their traditional calling.[7] In Rampur, the bulk of the Brahmans are engaged in secular occupations, while even those who practise the priesthood often also engage in subsidiary occupations such as agriculture and moneylending.[8] In Bira-Narsinghpur in Orissa, only 25 per cent of the total population of Brahmans seem to follow their traditional calling.[9] In Patal, mendicants and temple priests do not follow their traditional occupations exclusively.[10] In Bengal, the percentage of Brahmans engaged in traditional callings was reduced from 33.59 in 1901 to 19.57 in 1931.[11]

As against this picture, in the village Ramapur, out of the total population of a little less than 3,000, the number of Brahmans is 500. In this village, the numerical strength of the Brahmans can be correlated with the demand for ceremonies of all kinds at the Ganges and with the existence of many temples and shrines in the area. Of these, 60 are Pandas (who officiate at the rituals connected with pilgrim-centers) and 150 are Mahabrahmans or Mahapatras (who officiate at the rituals connected with the cremation of a dead body).[12] From the above data, it is clear that wherever the number of Brahmans is large either they have taken to secular occupations other than their traditional calling or there is an extension of the clientele due to external factors.

The role of a Mali in the rituals is minor and he combines this occupation with two others. He acts as a physician for the villagers and cultivates his own land. In the worship of local goddesses he officiates as a priest, and in the Sanskritic rituals officiated by Brahmans he is expected to supply followers. The latter two activities of Mali are not required regularly. In Gamras, there is only one family of Mali caste and its household head is engaged in these traditional callings. Similarly, in Karimpur, the only Mali family and in Patal all Mali families are so engaged.[13]

Begging is another occupation connected with the religious beliefs of the people. It is believed that spiritual merit can be earned by giving alms. A beggar cannot, however, be assured of receiving alms. The Faqir of Gamras, being a Muslim, had to leave his traditional occupation because the village is predominantly Hindu and, generally speaking, poor.

The uncertainty of income in these occupations creates similar problems for these castes. Therefore, these occupations have been called *akashivritti* (occupations with uncertain income) by those who practise them. Families which depend on these occupations are hard-pressed in normal circumstances. If there is a large number of families of these castes in a village, the problem of subsistence is all the more aggravated.

In the second category, I have put those castes which depend on agriculture. They may be either non-cultivating owners of land or cultivators, but all enjoy the common advantages of agriculture. On their lands are grown the important food crops and therefore they are reluctant to leave agriculture unless it becomes impossible to make ends meet.

The Kshatriyas or Thakurs were traditionally rulers and warriors. Now, as a caste, they do not wield either political or administrative power. As the rulers of land, they were owners of land also, so the easiest shift in their traditional calling was toward non-cultivating ownership of land. As landlords or zamindars they could perform pseudo-Kshatriya roles. This occupation may, therefore, be regarded as a traditionally permitted occupation.

In Gamras, all Thakur families are engaged in agriculture, but not all of them are non-cultivating owners of land. In Madhopur, 82 per cent of the total land is held by Thakurs as landlords and they own a large percentage of the remainder under one sort of title or another.[14] In Bisipara, warriors were landlords.[15] In Malabar, Nayars were landlords and gave land to the upper non-polluting castes for cultivation.[16]

The Lodh caste has been engaged in cultivation in general and the Kachhi caste in the cultivation of vegetables. As they are not engaged in any other kind of occupation, cultivation may be treated as their traditional calling, but in fact no occupation connected with agriculture can be regarded as the exclusive calling of any caste. This is not the case with the occupations of Brahmans, Malis, and most of the other castes.

In Gamras, all 14 families of Lodh caste depend on agriculture. In Karimpur, all 26 families of Kachhis and the single family of Lodh caste are engaged in agriculture.[17]

In the third category, I have included Ahir and Gadariya castes whose traditional occupations are the keeping of cows and of sheep and goats, respectively. For these occupations availability of pasture is very important. If more and more land is brought under cultivation by non-cultivating castes, this encroaches on pastures to a very great extent. Moreover, if the economic condition of the village is not satisfactory, they cannot afford to keep milch-cattle and goats and pay for the services of Ahirs and Gadariyas. It is common knowledge that all over India a major portion of pastures has been brought under the plough. Both situations have resulted in economic hardship for these castes and consequent loss of their traditional callings. In the absence of adequate facilities for the prevention and cure of diseases of cattle, goats, and sheep, it is highly uneconomic for these castes to keep a large number of these animals themselves. Still, wherever sufficient pastures are available they have continued to follow their traditional callings.

In Gamras, no Ahir follows his traditional calling. The Ahirs of Madhopur cultivate the land of their Thakur landlords.[18] Later Ahirs were reported to be leaving for new pasture land.[19] In Karimpur, four of six Gadariyas had no sheep and the majority were engaged in cultivation.[20] The shepherds of Rampura changed from keeping sheep and weaving blankets to farming. In the neighbouring village of Kera also most of them have taken to agriculture.[21] In Shamirpet, although some of the shepherds cultivate small land holdings, the major source of their income is their traditional occupation of keeping cattle herds.[22]

In Bengal, the percentage of Goalas engaged in their traditional calling of cow-keeping and in the milk trade was reduced from 41.45 in 1901 to 24.77 in 1931.[23] Thus, it is apparent that cowherds and shepherds are leaving their traditional callings.

In the fourth category, I have put Kayastha[24] and Vaishya castes of Hindus and Pathan and Kunjara castes of Muslims. The traditional occupations of these two Hindu castes are secretarial work and business, respectively. They have been included in one category because both of these services forge links between the village and the outside world and both of them are non-agricultural, secular occupations.

The traditional occupations of Pathan and Kunjara castes of Muslims are moneylending and selling of fruits and vegetables. These occupations by their very nature cannot be parts of the network of the *jajmani* system, as are the occupations of Kayasthas and Vaishyas, because these occupations do not meet the essential needs of the villagers. Also, all of these occupations are non-ritualistic. Therefore they have been included in the same category.

In Gamras, there is nobody representing the Vaishya caste. However, among the Muslims of the village, there is one family of Pathan, whose traditional calling is moneylending. A poor immigrant Muslim moneylender cannot operate in his calling in a predominantly Hindu village. There is one family of Kunjara (Muslim) caste in the village. His traditional calling is the selling of fruits and vegetables. His commodities are not in demand in a small, poor village like Gamras. Both of these men have given up their traditional callings.

In the fifth category are included Nai, Kahar, and Dhobi castes. Their services are required by upper castes regularly, and unlike the services of Kayastha and Vaishya castes their services form part of the network of the *jajmani* system. Besides the personal services of hair-cutting, carrying of water and washing of clothes, respectively, these castes perform certain occasionally required ritualistic functions also, but their livelihood depends primarily on their personal services. Therefore, these castes have been included in this category.

The Nai has an advantage over all other castes of this category because his services in the rituals are more regularly required than those of Kahar and Dhobi. The Brahman and Nai go together in every Hindu ritual. There are several sayings to this effect in the village of Gamras. In this village, only one out of seven families of Nais does not follow the traditional calling. In the village of Karimpur, there is only one family of Nai caste and its head follows the traditional calling exclusively.[25] In Madhopur and Patal, the Nais do not follow their traditional callings exclusively.[26] In Khalapur, 37 per cent of the Nais follow their traditional calling exclusively and 22 per cent practise agriculture besides their traditional calling.[27]

The functions of the Kahar are drawing and carrying water from the well to the house of his client, serving water at feasts given by his client, and removing the leaf-plates from which the guests have eaten at a feast. They also serve as palanquin-bearers. The existence of this caste or any other caste performing similar functions has not been reported either by Srinivas or by Beals who worked in South India. In Gamrass there is only one family of this caste and its head does not perform the functions either of water-carrier or of palanquin-bearer. These functions are not required in the village, because the level of water in the wells is not very low and there is no family in the village which is wealthy enough to employ the Kahar to carry water. Palanquin-bearing is obsolete because other more efficient and cheap means of transport are available. However, the Kahar's services are still required at feasts. The other village from which the Kahars have been reported is Karimpur.[28] There most of the men of the 11 families of Kahars are employed as day labourers; others cultivate their own fields.

The Dhobis cannot continue in their traditional calling of washing clothes if the villagers do not feel the need of putting on clean clothes in their day-to-day life. Moreover, a poor person, having only one set of clothes, cannot afford to hire the Dhobi. The Dhobis of Gamras, however, have the advantage of living in the vicinity of a big city—Kanpur—where they have extended their clientele. None of them has left the traditional calling. In Karimpur there is only one family of the Dhobi caste and it is engaged in its traditional calling.[29] Madhopur is a big village with a large population of Thakur landlords. To cope with the demand of a large number of *jajmans* or clients, most of the Dhobis come from neighbouring villages.[30] There is only one family of Dhobi in Rampura. A second family comes from another village to serve the clients of this village.[31] In Patal, two, out of eight Dhobi families, do not follow their traditional calling.[32] In Khalapur (Uttar Pradesh), all Dhobis are engaged in their traditional calling. 15 per cent of them are engaged in other non-agricultural pursuits.[33]

In the sixth category have been included the Lohar (blacksmith), Barhai (carpenter), Sunar (goldsmith), Julaha (weaver), Teli (oil-presser), Bharbhuja (grain-parcher), Bena (fan-maker), Kumhar (potter), and Kasai (butcher) castes. Each of these castes is engaged in manufacturing of some kind. Some of the commodities they make are also being manufactured in large-scale industries so the local producers are facing competition. The result is obvious: they have to leave their traditional callings.

The functions of Lohar and Barhai are required in repairing and manufacturing agricultural tools and implements and in building houses. These functions are closely linked to one another and usually are performed by the same person. In Gamras, five of eight families of Lohars are engaged in their traditional calling. The Lohars in Madhopur are economically better-off. In their spare time they cultivate their land-grants.[34] In Patal, all four families of Lohars are engaged primarily in their traditional calling.[35] In Khalapur, 28 per cent of the Barhais follow carpentry exclusively, while 25 per cent follow other occupations as well.[36] In Karimpur, the Barhais are all engaged in their traditional calling, but some are engaged in agriculture as well.[37] As the occupations of Lohar and Barhai are closely linked with the traditional techniques of cultivation, members of these castes cannot be dislodged from their traditional callings unless the tractor replaces the plough. Because of this and also because they receive land-grants from their rich clients, the easiest shift, in case of necessity, is toward agriculture. Both Sunar families of Gamras are carrying on their traditional calling, but they feel that the vicinity of Kanpur has adversely affected them. In Karimpur, most of the goldsmiths found it worthwhile to migrate to cities. The two families of goldsmiths which are still living in the village have taken up moneylending in addition to their traditional calling. Abandoning the traditional calling by the village goldsmiths results from the fact that the villagers have a wider choice of designs of ornaments in the shops of the cities. They prefer to go to cities instead of patronizing the local goldsmith.

In Gamras, both families of Julaha caste have left their traditional calling. In Khalapur, only 12 per cent of the weavers follow their traditional calling exclusively, while 13 per cent follow some other occupation as well.[38] In Shamirpet and Patal, the weavers have practically abandoned their traditional calling.[39] In the West Bengal village studied by Jyotirmoyee Sarma, however, the Tanti weavers are still engaged in their occupation. The young men in their families are receiving education and seeking jobs in Calcutta. Here, they do not face any direct competition from the large-scale industries because they weave on the orders of Mahajans (businessmen).[40]

Only two of 19 families of Teli caste are still partially engaged in oil-pressing in Gamras. In Karimpur village, all four Teli families are engaged in their traditional calling,[41] but in Madhopur and Patal no Teli follows his traditional calling.[42] In Rampura, except in two families, all oil-men are labourers, servants, or petty traders.[43]

In this category of castes the Julahas and Telis have been affected most adversely because they are fast losing their traditions, weaving and oil-pressing, respectively, in competition with large-scale industries. Mahatma Gandhi's movement for using *khadi* (hand-spun and hand-woven cloth) has, however, stabilized the occupation of weavers in certain parts of India.

In Gamras, there is only one family of Bharbhuja or Bhurji (grain-parcher) caste. A very important common observation of anthropologists is that the number of Bhurjis is very small in the villages studied by them. In Karimpur, there is only one family of grain-parcher caste, but because it is too big to subsist on the income of its traditional calling the men are engaged in agriculture as well.[44] In Khalapur, 20 per cent of the Bhurjis follow their traditional occupation exclusively, while 17 per cent follow some other occupations as well.[45] The goods manufactured by fan-makers, basket-makers, and potters are not very much in demand. In Gamras, there is only one family of Bena (fan-maker). The potter comes from another village. In Rampura, the regular immigrant basket-makers follow their traditional calling.[46] In Patal, the basket-maker and mat-maker do not follow their occupations exclusively.[47] In Klahapur, 36 per cent of the potters follow their traditional calling along with some other occupation and nobody follows it exclusively.[48] In Sirkanda village, all of the artisan (Shilpkar) castes depend primarily upon their crafts.[49] The services of the Muslim butcher (Kasai) of Gamras are required by meat-eating families of the village and its neighbourhood. He is not facing any competition from large-scale industries, and there are very few butchers in the rural areas, so he has a virtual monopoly of his trade.

In the seventh and last category, I have put Chamar, Pasi, and Dhanuk castes. Their occupations are unclean. In such occupations sufficient regular income for maintaining the whole family is not easy if the caste is populous. More than two families, I should say, in a medium-sized village cannot make ends meet. In certain cases, it has been reported that unclean occupations are being abandoned in order to raise the caste status of those who traditionally followed them.

In Gamras, only two Chamars are engaged in their traditional callings and those two are old residents of the village. According to Russel, writing in 1916, fewer than one-seventh of the Chamars were following the traditional callings.[50] Briggs also stresses that they were not leather workers.[51] Wiser and Mathur report similar situations operating in their villages.[52]

Pig-rearing is a common occupation of Pasi and Dhanuk castes. Proper handling and adequate contacts for selling bristles are required in this endeavour. In Gamras, no Pasi family is engaged in pig-rearing. The only Dhanuk family of the village is, however, engaged in callings traditional to this caste. The Dhanuk widow's son-in-law, who lives in Kanpur, helps her to sell bristles in Kanpur. In return, for regular services of scavenging she has received a land-grant from her Thakur *jajmani* family. This is the only family served by her in this respect. In Karimpur, the Dhanuk and Bhangi families are engaged in their traditional callings primarily, but they also engage in agriculture. In Rampura, 15 out of 30 untouchable families are cultivators and fifteen are coolie labourers.[53] In Shamirpet, the untouchables are employed in agriculture either as cultivators of their own land or as farm labourers, or they work at non-farm labour.[54]

III

Directions of Occupational Mobility

Rural Occupations

In a peasant society land is valuable for reasons besides economic ones. On the economic side, ownership or cultivation of land provides direct subsistence in the sense that people produce or get the foodstuffs without depending on anybody else. When a person cannot subsist on his traditional calling, land provides the best alternative to it. In the *jajmani* system, a piece of land is often granted by landholders to families which offer them services of various kinds, especially religious or secular ceremonial services or both.[55] Besides, the families which have any surplus money try to acquire land from the families which own uneconomic holdings[56] because there is no entrepreneurial system available to them where they may invest their surplus money. Also, ownership of land may convey political authority and superior status in the community. These social factors further impel the villagers to acquire land. Those who cannot acquire land for some reason or other search for jobs on the land of others, such as cultivation on batai (sharecropping) or field labour.

Generally, non-cultivating ownership of land is associated with the Thakur castes, cultivation is associated with Lodh and Kachhi castes, and field labour is associated with untouchable castes such as Chamars and Pasis. This simple association of occupations to castes is a real one but the occupations cannot be regarded as traditional for and exclusive to the castes which practise them. In a peasant economy based on land such rigidity is impossible; otherwise, if no other avenues were open, either the surplus population would starve or would break the system itself. The adjustments and re-adjustments of the economy are possible only by keeping certain avenues open to all castes and groups. Agriculture has been treated in this way. Under these circumstances dependence of families on agriculture is likely to increase.

From Table 3 it is clear that 138 families (88.4%) out of the total of 157 depend on agriculture either exclusively or partially. Of the 19 families which do not depend on agriculture at all, the Lohar, Sunar, Bhurji, Dhobi, Chamar, Bena, and Kasai families are engaged in their traditional callings (except that one Chamar is exclusively engaged in business), while the Brahman, Julaha, and Pathan families are engaged in callings other than traditional. Agriculture is a partial source of livelihood for about half the families in the village. This overwhelming dependence on agriculture is reported from elsewhere also.[57] Thus, the primary direction of occupational mobility is toward agriculture.

For the purpose of finer analysis, dependence on agriculture has been classified into several categories in Table 4, i.e., non-cultivating landownership, cultivation of land wholly or mainly owned, cultivation of land wholly or mainly unowned, and field-labour.

Besides agriculture, there are other rural occupations in which the families of Gamras are engaged. These are grazing of cattle, masonry work and service and general coolie labour.

Table 3
Dependence of families of Gamras on agriculture

Categories	*Name of castes*	*Dependence on agriculture*		*No dependence*
		Exclusive	*Partial*	
A.	Kanyakubja Brahman	14	9	3
	Mali	x	1	x
	Faqir	x	1	x
B.	Thakur	7	12	x
	Lodh	3	11	x
C.	Ahir	10	5	x
D.	Kayastha	x	4	x
	Pathan	x	x	1
	Kunjara	1	x	x
E.	Nai	1	6	x
	Kahar	x	1	x
	Dhobi	x	2	5
F.	Sunar	x	x	2
	Lohar	3	4	1
	Teli	12	7	x
	Bhurji	x	x	1
	Julaha	x	x	2
	Bena	x	x	1
	Kasai	x	x	1
G.	Chamar	8	12	2
	Pasi	x	11	x
	Dhanuk	x	1	x
	Total	61	77	19
	Percentage	38.8	49.6	11.5

The most striking feature about Gamras is that of the total of 138 families, 52 (37%) depend on cultivation of their own land. Among landowners, who either do or do not cultivate their land themselves, there are only two families of untouchable castes: one Pasi and one Dhanuk. None are Muslims (see Table 4). In the third and fourth categories, the number of families of clean castes aside from Telis is very small. Two Dhobi families in the first category bought land with surplus money, while Pasi and

Dhanuk families got grants of land for performing certain services. In the Dhanuk family, there is no male, so the land is given to others on share-cropping, while the Pasi, who cultivates his own field, is employed as watchman in the temple of the old zamindar of the village. These categories of agricultural occupations are arranged in a descending prestige hierarchy in the view of villagers; therefore, generally speaking, there is a correlation between the descending order of rural occupations and the castes of Gamras. The exceptions to this generalization are explained by unusual circumstances. Except for one family each of the Brahman and Thakur castes, nobody from upper castes is engaged as a field labourer. The exceptions are due to extreme poverty. Among the non-agricultural rural occupations, grazing of cattle is the only occupation which is traditionally associated with Ahir caste, but there is no Ahir engaged in that occupation in the village. Since the families of other castes which follow this calling are only partially dependent on it, this is not regarded as an infringement on the traditional calling of Ahirs.

Table 4

Category-wise distribution of families in the various rural occupations

	Categories							
	A	*B*	*C*	*D*	*E*	*F*	*G*	*Total*
Rural agricultural occupations								
1. Non-cultivating ownership of land	10	4	4	2	5	1	1	27
2. Cultivation of land wholly or mainly owned	13	—	12	10	4	12	1	52
3. Cultivation of land wholly or mainly unowned	—	—	2	3	—	9	14	28
4. Field labour	1	—	2	—	1	—	5	9
5. General labour	1	1	3	—	—	4	13	22
Non-agricultural* rural occupations								
1. Watchman	—	—	—	—	—	—	1	1
2. Grazing of cattle	—	—	1	—	—	—	1	2
3. Masonry work	—	—	—	—	—	—	2	2
Total	25	5	24	15	10	26	38	143*

* Denotes the non-exclusive dependence on non-agricultural occupations. The five families engaged in such occupations are also engaged in some kind of agricultural occupation as well.

Commercial Occupations

Commercial occupations are also hierarchically viewed by the villagers as indicated by their placement in descending order in Table 5.

Table 5

Number of families of castes depending on commercial occupations in Gamras

Commercial occupations	*Castes*							
	Brahman	*Kayastha*	*Lodh*	*Kahar*	*Teli*	*Julaha*	*Chamar*	*Total*
Shopkeeping	2	—	—	1	1	—	1	5
Moneylending	—	3	—	—	—	—	—	3
Wood-cutting	—	—	3	—	—	2	—	5
Total	2	3	3	1	1	2	1	13

In Table 5, there is also a correlation in the descending order of castes and commercial occupations. Nobody from the untouchable castes except one Chamar is following such occupations. Because that Chamar stayed in the Andaman Islands for more than 20 years, his outlook on life changed. There he was working as an orderly. When he came back with his savings he did not like either his traditional calling or cultivation, so he started a business.

Urban Occupations

The third direction of occupational mobility is toward urban occupations or rural-urban occupations. By urban occupations I mean those for which a person commutes to the town daily and depends for income on the town only, e.g., the jobs of secretary or clerk, bus conductor, peon, and industrial worker. By rural-urban occupations I mean those occupations in which a person commutes to the city either occasionally or daily and depends for income on both the town and the village, e.g., carrying and selling milk in the city, cart-driving and *ekka* (horse-driven passenger cart) driving. Persons engaged in these jobs carry either goods or human beings to the city. These occupations would not have arisen had the village not been situated in the proximity of a town.

In Table 6, urban occupations have also been presented in a descending order of their status-significance to the villagers. Generally speaking, in this table also, there is a correlation between the descending order of castes and that of urban occupations. As education is concentrated in the

Kayastha, Brahman, Thakur, Ahir, and Teli castes only, the lower castes cannot get into jobs requiring literacy. For getting into other lower urban occupations like that of peon and industrial worker one must have some initiative and drive and, if possible, some urban contacts. The lower castes usually lack both and it is therefore difficult for them to get even these occupations. They avoid moving out of the village as long as it does not become impossible for them to make ends meet there. Even when they move out they do not break their links with the village.

Table 6

Category-wise distribution of castes in urban and rural-urban occupations in Gamras

	A	*B*	*C*	*D*	*E*	*F*	*G*	*Total*
A. Urban occupations								
Secretarial	—	2	—	—	—	—	—	2
Bus conductor	1	—	—	—	—	—	—	1
Peon	1	—	1	—	—	—	—	2
Industrial worker	—	1	—	—	—	—	—	1
B. Rural-urban occupations								
Carrying and selling milk in the city	3	—	—	1	1	—	—	5
Cart-driving	3	—	3	2	—	—	—	8
Ekka-driving	—	1	—	—	—	1	—	2
Total	8	4	4	3	1	1	—	21

Conclusions

1. Perfect correlation between castes and their traditional callings can be found only in an ideal community whose economy is insulated; where the total population of the village and the total natural resources available for exploitation, the population size of each functionary caste, and the population size of the castes whom they serve, are evenly balanced. Such an ideal village probably does not exist. If nothing else changes, at least the balance of population is occasionally disturbed, forcing people to leave their traditional callings for adequate subsistence.
2. If the proportion of families of a particular caste is larger than the number which can be maintained by the families of other castes to whom they offer their services, some families are forced to abandon

their traditional callings. However, when such castes succeed in increasing their clientele outside the village, the balance of population is tilted in their favour. In such a situation the traditional callings become remunerative and the families remain attached to them.

3. In the absence of such an extension of clientele, the castes whose services are not regularly in demand to a great extent and which have to compete with urban manufacturers, are forced to leave their traditional callings. This does not mean that all families of the caste leave, but a majority of the families does.
4. A largely insulated economy and occupational specialization within the *jajmani* system create a situation in which the main avenue open to all castes after leaving their traditional calling is agriculture. The social significance of the ownership of land, granting of land to the families which offer some kind of service regularly, and lack of opportunities for the investment of surplus money, have created a situation in which agriculture never remained the specialized monopoly of any caste. The various agricultural occupations are hierarchically ranked by villagers. The higher occupations are those in which no manual labour is involved and the lowest those involving manual work for others. Therefore, the upper castes like to be non-cultivating owners of land. The families which have surplus money have been investing it in the purchase of land. The functions of untouchable castes are neither remunerative nor are they required regularly. As a consequence they are generally poor. The poor families in all castes move toward manual field labour. The untouchables move to general coolie labour and masonry work as well. Some untouchable families may receive land-grants from their *jajmanis,* but usually they cannot depend on these to make both ends meet.
5. The pressure of population on land forces people to bring more and more land under the plough, and the easiest way is to start the cultivation of pastures. This situation forces the cowherds and shepherds to abandon their traditional callings. Since cattle are kept by all castes, and as Ahirs leave their traditional calling, other castes can acquire these occupations without much difficulty.
6. The traditional occupations of other castes are not usually adopted. Following the occupations of castes lower than one's own involves loss of social status. Since the occupations connected with the manufacturing of goods are not ritualistic, in exceptional circumstances they may be followed by various castes to fulfil the needs of the vil-

lage. Carpenters and blacksmiths are the only caste groups which have been found interchanging occupations. These occupations go with one another and are socially at a par, hence this interchange does not involve any social problem.

7. Besides agricultural occupations and traditional callings of the various castes, there are very few rural occupations available to people in the village. The jobs of general labourer and mason are too low in the occupational hierarchy of the village to be followed by the high castes. The lower castes do not stand to lose anything.
8. As and when the insulation of a village is broken, commercial occupations (such as running shops to cater to villagers' desire for goods imported from outside) become profitable. This depends upon the values villagers place on urban goods in comparison to those locally manufactured and produced.
9. Urban contacts open up new occupations to villagers. Villages which are in the vicinity of a city get the opportunity to engage in and develop rural-urban occupations. In these occupations also there is a hierarchy. Most of these occupations require some kind of investment of money. The untouchables are again at a disadvantage because of their poverty. With regard to urban occupations, the people living in such villages have a double advantage. They have better opportunities for employment and enjoy cheaper living in the village. Yet, the higher or better occupations cannot be acquired without education, and here the higher castes and rich families have an advantage over the untouchables and the poor. The Brahman and Kayastha castes, being traditionally associated with literary pursuits, have an initial advantage.
10. Surplus money plays an important role in mobility toward higher occupations of any kind. It can be invested in purchasing new land, in commerce, or in education. The choice depends ultimately on values and comparative expectations of returns. Now after the abolition of landlordism or *zamindari* in most of the states, it is not very profitable to invest surplus money in land unless one is interested in doing the cultivation himself. Consequently, the most likely directions of mobility for the families which have any surplus money are into commercial and urban occupations.
11. The actions of the state also have a bearing on occupational mobility. Extension of educational opportunities to wider areas is likely to affect the movement toward urban occupations, as has happened in

Mysore.[58] Provision for free education to the untouchable and backward castes will bring about further changes. Similarly, various kinds of land reforms will restrict the mobility of the several castes toward rural and especially agricultural occupations.

In brief, we can say that there are one or more occupations which are traditionally prescribed for each caste. But for maintaining the stability of the system certain occupations in the field of agriculture are traditionally permitted to all. Movement toward the traditionally prescribed occupations of other castes, it seems, is not accepted by the society. However, there is restricted movement toward occupations which are quite close to one's own traditional calling or which do not involve any substantial gain or loss of status, or which are secular in character, e.g., weaving. External contacts have added two new dimensions to the occupational pattern of a village—commercial and urban occupations. Agricultural, commercial, and urban occupations are not caste-bound and therefore are open to all castes. Since all of these occupations are hierarchically viewed by the villagers, the upper castes try to move into the higher occupations. The ultimate choice depends on the value and surplus money of each group. The new far-reaching legislative measures of the state and the abolition of *zamindari* on the one hand and of untouchability on the other, are likely to affect the directions and range of occupational mobility of the various castes. Thus, there is every possibility that opportunities for occupational mobility throughout rural India will be equalized in times to come.

Notes

1. Fieldwork in Gamras between April 1954 and December 1955 is reported in full in the author's unpublished doctoral dissertation, Lucknow University, 1956, which was written under the supervision of Professor D.N. Majumdar. The present paper was prepared for presentation before the South Asia Colloquium, University of California, Berkeley, while the author was a visiting scholar from India under sponsorship of the Institute of International Education during 1959-60.
2. Miller, 1954.
3. Bailey, 1957, p.39.
4. Gamras is a pseudonym.

5. Mathur, 1958.
6. Wiser, 1936, pp. 146-147.
7. Opler and Singh, 1972b.
8. Srinivas, 1955, p.4.
9. Ray, 1956, p. 12.
10. Mathur, 1958, p. 49.
11. Bose, 1959, p. 20.
12. Opler and Singh, 1952b.
13. Wiser, 1936, pp. 146-147; Mathur, 1958, p. 49.
14. Opler and Singh, 1952b.
15. Bailey, 1957, p. 266.
16. Miller, 1954.
17. Wiser, 1936, p. 30.
18. Opler and Singh, 1947, p.479.
19. Opler and Singh, 1952a, p. 10.
20. Wiser, 1936, p. 42.
21. Srinivas, 1955, p. 3.
22. Dube, 1959, p. 64.
23. Bose, 1955, p. 19.
24. Wiser has created confusion by accepting Kayasthas as representative of Kshatriyas in the village of Karimpur, and listing military service as their traditional calling (Wiser, 1936, pp. 24-26). Kshatriya is a varna, while Kayastha is a caste or jati, and the traditional occupation of Kayasthas is secretarial work.
25. Wiser, 1936, pp. 146-147.
26. Oper and Singh, 1947, p. 480; Mathur, 1958, p. 49.
27. Mahar, 1958, Table A.
28. Wiser, 1936, p. 41.
29. *Idem*, p. 49.
30. Opler and Singh, 1947, p. 486.
31. Srinivas, 1955, p. 8.
32. Mathur, 1958, p. 52.
33. Mahar, 1958, Table A.
34. Opler and Singh, 1947, p. 482.
35. Mathur, 1958, p. 49.
36. Mahar, 1958, Table A.
37. Wiser, 1936, pp. 146-147.
38. Mahar, 1958, Table A.
39. Dube, 1955, p. 65; Mathur, 1958, p. 49.

40. Sarma, 1955, p. 164.
41. Wiser, 1936, p. 30.
42. Opler and Singh, 1947, p. 485; Mathur, 1958, p. 49.
43. Srinivas, 1955, p. 7.
44. Wiser, 1936, p. 42.
45. Mahar, 1958, Table A.
46. Srinivas, 1955, p. 7.
47. Mathur, 1958, p. 49.
48. Mahar, 1958, Table A.
49. Berreman, 1959, p. 108.
50. Russel, 1916, Vol. 2, p. 406.
51. Briggs, 1920, p. 226.
52. Wiser, 1936, pp. 48-49; Mathur, 1958, p. 49.
53. Srinivas, 1955, p. 7.
54. Dube, 1955, p. 58.
55. Rural, commercial, and urban occupations have been oriented in three hierarchical orders separately, because it has been found that all villagers do not view these occupations in the same way. For some, urban occupations are better than rural; for others commercial are best; for still others rural occupations are best.
56. Bailey, 1957, p. 240.
57. Beals, 1955, p. 88; Srinivas, 1955, p. 3; Sarma, 1955, pp. 169-171; Dube, 1959, pp. 71-72; Government of India, 1956, pp. 5-6.
58. Srinivas, 1955; Beals, 1955.

References

Beals, Alan R., 1955, "Interplay among Factors of Change in a Mysore Village" (in *Village India*, McKim Marriott, ed., Memoirs, American Anthropological Association, No. 83, pp. 78-101).

Bailey, F.G., 1957, *Caste and the Economic Frontier* (Manchester: Manchester University Press).

Berreman, G.D., 1959, *Kin, Caste and Community in a Himalayan Hill Village* (Ms.: Ph.D. Dissertation, Cornell University).

Bose, N.K., 1959, *Modern Bengal* (Reprint No. 10, Institute of International Studies, University of California, Berkeley).

Briggs, George W., 1920, *The Chamars* (Calcutta: Associated Press).

Dube, S.C., 1955, *Indian Village* (London: Routledge and Kegan Paul).
Government of India, 1956, *Village Artisans* (P.E.O. Publication No. 5, New Delhi: Manager Publications, Government of India).
Mahar, Michael, 1958, Paper presented at the Annual Meeting, American Anthropological Association, Washington, D.C.
Mathur, K.S., 1958, *Caste and Occupation in a Malwa Village* (Eastern Anthropologist, Vol. 12, No. 1).
Miller, Eric J., 1954, *Caste and Territory in Malabar* (American Anthropologist, Vol. 56, pp. 410-420).
Opler, Morris, and Rudra Datt Singh, 1947, "The Division of labour in an Indian Village" (in *A Reader in General Anthropology*, Carleton S. Coon, ed., New York: Henry Holt and Company.).
—, 1952a, *Economic, Political and Social Change in a Village of North Central India* (Human Organization, Vol. 11, No. 2).
—, 1952b, *Two Villages of Eastern Uttar Pradesh (U.P.), India: an Analysis of Similarities and Differences* (American Anthropologist, Vol. 54, pp. 179-190).
Ray, Ajit, 1956, *A Brahman Village of the Sasna Type in the District of Puri, Orissa* (Man in India, Vol. 36, No. 1).
Russel, R.V., 1916, *The Tribes and Castes of the Central Provinces of India* (4 Vols., London: Macmillan and Company).
Sarma, Jyotirmoyee, 1955, "A Village in West Bengal" (*in India's Villages*, Calcutta: West Bengal Government Press).
Sharma, K.N., 1956, *Urban Contacts and Cultural Change in a Little Community* (Ms.: Ph.D. Dissertation, Lucknow University).
Srinivas, M.N., 1955, "The Social System of a Mysore Village" (in *Village India*, McKim Marriott, ed., Memoirs, American Anthropological Association, No. 83, pp. 1-35).
Wiser, W.H., 1936, *The Hindu Jajmani Systems* (Lucknow: Publishing House).

16 Stratification among Tribals in Gujarat

PRADIP KUMAR BOSE

The tribes in Gujarat today are equally affected by the processes of planned and unplanned change and by the continuous structural and institutional shifts in rural India. They are stratified in terms of control over resources. Furthermore, during the process of industrialization, major alterations in the pattern of stratification are inescapable. Old resources acquire a new significance, and new resources are to be managed and controlled effectively to survive in the severe competition over the control over resources. In this, tribes cannot remain isolated any longer and changing stratification is consequently appropriate for the study of tribes.

Stratification of Indian Society

In the study of stratifications in Indian rural society, scholars have distinguished two kinds of hierarchies. The first is referred to as 'sacred', 'ritual' or 'pollution' hierarchy, with Brahmins at the top, untouchables at the bottom, and intermediate groups ranked according to certain principles of purity-pollution. The second kind of hierarchy is referred to as 'secular', or 'politico-economic' with the most powerful economic and political group (e.g., large landowners) at the top and least powerful economic and political group (e.g., landless labourers) at the bottom. Of the two kinds of stratificatory approaches mentioned above, one comes across very few studies on the stratification of rural society based on secular dimensions; besides, even these few studies are confined to an analysis of caste society.

The studies on tribes are far removed from this kind of treatment. The reasons are not far to seek. First, is the continuation of the colonial tradition of collecting ethnographic materials relating to the life-cycle rituals, customs, etc., of the tribals by anthropologists. The second reason is the lack of a precise definition of tribe. The term 'tribe' has been variously understood as 'nation', 'society', 'race', etc., as in the beginning no anthropologist bothered to define clearly the term tribe so long as they could locate and differentiate one group from the other as was the case in Australia, Melanesia and North America. In India, the situation was entirely different but in anthropological studies the understanding has been that a tribe is: (1) geographically and culturally isolated; (2) relatively non-hierarchical and non-differentiated; and (3) with a low level of techno-economic development (Dube 1977: 2; Beteille 1977: 12).

However, it is obvious that, on none of these counts can the majority of people in India who are known as 'tribals' be characterized as such. Nor can one characterize tribe as 'society' or 'nation' having well-defined linguistic and political boundaries. The cultural boundary of a tribe is much less well-defined (Beteille 1977). It is for these reasons, that the 'tribe' of an anthropologist's ideal type can be rarely found in India, and why some scholars have preferred to consider it as a thing of the past and instead drawn our attention to tribes in transition (Desai 1979; Desai 1977; Dube 1977; Beteille 1977). However, in this paper, we shall continue to use the word 'tribe' as defined in the Government Schedule.

This transition is seen by anthropologists as the shift of tribal people to *jati* society (Mandelbaum 1970: 573-619; Sinha 1958). According to Mandelbaum, "the direction of tribal change in India is clear and predictable. Virtually all tribes are now shifting toward Jati characteristics, a movement which has greatly accelerated as communications have improved and external forces have impinged more closely" (1970: 593). If this is so, the significant question will be: Should one study the stratificatory system of tribes within the broad framework of the caste system or what is known as ritual hierarchy or is there another alternative in terms of a secular hierarchy? In this paper, our contention is that the change among the tribes can be best understood now not within the context of caste, i.e., how they are moving towards *jati* society, but on the basis of a secular principle, i.e., class.

The phenomenon of tribes in transition is nothing new in Indian history. As Kosambi (1975:27) noted, "the entire course of Indian history shows tribal elements being fused in general society", and the process still continues. However, there is a difference. In earlier times, when tribes came in contact with Hindus, the caste ideology was the dominant ideology of the economic system and, willingly or unwillingly, tribes had to assume a rank in the overall caste system. However, in modern times, caste ideology is no longer the dominant ideology, tribes are directly interacting with the market network, the regional and the national economy, without the mediation of caste, and are adopting characteristics of the commercial capitalist system. Modern technological development and the growth of the market network is beyond the boundaries of the caste system; on the contrary, castes are decisively influenced by them and so (as we shall see) are the tribes.

It is in this context that the study of stratification among tribes, in terms of secular hierarchy, becomes meaningful. The tribes in Gujarat today are equally affected by the processes of planned and unplanned change and by the continuous structural and institutional shifts in rural India. They are stratified in terms of control over resources. Furthermore, during the process of industrialization, major alterations in the pattern of stratification are inescapable. Old resources acquire a new significance, and new resources are to be managed and controlled effectively to survive in the severe competition over the control over resources. In this, tribes cannot remain isolated any longer and changing stratification is consequently appropriate for the study of tribes.

Is There a Separate Tribal Economy?

Gujarat ranks fourth in tribal population among the states of the Indian Union. The first three are Madhya Pradesh, Orissa, and Bihar, respectively. Within Gujarat itself, the scheduled tribe population is 37,34,422 which constitutes about 14 per cent of the total population of the state. Of the total scheduled tribe population, 94.88 per cent are distributed in the seven districts, viz., Surat, Valsad, Panchmahals, Bharuch, Vadodara, Sabarkantha and Dangs, and they are mainly confined to the eastern belt of South Gujarat. Nearly 94 per cent of tribal population in Gujarat live in villages, and they are naturally affected by the agrarian change taking place therein.

The eastern region, where the tribes are concentrated, consists of mountainous tracts and forests. At the beginning of the last century the tribes were mainly shifting cultivators. As one British district officer wrote in 1854: "They rudely till the soil, but are very migratory and unsettled cultivators" (Breman 1974: 30). However, with the pacification by the colonial rulers and the introduction of the *ryatvari* system, the tribals gradually came in contact with the plains Hindus and the process of land alienation started—as lower tax was imposed on plots tilled by tribal cultivators—and a majority of them became tenants (Breman 1974). That is how the region opened up and more frequent contacts with non-tribals got established. In the plains, on the other hand, the process of tribal assimilation into Hindu society started much earlier and tribes like Kolis and Dublas were incorporated into the caste system.

At the turn of the century, we find that tribes like the Bhils (the largest tribe in Gujarat) were occupied in settled agriculture (Enthoven 1920) and the Dublas were well-entrenched as *halis* or agricultural labourers of the better class cultivators (Shukla 1937; Enthoven 1920). In the 1930s, we find that the Chaudharis were settled in villages with differential landholdings and a sizeable percentage of them were agricultural labourers (Shah 1978a). The Naikas of Naikdas, who were well-known in the early 19th century for their predatory and lawless habits and their love for independence, were found to be working mostly as agricultural labourers in the early 20th century (Shah 1959). Without multiplying instances, we can say that this transformation was caused mainly by the changed agrarian policy of the colonial rulers. As more and more land was brought under cultivation, the possibilities of bringing still more land in Gujarat was almost exhausted by 1911. We find that the gross cropped area in Gujarat, which was 44 thousand acre in 1911, increased by only 4,000 acre in 1941 (Desai 1948: 46). As Desai noted (1948: 50), because the rate of increase in population was greater than growth rate of cropped area in that period "new avenues of support for the rapidly rising tide of rural population will have to be sought elsewhere than extension of ploughed lands". As a corollary to this, the tribes were gradually drawn into settled agriculture, either as cultivators or as labourers.

In the post-independence period, the tribes in Gujarat were drawn into an environment of modernizing and productivity-oriented agriculture at a much faster rate. In this period, the growth record of agriculture in Gujarat appears to be quiet impressive when compared with the all India record. The compound growth rate for all crops during the 22 years, from 1951-52 to 1972-73, was substantially higher for Gujarat (4.44%) as compared to all India (2.51%). This is all the more significant because the compound growth rate of area under cultivation for all India was 0.93 per cent whereas for Gujarat it was only 0.43 per cent. The compound growth rate of productivity for Gujarat was substantially higher (3.05%)

as compared to all India (1.21%).

Inter-state comparison of growth rates also bears out the impressive performance of Gujarat. In the period prior to green revolution (1952-53 to 1964-65) the compound growth rate achieved by Gujarat (4.55%) was quite close to Punjab's which had achieved the highest growth rate of 5.56 per cent. Again, in Punjab, the area under cultivation increased at 1.90 per cent, whereas in Gujarat it increased by 0.45 per cent in this period. The compound growth rate of productivity achieved by Gujarat (4.09%) was the highest among all the states (Pathak *et al.* 1979).

Two major factors contributing to the increased agricultural output have been increase in yield, and crop-pattern changes. Increasingly the land was being brought under cash crop cultivation and there was a negative increase in the area for foodgrains (Pathak *et al.* 1979). Consumption of fertilizers like nitrogen per hectare of gross cropped area increased from 0.66 kg in 1959-60 to 13.48 kg in 1973-74. Similarly, the number of oil engines per thousand hectare of net sown area increased from 1.48 to 38.38 for the period 1950-51 to 1971-72. For the same period, the number of electric motors increased from 0.10 to 5.01 per thousand hectare of net sown area. Simultaneously, the pressure of rural workers on land also increased considerably. Total rural workers per 100 hectare of gross cropped area increased from 63 to 82 between 1951-52 and 1970-71. All these factors, combined with decline of large holdings (25 acre or more) in terms of area and number (Vyas 1975), virtual absence of bonded labour (Shah 1978b), tenancy reform, and improved communication system, have brought a capitalist agrarian system in Gujarat and tribals are not isolated from it. This is exemplified by the fact that, of the total tribal workers in the seven districts mentioned above, the proportions of cultivators and agricultural labourers respectively are as follows: Valsad (0.46: 0.41), Surat (0.35: 0.52), Bharuch (0.26: 0.67), Vadodara (0.33: 0.59), Panchmahals (0.86: 0.10), Sabarkantha (0.82: 0.12) and Dangs (0.70: 0.20). Less than 1 per cent of all the tribal workers are engaged in occupations like livestock, forestry, fishing, hunting, etc., which were supposed to be the traditional occupations of the tribals.

However, it must be stressed that there is considerable inter-regional variation in agricultural development in Gujarat. Even within a district, talukas are unevenly developed, but the studies show that there is no pattern in the unevenness nor can it be attributed to the concentration of tribals in the talukas (Pathak *et al.* 1973).

If we go a little deeper and study the case of Bharuch district, in which 13 per cent of tribal population of the state live, we find the degree of unevenness between the tribal region and the non-tribal region is quantitative and not qualitative. In agriculture, we find that the area sown under food crops in the tribal region decreased by 5.3 per cent between 1968-69 to 1970-71, in the non-tribal region for the same period it decreased by 3 per cent. Area under cash crops, in the tribal and non-tribal regions, increased during the same period by equal percentages.

This shows that the tribals are entering the market network through cash crops in the same fashion as the non-tribals. The numbers of diesel oil engines and electric motors with pumps in the tribal region are 14.8 and 2.0 per thousand hectare, respectively; in the non-tribal region the respective numbers are 4.2 and 1.7. These facts are still more significant because in the tribal region 9.7 per cent of gross area is irrigated, whereas in the non-tribal region it is 14 per cent. Regarding the use of inputs like improved seeds, chemical fertilizers, etc., the tribal region is not lagging behind. For instance, between 1971-72 and 1972-73, quantity of improved seeds distributed per hectare of gross cropped area in the tribal region increased from 3.07 kg to 3.53 kg; in the non-tribal region it declined from 4.68 kg to 4.29 kg. Per hectare use of chemical fertilizers in the tribal region increased by 35 per cent for the same period, whereas in the non-tribal region it increased by 44 per cent (Directorate of Evaluation, 1976).

Same is the case with Surat district, where 23.3 per cent of the state's tribal population live. The tribal talukas, i.e., the talukas having more than 50 per cent tribal population, like Vyara and Valod are more developed than, for instance, a non-tribal taluka like Olpad. The point that we want to make is not that all the tribal regions are highly developed but that these regions are generally not isolated from the main trends of development. If we consider some key economic indicators, as above, we will find that the tribals have entered into a complex system of production and market network at different levels and this has produced distinctions based on land and wealth in the same manner as is observed in the macro-society. So what is happening in a tribe can only be described by recognizing that the tribe has been incorporated into the wider political and economic structural system.

An interesting feature of this development has been the way the traditional market institutions have acquired new meaning among the tribals. It is well known that traditionally tribes placed little value on surplus accumulation and on market trading (Sinha 1958). As Mandelbaum

(1970: 312) noted, "since a trader can scarcely treat customers and suppliers as kinsmen, tribesmen do not usually make good traders". But recent study (Punalekar 1978) of 48 weekly markets in tribal region of Gujarat has shown that the tribals are no longer at the buying end but are participating in the weekly markets as sellers of commodities and services. Not only are the tribals entering trade but as buyers they are being exposed to various influences in the market and are also becoming sharply aware about the economic disparities among themselves. The study shows that the weekly market has brought the tribals into the orbit of the wider society, has influenced their needs, and is now also making them aware of their own inequality.

This is because agrarian development has not raised the standard of living of all the people, nor is it egalitarian. On the contrary, as a consequence of this type of capitalist development inequality and poverty increase. According to an NSS consumption survey conducted for 1968-69, nearly 50.33 per cent of the rural population was found to be below the poverty line in Gujarat. The situation is not different in the tribal regions, and in the tribal regions of eastern hilly areas 83 per cent of population among agricultural labourers live below the poverty line (Government of Gujarat, 1974). Similarly, the percentage of agricultural labourers among the tribals is also steadily increasing as is the case in the non-tribal society.

In the next section, we shall deal with the nature of stratification among the tribes in Gujarat to show that, over a period of time, the control over resources and privileges has been transferred into a few hands among the tribals. Thus, the same kind of inequality and stratification which one is likely to observe among the non-tribals prevails among the tribals as well.

Secular Stratification among Tribals

The following account is based on three studies covering all the tribal talukas in the seven districts of Gujarat, viz., Surat, Valsad, Bharuch, Panchmahals, Dangs, Sabarkantha and Vadodara (Shah 1976, 1977; Bose 1978). The information was collected through survey method from the 111 randomly selected villages with more than 50 per cent of the tribal households. In all, 2,288 heads of tribal households were interviewed.

It was found that, in all the districts, four distinct classes of peasants have emerged among the tribes. They are rich peasants, middle peasants, poor peasants, and agricultural labourers. In no region has a single tribe solely occupied a particular class position; but they are generally distributed among all the four classes. However, some tribes are in better position than the others. For instance, in Vadodara, none of the Nayakas is rich peasant, 30.3 per cent of them are labourers and 54.5 per cent are poor peasants, while all the rich peasants in this district belong to the Bhil tribe. But, from the same tribe, we find 35.4 per cent are middle peasants and 1.6 per cent are rich peasant, and 10.5 per cent are agricultural labourers. Again, in Sabarkantha in which 97 per cent of the district tribal population belong to Bhil tribe, we find that 11.6 per cent are agricultural labourers, 65.1 per cent are poor peasants, 21.7 per cent are middle peasants and 1.6 per cent are rich peasants. A similar pattern has also been observed in the other districts.

At the bottom of the stratificatory system are the tribal agricultural labourers. A majority of agricultural labourers are landless, a few of them have less than one acre of land of poor quality—which virtually means having no land at all—and like landless labourers they also live by selling their labour power.

The wages of agricultural labourers, in spite of the Minimum Wages Act, differ from region to region and also from season to season. A labourer gets anything from 75 paise to Rs. 3.50, depending upon the nature of work and availability of labour force. Work is not available throughout the year, and during the lean periods some of them are employed in forest work, or in road construction. In the regions where productivity of land is very low, as in Dangs, nearly 92.5 per cent of the labourers at one time or the other work outside agriculture. On the other hand, in the relatively developed region like Vadodara the respective percentage is 15. During the lean season labourers have nothing to depend upon if they cannot find work outside agriculture, as moneylenders these days do not give loans to them. Earlier, a labourer could get small sums from the moneylenders by mortgaging his labour and by promising to work at low wages during the peak seasons, but now, due to various laws, moneylenders refuse to take such risks. The percentage of agricultural labourers among the tribal households in the different districts vary. In Panchmahals, it is 5 per cent, in Sabarkantha and Vadodara it varies from 11 per cent to 13 per cent, in Surat, Valsad, Bharuch and Dangs the variation is from 25 per cent to 30 per cent. The strength of agricultural labourers mainly depend on the development of the resources in the tribal regions, and generally in the more developed regions the percentage of labourer is higher.

The class of poor peasants among the tribals generally own between

1 to 5 acre of land. The land owned by them cannot be called as economic holding and it is not sufficient for their subsistence. That is why part of the time they work as agricultural labourers at daily wages. Their family members also participate in cultivation and agricultural labour. The poor peasants are the largest single class in almost all the districts. It is around 65 per cent in Panchmahals and Sabarkantha, around 50 per cent in Valsad and Vadodara, and nearly 40 per cent in Bharuch and Surat. Very few of them have wells or engines in their farms; they depend mostly on animal dung as fertilizer and generally grow food crops instead of cash crops. Use of improved seeds in this class of people is limited, principally because of the shortage of cash.

The third class among the tribal households is that of middle peasants. They generally own between 6 to 15 acre of land; their family members participate in labour; but in peak seasons they employ hired labourers. They rarely work as agricultural labourers and they produce some, though not much, marketable surplus. The percentage of middle peasants in all the districts vary from 25 per cent to 35 per cent except in Valsad and Sabarkantha where their percentages are 17 and 50, respectively. They produce mainly foodcrops, but also produce some cash crops like cotton, groundnut, etc.; use mainly animal dung as fertilizer but their use of chemical fertilizer is more than that of poor peasants. Quite a few of them have wells and engines in their farms. Their use of improved varieties of seeds is higher than that of the poor peasants.

The rich peasants are statistically in a small minority. Their percentage is less than six in all the districts except Dangs; but as a class it is very important in understanding growing inequality and stratification among the tribes. As a class, they are the largest single users of chemical fertilizers, improved seeds and irrigation water. They generally own more than 16 acre of land, most of it of good quality, and they depend mainly on wage labour. Though sometimes their family members also participate in essential labour, mostly they participate in supervisory labour. Female members of these households do not take part in field labour but are confined to household chores. As producers they produce the largest marketable surplus and generally concentrate more on cash crops than on food crops. They are well informed about fluctuations of prices of crops in the market.

Though the extent of stratification in different districts differs, for instance Bharuch is more stratified than Panchmahals in which only 5 per cent of tribal population are agricultural labourers and 2 per cent are rich peasants, in Bharuch there is almost an even percentage distribution of the landless, middle and poor peasants. Similarly, one can say that Surat is more stratified than Bharuch and so on. But the above facts clearly show that the classes among the tribes are emerging whatever may be their variations and these classes are in no significant way different from the classes one finds in non-tribal regions of Gujarat (Punalekar 1979) or in Bengal (Bose 1978), Kerala (Gough 1968) or Tamil Nadu, (Djurfeldt and Lindberg 1976), except for one significant fact that in Gujarat there is no landlord class which rents out land, generally do not take part in essential labour, and exploit chiefly by land-rent. As a logical consequence of this stratification, one can assume that it is the class interest which will predominate, instead of tribal solidarity. And other studies have shown this to be true. A study of land alienation among tribals of Gujarat has shown that 68 per cent of the tribal landholders have mortgaged their land with the tribals, and tribal rich peasants do not hesitate to exploit their own people who are economically weak (Masavi nd: 18-19). They are as clever and unscrupulous in their dealings with poor tribals as anyone else.

For instance, in Gujarat, transfer of land from tribals to non-tribals is prohibited without the permission of the collector. The tribal rich peasants take advantage of this act. A common way of mortgage transaction in tribal areas of Gujarat is known as 'land given on word' and the transaction is carried out in two alternate ways: In the first, the mortgagor is required to pay back the loaned amount within a stipulated period and, for that period, the right of cultivation of the mortgaged land remains with the mortgagee. Or, the mortgagee cultivates the land for a mutually decided period and returns it afterwards. In the later case, the debtor has not to repay his loans as the mortgagee is cultivating his land and selling the produce. It is evident that the first instance is more beneficial to mortgagee than the second. The study by Masavi shows that tribal rich peasants in the developed regions prefer the first type of transaction than the second.

Regarding the governmental benefits for the tribals, it is the rich peasants who corner most of the benefits. The different schemes of the Government, to help the tribals in terms of loans to buy cattle, engine, etc., or in the form of manure and seeds, benefit mainly the rich peasants and to some extent the middle peasants. But marginally the poor peasants and labourers do not get any benefit at all. For instance, in Vadodara 44.4 per cent of rich peasants as against 18.8 per cent poor peasants received loans from the government. In Bharuch 61 per cent of the rich peasants, as against 8 per cent of poor peasants, received loan; in Panchmahals the respective percentages are 63 and 12 (Shah 1976; Bose 1978).

The stratification is more clearly evident if we study the number of school-going children of different classes. For instance, in Bharuch and Panchmahals, only 16 per cent of children (6-12 age-group) of labourers as against 65 per cent children of the rich peasants attend school. Similarly, in the other districts, the percentage of students from the labourer families in the above-mentioned age-group are the lowest. In the tribal households it was observed that the poorer the class is, the less literate its members are.

As a result, we find that there are two distinct kinds of life-style among the tribals. Sons of the rich go to schools and colleges, and in their dress, fashion, and life-style try to imitate the urban upper class; whereas the poorer people follow more traditional ways of living. In marriage ceremonies, the rich tribals have adopted upper class values. For instance, rich Chaudhuris, in their marriages do not invite indigenous dobru (a traditional instrument) player, nor do they invite orally and symbolically, which is known as *punj mukari* as was their traditional custom. Instead, they call for 'Bhajan Mandalis' and invite through printed cards imitating non-tribal upper class (Shah 1978a). They consider that these new customs add to the prestige of the family, and even the lower classes who cannot afford to adopt the new customs consider them desirable. Similarly, all the tribals aspire to educate the children upto the college level and hope that they will get government jobs. In short, they all in principle adopt urban upper class values though the richer section is really able to adopt them.

In political power and authority, we find a clear reflection of the stratificatory process noted earlier. The political leadership among the tribes in Gujarat is from the richer classes of the tribals. These leaders are economically better off, better educated, and more exposed to the outside world. Consequently, there is a wide gap between leaders and masses which is in no way different from the gap found in non-tribal society (Shah 1973).

Tribal Stratification: Political Dimensions

In this context, the relevant question will be whether there is anything like 'tribal identity'. In a sense, one can speak of tribal identity in the context of different protective measures for the tribals by the government. That is, the tribals apparently try to project themselves as one vis-a-vis other sections of the society on the various issues of protective legislation.

However, on closer inspection, this 'identity' turns out to be an illusive one. This is the same kind of manipulation by upper class tribals in ethnic symbols and idioms to serve the upper class interest—as one finds it happening among the various castes.

In a study of tribal leaders of Gujarat, Shah (1973: 1443) has observed that "the (tribal) leaders are more concerned with the interests of their own elite class rather than with those of their constituents. They are more interested in seeing an *adivasi* (needless to add one of their own class) as a cabinet minister in the state, to secure more reservations in white-collar jobs, to organize co-operative banks which can support *adivasi* entrepreneurs, to start a university for tribals and so on. They make these and other demands in the name of the *adivasis*, but in practice, their concern for the ordinary *adivasi* is only secondary. The ordinary *adivasi*... belongs to a class different from that of his leader."

Similarly, we find that in the relations of production, a tribal labourer is not treated preferentially by the tribal rich peasant than a non-tribal labourer. They all get the same wages and are treated similarly. The immediate problems perceived by the labourers are of the nature of low wage rates, adequate food and clothing, shortage of agricultural implements, etc. Whereas the rich peasant's problems are of better credit facilities, land-revenue, supply of canal water, scholarships for higher studies, etc. These problems are clear manifestations of the awareness of respective class interests by each class, and obviously they are in conflict. It is true that, under the present situation, the interests of specific economic classes await a fuller formulation and articulation for the simple reason that class consciousness is lagging behind. But what we have tried to show is that homogeneity of economic and social situation binds a cross-section of individuals belonging to the same tribe in different classes. It is in this sense that we have preferred to divide the tribals into four classes, rather than four strata. As Mitra (1977: 94) has pointed out: "Even among individuals or groups supposedly belonging to the same class, significant disparities in attitudes and patterns of behaviour are only natural at any point of time. Notwithstanding the heterogeneities which hit the eye, it is the presence or otherwise a common set of interests which ought to be considered to be of greater relevance. It should be enough if there were a convergence of the basic interests of the constituents of a class even when its actual formation is still a prospective event. This convergence of class interests may in some cases be overt, in other cases tentative and subterraneous."

It is true that there is no clear manifestation of class consciousness on the part of the tribal agricultural labourers, and they are often duped by the upper class tribals in the name of 'tribal development', 'tribal backwardness', etc., which in effect serve the latter. But it seems that these are short-term alliances. Because the same upper class tribals on the question of higher wages to labourers align with their non-tribal counterpart to suppress the labourer. This is their long-range interest. And realization is beginning to dawn on the part of agricultural labourers that there is a contradiction when they are mobilized on the slogans of 'tribal development' and when they mobilize themselves on wage issues. In the near future, it is the long-range interest which will play a predominant part in the relations between the classes and angularities, and egocentricities of individual positions will tend to wear off resulting in a more crystallized class formation. It is this aspect of the tribes that will be of interest to sociologists and anthropologists in the future. And it is in this context that an analysis of tribal change on the basis of caste principle will be inadequate. Principle of class will give a more meaningful and comprehensive account of tribal change as the tribals interact in terms of class interests in a class-divided society.

References

Beteille, Andre; 1977, "The Definition of Tribe", in Romesh Thapar (Ed.), *Tribe, Caste and Religion in India*, Delhi: Macmillan.

Bose, Pradip Kumar, 1978a, "Stratification among the Scheduled Tribes in the Vadodara, Sabarkantha and the Dangs Districts of Gujarat", Surat: Centre for Social Studies, Mimeo.

—, 1978b, "Proletarianization of Agricultural Labourers: A Sociological Study of some Villages in Bengal", *Indian Journal of Labour Economics*, Volume 20, No. 4.

Breman, Jan, 1974, *Patronage and Exploitation: Changing Agrarian Relations in South Gujarat, India*, Berkeley: University of California Press.

Desai, A.R., 1977, "Tribes in Transition", in Romesh Thapar (Ed.), *Tribe, Caste and Religion in India*, Delhi: Macmillan.

Desai, I.P., 1978, "Tribal Problem in India: A Perspective", Surat: Centre for Social Studies, Mimeo.

Desai, M.B., 1948, *The Rural Economy of Gujarat*, London: Oxford.

Directorate of Evaluation, "Benchmark Survey of Indicators of Social and Economic Development of Tribal Area of Bharuch District", Gandhi Nagar, Mimeo.

Dube, S.C., 1977, "Introduction", in S.C. Dube (Ed.), *Tribal Heritage of India*, Volume I, New Delhi: Vikas.

Djurfeldt, Goran and Staffan Lindberg, 1976, *Behind Poverty: The Social Formation in a Tamil Village*, New Delhi: Oxford.

Enthoven, R.E., 1920, *The Tribes and Castes of Bombay*, 3 Volumes (Reprinted), Delhi: Cosmo Publications, 1975.

Gough, Kathleen, 1968, "Peasant Resistance and Revolt in South India", *Pacific Affairs*, Volume XLI, No. 1.

Government of Gujarat, 1974, Draft Fifth Five Year Plan 1974-79, Gandhinagar.

Kosambi, D.D., 1975, *An Introduction to the Study of Indian History*, Bombay: Popular Prakashan.

Mandelbaum, David G., 1970, *Society in India*, Bombay: Popular Prakashan.

Masavi, Mustaali, nd, "Problems of Land Alienation among Tribals of Gujarat", Ahmedabad: Tribal Research and Training Institute, Gujarat Vidyapith, Mimeo.

Mitra, Ashok, 1977, *Terms of Trade and Class Relations: An Essay in Political Economy*, London: Frank Cass.

Pathak, Mahesh T., M.D. Desai and A.S. Charan; 1973 "Development of Agriculture in Gujarat: Facts and Issues", *Artha-Vikas*, January-July.

Pathak, Mahesh T., Mahendra D. Desai and Haribhai F. Patel; 1979 "Agricultural Development in Gujarat: 1949-50 to 1974-75", Gujarat Agro-Economic Research Centre, Sardar Patel University, Mimeo.

Punalekar, S.P., 1978, "Weekly Markets in Tribal Talukas of Surat: Valsad Region", Surat: Centre for Social Studies, Mimeo.

—, 1979, "Socio-Economic Survey of Rural Households of Olpad Taluka", Surat: Centre for Social Studies, Mimeo.

Shah, Ghanshyam, 1973, "Gap between Representatives and Constituents: An Aspect of Tribal Society in Gujarat", *Economic and Political Weekly*, Volume VIII, No. 31-33.

—, 1976, "Stratification among the Scheduled Tribes in the Bharuch and Panchmahals Districts of Gujarat", Surat: Centre for Social Studies. Mimeo.

—, 1977, "Stratification among the Scheduled Tribes in the Surat and

Valsad Districts of Gujarat", Surat: Centre for Social Studies", Mimeo.

—, 1978a, "Socio-Economic Conditions of Chodhries: A Restudy", Surat: Centre for Social Studies", Mimeo.

—, 1978b, "Agricultural Labourers: Are they Bonded"? Surat: Centre for Social Studies, Mimeo.

Shah, P.G., 1959, "The Naikas-Naikdas: A Gujarat Tribe", Bombay: Gujarat Research Society.

Shukla, I.B., 1937, *Life and Labour in a Gujarat Taluka*, Calcutta: Longmans, Green.

Sinha, Surajit, 1958, "Tribal Cultures of Peninsular India as a Dimension of Little Tradition in the Study of Indian Civilization: A Preliminary Statement", *Journal of American Folklore*, Volume 71, 504-518.

Vyas, V.S., 1975, "Structural Change in Agriculture and the Small Farm Sector", Presidential Address at the 7th Annual Conference of Gujarat Economic Association, Valsad.

17 Struggle of the Chamar Peasants for the Removal of Social Disabilities in a Feudal Estate (Uniara Thikana) in Rajasthan, 1946-47

VIJAY KUMAR VASHISHTHA

The All India State People Bairwa Mahasabha, Indore, was organized in 1941 for uniting the Bairwa community (Chamars) and for ameliorating their social conditions. On its persistent pressure the Chief Secretary of the former princely State of Jaipur, by way of memorandum and deputation1, directed the jagirdars and the state officials in January 1943 for not exacting *begar* (forced labour) from the depressed classes. He ordered to pay them wages according to the then prevailing rates; and also instructed to allow them the right of cultivation, feasting people of their own community with sweets and food cooked in *ghee*, and the use of gold and silver ornaments in accordance with the Jaipur State Council Resolution of 10th March, 1926.[2] The publicity of these liberal measures by the All India State People Bairwa Mahasabha[3] stirred the Chamars of Uniara *thikana* and others in the Jaipur State to turn to agriculture and cattle-rearing as they believed that their occupational mobility would enhance their social status. The Chamars who abandoned their unclean traditional occupations generally designated themselves as Bairwas, though this new emerging caste continued to be returned along with the Chamars in the decennial census and government reports till 1956 when they were listed as a separate Scheduled Caste under the Indian Constitution.[4]

Occupational and Social Mobility of Chamars in Uniara Thikana

The Uniara *thikana*, situated about 134 km to the south of Jaipur, was ruled by Rao Raja Sardar Singh (1913-1969 A.D.) under the former Kachhawa princely state of Jaipur in Rajasthan. The Uniara chief was the head of the Naruka branch of the Kachhawa Rajputs and his common lineage with the ruling house of the Jaipur State gave him a certain leverage in the state bureaucratic circles. He enjoyed, as in case of other *thikanas*, autonomy in the internal administration, but maintained authoritarian control over his subjects by his police and judicial powers and through his domineering influence in the Jaipur *durbar*. According to the figures of 1938, he paid as annual *mamla*, Rs. 38,335 to the *durbar*.[5] The total population of the *thikana* in 1931 was 36,363 which rose in 1941 to 40,609, and in 1951 to 69,255. The predominant numerical strength of the Minas in the *thikana* gave them an edge over the Chamars.[6] The conservative attitude of the Rao Raja towards the Chamars in defiance of the progressive measures of the Jaipur government as well as the demands of the national leaders for social justice brought him in conflict with them in 1946-47.

The Chamars of the Uniara *thikana* abandoned their unclean traditional occupations and instead they adopted agriculture and cattle-rearing as their new economic pursuits. Due to the liberal social policy of the Jaipur State and the efforts of the All India Bairwa Mahasabha between 1943 and 1946, along with this occupational mobility, the Chamars stopped performing *begar* (forced labour) for the Rao Raja and his officials and took to all those symbols of social status which were denied to them for ages. They began to keep cows and buffaloes, used *ghee* and sugar on festivals and death feasts; several of them built *pucca* houses with doors and wore good clothes, while their womenfolk began to wear gold and silver ornaments and *sanjabdar ghagras* to the great resentment of the Rao Raja and well-off peasants belonging mainly to the Mina, Gujar, Mali and Jat castes. This created social tension in Uniara *thikana* during the period under review.

(a) Resentment against the Chamars

Occupational and social mobility among the Chamars was opposed by the Rao Raja, the Minas and the zamindars in general on several counts. The transformation of the status of Chamars from *begaris* and agricultural labourers to tenant-cultivators, and above all, their donning clean clothes and assumption of social symbols apparently placed them at par with the zamindars. It was also feared that the Chamars would pollute the upper castes by selling milk and *ghee*. The occupational mobility of the Chamars deprived the Rao Raja and the zamindars from the privilege of employing them as agricultural labourers specially when there was dearth of agricultural labourers all over the princely state of Jaipur because of their steady migration to British provinces in search of better employment during the Second World War.[8] The Rao Raja decided to exact *begar*, to deprive the Chamars of their newly acquired social symbols, and to eject them from their lands and thus to force them to revert to their traditional occupation of removing carcasses. His promptings brought the zamindars into conflict with the Chamar peasants and forced the latter to struggle against the social disabilities and discrimination in 1946-47 under the aegis of the All India State People Bairwa Mahasabha, and with its branch in Jaipur city, which was established in July 1944.

(b) Atrocities on the Chamars

The Mina, Gujar, Jat and Mali peasants of the villages of Nimolia, Sardarpura and Raghunathpura, in their joint panchayat session at Nimoli village on 9th August, 1946, resolved to prevent the Chamar peasants from using good clothes and their womenfolk from wearing silver and gold ornaments and red gaudy *ghaghras*. They called upon the Chamars of Nimola to stop using these social privileges as they were not entitled to them and to stop cultivation of land. On the refusal of the Chamars to abide by this command, about 150 zamindars attacked their houses, beat them up and their womenfolk and robbed the latter of their silver and gold ornaments.[9]

The indifference of the Rao Raja and his police force to the complaints of the atrocities on Chamars emboldened the Minas of the villages of Sada, Baski, Gumanpura and Soorajpura to unite against the Chamars of Sada and other neighbouring villages between 15th August and 21st November, 1946. The Chamars of Sada showed resistance in putting off their ornaments and made it plain to the law-breakers that it could only be done by the order of the Jaipur *raj*. The Minas declared themselves as the *raj*; and in retaliation they attacked the Chamars of Sada, Nagar, Gorda, Cakod, Manpura, Santpura, Banetha, etc. The Minas beat up the Chamars, their women and young girls with *lathis* and robbed the women of their silver and gold ornaments. They destroyed the standing crops, dismantled several of their *pucca* houses or broke their doors, and insisted upon a ban on cultivation. The Minas and Jats were conspicuous in inflicting similar atrocities upon the Chamars throughout 210 villages of the Uniara *thikana*.[10] The fields of the Bairwas were occupied and cultivated forcefully in Ghuari, Balapura and Chodki.[11] Guman Singh, a chhutbhai jagirdar of village Gudeliya under the Uniara estate, also supported the zamindars by ill-treating the Bairwa community and preventing them from using ornaments.[12]

The zamindars, with the avowed support of the Rao Raja, his *chhutbhai* and *thikana* officials and police, oppressed the Chamars, snatched off their social rights, ejected several of them from their lands, forced them to perform *begar* and robbed their women folk.[13] The indifference of Rao Raja to the sufferings of Chamars even after receiving the complaint regarding the incident of Nimoli emboldened the zamindars to commit atrocities on the Chamars all over the Uniara *thikana*. The tehsildar of Nagar was a party along with the Minas in the demolition of two *pucca* houses of the Chamars, and in inflicting atrocities on them. The patwari of Gorda had pressurized Chitter Chamar to surrender his ornaments to the Minas by torturing him in a stock (*kath*).[14] The *thanedar* had showed procrastinations in registering the complaints from Chamars, while Babu Kanwarbehari, an employee of the Uniara *thikana*, employed 50 Chamars in *begar* for the repair of the Uniara *thikana* palace in open defiance of the order of Jaipur State.[15] This spread panic among the Chamars who formed a small percentage of population in the Uniara *thikana*. Therefore, they approached Harishankar Siddhanta Shastri, General Secretary of the Jaipur branch of the All India State People Bairwa Mahasabha, for prompt action to safeguard their social rights, life and property.

Struggle of Chamar Peasants against Social Disabilities

Harishankar Siddhanta Shastri was born in a Bairwa family on 3rd July, 1918, and had studied in the St. Paul Missionary School at Jaipur. He turned into a staunch Arya Samajist and a Gandhian to the core. Shastri started working for the betterment of his caste-fellows from the age of 15, and was instrumental in persuading the Jaipur State for the restoration of their social rights. In July 1944, he assumed the charge of the General Secretary of the Jaipur branch of the All India State People Bairwa Mahasabha, with the objectives of uniting the Bairwas, propagating education among them, and improving their socio-economic condition.[16]

Hari Shankar considered the social rights of the Chamar peasants of Uniara *thikana* as a matter of their civil liberties. He decried atrocities on the Chamar peasants and denial of civil liberties which were enjoyed by others specially at a time when all the reformers and nationalists were working for the upliftment of the depressed classes.[17] Shastri declared that the Rao Raja was solely responsible for the atrocities on Chamar peasants as he had not taken any measures for giving them protection and punishment to the law-breakers. He, therefore, demanded during August 1946 and February 1947: (i) to punish those who were responsible for inflicting cruelties on the Chamar peasants, and (ii) to obtain assurance from the Jaipur State authorities that in future social rights of the Chamars would not be interfered with by the Minas, Gujars, Malis, Thakurs, and Jats.[18]

(a) Struggle of the Chamar Peasants in Uniara Thikana

Harishankar Siddhanta Shastri visited several villages of Uniara *thikana*, and this infused confidence among the Chamar peasants and urged upon them not to migrate due to any pressures, and mobilized them for safeguarding their civil liberties. Under his guidance they appealed several times to the Rao Raja for providing justice during September and December 1946. A deputation of 2,000 Chamar peasants met the Rao Raja at Uniara on 3rd September, 1946, and complained about their being robbed of their ornaments and for not being allowed to cultivate by the zamindars.[19] On realising that no remedial measures were being taken by the Uniara Rao, the representatives of the Chamar peasants from the villages—Nimola, Sada, Nagar, Kakod, Amba, Rubas, Bhanpura, Gotha, Lamba, etc. submitted (on 30th September, 1946) a memorandum to a senior officer (superintendent of police), Uniara, and to the Jaipur authorities and the Political Resident narrating their woeful sufferings in the *thikana*. They pleaded that the leaders of Mina, Jat, Gujar and Mali castes be instructed to maintain peace and not to interfere with their civil liberties such as wearing of ornaments, building of *pucca* houses, etc.[20]

On receiving reports regarding the cruelties inflicted by the Minas and other zamindars on the Chamars between October and November, 1946, Harishankar Siddhanta Shastri censured the Rao Raja for not taking remedial measures, and for prohibiting the Chamars from exercising their civil liberties which were enjoyed by other sections of the population. On 21st November, 1946, he submitted a letter to the Rao Raja demanding time to meet a deputation of the All India Bairwa Mahasabha, and simultaneously he sent a telegram to the Maharaja of Jaipur informing him about the cruelties on the Chamars in Uniara.[21]

The Rao instead of giving any relief to the Chamar peasants managed the escape of the culprits from Sada and the neighbouring villages when the Jaipur State police came to arrest them on 26th December, 1946. Similarly, he abused the representatives of the All India Bairwa Mahasabha when they met him at Sada. He made it plain to them that the Chamar peasants should confine themselves to the traditional occupation of removing carcasses and should not aspire to cultivate land which even their forefathers had not done. He declared that agricultural profession was meant for the zamindars. He also expressed his determination, namely, not to permit the Chamars to use ornaments, and to till the land in Uniara *thikana*, in defiance of the State directives. This caused a great dissatisfaction among the depressed classes, and convinced the workers of the All India Bairwa Mahasabha that they had no alternative but to approach the Jaipur State authorities to mitigate discontentment in the *thikana*.[22]

(b) Favourable Public Opinion for the Struggle of Chamar Peasants

Harishankar Siddhanta Shastri mobilized various agencies to build up public pressure on the Jaipur State authorities, the Minas and other zamindars and the Rao Raja, to secure justice for the Chamar peasants through various agencies. The central organization–the All India Bairwa Mahasabha, Indore, passed a resolution against the Rao Raja on 6th September, 1946, and circulated a pamphlet in support of the struggle to build up public opinion and to infuse confidence among the Chamars.[23] In October, 1946, several letters were sent to Jawahar Lal Nehru, the Prime Minister of National Government, Mahatma Gandhi, and to the Chancellor of the Chamber of Princes, the Nawab of Bhopal, with an appeal to safeguard the social rights of the Chamar peasants in Uniara *thikana*.[24] Along with this, Harishankar Siddhanta Shastri, with the support of the All India Bairwa Mahasabha, Indore, tried to infuse confidence among the Chamars of Uniara by assuring them of the support of the six crore strong depressed classes in their struggle for civil rights.[25] He appealed to the Minas and other zamindars of the *thikana* for allowing the Chamar peasants to enjoy their civil liberties and allow them to live peacefully.[26] Moreover, he won sympathy of the Jaipur Rajya Prajamandal workers and the public in general in favour of the Chamar peasants by publishing reports, from time to time, about the atrocities in the Uniara *thikana*, in the newspapers such as the *Jaipur Samachar*, *Lokwani* and *Bazm-E-Adab*. The Holkar State, Indore, in its special meeting at Indore on 19th February, 1947, condemned the highhandedness of Minas in Uniara *thikana* against the Chamar peasants. It appealed to the Rao Raja to change his hypocritical attitude towards the Bairwas and requested the Jaipur State to accept their demands, and to remove all their grievances.[27] This growing wider support from outside the Uniara *thikana* and from the neighbouring states legitimized the Chamar struggle, and thereby strengthened the hands of Harishankar Siddhanta

Shastri to approach the Jaipur government for an amicable settlement.

(c) Appeals to the Jaipur Maharaja

Harishankar Siddhanta Shastri collaborated with the central organization of the All India State People Bairwa Mahasabha to take up the matter seriously with the Jaipur government. Master Jhuntalal Jawaharlal, the president of the central organization of the All India Bairwa Mahasabha, Indore, appealed to the Maharaja of Jaipur and his officials regarding the woeful sufferings of the Chamar peasants (several times in September and October, 1946). He threw an unsuccessful ultimatum to launch a *satyagraha* in case of their failure to stop atrocities on Chamar peasants in Uniara *thikana*.[28] The oppression on Chamar peasants continued. Master Jhuntalal found it difficult to pursue negotiations with the Jaipur government because of his involvement in resolving the problems of Chamars in Ratlam, Kota, Bundi, Karauli and other places. He entrusted the responsibility of further negotiations with Jaipur State authorities to Harishankar in October, 1946.[29]

Harishankar addressed the Jaipur State authorities afresh about the grievances of Chamars in the Uniara *thikana* during October and December 1946. He complained to the Prime Minister of Jaipur government that the Minas, Jats, Gujars, Malis and Thakurs had beaten up the Chamars of Uniara, Amba, Nagar, Kakod and Sada villages, and forcefully snatched their silver and gold ornaments, and destroyed several of their *pucca* houses on the plea that the Chamars had no right to live and use ornaments like them. He appealed to the Prime Minister to take strong action against the ring-leaders responsible for this "kind of dacoity".[30] On behalf of the Executive Members of the All India Bairwa Mahasabha, he further pressed upon his demands in a memorandum to the Chief Secretary, Inspector-General of Police, and Home Minister on 16th December, 1946, demanding punishments to the ring-leaders, restoration of gold and silver ornaments to the legal owners, compensation to the Chamars for their losses, unconditional release of the Chamar leaders, and above all an assurance that social rights of Chamars would not be inferered with by Minas and other zamindars.[31]

The persistence of the All India State People Bairwa Mahasabha, at last, moved the Jaipur government to agree to its demands on 14th December, 1946. However, the Rao Raja refused to implement the same, and abused and misbehaved with the four member delegation of the All India Bairwa Mahasabha at Sada village (in Uniara *thikana*) on 26th December, 1946. He reiterated his resolution not to permit the Chamars to use ornaments and to cultivate land in his *thikana*.[32]

The All India Bairwa Mahasabha assured of the support and sympathy of the Jaipur government took the cudgels against the Rao Raja. Jhuntalal Jawaharlal, the officiating vice-president of the All India State People Bairwa Mahasabha, Indore, rejoined the struggle of the Chamar peasants of Uniara *thikana*, in January, 1947. He appealed to the Prime Minister of Jaipur to advice the Rao Raja to respond sympathetically to settle the dispute by negotiation lest the *Bairwa Samaj* would migrate elsewhere from Uniara *thikana* to seek peaceful settlement.[33] This threat woke up the Jaipur government from its slumber as the migration of the Chamar peasants was likely to create adverse public opinion in the political circles throughout the country. It, therefore, threw the Rao Raja off its neck and took concrete and firm action for the redressal of the grievances of the Chamar peasants.

(d) Success of the Struggle and its Impact

The Jaipur government issued orders to the Rao Raja and the state police to give protection to the Chamars in the Uniara *thikana*. Action was taken against zamindars who had harassed and misbehaved with the Chamars. The state police officers along with the help of the *thikana* constables started investigation of the atrocities on Chamar peasants in Sada and Nimolia villages which gave a feeling of security to the Chamars. The relations between the zamindars and the Chamars became "quite normal" by February, 1947. There were no complaints from the Chamars for being deprived of civil liberties in Uniara *thikana*, and the seven months' struggle ended with complaisance.[34]

The concerted measures of the central and the Jaipur branch of the All India State People Bairwa Mahasabha infused cohesiveness among the Chamar peasants of Uniara *thikana*. This caste solidarity emboldened them to stick to their social rights, prevented their migration from Uniara *thikana* out of fear of oppression by the zamindars, and stopped reprisals. The four Chamar peasants of Sada village successfully resisted the pressure of the Minas, Jats and Malis for withdrawing police reports against them. In 1951, the Chamar peasants of village Bandhya, tehsil Sawai Madhopur, organized themselves successfully and used the good offices of the Rajasthan State government against the efforts of Minas to deprive them of their ornaments and land.[35]

Harishankar Siddhanta Shastri played a major role in the struggle of the Chamar peasants in Uniara *thikana* during 1946-47. He achieved success in the removal of social disabilities. He successfully politicized the Chamar peasants, and compelled the Rao Raja for the removal of their grievances. Public opinion in favour of Chamars was created by circulating pamphlets and utilizing the media. And at the top of this, he collaborated with the central organization of the All India Bairwa Mahasabha, Indore, and others, for pressurizing the Rao Raja and the Jaipur State authorities to stop social oppression. His perseverance in conducting the struggle for about seven months made all the efforts of the Rao Raja futile to camouflage the misdeeds of Minas and other zamindars. Shastri proved Rao Raja's complicity in the atrocities on the Chamar peasants. Such was the movement that the Rao Raja lost public sympathy all over the country and the support of the Jaipur *durbar*. The Jaipur government censured the Rao Raja for his retrogressive measures and restored the social rights to the Chamars. It further demonstrated its progressive attitude by passing the Harijan (Removal of Social Disabilities) Bill, 1947, granting the Harijans the right to use public wells, *dharmashalas*, schools, public vehicles, temples and other common places.[36] Harishankar Siddhanta Shastri praised this progressive step which secured full civil rights to the depressed classes. Shastri suggested to the Jaipur State authorities to give wide publicity to this Bill by beats of a drum in rural areas for the benefit of the depressed classes and for the general information of the people.[37]

Notes

1. G—20, File No. 30, Pt. IV, Mehkma Khas, Jaipur, 1938, *Rajasthan State Archives, Jaipur Branch* (hereafter abbreviated as RSAJ).
2. *Ibid.*, Copy of Memorandum No. G—20—30 R.D., dt. 13 January, 1943, from the Chief Secretary to the Government of Jaipur to the Secretary, All India State People Bairwa Mahasabha, Indore, *Private Papers of Harishankar Siddhanta Shastri, Jaipur*. (Hereafter abbreviated as *Shastri Papers*).
3. Notification through the All India State People Bairwa Mahasabha, Indore, and Publicity District Board, Jaipur State, Nd., *Shastri Papers*.
4. *Census of India*, 1961, Vol. XIV, Rajasthan, Pt. V-A.pp. IX, 473.
5. *Rajputana and Ajmer Merwara: List of Princes, Chiefs and Leading Personages*, seventh edn., Government of India, Simla: 1938, p.82.

6. Swami Prakash Chandra, *Census of India: Jaipur State, 1941*, Pt. I, Report, Ajmer nd. p. 47, Pt, Yamuna Lal *Dashora, Census of India: Rajasthan and Ajmer, 1951 Census*, Vol. X. Pt. I-A. Government Press, Jodhpur, 1953, p.71.
7. Letter from 17 Chamar peasants of Uniara Thikana to General Secretary, Bairwa Mahasabha, Jaipur dt. nil., August 1946, *Shastri Papers*; Ramnath of Gurhi to General Secretary, Bairwa Mahasabha, jaipur, dt. 19 November, 1946, *Shastri Papers*; Harishankar Siddhanta Shastri, General Secretary, All India State People Bairwa Mahasabha, Jaipur to Chief Secretary, Government of Jaipur, dt. 15 October, 1946, *Shastri Papers.*
8. File No. 5/7, List No. 7, Jaipur Government, *Deposited Records, RSAJ*; Munshi Rampratap Khunteta, *Census of India, Jaipur State 1931* (Report), 1932, p. 109; pt. Yamunalal Dashora, *Census of India, 1951, Vol. X. Rajasthan and Ajmer*, Pt. I-A. Report, Government Press, Jodhpur, 1953, p. 223.
9. Letter from 17 Chamar Peasants of Uniara Thikana to General Secretary, Bairwa Mahasabha, Jaipur dt. nil., August, 1946, Shastri Papers.
10. *Ibid.*, Sheoram and Bhura Chamar of Sada to Secretary, All India State People Bairwa Mahasabha, Jaipur. dt. 21 November, 1946, Shastri Papers.
11. Ramnath of Gurahi to General Secretary. Bairwa Mahasabha, Jaipur, dt. 19 November, 1946, *Shastri Papers*; File No. 90 p. NWER/C.V., S.No. 346, Jhunjhunu Section, Revenue 4 (1946-47), *Deposited Records, RSAJ.*
12. File No. 90/NWR/C.V. S.No. 346, Jhunjhunu Section, Revenue 4 (1946-47), Deposited Records, *RSAJ.*
13. Harishankar Siddhanta Shastri to Chief Secretary to the Government of Jaipur, dt. 16 December, 1946, *Shastri Papers.*
14. Letter from 17 Chamar Peasants of Uniara Thikana to General Secretary, Bairwa Mahasabha, Jaipur, dt. nil., August, 1946, *Shastri Papers.*
15. Hardeo s/o Bhuwan of Uniara to Secretary, Bairwa Mahasabha, Jaipur dt. 19 November, 1946, *Shastri Papers.*
16. File No. 5/7, List No. 7, Jaipur Government, *Deposited Records, RSAJ.*
17. Harishankar Siddhanta Shastri to Private Secretary to Rao Raja Sahib Bahadur of Uniara, dt. 1 October, 1946, *Shastri Papers.*

18. Harishankar Siddhanta Shastri to Chief Secretary, Jaipur Government, dt. 16 December, 1946, *Shastri Papers.*
19. *Lokwani* (Jaipur), 8 September, 1946.
20. Representation from the Chamar peasants of Nimola, Sada Nagar, Kakod, etc., to Prime Minister, Jaipur, Senior Officer, Uniara, Political Resident of Jaipur and Others, dt. 30 September, 1946, *Shastri Papers.*
21. Harishankar Siddhanta Shastri to Private Secretary to Rao Raja Sahib Bahadur of Uniara, dt. 1 October, 1946; Harishankar Siddhanta Shastri to Rao Raja of Uniara, dt. 21 November, 1946, *Shastri Papers.*
22. File No. 90/NWR/C.V., S.No. 346, Jhunjhunu Section, Revenue, 4, *Deposited Records* (1946-47), RSAJ.
23. Resolution passed in the emergent meeting of the All India State People Bairwa Mahasabha, Indore, dt. 6 September, 1946; Pamphlet issued by the All India State People Bairwa Mahasabha, Indore, dt. 21 September, 1946; *Shastri Papers.*
24. Jhuntalal, President, All India State People Bairwa Mahasabha to Nawab of Bhopal and others, dt. 10 October, 1946, *Shastri Papers.*
25. Printed Pamphlet in Hindi, issued under the joint auspices of Master Jhuntalal Jawaharlal, President, All India State People Bairwa Mahasabha and Harishankar Siddhanta Shastri, dt. nil., *Shastri Papers.*
26. *Jaipur Samachar* (Jaipur), 5 November, 1946.
27. Resolution of Bazm-E-Adab, Holkar State, Indore, 19 February, 1947, File No. 90/NWR/C.V. Jhunjhunu Section, Revenue 4, *Deposited Records, RSAJ.*
28. Master Jhuntalal Jawaharlal to His Highness Maharajadhiraj Sawai Mansingh of Jaipur, dt. 9 October, 1946, *Shastri Papers.*
29. Master Jhuntalal to Siddhanta Shastri, dt. 9 October, 1946; Mangilal, Member, All India of All India State People Bairwa Mahasabha to Harishankar Siddhanta Shastri, dt. 2 December, 1946, *Shastri Papers.*
30. Harishankar Siddhanta Shastri to Chief Secretary, Jaipur Government, dt. 14 October, 1946, *Shastri Papers.*
31. Letter from Harishankar Siddhanta Shastri to Chief Secretary, Jaipur Government and others, dt. 16 December, 1946, *Shastri Papers.*
32. File No. 90/NWR/C.V.S. No. 346, Jhunjhunu Section, Revenue 4, *Deposited Records, RSAJ.*
33. *Ibid.*
34. *Ibid.*

35. Director of Backward Class, Welfare, Rajasthan, to District Magistrate, Sawai Madhopur District, Sawai Madhopur, and copy to the General Secretary, Depressed Class League, Jaipur, dt. 26 September 1951, *Shastri Papers.*
36. *Jaipur-Legislative Council Debates*, First Session, August-September 1947, Vol. V.
37. Harishankar Siddhanta Shastri, *A Brief Report of All India State People Bairwa Mahasabha, Bandikui, Syaliyawas, Conference, Bairwa Mahasabha*, Bandikui and Syaliyawas, nd., p. 5 (Resolution No. 1).

18

Social Mobility and Status-Identification among the Scheduled Castes

A Synoptic View

NANDU RAM

A number of constitutional safeguards have been provided, after independence, to the scheduled castes (and also to the scheduled tribes) under the "policy of the protective discrimination"1, popularly known as the reservation policy. These safeguards are primarily in the areas of their social welfare: protection from all sorts of exploitation and discrimination, and their overall social and economic development. The reservation given in the areas of education, employment in public sector jobs (recently in the private sector also), and representation in the parliament and state legislatures is to protect the interests and to facilitate social and economic development of various scheduled castes in the country. Though the whole scheme with the concurrence of the centre has been adopted as a national policy, the state governments are empowered to implement its various provisions in their own ways but within the overall directives laid down by the central government.

The Present Study

It is apparent by now that a small number of persons belonging to the different scheduled castes have benefited from several provisions of the reservation in education, employment in government departments, and representation in the parliament and state legislatures. These persons have certainly availed themselves of opportunities to occupy different and, in some cases, probably better socio-economic positions. Thus, they are socially mobile in comparison to the scheduled caste masses in general and the generation of their fathers in particular. Such persons have also improved their status both in the caste and class hierarchies. However, the nature and levels of their social mobility are not very clear. In other words, it is not very certain whether their improved status in the class structure has affected, in the same magnitude, their status in the caste system. It has, therefore, been proposed in this study to inquire into the specific nature and levels of their social mobility both in class structure and caste system.

Such an inquiry is reinforced by the fact that an analysis of social mobility in India, at present, is to be related to the analysis of changes taking place in one's status in the class structure as well as in the caste system—the two regulatory structural elements of the Indian society. Besides measuring the determining factors and indicators of such changes, this study also intends to examine the congruity between the status of the mobile scheduled castes acquired in both the class structure and caste system and the status-anxiety, if any, in case any incongruity exists between the two.

Further, social mobility is related to the identification of the status of a person. The nature, amount, and degree of social mobility acquired by him are to be exhibited to others so that they may recognize the mobility of his status in the existing social hierarchy and accept him as their equal if his acquired status is identical to that of their own. Therefore, this study finally examines the nature and levels of status-identification among the mobile persons of the scheduled castes. In other words, it has been questioned whether such persons identify with their status in the caste system or in the class structure or outside both the systems.

Theoretical Framework

A number of studies have analyzed social mobility through both single and multiple approaches. Studies based on a single approach[2] argue that occupation is the sole criterion for determining one's social status. But the adherents to the multiple approach[3] find the single approach inadequate for analyzing social mobility. Hence, most of the studies analyzing the phenomenon do not help provide a precise and compact model for measuring the actual nature and degree of social mobility taking place in India. Therefore, attempts have been made, in this study, to measure and analyze social mobility and the status-identification of the mobile persons of the scheduled castes through a theoretical framework based on the multiple approach. More precisely, the framework is based on two sets of four theories which have been accepted as interrelated for the present purpose. These theories are: the theory of social mobility propounded by Lipset and Zetterberg[4], the theory of status-congruence formulated by Homans[5], Merton's theory of reference group behaviour[6], and the theory of ethnocentric and contra-identification advanced by Paranjpe.[7]

The theory of social mobility is based on a multiple approach, according to which the mobility of a group or individual is determined both by its shift and the ranking of multiple dimensions like occupations, consumption patterns, and social power along with the social class "...composed of the individuals who accept each other as equals and qualified for intimate associations.[8] " The adherents to this theory accept that in a society there is a possibility of having a higher rate (and degree also) of mobility in one dimension and a lower in others. Therefore, the derivation of more qualified and accurate conclusions about social mobility and social stratification is possible only through a multidimensional approach in which one has to consider together all the possible dimensions of status-achievement. Besides, two sets of methodological approaches have been suggested in the theory to measure social mobility. In the first set, it is suggested to compare (i) the present status with that of the past; (ii) the mobility in one area or country with that of another; and (iii) one model of mobility with another expressing equal opportunity. In the second set, it is envisaged that we might adopt the conventional method of ascertaining mobility by comparing father's and son's positions. Social mobility is caused by (i) the supply of vacant status, and (ii) the interchangeability of ranks. Finally, the theory winds up with findings regarding the political consequences of social mobility.

Likewise, the theory of status-congruence envisages that one may acquire similar or equal status in two different domains. If two officials employed in the same cadre in an organization equal each other in terms of salary, authority, prestige, etc., their status in these domains is congruent. But if one of the two differs in these domains, his status is incongruent to that of the other. In such a situation the one with an incongruent status may suffer from status-anxiety. Further, according to the theory of reference group/individual behaviour, a person adopts a style of life and the behaviour patterns of his superior in anticipation of acquiring a status equal to him. In this process he accepts his status inferiority and tries to raise it to the level of that of this referent(s) through *anticipa-*

tory socialization. And finally, according to the theory of ethnocentric and contra-identification, persons hailing from traditionally high-ranked caste(s) may be ethnocentric and those with low caste(s) may believe in an identification contrary to that (contra-identification).

In the present study, we have partially adopted from the said theory the multidimensional approach and the conventional method (comparison of father's and son's earlier and present positions) of measurement of social mobility. More precisely, we have included in the framework, developed for this study, the dimensions of education, occupation (government employment in various cadres), income, expenditure pattern, and social power. We have also adopted the dimension of "social class" in the second part of the study where we have examined the achievement of status and its identification. We have, however, included these dimensions in the framework for measuring social mobility in the class (socio-economic status) structure.

The causes of social mobility in terms of the supply of vacant status and the interchangeability of ranks as envisaged in the theory are not directly relevant in the case of the sponsored social mobility[9] among the scheduled castes. In fact, their mobility is greatly facilitated by the government policy of "preferential treatment" or "protective discriminations" meant for them though the policy does generate some spirit of competitiveness or contest mobility among them to fill the vacant statuses or positions in the class structure. This also helps them to claim a higher status in the caste system in which no vacancy of statuses exists. Hence, there is no question of "demand and supply" of vacant statuses and "interchangeability of ranks" in the caste system.

It is, however, easier to acquire and improve social status in a class structure than in the caste system. Certain types of changes have also taken place in the caste system in recent times but these are less pronounced in the case of improvement in status of the scheduled castes in the caste hierarchy. Since some members of these castes have improved to some extent, their status in the class (socio-economic status) structure as mentioned above, they may or may not witness the same magnitude of change in their caste status. Such a discrepancy in status has been analyzed through the theoretical formulation of status-congruence.

Social mobility takes place within the systemic framework of status acquired by certain reference groups or individuals. In other words, people get socially mobile by adopting the style of life, behaviour pattern and value system of certain groups and individuals though their improved socio-economic status and material condition play a significant role in it. This also works in the case of social mobility both in class structure and the caste system.[10] We have, therefore, included this in the framework for analyzing the social mobility taking place among the scheduled castes. Again, there are both positive and negative consequences of social mobility. Positively, social mobility results in the acceptance and assimilation of the mobile groups or individuals in the status of the referents. Thus, the mobile groups or individuals may identify themselves with a "social class" or status acquired by their referents or even beyond that. But at the negative level, if they find incongruity between different sets of status acquired by them and that of their referents, their social mobility may result in status-anxiety or alienation towards the social system and the process of social mobility.

Without contesting the views about the political radicalism or conservatism among socially mobile persons or groups,[11] we have excluded from our framework the political consequences of social mobility partly because these are out of the purview of the present study and partly because the government officials are not supposed to actively participate in politics though they may hold an independent opinion about the government or political system as such. Hence, we have measured the consequences of social mobility among the scheduled castes in terms of the levels of their status-identification, especially within the theoretical explanations mentioned above.

Thus, in the first set of the present framework, the two theoretical formulations about social mobility and status-congruence have been adopted to analyze social mobility among the scheduled castes within the class structure and caste system. Similarly, in the second set the formulations about reference group/individual behaviour and ethnocentric and contra-identification have been included to explain the status-identification among the scheduled castes as a consequence of their social mobility. Since improvements in status in the class structure and caste system, the congruity between the two, and consequences like status-anxiety and different levels of status-identification have been analyzed as various aspects of social mobility, the above mentioned four sets of theoretical explanations have been well-integrated in a single framework for the purpose of our study.

Method of Study and Data Collection

The major orientation of the present study is towards a quantitative measurement of social mobility, but the qualitative analysis has also found a headway. Besides the specific theoretical framework, a number of items relating to the background of the mobile scheduled castes under the study have been treated as independent variables and their social mobility in the class structure as the dependent variable. Similarly, various dimensions like education, job-cadres, income, expenditure patterns, and social power, which influence their social status vis-a-vis changes therein, have been accepted as independent variables, while the "achievement" of status in the caste hierarchy has been treated as a dependent variable. Finally, at the level of the consequences of social mobility, status-identification has been considered as a dependent variable and the background and social mobility (changes of status in both the class structure and caste system) as independent ones.

Socio-economic status of the mobile scheduled castes and that of their family of procreation and of orientation, and the social distance between them and their non-scheduled caste acquaintances have been measured through the Kuppuswamy[12] and the Bogardus[13] scales with suitable modifications. Similarly, caste status and changes, if any, have been measured through a scale devised on the basis of the opinion of twenty "knowledgeable" persons of the non-scheduled castes. Finally, mobility indices have been constructed with the help of various items included in the framework for measuring the degree and directions of social mobility.

The study is restricted to the scheduled caste government employees located in Kanpur city. Out of nearly 600 scheduled caste officials employed in different jobs both in the Central and State government offices in the city, 240 (40%) were interviewed during 1973-74. The selection of the respondents was made through a stratified random sample from each cadre ranging from class IV (16.7%) to class I (1.7%) administrative jobs. Those employed in other cadres were from lower (16.6%) and upper (40.4%) clerical and lower technical staff (7.9%), technical and non-technical supervisory (class III) staff (13.3%), and technical and non-technical (class II) officers (3.3%).

Further, from the point of view of the social composition of the sample, more than 50 per cent respondents belonged to the Chamar (137) caste, followed by the Kori (35), Pasi (20), Dhobi (17), Balmiki (11),

Khatik (8) and other scheduled castes (12). In all, about 70 per cent of them hailed from villages and the rest from towns and cities including the city of Kanpur. Those hailing from outside Kanpur city had not completely shelved linkages with the places of their origin as they used to visit there and observed certain rights and obligations to their kith and kin.

Most of the respondents were literate, and about 40 per cent were educated upto graduation and post-graduation levels. About 25 per cent of them belonged to the Chamar caste and the others were of the Kori, Pasi and Dhobi castes. Coming from a younger age-group of 19-25 years, most of them were married and hailed from joint families living either elsewhere or in the city. Again, a large majority hailed from families with low socio-economic status and were living in localities of both scheduled and non-scheduled castes in the city though most of them faced prejudices and discriminations of various kinds in renting accommodation in the latter's localities. Their higher educational achievement and official positions did not help them much in their endeavour.

Social Mobility: The Dimensional Framework

Within the framework of the multidimensions of social mobility, almost all the respondents (98.7%) were upwardly mobile and the average scores of their mobility, along all the five dimensions, were higher (23.2) than that of their fathers (8.1). As the majority was employed in the lower and upper clerical cadres, their average mobility scores were obviously lower than of those employed in higher cadres (supervisors and officers) of jobs. Similarly, the average mobility scores of the fathers of those employed in higher cadres of jobs were more than that of the fathers of those employed in the lower cadres. A general conclusion, then, could be drawn that the upwardly mobile persons of the scheduled castes hailed from the families of procreation with a better socio-economic status. It is, however, clear from Table 1 that the fathers of those employed in the lower (for instance, the lower division clerks) and the lowest (like sweepers) cadres had secured a relatively higher average of mobility scores than the fathers of the upper clerical and lower technical staff.

The only reason for such a discrete variation in the averages of mobility scores can be given in terms of the multidimensionality of social mobility where fathers of these respondents had acquired better position in one dimension or the other than the fathers of those employed in relatively superior cadres of jobs.

Table 1

Average mobility scores of the respondents and their fathers

Job-cadres of respondents	*Average mobility scores**		
	Respondents	*Fathers*	*Variance*
1. Sweeper (IV)	11.3	9.1	2.2
2. Non-sweeper (IV)	17.9	7.4	10.5
3. Lower Division Clerk	21.6	8.5	13.1
4. Upper Division Clerk	22.9	7.8	15.1
5. Lower Technical Staff	23.6	7.8	15.8
6. Supervisory Staff	29.9	8.9	21.0
7. Officer (II)	31.4	8.9	22.5
8. Officer (I)	37.0	10.7	26.3
Total	23.2	8.1	15.1

* Average scores have been calculated by aggregating scores obtained separately by the respondents and their fathers along all the five dimensions of social mobility and then divided by their numbers.

Further, the average amount[14] of social mobility of the respondents was 21.9 on a 100 point scale, though in some cases it ranged between 30-44. It was, however, correlated[15] with their age, job-cadres, service seniority (total length of service) and socio-economic status of their family of procreation. That means that the higher the job-cadres in which they were employed, the more the amount of social mobility they obtained in a multidimensional framework and so on (for details, see Table 2). But other variables like their caste and the rural-urban background were not correlated with the amount of their social mobility. For instance, the average amount of upward social mobility was highest (25.7) among those belonging to the Khatik caste, and the respondents from among the Chamar, Kori and the Pasi castes lagged behind though they had otherwise done well in Uttar Pradesh.

But these findings were not coherent with caste status of the respondents in the caste-hierarchy as the Kori caste was assigned (by the "judges") the highest status in the hierarchy of the scheduled castes. However, those belonging to this caste were in the third position with regard to the average amount of their social mobility.

Table 2
Job-cadres of the respondents and amount of their social mobility

Job-cadres	*Amount of social mobility*			*Total**
	Low (0-14)	*Medium (15-29)*	*High (30-44)*	
Sweeper (IV)	3	3	—	6 (12.4)
Non-sweeper (IV)	16	16	—	32 (14.5)
Lower Division Clerk	7	31	2	40 (20.1)
Upper Division Clerk	4	88	4	96 (22.0)
Lower Technical Staff	2	17	—	19 (22.4)
Supervisory Staff	2	13	17	32 (29.0)
Officer (II)	—	2	6	8 (33.3)
Officer (I)	—	1	3	4 (33.3)
Total	34	171	32	237 (21.9)

X^2 = 146.6, df = 14, P. < .001, C = .618

* All the three downwardly mobile respondents have not been included in this table. Figures in brackets denote the average amount of social mobility.

Since the social mobility measured in the multidimensional framework pertains to the mobility in the class structure (whereas class structure is analogous to the socio-economic status based on education, occupation, income, etc., and excludes the social relational and cultural aspects), we have introduced a new concept of "total" social mobility. That is, a total social mobility had occurred among the respondents because they had obtained much higher scores and amount and degree of mobility than that of their fathers. Similar was the case of the direction of their social mobility (except for three cases who witnessed downward mobility).

Social Mobility in the Hierarchical Domains

Indian society has imbibed both the caste system and other primordial social categories and class structure. Without going into their complementary and contradictory nature, we may agree with the view that with its all pervasive emphasis on a hierarchical gradation of different segments (castes and sub-castes) and other characteristics like endogamy, purity-pollution, the separation of and repulsion to other segments, interdependence, and socio-religious disabilities of certain castes, the traditional caste system has undergone a series of changes in the recent times. Although its overall ethos is not completely altered, members of various castes and sub-castes have succeeded in improving their lot by claiming and getting their claims accepted for the status of a higher caste(s). In other cases, they have not cared much for their caste status and have tried to improve their overall position through other channels like education, modern jobs, political power, etc., which, in turn, has certainly influenced their caste status.

On the other hand, the class structure, especially people's perception of it, is a later elaboration, though many social scientists have located the presence of different social classes concomitant with the existence of society in India. Notwithstanding its antiquity, class structure has provided numerous opportunities to the people of different castes and communities to improve their lot. This has helped them not only to improve their socio-economic position and thereby a rise in their class status, but also to claim and in many cases to get their claims legitimized and socially accepted for a higher status and rank in the caste hierarchy. In certain cases, even traditionally most downgraded scheduled castes have tried to raise their caste status through various ways and means. This trend continues even today though people in general and the scheduled castes in particular utilize more secular channels like education, white-collar employment, improved economic condition, political power, etc., to raise their caste status.

In the above context, we have examined the status achieved by and accorded to the respondents in both the class structure and caste system. Besides the quantitative explanation of class in terms of the socio-economic position accepted earlier in this study, we have adopted it here in a broader sense where it refers to a category of people having an equal liking and disliking and social and cultural standing. Thus, we have found that most of the respondents had achieved a "middle class" status though their understanding of the middle class as a conceptual category was not very clear. In fact, their understanding of the middle class was guided more by socio-economic similarities rather than other attributes of class. This was evident from the fact that a large majority (77%) of the respondents including lower and upper division clerks, lower technical staff, peons, etc., like the administrative officers, claimed to have achieved middle class status. Only 17.5 and 5.5 per cent claimed to have acquired the status of lower and upper classes, respectively.

Their understanding of the middle class was also vague because a mid-

Table 3

Socio-economic status of families of the Respondents and the interaction with their non-scheduled caste acquaintances

Socio-economic status of family	*Interaction with the non-scheduled caste acquaintances*												*Total*
	Attending ceremonies				*Taking meals/refreshments*				*Kitchen entry*				
	None	*Some*	*Most*	*All*	*None*	*Some*	*Most*	*All*	*None*	*Some*	*Most*	*All*	
Low	67	90	13	18	65	93	16	14	124	42	10	12	188
Medium	9	21	9	9	11	23	6	8	27	11	6	4	48
High	—	1	3	—	—	2	2	—	1	1	2	—	4
Total	76	112	25	27	76	118	24	22	152	54	18	16	240

df = 6, X^2 = 30.0, P<.001, C = 333, X^2 = 13.9, P<.05, X^2 = 14. P.<05

C = 234; C = .236

dle class in real sense has a long historical standing and distinct cultural moorings. The middle class is not a homogeneous entity. Rather, it is constituted of professionals, middle peasants, traders, white-collar workers, etc. Therefore, some social scientists have preferred to use the term "middle classes". In the case of the respondents, the divergences were noted in their claim of "middle class" status and also it was not similar to the status of the middle classes in general because no congruity existed between their class and caste statuses. We have9, therefore, called their middle class status as the "new middle class"[16] because they are not easily accepted by members of the old middle classes due to their "stigmatized" caste background.

The status of a person in India at present is determined on the basis of his birth in a particular caste or community and his socio-economic standing besides his interaction with others. His status, determined exclusively on the basis of his birth in a caste or community, is possible only at the theoretical (ideological) level, and that too in rural areas. Change in such a status is possible only in the next life or if he renounces this world and becomes an ascetic (*sanyasi*). Contrary to this, in urban areas, the status of a person is largely determined on the basis of his socio-economic position, and his caste or community background also influences it in one way or other. In fact, in an empirical situation, change in his status in the caste system is possible on the basis of his material conditions and his interaction with others, though such a change may not completely alter the status based on birth in a particular caste or community.

We have measured changes in the status of the respondents on the basis of their interaction with others. On the basis of socio-psychological indicators like social perception and social interaction, we recorded a considerable change in their status in the caste system. A large majority (87.5%) of them perceived changes of one type or the other in their caste status. Even most of the sweeper respondents (71.4%) observed changes of some types in their status in the caste system. Thus, those who perceived changes in their caste status were employed in all cadres of jobs in the sample except class I officers who had already improved their status in the caste system.

Again, a large majority of the respondents found that changes occurred in their caste status on the basis of their interaction with their non-scheduled caste acquaintances. Such interaction pertained to their attending ceremonies, taking meals/refreshments occasionally, and entering the kitchen of their acquaintances in the city. Such interaction between them and their acquaintances took place irrespective of age, caste, cadres and seniority in the jobs and rural-urban background of the former. But the socio-economic status of their family of both procreation and orientation was highly correlated with all the three forms of interaction between them and their acquaintances. Thus, we noted that changes of one type or the other had occurred in their status in the caste hierarchy, though there were certain reservations about their being freely accepted by their acquaintances and others.

Social Status in a Multiple Status-Hierarchy

We have mentioned earlier that status of a person in Indian society is determined on the basis of his birth in a particular caste or community and his socio-economic position and social interaction with others. Such a status is regarded as his social status (consisting of status both in the caste system and the class structure), and can be explained in terms of a composite evaluation by him and others and his self-awareness of such an evaluation. This can also be treated as composite and individual status contrary to the status of his group (caste). More precisely, a comprehensive evaluation of social status of the respondents was made through the subjective, composite (based on objective criteria like education, job, income, etc.) and group (caste) criteria.[17] Such criteria of status-evaluation obviously pertained to their social status in a multiple status-hierarchy[18] of caste system and class structure.

The respondents' perception about their own social status was examined in their neighbourhood in the city as the neighbourhood consisted of people of the same or different castes and communities. Neighbourhood is a unit of interaction where social situations are agglomerated at a given point in time. We have found that a considerable number of them (57.9%) had achieved a middle level social status in their neighbourhood. The percentage of those having a "high" social status was also quite noticeable (31.7%) contrary to only 10.4 per cent with a low social status in their respective neighbourhoods. Hence, 15.8 per cent suffered from status-anxiety resulting from an incongruity between their caste and class statuses and their low social status in the multiple status-hierarchy found in their urban neighbourhood.

A majority of the respondents, with their improved class status, had established a diagonal interactional relationship with their non-scheduled caste acquaintances, though this might have existed even earlier in some cases. This helped them perceive the enhancement in their caste status though the reverse is not ruled out where the improved class and caste statuses would have guided their diagonal interactional relationship. But as pointed out earlier, they and their acquaintances had certain reservations in their interaction and free acceptance of each other perhaps because of their caste background. Therefore, the respondents had not acquired "complete" social mobility in terms of congruity between both types of statuses and changes in their social status in an overall stratification system consisting of the caste system and class structure.

Status-Identification: A Framework of Ambivalence

The process of identification has been dealt with from the psychological and sociological points of view. Psychologically, the phenomenon of identification is related to the self. The formation of an individual's self and his personality is related to his identity which has both subjective (private) and objective (public) aspects. But in sociological literature the identification of a person is related to his adjustment in his social surroundings and, thus, in his social status. Such identification always exists in comparison to a certain group or individuals who may sometimes serve as referents of the identifier but generally it is directed towards those who are inferior.

The nature and levels of the status-identification of the respondents have been measured within the theoretical framework of ethnocentric and contra-identification. At the ethnocentric (caste) level, we have measured their identification in terms of the disclosure of their caste background to a visitor, the adoption of caste surnames and of the behaviour of reference group/individual belonging to their own caste. Similarly, at the level of contra-identification, the same indicators like the respondents' identification to a visitor, the adoption of surnames other than that of their caste, and the adoption of behaviour of a reference group/individual(s) drawn from another caste (including the other scheduled castes) have been taken into account. In this we have also included class identification to compare the levels of their status-identification within the caste and class hierarchies. Finally, we have measured the crisis of their status-identification.

A large majority of the respondents (90.8%) had, thus, identified themselves at the level of contra-identification in which they mentioned their names, educational qualifications, job-cadres, residential localities (*mohalla*), and the names of the offices in which they were employed. A few (5.8%) identified themselves as a "human beings", contrary to others (9.2%) who did not hesitate to identify as members of their respective castes. Their self-identification vis-a-vis a visitor did not correspond to their social background, though their adoption of surnames was correlated with their job-cadres, age and job-seniority. Other variables like caste, residence and socio-economic status of their family were not correlated at all with the levels of their status-identification, and the probability of correlation was also very low (at $>.05$ level of significance).

Finally, status-identification of the respondents was measured in terms of their imitation of ritual practices (sanskritization),[19] consumption patterns, and development-orientation (reference to activities related to their material progress) of their reference group/individual(s). A large majority (87.5%) did not emulate the ritual practices of others at all. There were only 20, 23, and 50 respondents who had adopted all the three types of behaviour patterns and life-styles of other individuals who served as their referents. But their number overlapped in the sense that those who adopted the ritual practices of others had also emulated their consumption patterns and activities relating to socio-economic development and vice-versa. Contrary to this, 10 per cent of the respondents strongly opposed the "hierarchical stratification" as they identified themselves at a non-caste-class level. They believed in a more egalitarian level of identification along the Marxist ideology (6.2%) and the Buddhist (4.1%) thought and way of life.

The mobile scheduled castes have remained in "semi-limbo"[20] situation as they are uprooted from their family and caste, and where would they go nobody knew. They have also been suffering from the "stigmatized identity"[21] of being 'untouchables'. Contrary to this, we have found that not only those who opposed the hierarchical identification and identified at the non-caste-class level, but even those who believed in contra-identification were, in fact, in an "identification dilemma". They were ambivalent to their identification as their kith and kin were still a part of the Hindu caste system and they themselves lived with their caste members, continuing their relations with them and availing of the reservation facilities meant for the scheduled castes. They also occasionally felt worried about their being scheduled castes, especially when they had to face various types of prejudices and discriminations. Hence, they were opposed to the ethnocentric (caste) identification.

Thus, the findings of our study suggest emergence of a new middle class consisting of the salaried persons among the scheduled castes. Such a middle class, which is an outcome of the "protective discrimination", is quite different from the old middle class in the country due to its specific social background and distinct historical origin. The members of the new middle class have not yet been fully accepted by the old middle class. In addition, a sizeable number of them suffer from status-anxiety resulting from an incongruity between their caste and class statuses. Moreover, they have an ambivalent identification due to dualism, that is, ethnocentric identification and, the contra-identification.

Our study provides a framework for the quantitative measurement of social mobility and status-identification. It suggests a comprehensive theoretical framework in which social mobility in the multiple status-hierarchy can be measured at both the quantitative and qualitative levels of analysis. Such a framework incorporates psycho-sociological indicators of status-identification of the mobile persons in general and the scheduled castes in particular. The present study also suggests a methodology to measure and analyze inter-generational social mobility and various levels of status-identification.

Notes

1. The term "protective discrimination policy" has been elaborately used by Lelah Dushkin in her "Scheduled Caste Politics", in *The Untouchables in Contemporary India*, M.J. Mahar (ed.), (Arizona, 1972), pp. 165-226.
2. A single approach emphasizes on the criterion of occupation for determining social status; see S.M. Lipset and R. Bendix, *Social Mobility in an Industrial Society* (New York, 1959); W. Lloyd Warner, *American Life* (Chicago, 1953).
3. A multiple approach includes more than one criterion for determining social status; see for instance, S.M. Lipset and Hans L. Zetterberg, "A Theory of Social Mobility", *in Transactions of the Third World Congress of Sociology*, Vol. III, (London, 1956), pp. 155-77; for both single and multiple approaches, see F. van Heek,"Some Introductory Remarks on Social Mobility and Class Structure", in *Transactions of the Third World Congress of Sociology*, pp. 129-43.
4. Ibid., pp. 155-77.
5. G.C. Homans, *Sentiments and Activities: Essays in Social Science* (London, 1962), pp. 91-102.
6. R.K. Merton, *Social Theory and Social Structure,* (Glencoe, The Free

Press, 1962), pp. 297-440.

7. A.C. Paranjpe, *Caste Prejudice and the Individual* (Bombay, 1970), pp. 106-38.
8. S.M. Lipset and Hans L. Zetterberg, op.cit., p. 159.
9. R.A. Schermerhorn, "Social Mobility of Three Minorities in India: A Qualitative Approach", in *Cohesion and Conflict in Modern India*, G.R. Gupta (ed.), (New Delhi, 1978), pp. 46-59.
10. McKim Marriott, "Multiple References in Indian Caste System", in *Social Mobility in the Caste System in India*, James Silverberg (ed.), (The Hague, 1968), pp. 103-14.
11. S.M. Lipset and Hans L. Zetterberg, op.cit., pp. 175-6; see also S.M. Lipset, *Political Man* (Bombay, 1960).
12. B. Kuppuswamy, *Manual of Socio-Economic Status Scale (Urban)*, (Delhi, 1962).
13. E.S. Bogardus, "Measuring Social Distance", in *Readings in Attitude Theory and Measurement*, M. Fishbein (ed.), (New York, 1967). While modifying the scale we have excluded those items which are not relevant in the context of urban situation in India.
14. The average amount of social mobility has been calculated as: $M = \sum \frac{X}{N}$, where X = total sum of the respondents' mobility scores after subtracting, in each case, the mobility scores of their fathers from their own; N = total number of upwardly mobile respondents; and M = average amount of social mobility of upwardly mobile respondents.
15. The correlations between independent and dependent variables have been calculated through $X^2 = \left(\frac{O - E}{E}\right)^2$, and the extent of such correlation or co-efficient of contingency has been calculated through $C = \frac{\sqrt{X^2}}{X^2 + N}$.
16. For details, see E. Franklin Frazier, Black Bourgeoisie: The Rise of a New Middle Class *(New York, 1966); C. Wright Mills,* The White Collar *(New York, 1966).*
17. In a "subjective" criterion, one's status is evaluated by oneself or by one's acquaintances. The "composite" criterion of status evaluation is the summation of "status-sets" achieved in various spheres like education, job, income, etc. and the "corporate" criterion is that

which attributes status to an individual and has its sanction in "tradition". The empirical and non-empirical bases of such status-evaluations can be seen in Satish Saberwal, "Status Mobility and Networks in a Punjabi Industrial Town", in his *Beyond the Village: Sociological Explorations*, (Simla, 1972), p. 114; see also T.H. Marshall, *Sociology at the Cross Roads and other Essays* (London, 1963), p. 197.

18. The analysis of multiple status-hierarchy in this study is different from that of Hazelhurst; see Leighton W. Hazelhurst, "Multiple Status Hierarchies in Northern India", *Contributions to Indian Sociology*, No. II, (1968), pp. 38-57.
19. M.N. Srinivas, *Social Change in Modern India* (Bombay, 1966), pp. 1-45.
20. Harold R. Isaacs, *India's Ex-Untouchables*, (Bombay, 1965), pp. 128-42.
21. Gerald D. Berreman, "Self, Situation and Escape from Stigmatized Ethnic Identity", in his *Caste and Other Inequities* (Meerut, 1979), pp. 164-77.

19 Open Education and Closed Society

A Study of Social and Educational Inequalities in Contemporary India

EHSANUL HAQ

The traditional Indian society has been characterized as a closed system because of the dominance of caste and religious factors. The coexistence of these factors operated in the society in such a way that a system developed which imposed segmental division of labour, rigid rules of hierarchically-arranged ascribed statuses, religious and civic disabilities and privileges, restrictions on social interaction, and on the choice of occupation. This type of system gave rise to a caste-based hierarchy with structured social inequality. It promoted a pervasive and deep-rooted culture of inequality with a very strong religious and ritual legitimacy. It delivered a socially unchallenged and non-competitive authority to Brahmana and other higher castes.

The caste and religious support gave such a strong authority to the priest that, even at the time of coronation, the king (550 BC) used to bow at least thrice before the Brahmana thereby accepting his subordinate position to his ritual, religious, and social supremacy. A passage in *Rigveda* confirms that a king or a monarch can secure an early mastery over his subjects and defeat his enemies only if he honours the Brahmana priest who, through him, used to extend his control over the state. This shows an absolute control of the priestly caste over society without any infringement from other castes because of his ritual, religious, non-secular, spiritual, divine, and ascribed status. A time came when the priestly profession became the preserve only of the priestly caste—the Brahmana. Even the non-Brahmana high castes like Kshatriya were debarred from this profession and assigned to rule and protect the territorial sovereignty.

However, caste, with its religious legitimacy, became such a crucial dimension of Indian traditional structure that it subsumed almost all the functions of society and made them contingent upon it, and the authority and superiority of the higher castes remained unchallenged for centuries. This type of social structure, based on caste, was so pervasive and deep-rooted in the organic structure of Indian society that it persisted throughout Indian history, from the Sanskritic period to the Mughal period (an apparently non-hierarchical system)—to the British period (a highly elitist system)—and to the contemporary times (a highly democratic system).

Every social system develops a tendency to exist, perpetuate and continue, and for this, it evolves its own mechanism. Our Sanskritic tradition in the same manner devised its methods to persist and perpetuate itself. The best tool devised and used for this purpose was the system of education. Since the higher castes attained a superior, pure, and legitimate position by claiming to have undergone the process of "salvation", they directly and indirectly controlled the society (Gore et al. 1967: 61). The task which they assigned for themselves was to strengthen the normative order and preserve their traditional authority by educating the society. This task was accepted to be the special privilege of only the Brahmana priests because they were not only higher in terms of caste position, but also well-read in Vedic language and literature. Their pursuits were solely the priestly profession and a theological career. Thus, they became the custodians of "Gayana Shastra".

Since the Sanskritic tradition was caste-based, and the Brahmana was (caste-wise) a superior being, a theologician, and well-read in Vedic education, he guided the society, in general, and the system of education, in particular. He prepared sacred texts, laid down social laws, and interpreted social relations and customs based on religious and caste ideology, which governed the subject-matter of education. Education thus became highly religion-oriented, personalized, authoritarian, ascribed, restricted, monopolized, esoteric and subjective, based on fundamental values which are ends in themselves (see the paradigm given below). It transmitted the idea of purity and pollution, religious and civic disabilities, and privileges of various castes, restrictions on social interactions, and the choice of occupation. It was ultimately meant to produce orthodox and uncritical subscribers to Hindu religious and caste ideology, and to prepare them for the transcendental world (Ghurye 1979: 1-28; Anderson 1966:79-90).

Paradigm showing the main features of traditional social structure, traditional and modern education

Traditional social structure	*Traditional education*	*Modern education*
Hierarchical and closed	Hierarchical and closed	Hierarchical but constitutionally open
Ascriptive and subjective	Ascribed and subjective knowledge	Achievement-oriented objective
Particularistic and self-oriented	Particularistic and self-oriented	Universalistic and collectivity-oriented
Non-secular and sacred	Religious, non-secular and sacred learning	Secular and profane
Authoritarian and non-competitive	Authoritarian and non-competitive	Democratic and competitive
Pre-eminence of Fundamental values	Transmission of fundamental values	Learning of operational values

Since, this kind of education was highly restricted, the lower castes were rigorously excluded on the grounds of purity and pollution. It was mainly on this basis that Eklavya, a competent Shudra boy, was not accepted as a disciple by Dronacharya, a Brahmana teacher of Sanskritic teaching and learning. The education became so ascribed, rigid, and restricted that even the non-Brahmana higher castes were unable to have full access to it. Thus, education became merely an apparatus and an instrument in the hands of the Brahmana for strengthening the traditional social structure, maintaining their superiority, and perpetuating inegalitarian values and culture. Thus, they remained for centuries as dictators of Hindu life and the repositories of learning (Galanter 1984: 7-17).

The exogenous contact with Indian tradition brought about some changes in the traditional society, and education became gradually more open, egalitarian, secular, objective, and formal (Singh 1973: 101-107). Yet, it served, by and large, the interests of higher castes and classes throughout Indian history. For instance, during the Sanskritic tradition, it was the Brahmana who benefited most; during the Mughal period, it was the nobility of Islam; during the British period, it was the aristocracy and the Indian feudals; and, during contemporary time, it is the elite from the higher caste and class background who monopolize and make use of the best available educational opportunities (Bendix and Lipset 1966: 449).

The Situation after Independence

Social and educational inequalities, continued despite the changes ushered into the Indian society before and after independence. In order to change this situation and transform the traditional social structure, new policies were formulated after independence based on a planned programme of scientific, technological, liberal and democratic frameworks of modernization. Many steps were taken to promote social and economic equality and justice, and to provide equal educational opportunities to all, irrespective of caste and class considerations. The Constitution (Article 29) guarantees that "no citizen shall be denied admission into any educational institution maintained by the State or receiving aid from state funds, on grounds of religion, race, caste, language or any of them". This was amended (1951) to "provide reservation of seats on the ground of caste". It was also added that "nothing shall prevent the State from making any special provision for the advancement of any socially and educationally backward classes or of the scheduled castes and scheduled tribes". The government is now intent upon demolishing social inequality as well as untouchability, and forbidding the enforcement of any disability arising out of them. The government is also trying its best to protect minority rights and ensure equality, individual liberty, and secularism and to prevent discrimination by promoting educational and economic interests of the weaker sections, especially the lower castes. The educational system is geared to function accordingly, but the results are not very encouraging because a great disparity in terms of educational opportunities still persists among various castes.

The paradigm given above shows a reciprocal relationship between traditional social structure and traditional education. It also reflects a conflicting situation. For example, the traditional education has undergone change giving rise to modern education but the traditional social structure has not changed to that extent. The continuity in the traditional caste-based inegalitarian socio-cultural system still seems to exert a strong pressure on modern education by offering a powerful resistance to the modernizing power of education. This paper examines this conflict and the emerging contradictions between the particularized traditional caste structure and the rational, liberal, modern education. It will explain the basic causes of educational inequality which lie in the structure of values pertaining to caste. It will also examine whether the constitutional objectives and the message of modern education can fully be achieved within the framework of continuing traditional values and culture in which modern education exists today.

Empirical Observations

In order to examine the problem, we have gathered empirical facts from some of the schools, colleges and universities of mainly the eastern parts of Uttar Pradesh. The paper is based on observations and some available quantitative data. The data collected show it explicitly that the traditional caste structure is now extending its control and monopoly over the modern education to strengthen its traditional control over power and resources. This is done in more or less the same manner in which education was maintained and used in the traditional society.

Table 1

Caste background and organizational structure of modern education (schools and intermediate colleges of Dobhi region of Sultanpur, U.P.)

(in per cent)

Caste Background	*Organizational Structure of Education*			
	President	*Vice-President*	*Manager*	*Total*
Brahmana	1	–	–	1
	(3.7)			(1.3)
Kshatriya	26	12	38	76
	(96.3)	(100)	(100)	(98.7)
Vaishya	–	–	–	–
Middle Castes	–	–	–	–
Lower Castes	–	–	–	–
Total	27	12	38	77
	(100)	(100)	(100)	(100)

Note: This table is based on data collected from nine educational institutions managed and financed by the government in Dobhi region of Sultanpur district, U.P., during the year 1978-1979. Since the establishment of these institutions, all 26 positions out of 27 have been occupied mainly by the Thakur caste.

Source: H.N. Singh (1979).

Table 1 reveals a positive correlation between the caste structure and the organizational structure of modern education. Since there has been an erosion in the religious and ritual authority of the Brahman as priest and the non-secular and religious content of education has undergone change, they now have only a marginal role in the management of educational institutions. The Kshatriyas (known as Thakur or Rajput), the next higher caste in the hierarchy, who were the ruling caste and economically and socially dominant, have taken over the monopoly of education. However, there has also been an erosion in the economic dominance of the Kshatriyas because of various measures taken by the government. To a great extent, however, they still continue their hold over society, and safeguard their socio-economic positions by entering into new areas like politics, administration, professions, and education. As shown in Table 1, the Kshatriyas have absolute control over the organizational structure of education in the region. They have occupied and still hold almost all the organizational positions. According to the 1901, 1921, and 1931 censuses of Sultanpur, the total population of the Thakur caste was, on an average, not more than 10 per cent of the total Hindu population. This shows that they had always been a very small group, but held the most powerful positions. As the 1901 census shows, 8.9 per cent of the Thakurs owned 76 per cent of the land in Sultanpur district.

Today they are influential agriculturists, local as well as national leaders, advocates, university and college teachers, and administrators. They are considered as 'zamindars' of those institutions which they control and use to strengthen their social status and exercise their influence. Thus, even today, education is being used as an apparatus of exploitation, discrimination, and manipulation, and of consolidating the traditional control over modern resources. It is because of the Thakur domination in education that we find a popular phrase in UP that "the Congress had abolished the zamindari in land and has created a zamindari in education... Such zamindars (landowners) are presidents, vice-presidents, managers, principals of schools and colleges... They are well-fed, well-clothed, and maintain their own cars, all on the profits from the institutions which they run. It is now recognized that running an educational institution can be an important means of social, economic, and political power" (Gould in Rudolph 1972: 94).

Since a caste has almost total control over the educational system, it tries to perpetuate itself by making the entire educational machinery as an instrument of power. For example, it controls and affects election of the members of managing committees, recruitment of teachers power and administrative staff, admission of students, distribution of various types of patronages and facilities, and the like. It is through the educational structure and educational process that the values pertaining to caste like untouchability, caste feeling, casteism, parochialism, caste superiority, caste hatred, mess discrimination, and the like, are transmitted, and, thus, education becomes a mechanism of the traditionalization of modernity. It is constrained to provide a conducive environment for social and national integration and modernization by uprooting traditional values.

The illustrations given here show very clearly how the caste-based structure of our society penetrates into educational structures and the process of teaching and learning. Table 1 shows the dominance of an upper caste in holding all powerful positions in educational administration. The system of education is controlled in such a way that this dominance gets reflected in the elected members of managing committees, recruitment of teachers and staff, and admission of students (Table 2).

Table 2

Caste background of members of managing committees, teachers, administrative staff and students in educational institutions

(in per cent)

Caste Background	*No. of elected members of managing committees*	*No. of teachers*	*No. of administrative staff*	*No. of students*	*Total*
Upper Caste (Only Thakur)	124 (98.4)	200 (86.6)	53 (43.1)	1468 (48.4)	1845 (52.5)
Middle Castes	1 (0.8)	29 (12.5)	63 (51.2)	884 (29.1)	977 (27.8)
Lower Castes	1 (0.8)	2 (0.9)	7 (5.7)	680 (22.4)	690 (19.6)
Total	126 (100)	231 (100)	123 (100)	3032 (100)	3512 (100)

Note: See Table 1.
Source: H.N. Singh (1979).

We observe that a majority of the members of managing committees, teachers, and students belong to the same caste to which the president, vice-president, and managers of managing committees of these institutions belong. As far as the selection of the administrative staff is concerned, their case does not strictly follow the caste lines because they are merely subordinates, as compared to the relatively autonomous and more influential category of teachers. We can see the same pattern of dominance in the organizational structure of higher education in the Dobhi region of Sultanpur district.

Table 3 shows that there is no representation of the middle and lower castes in educational administration except for 12.7 per cent of the teachers who belong to the middle castes. During 1985, the total enrolment of lower caste students in higher education was only 9.05 per cent (much below the reserved seats) as against 90-95 per cent of the students from the upper and middle castes.

Table 3

Caste background and organizational structure of modern education (PG College of Dobhi region of Sultanpur, 1985)

(in per cent)

Caste Background	*Organizational Structure of Education*			
	President	*Manager*	*Members of Managing Committee*	*No. of Teachers*
Upper Castes	1	1	20	48
	(100)	(100)	(95.2)	(87.3)
Middle Castes	—	—	1	7
			(4.8)	(12.7)
Lower Castes	—	—	—	—
Total	1	1	21	55
	(100)	(100)	(100)	(100)

Note: In the upper caste category, president, manager, and one member of the managing committee belong to the Brahmin caste and the rest of them belong to the Thakur caste.

Source: P.G. College (1985).

In another district of UP, namely, Ghazipur, we also observe such a pattern of dominance. Table 4 shows that the upper castes excel the middle ones in occupying all administrative and teaching positions. It is through administrative control that the recruitment of teachers in the PG college seems to have taken place along caste lines. A majority of the teachers (77.3%) belong to the Thakur caste, including the previous principal and the present secretary of the college. It is because of this reason that the college is sometimes referred to by the name of the dominant caste, "Thakur College". Similarly, in Mysore, there is a powerful organi-

Table 4

Caste background and organizational structure of modern education

(P.G. College, Ghazipur, 1985) (in per cent)

Caste background	*Organizational structure of education*									
									Students	
	Presidential positions[a]	*Secretaries*[b]	*Treasurer*	*Members of managing committees*	*Principal*	*Teachers*[c]	*Nonteaching staff*	*Class IV staff*	*Under-graduates*	*Post-graduates*
Upper Castes	2	3	—	1	1	68	11	1	467	116
	(66.7)	(100)		(14.3)	(100)	(77.3)	(42.3)	(1.8)	(35.6)	(41.8)
Middle Castes	—	—	1	6	—	20	14	44	612	98
			(100)	(85.7)		(22.7)	(53.9)	(81.5)	(46.5)	(35.1)
Lower Castes	—	—	—	—	—	—	1	9	170	49
							(3.8)	(16.7)	(13.1)	(17.4)
Others (Muslims)	1	—	—	—	—	—	—	—	64	16
	(33.3)								(4.8)	(5.7)
Total	3	3	1	7	1	88	26	54	1313	279
	(100)	(100)	(100)	(100)	(100)	(100)	(100)	(100)	(100)	(100)

Notes: a. Presidential positions include the president, senior vice-president, and junior vice-president.
b. Secretaries include secretary and two joint secretaries.
c. Office bearers as well as teachers mainly belong to the Thakur caste.

Source: P.G. College (1985).

sation known as the Karnataka Lingayat Education Society, which controls a number of educational institutions in the state. In order to make this organisation apparently secular, it was renamed as the Karnataka Liberal Education Society, but it is still popularly known by its caste name because of the continuance of Lingayat domination. In spite of the secularization of the Society by name, most of its members and staff under its control belong to the Lingayat caste (Madan and Halbar 1972: 133).

In such a situation, not only the organization or the institution, but also the teachers and others, are sometimes referred to by their castes. For instance, in the Thakur-dominated educational institutions, and also in highly advanced liberal centres of higher learning, a teacher from the higher caste is frequently called as "Thakur Saheb" and "Pandit Ji", and those from the lower castes as "Babu Saheb" or "Munshi Ji". Since the former are socially dominant, they do not object to be addressed by their ascribed position because it serves their caste interest and they feel honoured, but when this is objected to by the latter, they are considered as suffering from "complexes".

Two Levels of Caste Control over Education

The domination and control of traditional caste structure over secular and modern educational institutions operates at two levels. First, there is the structural level. From the apex to the bottom, the caste dominance persists and manipulates educational structure along caste lines in order to strengthen its traditional control. Second, there is the level of process where the educational structure itself becomes a source to provide a fertile ground to make the educational process effective. This functions in such a way that the caste is preserved, and its interests are served.

Since education performs as an agency of both selection and socialization, the caste-based discrimination not only influences the selection of teachers and students, election of the members of managing committees, and distribution of privileges, but also the process of teaching and learning which is considered a main source of continuity, a torch-bearer of traditional as well as modern values. A teacher is product of certain social conditions. He or she becomes an agent of preserving and promoting traditional values like purity-pollution, ascription, structured social inequality, caste ideology, caste culture, caste and communal loyalties, non-secular and particularistic values, caste-based discrimination, and socialized inequality through the process of teaching and learning.

We have observed numerous such examples in and outside the classroom situations. For instance, in one of the schools it was observed how classroom teaching becomes a source of perpetuating caste-based discrimination. In one book-craft class, all the boys were assigned to prepare files. A lower caste boy somehow did the job most skilfully in a professional manner. The teacher was very impressed but rewarded the boy with the remark that "after all, you are the son of a cobbler". Similarly, in some of the schools, it was observed that the upper caste teacher invariably prefers the boys from the higher caste for tasks of bringing him water, tea, foodstuffs, and the like, while for other services, such as cleaning, sweeping, and furniture arrangement the lower caste boys are preferred. This shows as if the former type of work, if rendered by the lower caste children, will make "Thakur Saheb" and "Pandit Ji" impure. This type of social situation reflects an emerging conflict because it contradicts the objectives of modern education and the constitutional directives. Some of the implications of such a classroom climate are as follows: First, it reflects sincerity of the student who obeys the instruction of the teacher, but insincerity of the latter who develops a prejudiced, discriminatory, and casteist attitude towards the lower caste learner in particular. Second, it promotes directly or indirectly a feeling of structured social inequality with respect to status and work. Third, it demonstrates that the less-skilled, low-paid, manual, less clean and similar occupations are meant only for lower caste people who are socially as well as economically inferior. Fourth, it transmits the idea of purity and impurity or untouchability to the minds of the young students. Fifth, it creates a feeling of hatredness and alienation not only among the learners but also among those who belong to other religious communities. For instance, it was observed that Muslim boys do not properly mix up with Harijan boys who are looked upon down in comparison to other caste children. This is partly because such a feeling is implanted in their mind, and partly because the upper caste boys look at the Harijan boys with a feeling of superiority.

Similarly, caste affects other aspects of education like politics, evaluation, interpersonal relationships, and so on. For example, when the same lower caste boy, mentioned above, reached the college in the same district, he was confronted with a similar situation of discrimination. He contested election for the post of student representative against a Muslim candidate and got elected, but the next time, when he contested against an upper caste boy, he lost. This shows that education, both formal and informal, creates a gap not only between a upper caste and a lower caste within the community, but it does also between the two communities, by generating a caste-basis for electoral loss and a communal basis for electoral gain (Beteille 1983: 184).

We have numerous such examples not only from the schools and colleges, but also from the centres of higher learning and research, especially in the eastern parts of UP. Not only teaching has become caste-infected, but hostel life has become caste-ridden, which is supposed to be a place of integrated living and learning. One may observe caste-based alliances in the selection of room-mates and peer groups among the hostel residents. Even the teacher-warden, who looks after his wards, makes decisions directly or indirectly on the basis of caste factor in terms of room allotment, reward and punishment, and the like, in order to seek caste-based support, especially during the time of crisis.

Similarly, the process of evaluation—another very important component of education—is not free from caste influences either. For instance, in one of the schools, the academic performance of a lower caste boy was found quite satisfactory. His teacher, who happened to be from the higher caste, became interested in knowing the caste background of the boy, assuming that he must be from a higher caste. The boy reacted in anger and said: "I happen to be a Chamar." The teacher mildly replied: "You do not look like a Chamar by appearance and performance." The boy answered: "Does a Chamar reflect some special features, like the horn of a buffalo?" The boy was ultimately downgraded. Similarly, at a higher level of education, especially in one of the colleges, a evaluation is so biased that invariably only a person from a higher caste tops the merit list. Even at other institutions of higher learning and research, including those located at central places like Delhi, where there is internal assessment, factors like caste, region, language, religion, ideology, and personal consideration do play an important role, resulting in subjective and biased assessment by the teachers.

Caste and Educational Inequalities: A Reciprocal Relationship

The caste-based discrimination and the higher caste domination over the educational structure are, to a great extent, responsible for the emergence of caste associations and united fronts consisting of teachers and students mainly from lower social background. These generate support from within to launch an organized protest against discrimination, maltreatment, harassment, manipulation, and victimization. It has also given rise to educational institutions dominated by the lower and middle castes, where upper castes are deliberately debarred, harassed, and victimized. This may continue until the structure of values undergoes drastic change, social and educational inequalities are minimized, and the traditional control over modern education discontinues. The preceding analysis may be summarized in the following paradigm:

		Education			
		Traditional	Modern		
Social	Traditional	- -	- +	1. Traditional	(-)
Structure	Modern	+ -	+ +	2. Modern	(+)

1. - - Existent category in traditional India.
2. + - Non-existent category.
3. - + Existent category in contemporary India.
4. + + Non-existent category.

1. The first type (- -) represents continuity with a harmonic and reciprocal relationship between the traditional social structure and traditional education in the past. They co-existed in the traditional society, where this reciprocity reflected hierarchy and closedness, ascription and subjectivity, particularism and self-orientation, religious and non-secular values, authoritarianism and non-competitiveness.
2. The second type (+ -) does not exist in contemporary India because we have neither the modern social structure nor the traditional system of education.
3. The third type (- +) also does not exist at present because the traditional social structure is not modernized to the extent to which education has undergone change.
4. The fourth type (+ +) does exist in contemporary Indian society, where the traditional social structure perpetuates but the traditional system of education is discontinued, giving rise to modern education which is constitutionally open, non-hierarchical, achievement-oriented, objective, universalistic, scientific, secular, democratic, and competitive.

We observe the continuance of the former and discontinuance of the latter in Indian society today. This co-existence of continuity and change creates disharmonic and conflicting type of relationships. The modernizing power of education is resisted by the continuance of traditional social structure, which is so pervasive and entrenched that it seems to accelerate the traditionalization of modern education (Rudolph and Rudolph 1967: 17-28). This contradicts our constitutional and national objectives, because the traditional caste hierarchy and structured social inequality result into educational inequality. This entire process is schematically depicted in Figure 1.

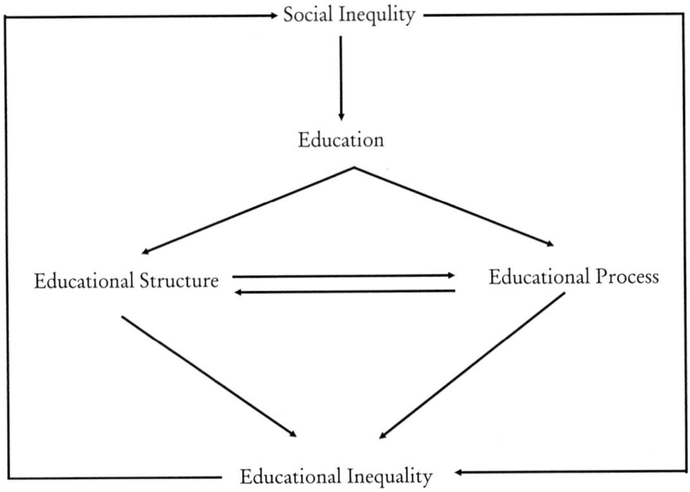

Figure 1

Here, educational inequality becomes an offshort of an overarching social inequality with an inherent structure of values opposed to the equalization of opportunities. In such a situation, the system of education is functioning under very strong social pressures. Hence, it cannot easily be an instrument of change and modernization. The Education Commission (1966: 4-5) has very strongly advocated that there is one instrument only, namely, education, "to be used to achieve the desired socio-economic and cultural revolution". The Commission further highlights the importance of education in national development, by saying that it is only through this instrument that "the destiny of India is being shaped in the classroom". But unfortunately, education in general, and the classroom in particular, are used as a new apparatus to preserve caste inequality and traditional control. Even today, it is not free from socio-linguistic, cultural, regional, and parochial forces. Education is being moulded by these factors in such a way that irrational values are transmitted and social inequality is reproduced. Education becomes an instrument to strengthen these roots because it is a part of the social reality in which it exists. We need a more powerful force to counteract the values behind these forces which are highly pervasive and deep-rooted in the structure of Indian society (Haq 1981: 145-165).

References

Anderson, C.A. 1966, "The Modernization of Education", pp. 66-80, in *Modernization: The Dynamics of Growth*, edited by Myron Weiner, Washington, DC: Basic Books.

Bendix, R. and S.M. Lipset, 1966, *Class, Status and Power*, London: Routledge and Kegan Paul.

Beteille, A., 1983, *Equality and Inequality*, Delhi: Oxford University Press.

Galanter, M., 1984, *Competing Equalities*, Delhi: Oxford University Press.

Ghurye, G.S., 1979, *Caste and Race in India*, Bombay: Popular Prakashan.

Gore, M.S., I.P. Desai, and S. Chitnis, 1967, *Papers in the Sociology of Education*, Delhi: NCERT Publication.

Gould, H., 1972, "Educational Structures and Political Processes in Faizabad District, Uttar Pradesh", in *Education and Politics in India*, edited by S.H. Rudolph and L.I. Rudolph, Delhi: Oxford University press.

Government of India, 1951, *The Constitution of India*, Government Publication.

—, 1966, *Report of the Education Commission 1964-66*, Government Publication.

Haq, E., 1981, *Education and Political Culture in India*, Delhi: Sterling Publishers.

Madan, T.N. and B.G. Halbar, 1972, "Caste and Community in the Private and Public Education of Mysore State". In *Education and Politics in India*, edited by S.H. Rudolph, and L.I. Rudolph, Delhi: Oxford University Press.

P.G. College, 1985, "College Records" (Unpublished), Ghazipur: P.G. College.

Rudolph, L.I. and S.H. Rudolph, 1967, *The Modernity of Tradition*, Delhi: Orient Longman.

Singh, H.N., 1979, "Caste, Land and Power", Mimeo, Delhi: Centre for the Study of Social Systems, Jawaharlal Nehru University.

Singh, Y., 1973, *Modernization of Indian Tradition*, Jaipur: Rawat Publications.

20 The Indian Institutes of Technology

Do they Contribute to Social Mobility?

C. RAJAGOPALAN AND JASPAL SINGH

The Indian Institutes of Technology (IITs) were intended to be a kind of model institutions designed to play a leading role in promoting engineering and technological education. This paper presents an analysis of the social background of the first year students at one of the IITs.

The data presented in this paper were collected through personal interviews, employing a formal interview schedule, of 237 students who represented 86.5 per cent of the total admissions in 1966 in the IIT under study.

As the IITs enjoy a special status, they are endowed with a constitution and organization different from that of the other engineering colleges in the country, and have been declared institutes of national importance, it may be of interest to know something about the students who succeed in securing entry to these institutes. There is a great demand for admission to the IITs, as evidenced by the number of applications for admission, but only a small percentage are eventually admitted. In 1965, the total number of applications for admission to the five IITs was 25,719. The number of students who appeared for the entrance examination was 22,776. Of these, only 2,133 or 9.37 per cent were qualified. The number of applicants in 1966 was higher than that in the earlier years. Admission to these institutes is based on an all-India joint entrance examination and is apparently free from all discriminations. Yet, in a vast country like India, the great range in social and economic conditions may have the unintended effect of making it difficult for certain sections of society to qualify for the facilities of education provided in these institutes. For instance, the localization of educational facilities may itself have the unintended consequence of actually restricting their use to that region. Or, the existence of certain educational facilities may not be known to most people. Also, as schools vary widely in the facilities they offer and consequently in the standards they maintain, belong to different denominations, and use different media of instruction, students from certain schools may be automatically eliminated in the competition for admission owing to no fault of their own. This is especially so when the competitive examination is modelled on the basis of standards maintained by the best schools. It is far from our intention to suggest that the standard of the competitive examination be brought down to enable the weak students to get through. Our aim is only to examine whether there is evidence that any such disabling factors are in operation against certain sections of society. How these factors can be eliminated is an altogether different question, and is in any case beyond the scope of this paper.

A study of the social background of these students is of interest for another reason. It is assumed that the IITs, by virtue of their unique status and numerous facilities, can attract the most suitable and talented students and train and convert them into engineers who are bound to be superior to the ones being turned out by the ordinary engineering colleges. If this is true, it is likely that the students graduating from these institutes will have a definite edge over their counterparts from other engineering colleges in matters of employment. Consequently, in a few years most of the important and top positions in the field of engineering and technology in the country may be controlled by them. In a country which has embarked on a process of rapid industrialization, therefore, what amount of power and influence the products of the IITs might wield can easily be imagined. If the IITs are engaged in producing a potential elite which is bound to play a very crucial role in the industrial and technological development of the country, the whole question of recruitment and of the elite becomes a matter of profound interest. A study of the social background of these students would disclose the social strata from which they come and the extent to which the recruitment conforms to the accepted goals of social transformation of our society.

The term "social background" has been used in this study in a very comprehensive sense and includes factors such as religion, caste, family, the rural or urban character of the native place of the students, the income, education and occupation of their parents, and the students' school background, i.e., the type of school attended, its media of instruction and the final qualifying examination passed before being admitted to the IIT. Factors like caste, religion, family and rural-urban background have been included because they are important principles of stratification in Indian society which has yet to completely shed its traditional character. As Indian society undergoes a change from its traditional orientation to a modern one, these principles of stratification are bound to lose their importance and be eventually replaced by criteria of achievement for social stratification; hence the relevance of factors like parental education, occupation and income being included in this study. The analysis of the school background is designed to discover whether certain kinds of schooling tends to act as a handicap in securing admission.

Of the 237 students interviewed, as many as 87.7 per cent were from urban areas, and only 8.1 per cent from rural areas. The remaining 4.1 per cent did not indicate the rural/urban character of their native place. It is clear that the bulk of the students belong to urban areas.

The rural-urban background refers to the student's native place, defined as his traditional home community. In actual fact, however, the student may be alien to his home community insofar as he may have been born and brought up in an urban area where his parents have been permanently employed. Further analysis of the data shows that this is substantially true. Out of 8.1 per cent of the students whose traditional home community is rural, as many as 5.5 per cent are more or less permanent residents of the city where the institute is located (this will hereafter be referred to as the "city area" and students from it as "local students"). It is possible that the remaining six students too, whose parents are not settled in city, are in fact residents of an urban area other than the city, so that not more than 2.6 per cent of the students belong to the rural areas.

Table 1 shows the nativity of the students in terms of the state of origin and rural/urban background. It will be seen that 59.5 per cent are local students, and of these all but two are urbanites. The actual number of people belonging to the city however is more if we add the 5.5 per cent from the rural areas whose parents have actually settled down in the city. In other words, as many as 65 per cent of the students are from the city itself. Another 22.4 per cent come from the three states adjacent to the city. Students coming from other states in northern and southern India form 8.0 and 5.1 per cent respectively of the students interviewed. It is quite clear that, judged by the state or origin of the students, the institute caters mostly to students from the city.

Table 1
Students by the state of origin and rural/urban background

State of origin	*Urban*	*Rural*	*No. response*	*Total*
The city	137	2	2	141
Three adjacent states	36	15	2	53
Rest of Northern India	17	2	—	19
Southern India	9	—	3	12
Foreigner	3	—	—	3
No response	6	—	3	9
Total	203	19	10	237

In the course of the interviews it came to light that of the five branches of engineering in which courses are offered at the institute, mechanical and electrical engineering were the most sought after. This is also borne out by the preferences expressed by the students in their applications for admission to the institute. When the students were asked why they chose the particular discipline, virtually all the students reading mechanical and electrical engineering replied that they were genuinely interested in these branches of engineering, while many of the students from the other three disciplines said that they did not choose these disciplines but had opted for them after having been refused places for mechanical and electrical engineering on the basis of the merit entrance examination. This is also attested by the fact that students on the top of the merit list are generally admitted to mechanical and electrical engineering courses except when their own preference is for some other discipline.

In view of the different degrees of prestige attached to the different branches of engineering, it may be interesting to see whether the rural/urban background and nativity of the students are factors that have helped or hindered them in getting admission to the preferred branches of engineering. The relevant data are presented in Table 2 which indicate that while the percentage of students not belonging to the city is as low as 17.5 in some of the more highly preferred disciplines, their percentage rises to 42.3 in the least preferred discipline. As a matter of fact the total intake of students is much smaller in the least preferred discipline compared to that in the other disciplines. In other words, students from the city have not only a better chance of getting admission into the Institute, but also of getting admission into courses of higher prestige.

Table 2

Students classified by engineering discipline and parents' present residence

Parental residence	Engineering discipline			
	Mechanical	*Electrical*	*Three other disciplines*	*Total*
The city	44	47	91	182
Three adjacent states	3	5	22	30
Rest of Northern India	2	2	9	13
Southern India	1	1	—	2
Foreigner	2	1	—	3
No response	4	1	2	7
Total	56	57	124	237

A religion-wise break-up shows that 90.3 per cent of the students are Hindus, 8.4 per cent Sikhs and the remaining 1.3 per cent Muslims. Of the three Muslim students, one is a foreigner. And the two Indian Muslim students are in the least preferred branch of engineering. It is also significant to note that there is no Christian student. Thus, the vast majority of the students are Hindus.

In view of the fact that the students come from different states, some of which have unique systems of caste nomenclature, it is difficult to make any comparisons of caste unless they are reduced to the Brahman/non-Brahman/scheduled caste classification. This is an oversimplification which may overlook differences between castes comprised within any of the categories.

However, the fact that the vast bulk of students come from the city and other adjacent states, where the caste systems are comparable to a certain extent, permits us to analyze caste by excluding the small proportion of students who belong to other states. Similarly, since only two religious groups are represented adequately in the sample, the analysis of caste can be done in the context of religion. This is presented in Table 3.

Table 3

Students classified by religion and caste

Caste	Religion			Total
	Hindu	Sikh	Muslim	
Brahman	52	—	—	52
Trading castes	142	6	2	150
Agricultural castes	2	6	—	8
Artisan castes	—	6	—	6
Miscellaneous	12	—	—	12
No response	6	2	1*	9
Total	214	20	3	237

* Foreigner

It is significant that there is not a single student from any of the scheduled castes or tribes. Brahman castes are represented to the extent of 21.9 per cent. The vast majority of the students are from the trading castes[1] which account for 63.3 per cent of the aggregate and artisan castes have a numerically small representation. In terms of religion, however, the agricultural castes have a much higher percentage among the Sikhs than amongst the Hindus. All students from the artisan castes belong to the Sikh religion and none to the Hindu. Thus, while the Hindu students are almost exclusively from the Brahman and trading castes, the Sikh students are more or less evenly distributed among the trading, agricultural and artisan castes. The two Indian Muslim students are also from a trading caste (Bohra).

Most of the students, i.e., 67.9 per cent, come from nuclear families. The second largest category, 22.8 per cent, are from potentially nuclear, residually joint families. Only 9.3 per cent come from joint families. That a large number of students come from nuclear rather than joint families, is quite consistent with the earlier finding that practically all the students come from urban areas and particularly from the city itself

Significantly again, all the students are males, with no girl getting admission in the year under review, although there is no bar against the admission of girls.

The educational level of the parents of the students is shown in Table 4 which reveals that the largest number of students, viz., 39.6 per cent, have fathers who have had college education. Next come those whose fathers have a post-graduate degree and they number 18.5 per cent. Students with fathers whose educational level is that of matriculation account for 17.7 per cent. The fathers of 10.6 per cent of the students have professional education, such as a degree in engineering or medicine. Only a small number of students, viz., 5.1 per cent, have fathers who are not even matriculates. A vast majority of the students, therefore, have fathers with varying degrees of college education, ranging from graduation to doctorates and professional degrees.

Table 4

Students classified according to their parents' education

Fathers' education	*Mothers' education*					*Total*
	Below matric	*Matric*	*College educated*	*Post-gradu ate*	*No response*	
Below matriculation	9	—	—	—	3	12
Matriculation	23	11	1	—	7	42
College education	23	26	22	2	21	94
Post-graduate	6	10	12	6	10	44
Professional degree	5	7	8	2	3	25
No response	3	6	1	2	8	20
Total	69	60	44	12	52	237

As regards the education of the mothers, with the exception of three cases, their educational level is lower than that of the fathers. As against 5.1 per cent of fathers with education of below the level of matriculation, the percentage of mothers with this level of education is 29.1. As a rule, the difference between the education of couples is not too wide insofar as in only 4.6 per cent of the cases of cohorts the father has the highest education, such as a post-graduate or professional degree, and the mother the lowest, viz., below matriculation. Our analysis thus conclusively proves that most of the students have parents who are fairly well, if not highly educated.

The fathers of the students are engaged in a variety of occupations and these have been classified under six heads. The fathers of the largest number of students, i.e., of 32.9 per cent, are clerks, assistants, stenographers, accountants, section officers, superintendents etc. The next largest number, i.e., 18.9 per cent are in higher administrative occupations such as gazetted officers, company managers, executives, secretaries to government etc. Third comes business, with 15.2 per cent of the fathers engaged in it. This includes retail as well as wholesale dealers, contractors, commission agents etc. The next largest category is the professions which includes engineers, doctors, lawyers, and chartered accountants who account for 13.9 per cent of the fathers. There are only 5.1 per cent and 4.6 per cent students whose fathers are in teaching and in the armed forces, respectively. It may, however, be pointed out that of the 12 teachers six are school teachers, while the rest are college or university teachers. Among those in the armed forces, except for one who is a junior commissioned officer, all the rest are commissioned officers of various ranks. The residual category consists of 10 fathers of whom three are non-cultivating land-owners residing in the city, one is an ex-cabinet minister, two are artists, one is a cabinman in the railways, one a traffic inspector and two railway inspectors. It may be pointed out that there is not a single student whose father is a farmer, labourer, artisan, craftsman, soldier, or in any other low-paid occupation. So, occupational background again indicates that insofar as occupation is an index of social stratification practically all the students come from the middle or upper strata of society.

Another index of social position is income. We have sought to find out the incomes of the fathers of the students from their occupations and the total family income including the income of other earners in the family to get an idea of the per capita monthly income in the family. Both these provide some idea of the economic background of the students.

Table 5

Students classified according to their fathers' occupation

Occupation	*Number of cases*
Clerical	78
Higher administrative	45
Business	36
Professional	33
Teaching	12
Armed forces	11
Others	10
No response	12
Total	237

The incomes of the fathers vary widely between Rs. 100 to Rs. 6,000 per month. The largest number of fathers, viz., 34.2 per cent, have monthly incomes ranging from Rs. 251-500.[2] Another 16 per cent of the fathers have incomes between Rs. 501-750, 11.4 per cent of the fathers from Rs. 751-1,000, 17.3 per cent from Rs. 1,001-2,000, and 3.8 per cent above Rs. 2,000 per month. There are only 5.1 per cent of the students whose fathers have an income below Rs. 250 per month. The distribution of fathers by income thus corresponds to a considerable extent with the occupational distribution. During the course of our investigation we found that in many families there are earning members other than the father. Since the majority of the students are members of nuclear families, it was thought that family income would provide a more accurate measure of the economic condition of the students than the father's income alone. However, in view of the fact that the families may vary in size, we thought it better to analyze the families in terms of the average per capita monthly income of its members so as to give due weightage to such variations. We have calculated the per capita monthly income by dividing the total income from all sources by the total number of members in the family. This is presented in Table 6. It is seen that in the case of 3.4 per cent of the students their families have a per capita monthly income of over Rs. 500 per month. In 36.7 per cent cases it is upto Rs. 100, which includes 9.3 per cent cases with income of less than Rs. 50. Judged by the national per capita income[3] all the students except very few come from families which have a per capita income much higher than the national average, and this reinforces our earlier finding regarding the social class status of the students.

Table 6

Students classified according to per capita family income from all sources

Income in Rs./month	*No. of cases*
Upto 50	22
51-100	65
101-250	77
251-500	51
501-750	2
751-1,000	3
1,001-1,500	3
No response	14
Total	237

It is clear that in terms of the objective criteria of education, occupation and income of their parents, virtually all the students belong to the upper and middle class. That this is substantially true is also attested by the students' own assessment of their class position. The students were asked two questions, viz., "How would you yourself rank the overall esteem of your family" and, "In your opinion, in what esteem is your family held in the place where you habitually live?" The results of their responses recorded a three-point scale are as shown in Table 7. It is clear that by either standard of assessment, not more than 1.3 per cent of the students can be said to identify themselves with lower class. Thus, even according to their own self-image as well as their conception of their image others have about them, virtually all of them belong to the upper or the middle class.

Table 7

Students classified by their subjective class identification

Response	*How would you rank the overall esteem of your family?*	*In what esteem is your family held in the place where you habitually live?*
High	105	117
Neither high, nor low but in between the two	123	113
Low	3	—
No response	6	7
Total	237	237

In our study we made an attempt to find out how many of the students come from families in which someone or the other is already an engineer. We tried to collect this information at two levels of family organization. At the widest level the information refers to a maximum of four degrees of relationship with the student considered as the ego, and at the narrowest level the first degree relations, viz., the students' fathers and brothers.

At the widest level our data show that 70.5 per cent of the students have some relative within the range of four degrees who is an engineer and the maximum number of relatives in the engineering profession which any student has is 10. In all, 167 students have in all a total of 451 relatives in the engineering profession, which works out to an average of

2.7 relatives per student. In view of the fact that nearly three-fourth of the students already have one or more relatives in the engineering profession, it is clear that the tendency for self-recruitment in terms of the wider family unit is quite pronounced.

With regard to first-degree relatives, we find that only 15.6 per cent students have such relatives in the engineering profession. In case of 8.4 per cent, the relative in the engineering profession is his own father, and in the 7.1 per cent it is his brother. There are, however, only two cases where both the father and one or more brothers are in the engineering profession. At the level of the nuclear family, therefore, the tendency for self-recruitment is much less marked than at the wider family level.

We may now turn to an analysis of the educational background of the students themselves with a view to finding out whether students educated in certain types of schools and with a certain language as the medium of instruction have an advantage over others in securing admission to the Institute. This is important especially in view of the fact that there are different types of schools in the country employing different languages as media of instruction, especially upto the high school level. Since the medium of instruction in the institute is English and the joint entrance examination is being conducted in English, it is likely that students educated through the medium of regional languages are handicapped in securing admissions. We have, accordingly tried to analyze the educational background of the students in terms of the type of school in which they were educated, the medium of instruction, and their maximum educational attainments before being admitted to the institute.

Table 8 shows the highest examination passed by the students before they were admitted to the institute. Three-fifth, or 60.3 per cent, of the students have passed the higher secondary examination. The remainder consists of those who have passed the Indian School Certificate Examination and Pre-Engineering FSc, in more or less equal ratio. As compared to the proportion of students passing the Indian School Certificate Examination to that passing the Higher Secondary or Pre-Engineering FSc in the country as a whole, or even within the city, it seems that the former have a definite edge over the latter for admission to the institute. It is also interesting to note that 77.3 per cent of those who have more than the required minimum in education such as FSc Pre-Engineering, are from outside the city. Thus, in order to successfully compete for admission, students from the rest of the country are required to have higher education than students from the city.

Table 8

Students classified according to the examination passed and the university

Examination	*ISC*	*City Board*	*Others Boards/ Universities*	*No response*	*Total*
Higher Secondary	—	131	9	5	145
Indian School Certificate	45	—	—	1	46
FSc, Pre-Engineering First Year of Diploma in Engineering	—	6	34	4	44
No response	—	1	—	1	2
Total	45	138	43	11	237

Table 9 shows the type of schools attended by the students. It is found that public schools contributed the single largest number of students to the institute, i.e., 26.6 per cent. The percentage of students from privately-managed schools (may be aided by government, and other than public schools) is 24.5. Schools run and managed by government or municipal committees etc. got in 18.9 per cent of the students. Another 29.0 per cent were from a mixed school background, having moved between government, private and/or public schools at primary, middle and higher levels of study. Judged by the proportion of public schools to the total number of educational institutions in India, or in the city itself, the higher percentage of students from the public schools indicates that the former have relative over-representation.

Table 9

Students classified by the type of schools they went to

Schooling	*Number of cases*
Public throughout	63
Private throughout	58
Government throughout	45
Mixed (public/private/government)	69
No response	2
Total	237

Table 10 indicates that 60.3 per cent of the students were from schools with mixed media of instruction,, one medium invariably being English. They may have received instruction in English and Hindi, or in English and their own regional language, or in English, Hindi and the regional language. Another 33.3 per cent had all their education in English only. Only 6.3 per cent were from vernacular medium schools. Thus, schools with English medium have contributed more than five students to every student from schools employing vernaculars as media of instruction.

Table 10

Students classified by the media of instruction in school at different levels

Level of schooling	*Medium of instruction*			*Total*
	English	*Vernacular*	*English + Vernacular*	
Primary	94	143	—	237
Middle	92	142	3	237
Higher	213	16	8	237
Throughout	79	15	143	237

It is evident from the foregoing analysis that the students represent, by and large, a homogeneous group insofar as their general social background is concerned. More specifically, in terms of cultural factors like religion and caste, there is a preponderance of the Hindus belonging to the Brahman and the trading castes. As regards the social class background, they represent preponderantly the urban upper and middle classes. The educational background reveals that students from public schools, with English medium, and qualifying for the Indian School Certificate Examination generally preponderate over others.

Conclusions

This finding seems to fit into a certain pattern. Even though admission to the Institute is based on an all-India competitive examination and no artificial restrictions have been imposed on any section from seeking admission, in actual practice admission appears to be determined by a set of socio-cultural factors. Among these the awareness of the existence of technological education, appreciation of its importance (perhaps more important), the ability to afford that education as well as the quality of education previously received seem to be crucial. These factors are not isolated, however, but are closely related to one another. Awareness of new educational opportunities holding possibilities of a good career is bound to be higher in the urban areas where these opportunities are generally concentrated. And within the urban areas awareness is bound to be higher at the upper rungs of the social hierarchy since individuals so placed are more educated than those at the lower rungs. For the same reason people from the upper strata are also in a position to select the best schools for their children. Since these schools are more expensive than the government-managed and other aided schools, they tend to draw their students from a select segment of society who can afford them.

In other words, even though no student is intentionally precluded from securing admission there are certain disabling and debilitating factors inherent in the structure of society which prevent certain sections from taking advantage of the new educational opportunities.

It has already been pointed out that the IITs are engaged in producing what may be termed as a class of potential elite, and our findings have established that this potential elite is itself being recruited from the higher strata of society almost to the neglect of the lower strata. Accordingly, IITs as educational institutions seem to make only a limited contribution to social mobility.

Notes

1. Bania, Arora, Bhatia, and Sood are undisputedly trading castes. Khatris have been classified by Hutton as trading caste. See J.H. Hutton; *Caste in India*; Oxford University Press, London, 1961; pp. 284.
2. The report of the Education Commission (p. 119) has pointed out that the fathers of 57.5 per cent of the students of the IITs in India have income exceeding Rs. 500 per month. According to our data the percentage of students whose fathers have similar incomes is 48.5. According to another study, the family income of 57 per cent of the sample was above Rs. 1,000 a month and only 7.1 per cent came from the income group below Rs. 500. The authors of this survey have pointed out that, "Considering the fact (given by the last census) that the average income of families in Delhi is approximately Rs. 300 a month, it is not impossible that the education in the Delhi University is the prerogative of the more affluent". See A. Ghosh, TCA Rangachar, and S. Chatterjee, "Sample Survey of Delhi University", *Yojana*, April 2, 1967, pp. 23-24.
3. According to the NCAR per capita income of an average Indian is Rs. 334.5 (Quoted by the Education Commission Report, p. 126.)

Contributors

Shirirama Indradeva, Professor of Sociology, Ravishankar University, Raipur.

Suvira Jaiswal, Professor, Centre for Historical Studies, Jawaharlal Nehru University, New Delhi.

Satish Saberwal, Professor, Centre for Historical Studies, Jawaharlal Nehru University, New Delhi.

Andre Beteille, Professor of Sociology, Delhi University, Delhi.

Sheo Kumar Lal, the late Professor of Sociology, Jodhpur University, Jodhpur.

Dipankar Gupta, Professor of Sociology, Jawaharlal Nehru University, New Delhi.

A.M. Shah, Professor of Sociology, Delhi University, Delhi.

Victor S. D'Souza, Former Professor of Sociology, Punjab University, Chandigarh.

R.K. Bhadra, Professor of Sociology, North Bengal University, Siliguri.

Pradip Kumar Bose, Professor of Sociology, Centre for Studies in Social Sciences, Calcutta.

V.M. Dandekar, the late Former Director, Gokhle Institute of Economics & Politics, Pune.

D.N. Dhanagare, Professor of Sociology, Poona University, Pune.

Jaganath Pathy, Professor of Sociology, South Gujarat University, Surat.

K.L. Sharma, Professor of Sociology, Jawaharlal Nehru University, New Delhi.

K.N. Sharma, Former Professor of Sociology, Indian Institute of Technology, Kanpur.

Vijay Kumar Vashishtha, Professor of History, MDS University, Ajmer.

Nandu Ram, Dr. Ambedkar Chair, Jawaharlal Nehru University, New Delhi.

Ehsanual Haq, Professor of Sociology, Jawaharlal Nehru University, New Delhi.

C. Rajagopalan, Former Professor of Sociology, Bangalore University, Bangalore.

Jaspal Singh, Professor of Sociology, GND University, Amritsar.

Index